Liberia

Liberia

AMERICA'S AFRICAN STEPCHILD

—⚋—

David Gene Reese

© 2017 David Gene Reese
All rights reserved.

ISBN-13: 9781494753436
ISBN-10: 149475343X
Library of Congress Control Number: 2013923452
CreateSpace Independent Publishing Platform
North Charleston, South Carolina

Table of Contents

Illustrations · vii
Preface · ix

Chapter 1   The Mulatto "Marineer" · · · · · · · · · · · · · · · · · 1
            Slavery in America · · · · · · · · · · · · · · · · · · · 9
            America's First Black Émigrés · · · · · · · · · · · · · 28
Chapter 2   Captain Cuffe and the "Province of Freedom" · · · 31
Chapter 3   The American Colonization Society · · · · · · · · · · 54
            Cultural Divisions among Free Black Americans · · · 69
Chapter 4   The Search for a Home · · · · · · · · · · · · · · · · 85
Chapter 5   Liberia Is Born · 108
            Tribes of Liberia · 113
            Tribal Conflicts, Wars, and Revolts, 1822–1980 · · · 117
Chapter 6   From Colony to Commonwealth · · · · · · · · · · · 137
            A "Peculiar" Special Relationship · · · · · · · · · · · 146
Chapter 7   From Commonwealth to Republic · · · · · · · · · · 161
Chapter 8   The Republic Established · · · · · · · · · · · · · · · 183
Chapter 9   A Scandal, Coup, and Mystery · · · · · · · · · · · · 212
            The Drowning of President Roye · · · · · · · · · · · 219
            Liberian Political Parties · · · · · · · · · · · · · · · · 232
Chapter 10 The 1870s: Coming of Age · · · · · · · · · · · · · · 235

Chapter 11	The Unknown Hinterland	253
Chapter 12	The Scramble	286
Chapter 13	The Barclays of Barbados	312
	Africa's Renaissance Man	319
	Liberia's Military	349
Chapter 14	One for the Record Book	360
	Indirect Rule	364
Chapter 15	Boss of the Whole Show	403
	The Poro and Juju	428
Chapter 16	"Uncle Shad"	441
Chapter 17	A New Era	470
Chapter 18	Growth without Development	492
Chapter 19	Master of Liberia	515
Chapter 20	After Tubman, What? A Summing Up	543
Chapter 21	Blood on the Sand: The End	556

	Epilogue	593
	Appendix A: Time Line	595
	Appendix B: Colonial Agents, Governors, and Presidents 1820–1980	613
	Notes	615
	Selected Bibliography	703
	A Note About the Sources	707
	About the Author	709
	Index	711

Illustrations, Maps and Figures

Illustrations
Captain Paul Cuffe and his brig *Traveller* · · · · · · · · · · · · · · · · 1
President Joseph Jenkins Roberts, first
    president of Liberia · 166
A coffle of slaves · 171
President Roberts's house, Monrovia · · · · · · · · · · · · · · · · · · 177
Ashmun Street with houses and a church, Monrovia · · · · · · · 192
Edward Wilmot Blyden holding a book · · · · · · · · · · · · · · · · 357
President General of the Republic of Africa Marcus
    Garvey on parade · 371
Poro society mask · 430
President William V. S. Tubman after being crowned
    "King of the Bassas" at a political rally · · · · · · · · · · · · · · · 442

Maps
1. Liberia · xiii
2. Distribution of major Liberian ethnic
    and language groups · 113
3. Liberian territorial claims conceded to Britain
    and France · 334

Figures
The flag of Liberia · 161
The great seal of Liberia · 181

Preface

THIS BOOK DIDN'T START OUT to be a book. It had its origins in a proposed article that would explore the reasons for the markedly different paths Liberia and neighboring Ghana took in the years following their respective military coups in 1980—led by Samuel Doe in Liberia and Jerry Rawlings in Ghana. Not surprisingly, when it came time to put pen to paper, it became obvious that whatever the reasons might be, they were not to be discerned—at least not by me.

In the course of my preliminary research, and having spent three years as the person primarily responsible for the World Bank's operations in Liberia (and Ghana—and ten years in other African countries), I had become increasingly fascinated by Liberia's history, particularly its origins and connections with the United States. It was, after all, this country's first colony (although never formally acknowledged as such by the US government), its first attempt to deal with the race problem, the site of the world's largest rubber plantation (Firestone's), the first Negro republic in Africa, ruled by American blacks and their descendants for almost two hundred years, and which historically enjoyed a "special relationship" with the United States. Sadly, following 1980, much of Liberia's history was one of devastating civil war. Only after the end of the war in 2003 did a glimmer of peace and stability, including the election in 2005 of the first woman president of an African country, manage to break through the dark clouds.

In my research I also discovered that, other than articles in various magazines and journals, there had been relatively little serious historical literature, with some notable exceptions (mainly about the civil war and the new government), over much of the past twenty-five years or so. I decided to try to write a relatively brief account, with emphasis on the period of Doe's government accompanied by a minimal background. I wrote the book. It turned out to be only an exercise, but hopefully one that would be a learning experience for me. At this point, I must acknowledge the encouragement and support I received from many friends and acquaintances, four in particular. The instructor in my creative nonfiction workshop at the Johns Hopkins University, Mary Collins, pointed me in the right direction. Sybil Kyi provided me much-needed support—all the way from Hawaii. Frances Swanson read proof after proof and still remained enthusiastic. Fuddy gave unstintingly her encouragement and succor over a seemingly interminable time. But for her, there would be no book.

I decided that in this current work I would try to help a reader, be he or she a serious scholar of African history, a student, or an average person interested in history, understand how and why Liberia came to be and what it experienced in its more than 150 years of existence before the coup in 1980. (The tale after 1980 would be a very different story.)

I wanted the work to be carefully researched, comprehensive, and sufficiently detailed to serve as a useful reference. But, on the other hand, hopefully, to be a welcoming read rather than a soporific chore. I wish I could say I had fully achieved these objectives. Only the reader can decide how far I succeeded.

In my quest, because I discovered a surprising wealth of interesting and colorful characters that left their imprints on Liberia, I chose a somewhat different approach from that of the usual history. I relied on these characters, to the extent possible, to carry the story forward. I realized this method had obvious shortcomings, particularly since it produced a series of mini–biographical sketches, but I felt the subjects sufficiently interesting in their own right to justify it. Another concern was how to include enough detail to provide background and color, stimulate interest, and facilitate understanding without smothering the reader. Additional background and details, separate from the main text and appendixes (and in different type), seemed to be one answer, though not a wholly satisfactory one. I also chose to cite quotations and references and furnish additional information in endnotes rather than disruptive footnotes in the text.

In any event, this is *not* a standard straightforward history of Libera. I realize, too, there must be unfortunate errors and omissions in it. But I would beg the reader to give pause to the words of Tai T'ung, a thirteenth century Chinese historian: "Were I to await perfection, my book would never be finished."

The first two chapters describe the remarkable individual, a mulatto born on a tiny island off the coast of Massachusetts, who can be said to be the "spiritual father" of Liberia, and the New England that shaped his life and thinking. The next two chapters detail the paranoia over race that gripped much of the United States before the Civil War, the rise of the idea of colonization, creation of the American Colonization Society, and the society's quest to find a home for a colony. Chapters 5, 6, and 7 trace the birth of Liberia and its progression from colony to commonwealth to independent republic. The succeeding three chapters chronicle the vicissitudes of the republic as it grappled with financial crises, tribal wars, scandals, and the emergence of a society based on inequality and discrimination.

Chapters 11 and 12 recount an epic expedition into Liberia's unknown hinterland and the territorial threats from European powers in their "scramble for Africa." The following three chapters mark Liberia's entrance into the twentieth-century world, and its economic failures, foreign intrusions, loans and concessions, as well as fraudulent elections and accusations of slavery. The remaining six chapters center on William Tubman's twenty-seven-year presidency, the iron ore–fueled economic bonanza and resultant "growth without development," the mounting unrest against the long-term rule of Americo-Liberians, and its conclusion in the bloody military coup in 1980.

PLEASE NOTE
All quotations from letters, journals, newspapers and other periodicals, books, etc., retain the grammar and spelling of the original works.

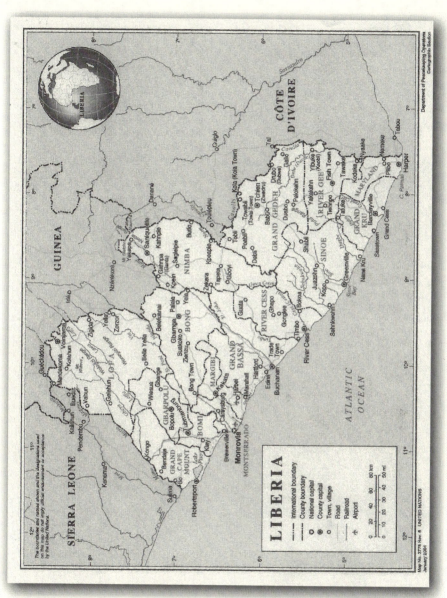

Map 1. Liberia. United Nations Map 3775, rev. 8 January 2004

CHAPTER 1

The Mulatto "Marineer"

Captain Paul Cuffe and his brig *Traveller*. Prints and Photographs Division, Library of Congress, DIG-ppmsca-07615

AN ENTRY ON 31 JANUARY 1811 in the brig *Traveller's* log reads;, "first part Of these 24 hours begins with Calm but Ends With high Winds and Squally. opend our four [fore] hatch + took out 1 barrel pitch...[also] Ship Bread and opened 1 barrel mess beef for Ships use."[1]

The Atlantic Ocean when aroused can be an unforgiving mistress. The 109-ton brig *Traveller* out of Westport, Massachusetts, pitched and heaved as it struggled against fearsome waves that threatened to devour the tiny vessel. The wind literally ripped through the sails and tore at the rigging. Rain in volley after volley of tiny, stinging bullets pelted the two figures barely visible, hovering in the stern as they wrestled with the helm. Two others fought to hold on to a line being whipped by strong gusts of wind. Another sat hunched on the deck retching into a bucket. Other crewmen worked intensely to plug leaks the wooden hull had sprung in the rolling sea.

Traveller was thirty days out of Philadelphia on a voyage that had until now been relatively uneventful. In preparation the vessel had been careened, the sails mended, rigging and lines checked. Before setting sail for Africa, they first would head with a cargo of barley to Philadelphia. They also would solicit the support of local Quakers for their venture that many would dismiss as impossible. Casting off their lines on January 1, 1811, the brig and its crew of nine had made their way down the Schuylkill and Delaware Rivers, past Wilmington and New Castle, into Delaware Bay, and on to the great Atlantic Ocean. Their destination—Sierra Leone, the British colony for freed slaves on West Africa's coast. Their mission—to further "the improvement of Africa" by establishing some kind of entity there that would trade in ivory and spices, rather than in slaves. That is, if such an enterprise looked feasible.

In many respects it was a daring voyage, but one that had long been a dream of the ship's owner. Sea travel in those times, at best uncomfortable, could be most perilous. Below deck, it was dark, space was cramped, and the air fetid. Food was boring and usually home to myriads of vermin. The usual victuals were ship's biscuit (appropriately called hardtack), salt beef, salt pork, cheese, and oatmeal. No fresh vegetables. The only fresh meat would come from the goats, sheep, or pigs on board. Slops were thrown overboard—carefully downwind. The toilet? A holed plank extending from the bow.

The most daring aspect, though, lay in the nature of the undertaking itself and the men carrying it out. The brig's owner, Captain Paul Cuffe, kept a log of the journey. His initial entry (in his own words, grammar, spelling, and punctuation, or lack thereof) read:

> Paul Cuffe account Book keep by himself Relative to his Voyage or Vissett [visit] towards Sierra Leone onboard the Brig traveller of Westport. Thomas Wainer Master her Crew Consisting of Nine in Number all peopel of Colour Except 1 Aprintace Boy [a Swedish lad by the name of Abraham Rodean] to Paul Cuffe: Paul Cuffe Considers himself as owner of the Brig and Supercargo.[2]

In the eyes of many whites, crossing the Atlantic in a 109-ton vessel commanded, navigated, and manned entirely by blacks was simply unthinkable. They just believed it couldn't be done. Even if Cuffe and his colored crew proved them wrong, other hazards threatened. Cuffe's destination, Sierra Leone, was a British colony. At this time the United States and Britain found themselves perilously close to war. (In fact the Nonintercourse Act, which had banned American trade with Great Britain, was reinstated in February 1811, and following a number of incidents, the United States declared war on June 19, 1812.) Either a British or American warship could intercept the *Traveller* and its crew. The color of the crew posed another risk. The 1793 US Fugitive Slave Law had stripped protection for any "dark complected" person from being taken by slave traders. And many such traders preyed on shipping in the Atlantic.

The voyage was daring in another sense as well. It marked an important link in a chain of events that in the United States would engender a "back to Africa" movement, split the nation's free black community, arouse both abolitionists and slaveholders—possibly hastening the onset of the Civil War—and capture the attention of the entire country for much of the pre–Civil War period. And out of this chain of events came the creation of Liberia, America's first colony and Africa's first black republic.

But for now, Captain Cuffe and his crew had their hands full just to survive. A wave washed John Masters (the husband of Cuffe's niece) overboard. The captain's entry in the ship's log on February 2:

> high Wind SSE and Stormy at 3 AM Wind + Sea Struck us Down on our beem end and Washed John Masters overboard but by the help of Some lors [loose] Rigin he Regain the Ship again Latd [latitude] per obser'n 34-26 and Longitude 34-09.[3]

The ship actually had rolled fully on its side so that its decks were perpendicular to the ocean floor. They risked being sunk as the yards of the tall masts dragged in the water. The storm continued to rage unabated. The wind shifted to west by south, pushing against the ship's stern. At four in the afternoon, Cuffe was forced to haul in the main topsail in the face of "Very heavy Sea [and] Sever gail of Wind."[4]

At last, though, the wind blew less fierce, and the sea grew less threatening. They soon began to spot other ships and welcomed, in Cuffe's words, "Pleasant Breezes…it begins to feel Like trade Wind. A heavey Dew and gentill breeze."[5] After noting "Weather Clear but Very Smoakey the Dust of Africa lodged on our Rigin We judged the Land to be about 25 Leagues [75 miles] off." They saw "birds, flying fish, black fish, and propoises [porpoises]…We had an Excellent fish Dinner for the first time Since We Sailed from America."[6]

Finally, on March 1, 1811, fifty-eight days after leaving Westport, the most welcome sight—land, green and inviting—came into their view. A triumphant but relieved Cuffe noted that his bruised and weary crew, and his somewhat storm-battered *Traveller* "at ½ past 8 o'clock…Came too in Sierra Leone Road Where was an English frigate of a Letter of marque [a privateer] + 2 vessels that was taken and brought in for tradeing in Slaves." Another two slave trade vessels, now hulks, lay on the shore.[7]

—⁂—

This Captain Cuffe, a fifty-one-year-old, half-black mariner, a ship owner willing to risk his vessel, crew, and himself in such a voyage, intrigued many on both sides of the Atlantic. The London *Times* later that year described him as being "of agreeable countenance, and his physiognomy truly interesting: he is both tall and stout, speaks English well, dresses in the Quaker style, in a drab-coloured suit, and wears a large flapped white hat."[8] Three years earlier Cuffe had become a Quaker—a rarity at that time for a man of color. He soon was a respected leading member of the Westport (Quaker) Meeting in Massachusetts. He also had become a ship builder, trader, owner of several vessels whose voyages ranged up and down the Atlantic coast, the Caribbean, even to the Caspian Sea—and one of America's earliest black entrepreneurs.

Biographer Sheldon Harris thought him not particularly handsome, but found his "features…fair and pleasant to the eye." Though "tending a bit toward portliness," he looked "every inch the country squire—except for his skin color"—a soft copper tone—and his facial features that reflected more his Negro origins than his [American] Indian. According to Harris, he was "essentially the sober Quaker In conversation with thee's and thou's heavily interlacing his every sentence. But interspersed with Cuffe's Quaker simplicity was the elegant but stylized and carefully developed speech pattern of the self-taught."[9]

Cuffe possessed an indefinable aura about him that bespoke integrity and inspired trust. Friends remarked that he was able to overcome "by native strength of mind, and firm adherence to principle, the prejudices with which descendants [of Africa] are too generally viewed."[10] He was, in short, "a man of remarkable dignity, initiative, tact, and piety, and the unselfishness of his efforts impressed all who knew him."[11]

Having now arrived at Sierra Leone, the "Province of Freedom,"[12] Cuffe had taken the first step on a long and arduous journey toward his vision of improving life for Africans, both in America and in Africa—one that would earn him the title of "spiritual father of Liberia."

It began on an island off the coast of Massachusetts.

The day Paul was born, January 17, 1759, dawned cold and raw on tiny Cuttyhunk Island. But Cuffe and Ruth Slocum scarcely noticed the icy wind blowing off Buzzards Bay. They had too much to do in welcoming the new son into their modest family. And the world was too busily occupied with wars and lesser things to take note of the birth of a mulatto boy born to a freed slave and his American Indian wife.

A haze of uncertainty hung over the Massachusetts colony where they lived. The English settlers in British North America had fought against the Indians and French in a series of wars over the previous seventy-five or so years. And now another was upon them. The defeat and death of French general Marquis de Montcalm on the Plains of Abraham in September 1759 assured British victory and the end of France's threat to George II's American possessions.

Although the French and Indian War ended the threat from France and opened the way for the colonies to wrest themselves from the grasp of the British crown, they faced an even more ominous threat, one that already was gnawing at the new country's very heart.

Slavery had become warp and woof in the North American colonies' economic and social fabric. Slaves were first introduced in 1619, as recorded by John Rolfe of Jamestown, Virginia, who noted, "About the last of August came in a Dutch man-of-warre that sold us 20 negras."[13] British ships soon dominated the lucrative trade and during succeeding years dumped thousands of African slaves on North America's shores. By 1760 every fifth inhabitant of Britain's North American colonies was black. Nine out of ten lived in Virginia, North and South Carolina, and Maryland, where they worked mainly on tobacco, rice, and indigo plantations as field hands. Almost a century later, more than 60 percent would work on cotton plantations.[14]

New England also had its slave population, who mostly worked as household servants in New York, New Jersey, and Rhode Island. Though slaves in the North numbered relatively few, Thomas Jefferson liked to remind his New England colleagues of their sinister role as "considerable carriers" in the slave trade. In fact, "at one point, earlier in the [eighteenth] century, approximately half the tonnage of New England shipping had been in transporting slaves, and the port of Boston prospered from the trade."[15]

"In truth, black slavery had long since become an accepted part of life in all of the thirteen colonies."[16] No fewer than a third of the members of the Continental Congress either owned or had owned slaves. Virtually all southerners of means did, including four out of the nation's first five presidents. George Washington and Thomas Jefferson each owned about two hundred. Even in Quaker Pennsylvania, the distinguished John Dickinson, one of the leaders in the Congress, owned eleven slaves—despite his Quaker mother and wife. And the respected, venerable Benjamin Franklin "had once owned two black house servants and had personally traded in slaves, buying and selling from his Market Street print shop."[17]

The sale of slaves flourished in Philadelphia and other cities—often mixed in with the sale of pine boards and other commodities. An advertisement, not unusual, appearing in Franklin's *Pennsylvania Journal* in January 1776 read:

> TO BE SOLD. A large quantity of pine boards that are well seasoned. Likewise a Negro wench; she is to be disposed of for no fault, but only that she is present with child, she is about 20 years old…and is fit for either town or country business.[18]

SLAVERY IN AMERICA

Servitude in America began early after the continent's discovery by Europeans. Spanish efforts to feed the demand for labor to grow sugar, their new American crop, by enslaving Indians largely failed. "The answer was in African captives... A cargo of seventeen Africans arrived in Hispaniola in 1505. Soon the Antilles sugar plantations were manned by African slaves."[19] British colonies in North America also faced severe labor shortages for their tobacco fields.

But in the early part of the seventeenth century, indentured servants, mainly recruited from the poor in London and other European cities, supplied most of the labor on tobacco and other farms in Virginia and in neighboring colonies. Many a colonial New England household depended upon them as household servants. They usually signed a contract for four to seven years of labor. In return they received passage to America, living necessities, and the prospect of freedom and land.[20]

The first Africans delivered to Jamestown actually were indentured servants. After securing his freedom, Anthony Johnson, one of the group, prospered as a land-owning farmer and employed at least one servant himself. According to court records, "Anthony the negro" declared in 1645, "Now I know myne owne ground and I will worke when I please and play when I please" (and, according to court records, be the master of a black servant).[21] Such mobility, however, lasted only until the end of the century. As slave traders delivered increasing numbers of black African captives to the colonies, the advantages to owners of exploiting their labors rather than employing indentured workers soon outweighed any moral inhibitions against slavery.

A Virginia act of October 23, 1705, declared, "All servants imported and brought into this County...who were not Christian in their native Country...shall be accounted and be slaves. All Negro, mulatto and Indian slaves within this dominion...shall be held to be real estate."[22] As Indian slaves became fewer and fewer, this act, in effect, limited lifelong slavery to Negroes and mulattoes and their offspring. The act also prohibited white-black marriages. A pernicious brand of involuntary servitude based on race now became part and parcel of an evolving New World culture—and a curse on American society for which there seemed no cure.

Rhett S. Jones, in Rosalind Cobb Wiggins's work on Paul Cuffe, suggests that the first English colonists in America believed "they were...the product of a centuries-long supernatural intervention that had placed them at the center of the world and charged them, under God's protection, with special responsibility to spread Christianity and civilization."[23]

Technological, organizational, and military superiority soon spawned the notion, bolstered later by the myth of white biological superiority, that "Europeans were destined to conquer Native Americans and enslave blacks."[24] Failing even more grandly than the Spanish before them to Christianize and civilize the Indians—and exploit their needed labor—the North American settlers also turned to Africans. The transition to enslaving inferior, un-Christian, uncivilized blacks proved easy.

As new settlers arrived, most colonies soon comprised a diverse lot—English, German, Dutch, Swedes—who needed a unifying identity in conquering a new world and its indigenous inhabitants, in forging a European-American culture, a new way of life. Race conveniently met this need. "Part of the consensus on which whites came gradually to agree over the course of the eighteenth century was the importance of race." They came to identify by race rather than their country of origin. Differences in language, religion, and customs of course remained, but the non-English settlers "generally accepted the basic Anglo-American tenet on race." And seventeenth- and early eighteenth-century white Europe shared the settlers' conviction of white supremacy, which in America "was made necessary and made possible by slavery."[25] But many Americans, especially in the South, feared this supremacy was frighteningly vulnerable.

Where young Paul grew up in Massachusetts, Negroes numbered fewer than five thousand, less than 2 percent of the colony's total population.[26] Most—like Paul and his family—were free blacks. Many farmed or worked on the water that framed his world, a world that centered on Massachusetts's Buzzards Bay. The sparsely settled area of large farms would grow rapidly in succeeding years to include the port of New Bedford (which in the nineteenth century would rule as the whaling capital of the world and flaunt its riches as arguably one of America's wealthiest cities).

Cape Cod lay to the east, while the sixteen Elizabeth Islands (including Cuttyhunk Island) stretched southwest like a finger from the cape to form the southern boundary of Buzzards Bay. Cuttyhunk, Paul's birthplace, was but a tiny sliver of land two and a half by three-quarters of a mile in size. Martha's Vineyard, his mother's home, was less than ten miles away to the south and east, and busy, prospering Nantucket lay a bit beyond.

To the west, neighboring Rhode Island, where free Negroes increasingly congregated, boasted one of New England's most prosperous and influential Quaker communities. In fact, by 1690 much of the area's "population consisted largely of Quakers [known also as Friends]."[27] The second half of the eighteenth century would see their small hamlets and scattered farmsteads rapidly grow and turn for livelihood to the sea—and, for God's work, to the evil of slavery.

It was an area of antislavery sentiments that would join with the other New England colonies to crusade against the detestable institution. Already in the 1750s, John Woolman, a Quaker cleric, was preaching against slavery as he visited monthly meetings (the Quaker term for church or congregation) up and down the coast, urging members to free their slaves. And in 1776 the Friends prohibited slave ownership among their members. By 1787 no member owned a slave.

A curious little book published anonymously in 1822 in Dublin, Ireland, contains one of the earliest accounts of Paul Cuffe's life. His brief biography is sandwiched between "The History of Prince Lee Boo" and "Some Account of John Sackhouse, The Esquimaux." Prince Lee Boo hailed from the "Pelew Islands" in the western Pacific Ocean. Sackhouse, born in Greenland, was an Eskimo. The account of Paul's life begins, "The following story of Paul Cuffe, will plainly shew how foolish the notion is which some ignorant people have, that those whose skin is black, or not of the same colour as their own, are inferior in sense and understanding to themselves."[28]

Paul's father, Cuffe Slocum, was born Kofi, probably in the area of present-day Ghana. Brought to Buzzards Bay in 1728 when about ten or eleven years old, he served as a slave of Captain Ebenezer Slocum, a Quaker and member of one of the area's prominent families. According to local records, on the fourteenth day of February 1742, he "sold a Negro man of about twenty-five years of age named Cuffe to Mr. John Slocum [his nephew] for $150."[29]

Cuffe Slocum's new Quaker master allowed him to earn enough through supplemental work to purchase his freedom. Within four years he was free. That year, 1746, he also wooed and married Ruth Moses, a Gayhead Indian of the Wampanoag tribe, who lived on neighboring Martha's Vineyard. They began a family that ultimately included six daughters and four sons. Paul was number seven. Life could not have been easy for a freed, uneducated slave, his Indian wife, and growing family. They worked as caretakers of the Slocum farms. Besides farming and fishing, Cuffe did some carpenter jobs, and he won a reputation as a hard worker and responsible black man.

By 1764 the uneducated ex-slave, now close to fifty years old, had taught himself to read and write and started keeping business journal accounts for his white neighbors in their various small enterprises.[30] Cuffe became an independent entrepreneur—ferrying, repairing boats, hiring other men for work in the coastal trade—and property owner. He achieved a level of success unheard of for an ex-slave. [31]

The property also included a farmhouse and outbuildings. Young Paul worked with his family on the farm, but with the area's rapid development, driven by whaling and shipbuilding, maritime pursuits soon captured his interest.

Cuffe Slocum died in Westport in March 1773, a prosperous, respected member of the small Westport Quaker community. Ruth, Paul's mother, lived on the family farm until she died fifteen years later.

Paul, only fourteen when his father died, already showed many of the traits that had enabled his father to reach the heights few believed a black man, particularly an ex-slave, could achieve. Paul's anonymous biographer noted that even as a young lad, he embodied that "determined spirit of perseverance and firmness of mind, which" enabled him to succeed "in his endeavours." And as long as "he maintained integrity of heart and conduct," Paul believed he "might humbly hope for the protection of Providence."[32] Possessed of a boldness that at times seemed to teeter on rashness—which his inherent steadiness and constancy tempered but failed to fully dampen—Paul's early life seemed to move from one daring adventure to another, weathering one calamity after another—but ultimately succeeding. One is tempted to believe that his hoped-for "protection of Providence" did indeed favor him in much of his life.

Unfortunately, reliable information on that early life is scant, and the accounts that are available, although they agree broadly, differ in many of the details. Rosalind Wiggins, who edited Paul Cuffe's logs and letters and has written about African Americans, particularly in New England, writes that Paul, not long after his father's death in 1773, embarked on his first venture on the sea. He shipped as an ordinary seaman aboard a whaling bark (or merchantman) headed for the West Indies. Either this or a subsequent voyage in 1776 provided Paul an unwelcome adventure that could have ended his career. The British navy captured the ship and threw him and his fellow crewmen into prison in New York. After three months, however, their captors released Cuffe and the others and allowed them to return home—due, according to one version of the story, to overcrowding in the prison, shortages of provisions, or just good luck...or perhaps the "protection of Providence."

By the time he turned sixteen, Paul became, as he put it, a "marineer." A career on the water came naturally. Cuttyhunk Island was long renowned for its ship pilots. Even as a seven-year-old, perched on his favorite vantage point atop Cuttyhunk's Lookout Hill, Paul often had watched the trading ships plying the waters off the southwest corner of Massachusetts where it borders on Rhode Island—"whaling ships, fishing boats sailing to the banks, and the Indian craft carrying furs in the southerly direction after the portage across the base of Cape Cod."[33] He doubtless dreamed of what might lie beyond.

Like his father, Paul received little formal education. He taught himself to read and write, studied arithmetic and navigation, managed to absorb a surprising amount of the sea lore that abounded in the area, likely heard stories from the crews of slavers' ships about the horrors of the Middle Passage, and learned about the life plantation slaves lived. He also would learn firsthand about life as a person of color, a mulatto son of a Native American and an African former slave. But he would discover, too, many willing hands that would reach out to him in friendship and help.

Probably the most helpful was William Rotch Jr., son of William Rotch Sr. and grandson of Joseph Rotch, prominent Nantucket merchant and whaling agent. The Rotches belonged to a prominent New England Quaker family.[34] They opposed slavery and the slave trade, provided support to others of like mind, and acted as useful channels of information about British colonization of blacks in Africa. William Sr. "was a Quaker of influence," so such information "soon circulated through" the New England communities of Friends. William Jr. was a "long-time business associate" who occasionally would embark on joint ventures with Cuffe.[35]

At the age of twenty, the now-confident "marineer" ventured into business on his own, or rather jointly with his older brother David—despite the Revolutionary War's being in full swing. They probably watched the flames rise from New Bedford as the town burned from fires set by British troops on September 5, 1778, in reprisal for privateering and the town's "storing seized goods and artillery and ammunition." Damages came to more than $500,000, and no whaling vessel left New Bedford for the next seven years.[38]

Undeterred, Paul and his brother decided to build a small boat to deliver needed supplies across the bay to blockaded Nantucket and Martha's Vineyard. They "dodged the British boats by night, taking goods across thirty miles of open ocean."[39] Not unless one has experienced a foul and blustery Buzzards Bay, when wind-whipped, angry waves threaten to demolish anything that comes before them, can one fully appreciate the two brothers' daring in setting out on these waters in a small, open craft.

However, they could not dodge local pirates who robbed them of boat and cargo. After they somehow escaped unharmed, older brother David, understandably, decided the seaman's life was not for him. But indomitable Paul set out once more—only this time to lose his cargo in a storm. After still another encounter with pirates, he finally completed a voyage to Nantucket, then to Saint Georges Bank. He returned with a boatload of prized cod. He was in business.

Now twenty-four, Paul married Alice Pequit, a Wampanoag Indian like his mother, on February 15, 1783. They purchased the small house he had been renting, and the couple settled down to raise a family. With his Native American brother-in-law, Michael Wainer, he built a boatyard near his property on the Acoaxet River in Westport.

Even though half white and a free man in a "liberal" Massachusetts, Paul Cuffe still suffered discrimination. People of color, whether free or not, could find few open doors when it came to education, employment, training, investments. They found that the white churches they attended were usually segregated and, in any event, allowed nonwhites little meaningful say in church affairs.

Yet, as Professor Rhett H. Jones points out, free blacks were "infinitely better off than slaves." They were at least in charge of their own family. A slave's family could be torn apart, its members sold away—one of the slave's greatest fears—on the whim of the owner. Parents "could not [even] pass on a toolbox, a Bible, or a musical instrument to their sons and daughters," or for that matter, any kind of property, "without permission of their owner."[38] In contrast, free blacks, particularly property owners, enjoyed a number of legal rights and social positions. While the white community refused to accept free blacks as equals, the American preoccupation with property rights under the law prevailed. For white property owners to deny such rights, even to free blacks, could jeopardize the underpinnings of their society. However, property rights, as Paul Cuffe discovered, did not convey the right to be free from discrimination.

—⚍—

Unwelcome demographic developments, moreover, increasingly rattled America's white-dominated society. In the eighteenth century, the black population in North America began to climb, and its rate of growth accelerated. Although not as rapid as the near-explosive pace of white expansion, the numbers caused alarms to sound for many Americans. Imports of slaves accounted for a significant part of the rise until the legal slave trade ended in 1808. But the natural increase of North American slaves, who fared far better than those in sugar plantation–dominated South America and the Caribbean, was the major factor.

By 1750 the yearly rate at which the population of North American blacks increased, excluding imports, had climbed to almost 1.5 percent; by 1800 it reached more than 2 percent.[39] "By the mid-1750s, one in every five Americans was a slave—nearly 300,000 out of a total population of a million and a half. And five thousand new captives arrived from Africa or the Caribbean each year."[40]

More alarming to most slaveholders, the number of free blacks in the United States swelled even more rapidly—by 80 percent between 1790 and 1800—due largely to the Revolutionary War, when the British freed many slaves, and to the success of the abolitionist campaign in the northern states.[41] The numbers of free blacks still were not large in terms of the total US population (only about 3 percent in 1800). Slave owners and other southerners especially feared free blacks; usually better educated than slaves, they were potential troublemakers and leaders.

Still, manumission was not uncommon, even in the South. George Washington, for example, in his will instructed the 124 slaves he owned outright in 1799 should be freed upon Martha Washington's death. (Martha owned an additional 194 slaves in her own name.) His estate would support the old and infirm among them, as well as orphaned children for as long as needed. Many other southern, and northern, slave owners followed Washington's example.

And starting in 1777 with Vermont, states in the North began adding to the free black population by abolishing slavery. The 1780 Massachusetts constitution declared all men free and equal at birth, and a 1783 judicial decision interpreted the provision as abolishing slavery. Pennsylvania passed gradual emancipation laws in 1780, followed by Rhode Island and Connecticut four years later, New York in 1799, and New Jersey in 1804.

On top of the swelling black population, a series of insurrections on land and uprisings on ships in the latter part of the eighteenth and early part of the nineteenth centuries fueled white anxieties. Armed slave resistance in British Jamaica and the bloody creation of an independent, slave-ruled Haiti in 1804 proved especially unnerving.

Even New Yorkers found themselves fearful. The city's African population in 1740 ranked second only to Charleston's. One in five were slaves, mainly domestic servants. Packed into three square miles at the southern tip of Manhattan, the threat they posed caused many a sleepless night for white residents. Earlier, twenty to thirty slaves, along with two Indians, in April 1712 set fire to a building and killed nine whites. Then on March 18, 1741, a suspicious fire reduced the governor's residence in Fort George on the southernmost tip of Manhattan to ash and rubble.[42]

> The following week, another fire broke out, followed by more than a dozen in the next three weeks...Van Sant's warehouse... Gerereau's cow stable...The home of Agnes Hilton. A haystack on Joseph Murray's property...The long-feared Negro uprising had begun. In response, almost every African American male over sixteen was hunted down and locked in the city jail.[43]

New York chief court justice Daniel Horsmanden headed the official investigation. Propelled by main witness Mary Burton, it found more than a hundred blacks guilty to varying degrees. Mary, a sixteen-year-old white indentured servant who worked for tavern and brothel owner John Hughson, "implicated every black brought into Horsmanden's courtroom, as well as four whites who were also sent to the gallows." Thirteen blacks were burned at the stake, eighteen were hanged, and more than seventy were "banished to the West Indies, Newfoundland, Suriname, and Spain."[44]

Mary had been promised freedom and one hundred English pounds for her testimony. But she did not stop there. She accused her employer, Hughson, his wife, and a prostitute named Peggy Carey of being part of the plot to kill all whites in the city. The three were hanged. She "then accused English schoolteacher John Ury of being a Jesuit priest in disguise and urging the slaves to violence. On the twenty-ninth of August, Ury was hanged."[45] The trials, which resembled those of the Salem witchcraft incident, ended only when Mary began accusing prominent New Yorkers. She received her freedom from indenture and one hundred pounds—and apparently left promptly for other parts.

But it was in the South that the fear caused white hearts to beat most violently. One of the first serious black insurrections occurred in South Carolina when a group of blacks, reputedly encouraged by Spanish missionaries, set out on September 9, 1739, for Saint Augustine, Florida, and presumably freedom, killing any whites they encountered. Forty-four blacks and thirty whites died. In the same year, South Carolina witnessed two other smaller uprisings. In Virginia a skilled blacksmith and slave named Gabriel, emboldened by slave resistance in Haiti, plotted a massive uprising involving some one thousand slaves. He set it to begin on August 30, 1800, when "all the whites were to be massacred, except the Quakers, the Methodists, and the Frenchmen;... they were to be spared on account...of their being friendly to liberty."[46] As the would-be rebels poised for their assault on Richmond, however, an unprecedented rainstorm poured down. Rivers and creeks flooded, blocking their march. They watched as their revolt "died under the weight of the water."[47] Gabriel and twenty-six of his fellow black plotters were executed.

Even after the American Colonization Society's founding in 1816 and Liberia's inception five years later, other plots followed. And with each report the fear would grow, and the pressure for relief from the rising paranoia increase.

A slave informant in May 1822 saved Charleston, South Carolina, from "what was probably the most well-thought out of all American slave rebellions."[48] The brainchild of Denmark Vessey, a former slave from Haiti who had purchased his freedom with $600 won in a street lottery, it resulted in forty-two plotters being deported and thirty-five executed. Twenty-two died in July in a ghastly botched hanging "when the platform they stood on was so low, their necks didn't break when they fell. Instead they slowly and agonizingly began to strangle. To resolve the unfortunate mess, the captain of the guard rode past each man and shot him in the head."[49]

Nine years later, on August 13, 1831, Nat Turner, a literate slave and radical preacher (termed by some a "cunjer man"), saw a halo around the sun. He took it as a sign from God for him to lead a revolt against whites to liberate their slaves. In response, early in the morning of August 22, he led a band of eight slaves to break into the house of his onetime owner, Joseph Travis, near Jerusalem in Southampton County, Virginia. With a hatchet they slaughtered the entire five-member family. An infant sleeping in a cradle escaped death, but only temporarily when the murderers remembered and came back to complete their job. The band, which had swelled to more than forty, moved farm to farm killing fifty-eight more men, women, and children over thirty-six hours.

Reports of the insurrection provoked near hysteria. The governor called up the militia. (A dispatch read, "The Fayette Artillery and the Light Dragoons leave here this evening for Southampton—the artillery to go in a Steamboat and the troop by land.") One report, probably exaggerated, stated that some three thousand armed white men, the militia, soldiers from Fort Monroe, and sailors from the navy were mobilized. Although the revolt ended in two days, vigilantes, mainly militia from surrounding counties, embarked on a vengeful massacre, killing hundreds of blacks, most of whom had nothing to do with the rebellion. Turner eluded capture until October 31 when a local farmer spotted him.

Before his life ended on the gallows on November 11, 1831, Turner dictated a confession while in prison awaiting his November 5 trial. A remarkable account of his life, his reasons for leading the rebellion, and grisly details of it, the confession was read in court and then published by the white lawyer to whom he confessed. The book, read widely, spawned a body of literature, including a 1967 Pulitzer Prize novel entitled *The Confessions of Nat Turner* by William Styron.

But what to do with free blacks? Most whites, and doubtless many blacks, in the United States firmly believed the two racial groups were simply too different to mix, to assimilate freely. Thomas

Jefferson, responding on August 25, 1814, to a query from Edward Coles, a fellow Virginian and secretary to President Madison, probably expressed the view of most whites. He wrote that blacks "are by their habits rendered as incapable as children of taking care of themselves...[They] are pests in society by their idleness, and the depredations to which this leads them [so that] their amalgamations with the other colour [whites] produces a degradation to which no lover of this country, no lover of excellence in the human character can innocently consent."

Regardless, he continued, "emancipation would come." But he "was convinced that if all of America's slaves were freed, they would have to be shipped out of the country."[50] Even Abraham Lincoln, while president in 1861, explained to a group of black leaders that in America (the United States), the difference between blacks and whites was greater "than exists between almost any other two races." And, due to "this physical difference," both races suffered.[51]

Although no doubt ambivalent, given the important role of slaves in the economy and their value as a commodity, most white Americans, including slaveholders, probably favored the demise---at least over time---of slavery. A significant number thought the institution would gradually wither away as the economy developed (although the rise of cotton production after the cotton gin's invention in 1793 would slow the process). Nevertheless, many, if not most, believed free blacks had to be resettled somewhere out of the country. Jefferson in 1781 outlined his solution—colonization—in elaborate detail in his *Notes on the State of Virginia*. Lincoln proposed a site in Central America.

—⚘—

While Cuffe could not have been oblivious to the controversies, fears, and schemes surrounding blacks, he centered his attention on work in the Quaker community and to transforming Paul Cuffe, half-black small boat builder and trader, into Captain Paul Cuffe, big boat builder and successful businessman who was well regarded among his Quaker neighbors. After all, they saw his prosperity as a mark of the Lord's favor. He stood out as an anomaly nonetheless. Intelligent, hardworking, responsible—and prosperous—but a black man? Hard to reconcile with their long-held beliefs.

Cuffe progressed from small open boats to larger and larger ones, investing the profits he realized from their trading voyages and the sale of a vessel when opportune. After a modest vessel he named *Box Iron* came a succession of increasingly larger schooners, culminating in 1795 with the sixty-nine-ton *Ranger*. To house his growing family (which would total two sons and five daughters), the increasingly affluent Cuffe purchased a new house and farm on the Westport River in 1797 for $3,500. (His farm, at 1504 Drift Road, was listed an historic landmark in 1974.)

He built a wharf, warehouse, and later a grist mill. Reminded of his own experience as a child denied formal schooling, Cuffe also built a school on part of his land. He gave the new facility to the people of Westport for use as a free school. Erected in 1797, "Cuff's" school—probably one of the first integrated schools in the United States—remained the town's sole educational institution for many years.

The mulatto entrepreneur continued to prosper. By 1806, when the 268-ton sloop *Alpha* was completed, he "owned one ship, two brigs, and several smaller vessels, besides property in houses and land."[52] The 109-ton brig *Traveller*, Cuffe's favorite, would figure in epic voyages to Africa. His ships mainly carried lumber and general cargo between New Bedford, Nantucket, and Martha's Vineyard. Some also could be found whaling and fishing off Saint Georges Bank in competition with many Yankee fishermen, and hauling cargo to Philadelphia; Baltimore; Wilmington, Delaware; the Caribbean; even to the Caspian Sea.

Cuffe himself captained many of the voyages. The *Liverpool Mercury* of October 11, 1811, carried an account of one of them, a 1793 whaling expedition in the Strait of Belle Isle off the northwest coast of Newfoundland. For some unexplained reason, he arrived with only ten crewmen aboard two boats. Several rival vessels were far better equipped in terms of crew, harpoons, and other gear. The custom in such situations was to combine the fleets to enable all the participants to share in the kills. Although some of the rival groups initially balked at joining with a black captain and black crew, they reluctantly relented. In the operation Cuffe and his blacks deeply impressed the white sailors with their diligence and enterprise. The combined fleets took seven whales on that trip. Cuffe and his crew killed six of the seven. Paul Cuffe himself killed two. He returned home heavily freighted with oil and bones.

The winter of 1795–96 witnessed a similar episode on a voyage to Virginia and Maryland described in the *Boston Weekly Recorder*. After sailing to Norfolk, Virginia, where he sold his cargo, Captain Cuffe navigated the *Ranger* up the Nanticoke River to bustling Vienna, Maryland, the customs district for the region. "His arrival filled the local populace 'with astonishment and alarm.' A vessel only commanded by a black man and 'manned with a crew of the same complexion, was unprecedented and surprising.' Local leaders feared Cuffe and his men were there to stir up mischief. Many suspected he was planning to lead a slave revolt."[53]

Since his papers were in order though, the local customs officer reluctantly allowed him and his ship to land. Cuffe acted with such "candor, modesty, and firmness" that he won everybody over. One of Vienna's most prominent figures even entertained the black sea captain in his home. Still, "the people in that area were astonished to see a black man with a black crew managing so well." Cuffe sailed back to Westport with three thousand bushels of Maryland corn that turned him a tidy profit of more than $1,000.[54]

But to the white man, Cuffe still was a curiosity, a freak of nature. He seemed so "untypical" of their image of a black man. He was sober, industrious, and civic-minded. In a society in which financial holdings were an important determinant of one's social standing, Cuffe was "America's first wealthy Negro."[55]

Cuffe, however, was no "Uncle Tom." According to one story, young Paul became Paul Cuffe when, presumably after his father died, he refused to accept Slocum as his surname. As a slave, his father followed accepted custom and adopted his owner's family name. Paul, however, refused. To adopt the Slocum name, he insisted, implied servitude. Instead he took Cuffe, his father's given name—and persuaded his three brothers to do the same.

He determined to prove himself in ability and deportment as a black man fully equal to the whites he encountered and insisted, as a matter of inherent rights, securing equal treatment under the law for himself and his fellow blacks. When he and his brother John became owners of property (his father's homestead), they found themselves also taxpayers. Like taxpayers universally, they objected, to the point that they were arrested for nonpayment of taxes. (They were released from jail on a writ of habeas corpus after a few hours.) But their objection was not mere carping; they objected to having to pay taxes while being denied the right to vote. Employing the same logic white colonists used against British rule, they argued in their 1780 petition that they were subject to "taxation without representation." Doggedly the two brothers fought their case layer by layer through the Massachusetts government machinery, until they managed to get the state legislature to pass the act of 1783 "by which negroes acquired legal rights and privileges in Massachusetts."[56]

Paul's heart over the years had spoken to him of the misery in which most black people—whether slaves in America, poor tribesmen in Africa, or even fellow free blacks in America—lived their lives. Cuffe, his early anonymous biographer wrote, "could not think of enjoying ease, when he reflected, that he might, in any degree, administer to the relief of the multitudes of his brethren, who were suffering under the yoke of slavery, and wasting their time in ignorance."[57]

A vision of aiding fellow blacks both in Africa and America had begun to form in his mind.

AMERICA'S FIRST BLACK ÉMIGRÉS

"**B**y the end of the American Revolution, 100,000 slaves had escaped bondage. Close to twenty thousand left with the British military while others fled in private vessels. Some returned to Africa." Others made it to the Caribbean, where many ended up again as slaves.[58]

In a New York City tavern, twenty-three-year-old Boston King also contemplated his future—as one of the first American black colonists who would return to Africa. King, formerly owned by Richard Waring, of Charleston, South Carolina, stood in the tavern jammed with blacks. The crowd quieted as it waited for one of the British soldiers to open the book, *The Book of Negroes*. It was a scene repeated "every Wednesday afternoon between May and November 1783." The brainchild of Brigadier General Samuel Birch, the commandant of New York during British occupation, the book contained some three thousand names. It included "every man, woman, and child who could prove their length of time [as a loyalist] with the British" forces against the American rebels in the war just ended. Each individual received a certificate, his ticket to freedom that enabled him or her to leave the States on a British vessel.[59]

King's name, along with his wife's, was entered in the book. He had served with British forces for four years, fighting in North and South Carolina and had taken a British warship to New York, where, like thousands of other black refugees, "he lived in crammed barracks."[60] Waiting to be evacuated, he worked at odd jobs, acquired a wife named Violet, and was abducted and sold back into slavery but "managed to escape once more and return to New York and to Violet."[61]

At last, they boarded the *L'Abondance*, bound for Port Roseway in Nova Scotia and resettlement. There, in 1783 the black refugees founded the largest of several Black Loyalist communities. Named Birchtown, out of gratitude for General Birch, its population swelled to 1,500–2,000 residents, reputedly the biggest settlement of free Africans in the world. Unfortunately, the area proved unsuitable for farming, and the winters proved devastating. [62]

The Sierra Leone Company, which had founded a "free" colony on the West African coast, primarily for former slaves, came to their rescue. The colony supplanted an earlier disastrous effort, by the Saint George's Bay Company, to provide a free settlement for the black poor of London identified by the abolitionist Committee for the Relief of the Black Poor. Many were Black Loyalists who escaped enslavement and fought for the British. For the 1787 send-off, the authorities swept together three hundred of them, plus a collection of clergy, white officials, and craftsmen needed to build the Sierra Leone colony. For good measure, they added, according to Africanist Sir Harry Johnston, "sixty irreclaimable London prostitutes, who were to…begin a new life under different conditions, as the spouses of some of [the] repatriated Africans."[63]

The company vowed to do a better job than its predecessor in resettling the remaining Black Loyalists. "In early 1792 fifteen ships entered the mouth of the Sierra Leone River, and eleven hundred black Americans [including Boston and Violet King] disembarked at what…[would come] to be called Freetown in the colony of Sierra Leone."[64] Although the reception of some British officials in the colony proved almost as chilly as the climate in Nova Scotia had been, they stayed on. Much to the despair of the authorities, their descendants would come to form an important segment in the colony's elite Creole society. After the British prohibition of the slave trade in 1807, captives rescued from slaving ships by the Royal Navy would join them.

While still in Nova Scotia, Boston became a Methodist preacher. He would later write in his memoirs that his thoughts, very much like Paul Cuffe's, turned to his "poor [indigenous] brethren in Africa," and he "thought what a wretched condition...those poor creatures" must be in "who never heard the Name of God or of Christ."[65] His devout wish to carry the Gospel to his poor African brothers had been answered by the Sierra Leone Company.

CHAPTER 2

Captain Cuffe and the "Province of Freedom"

—⚘—

PAUL CUFFE MUST HAVE KNOWN about Sierra Leone from his many Quaker friends or by his association with the cluster of free blacks residing in nearby Newport, Rhode Island. He was very familiar with Newport, especially the wharf areas, and the "shops along Thames Street, the main mercantile thoroughfare," where blacks congregated.[1] Perhaps he had encountered someone from Rhode Island's famous Black Regiment or Brigade, so-called Black Loyalists who had fought with the British. He also would have heard of William Thornton, of Tortuga in the Virgin Islands, who became a United States citizen in 1788. Thornton in 1787 outlined his ideas before the Free African Union of Newport for resettling free blacks. Established in 1780, the Union was one of the earliest organizations created to aid African Americans.[2] Thornton's message also was spread to other black organizations on the East Coast, including the African Union in Boston and others in New York and Philadelphia. Even as early as 1733, Yale president Ezra Stiles and Congregational clergyman Samuel Hopkins were advocating the colonization of free American blacks in West Africa.

Cuffe's connections with the many Friends who lived in the area, especially his commercial and personal ties with the Rotches, would expose him to the antislavery world. Abolishing the slave trade was one of William Sr.'s principal preoccupations. They knew of the noted British philanthropist Granville Sharp, the driving force behind the "Province of Freedom" in the Sierra Leone experiment. Closer to home, in April 1808 Cuffe became a member of the Westport Friends Monthly Meeting. Here "white men such as Benjamin Rush and Anthony Benezet, along with the Pembertons, had for years been concerned with antislavery aims."[3] James Pemberton, an "elderly Philadelphia Quaker" was "a key member of the Philadelphia Yearly Meeting" and "an early member of the Pennsylvania Society."[4]

In any event, Paul Cuffe apparently had for some time been turning over in his mind an idea he had—one that soon took on the trappings of a dream. In a letter in June 1809, he wrote that "for some years [he] had it impressed on [his] mind to make a voyage to Sierra Leone in order to inspect the situation of the country" in the light of his "feeling a real desire that the inhabitants of Africa might become an enlightened people…in the true light of Christianity… and be benefited both with agriculture and commerce."[5]

He envisioned establishing an association in Sierra Leone that would trade in ivory and spices—rather than slaves—in order to further "the improvement of Africa." Local Africans and those who had been dispersed overseas (whom Cuffe called members of "the nation of Africa") would run the operation.[6] And, much to his satisfaction, he had received a letter in June the previous year from James Pemberton. In his letter, Pemberton related that Zack Macawly (Zachary Macaulay), the Sierra Leone Company's former governor, had said that, if Cuffey should "make a voyage to Sierra Leone," although the company had handed over the colony's governance to the British Crown, he (Macaulay) would "take care that he will receive every encouragement which the Governor can afford."[7]

―᠁―

Lincoln, Jefferson, Madison, and many other American leaders believed resettling Negroes from the United States in colonies could play an important role in excising the cancer of race that afflicted the country. Jefferson reportedly thought suitable locations might be found on the Pacific coast or in the new, relatively unknown Louisiana territory. Lincoln, in a curious meeting at the White House during the Civil War, outlined his thinking to a committee of colored men who opposed colonization. He explained that Congress had appropriated a sum of $600,000 for colonizing slaves freed in the District of Columbia, thus "making it [colonization] his duty, as it had for a long time been his inclination." The proposed location: Central America, the Isthmus of Chiriqui.[8]

"Why, he asked the group rhetorically, "should the people of your race be colonized?" Lincoln continued, saying that "a broader difference" existed between blacks and whites "than exists between almost any other two races." And, "this physical difference is a great disadvantage to us both, as I think your race suffer very greatly, many of them by living among us," while whites also "suffer from your presence. In a word we suffer on each side." Although Honduras, Nicaragua, and Costa Rica protested, the Central American locale, Lincoln asserted, was a good site for the proposed colony because it was "within reach of the country of [their] nativity." It was, in his view, "a very excellent one for any people, and with great natural resources and advantages."[9]

Although not recorded, the president apparently failed to convince the delegation of the merits of colonization. In fact, the majority of blacks in the United States by this time shared their opposition.

Pemberton reported that Macaulay now was secretary to the "recently established 'Africa Institution.'" (The Africa Institution was formed in 1807, a month after the British Parliament had passed a bill outlawing the slave trade, "to promote the civilization of

Africa."[10] It replaced the London Abolition Committee that Quakers organized in 1787.)[11] Macaulay fully realized that its objectives "would be much advanced if any Free black people from... [North America] of good conduct [and] religious principle could be induced to offer their personal assistance."[12]

Captain Cuffe also sought the advice and support of his fellow Friends, many of whom had established themselves as successful international businessmen operating in a network linking Philadelphia, New Bedford, New York, Liverpool, London, and even West Indian ports. Cuffe's Westport Monthly Meeting, as well as the New England and Philadelphia Yearly Meetings, furnished him letters in support of his endeavor: to see whether or not it was feasible to create the sort of trading community he had in mind in Sierra Leone, with its goal "the improvement of Africa."[13]

Having now safely arrived in Freetown, Sierra Leone's capital, Captain Cuffe and his men must have felt not only a wave of relief but, to the extent their Quaker demeanor allowed, satisfaction and pride on their accomplishment. They busied themselves unloading and selling their cargo. Cuffe noted in his log June 8, 1811, that they spent the day landing flour and ship's cargo, and bartering for elephant "teeth." For 316 ivory tusks, weighing 2,352 pounds, the captain would exchange two yards of cloth per pound of ivory.[14]

The colony's current governor, E. H. Colombine, invited Cuffe to dinner where "an Estensive observation took place on the Slave trade and the unsecksulfeness of the Colony in Sierra Leone." The black captain again would dine and breakfast—and discuss Sierra Leone and the slave trade—at the governor's table before leaving the colony. He also met local African chiefs whom the British in true monarchical fashion crowned as kings. King Thomas Crane, "an old man greay headed," came on board the *Traveller*. Cuffe "served him With Victuals But," lamented the captain, "it apeared that there Was rum Wanting but none Was given." Cuffe also went to visit the king of Bullom Shores, King George. The dutiful Quaker presented each with a Bible and several pieces of Quaker literature.[15]

Cuffe planned to organize a prototype cooperative society, owned and managed by Africans. The association would trade local products such as ivory, palm oil, and camwood (used to make red dye) with the United States and Britain and other countries, and also develop a capacity to produce other items for export, particularly whaling and agricultural produce. With that in mind, he spent considerable time during his Sierra Leone sojourn searching out possible sources for new production, such as suitable mill sites, using local Guinea grass for cattle fodder, and even exploring the feasibility of introducing sericulture (raising silkworms to produce silk).

If the initial prototype society succeeded, additional ones could be organized in Sierra Leone and spread eventually across all of sub-Saharan Africa. Cuffe reasoned that if Africans had sufficiently attractive economic opportunities, they would be able to improve their lives and abandon the slave trade. Although both Britain and the United States had outlawed the trade and stationed naval forces along the coast of West Africa to intercept slave ships, slave trading remained an active virulence the civilized world could not ignore.

Slave trading centers and barracoons (slave barracks) dotted western Africa's coast. The early settlers, frequently assisted by British and American warships, clashed repeatedly with slave traders and local chiefs, their suppliers. Both parties violently opposed settlers bent upon destroying their lucrative livelihood. Cuffe added a further note underlining the difficulty in getting African chiefs to give up the slave trade, especially in the absence of economic alternatives. He wrote in a letter to Nathan Lord of the Andover Theological Seminary in 1815 "that in conversing with the African chiefs," he realized "it was with great reluctance they gave up the slave trade saying that it made them poor and they could not git things they used to git when they traded in slaves."[16] It would be well into the nineteenth century before Liberia could declare itself wholly free of any slave trading.

Cuffe's plan today appears anything but revolutionary. The idea of settling blacks in Africa was hardly novel. The British pioneered with Sierra Leone. But, the notion of the settlers redeeming "Africa from the evils of the slave trade" by helping Africans develop a viable economy as an alternative and introducing them to "the blessings of Western Christian civilization"—and, once "firmly established," becoming "missionaries to spread Western civilization and Christianity throughout all of Africa"—added a vastly different dimension, one that would fuel future back-to-Africa movements.[17]

More basically, having black people organize, own, and manage such an operation in the context of eighteenth- and early nineteenth-century Africa appeared radical and unworkable to many, if not most, whites. Nevertheless, Cuffe managed to enlist a suitable collection of Sierra Leoneans (all of whom were black immigrant settlers), and the Friendly Society, "A Society for the Purpose of Encouraging the Black Settlers of Sierra Leone, and the Natives of Africa generally, in the Cultivation of their Soil by the Sale of their Produce," was born.[18]

> The newly formed group promptly drafted a petition calling for encouragement to all our Breatheren who may Come from the British Colonies or from america and Become farmers in order to help us Cultivate the Land...to our foreign Breatheren who may have Vessels...to Establish Commerce in Sierra Leone... [and to] all those who may Establish whalefishery in the Colony of Sierra Leone.[19]

Cuffe's plan to trade in Sierra Leone, however, had to wait on the receipt of a license from London. He had expected it to have already arrived in Freetown. The permit would come from the British Privy Council through the Africa Institution in which Quaker Friend William Allen, who became one of Cuffe's closest friends, was a leading participant. But now he could do little more than wait. As weeks dragged on into months, however, Cuffe, crestfallen, gave up and readied the *Traveller* for the trip back home. He could sense his dream slipping away, turning to little more than a wisp of smoke that might have wafted up from the pipe of a fellow seaman—not one of his crew, of course, since he himself assiduously avoided tobacco and strong spirits and would allow none of his crew these pleasures.

But literally at the last moment, the long-awaited license arrived. William Allen, in a letter written March 7, 1811, notified Cuffe that Britain's Privy Council had granted him a six-month trading license.[20] With it also came an invitation to visit London and elaborate his proposed project to interested parties there. Cuffe by now was well known among the Friends and other abolitionists in Britain. And his voyage had stirred up much curiosity about this unusual man—educated, articulate, successful, and black—in an even wider audience.

A now buoyant captain and crew finished unloading the *Traveller* and reloading her with goods for England. On May 10, 1811, they sailed out of Freetown bound for Liverpool. The voyage took two months. Their arrival on June 12 sparked sufficient interest to merit notice in the *Times* of London and to attract crowds of curious onlookers.

> The brig Traveller, newly arrived at Liverpool, from Sierra Leone, is perhaps the first vessel that ever reached Europe, entirely owned and navigated by Negroes.

[The article goes on to note Cuffe's lineage and give a brief account of his life and mission:]

> When Mr. Clarkson's History of the Abolition of the Slave Trade fell into his [Cuffe's] hands, it awakened all the powers of his mind to consideration of the obligation and the duties he owed to his people. With the views of benefitting the Africans, he made a voyage to Sierra Leone, and with this same object has come to England.[21]

The black Quaker sea captain made his way to London where he stayed with William Allen virtually as a member of the family. Within a little more than three months, he managed to impress a wide circle of highly placed and influential Britons sufficiently to win their backing for his venture. Though he does not betray his feelings in his journal or letters, Cuffe must have enjoyed a great sense of accomplishment, and, notwithstanding his Quaker-bred humility, a modest measure of pride and satisfaction in what he, a black man, had been able to achieve in a white man's world. It doubtless was with a much-lightened heart that he returned to Liverpool and made ready to return to Sierra Leone.

He would remember these months fondly and with gratitude for the treatment—the affection and respect—he received during his stay in England. Years afterward, drawing upon the scriptures, he lovingly wrote to his English hosts, "I was a stranger and you took me in."[22] For him it was a redeeming experience. But he also would remember the contrast between his treatment in England and the treatment that white society generally meted out to men of color in America.

On September 20, 1811, Cuffe and his crew sailed back to Sierra Leone. The *Traveller*, laden with British goods, hove into Freetown on the twelfth of November. They spent the next two months disposing of their cargo and procuring items to carry back to America. Cuffe devoted much time working with his Friendly Society.

The time in Sierra Leone, though, posed difficulties for Cuffe and his men. The colonial administration proved less than friendly. Many of the men became ill. (Cuffe serves up a detailed description of the leeches used to treat his nephew, Thomas Wainer, who suffered an unspecified but serious and persistent malady.) After the sick recovered sufficiently, the *Traveller* was loaded, and on February 20, 1812, Cuffe and his colored seamen departed for home. Fortunately, the voyage back proved to be far less exciting than the outward trip. As the brig neared home, however, Cuffe received disturbing news from passing ship captains. Cuffe and party had been away for more than a year. In that time, relations between the United States and Great Britain had deteriorated to the point that the two nations were on the edge of war with one another. Congress had banned trade with Great Britain.

A US revenue cutter intercepted the *Traveller* not far from Westport. In a letter Cuffe related how on April 20 he "arived off" the American coast. Upon being informed about the US embargo on trade with Britain and ban on importing British products, he left his *Traveller* at sea and took

> a pilate Boat to the office to See what Safe Steep might be taken. But before I Reached the Traveller the Revenue Cutter…took hur… in and Libelled her for Condemnation for Coming from an English Colony With a Cargo. I was under the Necessetty of proceeding to Congress for Redress which was a Distance of a bout 500 miles.[23]

Once again Cuffe's enterprise appeared doomed and his dream threatened. He resolved to take his case to Washington, DC—to the secretary of state, even to the president of the United States. A colored man? Unheard of! Impossible! But Cuffe immediately began preparing for his mission by activating his network of Quaker Friends. He obtained letters of support from prominent traders and religious and political leaders. In Rhode Island, for example, they included the governor, a judge, and a former member of Congress. In each city he visited on his way—New York, Philadelphia, Baltimore—he got support from leaders, churchmen, and educators who established societies for "promotion of the good of Africa." He stayed with Friends everywhere.

Travel was not easy—especially for a man of color. On April 25, 1812, Cuffe started out on this memorable journey. He made his way from Bannister Wharf at Newport to Providence, Rhode Island. Here, he enlisted the support of Obadiah Brown and his father, Moses (members of the prominent Quaker family for whom Brown University is named), and other important Rhode Island personages.[24] After spending two days in Providence and another in New Haven, Connecticut, Cuffe wrote in his journal (again, in his own spelling and punctuation) that he

> arived at New York Stage office 4 oclock this morning. Paid passage to Philadelphia $8. Set off at 5 oclock Arived at John James in Philadelphia at 8 in the Evening. [He and Friend James dined at a tavern that was the stage stop, where] the Servent came and towled me my Dinner Was Ready in the other Room. I told him as I Rode With the Company I Could Eat With them So We all Set Down and Eat at one tabel. This is the only objection I meet With. There apeard to be a Southward man there not of the Best Caretor [character] Who Seemed to be Goodeal tried But We got through Well.[25]

The traveler rose at four o'clock the next morning only to find the stage had left an hour earlier. He managed to get on the mail coach at seven o'clock and arrived in Baltimore, 120 miles distant, at 5:00 a.m. the next day. Fare: eight dollars. "At 6," he continued, "Left Baltimore for Washington paid 4$ for a passage 42 miles and paid half Dollar for 1 hour Lodging." Cuffe arrived finally in the nation's capital eight hours later on May 1, 1812. He summarized the trip thus: "I left Providence at 10 Sunday morning arived at Washington" after eighty-five hours, "or 3 day and 13 hours" of travel, plus fifteen hours stopped "by the Way."[26]

Cuffe stayed in Washington with another Quaker, Samuel Hutchinson, who accompanied him to his interviews.

His journal entry May 2, 1812, reads, "Made the inquirey Which a peared to be most advisebel and at 11 o'clock Waited on the President [James Madison] accompenied With my friend Samuel Hutchinson." After leaving the president, Cuffe and Hutchinson called on "the Sectary [secretary of the treasury, Albert Gallatin] and the others for whom he had letters. Everyone he met gave him favorable considerations and assurances "of an answer on Sunday 12 o'clock." Cuffe, the tourist, visited the House of Representatives and found its "Construction Was magnificent." Summing up, he reported, "This Day Was a Very Rainey Day but I got Very Well Long With Business All Peopel apeared Very freindly indeed."[27]

Although the black sea captain must have greatly impressed those he met, his rather bland, matter-of-fact journal entries (he labels them "transactions") betray nothing of himself but the most modest and unpretentious of men. He described his meeting with Secretary Gallatin in his May 4 journal entry:

> The Sectary Very openly and freely invited us to Set Down. He then told me that all of my property Was Remitted or to be Restored to me With out Reserve. I thanke him for his Services. He then observed to me anything the government Could do to Promote the Good Cause that I was Presuing...they Would Certenly be alwas Readey to Render me their help.[28]

Not only did Cuffe manage to retrieve his boat and cargo that had been seized, he managed to obtain assurances from the highest levels of the US government of support in his efforts to bring down the slave trade and lay down the foundation for colonization. Contemporary descriptions of Cuffe somehow fail to capture the power of his personality and the gift this remarkable black sea captain possessed for gaining the confidence—on even brief acquaintance—of highly placed white gentlemen.

Cuffe's trip back to Westport probably proved as strenuous as his journey outward to Washington. But apparently basking in the warmth of his success in the capital, he refused to let anything disturb him, not even another attempt by a white fellow traveler to "put him in his place." Cuffe relates in his journal that he left Washington the morning of May 5. Having arrived and boarded the stage before the other passengers, he took the back seat when

> in Came a busseling powder headed man With Starn Countenance [who ordered him to] 'Come away from the Seat.' I was no Starter and Set Still...He then said "I wants to put my umbrella in the Box." I arose he put his umbrella in. He then Saith "You must go out of this for there is a Lady Comeing in." I...took my seat. He took his beside me but Shew much evel Contempt. At Length the Women and Girl made their appearance. I then arose and invited the Women in the after Seat Saying "We always give away to accomadate the women."[29]

Not the end of the story, though. Stopping at a tavern on the way to Baltimore, Cuffe encountered William Hunter, a member of Congress. Hunter apparently knew, or knew of Cuffe and engaged him freely in conversation. This was not lost on Cuffe's fellow passenger who, when back on the coach, "became Loveing and openly accosted me, 'Captain take the after Seat.'" The black captain thanked him but politely declined.[30]

Cuffe had rescued his African goods. Selling them was another thing. The war that for several years had threatened finally exploded into actual hostilities when on June 19, 1812, the United States declared war with Britain. Not every state agreed. Caleb Strong, the governor of Massachusetts, proclaimed a day of fasting to protest a war "against the nation from which we are descended." Connecticut acting governor John Cotton Smith vowed to curb any support for the war, which he claimed was unconstitutional. New England merchants continued to supply the British in Canada in defiance of the US trade ban. But trade still was limited, and the economy struggled. Paul Cuffe felt the financial pinch. Of even greater concern, however, his Africa project languished.

Nevertheless, the unrelenting Cuffe, emboldened by his earlier success in Washington, decided to make an even nervier move: a proposal for sending black Americans to Africa. After enlisting support from prominent Quakers in Washington, Philadelphia, Providence, and New Bedford, he addressed a memorial petition to Congress. The petition, dated June 16, 1813, asked for that body's permission, if the British government also agreed, for a vessel to transport from the United States to Sierra Leone "such persons and families as may be inclined to go, as also some articles of provisions together with implements of husbandry and machinery for some mechanic arts and to Bring back such of the Natives productions of that country as may be wanted."

He explained that he felt a moral imperative to help curb "the practice of his bretheren of the African Race in selling their fellow creatures into a state of slavery for life" and to give his "time and his property in visiting" Africa "to promote the improvement to civilization of the Africans."[31]

Given the ongoing war with Britain and the fact that Sierra Leone was a British colony, the likelihood he would be given approval was scant. Still he plowed ahead. He left for Washington in December 1813 carrying his petition and letters from leading New Bedford business figures to the Massachusetts congressional delegation. Cuffe also sent his plan to "the People of Colour in Baltimore and Philadelphia, New York and Boston."

Cuffe's petition, "introduced in the form of a bill, quickly passed the Senate." In the House, however, the bill stirred up "a much heated debate." Supporters argued it would hasten "the emigration of blacks, a part of our population which we could well spare." Opponents, though equally "anxious to rid the country of blacks," objected that Cuffe's plan would aid "the British enemy" (with whom the country, after all, was still at war). "The bill was finally defeated in the House of Representatives by a vote of 65 to 72."[32]

His petition was not without precedent. Four Massachusetts slaves in 1773 tried—and failed—to persuade the Massachusetts General Court (the colony's legislative body) to pass legislation allowing slaves to be paid for their labor one day each week so they "could procure money to transport [themselves] to some part of the Coast of Africa, where [they proposed] a settlement."[33] After the Revolutionary War, a committee of "African Lodge No. 1" in Boston, headed by Grand Master Prince Hall, petitioned the Massachusetts legislature in 1787 to assist them and other free blacks to return to Africa.[34] The legislature also turned down their request.

Even though his appeal failed, it further enhanced Cuffe's reputation and stature as a reformer. But his African dream once again would at best be delayed indefinitely—perhaps even permanently. He busied himself trying to sell the goods he had brought back from Sierra Leone, difficult because of the anemic market induced by the War of 1812. The financial difficulties of a business associate, a Friend, worried him. He labored at rebuilding the Westport Friends meeting house and occupied himself with family, orphan children, and education for blacks.

―⁂―

But on December 24, 1814, the sky brightened for Cuffe. Negotiators John Adams and British lord James Gambier shook hands in Ghent, Belgium, after signing the treaty ending the War of 1812. When news of the signing finally reached the American coast on February 11, 1815, Cuffe's spirits revived—even if his financial condition didn't. He had been forced to agree to the sale of the largest vessel in his fleet, *Alpha*, at a loss. The economy remained moribund. Family illness and sadness also threatened but failed to dampen his resolve. He set to work planning for his delayed voyage, this epic voyage that would inaugurate his dream of rescuing Africa and Africans—wherever they resided in the world.

In April 1815 he wrote John Murray Jr., a member of the New York Friends Meeting and Abolition Society, "I have written to the London African Institution [that was expected to finance six to eight of the immigrants] and have to wate for their answer before I can proceed with propriety which I think may be in time to Sail in the 10th mo. [October 1815]."[35] Cuffe also waited for the usual letter from the Westport Monthly Meeting of Friends giving their support. (It didn't arrive until November 16.)

Interest in the endeavor grew, however, and letters streamed in to Cuffe. One correspondent inquired about employment on one of his vessels. The captain probably scared him away when he listed the qualities he expected in each of his crewmen: "temperate in all things—not to Swearing, Tatling, drunkeness nor quarelsom." Hardly the picture of the typical nineteenth-century seaman. Men at the recently founded Andover Theological Seminary in Andover, Massachusetts, also took a keen interest. One of them, Samuel J. Mills, would later become known as the "father of foreign missions" and play a key role in the creation of the American Colonization Society and the founding of Liberia.

Among the black applicants seeking to go to Sierra Leone, Cuffe chose thirty-eight: nine families, eighteen heads of families, and twenty children whose ages ranged from eight months to eleven years. They came from Philadelphia, New York, Newport, and the largest number from Boston. He looked for those who possessed skills that could contribute to the Friendly Society. He later reported to William Allen, however, "The people I took over to Africa were all common labers [laborers], they were no mechaniks but are inclined to cultivate the land."[36]

Cuffe elaborated on his aims and thinking in a letter dated April 19, 1815, to Nathan Lord of Andover Theological Seminary. In it he wrote,

> My wishes is that good may grow out of all that I do in order to improve my fellow Countrymens condition. Firstly, we are the decendance [descendants] of that country [Africa] brought away by violence, sold in hard slavery, deprived of enjoying our liberty the natural rites of man. Now if we could return into the country of our ancestors and carry the seeds of civilization in return for this great ingery [injury] that she has so long groaned under and thus for her to injoy a peaceable prevelige of agriculture and Commeras as the other historyen Nations do injoy it doth feel to me that this would be the greatest blessing that that countery could be favored with.[37]

On December 10, 1815, the *Traveller* once again set sail for Freetown, this time heavily laden with thirty-eight crowded and scared passengers, including twenty children. According to a letter Paul Cuffe sent his friend William Rotch Jr. after he arrived in Sierra Leone on February 3, 1815, their fright was well justified. Cuffe wrote that he had arrived safely "after a passage of 56 days. I Exspearenced 20 days of the most Trimondous weather that I have ever remember exspearencing of. The Ship and Crew Seemingly were in jeopardy, but through mercy we ware preserved."[38]

For Cuffe's voyage, an invoice noted that provisioner E. J. Winchester put the following provisions aboard the brig: "twenty bbls No 1 Beef, One ditto Mess Beef and six bbls No 1 Pork, the quality we most sincerely believe may be relied on as very good." Since the cost of the voyage would come out of his pocket, Captain Cuffe understandably took particular interest in the prices of the provisions: pork $25 per barrel (total $150), No. 1 beef $12 per barrel (total $240), and one mess beef $15 per barrel (total $150). Including inspection fee and truckage, the total came to $410.[39] The captain also purchased an extensive list of articles for the ship's medicine chest. The items, the cost of which totaled $21.71, offer a fascinating window on early nineteenth-century medical practice. They included such items as "½ Flowers Sulphur, 52 oz Powd [Powdered] Rhubarb, 24 Tartar Pukes, 2 oz Laudanum Pills, 10 doz Merc[cury] Pills, 3 oz Chamomile, 1 oz Paregoric + phl [phial], 10 doz Soap Pills, 12 oz Cream of Tartar, 2/20 Blister plasters, 1 Bottle Castor Oil, 12 oz Sp [Spirit] turpentine, 8 papers Snak Root, 1 Dnis Syringe, 1 Lock and key."[40]

Captain Cuffe noted the passengers "was well received both by the Govenor [of Sierra Leone] and the Friendly Society." However, the authorities had not permitted him to land his cargo of "tobacco Soap candels nor navel Stores, and the duty on the few items he was allowed to land proved so high, he complained, "the expenses of the Voyage will fawl Very heavy on me."[41] "The

Africa Society in London had only agreed to cover the expenses of eight passengers. Cuffe paid for the other thirty, probably at least $4,000, out of his own pocket."[42]

The government allocated each family a lot in town and fifty acres of land two miles from town to farm. The warm reception they received bolstered Cuffe's hope that the new group would be able to help expand Friendly Society trade. (However, they needed, according to Cuffe, "men mecanicks," specifically a millwright "to Construct and manage a Sawmill also a rice mill," and a watch repairer.)[43]

The *Traveller* and Captain Cuffe arrived back in New York on May 28. The fifty-four-day voyage was easy compared to the outward one, although the trip proved disastrous financially for Cuffe. But he still began to think about another voyage—and an even greater scheme. Biographer Sheldon H. Harris maintains that sometime during "1816—the precise date cannot be determined"—Cuffe's vision had taken on "an even greater dimension, for it now became a mass emigration plan for blacks."[44]

Cuffe wrote to a friend in September that "a thought [had] passed [his] mind whether the America's Government, at Some future day when the liberation of Slavery become more General, Would not be prevailed upon to Settel a Colony in Africa, where this peopel Could be Colonized in from time to time as the occasion may require."[45]

Pressure was rapidly escalating to do something before the South exploded in a holocaust of black and white. A growing paranoia hung like a blanket of fear over much, if not most of the nation. Not even New York City was exempt. Cries for action to resolve the "race problem"—no longer just slavery—mounted with growing urgency. In addition to Cuffe, a number of clerics, apparently inspired by the Second Great Awakening, took on the cause.

A New Jersey Presbyterian minister named Robert Finley, moved by the plight of free Negroes, concluded that their salvation lay in resettlement outside the United States. Samuel C. Aiken, who had succeeded Mills and Nathan Lord at the Andover Theological Seminary, wrote Cuffe on July 23, 1816, asking for "all information possible respecting that part of our race, with whom the dealings of God have apparently been very mysterious, I mean the Africans." He underlined the urgency of taking action, saying,

> It is certain that something must be done and done soon for our African brethren in his country. They labour under a cruel and insupportable burden. They are rapidly multiplying without the means of instruction, and without those enjoyments and comforts of life, which but they are deprived of, but which they legally inherited from the Common Father of us all.[46]

Mills and Finley joined forces in a growing conviction that colonization was the only answer. Cuffe agreed. In a letter to Mills, he chided southern slave owners for their support of slavery and immoral behavior with their slaves but was hopeful that colonization could do some good and prevent the bloodshed and violence he felt were imminent. He had heard "by the publick paper that The Southern Slave holders [were] much alarmed on account of the Africans rising," and added that he "thought it would have Been prudent for them to have Early Seen to this."[47] These alarms, however, would only intensify with each passing year. And with each report, the fear grew.

> Years later in 1831 George Washington's niece and Martha's granddaughter, Eleanor Custis Lawrence, of Woodlawn, Virginia, vividly captured something of this unrequited fear. She penned an appeal to the mayor of Boston, Harrison Gray Otis, to suppress William Lloyd Garrison's abolitionist newspaper *The Liberator* after Nat Turner's aborted uprising. Her

fear was palpable when she warned, "It is like a smothered volcano—we know not when, or where, the flame will burst forth, but we know that death in the most repulsive form awaits us."[48]

Colonization—resettling blacks from America to Africa in a back-to-Africa movement—was rapidly gaining momentum. Finley and Mills launched a campaign to obtain support for a plan to ship free Negroes to Sierra Leone. Their efforts finally paid off when a group of prominent Americans met in Washington in December 1816 to form the American Society for Colonizing the Free People of Color of the United States.

They corresponded with Paul Cuffe to benefit from his wealth of experience and sage advice as well as to solicit his support. Cuffe wrote Finley a lengthy letter on January 8, 1817, answering questions about Sierra Leone and other possible sites for colonization. Cuffe noted that Sierra Leone area might be satisfactory for "small beginnings," but for a "general removal of the People of colour," the southern part of Africa looked "most favourable." Also, "the great River Congo which lieth near the Equator it is said...has extensive Population, and land fertile." The best arrangement to "draw off the coloured Citizens" would be "a spot fixed on the coast of Africa, and another in the United States of America." This second site, somewhere west of the Louisiana Purchase, would serve "those who felt no identity with Africa."[49]

Cuffe jumped at Finley and Mills's request that he accompany them "in going to England and Africa to seek a Place where the People of Colour might be colonized" and to help "in any way, which may forward" the plan for colonization.[50] After all, that was what his dream was all about. He commenced to busy himself with preparations for this all-important trip. But Paul Cuffe was not destined to see his promised land, a colony in Africa of American blacks; Liberia was still far away.

—⚉—

Cold winds blowing off Buzzards Bay and up the Westport River to his farmhouse, which usually braced him and boosted his spirits, seemed instead this winter to seep into his bones and innards, sucking out his vigor. Even the summer of 1816 failed Cuffe. He wrote in a postscript to his esteemed friend William Allen, "We have experanced a Very cold Summer past. We had frosts every month in the Summer."[51] (This was the notorious "Year Without a Summer.") And the sharply negative reactions of many free blacks, provoked by the establishment of the American Colonization Society at the end of 1816, must have saddened him.

Cuffe busily occupied himself with correspondence about colonization and the more immediate mundane concern of bringing his accounts up to date, insuring there were no unpaid bills. He wrote good friends, conveying his gratitude and affection to them. It was apparent that Paul Cuffe was failing. But the dream still possessed him. In his next-to-last letter, left unfinished, he wrote to good friend James Forten that he had "been asked the question again and again concerning Colonizing the free Peopel of Colour."

Continuing, he said, "If the free peopel of Colour would exert themselves more and more in industry and honesty, it would" help greatly toward liberating those still enslaved. He concluded with a prayer. "May the father of all mercies and the god of peace to influence the hearts of the Sons and daughters of the race of Africa, that they may Stretch forth their arms to God, and unite in celebrating."[52]

His large family gathered about him. Admirers and other well-wishers sent messages of hope. But Captain Paul Cuffe, successful black Quaker sea captain and dreamer of a better world for Africans and people of color wherever, died September 7, 1817. Lengthy, laudatory obituaries appeared in newspapers.

One obituary read,

> At Westport on the 7th inst. PAUL CUFFE, a very respectable man of colour, in the 59th year of his age. A descendant of Africa, he overcame by native strength of mind, and firm adherence to principle, the prejudices with which her descendants are too generally viewed. Industrious, temperate and prudent, his means of acquiring property, small at first, were gradually increased; and the strict integrity of his word gained him numerous friends, to whom he never gave occasion to regret the confidence they had placed in him...Grave, humble, and unassuming in his deportment, he was remarkable for great civility and sound discretion...He has left a widow and several children to lament the loss of an affectionate husband and parent.[53]

After a well-attended funeral service, he was buried in the graveyard adjacent to the Westport Meeting House. He lies in a somewhat obscure location near a stone wall at the far edge of the property. But at the front and side of the meetinghouse stands an imposing rectangular stone memorial erected in 1913 by his great-grandson Horatio P. Howard. The inscription reads, "In memory of Captain Paul Cuffe, Patriot, Navigator, Educator, Philanthropist, Friend and Noble Character."

Paul Cuffe reputedly left an estate of $20,000 (a very large sum in today's dollars) and a reputation of being one of America's earliest black entrepreneurs. But he also left a less tangible, more precious legacy: a dream of the slave trade's destruction, of the end of slavery in the United States, of the reawakening of Africa with the return there of black American settlers, and of the acceptance in this country of all its people as equals. It was an unfinished dream. But he—a self-educated half black—had taken on the charge as his life's mission. The task now would fall to the newly created, but white-dominated American Colonization Society. Many believed resolution of America's "Negro problem" lay in the balance. But it would turn out to prove a quest not easily achieved, a struggle that would not end quickly—or even finally.

CHAPTER 3

The American Colonization Society

—⚒—

ON DECEMBER 21, 1816, SNOW covered the ground in the city of Washington in the federal District of Columbia. It was Saturday, the sky still overcast and hinting of possibly more snow. The notice in the *National Intelligencer,* Washington's principal newspaper, read, "A meeting of those gentlemen who are friendly to the promotion of a plan for colonizing the free blacks of the United States, is requested at Davis's Hotel, in the city of Washington, on Saturday the 21st day of December, at 11 o'clock, A.M."

—⚒—

Davis's Hotel on the northwest corner of Sixth Street and Pennsylvania Avenue NW stood not far from the Capitol (still not fully restored from the 1814 British invasion) in an area bustling with activity. Hotels, taverns, restaurants, shops, and boarding houses lined the avenue, Washington's Main Street. Shoppers crowded nearby Center Market, the city's largest and most diversified mart. Nearby, a handsome new brick building at the northwest corner of Pennsylvania Avenue and Third Street shortly would house the Saint Charles Hotel.

The Saint Charles would cater to a prestigious group of customers, especially from the South. This was understandable, since visitors could keep their slaves in a series of six arched basement cells, each thirty feet long, complete with heavy iron door and iron rings embedded in the walls. Before the trade became illegal in the District of Columbia in 1850, these and four other known slave pens in Washington held most of the slaves purchased in the city. The captives were frequently sold at auction, together with furniture, carpets, and household goods, at the regular auction houses of the city. After 1850 the Saint Charles even guaranteed to reimburse owners at values ranging from $200 to $2,000 each, depending on age, sex, skill, and health for any of their slaves who escaped.

On this Saturday morning in 1816, the array of prominent white gentlemen filing into Davis's focused on the nation's free blacks. The Reverend Robert Finley stood at the side of his bother-in-law, Elias B. Caldwell, greeting each one warmly. Caldwell, with whom the reverend was staying, lived not far away in an imposing home on Pennsylvania Avenue across from the Capitol. He was clerk of the US Supreme Court, appointed while the court still sat in Philadelphia. After moving to Washington, he gained prominence during the War of 1812 when he rushed back from the battle at Bladensburg to save the court library, moving it to his home.

Finley and Caldwell were the prime architects of this day's meeting at the hotel. Finley was highly esteemed and widely recognized as one of the nation's leading preachers. To those who met him, he "projected an air of Christian love and benevolence, utterly devoid of artifice or pretense." His nineteenth-century biographer, Isaac V. Brown, painted him as a virtual saint: "He possessed in a remarkable degree, the faculty of inspiring confidence, esteem and regard for him, in the minds of others, young and old, cultivated and plain, acquaintances and strangers."[1] The contrast, when compared with the mien of many of the distinguished and powerful filing into the room, could not have been starker.

Brown found the reverend's physical presence equally compelling:

> [His] person exceeded the ordinary size of men; he was about six feet in stature; erect and well proportioned; wide across the shoulders and deep throughout the breast; grave and contemplative in his appearance; deliberate and dignified in his movements. The lineaments of his face were peculiar, and the expression of his countenance was striking. His hair, naturally black, was considerably whitened by the lapse of years and the toils of life. His forehead was unusually capacious and commanding. His eyes were blue, marked with a mixture of mildness and severity. His cheek bones were high and prominent. His nose, above the common size, was on the Roman model. His whole mien exhibited traces of Scotch extraction.[2]

Roberet Finley, age forty-four, now stood at the threshold of an undertaking that would define his life. He had realized that to fully validate his time on this earth in God's eyes, he must undertake "some great and benevolent scheme," one "that would make a deep impression—set a noble example—assume a national character," one that would help "largely to mitigate the sufferings of some aggrieved portion of the human family...He fixed his eye...on the colored people in these United States."[3]

It had been an ardurous journey, but he had finally arrived.

Finley started life in a devout Presbyterian family of Princeton, New Jersey, on February 15, 1772. His father, James, a Glasgow yarn merchant before immigrating to America, supplied clothing for Washington's soldiers in the Revolutionary War. Soon after arriving in the United States, James became a friend and admirer of Reverend John Witherspoon, the distinguished theologian, anti-slavery activist, and long-time president of the College of New Jersey (later Princeton University). In turn, Witherspoon would prove to be an important influence on young Robert. Scholarly, precocious Robert entered the College of New Jersey when only eleven years old. "For a youth of his age," he was seen to be "uncommonly grave and judicious in his deportment." [4] After graduating with a bachelor of arts degree when sixteen, he began teaching in the Princeton grammar school.

He studied theology and obtained his doctor of divinity degree from the college. On June 16, 1795, at the age of twenty-three, he was ordained pastor of the Basking Ridge Presbyterian Church in New Jersey. It was the start of an illustrious career that would bring him to the forefront of the American religious scene.

Finley continued to minister to his Basking Ridge congregation for almost twenty-two years. Besides the renown he would gain from preaching, Reverend Finley also expanded a class of ten boys taught in his home into the Basking Ridge Academy. Isaac Brown wrote that "for popularity, usefulness and real excellence during twenty years," many believed "no classical seminary on this continent" had ever surpassed this academy.[5] (Finley could not have guessed that one of his students, from a prominent Princeton family named Stockton, would play a seminal role in bringing to life what became Finley's passion —Liberia.)

The young reverend, caught up in the Second Great Awakening's evangelical imperative to save souls, embarked upon preaching tours and revivals, traveling from church to church. He vowed to visit all families "living in the mountains and barreen out-skirts of his congregation, " sometimes on foot for three or four days at a time in the winter of 1815-–16. He felt compelled to deliver his message of "sin and "danger" but "pardon and salvation, through the blood of Christ." So strenuous were his exertions that in the spring of 1816 "his nervous system presented evidence of great debiity and disorders."[6]

Still he was driven by a compulsion to do greater works.

> The Second Great Awakening was the second of three or four waves of religious revival in North America in the eighteenth and nineteenth centuries. It began around 1790 and lasted until the middle of the nineteenth century. During this time, Protestant ministers led widespread revivals. Their powerful preaching prompted a deep feeling of personal spiritual guilt and redemption in individuals and the need for personal commitment. The movement was closely related to other reform movements, notably temperance and the abolition of slavery. It also spurred a remarkable outburst of missionary activity, directed particularly to Africa and Asia. The First Great Awakening marked the first time African Americans accepted Christianity in large numbers.

"The longer I live," Finley wrote a friend in February 1816, and "see the wretchedness of men, the more I admire the virtues of those, who…labor to execute plans" for their relief. For a free black, "everything about his condition including his color is against him."[7] *And* Finley's "great and benevolent scheme"? Founding a colony for people of color. He explained to friends that he had been meditating on such a scheme for years. He recognized, however, that colonization was "considered by most men so visionary a project that no good could be expected from a public meeting."[8]

Finley opened correspondence with Cuffe (although there is no record of their having ever met in person). He also explored the idea with friends in Princeton, New York City, and Philadelphia. He argued, "We would be cleared of them; we would send to Africa a population partially civilized and Christianized."[9] They would better both their lives and the lives of their brother blacks. The Basking Ridge parson published his plan in a pamphlet, *Thoughts on the Colonization of Free Blacks*, which caught the attention of a number of influential persons, including President Madison and members of Congress.

Finley enlisted his brother-in-law Caldwell and "Star Spangled Banner" author Francis Scott Key to help drum up support. Washington's *National Intelligencer* newspaper helped spread his word, even affording him an office to use when in Washington. In a December 16 account, the paper reported on a meeting held in Princeton on November 6, 1816:

> The Reverend Mr. Finley read a paper purporting to be a memorial [statement of facts] and petition to the Legislature of New Jersey...[that tended to] show the expediency and practicability of colonizing on the coast of Africa or elsewhere, the Free Blacks in the different States, who may feel disposed to emigrate to the land of their fathers.[10]

The meeting resolved that the New Jersey legislature should lobby Congress to adopt some plan for colonizing free blacks. Toward the end of November 1816, Finley headed for Washington, DC, where he discussed his scheme with important public officials, including President James Madison. Virginians especially were enthusiastic. The Virginia House of Delegates—doubtless influenced by their westward-looking Thomas Jefferson—had resolved that their executive, John Mercer, correspond with the president of the United States to obtain territory "upon the shore of the North Pacific, or at some other place...[not within the United States or its territory] to serve as an asylum for...persons of color now free, and [for those freed in the future]."[11]

The stage was set for the December 21 meeting in Davis's Hotel. Like other expectant fathers, Reverend Finley doubtless felt nervous about the birth of his bold endeavor, an American colonization. The Honorable Henry Clay, distinguished senator from Kentucky, was called upon to chair the conclave. Thomas Dougherty, Esq., was appointed secretary. The chairman opened the meeting with an address, followed by a long speech from Reverend Finley's brother-in-law. Clay eloquently declaimed,

> Can there be a nobler cause than that which, while it proposes to rid our own country of a useless and pernicious, if not dangerous portion of its population, contemplates the spreading of the arts of civilized life, and the possible redemption from ignorance and barbarism of a benighted quarter of the globe?[12]

A report a scant two years earlier (that turned out to be false) that blacks were plundering and burning when Washington's population fled the British probably fired the imaginations of some in the meeting.

Caldwell, however, underscored the project's missionary aspect, how it would, through the repatriated black Americans, introduce civilization and the Christian religion into Africa. "It is the hope of redeeming millions of people from the lowest state of superstition and ignorance, and restoring them to the knowledge and worship of the true God."[13] Various friends of the project presented their views. Resolutions called for a committee to draw up a constitution, another to present a memorial to Congress.

To insure that the purpose of the enterprise not be misconstrued, two prominent southern slave owners, the Honorable Robert Wright and John Randolph, offered remarks the assemblage adopted unanimously: "all connections of the proposition with the emancipation of slaves, present or future, is explicitly disclaimed."[14]

Befitting the magnitude of its mission and the importance of its members, the American Society for Colonizing the Free People of Color of the United States was formally organized in the Hall of the House of Representatives on December 28, 1816. The society's basic objective, according to the second article of its constitution, was

> To promote and execute a plan for colonizing (with their consent) the free people of colour residing in our country, in Africa, or such other place as Congress shall deem most expedient. And the Society shall act to effect this object in cooperation with the general [federal] government, and such of the States as may adopt regulations upon the subject.[15]

The society elected a slate of officers that reads like a Who's Who of southern aristocracy. As president the society chose the Honorable Bushrod Washington, associate justice of the US Supreme Court, squire of Mount Vernon, large slave owner (though he reportedly favored abolition), and George Washington's nephew. The thirteen vice presidents included Senator Henry Clay of Kentucky, Secretary of the Treasury William H. Crawford of Georgia, John Taylor of Virginia, General Andrew Jackson of Tennessee (who actually opposed colonization and was included without his consent), and Reverend Finley. Elias Caldwell was selected to serve as secretary. Congressmen Daniel Webster and John Randolph, Francis Scott Key, and president-to-be John Tyler were prominent members.

Conspicuously absent was any person of color. Not even Paul Cuffe attended the meeting. White southerners, dominated by large slaveholders, occupied many of the key positions in the organization. Clay's six-hundred-acre Ashland home in Kentucky, for example, employed fifty slaves, and John Randolph of Virginia "owned more than 8,000 acres of land, nearly 400 slaves."[16]

As one might imagine, the new society did not inspire a uniformly favorable reaction. Soon after the Washington meetings, the editor of the *New York Courier* wrote a piece in Negro dialect, which he signed "Sambo." In it he "suggested that if colonization was such a fine idea, why did not Henry Clay return to England or wherever his ancestors came from; he also suggested that Negroes remain in the United States and whites sail to Africa, and even proposed that blacks form an organization to facilitate the white exodus."[17]

The Reverend Finley, who would come to be called the "Father of the American Colonization Society," nonetheless could at last see his handiwork done. But it would be more than four years before one could actually count any significant results on African soil. After his success in Washington, he headed back to New Jersey, where he busied himself in helping organize a state auxiliary to the national colonization society.

Always prepared to take on noble and benevolent causes, even if difficult, Reverend Finley in April 1817 accepted the presidency of the University of Georgia (also known as Franklin College in those early years). Upon arriving in Athens (which clearly at that time did not yet live up academically to its Greek namesake), Finley was dismayed to find the college "at its last gasp—forgotten in the public mind, or thought of only to despair of it—neglected and deserted—the buildings nearly in a state of ruins—and the Trustees doubtful whether it can ever be recovered." The students numbered twenty-eight. And instead of his "large congregation," he now preached "to about fifty people."[18]

But the indomitable parson still could write a friend, "I thank the Lord my spirits do not sink, nor is my heart discouraged."[19] He undertook a whirlwind tour of the state to drum up support for the university. Unfortunately this time divine providence would not allow him to complete his task. Finley contracted a fever and died October 3, 1817, only one month after Paul Cuffe. He was buried in Athens in today's Jackson Street Cemetery. Ironically, neither of the two spiritual fathers of Liberia lived to see its founding. At the society's first annual meeting on January 1, 1818, Bushrod Washington, president, and Elias Caldwell, secretary (and Finley's brother-in-law), paid tributes to both Cuffe and Finley.

During its first years, the Colonization Society moved slowly and hesitatingly. Money was the problem. The society expected to obtain funding from the federal government to dispatch free blacks to Sierra Leone in following up on Paul Cuffe's work there. Such funds that it did receive came from a highly diverse collection of reformers—"temperance men, tract dispensers, strict Sabbath day enforcers, enemies of vice, and emancipationists who believed that combining transportation out of the country with liberation" would make it easier for those owners who were given over to freeing their slaves to do so.[20] The society mainly busied itself with investigations and exploratory missions and seeking free blacks willing to be trailblazers in the back-to-Africa movement.

To search out a suitable site, the organization in November 1817 enlisted an exceptional young cleric, Samuel John Mills, to explore Africa's western coast. Mills was born in Torringford, Connecticut, on April 21, 1783. While a student at Williams College in August 1806, he became inspired during a small prayer meeting with the idea of sending missionaries abroad. Two years later he organized a "Society of the Brethren," the first missionary society in the United States. Although its existence was kept secret, the membership grew and spread to other colleges. And in

1810 the American Board of Commissioners for Foreign Missions was established, earning Mills the title of "father of American foreign mission work."

After graduating from Andover Theological Seminary in 1812, Mills served as a missionary in the American West and Southwest and sparked the creation of the American Bible Society in May 1816 to distribute Bibles. Mills and Ebenezer Burgess sailed for Africa in early 1818 and spent two months reconnoitering part of Africa's west coast for the Colonization Society. They first visited England, where the Duke of Gloucester, chairman of the African Institution, received them warmly and gave them useful information about possible sites and a letter of introduction to the British governor of Sierra Leone, who proved equally helpful. From Freetown the two sailed north to the Gambia River and then to the southeast, where they visited Sherbro Island. There they met John Kizell, Paul Cuffe's partner in Africa. On their return voyage to the United States, Mills, however, became ill, and on June 16, 1818, he died at sea—one of what would be many American Colonization Society casualties.

Burgess returned to Washington October 22 and presented their lengthy report to the society. The president, Justice Bushrod Washington, in his address to the society January 8, 1820, asserted boldly that the report "must have satisfied every impartial mind that a territory upon the west coast [of Africa] sufficient in extent, and unexceptionable as to the fertility of its soil, the healthiness of its climate, and the abundance of its present products to supply the first wants of the Colony, may be obtained upon the most reasonable terms."[21]

Luckily, Washington—and Mills and Burgess—would not have to later face the society's first settlers who might well have wondered if they had been talking about the same continent on which the settlers had landed. But the society, encouraged sufficiently, decided to move ahead with the project.

The society's fortunes changed for the better when on the first of March 1819, the US Congress passed an act declaring slavers to be pirates, subject to the death penalty. Liberated captives would be turned over to the federal marshal of the District of Columbia or to some other agency for resettlement in Africa. The law appropriated $100,000 to maintain a naval presence off the African coast to intercept slave ships and to "effect arrangements" for resettling any Africans who were rescued. It was understood that President James Monroe would designate the American Colonization Society as the unofficial agency to implement the resettlement. The legislatures of Maryland, Tennessee, and Virginia lobbied hard in favor of the society.[22]

Almost a year would pass before the organization submitted a memorial (statement of facts and petition), written by a committee that included Francis Scott Key, to the Congress on February 10, 1820. The memorial made the case for colonization on two counts:

First, naval power alone, regardless of how considerable, could not stop the slave trade. The second point played on the fear already gripping the country of "the number of free people of color in the United States, and their rapid increase." If they continued "to increase in the same ratio," they would, "in the course of even a few years," make up a large part of the population.[23]

The committee pointed out that colonization would reduce the slave trade, as demonstrated by the British colony of Sierra Leone, and provide an avenue for reducing the nation's free black population. For the scheme to work, however, it was "most important...the Civilized people of color of this country...be connected with such an establishment." Their "industry, enterprise, and knowledge of agriculture" were necessary "to bring the benefits of civilization and Christianity to their African brothers." The memorial concluded by requesting authority for the government to provide financial and other aid to the Colonization Society to finish purchasing the land in west Africa "already stipulated for with the native kings and chiefs of Sherbro" and for establishing a colony there. In closing, the memorialists also asked that the society be incorporated by an act of Congress.[24]

The society's plan came close to floundering when Secretary of State John Quincy Adams argued that the law did not give the president authority to purchase land for a colony. Attorney General William Wirt, however, offered an opposing opinion that President Monroe readily accepted. He not only agreed to the recommendation regarding purchasing the land but made available vessels, a navy surgeon, and supplies as well.[25] Without the aid of the government, the society would have been hard pressed to finance its program; the panic of 1819 had dried up much of the private funding it had hoped to raise. Now, finally, the American Colonization Society was in business. But would it have any customers?

When Reverend Finley had returned to Princeton from the Colonization Society meetings in Washington, he stopped in Philadelphia to sample the sentiments of black leaders there. James Forten, a wealthy black sail maker friend of Paul Cuffe's, was one of them. According to Finley, Forten heartily supported colonization, arguing that blacks in the United States "faced a peculiarly oppressive situation...neither riches nor education could put them on a level with whites, and the more wealthy and the better informed any of them became, the more wretched they were made; for they felt their degradation more acutely." Moreover, Forten "gave it as his decided opinion that Africa was the proper place for a colony." Settling in any site close to whites would soon bring the blacks face to face again with the same "peculiarly oppressive situation."[26] Bishop Richard Allen, founder and first bishop of the African Methodist Episcopal Church (AME)

and another of Cuffe's friends, reportedly agreed fully, speaking "with warmth on...oppression that they suffer from the whites." He also "spoke warmly in favor of colonization in Africa—declaring that were he young he would go himself."[27]

Some days later, on January 24, the free Negroes of Richmond, Virginia, voiced the first public statement by free blacks on the issue. They endorsed colonization but expressed their preference to be "colonized in the most remote corner of the land of our nativity [the United States] to being exiled to a foreign country." Lott Cary, a prominent minister of the Baptist Church in Virginia and founder of the Richmond African Missionary Society, supported colonization in Africa. "I am an African [he explained], and in this country, however meritorious my conduct and respectable my character, I cannot receive the credit due either. I wish to go to a country where I shall be estimated by my merits, not by my complexion."[28] (In 1820 Cary departed for Africa, where he would serve as acting governor of Liberia in 1828.)

The Reverend Finley must have been elated at the friendly reception colonization and his American Colonization Society elicited from most black leaders. His euphoria, however, proved short lived. And had he been better schooled in the dynamics of black society in America, he would not have been surprised.

Late in January 1817, an estimated three thousand black men, virtually every black man in Philadelphia, attended a mass meeting at Reverend Allen's Bethel Church. They totally repudiated the idea of colonization. They also renounced the colonization society's founders for "the unmerited stigma attempted to be cast upon the free people of color...that they are a dangerous and useless part of the community."[29] When the chairman, "the same James Forten whom Finley had met with earlier," called for a vote on colonization, not one "aye" in favor was heard. The "nays" were so loud it "seemed as it would bring down the walls of the building." Another huge anti-colonization meeting on August 10 reaffirmed the opposition of Philadelphia's free blacks. Blacks also gathered in other major cities in the North to protest colonization.[30]

CULTURAL DIVISIONS AMONG FREE BLACK AMERICANS

Many supporters of colonization were surprised that America's blacks did not speak with the same voice on the subject. However, Professor Rhett S. Jones of Brown University maintains that the people of color in America enjoyed no common culture. The part of the country they lived in, as well as "different occupations, backgrounds, and religious and other beliefs produced a people who had different lifestyles."[31] They held different values, different views of the world and of how to deal with the race problem, particularly colonization. In the North, leaders had few direct links with the mass of free blacks. "Most prosperous blacks ran thriving businesses, including hotels, restaurants, barbershops, cabinet-makers' shops and the like. They often owned slaves and hired free blacks, and even white workers."[32]

The southern dialect, drinking, gambling, flamboyant dress, "sauntering gait, unrestrained singing and laughing" of the mass of Negroes in the cities, many of them recent arrivals, "set them apart from 'respectable' black society."[33] Similarly, free blacks living in the lower South "were more likely [than their black brethren elsewhere] to be skilled and prosperous and to enjoy the support of white patrons."[34]

But in the Chesapeake Bay area, where the largest number of free blacks lived, two-thirds resided in the countryside and worked in the lowest manual jobs such as laborers, mostly for whites, sometimes for Indians.[35] Moreover, while most blacks opposed slavery, some, mainly in the southern ports of New Orleans, Pensacola, Mobile, and Charleston, actually owned slaves themselves.

The most fundamental distinction though—one that cut across color, education, occupation, economic status, etc.—among free blacks turned on the acceptance or rejection of the cultural system constructed by white European Americans. The values of democracy, love, success, and happiness formed its foundation. It taught that "to achieve democracy, one ought to vote; to be successful, one ought to work hard."[36] Clearly the majority of blacks found this system of values irrelevant to their situation. But Paul Cuffe and other leaders and most members of the black elite believed in it.

Not only did they tell fellow blacks to work hard, practice thrift, discipline themselves, save their money, and educate their children, but they also followed these norms themselves. They argued that the best way for blacks to get ahead was to emulate whites; not only would this win them the respect of whites, but it also was the most certain route to success. Unsurprisingly, when such men advocated a return to Africa, it was with the idea that blacks who returned would teach Africans white ways. Christianity, hard work, democracy, civilization, and discipline were what blacks everywhere needed. The organizations that African Americans established, while they considered the special needs and poverty of most free blacks, were modeled on white organizations. In this spirit African Americans founded Masonic orders, schools, churches, and a variety of self-help institutions.[37]

Finley had met with black leaders, members of a small free-black "elite." What he and Paul Cuffe and others had not appreciated fully was that even this community did not speak with a single voice. Many of the black elite supported colonization and the American Colonization Society. Forten and Allen did, "but as the majority is decidedly against me," Allen wrote Paul Cuffe, "I am determined to remain silent, except as to my opinion which I freely give when asked."[38] Most of Philadelphia's relatively well-to-do black elite usually supported the back-to-Africa movement—but for recently freed slaves, not for themselves. Few had any desire to return to Africa themselves.

While the debate ignited controversy among the free black community, the American Colonization Society struggled along. After three years it still had landed not a single colonist in Africa. But President Monroe soon came to the rescue. In January 1820 he appointed Samuel Bacon as the US agent to oversee the repatriation of slaves liberated from traders by the navy; John N. Bankston was to be his assistant. Bacon, like most of the personnel dealing with American colonization, particularly those in the field, was a Protestant clergyman driven by a missionary spirit. Born in Sturbridge, Massachusetts, on July 22, 1781, he graduated from Harvard University and was ordained in the Episcopal ministry. The society appointed Samuel A. Crozer of Delaware County, Pennsylvania, as its agent. Bacon was ordered to load the US-chartered *Elizabeth* with the stores, materials, and artisans needed to construct barracks for three hundred people. For good measure the president also ordered the US frigate *Cyane* to accompany the *Elizabeth*.

On January 19 the *Elizabeth*, carrying Bacon, his brother Ephraim, and others, arrived in New York, where they continued preparing for sailing on the thirty-first. Notice had been given that the emigrants should assemble at the old African Zion Church at 1:00 p.m. and proceed to the ship. Throngs of local residents, excited at the prospect of seeing off the first contingent of black colonists to Africa (since Paul Cuffe's voyage), crowded the streets in such numbers that an alarmed Bacon recorded in his journal that they "with difficulty had prevented" the crowds of people "from trampling each other to death."[39]

The church, "weak and insecure," would not hold all the people by "2 or 3000." Bacon and the others told the crowd the service would be held on board the ship "at the foot of Cedar Wharf North River." He added that the wharf "was filled in 10 minutes." Bacon continued that he "made a short sermon from the balcony of a tavern & dismissed them immediately

& entreated them to go home. Some did but most of them remained." So, he "sent the women & children [passengers] over, quietly to the ship & then before the crowd...knew it or suspected it all got onboard."[40]

The loaded ship and eighty-six American emigrants (all the Colonization Society could enlist at that time, possibly because of a shortage of funds) and the three agents finally sailed on February 4. But not before another incident occurred. Bacon again: "Febry 4th Just as we were leaving the wharf 2 constable came on board & took away, John Inwarden & wife on a charge of theft [even though] they came well recommended."[41]

All of the eighty-six passengers but one listed themselves as freeborn. Forty came from New York; twenty-eight from Philadelphia. Nine named Virginia as the state from which they emigrated, and two each listed Maryland and the District of Columbia. Ages varied from infant to sixty-six years. More than half were between the ages of twenty and forty, six were below the age of five, and three were fifty years or older. Occupations of the nineteen who listed them included six farmers, three carpenters, a nurse, tailor, ship's carpenter, potter, seamstress, shoemaker, smith, hatter, and turner. There was one schoolteacher, Daniel Coker, a black Methodist minister from Baltimore, Maryland, who later would distinguish himself as a leader among the "people" (as the black immigrants were referred to).[42]

Twenty-nine-year-old Elijah Johnson from New York kept a journal on the Atlantic crossing. In his entry of February 6, 1820, he records "a long storm in the seas; I [Johnson] hope that it will soon be over—after the raging night it became calm—In the afternoon we [saw] a schooner raider which had lost her mast, which caused both Agents and people to rejoice that it was not us."[43] Johnson would emerge later in the nascent colony on Cape Mesurado that would become Liberia as one of the leaders most respected by both the People and the agents.

Although Johnson remarked in his diary how "the people are much pleased with the Agents,"[44] Bacon, when scarcely out of New York, realized all was not well. He confided in a February 24 entry in his journal, "I have great anxieties about our people whether they will submit to proper regulation...A disorderly spirit manifested itself among them, several fight & threaten that they will not submit to be governed by white men. Others complain that they have been deceived, as they say they do not appear to comprehend the nature of the thing."[45] The grumbling and disaffection among the emigrants that continued during the rest of the voyage fueled Bacon's mounting anxiety.

The contentious band of would-be Liberians landed March 9, 1820, on Sherbro Island at a place called Campelar, about seventy miles down the coast from Freetown, Sierra Leone. Mills and Burgess had identified the site located on the Sherbro River on their reconnaissance mission. Here John Kizell, Paul Cuffe's partner, owned land and several houses. Kizell agreed that the colonists could reside there temporarily until they acquired their own land.

Crozer, the Colonization Society's agent, would acquire the land for the new colony and oversee its establishment and operation. Still only in his early twenties, he showed the same youthful idealism and zeal—even the willingness to suffer and, if need be, die for a religious cause—that distinguished most, even older men attracted to the African endeavor. In a letter from Philadelphia to his sister dated January 20, 1820, he wrote, "My dear Sister—Do not let one painful thought flit across your mind concerning me...If it is the will of god that I should die in Africa consider how much I shall gain—let your prayers be with me, but pray with a cheerfulness of spirit."[46]

An entry in an old journal thought to be Crozer's captures his unbelievably buoyant mood as the group waited aboard ship before landing on the island negotiated with Kizell:

> [We] lie in a very pleasant situation in the middle of the river Sherbro, which is here about 10 miles wide about 10 or 12 miles below Jenkens. the weather is very fine & we enjoy the land breeze in the morning and the sea breeze in the afternoon. the night is perfectly cool and pleasant. if Africa is always as pleasant as this I shall be satisfied indeed. I have now cashmire pantaloons on me which is not uncomfortable. I never felt more agreeable in my life than at present after the [unintelligible] and bustle of a voyage with a number of unruly disagreeable passengers.[47]

Alas, the colonists upon landing found Africa anything but pleasant and agreeable. Conditions proved devastating. Kizell's land was low and marshy, surrounded by dense thickets and stands of mangrove trees. The water supply, inadequate, soon turned bad. Crozer couldn't get the local chiefs to agree to sell land for the colony. (Rumor had it that the British governor of Sierra Leone discouraged the chiefs from selling land to the American colonists.) Fevers (mainly malaria but probably yellow fever as well) struck down one settler after another. The officers of the US escort ship *Cyane*, after completing a topographical survey, declared the island unhealthy and possessing little fertile soil. They recommended the settlers move elsewhere. But Bacon was reluctant to move.

Relations between the two agents and the people continued tense and rancorous. Bacon worriedly recorded that,

> [We] are at this moment in great anxiety to get the palaver [meeting with the local king to obtain land for the colony]... over so as to know what to depend on. the people are very much dissatisfied with this Island on account of the great scarcity of & bad quality of the water. A variety of notions are afloat in their heads. Some trust so seriously on their strength &...their tempers that they think we ought to go armed & keep a constant

guard every night. Others on the contrary are for incurring & puting at defiance all of their power & hatred, by forcibly taking possesion of territory regardless of right or palaver. A general spirit of extravagance, waste & complaining continually disturbs us.[48]

The women in the immigrant group particularly vexed him. He complained they were "full of evil speaking, nothing satisfies them." Many "would not be satisfied [even] in heaven, [and] if they could have their way they would destroy all our stores in a few days & we should then have to starve & die. But thank god he uphold me with a strong hand & I shall not fall."[49]

Bacon's journal entry the following day suggested he might be close not only to falling, but more likely verging on paranoia. The people, he wrote, complained "for the want of good fresh water because I [Bacon] stopped here; because I did not take possession of the land by force; because the people are sick; because there is no fresh meat, no sugar, molases, flour & other luxuries of life; because I do not give them better tobacco," and so on.[50]

Bacon had his complaints, too: the people had "stolen & sold some of our soap, stolen part of the molases & indeed every thing within their reach falls a sacrifice to—not the natives—but to our own Christians. I never knew so much lying, stealing & abusing & hipocrisy as amongst these people."[51] Moreover, sickness was taking its toll. Reverend Coker recorded that "many of our people are very sick amongst whom is Mr. Bankston, Mr. Crozer & Mr. Townsend [a US Navy midshipman from the *Cyane*]. Their disease is the fever a disease consequent on constitutions not naturalized to this climate." He went on to note that Bacon and he "had thus far been blessed with health for which we have to thank God...though we are surrounded with many cares & anxieties."[52]

Bacon's journal on April 7, 1820, read, "God help us."[53]

On April 15 Crozer—despite his "cashmire" pantaloons—was dead, at age twenty-three. Townsend, the young naval officer, "was taken ill with fever the 7th of April owing to fatigue and exposure to the heat of the sun." He "died on the 17th the day after Crozer died." [54] Bacon's health began to weaken although he managed to carry on—but obviously feeling the stress. In his journal April 9 he lamented,

> I am Doctor, nurse, caterer, cook, waiter, preacher & ruler for 35 sick & the rest of the well ones...This is a real intermitting fever as described by Dr. Buchan. I recommend & when I can get them to take it give them an emetic, I then give bark [presumably quinine] in port wine, when the fever is off; fresh meat broth, Panada [a thick sauce or paste made from bread crumbs, milk, and seasonings] & wine & water...as far as I am able to procure them.

He asks the Lord to "spare my health that I may be useful to this people! If death were to release me from trouble or trial it would be happy for me but it would...be awful for this people."[55]

Relations between Bacon and the people reached a low point on April 10 when he was handed a "Paper" signed by ten of the settlers expressing their disaffection and inclination "to take the management of matters in their own hands." The petition read in part,

> Be it known to you that our minds are much distressed seeing that we come so far short of what was promised us before we left our native shores, we have now arrived at the trying point we are sick, almost naked and really do suffer for the want of such things as was said to be in store for us.[56]

Bacon had failed to work out arrangements for getting his people settled. They wanted direction and reassurance from Bacon, their leader. As they sensed that he soon would be leaving because of his deteriorating health, their anxieties mounted into desperate fears. They prayed "in God's name" that Bacon tell them "how [they] were to Act and what [they] were to do on or before" he departed, as they expected him to do because of his health. In conclusion, the petitioners wrote,

> We wish the palaver to go on as soon as possible that we may have something to depend on for our support, for if we stay here till the rains are over without any place to clear or plant it may be attended with dreadful consequences to us and our friends who are coming on, we would be glad if you could give us a firm answer that we may seek for ourselves if Nothing can be done for us.[57]

―――᙭―――

Bacon suspected that Kizell was "at the bottom of this disaffection [sic]." Convinced that he kept putting off the palaver purposely, the reverend determined to see King Couben (another local chief) himself. Seriously ailing but feeling responsible for the plight of his charges, despite his using "every excertion to get them comfortably settled," the intrepid Bacon embarked upon his journey:

> I started in a krou [Kru] canoe with two men, at 10 AM & arrived at Coubentown in the afternoon of the same day. [The king] received & treated me cordially. I had some private conversation with him in which I endeavoured to draw from him his views. He promised to favour us. Said I must stay all night. Killed a kid & gave me good food. I slept in his own bed, he held a palaver next day with his head men & the result was that he would send for King Dorra & have the palaver [about

a colony site]. King Dorra owns the land we want. Couben sent his big canoe with 8 men to take me back in company with his three sons...The agility & athletic exercises of the boatmen on their oars was surprising.[58]

The Reverend Bacon's journal ends abruptly, and his handwriting betrays a failing body. Help from King Couben apparently never materialized.

Bacon's illness worsened, and he was removed to Kent, Cape Shilling, near Freetown, where he died May 3, 1820—perhaps happy after all to escape the trials and tribulations of Africa. The last agent remaining, John Bankston, also died not long after Bacon. Fifteen of the "people" died, another three the following year. Thirty-year-old Nelly Binks, the nurse, died. Philadelphian John Augustine's entire family—John, age thirty; Nancy, age twenty-five; two daughters, two and four years old; and an infant—all died in that first harrowing year.

The Society's Fourth Annual Report included a doctor's views on the causes of the deaths in the settlers' first year. He attributed "the mortality among the settlers to the extreme sultry heat of the climate, to their confined local situation, to indulging in eating freely of tropical fruits, and particularly to the impurity of the water." For good measure, he added "idleness, inattention to cleanliness and depression of mind...and lack of medical...[attention] and nursing."[59] Bacon had come to similar views on the causes of the widespread sickness and many deaths. He attributed them to "a sudden change of climate...2nd nonrestrain & unlimited indulgence in the fruits of this country...3rd exposure to heat & dews & hard labour & working in the water...4th sloth & laziness...5th sleeping in huts without floors & some on the ground & a refusal to take medicine when prepared."⁶⁰

—⋙—

The would-be colonists had been in Africa scarcely two months. With Bacon, Bankston, and Crozer dead, the Reverend Daniel Coker, the black minister from Baltimore, took charge. Born in Maryland in 1780 to an indentured Englishwoman and an African slave, Coker escaped to New York. There he joined the Methodist Church and became associated with Francis Asbury, Methodism's bishop and principal leader in America. Returning to Maryland and enslavement, he worked to purchase his freedom and became active among the African American community in Baltimore. He was ministering to black Methodists in 1802.

Coker at thirty-five years of age could already boast a distinguished ecclesiastical career when he sailed to Africa. In 1810 he published a pamphlet titled *A Dialogue Between a Virginian and an African Minister*, the first such publication by a black Marylander. He led a delegation to a meeting in Philadelphia where the African Methodist Episcopal Church, the first black denominational organization, was organized on April 9, 1816. The next day Coker was elected the first bishop of the new church but declined the honor in favor of the Reverend Richard Allen of Philadelphia. Sometime after being expelled from the church for a year for some undisclosed transgression, Coker signed onto the *Elizabeth* for the 1820 voyage to Africa.

And now he found himself by default the leader of a band of increasingly sick and dispirited strangers in a foreign land without a home in which to settle. Coker appealed to Governor MacCarthy, who agreed to allow the immigrants to settle temporarily at a site on Fourah Bay near Freetown until the colony could acquire its own land. Coker and many of the people moved to the new location; some elected to remain at Sherbro. As sickness continued to make deadly inroads and morale in the divided group plummeted, America's first colonization endeavor appeared destined for certain disaster.

But back in Washington, the society, undeterred, chartered another vessel, the brig *Nautilus*, and enlisted eighteen men, nine women, and twelve children to join the initial group, The roll of emigrants published by the US Congress counted thirteen men, ten women, and ten children, for a total of thirty-three.[61] President Monroe appointed the Reverend Ephraim Bacon, Samuel Bacon's brother, and Jonathan B. Winn to serve as US agents; the Colonization Society appointed as its agent the Reverend J. R. Andrus, and a young man, Christian Wiltberger, as assistant agent. Wives accompanied Ephraim Bacon and Winn. Andrus and Wiltberger were unmarried.

Relatively little is known about Winn and Andrus, even less about Wiltberger. He probably hailed from New Jersey. The diary he kept reveals him as being essentially of the same cloth as that of his fellow Christians, inspired presumably by the Second Great Awakening to resolute faith and good works.

He wrote that "from the time [he] was first brought to the knowledge of the truth," he had "a strong desire to go among the heathen."[62] He managed to get appointed an Assistant Agent of the American Colonization Society. After learning in early October 1820 of the deaths of Bacon, Bankston (his good friend), and Crozer "and a number of the Coloured people," he said, "This appears to me like a misterious providence, but I still felt that all was right, that the Lord had permitted them" to do "what he had for them to do there and then took them to himself."[63]

Wiltberger added that his father "would rather [he] not go to [Africa]," his mother "gave him up to the Lord," and his "Christian friends were generally opposed to it." But, he "felt willing to suffer any thing for him [Jesus] who suffered so much" for him, and even if he "should die in Africa [he] had a sweet sensation in thinking that all things would work together for [his] good."⁶⁴ The coming months would put Wiltberger's strong faith to the test.

The *Nautilus*, under the command of Captain George Blair, sailed from Hampton Roads, Virginia, on January 23, 1821. Young Wiltberger noted the day in his diary. "This morning at 7 we put down the [Chesapeake] Bay having a fair wind from (NW)." He also noted that "by 11 most of the people were sick," and in a letter to his father observed, "some were sick all the way, we had a very rough time, and hard winds, foul winds and calms all the way."⁶⁵

The fourth day out, during a gale, "Mrs. Coker's child [born shortly after she boarded the ship] die…and the next day, [January 27th] "at 12 oclock…was committed to a watery grave."⁶⁶ Mrs. Coker was joining her husband, Reverend Daniel Coker. Every passenger aboard, even Wiltberger, became unwell. He complained that he "was taken this Evening with a pain in my bowels. I took a little raw brandy which removed the pain."⁶⁷ He still had twenty-six more days to go.

At last, on Thursday, March 8, 1821, after forty-four days at sea, Wiltberger happily wrote:

> This [morning] we can see cape Sierra Leone & the Mountain near—It is remarkable that Mungo Park [an eighteenth-century explorer], Rev. Mesrs Mills & Burgess, the expedition that came out last year; and our vessel have all arrived at Sierra Leone in the month of March. At 10 oclock 12 Krusmen [local African tribesmen who lived on the coast] came on board. They were naked except for a piece of cloth round their waist. Several of them had papers of recommendation to show. They appear very happy and intelegent and could talk a little english. A Pilot also came on board.⁶⁸

Winn immediately dispatched a letter to A. Grant, the acting Sierra Leone governor during Governor MacCarthy's absence. The agent announced the arrival of the *Nautilus* and in most deferential language sought to confirm the earlier offer of a temporary site for the new settlers.[69] Grant responded the same day, in equally diplomatic language, that he would experience pleasure in "carrying out the wishes" of his government "by rendering you every possible assistance" and invited Winn to breakfast the next morning. At that time, he said, they could discuss "particulars reflecting these glorious purpose our countries have in view." Ominously, he said nothing specifically about a place for the people.[70]

The *Nautilus*, doubtless a bit tired and weather beaten after suffering the Atlantic's winds and waves in the long crossing, anchored for a well-deserved rest in Freetown Harbor.

Aboard the ship the new arrivals received several visitors. They reported that about twelve people, including Reverend Coker, were at Sierra Leone, the rest still at Sherbro. (Wiltberger thought only about sixty of the eighty-six immigrants who came out on Elizabeth were still alive.) All spoke "in great disapprobation of Kezzell," their Sherbro landlord. One visitor had some palm wine brought on board, and Wiltberger found "the taste was very agreeable." He later somewhat mellowly observed, "It is hot in the sun, but in the house it is quite pleasant. The houses generally are one story and thatched roofs except those the white people live in, some are two stories, fruit is quite plenty, and very cheap."[71]

In a later entry, however, he describes less pleasant aspects of life in Sierra Leone. Some kind of pest, presumably ants or termites, "forced inhabitants to abandon their houses, but when they [the pests] eat every thing in the house they will leave it and permit the inhabitants to take posesion again. There is also a reptile here called the Santapee [presumably centipede] about 3 inches long, having 100 feet the bite of which is very painful. And also the Scorpion will bite."

The young American observer added,

The horses are small and also the cows, chickens & goats. There appears to be no religion among the white inhabitants of the town. They appear very thoughtless & careles & putting far off the evil day. There are many Mahomedans in the place. The water is good, [and] between sunrise and 10 oclock is the most appropriate part of the day.[72]

The next day, after calling on the acting governor, Brothers Winn, Andrus, Wiltberger, and the *Nautilus*'s captain had a long palaver with Coker about the probability of establishing a colony at Sherbro and about the health of the people. Anxious to settle the matter of a temporary site for the colony, the agents—except Wiltberger, who stayed aboard the *Nautilus* to keep an eye on the people ("on account of some impudent conduct yesterday")—had breakfast with acting governor Grant. Winn, however, confided to Wiltberger that Grant at breakfast "had frankly told them that" for them to establish a colony on [at] Sherbro "would be very unpleasant" for the British in Sierra Leone. In particular, "it would be hurtful to the interests of the merchants of the colony [Sierra Leone]." The merchants "also stated that in case of war between the two Governments, it would place each Settlement in a disagreeable situation."[73] But if the colonists "would abandon the idea of settling there, he [Grant] would" give them every assistance in settling anywhere else. He "mentioned particularly Cape Mount [in present-day Liberia] on the coast of Guinea."[74]

Peter Duignan and L. H. Gann of the Hoover Institution claim the governor, Charles MacCarthy, "suspected that the [American Colonization] society was a mere cloak for the real purpose behind the American colony: to injure British interests, most notably trading." Despite the complaints of British traders and the government's attempts to subdue it, American trade with West Africa thrived. MacCarthy, a professional soldier, "able, conscientious, and conservative," made every effort "to eliminate

Americans and make the areas complete British monopolies."[75] He even had "requested permission from London to seize the island of Sherbro in order to forestall the suspected American peril."[194] Although Winn insisted "the Colonization [Society] had a claim on Sherbro & were unwilling to give it up," the agents reluctantly agreed in the face of "insurmountable obstacles we would relinquish all ideas of settling at Sherbro."[195]

After more than a year, the American colonists once again found themselves still without a home.

CHAPTER 4

The Search for a Home

—⚏—

IN THE FACE OF THE Sherbro debacle, it was agreed that Ephraim Bacon and Andrus should take the schooner *Augusta* down the coast to select a suitable place for a settlement. Winn opened negotiations with acting governor Grant for a temporary place to settle.[1] Of two locations offered, Winn decided on Fourah Bay, about one and a half miles above Freetown.

When Winn balked at the £500 annual rent, Grant, "ancious that we should be accommodated," agreed to an arrangement in which the society would pay only £260 (equal to about $1,040) per annum. The deal included houses and land, which the people could immediately go to work on since it was the season for planting.[2] The two agents noted how much they were "indebted to Governor Grant," who showed good will and friendship to them."[3]

Andrus and Bacon had planned to leave on their search for a permanent home for the colony on March 20, 1821, expecting to be gone three to six weeks. Bacon's journal records their trip in detail.

They "contracted with William Martin, a yellow man, to navigate the vessel [the *Augusta*], and John Bean as mate—Moses Turner, 8 native sailors and 5 Kroomen."[4] But as Bacon discovered, getting things underway in Africa often proved difficult. March 22 came, and they still had not left. He complained they "had much trouble in getting the Captain and Crew on board, some of them after receiving a months advance pay, are spending their time in dissapation; and indeed, dispatch of business is not common in Africa."[5] He wrote that, finally at five o'clock, "all hands are on board, some of the sailors intoxicated; the Captain appears to make unnecessary delays, and I fear I shall have trouble with him. But I expected to find trouble in Africa."[6]

At last they got underway. Five days and 250 miles down the coast, Cape Mount came into view. Bacon and Andrus, though, didn't bother to seek a meeting with the local ruler, a King Peter—according to Bacon, "one of the most powerful and warlike Chiefs of West Africa, and more deeply engaged in the Slave trade than any of his neighbors."[7] They continued on about fifty miles farther south to Cape Mesurado, where they anchored in the mouth of the Mesurado River. The two agents found the land along the left bank of the river "inviting. The natural growth is luxuriant and abundant; many of the trees attain to a large size, and present every indication of a strong and fertile soil."[8]

Could this possibly be the place for the colony's home? Andrus and Bacon decided they should try to see the local headman, another King Peter. They "attempted to obtain a palaver with him, and for this purpose went on shore with a present."[9] Unfortunately this King Peter wanted none of it. He sent a messenger to tell them there would be no interview. He feared any intrusion of foreign settlers. Ominously they saw a schooner flying the French flag lying offshore waiting to load a contingent of young African men bound for the Americas. (This same King Peter, however, would later in the year play unwilling host to two other Colonization Society representatives, Lieutenant Robert Stockton and Dr. Eli Ayres. They would prove more persuasive.)

Following this disappointment, the *Augusta* weighed anchor once again the evening of March 29. As it resumed its journey southeast along the coast, the explorers found the country "delightful...all the way to the St. John River." They anchored on

April 1 and were "soon surrounded by canoes and a number of natives."[10] Andrus and Bacon discovered that the local chief, a "prince" named Jack Ben, recently had been promoted from principal headman to king after the ruling chief, King John, died. Seeking an audience, they sent him a small present.

The next morning ten or fifteen canoes showed up with natives wanting to barter "fowls, oysters, eggs, palm oil and palm wine, cassada [cassava], yams, plantans, bannanas, limes and pine apples for tobacco, pipes, beads, &c." Bacon noted that "fowls are sold for one leaf of tobacco or one pipe each; oysters are very large and fine, half a pound of tobacco will buy one hundred, they are larger than the Bluepoint oysters."[11] They left the schooner to explore the surrounding area with a "Krooman, by the name of Bottle Beer" as their guide. Bacon in his journal relates the story:

> When we came to the left bank of the [Grand Bassa] river, we saw no canoe or other means of crossing over as we had thought, but Bottle Beer proposed to carry us over, and placed himself in a suitable position, and told one of us to sit upon his shoulder, when Brother Andrus seated himself with one leg over each shoulder, then Bottle Beer walked deliberately through the river, carrying his burden safely to the other bank, and returned back and proposed to take me. I told him I was so fat and heavy that he would let me fall into the water, he put his hands upon his arms and legs and said, "Me strong, me carry you, Daddy." At length I seated myself likewise upon Bottle Beer, and though he was not as heavy a person as myself, he carried me safe over without wetting me.[12]

Fortunately the river was but half a fathom deep.

They then walked to Bottle Beer's town, really just a little cluster of dwellings home to no more than sixty to one hundred inhabitants, then on to Jumbotown, which boasted a population of several hundred. After meeting Jumbo the headman and shaking hands with many of the natives, the group returned to the *Augusta* where Brothers Bacon and Andrus "dined on fish and oysters sumptuously." But, despite their several messages requesting a palaver, the king remained unresponsive. Their mission began to look like another failure. They had yet to give up, however.[13]

The following morning at six o'clock, they set out again for Jumbotown with four boatmen, two interpreters, and "five natives, two of which were Headmen," in two canoes.

After spending the night in Jumbotown in a native hut with their "clothes drenched in perspiration," and "without any covering but… [their] wet garments," their cottage "having no door," and "several hundred natives, within twenty yards, drumming and dancing until one or two o'clock in the morning," they arose the next day, not surprisingly, feeling "somewhat the worse for our hard lodging."[14]

The two agents and Davis, their interpreter, returned to the schooner and continued to wait. They heard from a headman that they could have land, but they had to meet with King Ben. Still waiting for word from him, Andrus and Davis decided to visit his predecessor's town. They found King Ben there; he at last agreed to a palaver the next day.

They also "saw the body of King John, who had been dead four moons, yet not buried; he was laid in state in a palaver-house, dressed in a fine robe, with a pair of new English boots on the feet: a brisk fire is kept burning in the room." They learned that his grave was "eight feet square," dug large enough to the purpose to admit "the body and the form upon which it lies, together with bullocks, goats, sheep, tobacco and pipes, as sacrifices."[15]

Bacon's reaction was, "O Lord when shall these superstitions cease."[16]

In his journal entry on Monday, April 9, 1821, Bacon described their meeting in Jumbotown, in the palaver house with King Ben:

> This morning the sea very rough. At 11 o'clock, we went onshore, with a present to the King, (as it is impossible to get a palaver with the authorities of the country without a respectable present "to pay service" to the King, his princess and his Headmen). [We met] his Majesty, King Jack Ben of Grand Bassa, together with several of his Headmen, with a large concourse of people. After shaking hands with them, we laid down our present, which consisted of one gun, some powder, tobacco, pipes, beads, &c. His Majesty said in broken English, "me tanke you."[17]

During another, even larger, palaver the next day, the king and his council stipulated as a condition for obtaining land that the agents "make book [agreement]…that the settlers and agents" would not in any way "assist the armed ships sent to the coast to suppress the slave trade."[15] Even though Andrus and Bacon pointed out the advantages to the Bassa people of getting out of the trade, which would soon be ended anyway as American and British warships captured all of the slave vessels, the king still insisted the condition be inserted in the "book." Reluctantly, the two agreed but felt relieved somewhat by their belief that the condition actually had little practical application; trying to end the slave trade by any means other than persuasion simply was not a viable course of action. Incurring the displeasure of the natives, given the colony's vulnerability at this point in time, would "cause the destruction of the whole of our expectations of future success."[19]

Andrus and Bacon chose a site for the colony. One more step remained. King Ben sent word that he would meet them in grand palaver to wrap up the deal. On Friday, April 13, the final palaver began with "more Headmen and Princes, as well as people, than at any time previous." The agents directed their interpreters "to tell them we wanted a large tract of land," thirty or forty square miles, which they described in detail.[20]

The assemblage readily agreed to the society's "having this tract...and directed their names to be set to the instrument." They all took hold of the pen and made their marks; then they cried aloud, "Palaver set! Palaver set!"[21]

In return, the Reverend Andrus as the society's agent agreed "to give certain stipulated articles annually, which will not cost more than 300 Dollars." Pledges of mutual friendship and agreement by each party not to make war on or trouble for the other followed. Bacon surmised that they had "at last succeeded in convincing them that we were their friends." But, Bacon and Andrus were certain they "could not have done [this], had it not been for the presence of Davis [their interpreter], and the entire absence of any display of military or naval force."[22]

At last the forsaken colony had a place in Grand Bassa for its home. Or did it?

―⚏―

The two explorers took, in their words, "an affectionate leave of the King and some of the Headmen." The following morning they were ready to start back to Fourah Bay, and with some difficulty got the horde of natives who had come aboard to barter their goods, mainly for tobacco, off the schooner. One of them sang a song of his own composition: "Whiteman gone, whiteman gone, whiteman gone—gone sabbyone, gone, gone, gone!"[23] Bacon did not record the tune.

After several stops, including Sherbro and Cape Shilling (where Samuel Bacon, Ephraim's brother, lay buried), the troop finally came into the harbor of Sierra Leone on April 26. What they found was distressing. Mrs. Bacon had fallen sick while staying with missionary friends at Regent's Town outside Freetown in her husband's absence.

Other passengers who came out on *Nautilus* also began to succumb to the African fever. Caleb Brander, age ten, who listed "Spells" as the extent of his education, died. Daniel Coker's entry in his diary of July 4: read,

"Heavy rains today attended with considerable wind. I feel light touches of fever/ or as we call it African fever." Two days later he noted, "This day Mr. John Adams from Philadelphia, a man of colour who came out on the ship Elizabeth, departed this life." And the next day, "This morning Mrs. Carey, from Richmond/ col'd/ who came out on the Nautilus departed this life." Reverend Coker added, "Several of our immigrants are indisposed. We have no Physician among us [although they could find some help in Freetown]."[24]

> Even the society's agent, Ephraim Bacon, who up until now had evaded the fever, could no longer escape. On the first of May, he wrote that "having exerted...[himself] overmuch, and suffered considerable anxiety of mind, and having moreover drank too freely of water, which is thought to be prejudicial to the health of white people in Africa...[he] was attacked with pain in the back part of the head, neck and back." After going back to the schooner and taking some medicine, Bacon suffered a chill, which "after about two hours ...was succeeded by fever." The fever continued until about nine o'clock in the evening, when the medicine began to take effect. The ailing Ephraim recorded that his stomach "being in a state for the reception of tonicks, and Brother Andrus," following "a small treatise of practice by [a] Dr. Winterbottom," gave him bark (quinine) "in as large quantities as [his] stomach would receive." The patient gratefully noted, "Brother Andrus followed that

plan during the night, and attended to me very kindly."[25] Such was the medical treatment at this time and place.

Mrs. Bacon, still sick in Regent's Town, grew sufficiently anxious about her husband that her physician thought it a good idea to move her to join Bacon at Fourah Bay. Mr. Johnson, their missionary friend, "sent six or eight of his captured people [natives rescued from slavers] with a palanquin...Those people were very affectionate; they would frequently remove the veil of the palanquin and view her with tender compassion, saying, 'Poor Mama sicke! White Mama sicke!'"[26]

During their exploratory trip, Andrus had decided that he should return to the States. Having discovered the want of missionaries in Africa, and the ardent desire of the natives to receive them, he had resolved to resign his appointment as agent to the Colonization Society, and return to these shores as a missionary, and "spend the remainder of his days in his Master's service, as had been his wish before leaving America."[27] Bacon thought well of Andrus's idea, noting he appeared "extremely well calculated for a Missionary"; moreover, the climate seemed to agree "with his constitution"; thus "his health ... [had] been better than that of any of the Agents."[28]

Andrus had booked passage to England, where he would find another vessel going to America. As the time for his departure drew near, however, Reverend and Mrs. Bacon's condition had not improved. In fact they had become so much worse Brother Andrus suggested that the two go in his place to the United States and he remain behind. Initially Bacon resisted the idea, but after consulting his doctor and Brother Winn, he "concluded to embrace the opportunity."[29] For Andrus it would prove a fate-ful decision. He even arranged for them the free passage he had been offered on a schooner that was sailing to Barbados.

After embarking on the schooner, "Mrs. Bacon was [again] taken extremely ill, and had she not obtained immediate aid would probably have survived but a short time. " An English surgeon, a Dr. Riche, came to her rescue. On Saturday, the sixteenth of June, 1821, they "sailed out of the harbour of Sierra Leone with the morning tide." That evening Bacon wrote that he "had no expectation of surviving...Death appeared fast approaching." When he awoke the next morning, he "was astonished to find...[himself still] in this troublesome world."[30]

For a time he was unable to speak, but with a Bible in hand, he soon found his voice. The two ailing voyagers gradually recovered. They finally reached Norfolk on the thirteenth of August 1821. Daniel Coker had noted that Brother Bacon had thought "of returning [to Africa] in the next ship out."[31] But, of course, he never did. In fact, Coker supposed Bacon "died on his passage home having left [Africa] very unwell."[32]

In the meantime, back in Fourah Bay, Coker recorded a cruelly ironic twist of fate:

July 28 Sat. Little did I think last Evening that I should have to enter on this journal so soon the death of my dear friend the Rev. Mr. Andrus...He expired about two oclock this afternoon. This dispensation seems to shed a veil of gloom over our prospects. But that we know that God done all things right, our duty is to submit may this sudden death be sanctified to my good.[33]

Andrus was laid to rest the next day in the burying ground in Freetown.

August proved nearly as deadly as July had been, and Coker feared the worst for his own family: "All my children continue sick. My oldest son Daniel is very sick/fever/..."[34] On the last day of the month: "This morning about 11 oclock Mr. Winn [the assistant US agent] departed this life." Despite his despair, Coker's faith stood solid. The day after Winn's death, the Baltimore minister relates how he opened his Bible without thinking to Psalm 146. *"I was so pleased with it I took up my pen and copyed it. 'Praise ye the Lord. Praise the Lord, O my soul.'"*[35]

Now, only Christian Wiltberger remained among the colonization agents. He became acting agent, although on July 13, he too had fallen ill. All thought of moving to Grand Bassa faded. The little band could do no more than remain in Fourah Bay—a colony still without a permanent home.

But help was on the way in the person of a remarkable young naval officer, who as a youthful student had attended Reverend Finley's Basking Ridge academy.

Lieutenant Robert Field Stockton, in command of the *Alligator*, left Boston on April 3, 1821, to patrol the waters off West Africa to intercept slave ships. Coker, in his diary entry of May 13, mentions the "American Schooner *Alligator* from Boston ...anchored in harbor of Freetown."[36] The *Alligator*, newly commissioned in March 1821, was the last of five twelve-gun schooners built specifically to combat slave traders and pirates. Stockton learned that the ship would be placed in service off the coast of Africa to combat slavery and help acquire land for the American Colonization Society settlement. Society representatives already had discussed the matter with him, and he relished the prospect of participating in the colonization endeavor; engaging slave traders and pirates would provide added spice. He lobbied the secretary of the navy, Seth Thompson, persuading him to pass over several more senior officers who also applied and give the assignment to him. It would be Stockton's first command of a vessel. And he itched for action.

Born on August 20, 1795, to a prominent Princeton, New Jersey, family, Stockton studied at Finley's Basking Ridge academy and entered the College of New Jersey (later Princeton University) when only thirteen years old. Appointed a midshipman at age sixteen and assigned to Commodore John Rodgers's flagship, the *President,* during the War of 1812, young Stockton, "by his coolness and military deportment won the title of 'Fighting Bob.'"[37] He was promoted to lieutenant in 1814 and sailed with Captain Stephen Decatur against the Barbary pirates.

During his tour of duty in the Mediterranean, the young lieutenant fought a duel with a British naval officer at Gibraltar because of the British officer's contemptuous treatment of him. And "it is said at one time he had accepted challenges to fight all the captains of the British regiment in the garrison."[38] A relative described him as "impulsive, yet self-possessed; brave and chivalrous; generous and noble; and had wonderful magnetic power over those who met him."[39]

"Bold, not afraid of assuming responsibility, in full sympathy with any daring enterprise, such as the [California] 'Bear Flag Revolt,' and ready to fight Mexico herself if necessary,"[40] Robert Stockton epitomized the archetypal agent of "Manifest Destiny," the promise that drove America's westward expansion in the middle part of the nineteenth century. A portrait, probably painted when he was in his thirties, projects a handsome young man in a naval officer's uniform with epaulettes, cradling a dress sword in his arms, a rather sharp nose dominating his face, a long forehead topped by a full head of dark, curly hair, sideburns reaching almost to his chin, his eyes suggesting a demeanor of calm confidence and resolve.

After his Liberian adventure, Stockton organized the New Jersey Colonization Society and served as the organization's first president. Stockton was promoted to captain in 1838, and in 1841 President John Tyler offered to make him secretary of the navy; he declined. With his friend, John Ericsson, the Swedish inventor of the maritime screw propeller, they produced the world's first screw-propelled warship, the USS

Princeton (the scene in 1844 of one of the most bizarre naval tragedies in nineteenth-century US history).

In the war with Mexico (1845–46), Stockton led American forces that captured Los Angeles and annexed California to the United States, served three years as a US senator, and was considered seriously as an 1856 presidential candidate of the American (formerly Know-Nothing) Party. He died in Princeton, New Jersey, on October 7, 1866.

Although Stockton is vaguely remembered as the man who acquired the land for America's first overseas colony and as one of the leaders in the Mexican War, his place in history has been largely forgotten. Few monuments or memorials commemorate his feats: the city of Stockton, California, and a tiny town along the Delaware River in New Jersey, renamed Stockton in 1853 by residents grateful to him for helping get the Delaware and Raritan Canal built, bear his name. Fort Stockton in Pecos County, Texas, and at least one naval vessel were also named in his honor. No statue, monument, or place name remembers him in Liberia except Stockton Creek (and an Ayres Branch—presumably for Dr. Eli Ayres—coming off the creek.

Coker again: "Fourah Bay [Sierra Leone] May 15th Tuesday We have been visited at our temporary residence by Captain Stockton and some of his officers. They appeared in words to be zealous in the cause [ending the slave trade]."[41] Stockton and the *Alligator* disappeared for several months on patrol looking for slave ships. He returned in November or December to meet Dr. Eli Ayres. Ayres, born in Shiloh, New Jersey, on May 9, 1778, was a physician recently appointed the Colonization Society's chief agent. He had been dispatched to Africa to help obtain the land for the colony and settle the colonists. He arrived at Fourah Bay courtesy of another US naval vessel, the schooner *Shark*, commanded by Lieutenant Matthew Calbraith Perry who later gained fame as Commodore Perry by opening Japan to the West in 1853.

—⚏—

With the arrival of Stockton and Ayres, events began to move quickly. Leaving the *Alligator* and his crew at Sierra Leone, Stockton, Ayres, Mr. Nicholson (a seaman), and a local Kru interpreter sailed off in the smaller *Augusta*. Ayres sought to acquire land farther north up the coast from Sierra Leone, but they also sailed south as far as Cape Mesurado to the locale that society agents Bacon and Andrus had found "inviting," and Sierra Leone governor MacCarthy had suggested. It was on what Europeans called the Grain Coast (because of the seeds, or grains, of the Malagueta pepper, one of the area's chief exports). The two Americans decided this was the place. But, with this decision following on such a disappointing series of failures, one wondered.

In December 1821, Stockton and his colleagues disembarked at Cape Mesurado to negotiate with the principal local chief, King Peter (who earlier refused Andrus and Ephraim Bacon an interview). Stockton and Ayres hiked some six miles inland to the king's village. Upon their arrival, one of the lesser native chiefs told them, "The King be fool—he no talk English—I his mouth, what I say, King say."[42] During the December 12–15 negotiations, the two American leaders asked for Dozoa Island and Cape Mesurado. The king, or his "mouthpiece," declined. King Peter reportedly would not sell the cape because "his women would cry aplenty."[43] (Although selling land generally was alien to Africans since they held ownership communally under the direction of the tribal chief, chiefs did on occasion sell land to foreigners.)

According to one account—perhaps apocryphal—surrounded by a crowd of hostile natives that the Americans feared would attack, "Stockton pulled out his pistol, cocked it and gave it to Ayres with the instructions to shoot if necessary. He then aimed another at King Peter's head. Having thus ensured an attentive audience, he lectured the company on the advantages of a settlement."[44]

Stockton's "gentle persuasion," or whatever, apparently worked.[45] The American Colonization Society on December 15 was granted title to "certain lands, viz., Dozoa Island [renamed Perseverance, Provenance, then Providence Island by the Americo-Liberian settlers], and also all that portion of land bounded north and west by the Atlantic Ocean, and on the south and east by a line drawn in a south-east direction from the mouth of the Mesurado River,"[46] a strip of land roughly 130 miles long and forty miles wide.

Besides King Peter, Ayres and Stockton also signed agreements with King George, King Zoda, King Long Peter, King Governor, and King Jimmy. Of the $100,000 appropriated, Congress earmarked $30,000 to purchase land. However, echoing a much earlier transaction involving Manhattan Island, only $300 worth of gifts, "muskets, beads, tobacco, gunpowder, clothing, mirrors, food, and rum," was required to close the deal.[47]

> Dr. Ayres jubilantly reported to the American Colonization Society that on December 15, 1821, "We have purchased a tract of country containing one million dollars' worth of land" for goods "not amounting to more than three hundred dollars."[48]
> The deed to the land listed the goods:
> Six Muskets, one box Beads, two hogsheads Tobacco, one cask Gunpowder, six bars, Iron, ten Iron Pots, one dozen

Knives and Forkes, one dozen Spoons, six pieces Blue Bolt, four Hats, three Coats, three pair Shoes, one box Pipes, one keg Nails, twenty Lookingglasses, three pieces Handkerchief, three pieces Calico, three Canes, four Umbrellas, one box Soap, one barrel Rum.

In addition, the deed specified the following were to be paid later:

Three casks Tobacco, one box Pipes, three barrels Rum, twelve pieces Cloth, six bars, Iron, one box Beads, fifty Knives, Twenty Lookingglasses, ten Iron Pots different sizes, twelve Guns, three barrels Gunpowder, one dozen Plates, one dozen Knives and Forkes, twenty Hats, five casks Beef, five barrels Pork, ten barrels Biscuit, twelve Decanters, twelve glass Tumblers, and fifty Shoes.

The price was never fully paid, and part of the initial payment was later taken back.

Finally, the Colonization Society had land. But the local Africans vigorously opposed the sale to these foreign invaders. And the prospect of a colony in their midst, peopled by men bent on eradicating the slave trade, and possibly even slavery itself, unnerved many of the natives. The chiefs especially, as Paul Cuffe discovered, had dealt profitably for many years in the capture, enslavement, and sale of fellow Africans to European and American slavers. They were not prepared to give up such a lucrative enterprise easily.

Upon returning to Fourah Bay, Ayres directed several immigrants (mostly single men) to ready themselves for departure. Two small schooners in January 1822 began shuttling the new settlers to what they thought would at last be "the Promised

Land." As they left Sierra Leone for their new home, they must have felt a heady mix of relief, excitement, anxiety, and apprehension. They sailed south and east along the coast—low-lying land interspersed with beaches, lagoons, and mangrove swamps, with a backdrop of rolling low plains ten to thirty miles deep. Farther inland, low, rolling hills were thick with tropical rain forests stretching as far as one could see, not unlike some of the Carolina coast. Few features broke the monotony until they came to Cape Mount, on the northwestern edge of what now is Liberia.

British adventurer Sir Richard Burton in 1861 took note of the mount, which "lies some ninety miles from Sherbro...a noble landmark, rising like a huge stud from the smooth front of the water before us." Burton also noted that the cape was "the last residence of the Franco-Italian slaver, Captain Canot," whose memoirs—actually written, according to Burton, "by some German 'cooker-up'"—were selling then "at a shilling."[49]

Some fifty or so miles farther down the coast, the settlers at last caught sight of Cape Mesurado, their new home to be. The American scheme, though, to locate a colony here was not the first. A Frenchman, one Chevalier des Marchais, had seized upon the idea some one hundred years earlier. The French government in 1725 and subsequent years dispatched him to report on the trading prospects of Africa's west coast and Cayenne (Guyana) in South America.

> Des Marchais apparently found Cape Mesurado much to his liking:
> [It] is a detached mountain [he reported], steep and high towards the sea, but less so on the land side. The summit forms a level plain, the soil of which is better than what is generally found in such situations. On the east is an extensive bay, bordered by good and uniform soil, which is bounded by

hills of moderate elevation, covered with trees. On the west is another great bay, which receives the River Mesurado [Saint Paul River].⁵⁰

Des Marchais goes on to describe a lagoon with two islands. The smaller, Perseverance or Providence Island, is where the initial band of American settlers would first land, and the larger, Bushrod Island, became the center of much of Monrovia's industry. (These are the names the colonists gave them. Bushrod was named for the American Colonization Society's first president, Bushrod Washington.) The French gentleman apparently got on so well with the local chief (who bore the same name as the chief with whom the Americans fared less well some one hundred years later) that the latter gave Bushrod Island to him. Des Marchais drew up a plan for establishing a French colony at Cape Mesurado, selecting as the site for his capital the actual plateau where the American colonists later built Monrovia. The French Senegal Company, to whom des Marchais submitted his scheme, never pursued it. Otherwise, the colony may well have been named Liberté instead of Liberia.[51]

When these American settlers neared their destination on Cape Mesurado, their Promised Land, shouts of "halleluiah" must have rung out. The local Dei tribesmen, however, did not open their arms in welcoming embraces. In fact, they proved sufficiently hostile that the colonists were forced to disembark on the nearby small Perseverance Island instead of the cape. The date, January 7, 1822, Liberia celebrated annually as Founder's Day until Samuel Doe overthrew the Americo-Liberian government in 1980.

The society had purchased the tiny island from an Afro-English merchant who owned a large trading concern on the coast. It was not a hospitable spot, Jehudi Ashmun later wrote, and "soon proved itself to be a most insalubrious situation. The only shelter it afforded...was to be found under the decayed thatch of half a dozen diminutive huts, constructed after the native manner of building; and the island was entirely destitute of fresh water and firewood."[52]

When Ayres returned from Sierra Leone on April 7 with the last remaining colonists, he was appalled at what he found: the "settlement in confusion and alarm," the colonists occupying only a "small and unhealthy Island, in the mouth of the Montserrado river."[53] This was not the Promised Land.

King Peter and his Dei warriors determined to expel these uninvited intruders before they put down permanent roots. The king enticed Ayres to a "friendly" meeting at his town but then held the society agent prisoner until he agreed to take back the remnants of the goods that had been advanced as partial payment for the land and relinquish any claim to it. Ayres, however, managed to ward off any immediate evacuation, alleging he had no vessel available. The ever-resourceful agent next worked out a secret deal with a subordinate chief, King George, who claimed jurisdiction over the northern portion of the cape. He allowed the settlers to cross the river and begin clearing the dense forest of tall trees, vines, and brush that covered much of the area acquired for the colony.

This encroachment by these strangers, whom the Dei knew were "entirely adverse to the slave trade," further inflamed the warriors. A skirmish ensued, in which a colonist and an English seaman died. "Old King Peter, the venerable patriarch of the nation," though, fared even worse. For his part in dealing with the intruders, "he was capitally impeached and brought to trial on a charge of betraying the interests of his subjects by selling their country."[54]

By April 25 most of the immigrants had been able to move ashore onto the cape; this is the date that Liberians mark as the colony's actual beginning. But it was not until July that they were "enabled to entirely abandon the Island, and place themselves beneath their own humble dwellings, on the Cape."[55] They built a storehouse and a frame house as the agent's residence. In another confrontation "the storehouse had taken fire, and most of the provisions and utensils of the Colony been destroyed."[56]

These clashes attracted the attention of probably the most powerful chief in the area—who carried the curious name King Boatswain. A Mandingo tribal leader, he had worked early in his career as a boatswain on various European ships. Although his Mandingo name was King Sao, he became widely known as King Boatswain or King Sao Boso or Sabsu. (The "Boso" or "bsu" came from the way his people pronounced "boatswain.")

> The Mandingo (Manding or Malinke) people were renowned as traders throughout western Africa. Muslims, they enjoyed a "fairly high degree of political and religious supremacy over the interior ethnic groups of the West Atlantic region."[57] King Boatswain presided over the Kondo (also Condo) Confederation to which the American settlers' neighbors, the Gola, Dei, Vai, and Loma, belonged. The confederation "stretched from the Lofa River to the vicinity of Cape Mesurado and from the coast far into the interior" with its capital in the town of Bopolu in the northwest area of today's Liberia.[58] Under Boatswain's leadership (1775–1836), the area around Bopolu probably reached its high point.

King Boatswain must have cut an impressive figure. Ashmun later described him as being "to a stature approaching seven feet in height, perfectly erect, muscular, and finely proportioned—a countenance noble, intelligent, and full of animation—he unites great comprehension and activity of mind, and what is still more imposing, a savage loftiness and even grandeur of sentiment."[59]

Through bloody wars in the interior, Boatswain "had thus been long acquiring a general influence, which gave him, even in the affairs of his neighbours, an authority little short of dictatorial."[60] He arrived on the coast "not, as he said, to pronounce sentence, between the coast people and the strangers, but to do justice."[61] And moreover, he brought along with him a force of warriors sufficient to give full effect to his decision.

He called the head chiefs, society agents, and principal settlers to a meeting to hear each party's grievances. After satisfying himself about the pertinent facts of the case, "he at length arose, and put an end to the assembly by laconically remarking to the Deys [Dei], that having sold their country, and accepted the payment in part, they must take the consequences...'Let the Americans have their land immediately. Whoever is not satisfied, let him tell me so.'"[62] He reportedly told the American agents and settlers, "I promise you protection. If these people give you further disturbance, send for me; and I swear, if they oblige me to come again to quiet them, I will do it by taking their heads from their shoulders, as I did old King George's on my last visit to the Coast to settle disputes"[63]

Why King Boatswain would come to the aid of the American Colonization Society's venture is unclear. The Mandingo traders would face potential competition from American traders once Liberia was established. More telling, his prosperous capital, Bopolu, depended heavily on exporting slaves, ivory, gold, and camwood (used to make red dye) from the north to the coastal peoples in exchange for salt, tobacco, guns, and various European goods. King Boatswain himself "raided towns and villages from Cape Mount to Grand Bassa, a distance of almost 200 miles, and sold his victims into slavery."[64] The American society's presence in Africa clearly posed a threat to him and his kingdom. The question was moot in any event. The king's warnings to the other tribal groups would prove hollow.

—⚘—

Despite Boatswain's assurances, many of the settlers remained fearful. Sickness, dismay, and weariness also took their toll. Supplies had dwindled. Ayres, the society's agent, and Christian Wiltberger, the assistant agent, were both ill. Some of the group wanted to return to Sierra Leone. Ayres offered passage back and temporary abode there while Wiltberger volunteered to remain on the cape with whomever among the settlers opted to stay. At this point, one of the group, a thirty-something New Yorker named Elijah Johnson, stepped forward, resolutely declaring, "Two years long have I sought a home; here I have found one, here I remain."[65]

His fearless determination somehow struck a chord among the wavering little band of settlers. Most resolved to stay. Sir Harry Johnston wrote, "He probably decided thus the fate of "Liberia.'"[66] Twenty-four (including women and children) who arrived on the *Elizabeth* and the *Nautilus* left for Sierra Leone in 1822. Four returned to the United States. The Reverend Daniel Coker and three family members numbered among those who decided to stay in Sierra Leone.[67]

Johnson, whose action won him instant fame as a national hero, went on to play a prominent role in the nascent colony. His experience as an artilleryman in the War of 1812 proved invaluable in the settlers' defense against subsequent attacks by their hostile neighbors. As the colony developed, he served in various important positions, including a stint as one of the delegates to the constitutional convention when Liberia declared its independence in 1847. He died in 1849, mourned as one of Liberia's earliest pioneers, a military leader and hero. His son, Hilary R. W.

Johnson, would be elected in 1883 as Liberia's first Liberian-born president.

Ayres and Wiltberger both left for the United States, doubtless happy to escape the fevers and tribulations of Africa. Once again the settlers found themselves without any official US or Colonization Society leadership. Upon leaving, Ayres wisely designated Elijah Johnson general superintendent of affairs and acting agent. Johnson took charge June 4, 1822. But his domain could be described as little better than pathetic: exclusive of women and children and four native Africans, he had only twenty-one persons capable of bearing arms, they were surrounded by hostile warriors, their stores nearly exhausted, and fevers ever threatening.[68]

Long-serving Colonization Society secretary Reverend Ralph Gurley, in his *Life of Jehudi Ashmun*, well summed up their plight:

> Few, destitute, and exposed to the treachery of savage foes, far away from the abodes of civilized man, this feeble company found shelter under the wing of Divine Mercy, and patiently awaited those aids and supplies, which their necessities demanded, and which they trusted the Almighty power, that had so long been their safeguard, would in due season afford.[69]

The Reverend Ralph Randolph Gurley was born May 26, 1707, in Lebanon, Connecticut. A graduate in 1818 of Yale College, he was licensed to preach as a Presbyterian but was never ordained. Nevertheless, he served as chaplain of the US House of Representatives for four congressional sessions. Gurley, one of the founders of Liberia acted as American Colonization Society agent and secretary for fifty years, from 1822 until 1872. During his first ten years as agent, the society's annual income rose from $778 to $40,000. President James Madison in his will bequeathed $2,000 to the society through him. As secretary, the society's chief executive, he built the organization and the cause of colonization into a national movement. Gurley edited *The African Repository and Colonial Journal*, wrote a *Life of Jehudi Ashmun* (1835), and visited Africa three times on society business. Gurley died July 30, 1872.

CHAPTER 5

Liberia Is Born

—⚭—

WHEN THE BRIG *STRONG* ARRIVED at Cape Mesurado on August 8, 1822, with a boatload of fifty-three new immigrants, the fate of the little community under Elijah Johnson's leadership still hung by a very slender thread. The society-chartered brig had left Baltimore on June 20 but encountered heavy gales for eight days, lost an anchor, and could not even safely land at the cape until August 13 and 14. It took four weeks to fully unload the passengers and cargo. The Reverend Jehudi Ashmun was in charge of the group.

Ashmun proved to be another of those exceptional characters whose faith and dedication were the lifeblood of the young colony. Born in Champlain, New York, April 21, 1794, the third of ten children, Ashmun began his religious studies at the age of fourteen and joined a church in July 1810.

A year later, at a prayer meeting, some remark made by a fellow attendee struck a sensitive chord in an already hypersensitive teenage Ashmun. He reported that after much soul searching, an "awful darkness enveloped him, and he was overwhelmed in guilt and misery."[1] Upon recovery, he knew that he must devote himself to serving God, and he decided to prepare himself for the Congregationalist ministry. In September 1812 Ashmun enrolled in Middlebury College.

Reverend Gurley described Ashmun, when a college-age young man, as "tall but spare," with "an air of striking dignity" and a "pale and emaciated countenance, [that] expressed the feelings of one who habitually communed with God, and viewed every object in the light of the eternal world." Inadvertently, Gurley drew a virtual caricature of the pious, somber nineteenth-century missionary, all of whose "thoughts and affections seemed occupied with religion." This "was the chief subject of his conversation"; moreover, "its truths were uttered by him with a manner and in a tone of such earnestness," he "convinced all in his presence, that to his mind they were of unspeakable importance." Furthermore, "that he was most benevolently anxious to extend their dominion over the minds of others."[1]

Due to financial difficulties, Ashmun transferred to Vermont University in Burlington in the autumn of 1815. In that year he also fell in love with a Miss C. D. Gray. But the following year, he lamented, "Into what an ocean of perplexities and sorrow...I precipitated myself and friends." He had, he wrote, "rashly given his heart to another...without asking counsel of the Lord, or depending on His guidance." He added later, "I wish to forget myself, to have my C. forget me also."[2] They broke up and went their separate ways. Ashmun was human after all. In October he moved to Hampden, Maine, to be principal of a newly established seminary, the Maine Charity School. He had six students.

Somehow he managed to swim safely away from his "ocean of perplexities," and he and CD were married in New York on October 7, 1818. He resigned his principal's post after a misunderstanding over his marriage, and the newlyweds embarked on a cruise from Maine to Virginia the next spring. As they sailed by Nantucket and continued across Buzzards Bay, "through the middle of the channel between Martha's Vineyard and Elizabeth Islands," one could believe Ashmun somehow aroused the spirit of the mulatto Quaker ship captain who had plied those waters two decades earlier.[3] In 1819 he landed a job editing the *Constellation*, a Baltimore religious weekly. Unfortunately, he didn't work out.

And after moving to Washington, in his next job as editor of the *Theological Repository,* an Episcopal Church monthly magazine, he suffered the same fate.

The two failures brought a despondent Ashmun to lament that he was "now twenty-five years of age; almost three years from College, [had] no profession; and [his] employment" since leaving college shaped him "to habits unfavorable to" acquiring a suitable position. He whined that he was "involved in debt, [possessed] neither books, nor money, and [had] a delicate and beloved wife to provide for."[4]

In looking back some years later, he noted how his "genius and habits, much of the time, were decidedly of the ascetic cast." He became "determined not only to forsake the gay; but even civilized world; and spend [his] life among distant savages." He had acquired that missionary "passion for the sacrifice."[5] Cuffe's spirit was at work. Ashmun soon found his destiny. In 1820, while in Washington, he became familiar with the American Colonization Society. In writing several articles in support of the society's work, he became intrigued with it. He started a newspaper, the *African Intelligencer,* which publicized the society's program. It soon failed. But he at last had found his calling, a mission that would satisfy his passion—Liberia.

Ashmun's fervent interest prompted him to write a *Memoir of the Rev. Samuel Bacon* (the society's first agent in Africa), published in Washington in 1822. Before long the society appointed him agent, and he and his wife prepared to sail to Liberia with the third contingent of would-be colonists. After seeing them settled in their new African home, the Reverend and Mrs. Ashmun were to return on the *Strong* to the United States. They little suspected it would be six years before that day would come. And that only one would make the return trip.

Less than a week after arriving at the fledgling colony, Ashmun on August 14 met with King Long Peter and King Peter, who apparently had survived his treason trial (for "selling" the land for the colony to the society). Immediately King Peter asked about the balance of the goods "to pay for the lands" for the colony under the agreement Stockton and Ayres extorted from him. Ashmun, taken aback since he thought the goods had already been given over, assured him that the next arriving vessel would bring instructions and (presumably) the goods. Not one to stand on ceremony, the king next asked the reverend for a gift, since "he [King Peter] would remain as he had been a friend." Moreover, he thought "that his age and rank, entitled him, according to the custom of the country, to some consideration, which he would be glad to have the Agent express by a present of whatever he had to spare."[6]

Ashmun, of course, agreed to send a gift, but according to biographer Reverend Gurley, he noted that "under smooth and friendly appearance, there lurked in the minds of many of the head men, a spirit of determined malignity, which only waited for an opportunity to exert itself for the ruin of the Colony."[7] Ashmun returned to the settlement and began organizing construction of defense works. It would not be long before that "feared opportunity" would arrive.

In fact, it already had begun to take shape as the Vai, Dei, and Gola—some of the settlers' nearest neighbors—banded together with the objective of evicting the unwelcome intruders. The native warriors would destroy the little colony and remove the threat it posed to their lucrative trade in slaves. European slave traders and Don Pedro Blanco, a notorious Brazilian mulatto, actively encouraged the native warriors. They, too, feared that the presence of the settlers and society agents, backed by the US Navy, would spell the end of their slave factories and depots along the coast.

Lieutenant Stockton and the *Alligator* already had left African waters when Ayres and Ashmun got wind of the developing plot. They appealed to the Mandingo leader, King Boatswain, who had intervened in the earlier dispute with King Peter, for help.

The appeal made sense. The Muslim Mandingoes, renowned as traders throughout western Africa, made up only a minor part of the area's indigenous population and claimed a relatively small enclave in the hinterland between the Gola and Kpelle. But the Americo-Liberians recognized them early on as one of the most powerful tribal groups in the entire region.

Even before all of the first settlers had made it onto Cape Mesurado, the site of the colony, in early 1822, the newcomers met with armed resistance from Dei tribesmen. A colonist and an English sailor were killed in the skirmish. From this unpromising start, the ensuing history of the Americo-Liberian settlers and the indigenous African tribes was riddled with revolts and lesser conflicts well into the twentieth century.

TRIBES OF LIBERIA

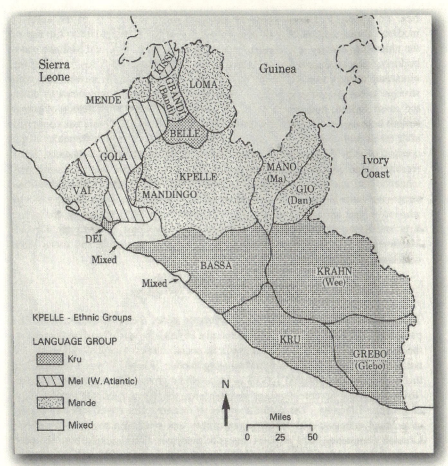

Map 2. Distribution of major Liberian ethnic and language groups.
Courtesy University of Indiana Press.

When the prospective settlers from America landed on the west African coast, they confronted a complex pattern of indigenous people divided into at least sixteen ethnic groups or tribes. Related linguistically to one of three major language groups—the Mande, Kwa, or Mei (also known as West Atlantic)—they shared some common characteristics. But each tribe was distinct. They differed markedly "in culture, degree of political cohesion and organization, ability and resolution to resist Americo-Liberian domination, and responsiveness to modernization."[8]

Adding to the complexity, tribal boundaries were fluid. Over history, the various tribal units migrated from one area to another in search of new agricultural lands or salt deposits. More often, according to Indiana Professor J. Gus Liebenow, they moved in response to "expansionist pressure from more powerful tribes," and later to escape "tax collectors, labor recruiters, and arbitrary rulers."[9] Liebenow adds, "Most of the nineteenth century was apparently marked by a constant series of movements, with stronger tribal groupings driving weaker ones farther into the rain forest or down the coast."[10]

The national boundaries later demarcated by colonial powers frequently sliced through tribal groups, isolating their members from one another. In modern-day Liberia, only the Dei, Belle, and Bassa lived entirely within the country. Large numbers of the other tribes resided in neighboring Sierra Leone, Ivory Coast, and Guinea.

The newly arrived Americo-Liberians first encountered the eight tribes who lived along the coast: the Dei (one of the smallest groups, who occupied an area that included Cape Mesurado, the site of the American colony), Gola, Kpelle, Vai, Bassa, Grebo, and Kru. Although their homeland lay some distance from the American colony, the Kru initially were the best known to the settlers—and to most foreigners—since they frequently worked as seamen on vessels. And, since many acquired some English, they often served as interpreters.

In the 1962 census, tribal people numbered 984,120—97 percent of the country's total population. In 1974 they numbered 1,445,828 (96 percent). Some rough approximations of the tribal groups' relative sizes might be gleaned from the two censuses and later estimates by the CIA and others. According to one source, of the country's total population, the Kpelle (20 percent) was the largest tribal group, followed by the Bassa

(14 percent), Gio (9 percent), and Kru (8 percent). The other twelve tribal groups, Americo-Liberians, and foreigners (particularly Lebanese and Syrians before 1980) accounted for the remaining roughly 50 percent of the population.[11]

―⁂―

It is difficult to judge the significance of membership in any particular tribe. Tribal groupings are not firmly fixed, nor are they historically rooted. At the least, such membership provides a sense of belonging to a particular group whose members share a number (although not necessarily all in every case) of common characteristics: language, a historical "homeland," similar customs and ways of viewing the world, recognition of mutual interests worth defending, solidarity and cooperation in a range of economic and social transactions, and, on occasion, a centralized political authority.

Each tribe, for example, traditionally possessed "a set of institutionalized beliefs" that defined which occupations "were proper and not proper" for the tribe, the proper occupation for each individual member—those okay for men, those okay for women, those for the old and young, for members of noble lineage, and for members with spiritual gifts.

With the arrival of the Americo-Liberian colonists, tribes began to be stereotyped in terms of occupations. For instance, the Kru would work only as seamen. The Bassa made good cooks and stewards, Loma the best soldiers. While the Kpelle supposedly excelled in agriculture, Mandingo never farmed, only engaged in trade. The Gola and Vai declined to work for others. And so on. As money displaced the traditional subsistence economy, the relative attractiveness of wages of course became the deciding factor, and the stereotypes became outdated.[12]

Because the Bassa and Dei were close to the early major Americo-Liberian settlements at Monrovia and Buchanan, they became involved with the settler society early on as artisans, clerks, and domestic servants. Many Vai, after initially resisting the Americo-Liberians, came to serve in the government, as officers in the army, and in the Liberian consular service. Some of the Grebo, largely mission educated, became teachers, ministers, and writers. The Kru (including several related groups) engaged in cash economic activities, mainly trading with Europeans, working as interpreters, middlemen, and coastal pilots. Due at least in part to their competition with the Americo-Liberians in trade, the Kru historically put up the most persistent resistance to the colonists.

In contrast, the tribal groups who made up the majority of Liberia's population occupied the more insular and remote hinterland. Mainly subsistence farmers, their first contacts with the Americo-Liberians came only in the twentieth century with the steady penetration of missionaries, mining, logging, and tree crop cultivation, as well as the construction of roads and railroads since the Second World War. The Kpelle, Liberia's largest tribal group, probably counted as its least acculturated until rubber plantations recruited tribal people to work as laborers and iron ore mines opened in their areas. Many Loma and Krahn made their contacts with modern life serving in the army.

*It should be noted these observations apply in large part to conditions before 1980. Doubtless some, if not many, have changed since then.

Liberia probably suffered at least fifteen tribal conflicts, wars, and revolts between 1822 and 1980. The last occurred in 1915. Most observers considered that the tribal hinterland had been pacified by 1925.

TRIBAL CONFLICTS, WARS, AND REVOLTS, 1822–1980

Colony (1822–39)
Dei, Vai, and Gola–Settlers War 1822
Dei and Gola–Settler War 1832
Bassa–Settler War 1835
Kru–settler "Fishman" conflict 1838

Commonwealth (1839–47)
Vai-settler battles 1839–40
Gola-Dei War (Gatumba's War) 1838–40

Republic (1847–1980)
Bassa-Government War 1851–53
Kru-Government War 1855
Grebo-Maryland War 1856–58
Grebo Reunited Kingdom Revolution 1875–76
Third Grebo War 1893
Grebo Troubles 1898–99
Kru-government battles 1909
Grebo-Government War 1910
Kru-government conflict 1912
Kru Confederacy–Government War 1915

(Sources include Jeremy I. Levitt, *The Evolution of Deadly Conflict in Liberia* [Durham, NC: Carolina Academic Press, 2005]; J. Gus. Liebenow, *Liberia: The Quest for Democracy* [Bloomington: Indiana University Press, 1987]; Frederick Starr, *Liberia: Description, History, Problems* [Chicago: privately published, 1913].)

Some sources include additional conflicts (some of which might duplicate those on the above list): Gola (1898–99), Kissi

(1903), Kru (1905), Loma (1905–7), Bassa (1906), Kpelle (1911), Krahn (1921).

More recently, the Liberian Civil War (1989–1997) had some tribal dimensions. Most, however, were more intertribal than Americo-Liberian–tribal.

Upon returning from his ominous meeting with King Peter earlier in August, Ashmun had thrown himself into preparing the settlement's defenses. Despite the fact that he had not been authorized by either the Colonization Society or the US government, Ashmun took command of the little band of settlers. He counted twenty-seven men deemed able to bear arms. His main hope resided in one brass and five iron cannons that lay dismantled and rusty. Under his direction the men readied the guns and muskets for action, drilled daily, and labored to clear away the forest and construct earthworks. The work for everyone was unremitting and harsh. Meager rations and incessant rain added to their misery.

And that ever-present scourge—African fever—struck often. At one point every man but one reported sick. Ashmun himself was prostrate, and his beloved wife, CD, languished. The reverend balefully wrote on the twelfth of September 1822,

> Rain falls in floods. The sick all seem better except Mrs. Ashmun... There is no rational hope of her recovery...[He beheld her] a female of most delicate constitution, lying under the influence of a mortal fever, in the corner of a miserable hut...on a couch literally dripping with water, which a roof of thatch was unable to exclude—circumstances rendering recovery impossible.[13]

CD died September 15.

Shortly before daybreak the morning of November 11, 1822, the pickets, who had been on guard through the night outside the settlement, began returning. Suddenly a horde of Golah, Dei, and Vai warriors burst forth from the forest wielding spears, war clubs, axes, swords, and bows and arrows, waving shields made of hides fastened to wicker or wooden frames, their faces and bodies made fearsome with paints, ungodly shrieks, and wild yelling.

Some carried muskets, most with percussion caps, but many with older flintlocks. The barrels were wrapped with brass wire or tightly bound cloth as a precaution against bursting—a frequent calamity given the lack of maintenance, unreliable gunpowder, and inferior quality of the weapons. (Europeans manufactured them specifically for the African market.) War belts carried musket balls made by melting down iron pots. As the overwhelmed colonists fell back, the invaders seized the outer defensive works. Ashmun's worst fears seemed to be materializing.

However, the colonists' arduous labors paid off. They managed to get their brass fieldpiece mounted on a platform into position. Firing at close range into the mass of invading warriors decimated their ranks. Ashmun, writing later, described the carnage: "Every shot literally spent its force in a solid mass of living human flesh. Their fire suddenly terminated. A savage yell was raised…and the whole host disappeared."[14] The little group of settlers had held off a force, Ashmun estimated, of eight hundred warriors—at a cost of four settlers killed and four seriously wounded.

Ashmun and the settlement had escaped destruction. But it would prove but a short interlude. The Dei, Gola, and Vai warriors would regroup and soon return, determined more than ever to crush the colony. Food and ammunition were virtually exhausted. Now only divine intervention could save the defenders and the settlement. An intervention, though hardly divine, did come—in the form of a British sea captain whose vessel had anchored off the cape. The captain generously replenished the colony's stores just in the nick of time. The very next evening, on November 30, the attackers began to gather once again, this time with a much larger force. Ashmun guessed it totaled around 1,200 men. Before daybreak they attacked on two sides.

But the colonists were ready. They manned all six cannons and fired them with deadly effect. Although they battled savagely, the invading warriors could not overcome the defenders' dogged resistance. With great loss, the attackers finally gave up the fight.

The next night, according to Ashmun, one of the settlers on guard detected some movement near his post and let off a brisk fire of musketry; several rounds of fire from the cannons followed. No response from the enemy natives. Only silence. But, luckily for the beleaguered defenders, the booming cannons in the night caught the attention of a British colonial schooner, the *Prince Regent,* lying offshore. The schooner carried a load of military stores—and an extraordinary, flamboyant Scottish adventurer. Captain Alexander Gordon Laing, a British army officer stationed in west Africa, would later gain notoriety when, in 1826, he became the first European to reach Timbuktu. Shortly thereafter he, as far as the rest of the world was concerned, vanished completely. His fate would remain a mystery until a French expedition discovered the truth eighty-five years later. He had been murdered by his guide upon leaving Timbuktu.

The British vessel and explorer proved most valuable to the colonists. Ashmun felt certain that the Africans would mount still another attempt to eradicate the colony. Laing, a skillful mediator, however, managed to secure a peace agreement in which the warring natives agreed to an unlimited truce between them and the colony and to submit any differences they had to the governor of Sierra Leone for future arbitration. (None were ever submitted.) Further good luck: A prize crew, who presumably had delivered a captured slave ship to Sierra Leone, also were aboard the *Prince Regent.* A midshipman named Gordon and eleven sailors volunteered to stay behind to help ensure compliance with the truce. The grateful settlers must have felt God was on their side. Not so for Midshipman Gordon and eight of the sailors, however. Within four weeks of the *Prince Regent's* departure, they fell victim to the African fever.

With their war-prone neighbors subdued—at least for the time being—Ashmun and the settlers turned to building their new home. Supplies, though, once more began to run low. But the group somehow managed to do with what they had until relief in the form of the US sloop *Cyane* arrived in March. The vessel's commander, Captain Robert Trail Spence, put his sailors to work helping erect buildings and recover the abandoned hulk of the colony's old schooner *Augusta*, which they refitted with six guns. Life at Cape Mesurado began to look up. Then the fever struck anew. It hit the *Cyane*'s crew so hard that Captain Spence felt compelled to put to sea. Unfortunately their departure came too late. Forty men, including the lieutenant, Richard Dashiell, and the ship's surgeon, Dr. Dix, soon died.

―――

In defending the settlement, Ashmun came to rely heavily upon a Baptist minister who had been among the *Strong*'s passengers. The Reverend Lott Cary (or Carey) was no ordinary black preacher. In fact a state historical plaque on a highway in Charles City County, Virginia, celebrates Cary's nearby birthplace and his role in history. The first African American Baptist missionary to Africa, Cary was born about 1780 as a slave on a plantation owned by John Bowry, a Methodist minister. Bowry in 1804 hired him out to a tobacco firm, the Shockhoe tobacco warehouse, in nearby Richmond.

In 1807, after tiring of what he admitted were three years of drunkenness, profanity, and rowdyism, Cary joined the First Baptist Church in Richmond. A sermon there about Nicodemus so stirred him that the illiterate slave determined to learn to read the story himself. With some instruction, but due more to his single-mindedness, Cary began to master reading, as well as writing. Although he spent any free time reading—mainly the Bible, but even Adam Smith's *The Wealth of Nations*—he didn't neglect his job at the warehouse.

Quite the contrary. He became so proficient, someone remarked that upon request he could produce any one of the hundreds of hogsheads of tobacco under his charge almost instantly. He managed the shipments, according to Ralph Gurley, "with a promptness and correctness which no person, white or black, has equaled in the same situation."[15] Shortly after Cary's wife died in 1813, his nine years working at the warehouse enabled him to purchase his and his two children's freedom for $850, even after regularly turning over a portion of his wages to his owner.

Cary soon was licensed to preach and rapidly developed a devoted following among the church's large black congregation and slaves on plantations around Richmond. He became renowned for his eloquent sermons in the white community as well. By 1815 his interest had focused on Africa and missionary work there, thanks in large measure to William Crane, his teacher in the Richmond school for blacks. Sometime after helping organize the Richmond African Missionary Society in 1815, Reverend Cary decided to go to Liberia.

Many of his friends and admirers were stunned. His warehouse employers reputedly had offered him a $200 annual pay raise if he would stay. But Cary remained steadfast. He explained,

> I long to preach to the poor Africans the way of life and salvation. I don't know what might befall me whether I may find a grave in the ocean, or among the savage men, or more savage wild beasts on the coast of Africa; nor am I anxious what may become of me. I feel it my duty to go.[16]

Cary also could not pass up the opportunity to vent his feelings about discrimination in the United States:

> I am an African and in this country however meritorious my conduct, and respectable my character, I cannot receive the credit due to either. I wish to go to a country where I shall be estimated by my merits, not by my complexion; and I feel bound to labor for my suffering race.[17]

Although initially he opposed the American Colonization Society, Cary—as a missionary sponsored by the Richmond African Baptist Missionary Society and the General Baptist Missionary Convention—left in 1821 for Liberia aboard the *Strong*. With him were his new wife and his children. But after landing at Cape Mesurado, his life took a different turn. Soon after arriving he helped save the colony by his determination to stay despite the appalling conditions the settlers faced, and he swayed others not to leave. His bravery in supporting Ashmun's defense of the settlement and rallying the colony's broken forces against the native attacks in November and December of 1822 made him a hero. The Reverend Cary also found the time and energy to found the first church in Liberia (Providence Baptist Church), preach regularly, establish a charity school for native children—and to marry once more following his second wife's death shortly after they arrived in Africa.

The dawning of May 24, 1823, gave new hope to Cary, Ashmun, and the rest of the settlers. The brig *Oswego* arrived loaded with supplies, including needed tools. Sixty-one new immigrants crowded her decks to view their new home. A recuperated Dr. Eli Ayres walked down the gangplank ready to resume his duties now as the "principal Agent and Physician in the Colony." However, the new hope proved short lived, particularly for Ashmun.

When he landed at Mesurado a year earlier, Ashmun had expected to find a Colonization Society or government agent on site. After seeing his group of emigrants off, he and his wife would then return to the United States aboard the *Strong*. But given the deplorable conditions prevailing in the settlement and the absence of official leadership, he assumed the position of acting principal agent. To stave off the colony's collapse, Ashmun purchased a small amount of supplies totaling slightly more than $1,400 by writing drafts on the US government and the society. Ayres brought unwelcome word that the drafts had not been honored since the government had not appointed him and the society had not authorized him to make such purchases. More disturbing, Ayres told him, "Society members and the Board suspected him of malfeasance." While they appreciated his services, they "had lost confidence in him."[18]

Ayres brought further trouble. One of his first acts as principal agent was to oversee a survey of the entire settlement and distribute or redistribute lots to all the colonists. Because of the turmoil attendant to the unsettled conditions and successive waves of emigrants, the initial allocation of land had been uneven. In the process of the subsequent redistribution, many of the earlier settlers found themselves dispossessed of holdings on which they had made improvements. They vigorously protested. Soon the colony was up in arms, beset with excitement, and verging on insurrection. Ayres's health conveniently again began to fail, and in December 1823 he prudently departed for the United States. Ashmun once more was left holding a very hot kettle of fish.

"Seeing the colony again deserted by the agent and in a state of discontent and confusion, [his wrongs forgotten, Ashmun]... remained at the helm. Order was soon restored but the seeds of insubordination remained." [19]

Even Cary, Ashmun's loyal lieutenant, turned against him and became leader of the malcontents, some of whom seized a portion of the colony's stores, a seditious offense. Ashmun was forgiving, however. In his report to the Colonization Society's board, he emphasized Cary's record of service to the colony and to himself personally, writing that but for "the unwearied and painful attention of this individual [Cary]—rendered at all hours—of every description—and continued for several months," this hand "that records the lawless transaction would long since been cold in the ground."[20] In the absence of any formally trained medical person, Cary had been appointed the colony's health officer. He undertook to study all the medical literature he could lay his hands on, "and devoted his time, almost exclusively to the sick and the afflicted." [21]

Cary realized he had lost his usual composure in the incident and now came forward declaring that "he had betrayed the trust reposed in him" and expressed his willingness to be useful in whatever way Ashmun might think fit. In addition, Cary, whom the Baptist Missionary Society sponsored, announced he would no longer depend on the Colonization Society for supplies. The two once again were fast friends.

But that was not sufficient to dispel the cloud that still threatened the colony, and Ashmun in particular. The supply of stores, always precarious, fell perilously low. To make matters worse, the *Cyrus* arrived from Virginia in February 1824 with 103 new immigrants. Ashmun had little option but to place the colony on half rations. Disaffected colonists railed against this further "act of tyranny." Opponents wrote letters back to the society's headquarters accusing him of various offenses.[22] One letter appeared in the *National Intelligencer*. The Colonization Society in Washington was aghast.

On March 15 Ashmun sent a letter to the board requesting that he be relieved of all his duties in Africa. The managers asked for an investigation. An ailing Ashmun decided to retreat to the Cape Verde Islands off the African coast to recuperate. But as luck would have it, in preparing to leave, he suffered a ruptured artery "in a bungling attempt to extract a decayed tooth." Blood gushed forth, and the bleeding continued for twenty-four hours. Ashmun came dangerously close to dying. He finally departed on his trip the first of April 1824.[23]

In late June Reverend Gurley left Norfolk aboard the US schooner *Porpoise* to make a first hand inquiry of the imbroglio. When they first met on July 24 Gurley immediately fell under Ashmun's charisma. He took little time to decide that Ashmun had acted in the best interests of the colony and the society and should be commended for his actions rather than censured. Gurley became a great admirer of Ashmun, writing somewhat floridly later, "The serene light of reason, of goodness, of meekness, softened the stateliness of sorrow, and threw a charm on the grandeur of his storm-shaken, but self-sustained spirit."[24]

He also brought with him a name for the new colony. Ashmun had named the settlement Christopolis but was not satisfied with it. He wrote asking the society's board if it had decided on a name for the town.[25] At the society's seventh annual meeting, General Robert Goodloe Harper of Maryland suggested the colony be named Liberia and its settlement on the cape, the principal town, Monrovia. The society agreed. Gurley, satisfied that he had helped mend the fissures among the colony's residents and set it on a more promising course, departed on August 24.[26] He also thought that he had healed the rift between Ashmun and the society's managers, but he was mistaken. They began recruiting a new agent.

To Ashmun's credit, he accomplished much for the colony. Virtually every landowner now could boast a shelter; many houses were well advanced in construction. Several roads were cleared and opened. A one-hundred-foot stone pier was built. A number of schools came into operation, including one for native children. Two large houses of worship were under construction. Ashmun organized a colonial militia that included "a voluntary corps of young men in a neat uniform."[27] He concluded an agreement with the principal chiefs securing "perpetual peace" in the area and guaranteeing free trade with natives in the interior and on the coast. Ashmun had decided the colony could be self-sufficient through trade with the natives. Gurley agreed, saying that Ashmun "had proved by actual experiment, that it was far more economical to subsist the Colony on African than American provisions."[28]

In a letter to a friend in 1823, Ashmun could write confidently, "We are now one hundred and fifty strong, all in health (I speak of the Colonists), have about fifty houses, including three store houses, and a heavy stone tower, fourteen feet high, mounting six pieces of ordinance."[29]

A steady stream of colonists continued to arrive from the United States. The *Cyrus* brought 105 new faces in February 1824, all healthy on arriving, but after four weeks, all sick. The *Hunter* with sixty colonists arrived in March the following year; other vessels delivered more settlers. The Colonization Society's toehold on Africa's western coast was rapidly emerging as an American colonial beachhead.

To complement this swelling population, Ashmun embarked upon a program of territorial expansion that would occupy the colony for most of the rest of the century. He purchased rights (although it would remain for Lott Cary to complete the transaction) to a sizeable tract along the south bank of the Saint Paul's River that the old nemesis of the colony, King Peter, claimed. Ashmun saw this "beautiful river" along which "in Africa's better days, innumerable native hamlets" had been scattered, "wasted by the rage for trading in slaves; with which the constant presence of slaving vessels, and the introduction of foreign luxuries, have inspired them."[30]

He and the society also realized the colony's growth called for a more formal statement of its governance. In July 1825 several American newspapers published a Constitution for the Government of the African Colony of Liberia. The document, brief and straightforward, consisted of ten articles. They spelled out the powers of and relationships between the society, the agents, and the settlers. Its provisions, however, did not apply to the African slaves (the "Congoes" or Congo people), freed by the US Navy from slave ships, nor to other native Africans, but only to American settlers. Only these Americo-Liberians could enjoy the privileges of citizenship—privileges their American homeland had denied them. The seeds that more than a century and a half later would help bring down Liberia's first republic had been sown.

Article 1 stipulated that all persons born in Liberia or who moved there to reside "shall be free and entitled to all the privileges, as are enjoyed by the citizens of the United States." Subsequent provisions confirmed the society's powers to make rules for the settlement's government, "until they shall withdraw their agents, and leave the settlers to the government of themselves" and to amend the constitution. The agents in Liberia would "determine all questions relative to the government of the Settlement," exercise all judicial powers, and appoint all officers not appointed by the society's managers. Article 5 prohibited slavery in the settlement.[31]

The pace of progress had quickened, though much more needed to be done. Slave raiders still stole men, women, and children virtually from Monrovia's doorsteps. Ashmun decided that forceful action was essential. Leading a band of twenty-five or so men, he launched a surprise attack on nearby Digby, where a Spanish-owned barracoon housed captured slaves. The small troop destroyed the structure and liberated the captives held there. Trade Town, a notorious slave center several miles down the coast, next came into Ashmun's sights. Two American warships joined in the attack on the town. The joint Liberian-American force landed, and soon the town was ablaze. Although they freed few slaves, they did blow up a powder magazine and kill a number of slavers and their African colleagues. "The slave trade on that part of the coast of Africa never recovered."[32]

But the man who had saved the nascent American colony from certain annihilation and helped put it on the road to survival, one of Liberia's greatest heroes, could not continue. Ashmun's physician advised him that the only hope for his recovery would be to return to the United States.

The entire colony held Ashmun in such esteem that his departure, though he supposedly would remain away only temporarily, provoked a great outpouring of affection. His loving friend Cary captured the mood describing how "J. Ashmun, Esq., went on board the brig *Doris*...escorted by three companies of the military, and when taking leave, he delivered a short address, which was truly affecting." Cary noted that nearly Monrovia's entire population (at least two-thirds) "were out on this occasion, and nearly all parted from him with tears." He thought "the hope of his [Ashmun's] return in a few months, alone enabled them to give him up...The brig sailed on the 27th May."[33]

Ashmun never returned.

―⚜―

The ailing clergyman landed at Saint Bartholomew's in the West Indies, where he decided to remain since he feared that to continue on would likely hasten his death. After a degree of recuperation, however, he took another vessel and arrived in New Haven, Connecticut, on August 10, 1828.[34] But he sensed that death was near. Gurley recounts that Ashmun said to a friend soon after his arrival in New Haven that he had come there to die. He died gently the evening of August 28, 1828, "in the thirty-fifth year of his age."[35]

The funeral took place the next day in the Central Church. Reverend Gurley reported that after the minister's eulogy, a poignant scene unfolded. He wrote,

A venerable, solitary female, entered the congregation, and with look which told what her tongue might in vain have essayed to speak, approached the corpse. It was the mother of Ashmun! Every heart in that vast assembly beat fainter, as they beheld this aged matron, who had traveled for several days and nights from a remote part of the country, in the hope of embracing her living son, pressing her lips and her heart upon the coffin which concealed all that remained of that son in death, forever from her sight.[36]

A large number of New Haven citizens and residents of nearby towns accompanied his body to the grave in the churchyard of New Haven. "A simple but beautiful monument erected by the Managers of the American Colonization Society...bears the name of Ashmun."[37]

Reverend Gurley remembered Ashmun as "tall—his hair and eyes light—his features regular and cast in the finest mould—his manners mild, yet dignified—and his countenance an expression of the gentlest affections softened the lineaments of a lofty, firm, and fearless mind."[38]

Ashmun looms large in Liberia's history. Many consider him the "founder of Liberia," whose greatness only Joseph Jenkins Roberts, the country's first president, can approach.

—⁂—

After his beloved friend left for the United States, Cary shouldered full responsibility for the colony—in addition to the indispensable duties he had performed since arriving in Africa. After serving as health officer, in 1824 he had become the physician of the colony. He had continued his missionary labors, establishing schools and churches, building meeting houses, baptizing converts. The Colonization Society's board had taken note of his outstanding work, particularly his medical service, and in the fall of 1825 invited Cary to visit the United States. The board members thought he could "strengthen the hands of those who had been laboring to sustain the colony," and because of "his influence among the free colored population of this country [the United States]...they would be favorable to their migration to the land of their fathers."[39]

The society made arrangements for Cary to depart for America aboard the *Indian Chief* in April 1826. Cary ardently wished to go, "to confer...with his friends of the mission in Richmond...and to wake up...the dormant energies of many of his colored brethren who he believed possessed talents to labor efficiently in Africa as teachers and preachers."[40] But the vessel sailed without him, carrying only a letter from him to friends in Virginia. Ashmun had enthusiastically endorsed the trip. However, the two, upon further reflection, had concluded that since the last immigrants had not yet recovered from the fever, it would be too risky for the settlement's only physician to leave. Better for Cary to postpone the trip.

Lott Cary, though disappointed, resumed his active life, optimistic as ever: "We dedicated our meeting house last October... Our native schools still go on under hopeful circumstances. I think the slave trade is nearly done in our neighborhood. The agent, with our forces, has released upwards of one hundred and eighty from chains, since the first of October."[41] In September 1826 he was made vice agent of the colony. Most important, Jehudi Ashmun had absolute faith in him. Even "on his death bed Mr. Ashmun urged that Mr. Cary should be permanently appointed to conduct the affairs of the colony, expressing perfect confidence in his integrity and ability for that great work."[42]

Ashmun's faith was not misplaced. Cary wrote his friend after he had arrived in Connecticut that "most of the work that you directed to be done, is nearly accomplished...The gun house in Monrovia, and the jail, have been done for some weeks; the mounting of the guns will be done this week, if the weather permits."[43] He reported similar progress at the other settlements and that the recently arrived colonists had recovered from their illness. A definite sign of progress, Cary enthusiastically described the colony's Fourth of July celebration, saying, "I have never seen the American Independence celebrated with so much spirit and propriety since the existence of the colony; the guns being all mounted and painted, and previously arranged for the purpose, added very much to the grand salute. Two dinners were given, one by the Independent Volunteer Company, and one by captain Devany."[44]

The black missionary still expected his friend Ashmun to return before the end of the rainy season. Even after October and then November rolled around, he still expected him, unaware that Jehudi Ashmun had succumbed to his infirmity in August. In fact, Cary never learned of Ashmun's death. Natives had robbed a factory belonging to the colony in Digby, one of the settlements. They even allowed a slave dealer to store goods in the same building and intercepted a warning letter from Cary to the slaver. The acting agent called up the colony's militia with the intention of launching a punitive attack on the African perpetrators. As part of the preparations, Cary and several others were making cartridges in the old agency building on November 8, when a candle apparently was accidentally knocked over onto some loose powder. Within an instant the whole cache of stored munitions exploded. Eight persons were injured; six died the following day; Cary and the remaining survivor lasted until November 10, 1828.

The two men who, more than anyone else, had saved the struggling colony of Liberia and placed it on a relatively secure course now were dead. Their loss staggered the colony, the Colonization Society, and Cary's Richmond African Missionary Society. The proceedings of the latter's annual meeting in 1829 lamented that "the loss which has been sustained cannot, in our estimation, be easily repaired. This excellent man [Cary] seems to have been raised up by Divine Providence for the special purpose of taking an active part in the management of the infant settlement." The proceedings concluded, "Lott Cary was among the most gifted men of the present age...Under more favorable circumstances, he would have been on a level with the most intellectual and honored of this race."[45]

After Cary's tragic death, the colony elected Colston Waring acting agent. Dr. Richard Randall, appointed by the Colonization Society to replace Ashmun, arrived in Monrovia on December 22, 1828, shocked to find Cary dead. In less than four months, Randall also would be dead. The colony once again faced a crisis in leadership; eight different agents and acting agents would serve in the next ten years. Nevertheless, despite the frequent changes in agents, Liberia had begun to prosper.

Trade flourished, and new settlers arrived in a seemingly endless flow. Between 1820 and 1843, some 4,571 immigrants went to Liberia (but because of the high death rate—20 percent—among them, especially in the first two years after arrival, only 1,819 remained in 1843).[46] And settlements other than the American Colonization Society's venture soon appeared. Following the American society's establishment in 1816, local societies, mainly state organizations, had sprung up in much of the country. The national society depended primarily on these local and state societies, churches, and individuals for financing, but still relied on the federal government for help in some areas. Any American could be a society member for an annual fee of one dollar, or a minimum contribution of thirty dollars for life membership.

The Maryland Colonization Society was incorporated in 1831. Mississippi followed suit in 1834, and societies were organized in Massachusetts, New York, New Jersey, Pennsylvania, Virginia, Louisiana, Georgia, and others. According to Fogel, 306 local societies, mainly in slave states, had been organized by 1832.[47]

These societies promoted colonization locally, helped fund the national society, and sponsored immigrants to settle in the society's Liberian colony. But some established their own independent settlements. The most notable and successful was Maryland's at Las Palmas, more than 250 miles down the coast from Monrovia, at Liberia's most southerly point. The first settlers arrived there in February 1834. At about the same time, the Young Men's Colonization Society of Pennsylvania and the New York Colonization Society in 1832 jointly sponsored the Port Cresson colony at Bassa Cove, less than one hundred miles down the coast from Monrovia. The initial settlers aboard the "good ship *Ninus,* laden with one-hundred twenty-six" brave souls arrived in 1834. The societies' agent, taking his cue from the dominant Quakers in the Pennsylvania group, adhered strictly to pacifism, including banning the ownership of guns. Unfortunately, the neighboring Bassa tribesmen did not follow the same persuasion. Within six months, they massacred the new settlers and virtually destroyed the colony. The sponsors revived the venture the next year at Bassa Cove under a "new and more realistic governor." It merged with Liberia in April 1839.[48]

In 1838 another group of thirty-seven settlers landed on the coast at the mouth of the Sinoe River, some 150 miles from Monrovia, to found a new colony, "Mississippi in Africa."

The colony's town received the name Greenville in honor of Judge James Green, who had emancipated from his plantation near Natchez a portion of the first group of immigrants from Mississippi. "Although started with enthusiasm, the Mississippi/Louisiana settlement in Africa failed to prosper, and in 1842 the sponsors were easily persuaded to merge their colony with that of the American Colonization Society."[49]

The American society wisely recognized that Liberia needed not only a new leader, but a new status as well. Allowing the colony greater autonomy also would reduce the financial burden it placed on the society. On January 5, 1839, the institution's board of directors adopted a new constitution for the colony, and befitting Liberia's new status, a new name: the Commonwealth of Liberia. It comprised two counties: Montserrado, which included the settlements of Monrovia, New Georgia, Caldwell, and Millsburg. The second county, Grand Bassa, with less population and more rural area, encompassed Bassa Cove, Marshall, Bexley, and Edina.

A governor, still appointed, replaced the agent as chief executive. To fill the post, The society named Thomas Buchanan, a Pennsylvanian (and cousin of future US president James Buchanan) the first governor. Born in Covington, Franklin County, on November 19, 1808, Buchanan served ably as the US agent of the Bassa Cove colony in 1836–37, but would serve Liberia only two years as governor before falling victim to the African sickness on September 30, 1841, at Bassa Cove. The settlement later was renamed Buchanan in honor of the commonwealth's first governor.

As lieutenant governor the colony had elected Joseph Jenkins Roberts. It was a providential choice. Roberts would emerge as one of the country's greatest leaders. He would guide a growing Liberia onto the international stage as governor of the commonwealth and into independence as the first president of the Republic of Liberia. They would be tumultuous years.

CHAPTER 6

From Colony to Commonwealth

—ɷ—

TWO YEARS EARLIER, ON APRIL 19, 1839, the crowd who gathered on Monrovia's waterfront had anxiously awaited the newly appointed governor's arrival. After all, he carried with him a very important document for the new commonwealth—the Constitution, Government, and Digest of the Laws of Liberia—which he had helped draft, and which the society on January 5 had adopted. Happily, when Governor Buchanan presented it to the settlers, their apprehensions soon dissipated. They accepted the new charter by unanimous vote, subject only to a minor amendment the society readily agreed to. Under the new government, power would reside in a governor, lieutenant governor, and legislative council, the latter two chosen by popular vote.

Buchanan quickly found himself confronted by two issues that threatened the new commonwealth. The slave trade, a bone in Liberia's throat since the first settlers arrived, stubbornly continued to flourish along the coast. The trade, carried out through a number of foreign-owned (mainly Spanish) barracoons or "slave factories," was too lucrative for local chiefs to relinquish easily. Hoping to eliminate the threat that the American colonies, backed by the US Navy, posed to their enterprise, the natives launched attacks against the settlers. The foreign slave traders, notably the notorious Don Pedro Blanco, naturally aided and abetted the African chiefs.

To deal with the problem, Buchanan relied heavily upon Roberts who already had proven himself an able leader in earlier operations against hostile natives. When a Gola tribal chief, Gatumba of Boporu, and an ally named Gotora, attacked settlements up the St. Saint Paul River from Monrovia in 1839, the governor dispatched Roberts with three hundred militia and several field guns on a punitive expedition. Gotora was killed, and "Gatumba's soldiers...after the first fierce conflict abandoned their stronghold and chief."[1]

Roberts concluded a treaty of friendship with the defeated chief. Among other things it called for him, Gatumba, to cooperate with the Liberians to end the slave trade. In succeeding years Roberts would find similar treaties of friendship and cooperation highly useful in extending Liberian claims to new territory. But, he would have to fight many more battles over the next ten years before he could claim Liberia free of the trade in human slaves.

A second issue posed a potentially more serious threat, one that ultimately played a large part in forcing the American government's hand in its policy toward the colony. Although the so-called "scramble for Africa" (to carve the continent into colonies or protectorates of European powers) would not begin in earnest until the 1870s, rivalry for African trade had been heating up for some time. British traders for many years had manned posts up and down the Liberian coast bartering trade goods for ivory, palm oil, camwood, and other local products. As the Liberian settlements grew and established themselves more securely, many colonists, including Roberts, also turned to trade in competition with the British merchants.

And as the colony grew, the government, in need of revenue, began to levy customs duties on trade falling within the territory it claimed. British traders, backed by ships of the Royal Navy operating off the coast, however, contested the colony's sovereignty over the territory and its right to control trade and collect duties.

As both Liberian and British trade expanded, collision was inevitable. Upon Buchanan's death in 1841 it fell to Roberts, now acting governor, to deal with this festering problem.

—⚉—

When the society formally appointed Joseph Jenkins Roberts, a thirty-three-year-old mulatto, governor in January 1842, he became the first nonwhite—although he was an octoroon, with only one-eighth Negro blood—to rule Liberia.

In Petersburg, Virginia, at the corner of Sycamore and Wythe Streets, stands a six-foot-long marker forty-two inches high, honoring Virginia's "Ninth President." Most schoolboys in the state that prides itself as the "cradle of presidents" can name eight: George Washington, Thomas Jefferson, James Madison, James Monroe, Zachary Taylor, John Tyler, William Henry Harrison, and Woodrow Wilson. But the ninth? The inscription on the marker reads, "Joseph Jenkins Roberts, resident of Petersburg 1809–1829. President of Liberia 1847–1851, 1868–1876."[2]

Born in Norfolk March 15, 1809, Roberts moved to Petersburg, Virginia, with his family while still a child. His father, James Roberts, was born free; Amelia, his mother, gained her freedom at the age of twenty-three. (The paternity of Joseph Jenkins, the oldest of her seven children, was not wholly clear; his biological father could have been James Roberts or possibly a white man.)[3] A contemporary described Amelia "as a woman of 'intelligence, moral character, and industrious habits.'"[4]

Roberts's father owned a variety of boats that plied the James and Appomattox Rivers. After the family moved to Petersburg, he began transporting goods from Petersburg to Norfolk on his own flatboats. Business apparently was good; he amassed a level of wealth unusual for a colored person of that time. When he died in 1823, he left his family two houses and land valued at $1,600 and other property, mainly four boats, worth $600.

The Roberts "came from the Negro elite of the Old Dominion."⁵ The entire family were ambitious achievers: After immigrating to Liberia, one of Joseph's brothers, Henry J. Roberts, returned to the United States to study medicine and became a successful physician in Liberia. Another, John Wright Roberts, was ordained a minister and rose to become bishop of the Methodist Episcopal Church in Liberia.

Young Joseph worked in his father's boating business and also apprenticed to a local barber named William N. Colson. (Barbering offered one of the most remunerative occupations open to free blacks.) On the back of the monument to Roberts described earlier is inscribed the following: "Joseph Jenkins Roberts worked 100 yards northwest of this spot"—in Colson's barber shop on Union Street.⁶ Although he might have attended a local school run by a Negro society or had some private tutoring, Roberts was mainly self-educated. Colson figured importantly in this process. Something of an intellectual, he lent Roberts books from his personal library and, along with several other prosperous colored friends, exerted a positive influence on the youth. Light-complexioned Roberts and brown-colored Colson became close friends and later business associates.

In January 1825 Roberts applied at the Petersburg clerk's office to be registered. "To become registered blacks had to show they were needed in the community's labor market." Once the court granted them this status, "they carried their legal papers with them, since they had to be presented upon demand."⁷ As Roberts worked on his father's boats and at Colson's barbershop, the clerk recommended he be registered. The clerk described him "as a lad of colour, 16 years old in March next—rather above 5 feet 6 inches high in shoes, light complexion, grisly or reddish brown hair."⁸

On February 9, 1829, six years after his father died, Joseph, his mother, and four brothers and two sisters boarded the *Harriet* in Norfolk's harbor. (Roberts had married early, but his wife had died.) They were part of a group of 160 emigrants bound for Liberia. The passengers coincidentally included another Virginian, James S. Payne, who would become Liberia's fourth president. A few days before the vessel landed at Monrovia on March 24, Joseph celebrated his twentieth birthday. He did not record what kind of a celebration it was.

As the Roberts family stepped off the ship and surveyed their new homeland, they could not help but wonder what they had ventured into. The little outpost of black Americans still suffered from the devastation that sickness, disease, hostile natives, shortages of supplies, and the loneliness of struggling in a strange land far removed from familiar sights had inflicted on them. Still, the worst appeared to have passed, and an air of cautious optimism could be detected—at least faintly.

The newly arrived family shared this air of optimism and refused to give in to what must have been a degree of disappointment, if not despair at the living conditions they found upon arriving in Africa—so different from those they enjoyed in Petersburg. They received their allotted plot of land, suffered the usual bout of African fever, and began to settle into their new home. Despite whatever misgivings they might have had, Amelia could write a friend "that they were 'pleased with the country,' and had 'not the least desire to return to Virginia.'"[9]

Quick-minded and ambitious, Roberts apparently had developed considerable business acumen working with his father and his barber friend Colson. With the colony now relatively stable and beginning to expand, he sensed opportunities for trade and business. Before long he and Colson were running a trading company they had previously begun or at least planned in Petersburg. "By the early 1830s they were transporting hides, ivory, cam wood, palm products, and other African goods to New York, Philadelphia, and other American ports. Roberts became as adept at trading with the natives as some of the best African tradesmen, and he established a company store in Monrovia in which he sold the products furnished by Colson."[10]

Colson turned out to be not merely a businessman intent on making money, but also a man of missionary bent. He saw this business venture as an opportunity to "do good" by bringing Christianity to the natives in Africa and determined to go there. The would-be missionary chartered a vessel in January 1835 and sailed with more than fifty immigrants to Liberia later that year. Sadly, Colson's reunion with his good friend and partner was cut short. Fifteen days after arriving in Monrovia, he suffered the same fate that befell many others before him. He died from African fever.

Despite his partner's death, Roberts's trading business continued to grow. But the young businessman began to be drawn to politics in the colony. He had caught the attention of Colonization Society officials when he wrote them protesting some of the colonists' taking part in the slave trade. Appointed high sheriff of the colony in 1833, when only twenty-four years old, Roberts took on duties that included supervising elections and controlling nearby tribes, which also involved leading expeditions to collect taxes or put down uprisings.

On one occasion, Roberts, by then a colonel in the colony's militia, led a seventy-man expedition to collect overdue debts from chiefs in Little Bassa. He managed to get the chiefs to agree to repay with land, which on April 12, 1838, the American Colonization Society acquired on Liberia's behalf. He soon gained a reputation for being a strong leader, but one who relied on diplomacy in handling problems, turning to force only as a last resort. And before long he became a popular figure countrywide.

As the commonwealth flourished, the British sensed a potential threat to their own expanding west African trade. The issue, however, transcended mere competition; it questioned Liberia's sovereignty and ultimately its very existence as a state. Even before Roberts had settled into his job as governor, it became increasingly clear that a showdown with the British was imminent. Not surprisingly, Roberts took center stage in a chain of events that would doom the commonwealth—but lead to its rebirth as a republic.

To the British and others, Liberia was puzzling. It was neither fish nor fowl—not a sovereign country nor a recognized colony of the United States but, instead, subject to rule by a civic society, a government proxy. The British government claimed that their traders "'had for a long series of years carried on an undisturbed trade with the natives,' at Bassa Cove, in particular. Therefore, the Liberians had 'no right now to insist upon their compliance with any'" ordinances of the so-called Government of Liberia.'"[11] The stage was set, and Roberts would show his mettle with a cask of palm oil in a supporting role.

Roberts won the case, impressing even his British critics.

> Soon after Buchanan became governor, Liberian authorities charged that John G. Jackson, master of the British schooner *Guineaman*, illegally loaded a cask of palm oil aboard his schooner. Roberts, then the commonwealth's chief justice, presided over the case, which turned on whether or not Jackson's action constituted trading—a narrow legal point. The real issue was whether or not Liberia had the sovereign power to make and enforce laws, particularly those dealing with trade.

A jury found the defendant guilty. Jackson was fined. He protested and "threatened to take the case to" the British government. Roberts's liberal education in the United States did not include the study of law. But his handling of the case, especially his charge to the jury, which many considered "a masterpiece," was "remarkable for its fairness and for its clear expression of the difficult legal points involved."[12] Even the British were impressed with this American-born mulatto, although they did not abandon their efforts to undermine the Liberian government's legitimacy.

Roberts seemingly had the knack for inspiring admiration, even from less-than-likely sources. Trying to muster support for the Liberian case, he made a quick trip to the United States in 1844. He was warmly welcomed. One of Virginia's most prominent planters (and owner of slaves), General John Hartwell Cocke, invited Roberts to visit him at his home. In a letter to the Colonization Society, the general effused that "there is no Governor on earth, I should entertain with more pleasure than the Chief Magistrate of Liberia."[13] When it came to the US government, however, the Tyler administration and Congress were too embroiled with the annexation of Texas, relations with Mexico, and the issue of slavery to worry about Liberia. Roberts came away empty handed.

A frustrated Britain turned to Washington for clarification. In 1843 the Foreign Office instructed its minister in Washington to inquire "as to the nature and extent of the connexion subsisting between [it and] the American Colony of Liberia" and the "degree of official patronage and protection accorded Liberia by the United States. And, if such protection was extended, requesting a definition of the geographical limits of Liberia."[14]

Abel P. Upshur, President John Tyler's secretary of state (who would die the next year, 1844, in the explosion on Stockton's warship *Princeton*) responded. His reply, couched in classical diplomatic obfuscation, said in effect that Liberia had no political relationship with the United States. But the US government held that Liberia occupied a "peculiar position" with "peculiar claims" on friendly relations with other countries. And, he cautioned, the United States would not be prepared to see it lose any of its territory "rightfully acquired" or be prevented from exercising its "rights and powers as an independent settlement."[15]

Upshur's answer left both the British and the Liberians still puzzled and failed to bring an end to the dispute. In fact, the dispute would mark only the beginning of a series of European assaults that would threaten Liberia into the twentieth century.

A "Peculiar" Special Relationship

From 1821, when the first black settlers arrived, until independence in 1847, Liberia constituted a political anomaly. While the initiative for its creation came from the American Colonization Society, the US government was heavily involved, given the two institutions' duality in both policy and membership. One of the primary objectives they shared was eliminating the international slave trade. Growing out of eighteenth-century enlightened thinking and the religious Great Awakening, Britain, having already abolished slavery, outlawed the trade in 1807 and stationed a naval squadron off the west African coast to intercept slave ships. In addition, it established Sierra Leone as a venue for resettling freed slaves, particularly American Black Loyalists following the Revolutionary War.

In accordance with the US Constitution, a law signed March 2, 1807, also banned the American trade after January 1, 1808, but enforcement was limited. The American Colonization Society was established in 1816 to colonize "the free people of color residing in" the United States, "in cooperation with the general government." Returning to the slave trade, Congress three years later passed an act stipulating that captives rescued would be turned over to the US marshal of the District of Columbia or to "some other agency" for resettlement. President Monroe designated the American Colonization Society as that agency. The act also allocated $100,000 for a naval presence to intercept slave ships and for the resettlement of freed captives. Thus, the US government officially had no direct interest in Liberia as a colony, except as a venue for resettling Africans rescued from slavers by the US Navy. The society administered the resettlement as a US government agent in addition to running its own show—colonizing free American blacks.

No act by Congress or by international agreement authorized the colonization societies "to exercise governmental powers," but in the absence of any other authority, they were forced to act as de facto government. The colony depended totally on them and the US government for its existence. The society's board of managers (or directors) in Washington handled the funding and governed the colony through their appointed agents. When Liberia became a commonwealth in 1839, a board-appointed governor replaced the agents. But sovereign power continued to rest with him (an elected lieutenant governor and legislative council had limited powers) until 1847, when Liberia became an independent republic.

The estimated cost of the colonization from 1817 through 1866 came to $2.6 million.[16] Funds came from local and state societies, churches, and individuals, who contributed one dollar yearly for membership. Agents also sold life memberships in the society for contributions of thirty dollars or more.

Questioning the legality of such an arrangement for governance, British traders strenuously protested Liberia's right to enforce commercial regulations and collect customs duties.[17] The British government took up the dispute in a note in 1843 to American secretary of state Abel Ashur, asking that Liberia's status be clarified. But his obfuscatory answer—Liberia had no political relationship with the United States, but occupied "a peculiar position" with "rights and powers as an independent settlement"—baffled both the British and Liberians.[18]

The American navy also played an important role in the US-Liberia relationship. Following the ban on the slave trade, US warships joined the British Africa Squadron in patrolling the west African waters. Some American ships were assigned to help the society find and acquire a suitable site for the colony. The US frigate *Cyane*, for instance, was detailed to accompany the *Elizabeth* across the Atlantic with the eighty-six original colonists on their epic 1820 voyage. The crew surveyed possible sites and otherwise assisted the settlers. Lieutenant Robert F. Stockton, commanding the US schooner *Alligator*, and society agent Dr. Eli Ayres together negotiated the purchase of land for the colony. From 1820 to 1860, the US Navy added 5,744 captives rescued from slave ships to Liberia's growing population.

Africa Squadron vessels called often at Monrovia, and US ships were dispatched numerous times (e.g., in 1843, 1876, 1910, and 1915) at the government's request to help in Liberia's conflicts with slavers and with tribes. This assistance usually proved crucial and ofttimes literally made the difference between life and death for the colony. In addition, the United States, when unable or unwilling to flex military muscle against foreign threats, employed varying degrees of influence, diplomatic clout, and financial help on Liberia's behalf.

Over the years, of course, many facets colored this relationship—historical, religious (particularly missionary work and education), cultural, military, and economic and financial. It was, however, a relationship inconstant at best. Its ebb and flow, broadly speaking, depended on the matrix of political, social, economic, and religious circumstances that defined US interests at any point in time. It has varied over the years from the highs of American interest in abolishing the slave trade, providing a home for freed blacks, and spreading Christianity in Africa up to the Civil War, followed by a period of American self-absorption and isolationism, which gradually gave way in the twentieth century to heightened interest in Liberia as a supplier of rubber and iron ore, and finally as an ally in World War II and the Cold War.

For the Europeans, trade was not the only issue. The Liberia on the original strip of land that Eli Ayres and Robert Stockton purchased from King Peter for the colony had vastly expanded during the ensuing years. Subsequent purchases between 1821 and 1845 added "strips of land along the coast and in the river valleys...often to forestall French or British incursions."[19] However, Indiana University Professor J. Gus Liebenow maintains that the purchases "were questionable and a source of continuing friction" since selling land, " in the sense of a permanent transfer of ownership...was an unknown concept in that part of Africa."[20] Besides the friction often generated with the various tribes, much of the territory would be the subject of protracted disputes with the British and French---who already were casting imperialistic eyes in its direction.

Treaties of friendship, such as the one Roberts extracted from the Gola chief Gatumba, provided another means for Liberian expansion. Besides cooperation with the Liberian authorities in the suppression of the slave trade, agreements usually included an element of protection for the subject chief or chiefs. Treaties stipulated that disputes be submitted to the Liberian government for arbitration. Since warfare between the various tribes raged almost continuously, these provisions greatly enhanced the central government's power over the tribes.

After the founding of the American Colonization Society in 1816, many state and local societies sprang up. A number of them sponsored freed slaves and other blacks to immigrate to the American society's Liberian colony. Some, such as the Mississippi and Louisiana, the Pennsylvania and New York, and the Maryland societies, established independent colonies. The story of "Mississippi in Africa," the one founded by the Mississippi and Louisiana state societies, though, has a singularly haunting quality.

Its origins lay in Jefferson County, Mississippi, which borders the Mississippi River between Vicksburg and Natchez. Prospect Hill was a once-thriving plantation in the county until 1845. But in the plantation's cemetery stands a curiously impressive marble monument commissioned by the Mississippi Colonization Society to honor former plantation owner Isaac Ross. The inscription on it reads, "His last will is graced with as magnificent provisions as any over which philanthropy has ever rejoiced and by it will be erected on the shores of Africa a monument more glorious than marble and more enduring than Time."[21]

Ross's last will stipulated that upon his death, his nearly two hundred slaves were to be freed, the plantation liquidated, and assets from the estate used to assist the freed slaves to emigrate to Liberia. After he died in 1836, however, his heirs contested the will in the Mississippi courts and legislature for more than a decade. Frustrated, angry slaves sparked a deadly uprising in which Ross's mansion burned to the ground in 1845. Sixty-nine emigrants from Mississippi, nonetheless, had arrived at Monrovia aboard the *Rover* in 1835. Judge James Green and Mary Bullock had freed forty-nine of them from their plantation near Natchez, Mississippi. Of the others, two were freeborn, and eighteen had purchased their freedom. None, of course, had belonged to Ross. But after his will was finally upheld, former Prospect Hill slaves came to make up the largest group of Mississippi emigrants.[22]

The two state societies, however, felt the American society did not give adequate attention to their emigrants (and also suspected the national organization of harboring abolitionist sentiments). In 1837 the state bodies purchased more than three thousand square miles of land at the Sinoe River, comprising the entire territory of the Sinoe tribe, to create their own colony. To sustain the venture, their members "pledged $14,000 annually."[23]

A determined group of thirty-seven settlers in 1838 landed at the mouth of the Sinoe River, some 150 miles down the coast from

Monrovia. Their town, which became the capital of Mississippi in Africa, was named Greenville in honor of Judge Green. But the largest number coming to Sinoe over the years hailed from Isaac Ross's Prospect Hill. "Although started with enthusiasm," the settlement seemed ill fated from the beginning.[24]

"The colony was underfunded" and frequently poorly administered. Moreover, to its detriment, it "did not enjoy good relations with the Liberian government in Monrovia."[25] Settlers and local tribesmen clashed frequently. While the Sinoes (one of numerous ethnic groups or "subtribes" belonging to the Kru, a major tribe in Liberia) were agriculturalists and friendly to the colony, a second group that settlers called "Fishmen" (obviously for their vocation) often proved hostile.

On September 10, 1838, the colony's governor, Josiah Finley, was murdered en route to Monrovia. The acting agent of the Mississippi colony reported that Finley had "left Greenville for Monrovia, on business, as well as for his health. On his way, he attempted to visit Bassa Cove. Landing about two miles below the settlement, he was robbed and murdered by the natives."[26]

The colony would have no officially designated leader for six years.[27] Finally, the two state societies gave up and decided to cast their lot with Liberia in 1842. Now christened Sinoe County, the colony joined Montserrado (Monrovia) and Grand Bassa as the third county in a now significantly bigger Commonwealth of Liberia. The following year, Liberian governor Roberts, in the company of Commodore Matthew C. Perry, commander of the US Navy Africa Squadron, visited Greenville.

In Sinoe, Roberts and Perry called together a council of Kru tribal chiefs primarily to decide a murder case. The chiefs, apparently welcoming Roberts's intervention. reached a broader agreement with the government that went well beyond the immediate case. They consented to give up their slave trading, allow and protect missionaries in their territories, and submit disputes among the tribes to the Liberian government for settlement. Of particular importance to the government, the chiefs also agreed to prohibit any foreign power from acquiring title to their land. Liberia would invoke such agreements numerous times to bolster assertions of sovereignty over areas it claimed. But to most tribal people, the agreements amounted to little more than expressions of good intentions, easily violated—and to Europeans, such as British traders, they were highly questionable bases for territorial expansion.

Governor Roberts nonetheless continued his program of enlisting the African chiefs in Liberia's expansion. Tribal leaders from the northern and western portions of Liberia in 1843 agreed to submit any disputes among themselves to the government in Monrovia before resorting to action on their own. The government, for its part, pledged "to promote the material and spiritual development of the indigenous people." In this vein Roberts introduced measures to help bring local Africans into the world of the Americo-Liberian settlers, such as "laws for the protection of ethnic apprentices and workers." By 1845 some three hundred African men had been enfranchised.[28] But any real progress in bridging the chasm between the worlds of the Americo-Liberians and indigenous peoples would wait more than a century.

Meanwhile, the British persisted in their attacks on Liberian sovereignty. In a January 18, 1845, message to the legislative council, Governor Roberts reiterated the British position, quoting a message from Commodore Jones of HMS *Penelope*. "The Liberian settlers [Jones wrote] have asserted rights over British traders on the coast which are inadmissible." These rights, "imposing customs duties and limiting the trade of foreigners by restrictions, are sovereign rights." Only "sovereign and independent states" could lawfully carry them out "within their own borders and dominions." His final barb: "I need not remind your Excellency [Roberts] that this description does not apply to 'Liberia' which is not recognized as a subsisting state."[29]

Roberts reacted cautiously. "'I feel,' he told the Council, 'that the position assumed by the British officers...will not be sanctioned by the British Government.'"[30] Two months later, however, the issue erupted. In April 1845 the British brig *Lily* sailed into Grand Bassa's harbor and seized a Liberian schooner, the *John Seys* (which belonged to Stephen Benson, who later would be elected Liberia's second president). An admiralty court in Sierra Leone acquitted the schooner of slaving charges, but the British continued to hold it for payment of court costs. And the court ruled that the Liberian flag the *John Seys* flew was not a national flag since Liberia possessed no sovereign rights as a state.

Roberts's reaction this time was anything but cautious. "I am decidedly of opinion that the Commonwealth of Liberia, not withstanding its connection with the Colonization Society, is a sovereign state, fully competent to exercise all the powers of government."[31]

Governor Roberts argued that while "the citizens of Liberia, as an infant Republic" had entered an arrangement or compact with the society for its management of "certain external concerns," neither the Liberians nor the society ever considered or intended this action to be a "surrender of sovereignty as a body politic."[32]

He argued it was not surprising that "an arrangement so novel and without precedent should in its operations experience some jarrings" in the minds of many. After all, they subscribed to the prevailing notion that for a colony to become a sovereign state, able to exercise the powers of sovereignty, it must have first been "in a state of political subjection to and dependence on a mother country before it became independent."[33]

But, Roberts insisted, in an innovative turn of legal theory, Liberia was different. It "never was such a colony; she never was in that state of dependence, and therefore needs no such process in order to become a sovereign state."[34] Other legal minds, notably the author of *The Political and Legislative History of Liberia*, Dr. Charles Huberich, have agreed with Roberts's theory.

The governor, nevertheless, realized that to dispel fully the confusion over Liberia's status, its unusual relationship with the Colonization Society must be altered. He told the legislative council that while "how far it is necessary to change our relationship with the Colonization Society...is a matter for deep consideration...in my opinion, it only remains for the Government of Liberia, by formal act to announce her independence—that she is now and always has been a sovereign state."[35]

The council referred the question to the financially strapped Colonization Society in Washington, which was anxious to reduce the burden of administering Liberia. On January 20, 1846, the society's board of directors resolved that "the time had arrived when it was expedient for the people of the Commonwealth of Liberia to take into their own hands the whole work of self-government, including the management of foreign relations."[36] They underlined that this was "a most important movement on the part of the Society...nothing less than a total severance of the Society from all political connexion with the colony and an entire withdrawal of control from all its affairs, both internal and external."[37]

When faced with the prospect of actual independence, however, many Liberians feared the worst. Opposition mounted. The American Colonization Society was accused of forcing the issue on a Liberia not yet ready. The governor even felt obliged to rebut an article in the *Liberia Herald* that complained, "the SOCIETY acted first and thus threw on the people of Liberia the necessity of acting." Roberts responded that it was the colonial legislature that first brought the matter to the society's board of directors, but since it was "a great way off, excited little fears for the consequences. But now the responsibility" was on the legislative council, "and they would fain throw it off."[38]

Five years of debate and discussion, ofttimes rancorous, had fractured the community. One faction led by colonial administrators favored independence. An opposition group, "rooted in Methodist lay leadership" and centered in Grand Bassa and Sinoe, feared an independent Liberia would not be able to survive. With only meager military capacity, the settlements would be exposed to even greater native and foreign attacks than they had experienced to date. And the colony's financial health was far from robust. Its reported income in 1846 totaled $8,525, and its expenses $7,538, leaving a slim surplus of only $987. Exports, mainly camwood, palm oil, and ivory, averaged $61,845 yearly, but imports ran some $78,915.[39] Most voters, however, simply were confused.

Roberts, nonetheless, plowed ahead. In a letter to the society's board on 19 October 1846, he reported that the Legislative Council on July 15 instructed him to set a date for submitting the independence resolution "to the people for vote." The date fixed was October 27.[40] A November 9 follow-up letter announced that the people's vote was in favor of the board's "suggestions" and recommended "the call of a convention to draft a constitution."[41] The society's directors in response suggested that Liberian commissioners come to Washington for "a full and free conference [with the society] before a constitution was framed"[42] to agree on arrangements for the transition to independence.

Roberts's tally of the October 27 vote suggested greater support for independence than perhaps warranted. According to Professor Carl Burrowes, only 269 of 600 eligible voters even turned out to vote. And only 52 percent of those who voted favored independence, while 48 percent opposed.[43] Despite the small turnout and the slim margin of those in favor, the governor and council decided to move ahead, and in its next session in January 1847, a still-divided Legislative Council took up the issue. Although it was feared that the body would be in for some rough weather, the governor later wrote, the members "after the first two or three days...adopted the proposals for independence "with great unanimity."[44]

The body called for the election of delegates to a constitutional convention. But Roberts's "great unanimity" cloaked deep divisions, which had been building over some time and had not disappeared.

―⁂―

An election in February selected eleven delegates—six from the county of Monrovia (Montserrado), four from Grand Bassa, and one from Sinoe—to begin drafting a constitution. The country would vote on the draft the last Monday in September. If voters rejected it, the delegates would make amendments or draft another version. If rejected again, the authors would keep repeating entire exercise until a version was adopted.

The delegates—Samuel Benedict, Hilary Teage, General Elijah Johnson, Beverly R. Wilson, J. N. Lewis, and J. B. Gripon from Montserrado County; John Day, Amos Herring, Anthony William Gardiner, and Ephraim Titler from Grand Bassa; and R. E. Murray from Sinoe—began their deliberations in Monrovia on July 5, 1847. Benedict, a leader in the opposition to the commonwealth's administration who had arrived in Monrovia only twelve years earlier, was elected president of the convention, and a Dr. Jacob W. Prout was chosen to serve as secretary—seemingly an unfortunate choice given the difficulties he had in keeping the minutes of the meetings.

Among the delegates, Benedict in the future would run unsuccessfully twice against Roberts for the presidency, while three decades later Anthony Gardiner would be elected president.

> Someone, possibly Prout, kept a journal of the convention's proceedings, but it was never published. Decades later it was decided to finally publish the document. But as fate would have it, through the carelessness of a servant of the individual preparing the manuscript, the journal was destroyed. However, someone else had kept a private account of the meetings that now was given over to an unnamed Englishman to take to England for printing. But the ill-fated journal never made it. The English courier died on the voyage, and the manuscript was never found among his possessions. The only account of the convention's work available is from the private Journal of Dr. J. W. Lugenbeel, then the US government agent for repatriated Africans, who attended most, but not all, of the sessions. He sent extracts from his journal in a letter to Dr. William McLain, secretary of the American Colonization Society at that time.[45] Fortunately for the convention, the jinx on the journal did not extend to the convention itself. The initial session got underway as scheduled.

Simon Greenleaf, a highly respected Harvard Law School professor, leading member of the Massachusetts bar, and president of the Massachusetts Colonization Society, had followed the Liberia experiment with close interest. In anticipation of the colony's independence, he had drafted a constitution, which he sent to the American Colonization Society. The society, after reviewing and forwarding the document to Liberia, asked that a clause be added declaring "all the property in Liberia held by the American Colonization Society, or their grantees...be respected as private property." Moreover, in an independent Liberia, "all the rights of the Society to property within the...[present] boundary should be inviolate, and arrangements...be made" for settling Africans rescued from slave ships and any "free people of colour" who immigrate from the United States.[46] The society wanted to ensure that it could continue to fulfill its mission of resettling blacks, even in an independent Liberia.[47]

Several delegates "indignantly denounced...so unreasonable a request on the part of the Colonization Society" to retain title to the colony's public lands.[48] Delegate Beverly Wilson also denounced the constitution Professor Greenleaf had drafted, and "boastingly asserted he could make a better Constitution himself. He stated that the People of Liberia do not require the assistance of 'white people' to enable them to make a Constitution for themselves."[49] Wilson subsequently presented to the convention what was, in US agent Lugenbeel's words, "almost an exact copy [of Greenleaf's draft]...as an original paper, drawn up by the honorable delegate himself...After the reading of this remarkable original (!) production the Convention adjourned."[50]

The Greenleaf/Wilson document omitted the controversial clause ensuring the Colonization Society's title to its lands. But a more fundamental issue still threatened to derail Roberts's independence train. From the very first, the majority of Grand Bassa and Sinoe County residents opposed separation from the Colonization Society. At a Grand Bassa county convention prior to the constitutional meeting, citizens adopted a resolution that included a threat in effect to cut its relation "to such parts of the [Liberian] Commonwealth" that pursued independence, and "to petition the American Colonization Society" to maintain its ties with and "continue their patronage" to the county.[51]

As the convention wore on, however, the Grand Bassa and Sinoe delegates ultimately decided that going along with the push for independence constituted their best course of action—at least for the time being. The convention delegates also finessed the land title issue by concluding it inappropriate to include in the constitution. Instead, the members thought the new government should resolve the problem directly with the Colonization Society. (An agreement on July 20, 1848, between the new Republic of Liberia and the society finally laid the matter to rest.)[52] The convention unanimously adopted the draft constitution with only slight modifications. The unanimity in the convention, though, was "only precarious." Some of the delegates, despite their votes in favor, would become leaders in efforts to block the constitution's adoption—and Liberia's independence.

Before adjourning on July 25, the convention adopted a national flag patterned upon the American banner. And to complete the march to independence, the convention also adopted a "Declaration of Independence" that each delegate duly signed. As Dr. Huberich points out, the document, by Hilary Teage, "has nothing in common" with the American declaration. It is a state paper, "not a declaration of political independence…[but] a statement of the reasons that Liberians had in coming to Liberia."[53] The declaration appeals "in the name of the great God, [their] common Creator" to Christendom's nations that they treat them with "sympathy and friendly considerations" and to "that comity which marks the friendly intercourse of civilized and independent communities."[54] Dr. Hubrich praises the declaration as a "historical and literary masterpiece… destined to arouse the lethargy of millions of Africans" to realize their "political destiny... in the history of the world." [55]

On a final note, the convention, still mindful of the American Colonization Society's seminal role in the country's birth, adopted a resolution expressing Liberia's "liveliest gratitude" to the society, to which "we [the people of Liberia] owe all the good which has been accomplished in us."[56] The document pledged "to maintain friendly feeling and correspondence [to] enable the American Colonization Society and American people to carry out their benevolent design in regard to the colored people of the United States, the Colony of Liberia, and the continent of Africa."[57] The convention's delegates also recognized that the friendship and material support of the United States would be crucial to independent Liberia—and wanted, above all, to preserve and maintain the "special relationship" between the two.

CHAPTER 7

From Commonwealth to Republic

—⚋—

On July 26, 1847, the declaration of independence was proclaimed and the Republic of Liberia was born. The twenty-fourth of August witnessed a wildly enthusiastic celebration of the momentous event with the unfurling of the republic's new flag. It was patterned after the American banner but with eleven stripes (for the eleven delegates, not including Prout, to the constitutional convention) and a blue field on which was set a single star, for Africa, a star one local poet declared that "after ages of wandering, has at length found its orbit."[1] A correspondent from the *Liberia Herald* covered the occasion.

The flag of Liberia

At daybreak, he reported, "booming cannons in Monrovia's Central Fort awakened the town's 1,000 residents. The streets soon filled with "all classes and descriptions of people...and unusual activity and bustle." Ladies waved their handkerchiefs. Shouts of "huzzah" vied with the sound of drums. As the official Flag Day ceremony got underway. Susanna Lewis, head of the committee of women who sewed the flag, delivered a "neat patriotic speech." In the Methodist church, overflowing with people, the Reverend James S. Payne delivered the address. Senator John Grip of Montserrado County read the Declaration of Independence, and Baptist pastor and editor of the *Herald*, Rev. Hilary Teage, led a prayer of thanksgiving.[2]

"During the ceremony presenting the flag, many eyes were suffused with tears. And indeed, who that remembered the past could forbear to weep? Who that looked back to America and remembered what we saw and felt there, could be otherwise than agitated?"[3] The American experiment seemed to be working. Paul Cuffe, Robert Finley, Jehudi Ashmun, and the other heroes of Liberia's creation would have been proud.

The British threat to Liberian sovereignty, however, still lingered. So much so, that when Her Majesty's sloop *Favorite* arrived in Monrovia's harbor during the initial days of the constitutional convention, a palpable wave of tension had swept over the city. But when independence was declared, Captain Murray, the sloop's commanding officer, acting on orders from Prime Minister Lord Palmerston, duly saluted the new flag and assured the government that British citizens would respect it. Dr. Hugenbeel remarked that it appeared Liberia now was sufficiently important to get the attention of the British government. Liberia would discover, however, a downside to that new attention. Guarantees in the world's political arena could prove ephemeral.

The new republic now faced the task of adopting a constitution and electing its leaders. A referendum on the proposed constitution was scheduled for September 27, 1847. The two parties, the Pro-Administration for adoption and the Anti-Administration opposed, began their campaigns in earnest.[4] But Liberia found itself largely in unexplored, uncharted waters. The proposed constitution, following its American model, made no mention of political parties. And as formal political organizations, the two parties had only recently come onto the scene. The settlers had limited experience in governing themselves. Protests over the allocation of plots for houses in the colony's early days, what came to be known as the Remonstrance of December 5, 1823, won them the right to elect the vice agent and two councilors to advise the Colonization Society's agent. Despite the 1824 Plan of Government, however, Ashmun never relinquished much authority and continued to dominate the colony's administration. Until the end of this first decade, settler participation was limited by and large to the right of assembly and petition, and electing the three officials—without major concern for issues.[5]

Following Ashmun's tenure in office, there was a gradual devolution of power to the settlers during the 1830s, as evidenced by the increase in the number of elected officials. Too, as the colony became more secure in its footing, elections increasingly turned on issues rather than on personal qualifications. Tensions understandably arose between various interest groups: the more liberal inhabitants of the coastal towns, particularly Monrovia, and surrounding Montserrado County, engaged mainly in commerce and trading, versus the more conservative residents of the predominantly agricultural settlements;[6] Methodist mission leaders and their followers versus colonial officials and their Baptist supporters, "who were more secular in world view, and employment"; the white officials who administered the colony versus an "emerging black leadership."[7]

One of the government's fiercest critics headed the local Methodist mission—the Reverend John Seys, a white West Indian with an "aristocratic pedigree." Seys, born March 20, 1799, arrived in Monrovia on October 18, 1834, after a series of assignments, including serving as a missionary to the Mohawk Indians. In November 1838 the Missionary Society of the Methodist Church, meeting in New York, resolved to establish a monthly or semimonthly newspaper under the direction of Seys and a committee of the Liberia annual conference. A printer arrived. The Methodist Episcopal Mission Press was established on Broad Street in Monrovia, and the first issue of *Africa's Luminary*, edited by John Seys, appeared in March 1839.

The Methodist clergyman's opposition to the commonwealth's administration initially stemmed from Governor Buchanan's refusal to allow missionaries to import goods duty-free. In the ensuing public debate, Buchanan's defenders rallied around him. They formed a group to support candidates in the election for the Legislative Council sympathetic to his position. Opposition on other issues widened the debate as the government's defenders, the Monrovia group, began to feel the sting of the assaults from Seys and his followers. The reverend's faction, largely dominated by the more conservative agricultural interests, became the Anti-Administration Party. They took aim on a broad range of the government's policies and actions—"health, relations with the tribal chiefs, foreign commerce, and taxation."[8]

Despite their attacks in the legislature, public gatherings, and in Seys's newspaper, punctuated by occasional outbursts of violence on the part of zealous followers, Roberts, now the governor, and the Monrovia faction still managed to keep control of the legislature until the republic came into being. But while the Anti-Administration Party had reluctantly accepted the decision to declare independence, it "vigorously opposed ratification of the proposed constitution and even threatened to have Grand Bassa secede from the new state."[9] Samuel Benedict and Seys led the assault.

Roberts and the Pro-Administration Party met the challenge. At independence they launched a spirited campaign in support of ratification. The Liberians who lived in the country's nine or so towns, particularly Monrovia and the surrounding Montserrado County, who made their living mainly in trade and commerce, and the majority of whom were mulattoes, formed the party's backbone. The party reputedly had a liberal bent, seen by some as even radical. They generally favored a relatively open Liberia in which foreigners shared nearly all the advantages that the country's citizens enjoyed.

The campaign began. The Anti-Administration Party's leader and candidate for president: Samuel Benedict. The Pro-Administration Party's champion of the constitution and presidential candidate: Joseph Jenkins Roberts. The results: Roberts reported October 9 in a letter to the American Colonization Society that the constitution had been adopted "by a large majority of the citizens of the Commonwealth."[10] Lugenbeel, once again, painted a slightly different picture of the referendum. Of the 272 votes cast, 214 favored the constitution and fifty-eight opposed. All of the 111 votes cast in Monrovia (Montserrado County) favored the constitution. In Sinoe County none voted in favor; thirty-seven opposed. In the community of Bassa Cove, in Grand Bassa County, nine voted for the constitution. Surprisingly, since this was the principal center of opposition, no votes were registered against. Similarly in Bexley, sixteen were in favor and zero against. And Edina registered no votes at all.

The answer according to Lugenbeel: those who opposed the constitution didn't vote. He judged that if those opponents had voted, the majority supporting the constitution would not even have exceeded fifty. He added wryly, "Thus you have a faint outline of the way in which things are working in the beginning of the Republic. It is all confusion, and almost anarchy...A strange set of people, some of the Liberians. But I hope it will all be O.K."[11]

On October 5 the electorate again went to the polls to select the president, vice president, and eight representatives and six senators from the three counties. Joseph Jennings Roberts was elected the first president of the Republic of Liberia and Nathaniel Brander vice president. Accounts of the presidential campaign are scanty, and no records of the voting have survived, although Lugenbeel mentioned that Benedict received only ten votes. Brander's election, while to a largely ceremonial post, saluted the pioneer settlers whose ranks were rapidly thinning. The vice president elect, now in his seventies, had arrived aboard the *Elizabeth* in 1820 and served the colony in various capacities, including supreme court judge and a brief stint as acting colonial agent. Roberts apparently trusted Brander sufficiently to act as president while he absented himself from Liberia for a lengthy European trip in 1849. Brander also happened to be the stepfather of the president's wife.

Joseph Jenkins Roberts. First president of Liberia, 1847. Prints and Photographs Division, Library of Congress LC---US26-1945.

The president-elect, now thirty-eight years old, was, as British African chronicler Sir Harry Johnston described him, "a slight-built handsome man with a very English-looking face, brown hair, blonde moustache and grey eyes." Johnston noted that as an octoroon, "his tinge of Negro blood was but slight."[12] Skin color at that time seemingly didn't matter. But in reality it did. And before long, it would become a major divisive issue in Liberian politics, pitting mulattoes such as Roberts against those with darker skin and more Negro blood.

By some accounts Benedict ran against Roberts again in 1849 but lost once more. After serving two terms, Roberts was reelected unopposed again in 1851 and 1853. Stephen A. Benson, Roberts's vice president in his final term, would carve out an impressive political career of his own as president of the republic from 1856 to 1864. Samuel Benedict reportedly joined in forming the new party but never managed to get elected president.

When Liberians awoke on January 3, 1848, expectations were high. The newly elected president would be installed that day and would usher in, so the people thought or at least hoped, a bright new era for Africa's first independent republic. President Roberts, for his part, doubtless fed on the prevailing optimistic spirit but could hardly ignore the enormity of the task that lay before him. Not one foreign power, not even the United States, had formally recognized the new state. Despite Captain Murray's assurances when the Liberian flag was raised, fears of possible encroachment at Liberia's expense, or even extinction, by the European powers still lingered. The native Africans still posed a threat. Periodic attacks on settlements and intertribal wars continued. Although the slave trade had largely been eliminated in Liberian territory, worrisome pockets, particularly in the area adjoining Sierra Leone, still remained. And the health of the Liberian economy and the government's financial situation could hardly be a cause for celebration. The new president made recognition by the international community and the acquisition of additional territory his chief priorities.

Roberts set sail for Europe in early 1849, bent upon obtaining recognition for the new state and negotiating trade agreements. To help, his second wife, Jane Waring Roberts, whom he married in 1836 in Monrovia, accompanied him. Well-educated and speaking "excellent French," Mrs. Roberts proved the ideal partner for her husband-president, "a man of intelligence and poise, slight and handsome, with olive skin and crisp hair...an excellent conversationalist," with the "manners of a gentleman."[13] Europeans wondered, could this strikingly attractive pair actually hail from darkest Africa?

Not surprisingly, they received an unusual amount of attention. In England the president received a seventeen-gun salute. Heads turned. Doors opened. Queen Victoria gave the Liberian pair "the most kindly reception"; the *Illustrated London News* of April 1848 carried an illustration of a reception on the royal yacht in their honor.[14] The Robertses moved on to the continent. The French in President Louis-Napoléon's Second Republic were fascinated. Leopold I cordially welcomed them to Belgium. They were feted in Holland and in Berlin. Britain recognized Liberia in 1848, as did France four years later, and by the time the United States extended recognition in 1862, most European powers had followed suit.[15]

Before returning home, President Roberts also managed to sign a commercial treaty (ratified by the Liberian Senate in February 1849) with Great Britain that put Liberia on a most-favored-nation footing and affirmed the country's right to levy duties. And before they departed a grand gesture affirmed the favor he and wife Jane had managed to capture from their British hosts."[16]

Sir Harry Johnston described the event: The Prussian ambassador in London gave a dinner for Roberts after he and Mrs. Roberts returned from their visit to the continent. Guests included the Reverend Ralph Gurley, longtime Colonization Society secretary; Lord Ashley; and the bishop of London. During the dinner Roberts described the slave trade thriving in the Gallinas, an area lying between Liberia and Sierra Leone. He avowed that the only way to end it would be for Liberia to purchase the sovereign rights to the territory from the ruling native chiefs. When asked how much money would be required, Roberts (blithely?) answered £2,000 ($10,000).[17]

Lord Ashley, perhaps enjoying a good cigar and imbibing more brandy than prudent, immediately offered to obtain the money. Next morning Ashley, true to his word, took Roberts to a bank on Lombard Street, withdrew £1,000, handed it to the president, and later arranged to raise the balance. Roberts used the money to purchase the lands, but the transactions with the array of native kings, chiefs, and headmen took almost nine years to complete. Ironically the territory was one of the thorniest issues in the long-playing dispute between Britain and Liberia and ultimately was lost by Liberia to Sierra Leone years later.

The Admiralty as a parting gift presented Liberia two vessels—the *Lark*, for use as a coastal transport, and the *Quail*, a small sloop of four guns to patrol the coastal waters in search of slave traders. "Roberts was conveyed home in triumph on the British man-of-war *Amazon*," and the queen herself signaled them from the royal yacht: "I wish you god-speed on your voyage."[18] The *Quail* had an interesting, if checkered history. Subsequently, the ship figured in a confrontation with one of Her Majesty's warships that aroused much ill will in Liberia.

Sir Richard Burton recounted the incident some years after, involving the vessel which he described as "an old schooner, now carrying three guns—one 32-pounder and two 12-pounder carronades...one of the two [vessels] that compose the 'Liberian Navy.'"[19] The schooner, according to the Liberian version of the incident, captured a small Spanish vessel, the *Buenaventura Cubano*, "collecting live cargo" in the Gallinas River on May 30, 1861. While the *Quail* was preparing to tow the vessel to Monrovia for trial, the HMS *Torch* appeared, hauled down the Liberian flag fluttering on the prize, and burned the ship. The Spanish crew were allowed to go to nearby Sierra Leone where a Spanish consul general resided. The Liberian government demanded compensation from Britain for destruction of the captured Spanish vessel.

And the story didn't end there. About a fortnight later, the Spanish warship *La Ceres* sailed into Monrovia's harbor "under the pretext of visiting the President." Then, on September 11, "without any warning she began firing...into the *Quail*."[20] The Spanish retreated when the *Quail* and Liberian harbor guns returned fire. The Spanish version, according to Burton, painted the *Buenaventura Cubano* as being innocently trading for palm oil when the Liberians attacked it, hauled down the Spanish flag, plundered the cargo, and scattered the crew. The *Las Ceres* was dispatched to Monrovia "for the purpose of demanding satisfaction" and fired on the *Quail* only after being fired upon by the harbor guns.[21]

—∞—

The Gallinas River and adjacent territory between Liberia and Sierra Leone was an area notorious for its slave trade. After Great Britain outlawed the trade in 1807 and positioned a naval squadron off the west African coast, the Gallinas developed into a busy illicit marketplace, a vast slave entrepôt where American and European slavers met their African suppliers. Fast-sailing schooners and brigs called at the mouth of the Gallinas River where an estimated two thousand slaves, mainly captives from the interior, were loaded aboard each year for the dreaded Middle Passage. The captives in the famous *Amistad* case doubtless passed through the Gallinas. Raids by British patrol vessels periodically disrupted the trade (one in 1849 by HMS *Albert* "broke up the slave factories...and carried off European traders and 1200 slaves to S'a Leone"), but only for a time, since the trade would start back up again after the British left.

A Coffle of slaves. Prints and Photographs Division, Library of Congress

An American visitor in 1839, startled by the enterprise's scale and organization, described Gallinas as "not only the centre of an extensive and lucrative traffic, but the theatre of a new order of society and a novel form of government." For most it was a terrifying place—"sluggish rivers oozing over treacherous bars, a shoreline of mango thickets and swamp, a delta pocked with spongy islands. 'Nothing more than a quantity of lagoons,' one slave trader wrote, 'shapeless and unproductive islands…a nursery for alligators, sea cow, and the hippopotamus.'"[22]

President Roberts, anxious to extirpate the noxious trade—and expand Liberia's territory—appealed to the United States as well as Great Britain for help in purchasing Gallinas. A major justification for Liberia's annexing new lands was eradicating slave trading. He posted an appeal not only to the US government but to the people as well for donations, pointing out that Liberia had managed to rid slavery from the territories it had acquired. Adding Gallinas to its domain would enable the entire coast "to be kept free from the demoralizing and wilting influence of the Slave trade."[23]

Accounts of Liberia's "purchase" of the territory differ. Burton, in his 1863 book, describes an "after dinner conversation" in 1848 "between Lord Ashley and Mr. Gurney [the Colonization Society's secretary] with Mr. President Roberts." In it "the wily negro [Roberts] persuaded them that by paying 2000£, slavery would be eradicated from the Gallinhas River and, 700 miles annexed to the Republic."[24]

Liberia, Burton wrote, subsequently claimed sovereignty over the territory by purchasing "the land and several points known as the Gallinhas…on 13th April, 1850," with, according to Burton, "money contributed mainly by the late Mr. Gurney, from Prince Mannah and other chiefs." He disputed Liberia's claim to sovereignty, maintaining that even if the African chiefs received the money, they would never agree to sell their land since the "negro never parts with his ground in perpetuity."[25] It is an idea alien to them. The dispute would not be finally settled until treaties in 1885 and 1903 established a division of the area and the Gallinas became part of Sierra Leone.[26]

Under Roberts's leadership, Liberia kept up a steady pace acquiring new lands on which to settle immigrants and to stop the slave trade. In January 1846, while still governor of the commonwealth, he purchased territory from four chiefs for $275. King John, Governor Peter, New John, and John Freeman signed the agreement.[27] The following year he reported two far more important purchases. One covered "the entire New Cess territory" in Grand Bassa County. With the purchase came a warning from Roberts to a Spanish slaver in the territory to desist from further operations.

The second parcel comprised all of the Little Cape Mount, a vital territory located up the coast northeast from Monrovia, toward Sierra Leone. The area ran "along the sea beach about 9 miles and 30 to 40 miles into the interior."[28] Based on a report that the English had "determined to possess themselves that country," Roberts feared Cape Mount would "be lost to Liberia forever, which," in his words, "would indeed be a great calamity."[29] In fact, the British in the same year did raid a slave-trading enclave that one of the slavers later made famous in his memoirs.

In his account of sailing past Cape Mount in his own 1863 book, Burton mentioned that it was "the last residence of the Franco-Italian slaver, Captain Canot, whose memoirs have been published at a shilling."[30] Although he fashioned himself "Captain Theodore Canot," his real name was Theophilus Canneau, and he was born in Florence, Italy, about 1803. His father was a captain and paymaster in Napoleon's army. The son sought adventure and drifted into slaving under the nefarious Don Pedro Blanco in Cape Mount, a busy slave-trading settlement. Burton relates the slaver's "conscientious endeavours to comfort and preserve his man warehouse." The loss of life aboard Canot"s ships, "one and a half per cent" was much less than the average aboard British emigrant vessels. He quotes a Dutch writer that "'the English slave-ships are always foul and stinking.'" (For the record, he adds that "ours [the Dutch] are for the most part neat and clean.'"[31]

Canot's descriptions of the slave trade in Cape Mount are vivid: "Hoops of bamboo were clamped round [the captives'] waists, while their hands were tied by stout ropes to the hoops. A long tether was then passed with a slip-knot through each rattan belt, so that the slaves were firmly secured to each other."[32] Among these wretched captives, able-bodied adults fetched only about ten dollars each, "children or inferior adults" from three to eight dollars, while those with a light skin, the "Mandingoes, Fula [tribes], and others, brought more."[33]

—⚑—

Independence bought little respite for the new republic from clashes with the native tribes. A *New York Times* correspondent described one: The night of November 5, 1851, Grando struck. Fishtown "was sacked and burned, and 9 of the inhabitants murdered. Grando commanded in person having about 300 troops—the garrison was taken by surprise. Among the murdered were 2 women and 4 children; the bodies were mutilated in a horrible manner. Homes ransacked. The village set afire."[34]

Grando had enlisted Boyer, the chief at nearby Trade Town, as an ally. Together commanding a force of some five thousand warriors, they next launched a general attack at midnight on December 11 on Bassa Cove. The Liberian defenders put up a stiff resistance, killing several of the assailants and wounding others. As the warriors "fled into the wilderness," the *Times* reported, "the air is said to have resounded with 'Nabo,' a cry of pain, the cannon of the Liberians having been well charged with slugs and grape shot."[35] Four days later the African natives renewed their assault in another and more desperate attack, this time "in great numbers." Again, the Liberian defenders repulsed the attackers "with the loss of from thirty to fifty killed and wounded, amongst them some of their chief warriors."[36]

President Roberts arrived at last with two ships, the *Dale* and the *Lark*, and seventy-five armed men. The arrival of these vessels forestalled further attacks—at least for the time being—while

Roberts rushed back to Monrovia to organize a stronger campaign. He returned to Buchanan (the newly renamed Bassa Cove) on New Year's Day 1852 with a force of about five hundred Liberians and an equal number of native troops. They routed Grando and his men from his headquarters in a well-fortified village surrounded by swampy lands. The Africans retreated to Trade Town, where they joined Boyer and his force. But to no avail. The Liberians attacked, and the campaign soon ended.[37]

Roberts's suspicion of British involvement went beyond a lone English trader aiding the uprising—particularly since a British vessel reportedly had landed the British consul at Trade Town, where he induced several native chiefs to sign statements denying they had sold their lands to the Liberian authorities. If the statements proved true, then Liberia would have had no authority over the areas where Grando, Boyer, and the other native chiefs were attempting to expel the settlers. As part of the conspiracy to free their traders from Liberian control, a British warship later docked at Monrovia to dispatch a message: the Liberian government had no sovereignty over Trade Town, and the Royal Navy would accordingly extend protection to British traders if needed. After President Roberts reported the incident to the British government, Parliament, apparently thinking better of the matter, decided not to support the actions of its naval officers.[38] But far more dangerous shoals lay ahead for Liberia's ship of state.

Despite such dangers from their tribal neighbors and threats of British and French territorial encroachment, the republic grew impressively under Roberts's administration. The Colonization Society, now freed from managing—and financially underwriting—the colony, could devote itself more fully to bringing new immigrants to Liberia. The country's population of 5,600 at independence in 1847 roughly doubled. Many owners freed their slaves to emancipate to Liberia. One freed slave, William C. Burke, sailed with his wife, Rosabella, and their four children from Baltimore in November 1853 aboard the ship *Banshee*. He wrote their former master and his wife from their new home, acknowledging "the receipt of your two letters, which gave both Rosabella and myself great comfort to hear from you all." The letter was addressed to "Col. R[obert] E. Lee of the US Army and Mrs. Lee."[39]

A *New York Times* article on 12 May 1853 took note of Liberia's rapidly expanding trade, and, as a sure sign of progress, that "a large number of new brick buildings [were] going up [in Monrovia]." One nineteenth-century American historian wrote glowingly about the many new settlements springing up, and how "agriculture, especially the cultivation of...rice, coffee, sugar, and cotton, [had] made rapid progress." English steamer lines established regular service to several coastal ports, and communications with America improved with the commissioning of a ship devoted to regular passage between the United States and Liberia.[40]

Sarah Joseph Hale (1788–1879), one of America's most prolific and important women of letters in the nineteenth century, described Liberia in her 1853 novel, *Liberia; or Mr. Peyton's Experiments*, in equally glowing terms. "The pretty town of Monrovia," she wrote, "excited...[a newly arrived immigrant family's] surprise and admiration. Its substantial, well-built houses, its churches, and its warehouses were superior to anything that they had imagined." The narrator goes on to describe capital streets "shaded with the singular and beautiful trees of the tropics" and "gardens filled with flowers and vegetables," as well as farms growing a copious and varied array of crops.[41] Although her descriptions were fiction and brightly colored by her enthusiasm for colonization, they were based on letters from actual settlers.

President Joseph J. Roberts's house, Monrovia. Prints and Photographs Division, Library of Congress LC---USZ62-107635

Several settlers from Indiana hoped to found a separate Hoosier community in Liberia. One, a barber, William W. Findlay, from Lafayette and Covington, Indiana, moved to Liberia on the *D.C. Foster* in the fall of 1850. Settling on a forty-acre farm on the Saint Paul River, he wrote Indiana governor Joseph A. Wright that he was "much pleased with this country" and did "believe that every colored man, that respects himself, as a man, would do well to come here, for truly I do think that it is a good country." However, he also rather matter-of-factly mentioned that "we have had some wars with the natives...The President [Roberts] had to take some two hundred men and go to Cape Mount, on the account of the native disturbances up there...They got the chief Boombo and about fifty of his men, and brought them down. And he will have his trial as soon as they can get the rest of the chiefs together." These native disturbances made it imperative to found settlements, "as the natives are all the time fighting and making slaves of each other" and "cannot be kept down unless there is a settlement."[42]

Even loyal Hoosiers, such as a free black barber named Samuel B. Webster, described their new homeland glowingly. Comparing Liberia's Saint Paul River with his beloved Indiana river, Webster wrote, "There are no parts of the Wabash, from its mouth to its head, that can in any way compare with [the Saint Paul's] beauty and fertility." He gushed that he had "actually seen, with [his] own eyes, large fields of sugar-cane," and had drunk "as fine specimens of coffee as the world produces." He also saw "rice, cotton, cassada [cassava], yams, chickens in abundance."[43]

One letter from an immigrant from New York offered a more sober assessment but still struck a positive note. He wrote that one coming to Liberia "would not find large cities with splendid buildings" but "only small villages" whose "buildings are generally quite plain, built of wood, stone, or brick. There are, however, some very neat brick buildings in Monrovia, and along the banks of the St. Paul's River." He did point out one deficiency: there were "only three horses in Monrovia," which were "only used for riding."[44] All transport was by human means.

In 1852 the president paid another visit to Europe. His itinerary this time included Holland, Prussia, and Belgium, where Leopold received him. European leaders continued to succumb to the mulatto president's "prepossessing personality, tact, and statesmanlike qualities."[45] In France, Louis-Napoléon, now Emperor Napoleon III, welcomed him and "presented him with arms and uniforms for the equipment of the Liberian troops."[46] During the year, France extended recognition to Liberia and signed a treaty of amity and commerce.

President Roberts returned to Monrovia, doubtless pleased with his continuing success abroad. He decided to make another run for the presidency, his fourth term, which he won unopposed. With the acquisition of the Cape Mount area, the president turned his attention to establishing a settlement there, one that appropriately would be named Robertsport. Unfortunately, an intertribal conflict began to pose a sufficiently serious threat to the new settlement that Roberts felt compelled to take military action. An article in the *New York Times* reported that "President Roberts left Monrovia of the 1st of March [1853], with 200 men under Gen. LEWIS, for Little Cape Mount, to arrest BOOMBO, a Chief, who has for a long time been carrying on a predatory war in that territory."[47]

The president decided not to run in 1855 for what would be a fifth term. Before relinquishing office, though, he was obliged to embark on one more foray to rescue settlers from warring African tribesmen. The *Chicago Daily Tribune* reported in February 1856 that "President Roberts, with the British consul, left Monrovia on the 26th of November [1855], and arrived at Sinoe on the 27th, when they went on shore and found that several of the inhabitants had been murdered." The president and British consul returned to Monrovia the next day with "several European ladies" evacuated from the fighting. In the meantime, "a voluntary corps was being raised to dispatch to Sinoe on the American schooner *George*." To Roberts it must have seemed business as usual.[48]

On January 7, 1856, he handed over the reins of government to President-Elect Stephen A. Benson, who had been serving as his vice president. Although still only forty-six years old, the retiring president had served Liberia in various capacities for almost twenty years. But "Old Soldier" Roberts wouldn't simply fade away. Following a brief stint as Liberian chargé d'affaires in Paris, he resumed his military career as a major general of the militia, which he headed for the next fifteen years. Later in the year, the former president traveled to the United States, raising money on behalf of the Board of Trustees of Donations for Education in Liberia.

That same year Roberts accepted a mission that would engage him for the rest of his life. Momentum had been gathering over the years to establish a seat of higher learning in the fast-developing colony. Helping to propel the movement, the same Simon

Greenleaf who helped draft the country's constitution, along with his friends, raised money for a higher education institution. After he approached then-president Roberts, the Legislature of Liberia in 1850 granted a charter to the Liberia College that was incorporated the next year. Roberts was appointed president of the college in 1856, and subsequently professor of jurisprudence and international law, posts he held until his death. Construction began of a three-story brick building on twenty acres of land supplied by the government on Monrovia's outskirts. The indefatigable Roberts set off for the United States on the first of several visits to garner support for the new institution. Americans contributed $22,000 and some four thousand books (six hundred from Harvard alone) for the school.[49]

On one of his money-raising trips in 1869, Roberts addressed the American Colonization Society on its fifty-second anniversary. The "father of the republic" briefly recounted the history of the colony and its achievements since the first settlers stepped off the *Elizabeth* in 1821, noting how "the slave barracoons at Momma Town, Little Cape Mount, Little Bassa, New Cesters, and Trade Town were demolished, and thousands of slaves liberated by the power of the little Commonwealth."[50] He pointed to the colony's territorial expansion, its growing population, and its humming economy and trade.

In his speech, Roberts declared the people of Liberia had made steady progress toward fulfilling "the great objects of their mission to Africa": establishing an "asylum" for people of African descent wherever they might be, ridding Liberia's coast of trading in slaves, and introducing the "blessings of civilization and Christianity among the heathen tribes" in Africa by means of Christian settlements in their midst.[51] In addition, he was persuaded that the republic had "indicated some ability, at least, for self-government and the management of their own public affairs."[52]

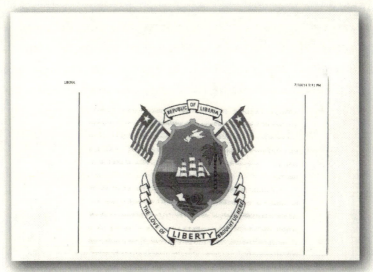

The great seal of Liberia.

The sailing ship (and the motto THE LOVE OF LIBERTY BROUGHT US HERE) represent arrival of the colonists. The dove is bringing a message from overseas (the US) granting independence. The spade and plow are the tools the colonists brought along. The palm tree symbolizes some of the region's main products.

His vision of the future also brimmed with optimism. "My own convictions," he declaimed, "are that Heaven has great things in store for Africa, to be conferred doubtless through the instrumentality of Liberia."[53] With its abundant resources, Liberia would continue "civilizing and Christianizing" until the rest of Africa were "brought within the scope of Christian civilization and incorporated in the Republic, thus forming an African nationality that will command the respect of the civilized world."[54]

In conclusion, the former president asserted that "Heaven's design" called for Africa's redemption, and with the development of its abundant natural resources, "she shall take rank with other States and Empires; that she shall have a literature and a history." He asked, "Is there any reason why all this may not come to pass?"[55]

Roberts's stirring speech must have been balm to the hearts of the Colonization Society's dedicated toilers in the vineyards of the Lord. His words abounded in the optimism, the idealism, the faith and missionary zeal of the men and women who brought forth and nourished Liberia in the previous fifty years. One can only wonder what his words and feelings might be when events less than a decade later would plunge the republic into a political crisis so threatening that he would be prompted back to lead the country once more.

CHAPTER 8

The Republic Established

—⚅—

JANUARY 7, 1856, BEAMED BRIGHT. The optimism Roberts had generated during his tenures as governor and president still invigorated the country and produced a seemingly unshakeable confidence in the future. After all, the colony had weathered a trying birth thirty-five years earlier, survived fevers, near starvation, attacks from hostile natives and foreign slave traders and bullying from European, particularly British, traders and governments. Now it appeared the worst was over. The economy was humming. Trade was thriving. Settlers had become successful farmers, traders, and businessmen. Some had become rich.

And the colonization societies continued to send new immigrants as quickly as the societies could charter vessels. Boatloads arrived each month. During 1848–54, the American society had transported nearly four thousand immigrants, in forty-one chartered ships, to settle in Liberia.[1] After a drop in 1855, the pace had quickened so that 538 would make the journey the following year. Although the lines of those waiting for passage continued to lengthen, ominous signs of possible disruption, especially if the United States fell into disastrous war, began to appear. But President Roberts, while on a European trip two years earlier in October 1854, was "so confident of the future" of Liberia he even asked the British foreign minister, the Earl of Clarendon, to consent to Liberia's annexing Sierra Leone. Roberts wrote later, "The proposition was received with some indications of surprise, and but little favour."[2]

During this January day, Stephen Allen Benson took the oath of office as the republic's second president. Benson, elected the previous May (Roberts decided, when he met opposition in his own party, that eight years in office was enough for him), was a natural for the job. Born in Cambridge, Maryland, May 21, 1816, he accompanied his parents when the family emigrated to Liberia in 1822. Local natives promptly initiated the six-year-old and his family into the rigors of life in the new colony when they captured the new arrivals and held them hostage for several months. After their release young Benson attended school, joined the militia in 1835, and was posted to Grand Bassa County. When he left the service, Benson remained in Grand Bassa where, working in trade and agriculture, he became a successful businessman. In 1842 Benson entered the political arena and won a seat representing Grand Bassa on the commonwealth's Colonial Council. After Liberia became independent, he served as a judge and then in 1853 was elected Roberts's vice president.

For the republic's sister settlement in Cape Palmas to the south, however, the new year unfortunately did not hold out as bright a future. Near-constant conflicts with warlike coastal neighbors, mainly the Grebo, Kru, and allied groups of the Lower Cavalla River, had taken its toll on the smaller independent colony, particularly following the death five years earlier of its outstanding governor, John Russwurm. And at the year's end, a particularly fierce battle would rock the colony and help push it from its independent status to joining the Republic of Liberia.

"The State of Maryland in Liberia," as it came to be known, was born out of the hysteria Nat Turner's 1831 uprising generated in much of the United States. Following Turner's failed Virginia rebellion, the Maryland General Assembly resorted to drastic measures to foil any similar disturbance.

The legislature enacted a law in 1831 directing that three members of the state colonization society be appointed commissioners whose duty would be to remove all free blacks from Maryland to Liberia. Anyone who offered resistance would face forcible expulsion from the state by the sheriff. The act stipulated $20,000 be appropriated in 1831 and $10,000 in each ensuing year for twenty years for their resettlement. Fortunately, fears subsided enough that the drastic measures were never enforced. However, the monetary provisions continued—much to the Maryland colony's good fortune—up to 1863, although at the reduced level of $5,000 yearly.

The first two groups of Maryland-sponsored emigrants sailed to Monrovia in October 1831 and December 1832. Because of differences with the American society over the status and rights of the emigrants, as well as other issues, the Maryland organization decided, however, to found a separate colony. The society chose a physician (an antislavery activist who had served in Liberia and written a popular book detailing the nearby Gallinas slave trade) to head its colonial effort. Dr. James Hall and a small contingent of emigrants sailed from Baltimore aboard the brig *Ann* on November 28, 1833. They first stopped at Monrovia to induce as many as possible of the settlers there to join their Maryland venture.

On February 12, 1834, the Marylanders landed at Cape Palmas. Located at a point where the Atlantic coast makes a sharp bend to the east, a promontory about seventy-five feet high rises on the cape. Given its prominent setting, it was well known to travelers. Visiting the Cape of Palms in 1863, British adventurer Sir Richard Burton described it as "a bold headland of red argillaceous earth, based upon black micabeous granite, tufted with cocoas and tapestried with verdure everywhere beyond the breaking of the waves."³

This new outpost avoided many of the mistakes the other colonies committed in their initial days. The local native Kru sold the desired land for the settlement without too much fuss. Hall arrived with a constitution to which each settler had to subscribe. Courts, public schools, and a militia were established soon after the first settlers stepped off the boat. The town (named Harper in honor of Marylander Robert Goodloe Harper, a president of the American Colonization Society) was laid out on the promontory, supposedly replicating Baltimore's city plan in miniature. A brass six-pounder mounted on the summit furnished some measure of security. Land for farms was allotted, and soon the new settlement began to flourish.⁴

After three years, when Hall's health failed, John Brown Russwurm replaced him as its first black governor. Russwurm, born October 1, 1799, in Port Antonio, Jamaica, to a white American father and a black Jamaican mother, grew up in Maine, where he attended Bowdoin College. He was one of the first blacks to earn a master's degree in the United States. Russwurm settled in New York City, and while still in his twenties helped found and edit *Freedom's Journal*, the first African American newspaper. Heavily involved in the colonization debate in the United States, he had planned to take medical training and go to Haiti.

However, he opted instead to go to Liberia, where he arrived in November 1828. Living in Monrovia, Russwurm served as colonial secretary and the first editor of Liberia's first newspaper, the *Liberia Herald*, from 1830 to 1835; he thus came to be regarded as the father of the Liberian press.⁵ He also worked as superintendent of schools for the colony (1830–36) and colonial agent for the American Colonization Society (1834–36).

The mulatto governor greatly impressed an American naval officer (later admiral), Andrew H. Foote, who served in the

US Africa Squadron. He noted in a 1854 manuscript how deftly Russwurm dealt with the local tribesmen. "Six kings of their own accord applied to Governor Russwurm and ceded their territories that they might be incorporated with the colony." Moreover, "every treaty contained an absolute prohibition of the slave trade."[6] Foote viewed the Maryland society's appointment of Russwurm as an essential step "to disgorge the colored men of Africa from dependence on foreign management."[7]

His consummate skill notwithstanding, Governor Russwurm could not prevent clashes between the settlers and the neighboring Grebo and Kru. Foote wrote about one such 1843 encounter in which he participated under Commodore Matthew C. Perry, commander of the squadron. Perry and his forces had come to aid the Liberia and Maryland colonies in their struggles with the natives and to punish the offending Grebo and Kru tribesmen for attacks on American shipping. Both Liberia's Governor Roberts and Maryland's Governor Russwurm closely followed the action as it unfolded.

Three American warships—the *Decatur, Macedonian,* and *Saratoga*—proceeded to Cape Palmas, where "natives attacked" an outpost "and suffered some loss in being driven off." The American officers "called together the chiefs and headmen," and some "palavering, and a great deal of lying on the part of the Natives" transpired. But a "conflict" for which the natives "had really prepared" broke out. In the ensuing "melee, the King was unintentionally killed, eight or ten men suffered [wounds] and the palisades and houses were burnt."[8]

The Americans afterward made landings "at towns along the coast, which had shared in the crime." Although "a few straggling shots were fired from the shore and from the woods," they didn't cause "any loss" to the American forces.[9] The loss to the natives, though, was substantial. "Four towns were burnt containing from fifty to one hundred houses, each neatly built with wicker work and thatched with Palmetto." Fortunately, the loss of life was minimal since "it was the Commodore's orders to destroy property but spare life."[10]

The highly esteemed Russwurm presided as governor of the colony from September 28, 1836, to his death, reputedly from "overwork and worry," on June 9, 1851, at Cape Palmas. Samuel Ford McGill served as acting governor until 1852 and governor to June 8, 1854. During this time Foote had observed "a movement" to declare the Maryland colony "as an independent state," a move he thought "requisite, [as] an element of the great achievement now going on."[11] The Maryland society agreed and in 1853 declared Maryland in Liberia the independent Republic of Maryland.[12]

The citizens of this new independent state of Maryland in Liberia elected William A. Prout governor. Prout, who took office June 8, 1854, found to his dismay that independence didn't solve Maryland's problems. His death in April 1856 at least spared him from the fierce fight between settlers and natives that erupted at Cape Palmas on December 22, and again on the borders of Sheppard Lake, a lagoon between Cape Palmas and the Cavalla River, on the eighteenth of January the following year. The Marylanders had launched a punitive expedition to chastise the Grebo but in the ensuing battle lost a number of men and guns.[13]

Once more it was Roberts—now former president and Major General Roberts, commander of the militia—to the rescue. He arrived with 250 men aboard the *Hirondelle*, the same small gunboat Napoleon III had sent Liberia as a gift five years previously.[14] The citizens, weary of having to depend upon outside intervention to fend off native attacks, finally decided it was time to consider joining their larger neighbor.

"President Benson," an article in the *Chicago Daily Tribune* reported June 3, 1857, "had sent a message to the Liberia legislature" on February 28, 1857, to the effect that "the people of the 'State of Maryland in Liberia'" had unanimously voted for annexation by Liberia. Maryland formally applied for admission as a county, sending Benson an act of annexation dated March 3, 1857.[15] Maryland in Liberia became the county of Maryland in the Republic of Liberia. Most Maryland settlers credited Roberts's rescue mission as the deciding factor in their applying to join Liberia.

Some 1,227 immigrants ultimately made it to Cape Palmas, but many Maryland blacks hesitated to join the venture since they sensed that the primary motivation of the whites who dominated the state colonization society was "to get rid of freed blacks." Aid from the sponsoring society also had gradually tailed off and stopped completely during the Civil War.[16]

—⚝—

With the addition of Maryland, Liberia now enfolded all of the original colonial settlements. The annexation of Maryland also brought the country's first hospital, Saint Marks, which opened in 1858 in Cape Palmas. The Americo-Liberians, still numbering little more than 10,700 souls in the entire country, now turned their attention to expansion into the vast, largely unknown hinterland. The interior was critical for Liberia. The coastal area, where most colonists had settled, "depended on trade with the far interior." It was also "essential for accommodating the massive influx of new immigrants expected from the US." And "many Americo-Liberians aspired to assimilate the huge native population to make "one people." [17]Thus, they eagerly sought to establish trade with the inhabitants and to enlarge the territory over which the government could claim sovereignty.

But, first, they had to shine some light on their unknown lands. Early in 1858 two Liberians, George L Seymour and

James L. Sims, set out to explore it. Seymour, born in Hartford, Connecticut, was a "passionate critic of Liberia's exploitation of interior peoples…and resolved to explore the far interior for the good of the Americo-Liberian colony."[18] He managed to gain financing for most of his expedition from a few liberal New York gentlemen, who probably looked at their outlay as a business investment.

He and two companions, Levin Ash and William Taylor, completed preparations and struck out for the fabled Mandingo capital Musadu on April 28, 1858. In their eight-month long trip they covered some 360 miles, but about twenty-five miles---only one or two days' walk---from their destination when they "were attacked, wounded and forced to abandon their mission."[19] Seymour was captured, and his American companion Ash "was captured, enslaved, and put on the market." [20] They eventually escaped and made their way back to the coast. Taylor stayed behind.

Sims, a native of Virginia, "about twenty-eight years of age, tall and thin, and of a dark brown complexion," also obtained private financing for his journey. Probably with an eye to trading in ivory he set out in January 1858. He built a house in the interior where he lived for several months until his return in 1859. He recorded his adventure in a "*Journal of travels to the interior of Liberia*,'" for which President Benson obtained "$50 from Treasury to finance 300 copies."[21] But both his and Seymour's accounts "became 'lost' soon after they were published. Portions of Seymour's journal were later found in obscure newspapers "and pieced together."[22]

Fuller exploration would have to wait until 1868, when a remarkable young Liberian, Benjamin Anderson, embarked on his journeys into the hinterland.

During his eight-year presidency, Benson was able to build on the momentum and optimism Roberts had brought to Liberia. On the foreign diplomatic front, England, France, Prussia, and Belgium had acknowledged the new government within a year after independence. Others had soon followed suit: Denmark in 1859, Italy in 1862, Norway and Sweden in 1863, and Haiti in 1864. Most important, the prize for which the republic had waited almost fifteen years finally came on October 22, 1862, when the United States formally recognized the colony it had initiated in 1821. The two countries signed a treaty of commerce and navigation in London on October 21, 1862. President Benson signed on behalf of Liberia. Lincoln appointed Abraham Hanson American Commissioner and Consul General June 3, 1863. He presented his credentials February 23, 1864. (The envoy's title and office were upgraded through the years to ambassador (and embassy) May 6, 1949.)

In his speech at the American Colonization Society's fifty-second anniversary meeting, Roberts highlighted Liberia's progress since its founding fifty years earlier: expansion to a territory of about six hundred miles of sea coast and "an interior over which she…[could] readily acquire an almost unlimited jurisdiction" whenever she was "prepared to occupy it." A population now of at least 600,000, composed of almost 15,000 emigrants from the United States and other "civilized" countries, about 4,000 Africans rescued from slavers, and more than 580,000 "aboriginal inhabitants."[23]

The republic could now boast four counties and thirteen towns and villages, "with their churches, schoolhouses, and comfortable dwellings."[24] Roberts's euphoria extended to the economy as well. Farms were turning out a wide variety of products for export, most notably sugar and coffee, camwood, and palm oil and kernels. Trade and commerce flourished. Even a nascent shipbuilding industry for the coastal trade was growing The capital, Monrovia, had made equally impressive strides.

Ashmun Street with houses and a school, Monrovia, 1893. American Colonization Society Collection. Prints and Photographs Division, Library of Congress LC---USZ62-129855

Edward Blyden in 1866 described coming into the harbor, where several vessels were anchored and warehouses hugged the Mesurado River's southern shore. Above the river, on a hill about one hundred feet high, stood the town. "Parallel with the river [were] four principal streets, River, Ashmun, Broad and College." Impressive residences lined each of the streets, occupied by the Americo-Liberian elite—the chief justice, future presidents, church ministers, and the like—and the president's house, courthouse, Ellis's Naval Hotel, post office, House of Representatives, the Baptist, Presbyterian, Trinity (Episcopal), and Methodist churches, and the "Methodist Seminary, occupying what may be called the acropolis." All were "substantial structures of stone or brick, and the dwellings two stories high." A "fine street intersects" the four streets "and descends" from the seminary "gradually a full mile to the sea-shore on the south."²⁵ The observer proudly pointed out Liberia College, located "about a mile in a south-westerly direction from the best built portion of the town." Sited on a "rocky eminence some three hundred feet high," the four-storied brick building was "surrounded by triple piazzas supported by light iron columns." And a cupola "command[ed] a fine view in every direction." He avowed the college was "indeed a noble institution," one that cast "lasting honor on the generous patrons in the United States to whom it [owed] its existence." Open for three years, the college could boast just twelve students, but expectations for the institution were high.²⁶

The Americo-Liberians had every right to be proud of their achievements. But the native Africans—whose numbers dwarfed the tiny handful of settlers—hardly shared this pride. The uninvited, unwelcome foreign, even though colored, intruders, with their zealous obsession to deliver the "benefits of Christianity and civilization" to the poor benighted, barbarous, heathen African, had taken his land, cut into his commerce, and earned the enmity of his chiefs and kings by eliminating their lucrative trading in slaves. And adding further insult, he (the native) was not even recognized as a citizen of the republic. He could not vote, hold office, utilize the legal system, or participate otherwise in the community. The settlers shared the same perceptions that "most whites held of blacks in America."²⁷ Colonial rule, be it white or black, was much the same everywhere in Africa.

Benson, reportedly the first Liberian president to speak several native languages, wisely recognized the importance of dealing with this issue and initiated at least the beginnings of a sensible policy. Unfortunately his efforts went for naught; his policy was not implemented. It was an open sore that would later eat at the very heart of the republic and ultimately contribute to its undoing.

Such divisive issues, though, were not confined to relations between the Americo-Liberians and the natives. Professor Liebenow notes that "the most divisive issue within the Republican Party concerned racial extraction." He maintains that Roberts, an octoroon, was denied a fifth term as president in favor of Benson because, although the latter also was racially mixed, "he was of darker complexion than was Roberts." Benson drew support from the poorer Americo-Liberians, who generally were purely of black ancestry, and the "Congoes," the descendants of the African recaptives rescued from slave ships. Both groups, according to Liebenow, "felt discriminated against by those of 'brighter' skin color."[28] One's skin color, and later the purity or extent of one's Negro blood, would become an issue so bitterly divisive, it would help spark an insurrection and play a role in deposing a president.

On January 4, 1864, Stephen A. Benson, after four terms as president, turned over his office to the newly elected Daniel Bashiel Warner. The old president returned to his coffee plantation in Grand Bassa County, where he died on January 24, 1865. Warner remembered his predecessor in his inaugural address, saying he "was regarded as one of the ablest men that have appeared among the negro race."[29]

Under Warner the country continued its peaceful climb. In fact, things were so peaceful the *Liberia Herald* reported that, in the June 1865 term of the Courts of Quarterly Sessions and Common Pleas (the principal court in each county), "no business was found for the Grand Jury" and "no Petit Jury was empanelled."[30]

A single blemish in Liberia's relations with the outside world, other than the wearying dispute with Britain over the Gallinas territory, had arisen with the rupture of diplomatic relations with France in 1858 over an incident involving the French ship the

Regina Coeli. The Liberian government had claimed the vessel was engaged in slave trading, but the French insisted it was only recruiting workers for sugar plantations in the French West Indies. The break, however, had been repaired and relations with France resumed in 1865. The dispute with Britain over the Gallinas territory, however, would drag on for years, until the British government forced Liberia in their 1885 and 1903 treaties to relinquish its claims to much of the area.

The burden of Liberia's foreign relations fell mainly on thirty-two-year-old Edward Wilmot Blyden, a young Liberia College professor who already had begun to make a name for himself as a writer, lecturer, and educator. Besides being appointed professor of Greek and Latin (in which he was self-taught), he had edited the country's premier newspaper, published a number of influential pamphlets, and been ordained a Presbyterian clergyman. President Benson had enlisted him as one of three commissioners to visit the United States in 1862 to promote colonization in Liberia, and President-Elect Warner tapped him to serve as secretary of state in 1864. Blyden, at the request of the college, resigned his government position the next year, to give his full time to his teaching job. Hilary R. W. Johnson took his place. But on July 14, 1864, only four months later, Blyden was back as secretary.

One piece of legislation enacted during Warner's first term, the 1865 Ports of Entry Law (also referred to as the 1864 Ports of Entry Act), provoked a storm of protest from both natives and foreigners and would remain a source of friction between the parties for years to come. The law required trade with foreigners be restricted to six "ports of entry"—Robertsport, Monrovia, Marshall, Grand Bassa, Greenville, and Grand Cestos River (and Nana Kru, Harper, and Cavalla were subsequently added). Each port, which was surrounded by a six-mile circular zone, included a government customs house. The government gave foreign traders two years to remove their goods from their establishments in the restricted zones.[31]

The outcry came immediately. The many native chiefs (and foreign traders) who had interests in the trade objected strenuously to the law and tried to prevent their goods being removed. They sought British support in a December 1, 1864, letter from the "Natives of Kroo Territory" to Major S. W. Blackall, governor and commander in chief, colony of Sierra Leone. (Liberian secretary of state Blyden also called on the same source for help. Liberia's only patrol craft, the venerable *Quail*, was laid up—not unusual—for repairs.)

Of the protesting chiefs, Prince Boyer of Trade Town in Grand Bassa, a well-known malcontent, proved the "most obstinate and unyielding." When he "threatened hostilities unless the Law was repealed," Warner dispatched "war materials" to Grand Bassa and sent someone to check on the defenses there. Boyer (and the other chiefs) backed down and duly delivered the disputed goods. He even sent an envoy to assure the Liberian government his intentions were "pacific."[32]

Warner in his 1865 annual address attributed "much of the obstinacy and disloyal conduct manifested by the natives to the mischievous interference on the part of foreigners with the native Chiefs."[33] Even Harry Johnston admitted that foreign traders, particularly British, "delighted in defrauding the [Liberian] government." Warner was elected as a Republican, the party dominated by mulatto traders. He supposedly introduced the measure in support of the True Whig party's policy of protecting Liberia from being overwhelmed by a "white invasion." Johnston concedes, "All things considered, perhaps [the law] was a wise measure." The government at that time could not afford to equip "more than six Customs-Houses," ensure law and order, and protect the goods there. Government finances, as usual, were precarious; duties, the principal revenue, were at 6 percent ad valorem, "an all time low."[34]

The controversy died down, but the determination of natives and foreigners to take a major role in the region's commerce would persist. And for them the Ports of Entry Law remained an irritation.

A more immediate threat loomed now. Immigration from the United States during the Civil War understandably had dropped sharply—only 169 newcomers made the trip in the four years from 1861 to 1864. Previously, Benson, while president, recognized the hazard Liberia faced if the supply of new settlers dried up. The colonization societies also recognized the danger. US president Lincoln received a letter on October 25, 1862, from Reverend J. B. Pinney, corresponding secretary of the New York State Society, urging the government to encourage "colonization of Negroes in Liberia,"[35] and in November [1862] Benson appointed three commissioners to go to the United States "to present the cause [for colonization] of Liberia." Besides Blyden, the trio included J. D. Johnson and Professor Alexander Crummell, one of Blyden's colleagues at Liberia College.[36] Blyden, on visits to the United States (and to other countries), would prove an invaluable asset in garnering support among the white populations, including official recognition for Liberia.

The three commissioners, in an effort to overcome the opposition of most American blacks to colonization, sent out a letter addressed "To the Free Persons of African Descent throughout the United States" cordially inviting them "to a home in that small but rising community" of Liberia.[37] The three carried their message during several months to most northeast cities—New

York, Washington, Philadelphia, Baltimore, Boston, Harrisburg (Pennsylvania), Portland (Maine)—to churches, colonization societies, and wherever else they could catch the ears of free black men (and presumably avoid the raging Civil War). En route to America, Professor Blyden had stopped in England where he even "endeavored to enlist the pen of Charles Dickens" to the cause.[38] But he met with no more success than he would achieve later in the United States.

Blyden addressed the annual meeting of the Maine State Colonization Society in Portland's High Street Church in July 1862. Attempting to sway his black listeners, he pointed out that, although they were free, American society still treated them most shabbily. Even "if the President of Liberia," he declared, "were to present himself at the door of one of the city [street] cars in Philadelphia, he would be told, perhaps politely and perhaps abruptly, to ride on the front platform."[39] But, despite the war's end the following year and the emancipation of slaves in the United States—and the persuasive powers of Professor Blyden— Liberia's worry only grew more urgent.

President Warner added his plea to the United States for more immigrants. "Our need for population," he entreated, "is immediate and urgent." Moreover, he suggested, "It is the most likely solution of the vexed negro question in the United States."[40] How could the United States, facing the overwhelming task of settling millions of freed slaves, ignore such a plea?

The American Colonization Society also joined the campaign, placing advertisements, distributing information, promoting Liberia as a virtual haven for American blacks. An information brochure, published earlier, highlighted Liberia's favorable employment climate, where schoolteachers could "get from three or four hundred" dollars yearly, good accountants "four to eight hundred as clerks in stores and mercantile houses," and "tailors, shoemakers, blacksmiths, carpenters, masons, bricklayers, cabinet makers, shipwrights, &c, &c.," could always find jobs paying good wages. Farming, in particular, offered great opportunity. And "each emigrant on his arrival" received a "town lot, or five acres of land." If accompanied by a family, he would be given additional land, up to ten acres, depending on the number of family members. When he had become financially able, the settler could buy additional land, "for $1 an acre."[41]

Given the high priority black Americans accorded education, the brochure's report that Liberian law required that all parents send their children to school provoked further favorable interest. Although the brochure admitted that quality of the schools varied from settlement to settlement, Alexander High School and Liberia College in Monrovia reputedly operated successfully. The society claimed boldly, "A parent who wants to educate his children can do it better in Liberia than in any other place."[42]

To still concerns about the sea voyage, the society's brochure explained that "the length of the voyage varied from thirty to fifty days," with "about forty days" the average, and boasted "the Society [had] never lost a vessel with emigrants on board!" The clincher was that for those unable to pay, the society would cover the cost of their passage and support them, supplying housing, provisions, and medical care, for six months after their arrival in Liberia.[43]

Potential emigrants could discern the living conditions they might face in Liberia from the society's recommended list of items to bring. While Liberia had no winter, "wearing flannel, or warm clothing" during the rainy season "greatly promoted health." Forget "large pieces of furniture, including tables and chairs"; just bring "a good mattress and bed clothes" and a table and cooking utensils, as well as "a keg of nails, a bale or two of domestics, and some money—$5 gold pieces preferably." The latter items would be useful in building their house and paying for any labor they might need in the first months of living in Liberia. A man should bring "the tools of his trade," a farmer, his "axes, hoes, spades, saws, augers, &c."[44]

In an effort to dispel the unfavorable information critics were spreading, the society even enlisted the *Liberia Herald*'s editor to refute claims "that Liberians [had] not say to eat but roots and wild animals." He countered with an impressively exhaustive list of "animals, fruits, and edibles [vegetables] as are in general use" in Liberia—"cows, bullocks, swine, sheep, goats, ducks, fowls, pigeons, turkeys," plus wild animals, fish and shellfish, more than a dozens different fruits, and twenty or so vegetables.[45]

The Colonization Society ended its appeal with a clarion call to the conscience of the American black community, particularly the "more enterprising and educated class"—of whom the society expected "to send out a large number." The call was aimed particularly at "the very intelligent and wealthy colored people" in America. The society thought they "would have some ambition to share in the splendid results, soon to be achieved" for Liberia "in laying the foundations for a great nation…and in redeeming an immense continent from Pagan darkness and barbarity."[46]

The appeal apparently worked. Some 527 American immigrants responded in 1865, the largest number in any single year since 1856. And on May 10, 1865, the brig *Cora* brought 346 black immigrants from the British Caribbean island of Barbados to settle in Liberia—an event that would greatly influence life in the republic. Whether or not these new colonists were "the very intelligent and wealthy" is not clear. Nonetheless, President Warner and Vice President James M. Priest doubtless felt relieved when they began their second terms in January 1866. It would, however, prove only a temporary respite.

Edward Blyden, himself a Caribbean immigrant who had arrived in Liberia as an eighteen-year-old in early 1851, welcomed them to their new home. He already was making a mark as secretary of state, and arguably would go on to become Liberia's most distinguished and world-famous intellectual, scholar, linguist, educator, author, diplomat, and politician (not to mention alleged adulterer and exile)—and probably one of its most complex, controversial, and colorful figures.

—⚌—

Born August 3, 1832, on the Danish Island of Saint Thomas (now one of the US Virgin Islands), Edward Wilmot Blyden could boast later of his pure and undiluted Negro blood. His father, Romeo, and mother, Judith Ann, were said to have been born on the Dutch Island of Saint Eustatius in the West Indies around 1794 and 1795. Blyden's grandfather, a member of the Ibo tribe, probably came from Nigeria as a slave. But his parents were freeborn. Edward, three of his brothers, and his father worked as tailors, an older brother as a shoemaker. His mother and two sisters were seamstresses. After a two-year sojourn in Venezuela, the family returned to Saint Thomas in 1844, and the twelve-year-old Edward began his training as an apprentice tailor, attending school in the mornings and working in the tailor shop in the afternoons. After five years of this arrangement, Blyden's life verged on a dramatic change, and he would find himself treading a path he could never have even imagined.

He joined the Dutch Reformed Church where the Reverend John P. Knox was pastor. Knox, intrigued by this smart, spirited black teenager, became Edward's close friend and mentor. The minister struck a responsive chord in the young Blyden when he encouraged him to become a missionary—which meant a missionary to Africa. But as far as Blyden was concerned, education stood paramount. Reverend Knox expected him to study theology at Rutgers University, the minister's alma mater, in the United States. Knox arranged a job for Blyden as a servant for a friend, handed Edward some old clothes and six dollars, and the excited young man was ready to go. But while he awaited passage, his father died on April 28, 1850. Edward hesitated to leave his mother, especially since one of his older brothers had died two years earlier. But he knew this was his great opportunity. Edward Wilmot Blyden sailed for America aboard the *Oxholm* on May 17, 1850.[47]

If New Jersey thrilled the newly arrived teenaged black from an obscure West Indian island, it also frightened him. Although New Jersey had ended slavery in its territory, the institution still prevailed not far to the south. And the Fugitive Slave Act cast a shadow of fear over any black man or woman, regardless of his or her status, since one might be kidnapped as a runaway slave. Disappointment overtook fear, however, when Rutgers, despite its distinguished alumnus John Knox, refused admission to his black protégé.

The refusal apparently stunned the young, sensitive Blyden, inflicting a wound that would never heal fully and that would affect his thinking and writing as he matured. Years later he confided that he found "the deep-seated prejudice against" his race "so controlling an influence in the institutions of learning, that admission was almost impossible."[48]

Perhaps even more devastating to the already wounded young man would be a subsequent experience in New York City, where he was spending some time after his Rutgers rejection. The Reverend J. B. Pinney, who would become another lifelong friend, invited Blyden to attend a church service. "The pastor, a D.D. [Doctor of Divinity] of eminent learning and ability," Blyden recorded, delivered the sermon. His subject—justification of the Fugitive Slave Act. The minister thundered, "Cursed be Canaan, a servant of servants shall he be unto his brethren." Taken aback, the young man later wrote, "This was the first of our hearing such weight given to that interpretation and application of Noah's malediction: and though not over eighteen years of age, we experienced as it were, an intuitive revulsion of mind never to be forgotten."[49]

"Discouraged by the difficulties" in his path, young Blyden "proposed to return to St. Thomas," and, as he wrote, "abandon the hope of an education."[50] However, he received a letter, this time from Mrs. Knox, urging him instead to become a missionary to Africa. She explained that the New York Colonization Society offered to furnish his passage to Liberia so he hopefully could attend the Alexander High School, then just beginning in Monrovia.

Blyden jumped at the chance. He sailed from Baltimore on December 21, 1850, for Bassa, Liberia, aboard the *Liberia Packet*. En route to Baltimore, Blyden went through Philadelphia, where he met William Coppinger, at that time the secretary of the Pennsylvania Colonization Society (and later the corresponding secretary of the American society). Blyden, writing years later, recounts how much he appreciated Coppinger's taking him to the foot of Walnut Street in Philadelphia to catch the steamboat to Baltimore. He confessed that he had been "in great fear of being seized for a slave under the operation of the Fugitive Slave law which at that time was causing great excitement in the country."[51]

In a letter to J. B. Pinney in February 1851, the callow and irrepressible youth described how the *Liberia Packet* first was delayed in its passage out of Chesapeake Bay and how later the vessel encountered a severe Atlantic storm. But "after two o'clock in the morning of the 25th [of January]," he wrote, "Cape Mount was visible," and "about 8 O'clock, we saw Cape Mesurado, on which stands the town of Monrovia." Scarcely able to contain his excitement, he told Pinney, "You can easily imagine the delight with which I gazed upon the land of Cyprian and Tertullian, ancient fathers of the Christian Church," and added, for good measure,

"Hannibal and Henry Diaz, renowned generals; yes, and the land of my forefathers." The following day, "which was Sunday," Blyden landed on "African shore...It was now my privilege," he gushed, "to gaze upon a delightful country—nay—to tread upon the land of my forefathers." Climbing up the "'heights of Monrovia,' everything I saw inspired admiration." It was a land teeming "with everything necessary for the subsistence of man."[52]

Blyden, so taken by everything Liberian, even went so far as to downplay the fear most persons held about snakes in Liberia. He explained to Pinney, somewhat glibly, that snakes were less common there than in some parts of the United States "on account of a species of ant, called drivers." These ants, he purported, "travel in large troops" that "attack reptiles," and are, he was told, "even troublesome to the famous boa constrictor." The attacker ants take on the snake after it has rendered itself "immobile" by "swallowing large prey." In an attempt to escape the ants, the poor victim assumes "all sorts of postures," but ultimately wears itself out in the struggle, making the snake's "death inevitable."[53]

In October 1851 Edward Blyden enrolled in Alexander High School, a project of the US Presbyterian Board of Foreign Missions. As principal of the new school, the board had appointed the Reverend David A. Wilson, recently graduated from Princeton University. In Wilson, young Blyden found a mentor and friend. In Blyden, Wilson found a promising young man whom he described in a letter to the mission board's corresponding secretary in New York, Dr. Walter Lowrie, as modest and respectful, with natural talents and attainment well beyond his years. In summing up, Wilson wrote that he had high expectations Blyden would make an able minister or teacher, fully competent to take the principal's place.[54] Edward Blyden was off to an impressive start, but on a career—as educator, scholar, writer, preacher, statesman, diplomat, and intellectual—that would reach far beyond anything Wilson could have imagined.

School opened in January 1852 with thirteen students, two about twenty years of age, the others ranging from twelve to sixteen. Wilson reported to Dr. Lowrie that Mr. James agreed to furnish Blyden "board & washing" for $112, which, with incidentals, would bring the student's total subsistence for the year to $150.[55] Blyden lost little time in applying himself with his customary zeal. He became a prolific and erudite letter writer, often lacing his epistles with bits in Latin. He wrote articles that began appearing in the *African Repository*. The *Liberia Herald*, for which he authored an editorial early in 1853 regarding unrest in Cape Mount County, signed him on as a correspondent. A detailed description of Roberts's campaign against Chief Boombo, in which Blyden participated in March of that year, appeared in the newspaper's letters to the editor.[56]

On July 26 he also began his career as a public speaker, delivering the Liberian Independence Day oration at Monrovia's Provident Baptist Church. He noted that even though "the day was exceedingly rainy, the large building was crowded."[57] And a report in the *African Repository* said that Blyden "acquitted himself to the admiration of that vast assemblage."[58] In early 1854 Roberts appointed him editor of the *Liberia Herald*, a post he held until 1856. And to round out his burgeoning multifaceted career, Blyden commenced teaching at the high school he still attended as a student. That year he received grades of 5 (perfection) in each of his Scripture, Behavior, and Industry courses, 4¾ in Latin, 4½ in Greek, and 4 (excellence) in Arithmetic.[59]

Blyden found time to get married in December 1856. In the same year, while still editor of the *Liberia Herald*, he published *A Voice from Bleeding Africa*, the first of many pamphlets he would pen. He had begun to acquire a reputation as a spirited defender of Africa and Africans, while (at least initially) praising colonization. Not surprisingly, when the school term opened in 1859, it was Principal Blyden, ordained a Presbyterian minister the previous year, now fully in charge. Principal Wilson, his prediction fulfilled, had retired.

—∿∿—

In April the following year, Blyden began a curious correspondence that lasted over sixteen years. His correspondent? William Gladstone, the chancellor of the exchequer and later prime minister of Great Britain. Blyden wrote Gladstone on April 20, 1860, congratulating him on his budget and speeches and on his "noble efforts in the cause of free trade," which Blyden hoped would "loosen the bonds" of his [Blyden's] people's enslavement.[60]

The letter, from a young and unknown high school principal in a scarcely better-known African country, apparently deeply impressed one of Gladstone's colleagues, Henry Brougham, the first Lord Brougham. It made such an impression that Brougham, a member of parliament, lord chancellor, and notable campaigner against slavery, referred to it in a speech he made before the House of Lords on April 25. Brougham remarked that he wished he could read Blyden's letter to his fellow MPs. Gladstone, who remained a faithful correspondent, never published it, nor any of the sixteen others that followed.[61]

Blyden, however, soon got his opportunity to meet Lord Brougham. The Presbytery of West Africa commissioned the young reverend to attend the Presbyterian General Assembly in Philadelphia in May 1861. The presbytery also empowered him to raise money in Britain and America for establishing a female educational institution in Liberia. He arrived in England on March 13, visited there and then Scotland. He met important people, gave lectures, made friends and useful contacts, and managed to elicit financial and material support for the proposed school. The youthful and engaging scholarly teacher had found his forte. Writing exuberantly to the Reverend J. J. Wilson in New York that he had "met with a good measure of success in this country," in which he "found many friends, especially among Quakers," he boasted, "Had I the time and the means I could raise large sums for Liberia."[62]

Among the Quakers in London and its vicinity whom Byden found "very kind" to him, were Samuel Gurney, an MP and prominent Quaker, "and his family." Blyden wrote, "Besides donations of books and other personal kindnesses, when I was leaving Mr. Gurney as a token of pleasure he felt (as he said) at having made my acquaintance, presented me with a splendid English silver watch, newly made I think to order." Mrs. Gurney presented him a matching silver chain for the watch.[63]

Before leaving England, Blyden remembered Lord Brougham (who would die seven years later); he presented "a walking stick made of ebony, and mounted with ivory and gold" to Lord Brougham "for his great service to Africa, and the Negro race."[64] Not surprisingly, Blyden delayed his departure for America. He would miss the Presbyterian General Assembly meetings—despite his new timepiece.[65]

Blyden arrived in Toronto April 23. There he joined his wife, who had preceded him to visit relatives in New York and Canada. On Sunday, July 21, Reverend Blyden delivered a sermon in the Presbyterian church on Seventh Avenue in New York. His subject, "Hope for Africa," came from his favorite Bible passage, Psalm 68:31, "Ethiopia shall soon stretch out her hand to God," As he stood in the pulpit and looked out over the congregation, and his thoughts turned back to that Sunday sermon ten years earlier—when he so vividly felt the "curse of Canaan" inflicted on him—he must have felt a trace of smug satisfaction.[66]

Before Blyden left the United States, the Reverend Dr. Joseph Tracy, secretary of the Trustees for Donations for Education in Liberia, the men responsible for Liberia College, asked him to meet with the group in Boston. They wanted to interview him for a possible appointment to the college. After a few rescheduling mishaps, Blyden, eagerly no doubt, managed to get to Boston. In view of his limited educational qualifications, no college, and his equally limited teaching experience, plus the fact they had heard talk of incoming president Warner's intention to tap Blyden for his cabinet, the trustees, however, hesitated to appoint him.

Two days before Blyden sailed from New York for home on August 10, 1861, Tracy gave him the good news. He had been appointed professor of the Greek and Latin languages and literatures at the new college. Ex-president Joseph Jenkins Roberts was appointed college president and professor of jurisprudence and international law, and Reverend Alexander Crummell, professor of intellectual and moral philosophy and of the English language and literature. Blyden arrived in Monrovia September 10 after spending nearly two months in America.

Liberia College was formally inaugurated on Thursday, January 2, 1862, with "impressive ceremonies." The chief justice of the republic, B. J. Dalton, delivered a "just and truly eloquent address," according to one attendee. Dalton presented the keys to the college to President Roberts, who gave the principal address. Professor Blyden delivered the second address, "mainly in defense of the classics."[67] The school did not open to its first students, seven in number, until the second of February the following year.

The Alexander High School Presbyterians understandably felt let down at losing the principal who had filled everyone with high hopes for the school. Blyden tried to placate them by promising he would "still be at their disposal and would return after one year at the College if the [school's] Board needed him."[68] The school, despite its bright promise, closed its doors after Blyden left, although the board hoped to restart the school at some different site in the future.[69]

Professor Blyden, still only thirty years old, assumed his teaching responsibilities at the college at a princely salary of $850 per annum, which the New York State Colonization Society paid from its Fulton Fund endowment. But, typically, it was not enough for Blyden. President Warner appointed him Liberia's secretary of state in 1864, and he remained on the college's faculty. During his tenure as secretary of state, he sharpened his negotiating skills in the ongoing, seemingly interminable discussions with Britain on territorial claims and the cascade of protests from both foreign and indigenous traders over the 1865 Ports of EntryLaw. His holding down both jobs, however, proved unsatisfactory as far as the college was concerned. The trustees induced him to resign the cabinet position in 1866 and gave him a temporary increase in his salary, plus a small loan "to aid him in erecting a convenient residence."[70]

Not one to sit on his hands, Blyden still found time beginning in January 1866 to fill the pulpit of the Presbyterian church in Monrovia and be in charge of another smaller church in nearby Junk Town without compensation. He finally wrote B. V. R. James, agent for the Presbyterian Board, on April 13, complaining that "*gratuitous* [italics his] devotion of life is nowhere considered obligatory in the Scriptures." And continued, "I cannot work for others for nothing and I will not do it. I am not willing to encourage the principle. God does not require it and men do not thank you for it."[71] In May 1866 the Reverend Thomas H. Amos was installed as pastor. The Reverend Edward Blyden, ever the instructor, preached the sermon at the installation. His theme: "The Duties and Responsibilities of a Pastor of a Church." Blyden, it was reported, presented his sermon "with that scholarly ability and eloquence for which he has already become distinguished."[72]

That scholarly ability and eloquence, however, could not hide concerns about money and health that marked much of Blyden's adult life. His complaints of "weak" eyes, "disordered state of [his] liver," and other maladies frequently led to his taking leave to recuperate and regain strength. And when he ran short of funds, which he often was wont to do, he usually turned to friends and employers. After all, he was, as historian A. Ayundale put it, an "African celebrity."[73]

—⚋—

Reflecting his growing fascination with Islam and the Muslim Africans, who occupied an important place in Liberia's interior and the surrounding lands but were largely ignored by Liberian scholars, Blyden toured Egypt, Lebanon, and Syria for three months from July to September 1866. And over the next four years, he "made the most of his opportunities," studying Arabic and "making friends with the Mohammedan traders who came to Monrovia from the interior."[74] On the same track, he progressively modified his vision of a "divine plan for the rebirth of Africa," in which "the civilized, Christianized and educated ex-slaves from the Americas," and even their slavery experience, "played a primary role." Instead, indigenous African cultures, "civilized" by the more tolerant Islam, would provide the foundation for the continent's reawakening.[75]

In addition, Blyden became nearly obsessed with color—skin color. He "developed an aversion to accepting mixed bloods, 'mulattoes,' as full 'negroes'" (or indeed as full humans!). He "even favored prohibiting interracial marriages later in life."[76] This preoccupation with color, however, attracted a following in Liberia far beyond Blyden.

—⚋—

While the black Americans who settled Liberia presented various shades of color, they came to be grouped into lighter-skinned mulattoes, often called people of color, and the darker Americo-Liberians. The mulattoes, usually better educated and better off financially, dominated the government and civil service. And the Republican Party, which commanded Liberian politics from the time of independence, came to be associated with the Monrovia-based mulattoes. Opposition, such as the True Black Man's Party, was largely ineffectual until a convention in Clay-Ashland of upriver farmers founded the True Whig Party in 1869. This new opponent, reflecting the resentment against mulatto Republican rule, drew its support mainly from black coffee and sugarcane growers in the upriver settlements and from the Congoes. (It also came to include many of the Barbados immigrants who arrived in 1865.)

This resentment fed on the mulattoes' social discrimination against them, their exclusion from political life, and economic policies that appeared to favor mulatto commercial interests.[77] And the frustration it generated over the years ultimately elevated the issue to a test of racial purity. The purity of one's Negro blood became as important as—even more important than—the degree of his "blackness."

In the May 3, 1867, presidential election, the Republican mulatto Reverend James Spriggs Payne defeated fellow Republican mulatto Daniel Warner. Blyden later fulminated that the mulatto Republicans could see only themselves worthy of wielding power, so they passed the top positions in church and state from one to the other in an unbroken circle[78]

When "pure" black, successful businessman Edward J. Roye threw his hat into the 1869 presidential ring, the True Whigs knew they at last had their candidate. Blyden gave him full support. Neither, however, had any inkling of the calamity that shortly would befall them and of the ensuing crisis that would threaten the very life of the republic.

CHAPTER 9

A Scandal, Coup, and Mystery

—⚬—

ROYE HAD ALREADY TURNED THIRTY-ONE and achieved success in business when he boarded the bark *Chatam* in New York City on May 1, 1846, bound for Monrovia, Liberia. The man who would become Liberia's fifth president also carried with him a bitter memory from his childhood in Newark, Licking County, Ohio, where he was born on February 3, 1815. Edward's father, John Roye, reportedly a freed slave from Kentucky, came north with his wife, Nancy, to settle in the newly created town of Newark. According to local records, he purchased a lot on the south side of the nascent town's square in 1810 and apparently prospered. But as Edward found out, regardless of being free and materially successful, blacks could never be wholly secure in the United States.

A three-member board of trustees governed Newark. For some reason not recorded, two of the trustees reportedly met on one occasion and issued an order requiring that all Negroes leave the town within twenty-four hours. Upon receiving this news, young Edward ran to the home of A. E. Eliot, the third member of the board, to plead for him to have the order stayed. Eliot, his son, and Edward raced to the town square where a large crowd of both whites and blacks had gathered, the latter begging not to be driven out of their homes. Eliot argued successfully that execution of the order be postponed and given further consideration. Fortunately, the measure was never carried out. But "young Eddie Roye must have walked away from the Square with a determination to find a land with freedom for 'men of colour.'"[1]

His father sold his property in 1822 and moved to neighboring Illinois. Seven years later he left the property acquired there to his young son, who had remained behind with his mother. Financially comfortable, Edward enrolled in Ohio University at Athens in 1832 or 1833 and after three years moved to Chillicothe to teach school for one year. Then he turned to making money. Striking out for the West with a supply of goods he had purchased for trading, he landed in Terre Haute, Indiana, in 1837. Here his business acumen flowered. Over the next seven years, he purchased a large two-story building within a few blocks of the town square, opened a trading store, and then bought more property, hired barbers for a barber shop, and opened Terre Haute's first bathhouse.

Notwithstanding his financial success, Roye decided to seek that "land with freedom for 'men of color'" he had determined to find as a child. In 1845 he left his business enterprises in Terre Haute to attend Oberlin College, intending to study French and emigrate to the French Caribbean island of Saint Domingo. But, as he would explain later in life, a fellow boarder at Oberlin persuaded him to change his destination to Liberia. The opportunities there for a black man with Roye's intelligence, education, and drive supposedly were boundless. And, in proof of his friend's assertion, not long after he walked down the gangplank in Monrovia, Roye had parlayed the trade goods he brought with him from the United States into a thriving business exporting African goods to England and the United States. After a few years, he became "the leading merchant and richest man in Liberia" and proudly sailed back to visit America on one of his own fleet of ships, the first vessels to carry Liberia's flag to European and American ports.[2]

Having established himself in business, Roye decided to try his hand at politics. A scant three years after arriving in Monrovia, he was selected speaker of the House of Representatives and then served as a senator from Montserrado County from 1856 to 1860 and as Liberia's chief justice from 1865 to 1868. In 1869 Roye won the presidential election with the slogan "internal expansion and economic development." Upon his inauguration on January 3, 1870, he outlined an ambitious program of financial reforms and educational and transportation improvements, even building a railway line which believed would greatly influence the "civilization and education of native tribes."[3] But financing was hard to come by.

Due at least in part to the of Ports of Entry Law, trade had dropped off, and government revenues were down. The economy was near stagnation. Clearly, opening up the interior to greater trade, coupled with public works to repair and extend the infrastructure, held the key. Equally clear, such a program would demand money—in considerable sums. Where would it come from? The republic's financial system was not up to the task of funding the major program Roye had in mind. Liberia would have to turn to a foreign source.

Breaking a long-held taboo against foreign borrowing, the legislature authorized President Roye on January 26, 1870, to negotiate a loan not exceeding £100,000 ($500,000) at an interest rate not more than 7 percent for fifteen years. Not less than £20,000 ($100,000) of the proceeds would be applied to the payment of existing public debt in Liberia, and another £20,000 would be deposited in the treasury as a basis for issuing paper currency.[4]

Given the dominant position Great Britain occupied in the financial world, and the close ties the two countries had developed, London was the logical source for the loan. Roye sailed from Monrovia in June 1870 to England (and subsequently to the

United States) to attend to "certain foreign interests"—Liberia's border complications, in particular. He anticipated while in London also giving his personal attention to negotiating the loan, thus saving the fees the government otherwise would have to pay someone else. For whatever reason, however, he did not pursue the loan and returned five months later empty handed. But not for long.

President Roberts later recounted the whole episode in his 1873 annual message to the legislature. Roye had charged David Chinery, at that time honorary Liberian consul general in London, to explore a possible loan. Roberts understood the president intended to convene the legislature to consider Chinery's proposals and, if deemed satisfactory, authorize appointing commissioners and taking any other actions needed. President Roye, however, did not convene the body, supposedly because "the general feeling" of the public "strongly opposed" a loan. He feared the legislature, if convened, would abrogate the enabling act and scuttle the whole enterprise. Instead, he simply plowed ahead, appointed Chinery, W. S. Anderson, and W. H. Johnson, the speaker of the House of Representatives, as commissioners and "vested them with powers wholly unauthorized by law" to negotiate the loan in London.[5] Roye appeared well on his way to achieving still another career success. But his good fortune would all too soon come to a mysteriously abrupt and tragic end.

In August 1871, Chinery and party concluded a £100,000 loan from a syndicate of banks—at 30 percent below par, and a 7 percent annual rate of interest, with three years' interest deducted by the lender, leaving a balance of £49,000—which was deposited in a bank to the account of the commissioners. The loan and interest was to be repaid in fifteen years, a total sum of £132,000. The British banks would make a payment of £70,000 upon the Liberian government's issuance of £100,00 in bonds.[6]

"Then," Roberts reported, there "followed a system of charges, peculations and frauds unparalleled, I presume, in any public loan transaction of modern times."[7] After the loan was secured, Roye proceeded, "before any money was paid in to the Treasury for any specific purpose and before the Legislature had either accepted the loan or taken any action in relation thereto," to draw drafts for himself and directed Chinery to purchase £10,000 worth of merchandise for the government's account, "without the slightest shadow of legislative authority." The goods that arrived at Monrovia were overpriced and of shoddy quality, "some almost, and others entirely, useless in Liberia."[8]

Upon his return to Liberia in October 1871, Roye faced a firestorm. News of the loan had incensed much of the populace. He was accused of embezzlement. And this incident, coming on the heels of another unpopular move on his part, so infuriated the public electorate that his fate was sealed. In the *New York Tribune*, June 9, 1871, a piece entitled "Liberia Not Prospering," explained. At the May 1869 presidential election, a proposed amendment to the constitution was also submitted for referendum. The amendment would double the president's and vice president's terms of office from two to four years, senators' from four to eight years, and representatives' from two to four years. These terms specified in the 1847 constitution were generally recognized as too short, especially given the unrest the Ports of Entry Law had generated among native Africans and the danger of "complications" arising "between the Liberian and British Governments."

Despite an overwhelming vote in favor (350 to 2) and the House of Representatives' decision to declare the constitution amended, the Senate withheld its approval. The two houses agreed to resubmit the proposal to the electorate in May 1870.

Following the voting on May 3, Roye "took charge of the ballot [box]," counted the votes, and announced the amendment passed. The legislators were up in arms. They declared his counting the ballots invalid since he "had usurped" a "Legislative function."[9] Over Roye's protests, another presidential election was held on May 2, 1871. Joseph Jenkins Roberts won, garnering an "almost unanimous vote unopposed." He would take office on January 1, 1872, at the end of the president's regular two-year term of office.

Roye adamantly insisted his term of four years would not expire until December 31, 1873, so when Roberts won the election handily, the *New York Tribune* correspondent reported there was "every danger of a conflict. The people are in rebellion against the Administration."[10] Many citizens remained deeply suspicious of Roye and feared he "intended" to secure "to himself supreme and uncontrolled power."[11] Roye's supporters prepared for action.

And drastic action was not long in coming. An insurrection was provoked in Monrovia after an attempt by armed supporters of the president to seize a building that the Saint Paul River settlements industrial society used for a bank. Anti-Roye forces overpowered his supporters. Several people were killed. The insurrectionists sacked the president's house and caught Roye as he tried to escape. The Liberian Senate and House of Representatives issued a proclamation that "the sovereign people of the Republic of Liberia" declared on October 26, 1871, President E. J. Roye deposed from his office."[12]

Not only was Roye deposed, he was imprisoned and charged with embezzlement. On February 11, 1872, the jury at a high court for impeachment found him guilty and remanded him to jail to await sentencing. But "at about 7:30 p.m. the alarm was given that he had escaped." And he was not alone. His son and fellow-prisoner, ex-treasury secretary R. F. Roye, also had taken leave. According "to the most reliable information," the two lowered themselves "down from the [prison's] back window" with a rope smuggled into the prison.[13]

Exactly what happened after that remains a mystery. According to one account, the elder Roye drowned attempting to escape to a British ship in the harbor. President Roberts said that he "tried to reach an English steamer anchored off Monrovia by removing his clothes to look like an ordinary Kruman boarding the ship for work." The "native canoe capsized and Roye drowned."[14] The younger Roye reportedly made it safely to England.[15]

An ironic variation on this story suggested that Roye was weighted down by British money—supposedly proceeds of the 1870 loan—tied to his waist. The money, according to the story, was stolen after his body was brought ashore. Edward Blyden, one of the president's closest friends and an ally in their "pure black" ardent opposition to Liberian mulattoes, claimed that Roye, after escaping from prison, was "waiting for a boat" when "a mulatto shot him and published he got drowned."[16]

However, many discounted Blyden's veracity. In fact, some suspected he had a hand in stirring up the trouble. After reading the New York newspapers' accounts of Roye's attempt to extend his term, Dr. Joseph Tracy, in Boston, who was well acquainted with Blyden, wrote that the *World*'s article painted "the contest as between the blacks, who go for Roye, and the colored, who support Roberts." He continued, "This looks as if the news came from Blyden." And Blyden was not one "to be relied on for accurate statements" on questions in which he had an interest, "especially on this question of black and colored."[17]

One of Roye's successors, Liberia's longest-serving president, William Tubman (1944–71), believed Roye was badly beaten and his nude body "dragged" through Monrovia's streets "to a spot in Ashmun Street" where he died. In his honor Tubman built a new True Whig Party building on the very spot and appropriately named it the E. J. Roye Building. Even the date of Roye's death is disputed. Numerous sources list it as February 12, 1872. But the date under Roye's presidential portrait that hung on the fourth floor of the Executive Mansion in Monrovia reportedly was February 11. The confusion presumably arose from not knowing whether he died during the night of the eleventh or in the early morning of the twelfth.

The *African Repository* published this local account of the episode:

THE DROWNING OF PRESIDENT ROYE

The following account from Liberia of the last days of President Roye will be read with melancholy interest. After mentioning that the High Court of Impeachment sat daily at Monrovia until the 11th February, when the jury brought in a verdict of guilty, it is stated:

President Roye "was taken back to jail to await the sentence of the court, but at about 7.30 p. m. the alarm was given that he had escaped; and, on search being made, it was found that not only he, but his son, E. F. Roye, late Secretary of the Treasury, who had been a fellow-prisoner, had also escaped. The most reliable information with regard to the escape is, that it was effected by means of a rope, which had been clandestinely conveyed into the prison to the younger Roye, and that with that his father and himself lowered themselves down from the back window of the prison. Having succeeded in effecting their escape, they proceeded to Krootown, in search of a boat to take them on board of the British mail steamer, which was then in port. The younger Roye offered £1, or $5, to be taken off, but the Kroomen refused it, informing him that orders had been sent to Krootown that no person should be taken off from there. He however made good his escape to England. President Roye also made application to other Kroomen to be taken off, but was recognized, and they gave information of his escape. Upon this chase was given and pursuit kept up, with varying success between the prisoner's chances of final escape and his pursuers' chances of capture, until on Sunday afternoon, between the hours of 2 and 3 o'clock, when President Roye, seeing that from his situation he must be captured, after divesting himself of his apparel, in a state of nudity, save a piece of cloth fastened around his waist, plunged into the sea, and made for a boat, (the Towns, of Liverpool,) lying off a short distance from the shore. He made several attempts to be taken or to get into this boat, until at last he sunk and was drowned. A bag of money, which the accused had fastened about his waist, facilitated, it was represented, his destruction.

 The news of this sad occurrence traveled with lightning-like rapidity throughout the town just as the hour for afternoon service had arrived. The day, the time/the circumstances, and the solemn nature of the event, made a strong and sad impression, which could not be concealed. The services in the various churches were suspended, no congregations in fact attending. The long-excited passions of the populace seemed to have lost all their recent vehemence on that holy Sabbath afternoon, as following in silence the lifeless body of him, once their ruler so lamentably misled, so deplorably ambitious, borne to the prison which, scarcely four and twenty hours before, he had left, animated doubtless by most sanguine hopes. So perished the deposed President B. J. Roye, fifth President of Liberia.

"The body of the deceased was, at his family's request, given up to them, and was buried on the next following afternoon."
(*The African Repository*, 48 [1872], 220–21)

After Roye's removal from office, the legislature announced an executive committee consisting of Charles B. Dunbar, General R. A. Sherman, and Amos Herring would head the government provisionally until arrangements for electing a new president could be made. Vice President James Skivring Smith made his way to Monrovia on November 2, 1871, and supposedly assumed his duties as interim president two days later. He served out the remainder of Roye's term that ended in December.

Smith, born in Charleston, South Carolina, in 1825, arrived in Liberia in 1833 and served as secretary of state from 1856 to 1868 and as a senator from Grand Bassa County from 1868 to 1869 before being elected vice president. Having governed as chief executive for only two months, he holds the dubious record of serving the shortest period of any Liberian president. Smith, though, did deliver the customary annual message to the legislature on December 4, 1871, even if some argue it was impossible for him actually to have assumed power since he belonged, as did Roye, to the True Whig Party, and all True Whigs were arrested. Whether or not he should be counted as having served as president is still debated.[18]

Even what happened to the money from the loan—how much actually reached Liberia—remains unclear. Some estimates run from £17,903 to £27,000. Sir Harry Johnston believed "a good deal...[seemed] to have disappeared with Roye, and a small sum" with one of the commissioners, W. S. Anderson, "who fled to St. Paul de Loanda" in Angola.[19] Of the £80,000 in bonds issued under Roye, the Liberian government disavowed some and cancelled others.[20] Not until 1898 did the republic finally admit to a loan of £70,000 to £80,000 and agree to pay a progressive annual interest rate of 3–5 percent on it.

Liberia now had sipped the deadly brew of foreign loans and corruption, and there was no turning back. A new "Africa fever" of debt, foreign intervention, and avarice, would join the old to plague the country and sometimes even threaten the republic.

―∽―

The year 1871 proved strange and tumultuous not only for Liberia and Roye but for his supposedly good friend Edward Blyden as well. In the summer before the president left on his English trip, a bizarre incident on May 5 involving Blyden seemed to portend Roye's downfall six months later. Henry W. Dennis, the agent of the American Colonization Society in Monrovia, captured the event in a letter dated 6 May 1871 to Dr. William McLain, the American Colonization Society's financial secretary and treasurer:

A "mob of some twenty-five or thirty persons, armed with clubs, loaded pistols and guns," gathered at Blyden's residence around "three o'c [o'clock]" in the afternoon. They broke into the house, took Blyden out, reportedly "dragging him out from under his wife's bed," and "put a rope around his neck," then proceeded to pull him through the streets to President Roye's home.[21] Poor Blyden was terrified. He feared what such a gang of ruffians might do. He presumably had no inkling of why this had happened.

The president, according to Dennis, was said to have arranged the whole business "for some improper intimacy" that allegedly had "been going on with Roye's wife." Dennis and ex-presidents Warner and Payne "denounced the [mob's] action" and succeeded in whisking Blyden away to Warner's house where the shaken accused told them he "will leave Liberia" and "probably never return here."[22]

Dennis thought perhaps the attack might have been more political than personal in origin. After all, Blyden was a black activist who sought "to arouse all the black skinned men against light colored men." But since the mob were also black men, he concluded that the president (who also happened to be black) personally was "at the bottom of this." Neither a constable nor any other officer would arrest any of the mob's leaders although "writs were issued to arrest some," including the acting secretary of state, W. A. Johnson.[23]

As for Blyden, everyone was asking where he was. He seemed to have disappeared.

Reverend J. B. Pinney, Blyden's close friend and corresponding secretary of the New York Colonization Society, reported that Blyden, contrary to some reports, currently was in Liverpool; he had left Monrovia as planned on the same steamer ex-president Roberts and his wife took to Madeira. Furthermore, the mob knew Blyden had resigned from Liberia College in April, effective June 1, a month before and not as a consequence of the attack, was traveling "for his health" with funds provided him, and "never promised to leave the country never to return." He had made all arrangements in advance for his trip, including "providing for his family in his absence."[24] The New York society had "appointed him to establish a High School for natives at Vesua, and furnished him with the funds."[25]

Pinney saw the genesis of the affair in "the growing animosity" for years "toward Professor Blyden chiefly for Political Reasons." He had, after all, cooperated with H. R. W. Johnson, Henry M. Johnson, Crummell, and Roye "for what is known as the Black Man's party," mainly "to bring natives" into the republic "as a component party...as soon as possible by treaties, schools, and missions."[26]

Reverend Pinney also thought that many "presumably hated" the gifted Blyden "because of his ability as a writer" and were jealous of his accomplishments. "To see him—a poor tailor boy from the West Indies—a Professor, with a good salary—a Secretary of State under President Benson and the right hand man of" Presidents Warner and Roye "was enough to make many full of hatred and malice."[27]

But Pinney concluded that his friend's real offenses were (1) "his bold advocacy of the Negro," (2) the fact that he "was going to start a High School for Natives," and (3) that he "had been invited to America."[28] As for Roye, Blyden's enemies had worked on his jealousy "to break a most intimate friendship of years," one that had produced "every creditable State paper of his administration." In a fit of jealousy, he "did his noble wife the grossest injustice" in regard to her "chastity." As a postscript, Pinney added that he learned the mob had been "fined [only] $5 each, the justice having gone with them to the Professor's house."[29]

Whether or not this bizarre incident was a cuckolded president's revenge or possibly an omen of further deranged behavior, it illustrated the heated atmosphere of color that clouded the Americo-Liberian political scene.

—⚏—

Thus 1871 turned out to be a watershed in Liberia's history and in Roye's and Blyden's lives. Both Liberia and Blyden lost their innocence. Roberts lost his confident optimism in the future of Liberia. And Roye lost his life. Liberia's image also suffered a terrible blow. Even before Roye's unseemly ouster and curious death, the front-page *Tribune* article trumpeted that some prominent men believed "Liberian independence was declared 25 years too soon. The people do not know how to appreciate their independence."³⁰ American society secretary Coppinger fretted that "other influential sheets" also "were carping...of the incapacity of the people of color to govern themselves, and the futile efforts of the Am. Colonization Society to bolster them up and make anything respectable out of them—even in Africa."³¹

In the wake of the Roye imbroglio, Blyden headed to Freetown, Sierra Leone, which offered a more hospitable climate. Presumably the high school for natives was put on hold. (After Blyden's brush with the Roye-sponsored mob, Dr. Tracy in Boston had expressed doubt also that Blyden would come to New York at all.)³²

Freetown, though, welcomed Blyden. He founded and edited a newspaper, the *Negro*, continued to study Arabic, and as he reported in a letter to William Coppinger in Washington, was "hard at work on Fulah" (the language of the Muslim Fulanis who occupied a large area in the sub-Saharan region from Senegal to Chad). He thought that in a few months, he "might be able to send a translation of the Gospel of Matthew for publication in England."³³ In addition, Blyden was appointed government agent of the interior; in that capacity he undertook several official government expeditions in Sierra Leone's interior, adding to his knowledge and understanding of the indigenous tribes.

In Liberia there had been much talk of civil war if Roberts were elected. But, in view of the reaction to Roye and the chastening of the True Whigs, really not so surprisingly, Joseph Jenkins Roberts, the old Republican warhorse, was once more elected president. Roberts likely heeded the call to return to the presidency more out of a sense of duty, a mission in his view to rescue Liberia from the political abyss on which the republic teetered precariously, than to confidently lead the country toward achieving the "great things" heaven [had] "in store for Africa, to be conferred," as he had declared only two years earlier, "through the instrumentality of Liberia."³⁴

Roberts's reelection, however, ignited a salvo from Blyden. In a letter dated September 8, 1871, to society secretary William Coppinger, marked "Private," the professor wrote, "our friends in America are mistaken if they think the mulatto and Negro can live in peace together." He continued his indictment of the mixed-race class, saying how "provoked" he was to think how they, "by being considered African should have so much power to damage Africa and the Negro race."[35]

In subsequent letters to Coppinger, Blyden pointed out how the mulattoes had placed obstacles to introducing Arabic studies at Liberia College and how they "unite to decry and depreciate every effort that tends to open up the interior." He concluded with an impassioned plea: "Their reign is a reign of terror. I beseech you with tears in my eyes, for the sake of Africa to save Liberia from them."[36] The Trustees of Donations for Education in Liberia suspended the college on April 2, 1876.

On his inauguration January 1, 1872, Roberts bemoaned the sad state to which political rule in Liberia had fallen and called for "a general renovation of [their] whole system." He found that "gross corruption, and a lavish misapplication of public funds" had reduced the country's financial position to a "deplorable condition." A presidential proclamation stressed that the "will of the people [was] paramount"; the three branches of the government must adhere to the constitution, each avoiding "any degree of encroaching upon the prerogatives" of the others; and only the legislative branch could submit changes to the constitution to the people.[37] Despite his acknowledgment of the government's failures, he wrote to the society in May, "I cannot rid myself of the belief that God desires to accomplish great a work in Africa and for Africa, through the instrumentality of Liberia."[38]

His words, while reassuring, cloaked a spirit that was flagging and a body that was weary. By the time Roberts's second term rolled around, the reelected president in his inaugural address on January 5, 1874, put forward a brave front. He said he had expected to be retiring, but his fellow citizens had "ordered it" otherwise, and he assured them that "no difficulty" would "deter" him "in the faithful discharge of duty."[39] He stressed, in particular, the need for the "elevation and Christian enlightenment of the aboriginal population," which was essential "to the stability and perpetuity" of the republic. They had to be "properly educated and trained" and introduced as coworkers in the construction of the political fabric now being erected.[40]

Once again, the rhetoric proved empty. Little was accomplished on these lines. And where indigenous people did become "Christianized" and "civilized," the results often proved not to the liking of the Americo-Liberians. The ever-restive Maryland Grebos, now Christian converts, in the 1870s proclaimed an independent Grebo Reunited Kingdom. Roberts clashed with these "acculturated native Africans," who "complained they had been deprived of their lands and brokerage (trade) rights by colonists."[41] Aided and abetted by foreign traders, they began trading directly with foreign ships, in violation of the Ports of Entry Law. Trouble clearly was brewing, and some colonists "withdrew themselves in fear of the native population."[42]

An economic depression added to the Americo-Liberians' miseries. And the president became very ill. In June 1875 he left for England for medical treatment, and the vice president, Anthony William Gardiner, took over as acting president. It was not an enviable position in which the fifty-five-year-old Gardiner found himself. Born in Southampton, Virginia, in 1820, he arrived in Liberia with his parents aboard the brig *Vorado* in 1831 when only eleven years old. They settled in Grand Bassa County, where Gardiner attended school and studied law. Politics soon beckoned. He attended the national convention in 1847 that drafted the republic's declaration of independence and constitution, represented Grand Bassa in the legislature, and served as attorney general under Roberts before being elected vice president in 1871.

And now the republic under Gardiner faced a serious crisis. The so-called Grebo Reunited Kingdom Revolution was gaining traction.

According to an October 12, 1875, *New York Times* dispatch, the Liberian consul claimed the Liberian army had "been victorious over the barbarian tribes" in all the five engagements that had been fought.[43] But the next report from Cape Palmas on November 2 proved far more sobering: "A Liberian force of 900 troops...attacked some native villages, but were repulsed...twenty-four killed and wounded." A follow-up report on November 25 was still more alarming. "Much distress... Some interior settlements are almost to a state of starvation."[44] In near desperation Gardiner sought help. William Coppinger, the American Colonization Society secretary, called on US president Ulysses Grant to order a "ship-of-war... to the neighborhood of the settlements, with a view of giving encouragement and support to the Liberians, and to chastise such natives as may be within the reach of its guns."[45]

The response came promptly from a sympathetic President Grant. The steamship *Alaska*, carrying twelve guns and currently attached to the European Squadron, would be ordered to Liberia. The American secretary of state also asked the British government to remove "a number of Englishmen" who were "trading guns, ammunition, and other means of war" with the rebel natives. The United States claimed its treaty with Great Britain for "suppression of the African slave trade...gave ample authority for Government interference for the protection of the Liberians."[46]

With American intervention, the rebellious Grebos finally were quelled in 1876. But it would not be the end of Grebo efforts to obtain freedom, at least in their trading relations with the outside world. Grebo nationalists, who "produced the prophet Harris, continued to take up arms until 1915."[47] And Edward Blyden was aghast that the United States sent a warship to aid "Liberia against the natives, and thus…pamper the miserable pretensions of a few men who have no love for Africa and whom the assistance provided will only place them in position to do more harm to the country."[48]

—⟪—

Roberts returned from his therapeutic English trip and left office on January 3, 1876. Less than two months later, he died, on February 21, 1876, after attending a colleague's funeral in a heavy rain. According to Sir Harry Johnston, "Roberts died from the chill."[49] One might suspect, however, that a worldly weariness and loss of zest, perhaps brought on by a dream that no longer visited him, contributed to the chill.

—⟪—

The Reverend John Maclean described the president six years earlier.

> Although a colored man, President Roberts is lighter in complexion than many white men, but has certain marks of his race. He is in this sixtieth year, a man of tall, spare frame, with a fine cast of head, and wears a heavy gray mustache, which gives him a military look. In speech, he is unusually clear and deliberate, with an easy style, that makes listening to him agreeable, and in manner he is very unpretentious.[50]

In Harry Johnston's view, "though Roberts had a strain of Negro blood in his veins, he was mentally and physically a white man." While this "perhaps gave him more weight at that time in the councils of Europe," it was "a circumstance which raised some jealousy about him amongst the pure-blooded Negroes in the Liberian State, and perhaps also in America."[51]

Johnston's observation struck at the very reason Blyden, Crummell, and the other "pure-blooded" blacks so violently opposed mulattoes such as Roberts. The reason, however, was not primarily jealousy, although such a human emotion doubtless figured in. The explanation lies rather in a far broader and more fundamental cause: the rising celebration of the African "race" in opposition to "dominant European [and American] paternalism" that Liberia's mulattoes represented. Blyden and Crummell ultimately extended their thinking to encompass a "Pan-Negroist ideal," which furnished "the main inspiration for the various 'Back-to-Africa' movements."[52]

When another Republican, James Spriggs Payne, who earlier had filled the president's chair for two years (1868–70), succeeded Roberts in 1876, Blyden, seldom at a loss for words when it came to mulattoes, again blasted them for thinking that "there are only a few men here who it is supposed ought to be in power, and they pass the Government from one to the other. Everything in Church and State, under their rule, proceeds in this circular manner.[53]

Payne would be the last president the Republican Party would manage to get elected. In fact, after he stepped down in 1878, the resurgent True Whig Party would never lose another presidential election up to Samuel Doe's coup that toppled the republic in 1980. Liberia, for most of this time, lived under this single political party, fueled by the Americo-Liberian leadership's "need," as Professor Gus Liebenow described it, "for solidarity in meeting the dual threats of tribal rebellion and European incursions."[54] On January 7, 1878, Anthony William Gardiner was inaugurated Liberia's ninth president.

LIBERIAN POLITICAL PARTIES

The Republic of Liberia's constitution, like its American model, made no mention of political parties. Nevertheless, opposing factions before independence evolved into the Pro- and Anti-Administration Parties. In the first presidential election in 1847, Pro-Administration Party candidate Joseph Roberts defeated the Anti-Administration Party's Samuel Benedict. The True Liberian Party, subsequently renamed the Republican Party, coalesced soon after independence. Dominated by the relatively better educated and more affluent mulatto traders (Roberts was an octoroon) it generally favored restricting foreign economic activities, opposed territorial expansion into the hinterland, and were more radical or progressive than their opposing Whigs. (There were of course, many exceptions to these generalizations, e.g., Roberts.) Nevertheless, They filled most important government positions; most had interests in business and commerce, centered in Monrovia.

Thanks to the minority mulatto community's political discipline and greater financial resources, coupled with the constitutional requirement that one must "possess" real estate to vote, the mulattoes held sway over Liberian politics in the first thirty years of the republic. (Most arrived in Liberia before 1832.} Noteworthy, the first five presidents of Liberia (Roberts, Benson, Warner, Payne, Roye) were wealthy traders. Fewer than one-third of the immigrants who arrived in Liberia between 1832 and 1843, however, could even "write" or "spell."

To oppose the lighter-skinned Republicans, John Henry Goode led creation of the True Whig Party in a convention in rural Clay-Ashland in 1869. The new party drew heavily for support from rural areas—the more recently arrived immigrants, Congoes, black upriver coffee and sugarcane growers, and others with primarily agricultural interests.

When these darker, often initially less affluent, Americo-Liberians and Africans protested against discrimination in public life and economic policies favoring mulattoes, race and skin color became a political issue. In the fiercely contested 1869 election, the True Whig presidential candidate, Edward James Roye, a successful businessman, defeated Republican incumbent James Spriggs Payne. Roye was a full-blood black, the first non-mulatto to be elected president.[55]

The election of Anthony Gardiner in 1877 marked the beginning of a string of Whig presidential wins, unbroken until the coup in 1980. It was only from 1848 to 1883 that Liberia enjoyed "intensive interparty competition."[56] Otherwise, it was one-party rule. The Whigs developed a highly effective system that reached its peak under Presidents William Tubman and William Tolbert, to sustain their rule. They employed patronage as a key weapon to keep "the party faithful in line."[57] To influence the general public, they would stifle public dissent, particularly in the press.

Then, they found they could control the election process itself, starting with appointments to the elections commission, the body that decided whether or not a party or a candidate "was entitled to a place on the official ballot." The Whig-controlled legislature also could simply declare opposition parties and candidates illegal, as it did to the Reformation and Independent True Whig Parties that opposed President Tubman's second term in 1955.[58] Finally, party zealots could outstuff the opposition at the ballot box or even resort to intimidating would-be voters. One of the most blatant examples of fraud-ridden and grossly lopsided election results was the 1927 contest between Charles D. B. King and J. R. Faulkner. It landed a place in *Guinness Book of Records* (1982).

After weathering the upheavals following Samuel Doe's coup and civil war, Liberia would see an abundance of political parties emerge. Their role in Ellen Johnson Sirleaf's election as president in 2006 and reelection in 2012 hopefully augurs well for democracy in Liberia.

CHAPTER 10

The 1870s: Coming of Age

—⚉—

SIR HARRY JOHNSTON, IN SUMMING up the 1870s, wrote that they "had not been a happy period for Liberia. Besides the loan and the Monrovia uprising there had been a terrible outbreak of small pox in 1871." Then came "more wars with the natives, chiefly the Grebos" in 1875–76. But perhaps the most abidingly annoying woe Johnston mentions is that "in the following year [1876] 'jiggers' or burrowing fleas also known as 'chiggers' [*Eutrombicula alfreddugesi*] were first introduced by a ship coming from the Portuguese island of Sao Thome to land or recruit Kru laborers." Since then, Johnston recorded, "the annoying little creature" had "spread all over the coast regions of Liberia, but," fortunately, was "not so abundant as it was a few years ago."[1]

By the end of the decade, the shape of the country's society and political establishment, "jiggers" and all, had by and large been drawn. While not frozen in time—many changes, especially in the economy, would alter Liberia's landscape—its outlines would in essence persist until Sergeant Samuel Kanyon Doe put a bloody end to Americo-Liberian hegemony in 1980. Immigration by 1880 had virtually ended. Some new colonists from Louisiana arrived in 1877, but the American Colonization Society, strapped for funds, offered little help. (The society halted active support of immigration in 1912–13 and was officially dissolved in 1964.) A trickle of individuals continued to come on their own; from 1865 to 1904, only 4,093 arrived from the United States, and some soon went back to America.[2]

Color, which had split the True Whig party and fractured the colonial establishment, already was headed for decline as a hot issue. Johnston offered a novel slant on the apparent decline of the lighter Liberians. "Some sixty years' experience," he wrote, "had shown that Negroes born in America, especially in the temperate climate of the United States, were scarcely less immune from African fevers than a people of European origin." Half-white mulattoes "suffered more than full-blooded Negroes, and quadroons more than mulattoes." As a result, mixed-blood individuals had gradually been dying out, and those of "a purely Negro type" had been increasing proportionately.[3]

While skin color faded, for whatever reason, as a defining issue, race and place of origin—America, Africa, the West Indies, or wherever—and wealth came increasingly to determine an individual's niche in the society fashioned by the Americo-Liberians. Liebenow made an exhaustive study of the "class and caste stratification" this colonial structure imposed on both native Africans and immigrant settlers[4] (I should point out here that not everyone shares Liebenow's view. Carl Patrick Burrowes dismisses the "Americo-Liberian ruling class...as a half truth," one that assumes "ethnicity has been the determinant social relation in Liberian politics.")[5]

Occupying the upper rungs of the social ladder were the black and mulatto immigrants (and their descendants), the Americo-Liberians, who had been born free, or who had purchased their freedom, or who had been emancipated in the United States. This group was augmented by the smaller but remarkably influential coterie of West Indians who had arrived in the mid-nineteenth century.

Lower down on the ladder were the "recaptives," the Africans rescued by the US Navy from slave ships. Although many hailed from present-day Nigeria, Ghana, and other countries on the Gold, Ivory, and Slave Coasts of West Africa, they all came to be known as "Congoes." The USS *Strong*, one of the ships engaged to transport free blacks to Liberia, brought the first, fifteen in number, to Liberia in 1821. They had been taken from a slaver off the coast of Georgia. By the time of the Civil War, when the United States recalled its antislaving West African fleet, it had settled some 5,744 recaptured Africans in Liberia.[6]

At the very bottom of the ladder, with hardly a foot on a rung, stood the great mass of Liberia's native residents, the indigenous Africans. From the first, as the record attests, rescuing and elevating—both spiritually and materially—Africa's uncivilized, un-Christianized black inhabitants was fundamental to the colonization rationale. This spirit, generated by the Second Great Awakening, drove many, maybe most, of Liberia's founders, early pioneers, and leaders with an amazingly powerful missionary force. Few of the country's religious or secular leaders, white or black, ever failed to proclaim this objective.

Conflicts between the colonists and indigenous Africans—over the slave trade, land, and trading rights—posed big obstacles, but this noble cause still proved a potent tool for the Americo-Liberian minority. It helped them establish and maintain dominance for 150 years. This missionary drive, however, stopped short of assimilation. Liberia's founders, according to Liebenow, did not expect to "swell their [ascendant] ranks by converting the 'heathen savages,'...but by encouraging" additional American blacks to emigrate.[7]

The 1866 obituary in the *African Repository* of the US naval officer who acquired the colony's initial piece of land reflected the typical settler mentality: "Much credit is due to Commodore [Robert] Stockton for his intrepidity in breaking down the savage opposition of the natives and in securing territory for the foundation of a Republic destined to diffuse the full tide of Christian glory upon benighted Africa."[8] The republic's first president, Joseph Jenkins Roberts, doubtless believed in good faith that the treaties he made with the local people would help redeem them from "heathenism" and "superstition and idolatry" and bring them "the blessings of civilization and Christianity."[9] These blessings, however, did not include citizenship and governance.

To what extent his successors shared his view is an open question. What clearly emerges, however, is that their missionary mind-set fit well into the colonists' general attitude of superiority vis-à-vis the local inhabitants. Even Edward Blyden, certainly one of the native Africans' most ardent champions, preached that American blacks returning to mother Africa carried a solemn duty to convert and educate the "uncivilized" local residents. His thesis of "provident return" contributed to the American colonists' patronizing and imperious attitude toward the native Africans. The society that soon emerged curiously mimicked, in some respects, that of the American old South from which many of the settlers had escaped. Liberia in many ways came to smack of antebellum Mississippi or nineteenth-century Rhodesia.

> An unintended consequence of Edward Wilmot Blyden's theory of "providential return"—his contribution to the back-to-Africa movement—was to reinforce the patronizing and imperious attitudes of the black colonists toward the native Africans. The colonists even adopted the notion of "the white man's burden." The society developing in Liberia, in fact, resembled the antebellum American South in many respects. The settlers usually referred to the Africans as "uncivilized," and the Africans referred to the black settlers as the "white men." A ludicrous example of the colonists' adopted white man's racism was one of the earliest laws enacted in the colony. The law restricted the movement of Africans by, among

other things, requiring them to carry torches at night to warn settlers of their approach.¹⁰

Even esteemed leaders such as President Roberts thought that the treaties the settlers made with the local people would help the latter improve their lives by adopting Christianity and becoming "civilized." James S. Payne, another Liberian president (1868–70 and 1876-78), called the Africans the "Barbarous Thousands" and exhorted the settlers to fulfill their responsibility to help civilize their less fortunate brothers.¹¹

The Reverend J. B. Pinney, Blyden's good friend and American Colonization Society official, on a visit to Liberia in 1833, reported back to the society that "the natives are, as to wealth and intellectual cultivation, related to the colonists as the Negro of America is to the white man." And, "their mode of dress," he wrote, "leads to the same distinction, as exists in America between colors." Thus, "a colonist of any dye (and some are of darker hue than the Vey, or Dey, or Kree, or Basso tribesmen)," would, if he were "at all respectable, think himself degraded by marrying a native." In fact, those Africans who have migrated to town are "menials…and I am obliged to say, that so little effort is made by the colonists to elevate them," in contrast to the efforts "usually made by the higher classes in the United States to better the condition of the lower [classes]."¹² (Ironically, while the colonists considered the Africans "uncivilized," many Africans viewed the alien Americo-Liberians as little more than liberated slaves, whose proper station in society was inferior to their own.

Not surprisingly, the settlers took measures to reduce the threats these "barbarous" hordes—as President Payne termed them—posed to the colonists' safety and society. Housing in the towns was de facto segregated. Private ownership of land, which replaced the traditional system in the settled areas, was being extended.

Ordinances against public nudity mainly targeted indigenous women who customarily went about bare breasted. While informal liaisons with tribal women, despite the social taboo, were not infrequent, as Harry Johnston put it, these unions "usually were kept in the shade." As a further means to maintain "the caste relationship, the tribal person lacked rights as an individual citizen... rather he or she was a member of an ethnically defined corporate group." As such they were subject to "a legal code" distinct from" the one "that applied to the settler citizen." For natives, their particular group was held accountable for acts of its individual members.[13]

The Congoes, technically settlers, occupied a preferred position relative to the native Africans. But they had not yet been blessed by Christianity and civilization, so the treatment they received differed markedly from that of the Americo-Liberian settlers. Unlike the Americo-Liberians, for example, they weren't given land in both towns and rural areas. In fact, Professor Liebenow relates that "they were long regarded as squatters or renters, rather than owners of land."[14]

Jehudi Ashmun, while serving as agent for the society and US government, described how the first groups of recaptives were formed into a separate and closely supervised community in which they followed a rigorous program. Ashmun noted a superintendent controlled "their hour of rising and sleeping," led "the family devotions," and instructed "them...in the principles of Christianity, from three to four hours, daily." Major T. Draper was "to be responsible for the good order, cleanliness, and good conduct of the boys [a derogatory term for the men]."[15] Their daily instruction in agriculture complemented the generous helpings of spiritual food the Congo settlers received.

Some of the Congoes after a time understandably began to mix with the natives resident in their areas. And, as Governor Joseph Mechlin Jr. (1829-34) wrote in 1832 to the Colonization

Society's secretary, "Our recaptured Africans of the Ebo and Passo tribes," have fallen into "the habit of procuring wives from the adjacent tribes...by paying a small sum to the parent of the girl" and, in contrast to their Americo-Liberian neighbors, bringing her "into the colony." But he hastened to add that the women thus obtained were "clothed after our own fashion, and we compelled them to be married."[16]

In any event, the discriminatory and restrictive status imposed on recaptives after a time dissipated. In fact, when the schism between "pure" Negroes and mulattoes opened in the settler society in the early 1870s, they found themselves occupying "a pivotal position in the factional arguments."[17] Their affiliation with the emergent True Whig Party and support of Edward Roye as president elevated them close to the level of the Americo-Liberians politically. As the line separating the recaptives and the Americo-Liberians blurred, many tribal Africans came to indiscriminately call both groups Congoes.[18]

Congo people and indigenous Africans did enjoy possibilities, though limited, to move upward in settler society. An individual might be adopted, or might marry into an Americo-Liberian family, or be born from one of the "in the shade" liaisons. Obtaining a formal Western education, or being admitted into Americo-Liberian social clubs bearing names such as the Crowds and the Saturday Afternoon Club or into fraternities and sororities (e.g., the United Brothers Friendship, the Odd Fellows, Free Masons, House of Ruth, Sisters of the Mysterious Ten, and the Order of the Eastern Star) also could count toward upward passage. Conversion to Christianity and "civilization"—that is to Western culture—nonetheless was the norm ultimately for full entry into Liberian society. And to be "civilized" was the term "invariably used...as a badge of distinction separating the Americanized settler from the indigenous tribal person."[19]

This cultural assimilation, of course, came with a cost. For an aspiring receptive or native to be admitted to civilized society meant adopting Americo-Liberian ways, lifestyles, norms, and values and jettisoning "much of his or her indigenous subculture."[20] As Liebenow points out, "the prescribed form of integration was decidedly on Americo-Liberian terms and conditional upon acceptance by the tribal person of various facets of the settler culture, and not the reverse."[21]

Curiously, these various facets were the very warp and woof of "the society across the Atlantic," the very society from which the American settlers had fled, the same society that had never accepted them fully. Thus, English, instead of any of the sixteen or more tribal languages, "became the preferred medium of communication in official circles, in most mission schools, and elsewhere."[22] Christianity, rather than Islam or any traditional African religion, offered the only way to salvation—and civilization. Monogamy, at least in name, replaced polygamy. Ownership of property was private instead of communal, and the "real" economy came to mean essentially a cash economy instead of the traditional subsistence one. The "political and legal institutions ...bore at least a formal resemblance to those of the United States." And the "foods, dress, art, and architecture of the Americo-Liberians" were generally "the desired legitimate norm."[23] And at the day's end, even if all the hurdles were jumped, cultural assimilation was no guarantee, only a prerequisite—and not always a sufficient condition---for upward social mobility.

As might be expected, the passage to become civilized proved easier for the tribes living in the coastal belt, notably the Bassa, Dey, Grebo, and Kru, who had the earliest contacts (and wars) with the American colonists. For the tribes in the hinterland, however, whose contacts and sustained interaction with the settlers came much later, the process was more difficult. The net result: this reluctance to assimilate local tribal people, coupled with the decline of immigration from abroad after the American Civil War, doomed Liberia to rule by a small Americo-Liberian minority—never as much as 5 percent of the population—until well into the twentieth century. Actually, the size of the real ruling group was even smaller since it was confined largely to an elite within the Americo-Liberian community.

The economy divided into two distinct parts. Most indigenous Africans followed a traditional subsistence agriculture that relied upon the slash-and-burn system of shifting cultivation. On plots they cleared from the forest, these farmers grew, mainly for their own consumption, rice, cassava, yams, sweet potatoes, beans, okra, eggplant, pepper, and peanuts, maybe some pineapples and sugarcane and coffee. They picked bananas and plantains, pawpaw, and other wild fruit. From wild palm oil trees, they took kernels and oil for cooking, and they tapped scattered wild rubber trees. Chickens, guinea fowl, and goats made up their livestock. Streams supplied them fish, and the forests various edible game. Any produce surplus to the family's needs might be bartered in local informal country markets. (Benjamin Anderson in his upcountry explorations also encountered towns and large markets where a variety of products were traded.) No roads or railroads cut through the countryside; only rivers and trails allowed transport.

The coastal Kru, Grebo, and Bassa farmed and fished, but trade (in both goods and slaves) provided their most lucrative employment. They, particularly the Kru, were well known as stevedores and fishermen all along Africa's west coast. Early settlers of the Mississippi colony marveled at their skill in daring the rough coastal waters in their primitive canoes. And the reliance European ships placed on them in landing, loading, and unloading their cargoes gave the tribesmen an enviable advantage when it came to trading—and a source of conflict with the American settlers even well into the twentieth century.

The badge of master traders undoubtedly belonged to the Muslim Mandingo who lived in the Liberian hinterland and beyond. Occupying much of the region between the Senegal and Niger Rivers, the Mandingo enjoyed "a fairly high degree of political and religious supremacy over" the other tribes residing in the west African interior. They also "effectively monopolized the trade" among these people and between the interior and the coast, including European traders.[24] They managed for many years to maintain their monopoly (which they jealously guarded from foreign incursions), despite Americo-Liberian determined efforts to break it. And even as recently as the twentieth century, Liebenow observed that they "still travel great distances across the Sahara and throughout West Africa in search of commercial opportunities."[25]

The other half of Liberia's dual economy lay mainly in the hands of the American settlers and recaptive Congoes. Paul Cuffe had envisioned a colony in which settlers would be organized into a cooperative society or societies that would procure commodities from the local inhabitants, in addition to whatever the settlers themselves produced, to trade with Britain, the United States, and other foreign powers. While in Sierra Leone he looked for suitable new products and means of producing them, e.g., mill sites, making cattle fodder from the local guinea grass, even introducing sericulture.

Cuffe expected that the settlers would include traders, entrepreneurs, and various craftsmen, but predominantly farmers. The members of the prototype organization he formed in Sierra Leone echoed his view, calling upon all their "Breatheren" to "Come from the British Colonies or from america and Become farmers in order to help us Cultivate the Land," and those "who may have Vessels" to come and

"Establish Commerce in Sierra Leone," including a "whalefishery in the Colony."[26]

Having goods to trade, Cuffe believed, would allow Africans to wean themselves off their lucrative trade in human beings. Unfortunately, their calls for immigrants mainly fell on deaf ears.

—⚍—

The first boatloads of immigrants to Liberia included relatively few farmers; on the first two vessels, the *Elizabeth* and *Nautilus*, for example, only seven of the thirty-two adults listed their occupation as farmer. The others were tobacconist, carpenter, ditcher, cooper, saddler, tailor, nurse, potter, schoolteacher, seamstress, smith, hatter, turner, shoemaker. All were born free. Most claimed they could read, write, or "spell." As the pace of immigration picked up, larger numbers of slaves who had been freed by their owners to go to Liberia appeared. Most probably they were little more than field hands, "unskilled laborers, and most were illiterate," if the experience of the Mississippi society's Sinoe River Colony in the 1840s is any guide. Those "who came with little or nothing, most of them took to agriculture—field Negroes."[27]

These immigrant vessels also brought numerous settlers who were literate, some educated, some fortunate because their "slave masters put something in their pockets—money."[28] Others had accumulated assets before embarking for the colony by working in assorted trades or by succeeding in various businesses. Upon arriving in Liberia, "those who were literate and educated went into international trade and commerce."[29] And later government service and politics.

Both local Africans and Europeans apparently viewed "these early Americo-Liberian traders as shrewd bargainers." From America and England, they procured "cloth, rum and tobacco," as well as other trade items such as bright-colored cotton cloth, beads, trinkets, guns, and hand tools. These they exchanged for food and other articles they needed themselves, and, for export, the palm oils, "camwood [used to make dye], cane sugar, palm kernels, rice, and the occasional ivory tusk that tribal traders brought to the coast.[30] A particularly bold Americo-Liberian trader might even hazard a perilous trip up a river into the unknown hinterland looking for local items to trade.

Some settlers became wealthy by trading. Between 1830 and 1840, the economy saw a group of "merchant princes" emerge—shipping entrepreneurs such as future president Edward J. Roye, who owned the *Eusebia Roye*; Francis Payne and Beverly Yates, owners of the *Liberia*; George Washington Young, owner of the *Mary Elizabeth*; and James B. McGill, owner of the *Eliza Francis* and the *Patsy*, among other vessels. The group was weighted with mulattoes (although with notable exceptions such as fully black president Roye) who usually were better educated and possessed greater resources than did other settlers.

Agriculture, nevertheless, probably provided the livelihood of the largest number of settlers. Despite the glowing reports sent to America (mainly to entice new settlers to emigrate)—fertile soil that would produce abundant yields of seemingly any crop, and idyllic living conditions—the farming life in Liberia was far from easy. Liberia lay some eight degrees above the equator in what geographers call humid and semi humid west Africa, home to one of the world's major tropical rain forests. Temperatures during the day usually ranged between eighty and ninety degrees and at night seventy to seventy-five degrees.

The initial settlements hugged the low-lying and swampy coast and the rivers with heavy growths of trees, shrubs, and vines—land difficult to clear and hard to cultivate. Torrential rains averaged more than 180 inches from April to the end of October, soils were subject to rapid leaching, and a formidable array of pests poised ready to devour whatever the farmer planted. Winds from the Sahara in January sometimes brought dust storms and drought. Tsetse flies carrying trypanosomiasis acted as a deadly barrier to keeping most livestock, except chickens, guinea fowls, and goats. Draft animals were few. Horses and mules found it difficult to survive. Cultivation depended on human labor.

It is no wonder that many, probably most, of these early settlers avoided farming if at all possible. Farming was hard. Bartering with the natives proved an easier way to make a living. Liebenow maintains that those who belonged to the upper strata of Americo-Liberian society especially disdained agriculture. Many, particularly "the offspring of illicit unions between slave women and white 'gentlemen,'" could boast of a good education, probably owned some property, and may well have enjoyed a certain social status prior to coming to Liberia. A good number had lived mainly in cities in America. They were not accustomed to the rigors of life in the Liberian countryside. The diet of the typical African cultivator did not sit well with them. Moreover, they "associated agriculture with the life of servitude they or their parents" may have endured. They clearly were not cut out for the life of a small dirt farmer in Liberia.[31]

Despite this general disdain for agriculture among educated Americo-Liberians, there were, of course, exceptions, usually among those "who settled some distance from the commercial attractions of Monrovia."[32] The Mississippi colony, situated on the Sinoe River and populated largely by freed slaves from Natchez, was an example. But the rescued Congoes proved to be "the most successful farmers of all."[33] Because they had not received the blessings of being civilized and Western educated, having not so much as glimpsed what life, even as a slave, in America was like—most had been torn away from their villages only weeks, or at most months before being deposited in Liberia—they found growing rice, yams, and the other crops in their new homes not too different from life in their own villages. Although subjected to spirited efforts on the part of their Colonization Society hosts to pry them away, they held on to their traditional religions and customs by and large. All in all, they found living in Liberia quite tolerable.

Too, as new settlements spread from the coast inland along the rivers, Americo-Liberians introduced cash crops. This proved particularly true along the Saint Paul River, where newcomers established farms upriver from Monrovia. As early as 1854, the *Liberia Herald* noted "how rapidly the quantity of sugar manufactured on the St. Paul's [River] is on the increase...When you enter the St. Paul's you can discover in every direction large cane fields; and persons who formerly prosecuted other avenues of employment, are now employed in cutting land to plant sugar cane."[34] Along with sugarcane, coffee, which indigenous Africans had long cultivated on a small scale, expanded rapidly. J. Milton Turner, the American minister and consul from 1871 to 1878, thought Liberian coffee the world's best. Among his detailed reports to Washington of the country's geography, resources, climate, soil, and ethnology, he sent a "careful study of the coffee growing potential of the area, urging that the crop's cultivation would benefit his own coffee-drinking nation and would also solve Liberia's economic difficulties."[35] To encourage production, the Liberian House of Representatives in 1873 passed an act "giving a bounty of five dollars to every planter-out of thousand coffee trees."[36]

Many of the Americo-Liberian elite took advantage of the opportunity. Secretary of State H. R. W. Johnson in 1873 reportedly had "within a comparatively few years raised him a coffee farm" that would "soon stand among the finest in the country." The previous year he had "set out 5,000 trees."[37] And a newly invented machine, a coffee huller, was successfully demonstrated in the United States before being shipped to Liberia, "where it [was] expected to make a revolution in the coffee trade." The demonstration, according to the report, was a colorful affair:

"The machine was gaily decorated with the flags of the United States and Liberia, and the background was enlivened with the gay dresses of several ladies who had come from Philadelphia to witness this new piece of machinery."[38]

Professor Liebenow notes that while the "educated Americo-Liberian" was ill prepared to till the soil himself, he happily took to the role of "absentee landlord of a plantation of sugarcane, rice, or coffee cultivated by poorer settlers or African recaptives."[39] Farms also employed native Africans as laborers. "The natives work very cheap, two dollars per month," Elder S. S. Ball, an African American who visited Liberia in 1848, observed. "Many of them live with the colonists bound to them for a term of years under what is called the apprenticeship system." But the "outrageously low" wages, nonexistent amenities, and masters who frequently abused the apprenticeship system and "could levee fines on their native workers without restraint" understandably often led to serious friction between the two groups.[40] The rise of these settlements focused on agriculture also threatened the economic and political power of Monrovia, the country's center of trading and commerce, and soon led to a division between the two competing interests.

While "the wealthy colonists live in fine style, houses of brick or pine," Elder Ball further noted, "the poor [settlers] often live in houses of bamboo made in the African style." But, "seldom you set down to dine with a gentleman that his table is not furnished with the best of wine and English or German ale. They have just as many servants as they wish, and as much distinction between rich and poor as in America."[41]

Not many "agreed with Lott Cary that Africa was their true home."[42] They considered themselves Americans and came to

Liberia with the mind-set of nineteenth-century white Americans. Not surprisingly, the tribal Africans who referred to these Americo-Liberians as "Kwee, or white people" called Monrovia "the American place."[43]

Americo-Liberian traders thrived. Production and exports continued to grow. Part of the increase came from expanded trading with "the interior tribes," who brought down larger "quantities of rubber, cam wood, and ivory" to the Liberian markets.[44] At the end of 1882, President Anthony Gardiner could report to the legislature "the exportable articles of coffee, sugar, rubber, palm oil, palm kernels, raw wood, &c., have never been shipped in such large quantities before."[45] Some of the success in "exporting coffee, sugar, and other commodities in the late nineteenth century," Liebenow maintains, also came from leasing plantations to foreigners.[46]

The salad days of trade-generated wealth, however, were numbered. Even by the late 1860s, Americo-Liberians found themselves beginning to be elbowed out of international trade by European and American merchants. In defense a Liberian government-formed trading combination was given exclusive rights to buy and sell all goods within the country. The government also passed the 1865 Ports of Entry Law that restricted foreign trade to six settlements (three more were later added), despite provoked protests and armed resistance of native and foreign traders—and governments.

The worldwide financial panic that began in 1873 (and only ended in 1896) further sharpened European competition in the African trade. The clear superiority of the new European steamships to the Liberian sailing schooners gave the competition a further edge. Liberians helplessly watched as commodity prices plummeted and the rise of Brazil's coffee and Europe's sugar beet industries ravaged their two major exports.[47]

Despite President Gardiner's optimistic report on exports, by the end of the 1870s, Liberian prosperity had largely played out, and the country "went into a steady economic decline."[48] Two other factors added to Liberia's distress: First, the burden of disastrous government loans contracted by successive administrations, most notably the 1871 British loan (Liberia's initial public debt). Second, the rising interest on the part of European powers in exploiting Africa's resources and trade opportunities as they began their scramble for Africa.[49]

The continuing world financial crisis compounded Liberia's plight. Confronted with a national deficit of $118,957—a sizable amount at that time for a country of Liberia's size—the government naturally looked to America for help. The United States, however, was preoccupied with the Civil War. Bankers had no funds available to make foreign loans, particularly in Africa. To investigate the origins of the deficit, the legislature in 1864 created a Special Committee on Public Accounts. It turns out, according to the committee, large sums of public monies, including US funds allocated for transporting and supporting recaptured slaves settled in Liberia, had been disbursed but not reported. Part of the money reputedly went for goods for speculation on President Stephen A. Benson's behalf.[50] Corruption and mismanagement at virtually every level of the government soon became so ingrained it was accepted as normal workaday practice.

—⚬—

Liberia's financial life was at best uncertain. Even in relatively good times, the government, according to Duignan and Gann, "was almost constantly insolvent." As a colony, Liberia relied financially on the American Colonization Society and the US government. With independence, the republic depended "entirely for revenues on import duties and uncertain taxes from an impoverished people."[51] And, when government expenditures outstripped revenues, as was all too often the case, and mismanagement and corruption ran rampant, the impact on government finances proved disastrous. Other than agriculture, Liberia was plagued by a lack of resources—at least known resources that Liberians could exploit. The country's economic potential had yet to be explored. Not only Liberia's, but most of Africa's interior still lay unknown to the outside world. The "Dark Continent" was simply dark.

Against this backdrop, the exploits of Benjamin K. Anderson, a nineteenth-century Americo-Liberian, stand out in bold relief. The Liberian government laid claim to vast tracts of land in the interior. But since few, if any Liberians, apparently had ever seen, much less visited, the far interior, the government could hardly succeed in establishing sovereign authority over them. Seymour and Sims's trips in 1858 covered a part of the area. And North Carolina Professor Tim Geysbeek credits them with providing "the first detailed descriptions of the region extending from the coasts of Upper Guinea to the savannas in what is today the Republic of Guinea."[52]

President Benson and others proposed further exploratory expeditions, but they would have to wait until thirty-four year-old Anderson came along.

CHAPTER 11

The Unknown Hinterland

—⚏—

"On the 14th February, 1868, I embarked…in a large canoe" on a journey to "Musardu, the capital of the Western Mandingoes," (today's Musadugu in the republic of Guinea). Benjamin Anderson recounted in his 1870 book describing his epic expedition to the unknown—*Liberia's Hinterland*. It was a territory in some respects not unlike America's Louisiana Purchase almost seventy years before, a great, unexplored area that piqued much curiosity and that many felt held the key to Liberia's future. Anderson would not return to "civilization" until one year and one month later.

—⚏—

Benjamin Joseph Knight Anderson's story began in Baltimore, Maryland, which in the nineteenth century offered blacks, even free blacks, little hospitality. Benjamin, born on January 4, 1835, to Henrietta and Israel Anderson—listed in the 1850 US census as a black illiterate laborer—was no exception. Young Ben, "brought up in the brickyards of Baltimore where he learned to make bricks…attended private primary schools" in the city. "But so strong was the race prejudice against Negroes obtaining an education…he was often sneered [at] and beaten by white men." Since the black youngster often fought back "by flogging some white lad," his mother, fearing the worst "might happen and thus cost his life," decided it was "best to leave America."[1]

Teenage Benjamin and mother Henrietta sailed from Baltimore on the *Liberia Packet* in December 1851, headed for Liberia. They arrived at Monrovia in April 1852 and settled in Virginia, up the Saint Paul River from Monrovia. Aboard ship a fellow passenger, Asbury F. Johns, an accountant, had become sufficiently impressed by Benjamin to hire him as a clerk in a business venture Johns started after they landed. Benjamin's salary of four dollars a month helped to support his mother, while Johns went on to become "one of the most 'wealthy merchants' in Monrovia" (for whom Benjamin later designed an imposing house, a "substantial structure of stone and brick," two stories high, in the city).[2]

Liberia the country—the area that was claimed by the settler government—fell into two distinct parts. The first was a strip of land roughly forty to fifty miles wide that stretched some six hundred miles along the Atlantic coast, from the disputed boundary with Sierra Leone in the west to the San Pedro River in the east. Here, the Americo-Liberians and recaptives, probably numbering in 1878 no more than twenty-five thousand souls, lived in settlements with names like Arthington, Bensonville, Brewerville, Caldwell, Clay-Ashland, Crozierville, Dixville, Harrisburg, Johnsonville, Louisiana, Millsburg, New Georgia, Virginia, Buchanan, Greenville, and Harper. They clustered along the coast and rivers, grouped into four counties: Montserrado, Grand Bassa, Sinoe, and Maryland. The oldest settlement and capital of the republic, Monrovia, could count an estimated thirteen thousand inhabitants; most settlements were far smaller. The Vai, Dei, Bassa, Kru, and Grebo, the original tribal residents, lived among the settlers in enclaves dotting the landscape.

The other portion of the country comprised a vastly larger, virtually unknown hinterland that reached into today's Guinea on the north, and the Ivory Coast on the northeast. Of the estimated seven hundred thousand to one million (some estimates were as high as two million) tribal Africans in Liberian territory in 1878, most by far lived in this interior. The largest tribal group, the Kpelle, occupied the central area extending northward into Guinea. Rain forest, crisscrossed by hills and interrupted by sluggish rivers and swampy lowlands, dominated the terrain. From May through October, torrential rain averaged more than 180 inches, while the thermometer registered between sixty-five and ninety-five degrees F on average during the year.

> Typically, a Kpelle village might range in size from ten to 150 round, one-room, wattle-and-daub huts, each topped by a conical thatched roof. Village populations could run from fifty to approximately six hundred inhabitants. Economic life revolved around slash-and-burn cultivation, most importantly of rain-fed rice. (In fact, the Kpelle word for "work" means "rice cultivation.") Besides rice, they grew cassava and a variety of other food crops: yams, potatoes, greens, peanuts, eggplants, okra, tomatoes, and fruits. Social life centered on the male Poro secret society and the comparable Sande society for females.

Five other tribal groups ringed the Kpelle area—the Gola and Mandingo on the east, the Belle and Loma to the north, and the Mano on the west. The remainder of the hinterland was peopled largely by Kisse, Mende, and Bandi in the extreme northeast along the Sierra Leone border, and Gio and Krahn on the west bordering the Ivory Coast. The populations of all but a few of the tribal groups also could be found in neighboring Sierra Leone, Guinea, and the Ivory Coast.

Even before the arrival of the Americo-Liberian colonists, competition for control of the trade routes between the coastal region and the hinterland led to clashes between rival tribal groups, most notably between the Mandingo and Gola. "Salt, gun powder, rum, tobacco, cloth, and beads"—largely supplied by European merchant ships—"were sold and exchanged for slaves and such hinterland products as ivory, gold, kola nuts, rice, camwood, and palm kernels and oil."[3] It was a lucrative trade. And the Americo-Liberian settlers arrived in 1822 at the height of the competition between the two groups.

> Two rival confederations emerged in the early part of the nineteenth century. The Mandingo Condo Confederation, headed by Chief Sao Bosa, controlled traffic to the coast through the Saint Paul River. Chief Zozu Duma, with headquarters at Kongba, led the Gola Confederation. The Gola managed to forge "a short-lived pan-ethnic confederation involving the Vai, Dey, Mende, Kissi, Loma, and Gbandi chiefdoms in the West Atlantic region, and by 1845 had wrested control of the Mandingo trade links between Bopolu and the coast."[4]

To Europeans and other foreigners, including most Americo-Liberian settlers, this was unknown, uncharted land. Europeans had plied the coastal waters of west Africa since the 1500s and established trading posts in many spots. However, the lack of accessible routes, the climate, fevers, and the hostility of many of the inhabitants discouraged efforts to penetrate the hinterland. It was for good reason the continent came to be called Darkest Africa—and the "graveyard of white men."

Toward the end of the eighteenth century, though, European and American interest in Africa—for enlightenment, evangelization, trade, adventure, or whatever—gained pace. In England Sir Joseph Banks in 1788 founded the Association for Promoting the Discovery of the Interior Parts of Africa, and explorations began in earnest. An obsession to find the fabled city of Timbuktu and to discover the source and route of the Niger River in west Africa matched the equally obsessed search for the source of the river Nile in the east. The explorers Mungo Park, Frederick Hornemann, Robert Moffat, Alexander Laing, Samuel and Florence Baker, John Speke, Richard Burton, and others became household names. And had it not been for the news-hogging exploits of Henry Stanley and the renowned David Livingstone in the 1860s and 1870s, Benjamin J. K. Anderson might well have enjoyed similar fame.

—⁄⁄⁄—

Anderson attended the Methodist Episcopal Seminary (later the College of West Africa), where he excelled in mathematics, so much so the professor often had him teach "the junior classes."[5] Anderson also became a skilled surveyor and was even appointed "Tutor in Practical Surveying and Plotting" at Liberia College (although he resigned shortly thereafter over some unspecified political issue). Later in his career, he served for a time in 1882 as Montserrado County surveyor and land commissioner. He excelled at mapmaking. In fact, the map he drew on his first expedition to explore Liberia's hinterland in 1868 "is best known and has been published several times."[6] And, according to friends, this remarkable young man also "developed an early taste for music," possessing a sweet and charming voice," and as a guitarist "was easily first among his peers."[7] At one time he also led his Methodist church choir.

Anderson enlisted in the militia (which every able-bodied male from ages sixteen to fifty was obliged to join) and in 1856 sailed off to fight a Kru rebellion in Sinoe, the site of the Mississippi colony. In the fighting Anderson took "pot slug" shrapnel in his left knee, a souvenir "which in after years caused him considerable trouble and inconvenience."[8]

After returning to Monrovia, young Anderson added "lawyer" to his credentials, practiced before the Supreme Court, and soon was headed on the path of public service. Obviously a rising star, he caught the eye of President Stephen Benson, who in 1861 appointed him comptroller of the treasury, and in April 1863 moved him up to serve as secretary of treasury and a member of the cabinet. He left office under something of a cloud in January 1864 a few days after Daniel Warner assumed the presidency. Although a special committee of the House of Representatives determined Anderson and the department committed a number of irregularities, no further action was taken.

While Liberia's deep interior remained largely unknown to the outside world until the mid-nineteenth century, some earlier travelers apparently passed through parts of it. Tim Geysbeek reports that a seventeenth-century Dutch trader describes a sizeable kingdom that covered much of the same territory Seymour, Syms, and Anderson explored. This kingdom, "ruled from far-inland," extended from present-day Freetown in Sierra Leone southeast to the Junk River. From there it stretched inland, perhaps 125 miles. While it is now a "celebrated tropical reserve in Guinea," Seymour and Anderson described it as lowlands and mountains, "open savanna, populous, prosperous, cultivated, and vibrant with trade."[9]

> In addition, several European explorers, notably Mungo Park, searching for the source and mouth of the Niger River, and Major Andrew Laing and Rene Callie, who visited Timbuktu, "had penetrated parts of the interior."[10] And a number of Liberians apparently made lesser trips before Seymour and

Sims. Numerous travelers covered the fifty miles inland to Boporu, home of the Mandingo chief Boatswain who had come to the aid of the first settlers in their encounter with hostile natives. Colonial governor Joseph Mechlin in 1831 traveled some forty to fifty miles inland to the source of the Junk River, and Governor and President Joseph J. Roberts reportedly followed the east bank of the Saint Paul's River inland for eighty miles.[11] Roberts and other officers also journeyed to various interior hinterland locations to conclude treaties with the chiefs and "promote peace and trade." Other Liberians made trading trips, while missionaries and scholars, such as Edward Blyden and Alexander Crummell, made forays into the hinterland to enhance relations with the natives.

Most of the journeys that Liberians and Europeans made, however, were "overshadowed by the lure" of the fabled town of Musardu (or Musadu), so-called capital of the western Mandingoes.[12] Reportedly "a key political center and commercial town, with gold and other natural resources, it had links to the Niger River and other trans-Saharan trade routes."[13] Duignan and Gann in their 1984 history remark that the location of Musardu hadn't been identified positively, but they thought it seemed "to have been close to, or identical with, the town now called N'Zerekore in Guinea, near the border with Liberia."[14] More recently, scholars such as Tim Geysbeek locate the city "about five miles northwest of Beyla in Guinea, northwest of the Liberian border town Yekepa."[15] None of the explorers, including Seymour and Sims, ever made it that far before Anderson came on the scene.

For the Americo-Liberian settlers (and most Europeans), the Muslim Mandingoes had "always excited the liveliest interest on account of their superior physical appearance, their natural intelligence, their activity, and their enterprise."[16] Physically handsome, proud, ofttimes even regal, large slave owners, horse breeders and riders, master traders, they presented a sharp contrast in the eyes of settlers and visitors with the other tribal Africans they encountered. Musardu, then, became the goal of Liberian exploration.

Daniel Warner, who succeeded Benson as president, also wanted the hinterland explored. And a wealthy New Yorker who shared their interest provided the means to make it happen. Henry Mansfield Schieffelin, whom Edward Blyden called "a great friend and benefactor" of "Colonization, Missions, Liberia and humanity in general," had been elected vice president of the New York Colonization Society Board of Managers in 1865 and also began serving as Liberia's chargé d'affaires in the United States. Schieffelin had sought for more than a half dozen years to realize such a project "to ascertain the capabilities of the country interior of Liberia."[17] He enlisted a friend, Caleb Swan, also of New York and also a man of means, to join him in financing the venture. An adventurous Benjamin Anderson volunteered to lead the expedition.

—ᴡ—

The aspiring explorer prepared for his trip with care. To make the observations essential to drawing a map with accuracy, he would carry the following instruments: "One sextant, by E. & G. Blunt, New York; one aneroid barometer; two thermometers—first, 133 degrees 2d 140 degrees, by B. Pike, New York; two small night and day compasses, by H.W. Hunter, New York; one tolerably good watch; one artificial horizon." He enlisted eighteen Kru men as carriers (a step he would later regret) and a headman named Ben He also engaged a "learned Mandingo" named Kaifal-Kanda, "for the conduct of the expedition" (another measure that would cause Anderson grief). Finally, Anderson took counsel from several individuals who supposedly possessed some knowledge of the country he would traverse.[18]

At last, "on the 14th of February, 1868," Anderson wrote, "I embarked [on the journey]...in a large canoe, loaned me by Dr. C.B. Dunbar for this purpose." Anderson would not return until the twenty-fifth of March 1869. He later explained that Musardu could, "by easy journeys, be reached in twenty-five or thirty days. I was obliged, however, from the delays and inconveniences incident to interior traveling in Africa, to occupy thirteen months."[19]

In his narrative, the explorer describes these many delays and inconveniences, beginning with having to wait three weeks in a nearby Dey village for the "learned Mandingo" to appear. During this time his Kru carriers, "being frightened by what the Dey people told them of the dangers of the road," deserted Anderson. Only Ben, the headman, remained. Anderson managed to hire "eighteen Congoes" as replacements, and the expedition finally got under way on March 6.[20]

Anderson would take a very circuitous route to reach Musardu, avoiding "the route usually traveled."[21] His friends in Monrovia had warned him of the hostility of the present chief and his people toward travelers, especially those such as Anderson who presented a potential threat to their trade monopoly.

The explorer records that as the little party marched along, their column stirring up clouds of dust—dust all pervasive, dust that invaded noses, ears, mouths, even eyes—the physical features of the country soon became "roughened by hills, valleys, and small plains." The hills grew "bolder and more conspicuous," running "toward every point of the compass."[22]

After about forty miles, they reached King Bessa's town, "in the western portion of the Golah country," on March 13. Anderson paints a vivid picture of the town, "located in a small, irregular plain, studded with palm-trees, and hedged in by hills in nearly every direction." At 480 feet above sea level, it was a comfortable departure from the oppressive, humid heat he had endured on the trail. Viewing the town through the eyes of a militiaman and surveyor, Anderson described its defenses in detail:

> It is strongly fortified with a double barricade of large wooden stakes; in the space between each barricade sharp-pointed stakes, four feet long, are set obliquely in the ground, crossing each other; this is to prevent the defenses from being scaled.... The points of access are flanked with four intervening gates, between the outside gate and the town itself. There are guardhouses to each of these gates, and people constantly in them night and day. To force without artillery this town would give some trouble.[23]

He was less favorably impressed with the town itself: about 350 "clay dwellings of various sizes," with about eight hundred to one thousand permanent residents, plus a varying number of transients, houses huddled so close together that "in some parts of the town scarcely two people can walk abreast." And, "in matters of cleanliness and health King Bessa can not be said to have seriously consulted the interest of his people."[24]

As for the king himself, Anderson thought him almost beyond redemption: he was "naturally avaricious," "drank day and night,"[25] and did his best to block Anderson's advance to Musardu. Even the gifts, the requisite "dash"—"three bars of tobacco, one double barreled pistol, one large brass kettle, one piece of fancy handkerchiefs, and one keg of powder"—Anderson gave him had little effect.[26] The chief was merely carrying out the policy mandated by the Mandingoes to guard their trade monopoly. Bessa would be only one of numerous obstacles Anderson would face in trying to reach the Mandingo capital.

The explorer soon encountered some of the Mandingoes' most lucrative trade goods. One morning in Bessa's town, Anderson "saw a slave with his right hand tied up to his neck, and fifty sticks of salt [a major trade commodity] fastened to his back, about to be sent into the interior to be exchanged for a bullock."[27] He later observed "six slaves chained together working" Bessa's farm. Later in his journey, at a market at Mohammadu, a town near Musardu, he observed a "number of slaves, especially children." One of them, "a pretty little Mandingo girl, about nine years of age, was sent to" his house so he "might purchase her. She cost 9,000 kolu, or about $15 in our money." Anderson declined, explaining that "Tibbabues," using the natives' name for Americo-Liberians, "never held slaves."[28]

He was surprised to see any Mandingoes as slaves since they seldom enslaved their own people. He also was surprised when the girl seemed disappointed, showing "that she preferred falling into" his hands, rather than those of her own people. The reason for her wanting to avoid a fellow Mandingo master became clearer when he learned the reputation Mandingoes had for being harsher on slaves than were other neighboring tribes, such as the Boozies (Loma). In contrast to Mandingo slaves, "nothing in dress, usage, or mark," Anderson noted, "distinguishes a Boozie slave" from a free person.[29]

The intrepid explorer finally made it to Boporo with two of his Congoes (the others had refused to go). Anderson managed to cow the minor kings along the route into allowing him to proceed. "I would talk," he wrote, "of nothing but soldiers, cannon, the burning of Bessa's town, and other [obviously frightening]

things."[30] They begged him not to report any adverse behavior back to Monrovia for fear of reprisals. Anderson quickly pointed out he also met many good, helpful, friendly people. Momoru, the king of Boporo, was one of those—"intelligent, and communicative," but at their first meeting, chagrined that the new Liberian administration of President Warner had not yet "sent him a book (a paper) expressive of the good feelings toward him, as had been the custom of" all prior administrations.[31]

Boporo intrigued Anderson. He described the town sitting on a small plain, about 560 feet above sea level, with a temperature ranging only up to seventy-eight to eighty degrees. Granite boulders covered the top and sides of the high hills rising above the town. He was impressed to see "the grave of King Boatswain, the present king's father"; Americo-Liberians still revered him as a savior of the nascent Liberian colony. Anderson also noted in the vicinity "beds of specular iron ore, which the natives break into fragments and use for shot."[32]

He saw that the town was an important trade center, with an estimated three thousand residents living in the town proper and another seven thousand or so in the suburbs, the surrounding villages and towns. The mixed population, whose livelihoods included "war, commerce, and the domestic slave trade," spoke as many languages as there were tribes present—Vey, Golah, Mamboma, Mandingo, Pessy, Boozie, Boondee, and Hurrah—although Vey was used for general communication.[33]

The Mandingoes, who followed Islam scrupulously, worshipped at a mosque in town. They exerted a "strong moral influence," but that obviously did not encompass slavery, "over the populace." The Mandingoes, Anderson said, had many slaves, so many in fact, their population supposedly trebled "the number of free persons." They were purchased chiefly from the Pessy (Kpelle), Boozie (Loma or Toma), and other tribes, and used mainly as carriers.[34]

Anderson found the pomp surrounding King Momoru's return to Boporo from visiting a nearby town particularly fascinating, and described the spectacle in some detail. The king "left the town [which he was visiting] May 10, 1868, accompanied by his courtiers, warriors, women, servants, and musicians"; there were two kinds of musicians, "those who performed on horns and drums, and those who sang the praises of the king, timing their music with a sort of iron cymbal, one part being fitted to the thumb of the left hand and beaten with a piece of iron by the right."[35]

The Liberian explorer also noted with favor that the native chief attempted "to practice our [Americo-Liberian] civilization," using "chairs, tables, beds, bedsteads, looking-glasses, scented soaps, cologne, &c." (He thought "imported goods superior.") Instead of the traditional African hut, the king lived in a frame house he had had built for himself. Momoru was anxious to learn and had taught himself a bit of English—despite, Anderson added, the absence of any "Christian school or church." Only a small Muslim school served the town.[36]

But the king still clung to old native beliefs. Concerned about the hazards, "distance, and dangers" Anderson would face in the interior, Momoru insisted they consult a "sand doctor." The two, "carried into a thatched hut," faced their "diviner." He began "spreading out a small pile of sand with his right hand" while invoking "the demon of the pile." An astonished Anderson recorded that "the whole thing was conducted without thunder, lightning, or anything else, except the rapid voluble utterances of our diviner himself." It was decided that it was okay for Anderson to go.[37] Despite the Boporo Mandingoes making "every effort to prevent his going," Anderson managed to leave for Musardu on June 14—with only three carriers, an interpreter, and a guide.

On his way Anderson would pass through Southern Kpelle territory, then traverse Belle land the first week of July, spend the next three months very slowly to reach Loma territory in early November. Along the way he would visit towns, filling his journal with descriptions of all that he saw and observations he made on the people, their customs and behavior. Not surprisingly, given the Liberians' abiding hunger for trade with the interior and beyond, the markets especially captured his attention. He was much taken with the Loma people, whom he called "Boosies" or "Boozies," the name (meaning "wild person") generally given them—but which they considered very offensive. Arriving in "Boosie territory," he proclaimed, "a coat of cleanliness, order, and industry strikes you," and one is welcomed "with hospitality and courtesy" into "large walled towns."[38]

On July 8, at one of these towns, Zolu's town, a salvo of musket fire announced Anderson and his entourage's arrival, and a band, "consisting of twelve large and small ivory horns, and a half dozen drums of various sizes and sounds," accompanied them to the marketplace. Here, the visitors found the crowd "astonished and overjoyed that a 'Wegee' an American should come so far to visit them in their own country." Anderson marveled that "a thousand strange faces" he "had never before seen, were gazing at" him with great curiosity.[39]

The "Wegee" attended a market "held at Zow, a very large town," where five to six thousand people would gather to trade by barter cotton, rice (the chief staple), cassava, and huge potatoes that "weigh six to eight pounds." Although barter was standard, "salt and kola [a brownish nut the size of a chestnut] function like a currency," so that prices of commodities were expressed in them.[40] Market days provided everyone an opportunity to dress up.

"The women," Anderson recorded, "wear blue and colored country cloth girdled tastefully around their waists, their heads bound round with a large three-cornered handkerchief of the same material." Completing the ensemble, "blue beads intermixed with their favorite" brass buttons "encircle their necks, their faces ornamented with blue pigment and smiles."[41] He thought many of them "very pretty."

Anderson found the Loma polite, almost to an extreme. They "thank you for the slightest favor," and even when you are doing something for yourself, such as "carrying a heavy burden on the road, you are heartily thanked." Anderson relates how his "nearly fagged out" Congo carriers would become annoyed with the "all thanks and no assistance."[42] He especially liked the "very clean habits" of the Loma, who bathed "regularly twice a day, night and morning, in warm water," which perhaps accounted for their being "exceedingly healthy."[43]

Apparently the "Wegee" visitor liked Zolu's town so much he did not leave until September 21. Possibly, another reason for his lengthy stay lay in the message his Loma hosts received from the Mandingoes in Boporu that they "were not to allow [Anderson] to go anywhere."[44] He and his party did finally depart for Bokkasab, a town of seven thousand divided into two parts: one Mandingo, the other Loma. A market every Saturday drew six to seven thousand persons. It boasted "an abundance of vegetables, rice, beans, potatoes, plantains, ground-nuts, etc."[45] Anderson also noted a number of other markets in the area.

While in Bokkasab he visited "a kind of convent for women" that consisted of "rows of long huts built low to the ground." Here, the women were initiated into a mysterious secret order, subjected to "a peculiar kind of circumcision," and taught "certain practices for health."[46] Normally, any man caught within the precincts was subject to death, "instantly inflicted by the women themselves." But Anderson came on a holiday, when the rules were relaxed.[47]

Belying the accepted view of the hardships and rigors explorers in Africa suffered, Anderson apparently enjoyed his trip, at least to such places as Zolu's town and Bokkasab. He stayed longer than three weeks in the latter, delayed not from "downright tyrannical opposition," but by the "kindness and generosity" of the people.[48] He confesses how every afternoon he would dress himself in his "Mandingo toga" and go visit friends. They would "fritter away the time in talking and singing," as he "musically entertained" them "with the beauties of 'Dixie.'"[49]

—⚜—

Dowilnyah, king of the Wymar Boozies, and reputedly one of the area's fiercest warriors, had heard of Anderson's arrival in the region. Curious about this foreign explorer, Dowilnyah dispatched messengers to invite the Liberian to visit him. Their appearance was anything but reassuring to Anderson. They "were tall black men, with red and restless eyes, tattooed faces, filed teeth, huge spears, and six feet bows. They also had a reputation which remarkably corresponded with their appearance."[50]

Considerable discussion about the wisdom of accepting the king's invitation ensued without any agreement. The messengers returned to Dowilnyah empty handed but were sent back again in a week. This time, Anderson summoned up his courage and set out to call on the persistent king. Dowilnyah at the time was staying in a village outside his own town, the capital. After alerting the king by firing their muskets, Anderson and his men entered the village. He was brought before the king, who, Anderson wrote, "sat on a mat...dressed in a gaudy-figured country robe; on his head was a large blue and red cloth cap, stuck all over with the talons of large birds."[51] Surrounded by his people, "all variously dressed in white, blue, striped, and yellow country coats," he busily tended to dispensing favors and settling disputes.[52]

Dowilnyah, aware of his fierce reputation, took pains—even trying to look "peaceful"—to reassure what must have been an apprehensive Anderson. But to no avail. His countenance, Anderson later wrote, still "was one of the most threatening and the blackest visage I had seen in a long time."⁵³ Then after the king seated him on a mat, iron horns and drums suddenly sounded, and "warriors rushed forth from their concealed places, performing all the evolutions of a savage and barbarous warfare."⁵⁴ After the din had quieted, the visitors, "being welcomed again and again to his [the king's] country," were shown to their lodgings.

—ẁ—

On November 6 Anderson records paying Dowilnyah, who still was in the village, a more formal call. He explained the nature of his visit and then handed over the presents he had brought—"a piece of calico, a music box, with which he [the king] was especially pleased; two pocket handkerchiefs, one pair epaulets, two bottles of cologne, one clasped knife, three papers of needles, one large kettle." Anderson noted the king "was delighted" and apparently completely won over by Anderson, whom he said "should always hold the first place in his [the king's] estimation."⁵⁵ He was anxious to see Anderson's revolvers, whose "fearful reputation," according to the explorer, "preceded" him "everywhere... [he] went." The king also had Anderson fire his percussion-cap muskets, which were far superior to the muskets ignited by a fuse, the standard weapon of virtually all the natives.⁵⁶

The king decided the occasion called for a celebration—a war dance. After downing "about a quart" of palm wine—fortunately "instead of blood"—he burst "forth with wild and prodigious leaps; a war-cap of leopard skin, plumed with horse-hair, covering his head; he was naked to his waist, but wore a pair of Turkish-shaped trousers. He had a spear in his right hand." Even scarier, "his black and lowering countenance had undergone a terrible change, which was heightened by the savage grin...his white teeth imparted to it." Now, he made "frantic gestures...amid the stunning plaudits of the whole town."⁵⁷

Dowilnyah now decided it was his women's turn "to give the finishing stroke to this happy business." Dancing it was. "The ladies of Wymar," Anderson had noticed, were so fond of dancing they spent "much of their time in this amusement." They were not, as he put it, "acquainted with the polite and delicate paces of their sisters at Monrovia." But for "downright solid-footed dancing" they could "not be surpassed." All were "fine, large, robust women," and they had "the happiest-looking countenances in the world."[58] The party presumably ended on a high note.

After a couple of days, possibly for everyone to recuperate, the monarch announced his intention to leave for his own town, Ziggah Porrah Zue, the Wymar country's capital and largest town. Anderson soon became a part of a royal procession, which "at ten o'clock...started, the king being attended by his friends, bodyguard, musicians, and women." About three o'clock the parade entered Ziggah Porrah Zue "amid the applause and gaze of the whole town" and made their way to the market space in the center of the town. Dowilnyah's uncle, the town's old chief, delivered a welcome speech, after which "every trumpet, consisting of forty pieces, sounded."[59] More speeches followed, each celebrated in turn by one of the three bands "of ivory and wood" in attendance.[60]

Festivities continued with war dances of each principal chief, topped off by Dowilnyah's "exhibiting his own warlike prowess."

The crowds thrilled at one of the town's "chief amusements... a 'jack upon stilts.'" A man "fantastically dressed, wearing a false face, and mounted upon stilts ten feet high, fitted to the soles of his shoes...danced, leaped, and even climbed upon the houses."[61] And, as he played the part of a kind of king's jester, his "clownish tricks and sayings" delighted the onlookers as well as the visitors. Anderson enthused that "every day we passed in this town was given to festivity and enjoyment."[62]

They finally tore themselves away from their "fierce" warrior host—and now good friend—to set out once more on their journey. Dowilnyah even provided protection on the trek, in the person of his nephew. Anderson could not leave Ziggah Porrah Zue, however, without first taking note of the celebrated market held each Sunday on the banks of the Saint Paul's River, "under the shade of large cotton (bombax) acacia-trees."[63] The array of commodities traded included "country cloths, cotton stripes, raw cotton, iron, soap, palm-oil, palm-butter, ground-nuts, rice, plantains, bananas, dried fish, dried meat, peas, beans, sweet potatoes, onions (shallots), snuff, tobacco, pipes, salt, earthen pots or vessels for holding water and for cooking purposes, large quantities of Kola nuts, slaves, and bullocks...generally brought to the market by the Mandingoes."[64]

―⟋⟍―

As the expedition got underway again on November 30, 1868, Anderson made some final observations on the country they had so far traversed and of the natives living there. In the 116 miles from Monrovia to Ziggah Porrah Zue, in Loma country, the land rose some 1,600 to 1,700 feet above sea level. The area where they now found themselves was densely populated with two divisions of the Loma: the Wymar and Domar. Anderson learned that one could distinguish members of one group from the other, a potentially useful bit of knowledge since the two often warred against one another. The Wymar marked "his face from the temple to his chin with an indelible blue stain," while the Domar eschewed tattooing of any kind.[65]

"The country was open," with "hill and plain covered with tall grass, canebrake, and wild rice, interspersed by short dwarfed trees" and dotted by "large plantations of rice, cotton, millet."[66] But they soon passed "through a district which was a solid mass of iron ore...A short reddish grass struggled for existence on this extensive plain of metal."[67] The iron in the deposits along the road "was so pure, that the road...was a polished metal pathway, smoothed by the constant tread of travellers."[68] Villagers busied themselves smelting iron in "furnaces...built of clay and of a conical shape, from five and a half to six feet high." The region also boasted elephants "plenty and large," but Anderson, when invited, declined to go on a hunt.[69]

The group on December 5 crossed over the Vukkah hills, a range marking the "boundary between the Boozies and Mandingo territories." They were, at last, in Mandingo country.[70] But stopping for the night in Mahommadu, the first Mandingo town, Anderson and his group complained of their being "entertained in a very pitiable manner," compared with what they "had been accustomed to in the Boozie country."[71] Nonetheless, several Mandingoes now accompanied them as they pushed on toward Musardu the following day.

Being able to see the "the features of the country" increasingly "distracted" them.[72] Where earlier "dense vegetation ... on each side of a narrow foot-path" had frequently restricted their vision, now they could see the sweep of the entire countryside. Anderson marveled that "the towns [were] visible for miles. The towns and villages seated in the plains, people on foot and people on horseback, [could] be seen at a great distance, and have more of light, life, and activity" than had been true in much of the lands they had traversed, "where the somber gloom of immense forests [concealed] such things."[73]

December 7, 1868, dawned in that magnificent splash of color only to be seen on the African savannas. And this particular sunrise was spiced with a touch of anticipation and a pinch of excitement. Almost a year had passed since Anderson set out for Musardu. Now, it loomed on the horizon. As they drew nearer, he could see the fabled town nestled "among gentle hills and slopes" at, as he would carefully measure, a comfortable two thousand feet elevation, "laid out irregularly, with very narrow, sometimes winding lanes." He judged it might be home to as many as seven or eight thousand people. In addition, several "villages and hamlets" strung like a rough necklace of stones and lions' teeth ringed the central town.[74]

As they approached the town's gate, Anderson wrote, "we fired our muskets," as was customary, "entered the town...and were led up a street, or narrow lane" to a square dominated by a mosque. Here the Mandingo king, Vomfeedolla, and the "principal men of the town" were gathered. Mandingo friends opened the welcoming program with "elaborate speech," explaining from where Anderson had come and for what purpose. One launched into a grandiloquent recital of the "power, learning, and wealth of the 'Tibbabues' [as they called Americo-Liberians]." Another friend "engaged to swear" for Anderson assured the assemblage that he "had come for no ill purposes whatever." Therefore he should be "treated in every way befitting an illustrious stranger" and the king's "particular guest."[75] Anderson, for his part, recalled that he began to feel uneasy, fearing the "high importance" being attached to the visit would "raise great expectations for dashes"—which would end in disappointment.

After visiting Dowilnyah, Anderson, upon meeting King Vomfeedolla, was somewhat taken aback. "Mild, gentle countenance...straight nose, broad forehead, thin lips, large and intelligent eyes, and an oval chin. Like all the Mandingoes, his skin [was] smooth, glossy black, [but he was] "rather below the general towering height of this tribe." Although, Anderson noted, "he is said to be a great warrior...the evidence around Musardu" [proved] "that if he is, he must belong to the unfortunate class of that profession."[76]

Finally, after an "infinite number of salaams and snapping of fingers," Anderson was lodged in a house in the king's courtyard.

Weary from the trek, and even more so from the excitement—and tedium—generated in the courtyard welcome, he retired for the night. But, scarcely had he laid his head down when a "harper" began to improvise, "in a tremulous minor key, that 'since Musardu had been founded such a stranger [as Anderson] had never visited it.'" The harp, "a huge gourd...had three strings," which when strummed produced "a noise, intrinsically disagreeable." Even more disturbing to Anderson were "the expectations it might be raising" when "the bard in his nocturne declared [Anderson's] many gracious qualities, [his] courage, [his] wealth, and [his] liberality," especially when "upon the last he dwelt with loud and repeated effort."[77]

Over the next several days, the visitors explored the town. They found the mosque, a quadrilateral structure, sited in the southwest quarter, surrounded by an eight-foot-high oval-shaped wall. Rafters, resting on the wall, supported a large, conical thatched roof. Anderson was surprised at the small size of the interior—thirty-two feet long, twenty-two feet wide, and nine feet high—which he estimated to be too small to accommodate more than 120 worshippers. Since he observed that Mandingoes followed Islam scrupulously, he assumed there was some arrangement to handle a larger number. He also heard from the town's "old men" of how it had suffered from wars that greatly reduced the town's "past power and wealth." They told him that what he "saw of Musardu was only the ruins of its former prosperity."[78]

Anderson was shown a large area outside of town, where an enormous marketplace, with sufficient space for eight to ten thousand people, had been. His guide pointed out the locations where each of the many products—country cloth, cattle, gold, salt, ostrich feathers, leather, ivory, cotton, tobacco, and an "infinite variety of domestic articles"—was exhibited for sale. But now it was "a barren space filled with weeds, grass, and the broken skulls and skeletons of enemies" felled in a "desperate battle" fought between western (Musardu) Mandingoes and eastern Mandingoes. The guide sadly mused how war had destroyed every vestige of this commercial activity.[79]

One of Musardu's current "wars and feuds" involved a Mandingo chief living at Madina, a large town three days' walk to the northeast. During Anderson's stay, a party of four Senegalese merchants and a Mandingo guide showed up at the town's gates seeking to trade. They had "two sturdy little jackasses, with enormous packs, containing...French blue baft."[80] However, they aroused the suspicions of the town and were turned away. But they persisted and finally were admitted. The guide, it turned out, served as a spy for the enemy Mandingo chief and used his employment to gather intelligence on the rival Musardu.

Because wars and similar outbreaks occurred so often, Mandingoes had learned not to keep close at hand anything "too bulky to be removed or concealed." Instead, they kept such items "out of reach, in some friendly Boosie town." Thus, Musardu supposedly contained little "but the war-horse, and articles easy to be hid or carried off." And Anderson remarked on the state of readiness in each house where one could see "muskets, cutlasses, powder-horn, war-belts, and war-coats, a powerful large bow, and four or five large quivers filled with poisoned arrows."[81]

These poisoned arrows, according to what Anderson learned, were particularly feared. The poison, a potion, made from a vegetable having "a bulbous root twice as large as an onion, and two kinds of small vines," would be "boiled in a pot to a thick or gummy consistency the color of...black." This substance was "said to be so fatal, that if it wounds so much as the tip end of the fingers, it [was] certain death." Anderson's source detailed the horrible death the poor victim suffered: "bleeding at the nose and ears; its nauseous attack on the stomach, and consequent spitting; the final despair of the individual in lying down, with his eyes set in a vacant death-stare." Anderson saw the weapon "as one of the most horrible means of barbarous warfare."[82]

The frequent or long-standing wars between the Boozies (Loma) and Barline (a Kpelle tribe) were a different matter. They seldom produced, in Anderson's words, "any sanguinary results," since they consisted "mainly in surprising" and taking prisoner "a few individuals" they "suddenly [came] upon," sometimes waylaying traders on roads. "These, together with some other petty annoyances, [constituted] their principal mode of warfare." The large walled towns were seldom taken; pitched battles seldom fought. Even then, in an open-field battle, "some war chief" would do most of the fighting "by way of displaying his individual prowess."[83] Anderson surmised that if these two groups did fight serious wars very often, the numerous large markets that dotted the countryside would not exist.

Without doubt, the Mandingoes impressed Anderson. Although they were "given to trade more than to manual labor," he still found them "very attentive to their farming interests." Around February or March, or sometimes sooner, they cut down the high grass and wild cane, which was allowed to rot for fertilizer. Then they planted "rice, potatoes, ground-nuts, onions, peas and beans, large gourds, corn, pumpkins, etc." Mandingo farmers also were said to be "the greatest tobacco-raisers and snuff-makers in the country."[84]

He was particularly taken with the Mandingoes' personal qualities—"quick and intelligent, easily to be managed by persuasion," and possessed of a "natural reverence for learning and mental superiority," which they respected whether it accorded "with their belief or not." He believed they offered "Liberia a more speedy prospect of assimilation and union than any other tribe" with which he was acquainted. On a personal note, he averred that none of them ever showed him any hint of "rudeness, or intolerance" or allowed any "difference of religion" ever to "diminish their respect, attention, and hospitality" toward him. As further evidence of Mandingo tolerance, he mentioned how one of his Congo carriers, a Baptist, prayed each morning—so loudly that few could fail to hear. The Mandingoes said nothing; they respected it as a prayer, though be it a Christian one.[85]

His enthusiasm perhaps waned a bit, though, when it came to attire. Men usually were dressed in "a pair of Turkish-shaped trousers, coming a little below the knees," and a shirt and a vest, large coat, or "toga worn over all." They wore sandals that were "sometimes beautifully worked," and a three-cornered cap, "made and worn with taste and utility." While men's dress generally passed muster, he "deplored" the way women wrapped "up their faces and bodies in a manner truly ungraceful, and unhealthy, too."[86]

But he marveled at how the Mandingo ladies of Musardu wore gold so "extravagantly." He noted that "their earrings [were] so large and weighty as to require a piece of leather to brace them up to their head-bands" so they wouldn't make "an unseemly hole" in their earlobes. Gold held a great interest for Anderson and for his Liberian compatriots, who keenly sought to find out the sources of this much-sought-after commodity. Anderson observed that gold was "absolutely abundant and would form a lucrative trade between Musardu and Liberia."[87] He also was intent on finding its source.

Anderson had been told that the "gold district of this part of Mandingo" was "principally in Buley," a "week's journey eastward." But this intelligence soon expanded to two weeks, "through hostile and dangerous districts." Then, other obstacles emerged, until he realized that "every difficulty was conjured up" in the hope of being "sufficient to extinguish all interest for further inquiry," or at least to intimidate him into not "going in that direction." Buley, by his own calculations, lay only four days' walk from Musardu. Moreover, Anderson decided his "Mandingo cousins" had doubtless "misrepresented the whole matter," since gold could be found not only in Buley, but right "in their own country."[88]

—⁂—

Anderson, the long-term visitor, "having now," in his words, "exhausted the time, as well as almost all the means which had been assigned to carry out this expedition…began to think"—reluctantly—"of returning home." Yet, he confessed that "there was nothing more contrary to [his] wishes." He wrote, "Had it not been that family responsibilities demanded my return home, I could still, with or without means, have prosecuted my journey eastward—a direction I have always had the presentiment contains the prosperity and welfare of Liberia."[89]

But at 8:00 a.m., Friday, December 25, the explorer and his Congoes at last began their journey home. From Musardu back to Monrovia, they followed much the same route they had taken on their outward trek, revisiting a succession of towns and markets. When the party reached King Dowilnyah's residence near Ziggah Porrah Zue, friends greeted him warmly, the dancing Wymar ladies "merrily fell to clapping and singing," and the "fearsome" king presented him several large country cloths and a "very large and heavy ivory." Here, he recorded, he "was obliged to spend some time" since it was "contrary to politeness" to rush away "from the town of a great chief." He stayed three weeks.[90]

After more stops, it was February 21 before Anderson reached Totoquella, where King Momoru greeted him "with every demonstration of joy and hospitality." As if in a kind of finale to his epic journey, the "musadu tebabu fin" ("the black European of Musadu"), as he had come to be called, was served a great delicacy at a dinner. Some of the king's people killed an elephant. So, instead of beef, the party, Anderson recounted, "dined heartily" on the elephantine part "regarded as a delicacy"—"the proboscis." The honored guest paid due respect to the poor beast, which, he noted, "had not yielded his life in a tame, unbecoming manner," but had smashed gunstocks, chased hunters, stamped and broken saplings, and "literally bent" one "musket barrel to an angle of ninety degrees."[91] He shuddered at the thought of what might well have been his fate had he accepted the earlier invitation to join an elephant hunt.

Benjamin Anderson and his small party arrived back in Monrovia March 25, 1869.

Anderson returned to Monrovia a hero. His exploits created a stir in Liberia and stimulated passing interest in Europe. But the saga of David Livingstone and Henry Stanley and other European explorers dominated the news. He penned a lively account of his journey, published in 1870, that also was "modest, clear, and concise," and, in the view of Liebenow, ranks "with some of the best literature in this genre."[92]

Although not publicized widely at the time, and nearly forgotten since, the exploration and Anderson's account of it were deemed "sufficiently important to warrant distribution by the Smithsonian Institution," and for Joseph Henry, the secretary at that time, to write a preface to the work.[93] Even the president of the prestigious Royal Geographical Society, Sir Roderick I. Murchison, gave a copy of the book to the society's library in 1870. A contemporary comment in the *African Repository* enthused that Anderson had introduced the reader "to the populous and thriving towns of Zolu, Zow-Zow, Salarghee, Fissahbue, and Bokkasaw."[94]

The now-celebrated explorer put aside his surveying instruments, and in 1870 the newly elected president, Edward Roye, tapped him to serve as secretary of the treasury once more. But after Roye was deposed in 1871, Roberts, who succeeded him, called on Anderson to undertake a second expedition. His principal objective this time would be to reach "the alleged gold-mines near Musadu." On this trip made in 1874 Anderson explored Liberia's forest in the northeastern part of the country but failed to discover any mines. And, unlike his initial foray, this adventure earned Anderson few plaudits. Harry Johnston "thought the geographical results were so vague and untrustworthy that it [was] scarcely worth mentioning."[95]

After precious little time back home with his wife, Anderson the following year went to war again, this time to fight against the Grebo Confederation in Maryland County. He gained a reputation as the militia's colonel of the artillery, according to his obituary, for his "work with the cannon then known as the eighteen pounder."[96] But he also suffered a tragedy at home during this period. After his first wife died, Anderson had married Mrs. Josephine Amelia Tredwell, a widow, in 1871. She, along with a newborn baby daughter, died in 1875, after Anderson left for Cape Palmas.

June 1877 found the perennial treasury secretary back in office in President James Payne's cabinet—accused "of failing to submit the annual report for his department" by political foes of the president bent on revenge. In December 1878 the House of Representatives impeached Anderson and then Payne for not suspending Anderson. The charges against the president were eventually dropped, but the Liberian Senate found Anderson guilty and ordered criminal proceedings against him. It is not known if the order was ever executed. Whatever punishment, if any, he received apparently had little effect on his public career.[97]

Anderson continued to advocate for an interior-oriented policy and became one of the directors of the Liberia Interior Association, an organization that "sought to forge trade links with the interior."[98] He also had his first brush with European imperialism when President Hilary H. W. Johnson dispatched him and Henry W. Grimes to Sierra Leone as special commissioners in 1884 to sign the infamous Havelock Draft Convention ending the long-standing, contentious dispute with Britain over Liberia's boundary with Sierra Leone. Johnson shared Anderson's vision that Liberia's destiny lay primarily inward and appointed him interior secretary in 1886. Anderson's attempts in this post to steer Liberian policy in this direction, however, met with only limited success.

Early in the next century, he would collide again with European imperialism—this time in the guise of a French army officer. Captain Henri d'Allone had come to west Africa in the late 1890s to survey his government's newly acquired lands, including areas that Liberia claimed. Presumably to legitimize France's actions, he attacked the credibility of Anderson's account of his explorations, setting off a debate that raged internationally in various articles during 1903–04.[99]

While Anderson's accomplishments went largely unnoticed in the outside world, his home country honored him. In recognition of his academic achievements, his prowess as an explorer, and his service to his country, Liberia College awarded him an honorary master of arts degree in the early 1880s and an honorary doctor of philosophy in 1903. The Liberian president conferred on him the title of knight commander of the Order of African Redemption. Although often called upon to serve his government in high positions, political success eluded him. He tried in an election for a seat in the House of Representatives, in the only recorded instance of his running for public office, but was "soundly defeated in the primary."[100]

Anderson painted a picture of what the interior of the country and its people were like—the first picture most of his countrymen, as well as the outside world, had ever seen. His detailed descriptions of exotic life (both people and places) and breathless adventures made for compelling reading. Although he opened their eyes to the potential the area offered in terms of trade and mineral resources, the government failed to follow up with necessary action. He reported extensive iron ore deposits, but their economic potential went largely ignored. It would only be in the next century that they would have a profound impact economically and politically on the country.

Anderson the explorer served the Liberian government equally well as a diplomat and trade representative, winning many friends for Liberia among supposedly hostile natives, most of whom welcomed the opportunity to trade with Liberians. He signed treaties by which chiefs placed their countries within the limits of Liberia and its government—although they appeared more expressions of friendship than accession. He recognized, too, that for trade to prosper, it would have to be protected. It was, after all, a country of "barbarians and semi-barbarians, and divided into so many warring interests."[101] Toward this end, four trading forts should be built: "two in Boozie and Barline" tribal areas that "would purchase country cloths, raw cotton, cam-wood, rice, palm-oil, etc.," and two in the "Mandingo country to secure "gold, bullocks, country cloths, and horses."[102] The natives, according to Anderson, would welcome the forts.

As a bow to the missionary spirit that seems to have inhabited every Americo-Liberian, he wrote that the forts would additionally "second and strengthen any missionary effort," and their "support, protection, and moral and material influence… would insure permanence and success."[103] He could have added, too, that an undertaking of this kind would go a long way in bolstering Liberia's claim to these territories by demonstrating the "effective occupation" the European powers laid down as requisite for annexation.

Benjamin Anderson, who "could claim to be the first outsider to see the forbidden city of Musardu,"[104] died in Monrovia on June 27, 1910, at the age of seventy-five.

—⚹—

This then was essentially the Liberia—a narrow coastal strip, peopled by settlers and tribal Africans, governed through a single political party by a handful of Americo-Liberians, overshadowed by a far larger and mostly unknown hinterland, home to a vast native population—that newly elected president Anthony Gardiner faced when he walked into his office in January 1878. Gardiner, a native of Virginia, was born February 3, 1820, in Southampton. Little is known of his early childhood years, except that in January 1831, he and his parents arrived in Liberia aboard the brig *Volador*. The family settled in Grand Bassa County where young Anthony attended school. After completing his law studies, Gardiner embarked upon a public service career, as a delegate from Grand Bassa County to the 1847 constitutional convention.

After President Roberts tapped him to serve from 1848 to 1855 as the republic's first attorney general, Gardiner was elected to the legislature representing Grand Bassa County. Following a legislative stint of sixteen years, he was chosen vice president in 1871 to serve under Roberts, who had again been elected president. Gardiner then took over the reins of office in June 1875 as acting president when Roberts took seriously ill and went to England for medical treatment. His tenure, however, lasted less than a year, until James Spriggs Payne was inaugurated in January 1876. Gardiner finally got his opportunity when Payne stepped down after completing his two-year term. Abandoning the Republican Party to run as a True Whig, Anthony Gardiner was elected Liberia's ninth president. Highly respected and popular with voters, he would be reelected in 1880 and again in 1882 for a third term that would be cut short by an encounter with British imperialism..

—⁂—

Harry Johnston described the 1870s as not being "a happy period for Liberia."[105] But the succeeding two decades, a coming of age for the republic, would prove no kinder., Six presidents, including Gardiner, would pass through the presidential mansion between 1880 and 1900. Two of them were born in Liberia, the country's first native sons. The others were born in the United States, in Kentucky, Maryland, and Virginia. Two were Protestant Christian ministers, one was a successful trader, and another owned a large coffee and sugarcane plantation. All of the six had significant experience in public service. All belonged to the True Whig Party. One of the group would die while in office, and two, Gardiner and William D. Coleman, would resign.

None, however, would satisfactorily handle the problem of President Payne's "barbarous hordes," the 95 percent of the people living within Liberia's borders but largely outside the country's social, political, and economic structures. Some observers, such as Harry Johnston, sensed that around this time (1880) public spirit in Liberia, given the disappointing decline in new immigrants, probably was looking more toward Africa in its orientation. But change would come ever so slowly.

Neither would any of them successfully bring order and discipline to the government's financial morass and achieve financial independence. Having once tasted the forbidden fruits of foreign borrowing and corruption, the country could never return to the innocent past. And they were powerless to fully protect Liberia from quite possibly the most serious threats to its continued existence as an independent republic. While Liberia escaped ending up a full course on the European imperialists' dinner menu, the country still would lose at least one-third of its territory to them.

The Gallinas, bordering Sierra Leone, had long been a festering source of dispute with Britain. And now, as Anthony Gardiner eased into his presidential chair, it seemed ready to erupt. The British colonists in Sierra Leone had grown restless, eager to join their imperial colleagues elsewhere in their quest to bring new lands (and trade) to Queen Victoria's African empire before other hungry Europeans struck first.

And Great Britain was not the only foreign power bent on acquiring Liberian territory. France had undertaken to revive its empire by annexing portions of land in various parts of the world, including west Africa. French encroachments on territory claimed by Liberia began in 1868 but did not appear to be a serious threat until 1891, when France annexed an area claimed by Liberia along the border with the Ivory Coast. The competition among the European powers had begun sweeping the African continent with growing fury. All that history needed now was a label for it—a shortcoming that Edward Henry Stanley, fifteenth Earl of Derby, the British foreign secretary, was about to remedy.

CHAPTER 12

The Scramble

—⚡—

SHORTLY BEFORE TWO O'CLOCK IN the snowy afternoon of November 15, 1884, Prince Otto von Bismarck welcomed the "nineteen plenipotentiaries, with fifteen assistants, representing fourteen great and lesser Powers...to the large music room" in his home at number 77 Wilhelmstrasse.[1] Chancellor Bismarck had convened the Berlin Conference on West Africa because of what Lord Derby, Britain's foreign secretary, termed an absurd "scramble for colonies" in Africa. All the major European powers attended. Even the Ottoman Empire was represented. The United States sent John A. Kasson, the American minister at Berlin. The Liberian president did not attend. No African attended.

Bismarck outlined in his brief welcoming speech the aim of the conference: "to promote the civilization of the African natives by opening the interior of the continent to commerce...the familiar '3 Cs'—commerce, Christianity, civilization."[2] The real purpose was to ease tension between the European powers over the partition of central Africa. British and Portuguese distrust of Belgian and French ambitions in the Congo and of German expansion in East Africa and the Cameroons had raised tensions to a dangerous level.

The conference, marked by dizzying diplomatic maneuvering, dragged on to a conclusion with the signing of the General Act of Berlin on February 26, 1885. The act guaranteed free navigation of the Congo and Niger Rivers, free trade in the Congo, and established rules for the acquisition of new territory. They required "effective occupation," which necessitated governing the territory, but excepted protectorates, the system of indirect rule employed by Britain, and also allowed spheres of influence. Although, as Thomas Pakenham writes, some people would come to believe "it was Berlin that precipitated the Scramble...it was the other way around...The race to grab a slice of the African cake had started long before the first day of the conference."[3]

Liberia already had experienced a taste of the scramble;. the country had been plagued periodically by British threats to the Liberian-claimed Gallinas territory. The Liberia-Sierra Leone border was nebulous at best. Liberian president Roberts insisted that he purchased the area for Liberia from native chiefs in a series of transactions from 1849 to 1856. But expansionists in Sierra Leone also claimed portions of this border area. The dispute came to a head in 1862; a trader, John Myers Harris, in 1860 established a trading post on the Sulima River in the Gallinas territory, and refused to acknowledge Liberian authority over the area where he was operating. An imbroglio involving the Liberian capture of two British schooners belonging to Harris transpired. Sierra Leone annexed part of the disputed territory. (In March 1883 the British government would annex the area west of the Mano River.)[4]

Clashes between rival tribes, smuggling, illegal trading, harassment of Liberian settlers, and Harris-fomented trouble ruled in the area, and figured in the Liberian government's passage of the 1865 Ports of Entry Law. After a joint commission failed in April 1863 to settle the dispute, Liberia dispatched troops to restore order. Their 1869 and 1871 forays, unsurprisingly, further damaged or destroyed property belonging to British traders, notably Harris. The traders claimed $80,000 (£17,000) or more in damages and appealed to the British government to get payment from Liberia. Some of the tribes there, notably the rebellious Vai, they argued, "were beyond the control of the Liberian government."[5] At the same time, these traders tried their best to thwart Liberia's efforts to enforce its laws, particularly trade regulation.

The Liberian government sought aid from the United States, requesting a vessel to control the belligerent natives along the coast. Washington agreed to order a cruiser to the area, but this had little effect. Two British gunboats in 1869 appeared in Monrovia's harbor, presumably as a reminder that the compensation earlier agreeed on had yet to be paid. They turned out to be a harbinger of what came to be called "gunboat diplomacy."

As the quarrel continued to simmer, Sierra Leone and Liberia sought arbitration. They agreed upon an international boundary commission presided over by US Navy commodore Robert W. Shufeldt. The commodore commanded the USS *Ticonderoga*, which was on an 1879–80 world cruise to search for new markets for American exports in Africa, the Middle East, and Asia. The *Ticonderoga* arrived in Liberia on January 15, 1879, and the body began its deliberations in the spring of that year. According to US State Department history, Shufeldt "successfully arbitrated the boundary dispute."[6]

But the British commissioners subsequently refused to be "bound by the decisions of the American arbitrator," who they claimed favored Liberia.[7] The commission ended May 12, and the commodore "returned from a fruitless mission."[8]

Shufeldt, though, did succeed in helping the Liberians quash another Grebo uprising in Maryland County. The rebellious chiefs in the fall of 1879 revolted against Americo-Liberian authority generally, but particularly against the trade restrictions imposed by the hated Ports of Entry Law. This time they even proclaimed themselves British subjects. But any hope of British intervention was in vain, and the rebellion collapsed once the *Ticonderoga* joined the USS *Essex* already standing offshore. Meanwhile, the dispute over the boundary smoldered on, seemingly beyond the reach of the two neighbors to resolve. Liberian commissioners relied on the agreements hammered out with the chiefs; the British relied on letters and statements also from the chiefs. Stalemate.

—⋘—

But that was about to change. The British Crown must have decided it was time for decisive action. It came in 1881 in the person of thirty-seven-year-old Sir Arthur Elibank Havelock, CMG—Sandhurst graduate, retired army captain, anxious to make his mark in the colonial service he had joined four years earlier. Appointed governor of West African settlements in February 1881, Sir Arthur would prove an able servant of the queen. And given the additional post of consul to Liberia, he would, as a later biographical entry noted, demonstrate "tact, firmness, and measure of diplomatic skill in the Liberian boundary situation."[9]

His firmness, though maybe not his tact, would soon become evident.

Havelock had been vested with "authority to visit [the Liberian government] with a view to effecting a solution of the long-pending" border problem, and investigate the claims of British traders for damages allegedly inflicted by Liberian troops fighting Gallinas tribes in 1871[10]

His visit had come sooner than most expected, and his approach to "effecting a solution" was not one the Liberians wished for.

As historians Duignan and Gann relate, "suddenly, on March 20, 1882," four British gunboats—the *Pioneer, Briton, Flint,* and

Algerine—"appeared without warning at Monrovia." Aboard the flagship stood Havelock, who came ashore and "served what amounted to an ultimatum on the Liberian government: he demanded that Liberia immediately recognize British claim to Gallinas "territory up to the River Maffa," (only fifteen miles from Cape Mount and about sixty-five from Monrovia) and pay the £17,000 (roughly $85,000) due British traders for damages from attacks by "tribes in the territory being claimed by Great Britain."[11]

—⁂—

On the Liberian side, the man Gardiner thought best qualified to meet Havelock's challenge was Edward Blyden. He had returned to Monrovia from London in 1880, after a four-year stint as Liberia's ambassador—the first, according to a British newspaper account, sent to Great Britain from a "negro state."[12] Now secretary of the interior in President Anthony Gardiner's cabinet, Blyden found that his experience in London and as secretary of state during 1864–66 would stand him in good stead.

In England Blyden had cut a wide swath, leaving in his wake scores of Victorian English men and women dazzled by this black man. A newspaper account of a visit to Brighton on August 31, 1877, gushed that the newly minted minister plenipotentiary of Liberia, although "from a pure negro stock, and...educated principally in Liberia...possesses talents of a high order, is a distinguished scholar, and has an intimate acquaintance with the language, manners, and customs, of the English race. His erudition and depth of thought...were displayed in articles" he contributed to *Fraser's Magazine*. The article goes on to report that Lord Derby, the foreign secretary, received him a few days earlier, and he (Blyden) would be presented to the queen at Balmoral "in a few more."[13]

The ambassador concluded his Brighton visit as the honored guest at a luncheon "in the company of two or three distinguished guests," where "the orchestral band of Mr. W. Devin, under his personal guidance, went through a short programme," that included, among others, "a selection from 'La Belle Helene' (Offenbach)."[14] The menu was equally imposing: "Tortue" soup; "Saumon, sauce d'hommard; Cabilaud, sauce d'huitres; Cotelettes de Mouton, printainier; Cotelettes de Veau, aux champignons; Quartier d'Agneau; Poulet roti; Jambons d'York; Gele dOrange; Crème de Fraise; Ananas, Peches, Abricots, &c.; Champagne, Claret, Burgundy, Hock, Port, Sherry."[15] The affair was quite civilized. Guests perhaps were surprised that Blyden (who had mastered Latin, Greek, Arabic, and several other languages) even knew how to use a knife and fork.

In the traditional exchange of toasts to the queen and to the president of Liberia, Blyden expressed his hope that "his present visit to England would tend to strengthen its friendly relations with Liberia," and it "would continue…to be a power for good in every corner of the globe."[16] He had not forgotten the warm welcome extended him in his earlier visits to England.[17]

Although President Gardiner must have been aware of Blyden's anglophile leanings—or probably because of them—he appointed Blyden and ex-attorney general W. M. Davis commissioners to deal with the crisis. They managed to get Havelock to cut the claims for damage by more than half and to recommend moving the proposed border to the Mano River. (Havelock apparently had been prepared in advance to concede these negotiating points.) A draft convention recorded their agreement.

Blyden and Davis reported back to Gardiner. The president promptly called a meeting of the cabinet that, doubtless prodded by Havelock and his gunboats, acceded to the demands, subject to Senate ratification. The legislative reaction would come quickly—but would not be what he would have liked.

Havelock likely saw the outcome as vindication of his "tact and firmness" and returned to Sierra Leone proud of his success. But the March 30 agreement was not yet a "done deal."

The Senate met in special session April 10 and 17. The members erupted in a storm of opposition, led by Vice President Alfred Francis Russell. They marched in a body to the president, to whom Russell reported the Senate's "unanimous opinion and advice against signing 'any convention or treaty ceding or relinquishing any of the public domain of Liberia.'"[18]

Suspicion immediately fell on Blyden as the miscreant. "It was said that the President, under pressure of the Cabinet, especially Dr. Blyden, had given the territory away to the British. Public meetings were called; excitement ran high."[19]

The April 27, 1882, *Monrovia Observer* captured some of the public's outrage: "England asks too much. To yield to the proposals of Consul Havelock would be national suicide. The people feel this throughout the length and breadth of the land and would rather see Liberia destroyed by British arms than make any such concessions. Let the might of England override the right of Liberia."[20]

Havelock merely dispatched messages to the president on June 15 and September 5 "demanding settlement on the terms dictated in March.[21] Gardiner opted to delay and let the legislature consider the matter in its December annual session. In his message to the legislature at the beginning of its regular session in December 1882, President Gardiner hailed Havelock's appointment to the long-vacant post as a measure of Great Britain's earnestness in removing anything that could cause "the least friction in the friendly relations so long existing" between the two countries.[22] He sent a copy of the Draft Convention to the Senate asking for its consideration "at the earliest date possible."[23] The tone seemed remarkably calm given the degree of heat the dispute had generated.

Perhaps this was because the president was an ailing man. Almost seventy, the tempest proved too much for him to weather. In fact, the secretary of state read the message on his behalf to the legislature. The American minister in Monrovia, John H. Smyth, reported the president was "believed to be threatened with paralysis."[24] Smyth's next dispatch to Washington announced that President Anthony W. Gardiner had resigned, effective on January 20, 1883, "on account of the incurable condition of his health."[25] Sir Harry Johnston claimed that Gardiner resigned from office over the trouble and "never recovered from the mortification caused by...Havelock's actions."[26] He died in 1885.

Vice President Alfred Francis Russell, a former Methodist missionary who emigrated from Louisville, Kentucky, at the age of sixteen, succeeded Gardiner. Two months later, in March, troops from Sierra Leone occupied the area west of the Mano River, and Britain annexed the Gallinas territory. Russell had hoped to be nominated (and elected) president in his own right once he completed the year remaining in Gardiner's term in January 1884. The Republican Party, however, thought otherwise. Despite his opposition to the Havelock-Blyden treaty, some Liberians still saw Russell as complicit in the country's loss of territory—a political opportunist who had attempted to use the incident to open the presidency to himself. In addition, the sixty-six-year-old Russell was of mixed blood (his mother, Amelia Crawford, was an octoroon), a minus in the minds of many voters. He retired to his extensive coffee and sugarcane farm and died April 4, 1884.

Gardiner doubtless felt he had been trampled by British imperialism in its scramble for African land. He also must have felt deeply wounded by the absence of local support for his handling of the dispute and likely left office with more than a little bitterness and remorse. The sole surviving signer of the republic's declaration of independence and constitution, he had served his country faithfully over many years—as its first attorney general, as vice president and acting president—and now would be its first president to resign voluntarily.

When Gardiner became president, Liberia stood at its territorial zenith—a seacoast of about six hundred miles stretching from the Gallinas territory in the west to the San Pedro River in the east, and a vast hinterland reaching as far north as Boporo and Musadu, in today's Guinea, and on the northeast well into what is now Ivory Coast. By the time the dust from the scramble finally settled, Liberia would have lost more than a third of its claimed territory.[27]

Although Liberia dispatched a protest to the various powers with whom it had treaty relations, none of them came to its defense, except diplomatically. Chester A. Arthur, the US president, in a reassuring message to the Congress, reported that the American ministers in Monrovia and in London had "endeavored to help Liberia" in its dispute. He thought the "prospect was good for a compromise."[28] But Britain and Sir Arthur were not prepared to compromise. The United States recognized the peril Liberia faced. But American policy was to avoid any serious confrontation over the issue: take whatever diplomatic action possible, but don't go so far as to risk a fight. The British expansionists, on the other hand, clearly "were ready to use force."[29]

For the approaching presidential election, the Republican Party turned to local-born Hilary Richard Wright Johnson, son of revered hero Elijah Johnson, one of the original settlers. The forty-seven-year-old Johnson had served as secretary of state in Edward Roye's disastrous administration. After Roye's downfall, he "emerged as a dominant figure in Liberian politics" and reigned as a "major player behind the scenes for the last quarter of the 19th Century."[30]

In an unusual twist, both the Republican and True Whig parties supported the popular Johnson in the 1883 election, leaving him without an opponent. When elected, Johnson became Liberia's first native-born president. After his election, he apparently experienced an epiphany. He announced that he had shed his Monrovian Republican cocoon and emerged a True Whig black butterfly. Johnson enjoyed wide popularity and would win reelection three times, serving from January 1, 1884, to January 7, 1892.

His popularity was soon put to the test when, yielding to American advice, he gave up further resistance and recognized the British territorial claims. The Liberian Senate reluctantly authorized the president to accept the British terms, and Havelock's successor, Sir Samuel Rowe, journeyed to Monrovia where the two parties signed the treaty on November 11, 1885. But it would not be until 1903 that the issue finally would be put to rest and the boundary firmly demarcated. "Sierra Leone, which had possessed but a few hills and swamps," now added the Gallinas region and a valuable coastline to its territory.[31]

Sir Arthur Havelock was assigned in 1885 to serve as governor of Trinidad. He would go on to compile a thirty-year distinguished career in Britain's colonial service as governor of Natal and Zululand, Ceylon, Madras, and Tasmania before he died in 1908. The Liberian legislature voted $1,000 for resigned president Anthony Gardiner to move back home to Grand Bassa. He died there in 1885, two years after leaving office.

Edward Blyden, whom many Liberians saw as "soft" toward Britain in the boundary dispute, was accused of having accepted a bribe from the British, though the accusation was never substantiated. During his sojourn in Sierra Leone in 1871–74, Blyden had become a highly respected and popular figure there. He founded and edited the *Negro* newspaper, and the colonial government appointed him government agent to the interior. The governor, Sir Arthur Kennedy, was sufficiently impressed to dispatch him twice on missions, some 250 miles into the hinterland, to the "King of Falaba [Fula], on a matter of considerable colonial importance."[32]

As a symbol of the esteem in which colonial Sierra Leone held Blyden, the government erected a statue of him in the center of Freetown (although the honor probably came more for his role as an early advocate of black nationalism rather than for his role in the boundary dispute). He clearly felt great admiration and affection for Great Britain. But his view (based on his pan-African philosophy) that the boundary between Liberia and Sierra Leone was largely irrelevant probably exerted a greater influence on his challenged approach to the issue.

Though no longer secretary of the interior, Blyden continued as president of Liberia College until 1885, when he ran unsuccessfully for president of Liberia. Dividing his time between Liberia and Sierra Leone, where he served as director of Muslim education, he would continue to add to his reputation as a scholar, teacher, and author and remained a prominent public figure.

Sadly for Liberia, the British settlement did not end her territorial woes. France, attempting "to regain the world position it seemed to have lost in 1871," also began "vigorously expanding its African empire."[33] And, unfortunately, Liberia lay in the path. The French already had established a series of protectorates on Liberia's eastern flank beginning in 1868 (which would be incorporated into the Ivory Coast and which France declared a protectorate in 1889). Thus, Smyth's report from Monrovia to Washington in 1879 that the French proposed a protectorate over Liberia seemed plausible enough to set off alarm bells.

Liberia's "honorary" consul general at Bordeaux, Leopold Carrance, a French citizen, had sent a dispatch addressed to the Liberian secretary of state in which such a protectorate was proposed. Carrance urged the Liberian government to agree, pointing out "the advantages to accrue to Liberia from such a relation with France"—although such advantages usually accrued more to France than to the "protected" Africans.

Edward F. Noyes, the American minister in Paris, discovered that the plot to enroll Liberia as a French protectorate was the work of a couple of entrepreneurial Frenchmen, not the French government. It turned out, as Noyes discovered, Carrance actually originated the proposal himself, probably in collusion with M. Huart, the Liberian honorary consul in Paris, to further their own interests. Huart himself was touting a concession scheme in which Liberia would grant "complete control over all mines and mineral resources in Liberia for a period of fifty years."[34] But he reportedly spent most of his time and energies on trying to induce the Liberian government "to create a decoration for which he would be eligible."[35]

Liberia, in Smyth's opinion, clearly "was a most desirable annexation for any nation hunting for African possessions."[36] As Duignan and Gann put it: Liberia was "the lamb" among "the wolves." For the time being, at least, the lamb seemed to have escaped annihilation at the hands of European imperialists. But the Germans had yet to be heard from. At the 1883 Berlin conference, Germany had shown little or no interest in acquiring an African empire. But in May 1884, Bismarck made an abrupt about-face. He ordered his imperial consul general for the west coast of Africa, Dr. Gustav Nachtigal, to seize the Cameroons, Togoland (now Togo), and South West Africa (now Namibia). Imperial Germany soon was on the move in western Africa. And Liberia was vulnerable.

According to author Thomas Pakenham, Bismarck's dramatic reversal of policy stemmed from a mistake. A senior German Foreign Office official, Heinrich von Kusserow, warned Bismarck to "beware France and Britain." They "were planning to share out the whole western Africa coast between them and had agreed not to levy customs duties on each other's nationals."[37] It turns out that Herr von Kusserow had rung the alarm bell mistakenly. He had wrongly read the French text of "an Anglo-French agreement on Sierra Leone."[38] Nevertheless, the fat now was in the fire.

An incident in 1881, luckily before Bismarck's change in policy, revealed just how vulnerable the lamb was. Liberian Krumen attacked and robbed the crew of the German ship *Carlos* after it had run aground on the Kru coast and sunk. The shipwrecked men came to Monrovia and reported the attack to the German consul. After the Liberian government failed to take action on the consul's complaint, on February 26, 1881, the German corvette *Victoria* appeared in Monrovia's harbor. Liberians understandably were anxious. The *Victoria*'s commander exacted a commitment from the government to punish the native wrongdoers and extract a $3,500 indemnity from them. Otherwise, the Liberian government would have to pay the amount to Germany.

Liberia apparently had managed to dodge, for whatever reason, the fate that later befell the Cameroons, Togoland, and German South West Africa. The offending Kru, however, were not as fortunate. On February 3, the *Victoria* "steamed out of the port of Monrovia," bound for "Nanna-Kroo, the place where the chief actors were who took part in the robbery and cruel treatment of the captain and crew of the German steamer."[39] In addition to the German consul, Gardiner and Blyden also were obliged to be on board the *Victoria*.

After the corvette reached Nanna-Kroo, President Gardiner ordered the town evacuated, after which the Germans began shelling it. "A Liberian officer, a German officer and 120 men, fully equipped, landed…and fired the town." The native culprits were brought to Monrovia to be tried in the court of admiralty, and the king and chiefs were held as hostages until their people paid the indemnity.[40] Although Gardiner and Blyden must have felt humiliated at having to serve as surrogates to the Germans, they probably concluded that it was a worthwhile sacrifice for avoiding possible German reprisal.

But this did not mean the Germans were free of imperial lust. They, "like the French and the British, at other times, have," as Sir Harry Johnston noted, "cast a longing eye on Liberia as a possible field for German 'colonization.'"[41] In fact, the German consul in 1897 settled a dispute over a claim for damage "to a German plantation at Cape Palmas by offering to the Liberian government a treaty placing the country under German protection."[42] Once the United States and Britain found out, the German government disavowed the consul's offer and transferred him elsewhere.[43]

But for the loss of the Gallinas territory to Britain, it appeared the European scramble for Africa had now passed by Liberia. At least, that is, until Liberian president Hilary Johnson in early December 1886 received a visitor, a Lieutenant P. Aroux, from the

French gunboat *Gabes*. As the two chatted diplomatically together, the French naval officer let drop that the *Gabes* had anchored for several days at Berribe, a tiny community well to the east of Cape Palmas—in territory "clearly and unmistakably Liberian."[44] Aroux failed to mention he had even negotiated a treaty with the Africans residing there—and another French naval vessel, *Voltigeur*, had been sent to Berribe to "protect" them.

After John Smyth, US minister in Monrovia, smelled French imperialistic designs, the State Department questioned France's intentions. The Foreign Office denied any "designs upon Liberian territory"; the territory belonged to France by virtue of old ties stemming from a treaty negotiated in 1868 by some French naval lieutenant named Crispin.[45]

US president Grover Cleveland's secretary of state, Thomas F. Bayard, argued that Liberia's claim to these lands flowed from purchases the American Colonization Society made in 1846. When Liberia gained independence, the society retained ownership to every other square mile, and thus Americans owned half of the disputed territory. Despite further diplomatic efforts, the French remained unbending, leaving Americans naively believing "that reason, right and argument would prevail over selfish national interests."[46] The more realistic concluded that for a second-rate United States to confront an aggressive France, one of the world's "foremost military and naval powers," would be a calamitous folly.[47]

President Cleveland, in his annual message to Congress on December 6, 1886, alluded to Liberia's vulnerability to European encroachment. He reminded Americans that the "distant community" was an American "offshoot" that owed "its origin to the associated benevolence of American citizens." While a "formal protectorate over Liberia," he continued, was "contrary to our traditional policy, "the United States had a moral "right and duty" to help preserve Liberia's integrity.[48] That "moral" help, however, usually translated into little more than a "stern" warning of the United States' right, "as the next friend of Liberia, to aid her in preventing any encroachment of a foreign power on her territorial sovereignty."[49]

Hilary Johnson's successor, forty-nine-year-old Joseph James Cheeseman, of Grand Bassa County, became president on January 4, 1892. Hoping for something more substantial to ward off any French transgression, he dispatched a commission, composed of Garretson W. Gibson, C. R. Branch, and T. J. R. Faulkner, to ask the US government to extend a protectorate over Liberia. The Liberians also wanted Americans dispatched to Liberia to reorganize and administer the country's customs, treasury, postal, education, agricultural, and police operations.

US president Benjamin Harrison and secretary of state John W. Foster could hardly have warmed to such a request, given the foreign involvements already on their plate—a conflict with Great Britain over Bering Sea fishing, a diplomatic crisis with Italy, an American-led revolution in Hawaii with an eye to US annexation. Cheeseman was elected twice more but died November 12, 1896, in Monrovia, a year before completing his third term as president. The boundary dispute with France still a threat.

Gibson, Gardiner's secretary of state, feared French designs on Liberian territory in the north and northeast as well. In 1879 he wrote Carrance, his "honorary" consul general in France, that the government was "actively engaged in annexing large tracts of inland territory [later part of French Guinea] with the view of reaching the Niger River." He reported the country to fabled Musadu, up to "nearly two hundred and fifty miles from the coast," already annexed.[50] The Liberian secretary of state also requested a $50,000 loan from the US government "to construct 'military posts' to Musadu," obviously with a view to forestalling the French. But the answer from Washington came back "no." The Liberian "government was so far in debt it would never be able to repay the loan."[51]

In May 1891 France occupied part of southeastern Liberia between the Cavalla and San Pedro Rivers and a large, though undetermined portion of the adjacent unexplored hinterland. Liberia claimed the territory based on purchases from tribal authorities between 1835 and 1860. The French, however, maintained the Liberian government had failed to effectively occupy the area it claimed—a requisite, emanating from the Berlin Conference, for annexation. In addition, French authorities argued that residents in the disputed area objected to Liberia's restrictions on their trade. (Nothing unusual, given the opposition among native African and foreign traders countrywide to the Ports of Entry Law.) Liberia conceded the area to France by treaty on December 8, 1892. The agreement established the Cavalla River, which flows southward into the Atlantic Ocean at Cape Palmas, as the boundary between Liberia and the Côte d'Ivoire.

Still, the hunger pangs of French imperialism had not been fully satisfied. The year before the 1892 treaty, France had moved again, this time claiming an extensive part of Liberia's hinterland that included most of the country Anderson had explored in 1868 and Liberia claimed to have purchased from tribal leaders in 1874. As part of the French imperialist wave, a French army captain, Henri d'Ollone, surveyed the area in the late 1890s and challenged Liberia's rights to portions of it. He charged that Anderson had fabricated his exploratory journey, alleging the explorer's itinerary on his 1870 map was "purely a fantasy" and saying his narrative should be "relegated to the rank of fables."[52]

The French captain maintained, with the European hubris typical of the time, that Anderson was "simply a black Liberian who could not possibly have traveled so far into the interior, calculated geographic coordinates and altitude, and written a book." D'Ollone thought the black Liberian had probably obtained some of the information from slaves and then got someone to write his account. The government, unfortunately, had not followed Anderson's recommendations for establishing a Liberian presence in the area, and d'Ollone asserted that he found no evidence of any Liberian ever having visited the area, and that "local people did not even suspect the existence" of Liberia.[53]

The captain's accusations fell onto receptive ears among some French writers. Then, a newspaper in Sierra Leone picked them up in 1903, and soon they appeared in Monrovian papers. The sixty-eight-year-old Anderson responded with vigor, and "for the next nine months the Liberian and Sierra Leonian press published more than two dozen articles designed to refute d'Ollone's accusations." Anderson smelled the odor of imperialism in the charges, writing that "the gentleman [d'Ollone] seems to be sounding the signal trumpet for a fresh grab of Liberian territory."[54] Edward Blyden, Liberia's most eminent intellectual, weighed in on Anderson's side. Even Maurice Delafosse, France's vice consul in Monrovia in 1897–1900, came to his defense. Other notables also supported him. They refuted and "exposed the political and racial motives behind" the French captain's allegations, and Anderson ultimately won the debate.[55] But, of course, it was to no avail. France already had added the territory, which included Musardu, to its possessions. Liberia finally agreed to French demands when President Barclay on

September 18, 1907, accepted the treaty negotiated in 1903 and conceded the land to France.[56]

—⚏—

Besides having to endure the loss of territory to European imperialists during the scramble, Liberian leaders also faced threats posed by its indigenous African people. From 1822, when the first colonists disembarked at what later would become Monrovia, clashes with native inhabitants became a regular, oft-recurring feature of settler life. Most clashes involved land and trade, in which slaves figured largely in the early days.

The conflict over land, exemplified in the very first acquisition of a site for the colony—achieved by holding a loaded pistol to King Peter's head—arose from the fact that African culture generally did not recognize transfers of land beyond the tribal community. Thus, critics could later claim that all of the territory acquired by the government over the years was obtained either by fraud or force, or both. Moreover, the government, in a Christian missionary spirit, extended what amounted to a protectorate over the tribal residents in these areas. As citizenship was limited to the colonists and their descendants (until 1907) tribal people were considered "subjects." And the government regularly intervened in indigenous affairs, tribal wars, and intra-tribal disputes. Monrovia seldom hesitated to step in to mediate, or, if need be, even take military action to maintain peace and order, and quell rebellions and other disturbances.

—⚏—

When President Cheeseman died in 1896, Vice President William David Coleman succeeded him. Coleman was an unusual character in the roster of Liberian presidents. A self-made man, successful in business and public service, he might well have stepped out of a Liberian Horatio Alger story. The story began July 18, 1842, with his birth to a free black family in Fayette County, Kentucky. After his father died, the eleven-year-old Coleman, his mother, and three other family members sailed to Liberia in December 1853.

Settling not far from Monrovia in Clay-Ashland, Montserrado County, William enrolled in the Presbyterian Mission School. But he soon dropped out for lack of funds. His family was too poor to support his schooling. Determined to obtain an education, he took a job during the day and studied at night. When Coleman was about sixteen, he became a carpenter. The bright, hardworking, ambitious youth soon rose to the position of master workman, and then, as he accumulated some wealth, he purchased a farm. Successful at farming, Coleman next turned to commerce, in which he proved to be equally successful as a trader.

Politics soon beckoned, and Montserrado County voters elected him to represent them in the House of Representatives, where he became Speaker in 1877. Two years later, in 1879, Representative Coleman moved up to become Senator Coleman. He remained in the Senate until he was elected as President Cheeseman's vice president in 1892 and again in 1894. Both he and the president belonged to the True Whig Party. When Cheeseman died in office, Coleman moved up to the executive suite in November 1896 to serve out the remainder of the deceased president's term. He seemed ideally suited to the job. The electorate agreed, electing him by a large majority to a two-year term beginning in January 1898.

—⚭—

Although President Johnson in 1885 had accepted the British-imposed boundary with Sierra Leone and President Cheeseman had accepted the French-imposed Cavalla River border with Ivory Coast, potentially explosive differences with the two European powers still lingered. Equally distressing, disturbances by the Kru and Grebo (including the so-called Third Grebo War) still simmered and threatened to erupt again. The government's ability to maintain law and order, particularly in the border areas and hinterland was questionable, and the country's finances remained fragile at best. European predators still prowled the area questing for more territory. Clearly, this was not the best of times for William Coleman to step in as president. In fact, the picture looked so perilous that in 1897 the German consulate (in fear of being left behind by Britain and France) offered to take Liberia on as a protectorate., of course politely declined.

As president, Coleman moved to improve Liberia's financial state, reorganizing the customs department and introducing bonded warehouses at the six ports of entry. Education also ranked high on the president's agenda. (He and Blyden collaborated in reopening Liberia College.) Most important, he believed that Liberia's future lay in the hinterland, in exploiting the resources there that Anderson's explorations at least had hinted at. An expanded government presence was essential.

Coleman proposed extending citizenship to tribal people in the Saint Paul River area, arguing that it was a vital step in establishing the government's authority in the area. However, the legislature, swayed by the fear of being swallowed up by hordes of indigenous Africans, refused. The president fared no better when he sought to settle a conflict that broke out in 1897 among Gola factions and with the Mandingoes over trade routes. Following the example of his predecessors, he tried peaceful negotiations between the warring factions. But when that failed, he resorted to military intervention. Unfortunately a number of Gola were killed. Coleman then hoped in mid-1900 to broker a general peace agreement among the various tribes. But it also failed. Finally, a presidentially convened peace conference brought together a large group of Vai, Gola, Mandingo, and Kpelle chiefs. However, the would-be peace conference ended in a short, bloody battle.

Heated debate erupted over Coleman's handling of the problem. Most True Whig Party supporters favored resolving intertribal disputes peacefully. It also touched a sensitive nerve in the wider settler community, which opposed any extension of the Americo-Liberian presence, particularly through the use of the military. They worried that such expansion might disrupt trade and commerce and threaten the peace, even jeopardize the ruling establishment's supremacy. They saw Coleman intent on exploiting the heartland's resources and opening the door to foreign investment and development, better integrating the tribal population into the republic's political and social fabric, even possibly extending citizenship to them. "'The Old Guard' feared that this would open the political floodgates and swamp the descendants of the settlers in a tribal sea." [57]

The criticism of Coleman and opposition to expansion intensified. Some of the most telling criticism came from Coleman's own political party, the True Whigs, including members of his cabinet, especially Arthur Barclay, secretary of the treasury, and Garretson Gibson, secretary of state. Even more potent was the "public stand...[of] T.W. Howard...the party's national chairman, and treasurer of the Republic," and his son, Daniel Howard, secretary of the party and governor of Montserrado County and later president of Liberia.[58] The leadership firmly believed the True Whig Party was essential for preserving Americo-Liberian unity and rule. So when the party spoke on such a vital issue, it must be, as Coleman and other national leaders discovered, with a loud, commanding voice.

Coleman bowed to the inevitable.

He submitted his resignation to the legislature, which ordered it to become effective at four o'clock on Tuesday, December 11, 1900, after Coleman's annual message to the legislature.

Since the elected vice president, J. J. Ross, had died, the speaker of the house, Robert H. Marshall, was next in line to succeed Coleman. But as Marshall was considered incompetent, the legislature repealed the 1873 presidential succession law and named the secretary of state, Garretson Gibson, president. He reluctantly accepted.

Coleman, the second Liberian president to resign his office, however, did not resign from politics. He ran, unsuccessfully, for president three more times—in 1901, 1903, and 1905—on the People's Party ticket. He died in July 1908 at the age of sixty-five at his home in Clay-Ashland.

Gibson, Liberia's fourteenth president, was an ordained priest. Born in Baltimore May 20, 1832, he was the last president of Liberia born in the United States. He and his family immigrated to Liberia in 1835. After studying in local mission schools, Gibson returned to Maryland to study theology. Ordained and back in Liberia, Reverend Gibson, besides serving as rector of the Episcopalian Trinity Church in Monrovia, was president of the board of trustees and president of Liberia College, and at one point chaplain of the Liberian Senate. He entered politics as a justice of the peace. When appointed in December 1900 at sixty-eight years of age, Gibson enjoyed the distinction of being the oldest president to serve Liberia. He broke his own record upon his election to a full two-year term (1902–03) at the age of seventy. He died in Monrovia April 26, 1910.

With an aged and respected reverend in the president's office, most Liberians may have rested easier, doubtless hoping the worst was behind them. At Britain's insistence an Anglo-Liberian boundary commission set straight the vague border with Sierra Leone established in the 1883 treaty between the two. The resulting 1903 agreement allotted £4,750 as reimbursement to Liberia for sums it paid for territory purchased in 1849 and 1856—a sale to Great Britain at a bargain-basement price. Despite leaving several issues unsettled, the agreement did nevertheless signal growing warmth in British-Liberian relations.

In fact, by the 1880s, despite the threats Britain posed over the years to Liberia's territorial integrity, and at times even to its existence, most Liberians came to prize the connections emerging between the two countries. They increasingly looked to Britain for advice. As important trading partners, the two countries enjoyed strong commercial ties. (The British pound continued to be used as currency in Liberia until President Edwin Barclay declared the US dollar the official currency in 1943.) President Roberts noted as early as 1855 that four British "steam-propellers" maintained regular service between England and Liberia.

Many Americo-Liberians, most notably the distinguished intellectual Edward Blyden, were practicing Anglophiles. Some Liberians possibly felt connected through Britain's neighboring colony, Sierra Leone, whose population of freed slaves was "essentially the same stock as Liberians."[59] And, Liberia's native Africans, allied with the many British traders in the coastal area, often looked hopefully to London for liberation from their Americo-Liberian overlords.

Perhaps the fact that the Americo-Liberians and the British were both colonialists provided a common link between the two, whereas, in contrast, the United States had no foreign colonies, historically eschewed acquiring any, and was more concerned with its own domestic affairs and expansion on the North American continent. And, although Liberia enjoyed a "special relationship" of sorts with the United States, the relationship proved tenuous. The "mother" country proved an inconstant partner at best.

A part of the bond that had evolved with Britain centered specifically on the queen. Sir Harry Johnston noted how, "throughout Liberia an extraordinary affection and reverence grew up... for Queen Victoria." He thought this feeling might have dated from President Roberts's celebrated visit to England in 1849. The British monarch showed her interest in west Africans, adopting or bestowing "her godmothership on Negro girls...one or two [of whom] settled in Liberia." Frequently, the wives of visiting Liberian officials were presented to the queen and came away with "photographs and kindly speeches." All of this royal attention, Johnston thought, resulted in a "kind of cult for the Queen of Great Britain."[60]

Queen Victoria's death on January 22, 1901, must have awakened most Liberians to the realization that a new era had begun. They now were living in the twentieth century, which would pose new challenges and grave threats. Yet Johnston in 1904 found their cult-like "affection and reverence" for the queen—perhaps as treasured memories—"still lingering." Her picture could be "seen almost wherever a Liberian settlement existed."[61]

—⚜—

As the nineteenth century came to a close, Liberians could look back on the seventy-nine years since the colony was born, with a mixture of pride, dismay, and hope. Pride, that the small community of settlers had withstood the African fever, near-starvation, and attacks from hostile natives and rapacious European powers—despite the loss to them of a third or more of the country's territory—and emerged as Africa's first and only republic until the middle of the century. Dismay, at the country's failure to resolve the native problem and the tear in the body politic that color and race had created, the corrosive impact of corruption and financial instability, and the country's inability to defend itself fully from the scramble for Africa. And finally, hope, that a new wave of inspired leadership would carry the country forward into a new, more promising twentieth century. But, it would fall largely to a remarkable group of Caribbean—rather than American—immigrants to ride that wave.

CHAPTER 13

The Barclays of Barbados

—⁕—

ON MOST WORLD GLOBES, BARBADOS is but a tiny speck, usually hard to find in the far side of the Caribbean Sea, some three hundred miles north of Venezuela. The Spanish in 1492 discovered the island—only twenty-one miles long and fourteen miles across at its widest point. The Caribs, the island's residents, reportedly were warlike cannibals. They once allegedly consumed an entire French crew who made the fatal mistake of landing there in 1596, barbecuing their captives and washing them down with cassava beer. The Indians proved no match for the Spaniards, however. They were enslaved and totally wiped out by smallpox and tuberculosis

After the Spanish abandoned the island, Britain claimed it for James I. Captain Henry Powell on February 17, 1627, landed eighty colonists and ten slaves to settle it. A dozen years later, the settlers established a house of assembly in 1639 (leading Barbados to boast it's being the world's third-oldest parliamentary democracy), introduced sugar growing, and imported Dutch-supplied slaves from west Africa.

From these African slaves, an exceptional colored population evolved. Work in the cane fields was brutal, and life dismal, but in 1838 Britain ended slavery on Barbados. Some seventy thousand newly freed slaves jammed the streets of Bridgetown, the capital, celebrating in song their liberation and their queen who had set them free:

> Lick an Lock-up Done Wid,
> Hurray fuh Jin-Jin [Queen Victoria].
> De Queen come from England to set we free
> Now Lick an Lock-up Done Wid,
> Hurray fuh Jin-Jin.
> —Barbados folk song

Many of the freed slaves took advantage of the excellent education that became available on the island. Soon a pool of educated blacks, no longer content to labor in the cane fields, began to fill many professional, government, and other upper-level jobs. Some gained prominent political office. But a drastic fall in sugar prices spelled economic ruin and social misery in most of the West Indies, inducing many to seek escape. Liberia became the goal. To promote their emigration, they formed such organizations as the Fatherland Union Barbados Emigration Society for Liberia and the Barbados Company for Liberia. Something must have worked. The American Colonization Society agreed to provide financial assistance. Between 1865 and 1869, some 2,394 immigrants from the British West Indies would make it to Liberia. Among them, the 346 Barbadans who arrived aboard the brig *Cora* on May 10, 1865, proved extraordinarily rich in terms of educated, talented individuals; some would found political and social dynasties in their new home. The Barclays were among the most prominent.

The immigrants from Barbados crowded the *Cora*'s deck, relieved at last to have reached Monrovia safely, happy to leave the crowded vessel, eager to see what their new home was like. Among the throng, a young lad named Arthur hung on his father's arm, wide eyed, excitedly taking in the sights of Liberia's capital as he and his family ascended the hill on which the town stood. They could see the town's fine homes, its churches, and government buildings, and in the distance, on a rocky prominence, Liberia College—which would figure prominently in shaping Arthur's life and the republic's future.

Despite these "fine" homes and public buildings, however, Monrovia to these new arrivals still exuded an unexpected scruffy air, compared to their venerable Bridgetown, Arthur's birthplace. The heat also seemed relentless, unbroken by the cool ocean breezes they enjoyed at home. Too, on the turbulent Liberian coast, they had seen no beach that could match the beautiful beaches Barbados boasted. But, it was the promise of a better life this new land held that beckoned the West Indians to the fledging Republic of Liberia.

A precociously bright and hardworking youngster, born the tenth of twelve children on July 31, 1854, to Anthony and Sarah Barclay, Arthur sold salt to help the family. But his education was not neglected. His oldest sister, Antoinette Barclay, tutored him until he entered the Preparatory Department of Liberia College, and soon he was promoted to the Collegiate Department. Four years after receiving a bachelor of arts degree in 1873, young Barclay was back at the college as principal of the Preparatory Department. Typical of many of the immigrants who never fully abandoned their calling in the church or in education, he later served the college at various times as professor, member and president of the board of trustees, and president of the college.

During his stint as Preparatory Department principal, he began to cautiously sample politics, serving during vacations as chief clerk of the House of Representatives. Apparently, he liked the taste. Now twenty years old, Barclay landed his first official position in 1874 as private secretary to President Joseph Roberts. Three years later he became a lawyer, called to the Montserrado County bar in 1877. His law practice advanced—by 1880 he had achieved the rank of counselor of the Supreme Court—and his political career gathered momentum. President Alfred Russell appointed him judge of the Court of Quarter Sessions and Common Pleas of Montserrado County in 1883. Russell's successor, Hilary Johnson, named him the county's subtreasurer in 1885.

Before long the ambitious West Indian immigrant had become a rising star in Liberia's political firmament and a man of growing influence in the True Whig Party. In 1892, he made it into the highest levels of government, when newly elected president Joseph J. Cheeseman tapped him to be postmaster general and then secretary of state and in 1896 named him to the cabinet's prize post, secretary of the treasury. He continued in that capacity after Cheeseman died and William Coleman assumed the office. He also gained a bit of foreign experience, representing Liberia at the Chicago World's Fair in 1893 and serving on diplomatic missions to England and France in 1901.

Doubtless he had seen enough to know what he faced when he entered the mansion as president of Liberia on January 4, 1904. He, his vice president, J. J. Dosson, and his fellow Americo-Liberians found themselves in a three-way vise that seemed to grow tighter by the passing day. European imperial wolves, notably France, still prowled the frontiers, hungry for more land to devour. Wars and rebellions erupted again and again between native tribesmen and their Americo-Liberian rulers—and themselves. The government's finances teetered precariously on the edge of an abyss of total ruin. The feeble leadership during the previous dozen years—a president who died in office, followed by one who resigned in response to public outcry against his policies, and, last, a seventy-year-old ordained clergyman—left a perilous legacy.

Barclay realized that without a strong president who took timely and decisive action, Liberia might well disappear as an independent country. To stave off foreign predators, the government would have to forestall any excuse they might find to annex Liberian territory. Monrovia's colonial treatment of its native Africans provided ample fuel for uprisings that the British and French readily seized upon as invitations to intervene. The government's scarcely discernible presence in the hinterland, where tribal rule and rivalries prevailed, offered further opportunities for imperialistic mischief. Moreover, the parlous state of the government's finances, as Barclay and other leaders well knew, would force it to seek help from abroad. And that help doubtless would not come without strings.

The new president took a deep breath and headed into the threatening storm. One of the first acts of his administration extended citizenship—at least in name—to tribal people in 1904, some sixty years after the republic's founding. They didn't get the right to vote, nor a ticket to participate actively in the country's political life. In fact, most Americo-Liberians still viewed their new African "citizens" as "wild savages" and an "uncivilized population."[2] Barclay reasoned that bringing the hinterland tribal people under the government's protection as citizens would bolster Liberia's defense against further European, particularly French, incursions.[3]

The president next took steps to improve the administrative system. The Department of Interior, created in 1868 during James Payne's presidency, became the Department of Internal Affairs. In addition, a new system of "indirect rule," modeled on British colonial administration, was introduced in 1907. It relied on traditional tribal authorities to maintain law and order as an extension of the central government. These measures hopefully would quiet British and French complaints of Liberian failure to exercise "effective occupation." They did relatively little to advance the conditions of the tribal population.

The president also looked to settle unresolved border disputes that might provide fodder for imperialist cannons. Despite the 1903 joint Liberian-British commission's delineation of the Sierra Leone border, several issues remained unsettled, and difficulties with France, despite an 1892 treaty, still lingered. Periodic threats of further encroachment persisted, and tensions remained high. And the financial nut proved even harder to crack. With the government almost broke, still burdened by the 1871 British loan—which had been in default for over twenty years—the government even found itself forced to borrow money for its operations from local German firms.

—⚹—

Looking for relief, since Barclay recognized that Liberia could not rely on America, he turned to England for help. Help came in the form of Sir Harry Hamilton Johnston, colonial Africa's answer to the Renaissance man: a noted British explorer, author, botanist, zoologist, artist, and colonial administrator who spoke many African languages, had traveled widely in Africa, and served as Britain's consul general and first commissioner for Nyasaland (now modern Malawi). Although Johnston's association with Liberia, including his efforts to promote joint enterprises, covered a relatively brief time, his impact had profound consequences for the country.

The crisis Barclay faced called for bold, if risky, measures. Given the threats Britain posed over the years to Liberia's territorial integrity, and at times even to its existence—not to mention the bad taste left by the 1871 loan—that the Liberian president would entertain thoughts of any joint enterprise seemed farfetched. But, his choices were limited. And Liberians saw an opportunity to use the British as a counter to the rival French, hoping to play off one against the other. And, in the final analysis, if forced to choose, they favored British imperialism over the French brand. Better the devil whose language they understood than the one whose words they couldn't pronounce.

On a personal level, too, there were connections. Johnston's brother, Alex, wrote later that President Barclay, in fact, "was from first to last...[Johnston's] friend, and constantly consulted him." After all, Sir Harry had "special knowledge of rubber trees and vines," a particularly valuable expertise for what lay in store for the Liberian economy.[4]

Africa's Renaissance Man

Born June 12, 1858, in South London, Harry Hamilton Johnston early in life showed artistic talent and a zest for travel and the study of languages. In 1881 an extended stay in Tunis as a twenty-one-year-old artist whetted his appetite for Africa south of the Sahara—the "real" Africa. He gave up a potentially promising art career and embarked on a study of Bantu languages, the predominant ethnic and linguistic group in sub-Saharan Africa.

Johnston become more interested in international affairs and politics than a career in painting and began writing pieces for the British press. He also solidified his commitment to the empire and believed wholeheartedly in the benefits of British imperialism for the lesser races of the world.

In April 1882 he sailed with the Earl of Mayo on a shooting trip to Portuguese Angola. At the trip's conclusion, rather than return home, Harry the explorer "struck out on his own." Trudging from village to village, earning enough to subsist on by "selling pictures he painted," this youthful Englishman must have stirred much curiosity and excitement in the forlorn and isolated African villages he visited.

In Uganda "natives called him 'The Lion,'" because his eyes were of "a peculiar magnetic green."[5] Later, in the Congo, Johnston earned the nickname Spider, for his "keenness in catching insects for his scientific collections."[6] In the course of his journeys in 1883, he met explorer Henry Stanley in the Congo (he would serve as a pallbearer at Stanley's funeral in January 1904), became acquainted with Sir Richard Burton, and later would be closely associated with Cecil Rhodes. Johnston began to make a name for himself. He led a scientific mission to Mount Kilimanjaro in 1884, became the intrepid explorer, artist, and natural scientist, and soon caught the fancy of England's Victorian romantics fascinated with "darkest Africa." London society in 1885, brother Alex wrote, "was inclined to make a lion of 'Kilimanjaro Johnston.'"[7]

He also caught the attention of the British Foreign Office, which appointed Johnston vice consul in Cameroon and the Niger River delta area in October 1886 and in January 1889 Her Majesty's consul at Mozambique. Harry Hamilton Johnston, at thirty-one years of age, was a rising star.

Johnston next was appointed the first commissioner for the British Central African Protectorate (renamed the Nyasaland Protectorate in 1903.) Wearing this hat, he introduced a system of local district administration coupled with central government departments. He also found time to raise a small army and to wage war against the slave trade that still flourished in East Africa.

In this military capacity, Johnston always carried a white umbrella, even into battles. It was said "he never lowered his beloved white umbrella," despite warnings from his officers that it made him a target for enemy gunfire. He "said he feared sunstroke much more than their bullets."[8] After Johnston defeated the native chiefs who were engaged in the business, the slave trade virtually disappeared in the protectorate.

Johnston returned to England in 1896 to be gazetted a Knight of the Bath, becoming the youngest member of any British order.[9]

After stints as consul general in Tunis and special commissioner in Uganda, Johnston returned to London in September 1901.[10] He asked not to be reassigned to tropical Africa since he feared for his health (having suffered six attacks of blackwater fever while in Africa). However, he soon fell victim not to some African fever or native spear, but to Foreign Office machinations. In 1901, at the age of forty-seven, Harry Johnston resigned from government service.

After unsuccessful runs for a seat in Parliament in 1903 and 1906, Johnston took to writing novels, in addition to travel books and works on the Bantu language. He also turned his attention back to Africa, this time to Liberia in particular. He disclosed in his autobiography that Liberia had begun to interest him back in 1882, when he was sailing off the African coast. He said he "never forgot the impression of the magnificent forest rising up so close to the waves."[11] And now opportunity knocked at his door. A British entrepreneur wanted Johnston to join his group in reviving a moribund company chartered in Liberia that held a concession to exploit the country's minerals.

Liberia's natural resources by the early 1880s had become an object of European attention, driven in large part by the restless energy the scramble for Africa generated. Exploitation, though, had lagged. The nature and extent of the country's resource base was largely unknown. The "belief in Liberia's mineral wealth," as Johnston put it, was "hypothetical." True, Benjamin Anderson in his explorations described extensive deposits of iron ore, but he failed to reach the mines of "fabulous wealth" he believed existed in the vicinity of Musardu or discover the "wonderful gold mines of Buley."[12] The lack of basic infrastructure—roads and particularly ports—the absence of government control in the interior, and the consequent tribal rebellions and wars that scared off wary entrepreneurs could explain the lack of exploitation.

Nevertheless, various parties, foreign and domestic, sought to obtain concessions to exploit the country's natural resources. While rubber occupied the interest of many investors, mining held out the possibility of even greater wealth. As early as 1861, the government granted the Liberian-owned Mining Company of Liberia a charter giving it valuable mining rights. Neither the company nor its successor, the Union Mining Company, however, could raise sufficient capital to carry on operations. Foreign interests, such as French and Spanish, unsuccessfully sought concessions as well. A group of Spanish banks in 1882 offered to extend a £400,000 loan to the government at 7 percent interest for fifty years—funds that could be applied to the long-in-default British loan—in return for a concession for mining, exporting timber, and cultivating "the soil."[13] The offer, however, came to naught. Even an American group in 1889 proposed—but never actually constructed—a railroad line.[14]

Until the turn of the twentieth century, companies, particularly those locally owned, found it difficult to raise capital to exploit Liberia's natural resources. For foreign ventures, another obstacle, perhaps even more telling, was a conservative bloc of the Americo-Liberian establishment. They stoutly opposed any opening up of the country, be it internally, by incorporating the native Africans, or externally, by allowing European or American economic ventures. Allowing either, they feared, could well doom Americo-Liberian supremacy. The disastrous British 1871 loan constantly reminded them, too, of the perils of foreign loans. Closed doors—economic, political, and social—they felt, offered the best insurance, at least for Americo-Liberians. Although these doors essentially remained closed, change clearly was in the air. The legislature in 1881 opened the economic door a whit by adding three more sites to the original six designated for trading in the Ports of Entry Law.

The presidential elections in 1885 brought the issue fully into the glare of public opinion. The two candidates, Hilary R. W. Johnson, seeking reelection on the True Whig banner, and Edward Blyden, once friends and schoolmates, had become rivals. Although Jamaica-born Blyden supported opening up the country to foreign investors, he accepted the Republican Party's nomination, the party that traditionally favored the closed-door policy. Johnson, of course, won the contest hands down, 1,438 votes to Blyden's 872. The view that Liberians, rather than foreigners, must take the leading role in the country's development continued to prevail but was waning. And by the time Barclay entered on the scene, it had become acutely clear that the country must try another path. It would be the path of foreign concessions and loans.

Among the abundant stands of Liberian timber, especially African teak and mahogany, a number of different varieties of rubber grew wild. Although none of the varieties was the high-quality *Hevea brasiliensis* native to Brazil, the Liberian rubber still enjoyed a reasonable demand, particularly in Europe. As early as 1887, an English trader was purchasing rubber collected by Liberian natives for export, and two years later, three other English enterprises followed suit.[15]

An 1890 article in the *African Repository* by the ex-mayor of Monrovia captured the wildly glowing expectations many had about concessions in Africa following the award to an English company for the right to develop the Liberian rubber trade. The author foresaw concessions attracting large enterprises that would open "the whole portion of West and Central Africa...to the advantages of civilization." The company also would enable Liberia to repay the 1871 loan, in which the English entrepreneurs admitted that "some of their unworthy countrymen did not deal honestly with Liberia."[16]

The trading activities, initially limited to collecting the wild rubber in coastal areas, soon expanded into the interior as well, and in 1894 the Liberia Rubber Syndicate was born. A decade later the successor Monrovian Rubber Company began building permanent buying stations, including six in the hinterland. The government collected royalties or export duties of about eight cents per pound. Half went to the company and half to the government, supposedly to service the 1871 loan.[17]

The Liberian Rubber Corporation, a British company, next acquired the concession, and would, in 1906, open the first interior rubber plantation at Mount Barclay. It would dominate Liberia's rubber industry for much of the first decade of the twentieth century. Rubber, Johnston predicted, probably would become a principal Liberian export.[18] No one, though, not even Johnston, could foresee the impact rubber would have on the country in the hands of Firestone Tire & Rubber, an American company that had just started up on August 3, 1900, in Akron, Ohio. Ironically, Firestone would two decades later assume the Rubber Corporation's Mount Barclay plantation and ultimately expand it to become the world's largest.

> With the concession door now wide open, the rush to exploit the country's mining resources also moved into high gear. An English syndicate, headed by one Lieutenant Colonel Cecil Powney, in December 1901 purchased the Liberian charter of a defunct company and transferred it to the Union Mining Company, which in 1904 became West African Gold Concessions, Ltd. The charter conveyed potentially valuable, wide-ranging rights that, according to Benjamin Brawley's *A Social History of the American Negro*, included the sole right to prospect and obtain gold, precious stones, and all other minerals in 50 percent of the country; acquire freehold land and take leases for eighty years in blocks of ten to ten thousand acres; import machinery and other things necessary

free of duty; establish banks in connection with the mining, with the power to issue notes; construct telegraphs and telephones; organize auxiliary syndicates; and establish a police force.[19]

An English syndicate approached the now "retired" Sir Harry Johnston to enlist him as director in the Liberian Development Chartered Company and in the Liberian Rubber Corporation (successors to West African Gold Concessions, Ltd.). The latter, which would become a subsidiary of Britain's Dunlop Rubber, held a concession to develop Liberia's rubber trade. The Foreign Office, including the foreign secretary, Lord Lansdowne, encouraged Johnston to accept the positions in the two British companies. They argued persuasively that the companies had, after all, been "formed to develop the very great, but latent natural resources in rubber and minerals of Liberia."[20]

Sir Harry believed, his brother Alex recorded, that besides advancing British interests, the companies—and especially himself—could help fulfill what he believed was his duty to safeguard Liberia's independence, which he thought was "clearly threatened."[21] The Foreign Office, according to Harry, shared his fear. They believed "if no attempt was made to strengthen British commerce in Liberia, the whole of the country" would "inevitably come within the French political sphere in West Africa, since the United States" at that period had "professed—or seemed to profess indifference as to its fate."[22]

During July and August 1904, Johnston traveled the whole of Liberia, primarily looking for possible port sites (but he found the country "not possessing a single natural harbor").[23] He also met the Liberian president, who offered suggestions for strengthening the Chartered Company and outlined a scheme for rubber operations.

The company had been busy, as well, sending an expedition in 1903 to investigate the country's flora and an additional six or more teams during 1902–04 to search for minerals. Johnston noted, "Powney already had found gold and diamonds." And he himself enthused, "I returned home, convinced of the great wealth of this curious little land."[24] He agreed to become managing director of both companies. Things began to move at an accelerating pace.

The British government agreed to support measures to improve Liberia's public administration and settle the country's borders with the neighboring French and British colonies. And taking a leaf from Britain's operations in China, they consented to recognize appointment of an Englishman as controller of Liberian customs.[25] This measure would help guarantee the availability of revenue for meeting government expenses—and for servicing foreign obligations—rather than finding its way into someone's pockets. The companies' agenda, in addition, included aiding the government to secure a loan from a British financial house to help meet public expenditures and the interest payments due the long-suffering British bondholders.

Johnston returned again to Liberia in November 1905, obtained the legislature's approval of the scheme and proposed measures, and in December started back to England.

As he later wrote in his autobiography, "[At] the moment I considered I had settled the fate of Liberia on very favorable lines, and," he continued, he "should have a task of great interest in developing her resources and steering her to affluence and good government."[26] He felt pretty good about himself, but bad news intervened.

Johnston felt confident he could win a seat at home in Parliament. He campaigned in 1903 to fill the one that Lord Salisbury's death had left vacant. Despite encouraging support and a laudatory article in the *Daily Mail*, however, he was defeated—but unbowed. He planned to run again in a general election that he expected, probably in early 1906. But, as fate would have it, the contest was called for December 1905, while Harry was en route home from Liberia. Despite vigorous campaigning by his wife and friends, he lost. Johnston believed firmly that if he had not been aboard a ship on the ocean somewhere between Africa and England at that time, he would have won.

Back in Britain, more bad news. The French Foreign Office's attitude regarding Liberia, Johnston recounted, had "changed markedly" during his trip to Liberia. While the US government raised no objections to the arrangements Johnston had worked out, the German government opposed them, and the French strenuously objected. Their foreign office abruptly deferred signing the border delimitation agreement hammered out with Liberia. Instead, the French accused the government of "interfering with tribes who believed themselves under French protection." They also declared that appointing a Britisher to head the Liberian customs service and awarding the Chartered Company a concession with "such unprecedented rights and privileges" violated French interests.[27]

As far as Johnston was concerned, the French became his enemies.[28] He thought the new British foreign secretary, Sir Edward Grey, at least partly responsible for this change in attitude. Grey, in contrast to his predecessor, was "quite willing to see Liberia come under French control." Without serious British opposition, France doubtless intended to settle on its own "favorable terms."[29]

The outlook for 1906 looked bleak. Liberia's finances continued to slide. Financial help became imperative. Despite serious misgivings, a foreign loan appeared the only route that would avoid bankruptcy. Sir Harry, again with the blessing of the British Foreign Office, came to the rescue.

And the government, despite Liberia's penchant for suffering major burns when playing with foreign financing, signed an agreement with Johnston's Liberia Development Company on

January 5, 1906. The company would secure a loan for "the benefit of Liberia" through a consortium of financiers, headed by the Emile Erlanger Company of London. Barclay, Johnston, Erlanger, and a British Foreign Office official, among others, meeting in London, agreed on a loan of £100,000 ($500,000) at 6 percent interest, to be paid in $30,000 installments annually until the entire loan had been retired.[30]

Part of the loan ($25,000) would meet pressing Liberian obligations, $125,00 would pay off domestic debts, and $35,000 would go to Johnston's Liberia Development Company as a loan. The balance ($315,000) would compensate Johnston's company for developing banking and constructing roads in Liberia. His company, in addition, would receive 10 percent of any excess over $250,000 in customs revenue each year. As security for the loan, a British chief and an assistant customs inspector would be placed in charge of customs revenues. The chief inspector also would act as financial advisor to the republic. Johnston and his bosses must have smiled broadly in their refined British manner.

This also would mark Liberia's initial, but far from last, adventure involving foreign experts to help run the country. The president and his fellow Liberians must have quickly discovered these helpers all too often came as mixed blessings.

Emmett Scott, a member of the 1909 American presidential fact-finding commission to Liberia, would confide later that the first "of the so-called [customs] experts sent to Liberia under the agreement...all but confessed his utter failure, after two or three months to understand what he was about."[31] The second, Scott continued, "developed into a somewhat capable official, although his chief claim to being called an expert was, it is said, that he had successfully raised oranges in California." He "probably had never been inside of a customs" house. And their pay far exceeded the salaries of Liberian officers; even the president's salary amounted to only half of what the chief inspector received.[32]

As might be expected, friction soon developed among the parties over the customs administration's operation. But the friction proved mild compared to the Liberians' outrage over Johnston and his Liberia Development Company's performance. The company—after constructing a scant fifteen miles of road in Careysberg District, buying a small launch for the Saint Paul River, and purchasing two automobiles—announced that it had exhausted its funds. Johnston and company spent $163,882 on "an ordinary dirt road?"[33] People were incredulous, and angry.

An investigation concluded Sir Harry "repeatedly ignored" President Barclay's requests "for an accounting by his company," And "he is said to have conducted himself in a supercilious manner," expressing his surprise the president would even make such a request—particularly since he (Johnston) denied any responsibility for how the money was spent. The nearly $300,000 advanced to the Liberian Development Company—a loan from the government of $35,000 and about $160,000 for road construction—was never adequately accounted for.[34] Professor Frederick Starr judged that about $200,000 of the funds raised on the government's credit "had been frittered away on badly designed schemes."[35]

Embezzlement had become the norm. And Liberia's financial plight only worsened. Contrary to the loan's objective of lessening Liberia's financial dependency, the public debt by 1911 climbed to almost $1.4 million. Moreover, The loan had proven insufficient to pay the demands of all of Liberia's creditors, and the revenue generated by customs receipts and "head money" (taxes paid by indigenous Liberian workers who left the country to work on foreign vessels or in foreign countries) was not enough to cover the government's operations. The country's heavy reliance on exports of coffee and palm oil, whose prices fluctuated widely, exacerbated the problem. And the misuse of funds was widespread. Even the British official in charge of customs could not pay his employees. Government supplies could only be procured on credit, and at distressingly high interest rates.[36]

This time there was no Sir Harry Johnston to come to the country's rescue. Too much bad blood had been spilt, and the Liberia Development Company was practically bankrupt. Late in 1906 the Liberian legislature "revoked or annulled its concessions."[37] The British Foreign Office saved a rubber concession and secured the company's continuation, but it was only as a mere "simulacrum [image] of a Chartered Company."[38] Not surprisingly, Barclay decided to dispense with Johnston and the company's services altogether. The Liberian government, Erlanger, and the company worked out a new, tripartite agreement in 1908. The government would apply the unspent balance ($150,000) of the loan to redeem its "floating indebtedness and Treasury Notes,"[39] which included the 1871 loan bonds. (It was "high time," the president declared, that Liberia began satisfying these long-suffering creditors.)

In the midst of this financial meltdown, Barclay had to face re-election as well. His two-year term as president would end January 1, 1908. Fortunately, he ran unopposed, and voters in the May 7, 1907, election also approved lengthening the presidential term from two to four years, a proposal that had been floated unsuccessfully several times earlier. Thus, Barclay would continue in office until 1912—assuming Liberia remained on the map as an independent republic.

Repeating what happened in 1871, the loan's failure ignited widespread protest and a political crisis and instability that foreign traders and Liberia's neighbors feared threatened their own interests. Adding further to these troubles, the long-festering border quarrels with Britain and France flared up once again. Differences with Britain were relatively minor (mainly navigation on the Mano River border with Sierra Leone). But the French, despite Liberia's acceptance of the December 1892 treaty that stripped the republic of lands bordering the Ivory Coast, continued trying to squeeze more concessions from a hapless Liberia.

Hoping to allay these threats, Barclay sent F. E. R. Johnson, at that time the attorney general, and James J. Dossen, associate

Supreme Court justice, to Paris in May 1904. En route, the two stopped in London seeking aid from the British government. The Foreign Office generously offered sympathy but little else. The French didn't even offer sympathy. Barclay's next gambit, in May the following year, was to appoint Edward Blyden, the old diplomatic warhorse and acclaimed intellectual, as minister plenipotentiary and envoy extraordinary to the United Kingdom and France.

After fleeing Liberia in the wake of the Roye episode in 1871, Blyden had established residence in Freetown, Sierra Leone, where he founded and edited the *Negro* newspaper. He also undertook several official government missions in Sierra Leone as its agent of the interior. But he still continued his ties to Liberia. Between 1875 and 1884, he served as principal of Alexander High School at Harrisburg, Liberian ambassador to Great Britain, minister of the interior, and president of Liberia College. But after running unsuccessfully for Liberia's presidency in 1885, Blyden devoted himself largely to Sierra Leone, except for a brief stint in 1892 when he reprised his posting as Liberia's ambassador to Great Britain.

Meanwhile, Blyden's reputation as one of Africa's greatest intellectuals continued to flourish. He traveled extensively, especially to the United States. On his seventh, and next-to-last, visit in 1889–90, he made a two-month tour of the Deep South. Conservative whites hailed him as "the heaven-appointed medium for helping to solve the (negro) problem."[40] They no doubt welcomed his conviction that the colonization of Liberia by blacks "was the only means of delivering the coloured man from oppression and of raising him up to respectability."[41]

Blyden and Alexander Crummell, another distinguished American Liberian intellectual, were both ordained Christian ministers. In the course of their work with the indigenous

Africans and scholarly study of their cultures and languages and of Islam, Blyden came to view Islam "as better suited to the needs of the African continent" than Christianity.[42] He resigned from the Presbyterian Church (to become what he termed a "Minister of Truth") in September 1886. A decade later, he was government agent of native affairs in Nigeria, teacher in Sierra Leone, professor at Liberia College, and, finally, from 1901 to 1906, director of Mohammedan education in Sierra Leone.

―⚏―

Blyden's instructions from President Barclay were straightforward: try to negotiate a settlement with the French, but if they insisted on a border that Liberians thought violated the 1892 treaty, he was to consult the American ambassador in Paris and Lord Lansdowne in London regarding possible arbitration by the two powers.

After a time, even Blyden, his dazzling resume notwithstanding, gave up on the French intransigence and American and British reluctance to enter the dispute, resigned in September, and retreated back to his home in Sierra Leone. President Barclay tried sending Sir Harry Johnston to Paris. The French refused to recognize him as an official negotiator.

It proved no easier for F. E. R. Johnson (now secretary of state) when the president dispatched him to deal with the problem in the summer of 1907. He found the French "hostile and unfriendly."[43] The climate was little better in London. The British told him they "had no designs against Liberia, but...believed the French were planning encroachment." If, the officials continued, "Liberia lost territory to France," Great Britain "would have to take new territory adjacent to Sierra Leone in her own defense."[44]

Secretary Johnson sent a distress signal back to the president, who hurried to London on August 29. There, Barclay underlined his fears of further aggression and proposed that "Great Britain and America...jointly guarantee the independence and integrity of the Republic." The British Foreign Office, not unexpectedly, turned his request down, maintaining that if Liberia got a "settled frontier [agreement] with France, and inaugurated certain reforms," the country would face no danger. But, if it did not make these reforms, "nothing would save it from the end which threatened."[45]

Told His Majesty's government would not discuss the territorial issues until Liberia had come to an arrangement with the French, Barclay and his secretary of state headed across the channel. Their French hosts handed them the draft of a treaty—an agreement that would rob Liberia of a large strip of Liberian territory, "situated in the richest and most prosperous districts."[46] An exasperated Barclay sought out US ambassador Henry White in Paris, hoping to enlist American support. The envoy, voicing his doubts that the United States would aid Liberia in this crisis, advised Barclay to accept the treaty, no matter how distasteful. Otherwise, he opined, France would seek even more territory at Liberia's expense.[47]

Wearied and dismayed, the Liberian president finally gave in to French demands. The treaty he signed on September 18, 1907, and the subsequent 1910 boundary demarcation handed over to French possession a "vast strip of land along the Guinea and Ivory Coast borders," land to which Liberia had long held historic claims.[48] The 1907 agreement also included the threat that if Liberia could not "maintain a frontier force to protect her boundary," the French would exercise "the right to place their own forces on Liberian territory for that purpose."[49]

A final insult, Professor Liebenow adds, "came over the deceptive wording of the treaty regarding the 'right' and 'left banks' of the Cavalla River, Liberia's largest river and the French-imposed border with Ivory Coast. The "Liberians," he continued, "were tricked into accepting French control over the entire river." When the two European powers finished their predations, the African republic had been stripped "of more than a third of the hinterland" it once claimed.[50] Concluding his disappointing mission, Barclay returned to Monrovia doubtless chastened but perhaps thankful that Liberia still lived, although its reduced size of some forty-three thousand square miles made it smaller than all but a handful of other African states.

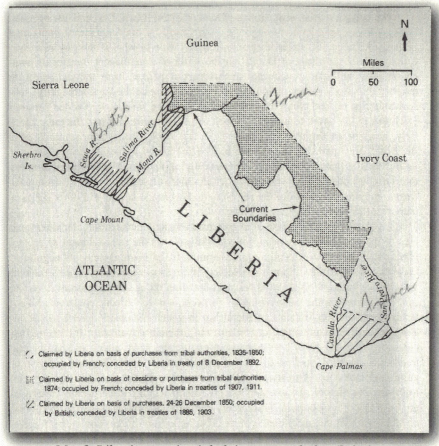

Map 3. Liberian territorial claims conceded to Britain and France. Courtesy University of Indiana Press.

Not long after Barclay returned, Great Britain's consul general to Liberia, Braithwait Wallis, sent the Liberian president a kind of "lest we forget" memorandum, a remarkably undiplomatic communication of four printed pages. The January 14, 1908, note begins, "I am directed to remind Your Excellency," so the cabinet and legislature also will know of "the vital and pressing necessity" for the reforms "His Majesty's Government" had discussed with Barclay in London. He disclaimed any British designs on Liberia's independence or territorial integrity; His Majesty's government only wanted that Liberia "should have such a stable and effective Government" that would "remove" any such danger. Without stating the obvious, he doubtless meant from France.[51] Wallis wrote that "the time had now gone by when Liberia could re-enact the part of a hermit kingdom, and that she must not lose a moment [in putting] her house in order, or be prepared at no distant date, to disappear from the catalogue of independent countries."[52]

The earlier appointment of two British customs officers had improved revenues, Wallis continued, but it was imperative to make further reforms by (a) putting the country's finances "in the hands of a European financial expert," (b) hiring at least three more European customs officers, (c) establishing an "efficient, well armed police force under competent European officers," and (d) reforming the judiciary.[53]

If the Liberian government initiated these reforms within SIX MONTHS (Wallis's capitals), the British government would be willing to help with them and would endeavor to settle the border problems. He didn't spell out the consequences if Liberia failed to follow directions. He didn't need to.[54]

Wallis ended his threatening message with the usual—and in this case particularly empty—diplomatic flourishes:

I have the honor to be, with great truth and regard,
Sir,
Your Excellency's most obedient, humble servant,
BRAITHWAIT WALLIS
His Britannic Majesty's Consul[55]

Barclay and the Liberian legislature got busy on the British demands. The legislature passed an act in 1908, establishing the Frontier Police Force, which came to be known as the Liberian Frontier Force (LFF), and later evolved into the Liberian Armed Forces. The five-hundred-man force's mission initially was to patrol the borders, keep order in the hinterland, and discourage foreign incursions.

During Barclay's visit in London, a Captain Mackay Cadell reportedly approached the president wanting to head up the frontier force that Liberia expected to organize. Although not actually hired by Barclay, Cadell, who had served in the Boer War in South Africa, showed up in Monrovia in January 1908, "ready for business." Despite opposition from many, Cadell was hired and given the rank of major, supposedly to mollify the British. He went to work, with two British assistants, building barracks on the edge of Monrovia.

Before long he had enrolled 250 men and bought uniforms, arms, and ammunition from Great Britain.[56] Suspicions began to be aroused when caps and other items came stamped with emblems of OHMS—"On His Majesty's Service"—hardly what one would expect to find on a Republic of Liberia uniform. Further investigation revealed that Cadell, in violation of Liberian law, enlisted sizeable numbers of Sierra Leonean and

British subjects, clothing "them in British uniforms with OHMS on their caps."[57]

Despite denials from Cadell, it turned out that seventy-one—probably more—of his troops were British subjects from Sierra Leone. (He was authorized to employ ten or more sergeants and buglers from Sierra Leone.) This revelation prompted France's vice consul in Monrovia to protest that the force actually constituted a "British army of occupation." Not to be outdone, he demanded an equal number of French nationals be added to it.[58]

Major Cadell proved to be more than just a thorn in President Barclay's side, constantly chafing under the president's supervision, resisting his authority. Sir Harry Johnston described him as "arrogant and condescending to the point of actually refusing to obey orders from...[Liberia's] president."[59] Finally, he proved too much, even for Barclay; the president and his cabinet agreed the British major had to go. However, rather than dismiss him outright, Barclay allowed Cadell the opportunity to resign.

In the meantime, on November 13, Consul General Wallis met with President Barclay to deliver a mysterious note, purportedly from the British government, warning that if any French subjects were appointed to direct, or even were enlisted in the frontier force, Great Britain would join with France "to disrupt and divide the Republic [of Liberia]."[60]

Cadell wasn't finished yet. The major precipitated a bizarre crisis when he announced in February 1909 that LFF soldiers who had gone unpaid planned to revolt—and, unbelievably, he would not stop it. Near panic swept through Monrovia's streets as rumors circulated of an impending coup, a gunboat lying offshore, a British occupation army ready to move. This time it proved no mere rumor. Instead of reprimanding the disobedient officer, the governor of Sierra Leone dispatched a gunboat and a detachment of West Indian troops "on the pretext of defending British lives and property."[61] American newspapers also reported the arrival at Monrovia of the gunboat and soldiers. Widespread doubt and despondency clouded the government's ability to continue its rule and even Liberia's ability to endure as a nation. Although the details remain a bit hazy, Johnston, in his autobiography, wrote that the Sierra Leone governor had gone on leave shortly after ordering the troop deployment. The acting governor, a better-informed, cooler-headed G. B. Haddon-Smith, however, countermanded the order.[62]

According to a fact-finding commission dispatched by President Roosevelt to Liberia in May 1909, Liberians believed that a plot among the British in Liberia and Sierra Leone aimed to "make it appear" Liberia was unstable and likely to fall and trigger British occupation and annexation.[63] (Some scholars, however, think the "actual existence" of a plot "more than doubtful," although many British in West Africa would have welcomed it.[64])

In any event, President Barclay refused to give in and reportedly "put down the mutiny by winning over most of the [LFF's] Liberian troops"[65] and sacking Cadell.

The American commissioners singled out the British officer for particular censure. He was found to have mismanaged funds, recruited British subjects into the force, and even to have threatened the Liberian president. "In short, he had acted as though Liberia were a British dependency and he himself superior to all Liberian law and authorities."[66] Cadell, according to Louis R. Harlan, Booker T. Washington's biographer, "possibly acted on orders from the British consul" in Monrovia.[67]

He noted, too, that the British Colonial Office, rather than the Foreign Office, had been "given control of the Liberian Frontier Force."[68] The two offices pursued different policies vis-à-vis Liberia. Where the Foreign Office "supported Liberian independence and integrity," the Colonial Office followed an "imperialist policy."[69] Cadell reportedly had served as a colonial officer in South Africa.

The commission concluded that had President Barclay not fired the British commander when he did, Liberia likely faced a classic case of gunboat diplomacy, with a "British gunboat in the harbor, a British officer in command of the frontier force and a large number of British subjects among the enlisted men, a British official in charge of the Liberian gunboat Lark [a vessel obtained through the UK government], a British regiment in the streets of Monrovia."[70] The French had added their unique Gallic contribution to the rapidly deteriorating scene by occupying a part of the Liberian hinterland, and they "reached for more." They were alarmed they claimed at the Liberian government's pro-British policies[71]

It is no wonder that Sir Harry Johnston later recounted in his autobiography: "The affairs at the opening of 1908 had got into such a condition of confusion, owing to French rapacity on the frontier and German intrigues for permission to establish great wireless stations...that I felt a strong disposition to go over to the United States, and endeavor to put before the American Government the whole situation."[72]

Johnston would be given his opportunity, and, fortunately, would find the American government he referred to a marked departure from the nineteenth-century model. It had shed its isolationist airs in favor of an active role, backed by a growing economic and military prowess, in shaping the twentieth-century world. Historians Peter Duignan and L. H. Gann described the change as "a veritable revolution...in American attitude toward the rest of the world following 1898, the year of the Spanish-American War."[73] And the hero of that war and symbol of this new era? Theodore Roosevelt—"Rough Rider," international activist, world traveler, explorer—who now occupied the White House. He had a personal interest in Africa, and his much-publicized 1909–10 expedition and book, *African Game Trails*, would kindle widespread public interest in the continent—and Liberia.

President Barclay, too, was sufficiently alarmed to try the United States once again. In May 1908 he dispatched still another commission, this one made up of ex-president Gibson, Vice President James J. Dossen, and attorney Charles B. Dunbar, to Washington to "plead for American financial and diplomatic assistance."[74] (They also would call in at Berlin to seek German support to protect Liberia from British and French territorial threats, and for replacing the British customs administrators, whose work had "caused much dissatisfaction.")[75]

America's most distinguished Negro figure at that time, Booker T. Washington, acted as host to the Liberian group, arranging accommodation at a white hotel, travel by train, and meetings with US officials in the State Department, as well as with President Roosevelt and the Republican Party nominee to succeed Roosevelt, William Howard Taft. Washington had laid the groundwork for the meetings, telling the president that Liberia needed "substantial American assistance."[76]

Roosevelt and Secretary of State Elihu Root listened to the Liberians with keen interest. They decided the United States must come to the aid of its African offspring. (Roosevelt would dispatch a fact-finding commission to Liberia to investigate and report back. He also urged Britain to cooperate with the United States in maintaining the status quo in Liberia until measures could be worked out to deal with the country's straits.

In a July 23, 1908, message to the US secretary of state, the British Ministry for Foreign Affairs insisted that Britain "had no designs" on Liberia's independence or integrity. The British advisors helping reorganize the country's customs and frontier police came at Liberia's request. Since there was no room for additional help in those two areas, the United States might look to possibly assist in other branches of the government. The message concluded that it appeared "the main risk to the future of Liberia" arose "from the inefficiency of...their own officers" in "administration...especially in...finance." If the author had included "corruption" as well as "inefficiency," the warning would have better pinpointed the sources of most of Liberia's woes—past, present, and future.[77]

Scarcely had the Liberians departed for home when Sir Harry Johnston appeared at the White House front door. Prior to becoming president, Roosevelt had become interested in Johnston's writings. When Roosevelt happened to meet one of Sir Harry's sisters who was visiting the United States, she told him her brother would gladly come to Washington to discuss African affairs with him. The president issued an invitation. And now, the autumn of 1908 found the renowned Africanist admiring the changing colors of the trees in Lafayette Square across Pennsylvania Avenue as he was escorted into the White House.

Johnston also met with the US secretary of state, Elihu Root, to discuss the Liberian crisis, including possibly replacing British with American control of the customs, settling the frontier dispute with France, and the absorption of the two British companies into a larger American undertaking. During the course of his visit, Johnston would tour (in addition to Washington, DC) New York, Philadelphia, Atlanta, the Tuskegee Institute in Alabama, and Latin America. The state dinners, interesting people, and other diversions proved heady for Harry. He was euphoric.

And now, topping it all, meeting the president of the United States, about whom he wrote, "I think I have never spent my time with any man more interesting [than Theodore Roosevelt]. He knew the things on which he spoke, yet by no means monopolized the conversation, either at banquets, at cosy meals, or in those retired duologues."[78]

―⚞―

Johnston's visit proved timely. It reinforced President Roosevelt's decision to aid the beleaguered African republic. Newspapers on February 12, 1909, reported the State Department had received a cable from Monrovia advising there was "great despondency" about the government's ability "to maintain itself and as to the future of Liberia as a nation." Further, a "British gunboat" had arrived to provide "protection to foreign interests and a company of soldiers...sent from Sierra Leone...for the same purposes."[79]

The month before, in January 1909, Secretary Root asked the president to request $20,000 from Congress for the commission's expenses. He underlined that the "condition of Liberia... [was] really serious"; it was very difficult "to control the native tribes or to conduct its own government in accordance with modern requirements." Root noted how the bordering French possessions and Britain's Sierra Leone were "continuously complaining" about Liberia's failure to maintain order. He cautioned that there was "imminent danger that the Republic," unless it received "outside assistance," would "not be able to maintain itself very long." Root surprisingly added, "Liberia is an American colony."[80]

The proposed commission would offer Roosevelt an opportunity to show off America's developing military might and act as a warning to the European colonial powers and to dissident African Liberians. To demonstrate this resolve, he dispatched no less than three cruisers, the USS *Birmingham*, *Chester*, and

Salem, a squadron more powerful than anything the Europeans had in Africa's waters, to transport the three-man commission. In addition to the commissioners—Roland Post Falkner, Dr. George Sale, and Emmitt J. Scott, a respected black educator and private secretary to Booker T. Washington—the entourage included George A. Finch, secretary to the commission; Major Percy M. Ashburn, medical consultant, who was a US Army specialist on tropical diseases and public health; Captain Sydney A. Cloman, military consultant; and Frank Abial, a specialist on African affairs.

Philander C. Knox, who had replaced Root at the State Department when Taft became president, laid out the terms of reference in a letter to the commissioners: They should address (1) border disputes and government's failure to control native tribes and keep order; (2) organization of the frontier police force and the preference of Liberians to employ "citizens or subjects of a Government that is not territorially interested"; (3) reorganization of fiscal affairs; (4) assistance to postal, education, and agricultural departments; (5) the judicial department; and (6) keeping open the possibility of future immigration to Liberia.[81]

The American delegation arrived aboard the USS *Chester* in Monrovia on May 8, 1909. Much to the disappointment of expectant Liberians, only the *Chester* steamed in. Another cruiser, the *Birmingham*, arrived five days later, having had to stop at Cape Verde Islands for repairs to her boilers. The *Salem* failed to show at all. (So much for Roosevelt's display of American naval might.) After a busy month, the commissioners completed their report, despite their complaints that the attention lavished upon them and the many social invitations they received interfered with their work.

The government, which cooperated heartily, offered fourteen suggestions for inclusion in the report. What they added up to was a remarkable request that the United States in effect virtually take over running their country. They included guaranteeing Liberia's independence and integrity; liquidating foreign and domestic debt by "taking over control of its financial and customs administration" long enough to "effect a reorganization" under US experts; supervising the organization of the police and the frontier force under American officers; using US good offices to secure "equitable execution" of the border agreements with Great Britain and France; and having American warships visit Liberia yearly or more often.[82] Of course, not all of the government's suggestions made it into the report.

The commission members concluded that while Liberia was not bankrupt, it was in serious jeopardy from mismanagement and the threat of further encroachment by both of its colonial neighbors, Britain and France. The French, "in pursuit of their policy of building up a great West African Empire...have been a thorn in the side of Liberia." And, as far as the British were concerned, despite the protestations of their foreign office that "Great Britain has no designs on Liberian territory," the acts of her officials in Sierra Leone suggested the contrary.[83]

They concluded, though, that the threat European colonialism posed was not as great as Liberia's chaotic economy and inadequate public administration. According to their report, the country imported most commodities, including food, while trade, industry, and agriculture languished.

The commissioners recommended that the US government help Liberia reorganize its finances and negotiate territorial settlements with European governments. However, they firmly recommended against US guarantees of Liberian independence or territorial integrity, upholding instead the traditional US policy of avoiding anything that might smack of an alliance. Liberia named an American to supervise the treasury, and Britain and

France accepted US proposals to resolve border disputes. To prop up the government's near collapse financially, the delegation also recommended the United States extend financial aid to the government while assuming control of Liberian customs to insure repayment.[84] The commission also recommended American investment in agriculture and in developing the hinterland and assistance in providing facilities for technical education. The Liberian government, however, did not favor any foreign involvement in the hinterland, and the recommendations regarding agriculture and education never gained support.

William Howard Taft, who succeeded Roosevelt as president in 1909, acted on the commission's report but opted for arranging private financing and establishing control over Liberian finances through private banks. To avoid charges by the European powers, particularly France, of American imperialism (a Paris newspaper, *Petit Bleu*, for example, carried an article in 1910 entitled "American Imperialism Even More Threatening for Europe," which the US ambassador forwarded to the State Department), it was decided to enlist them as financiers. The French agreed, provided that they were guaranteed equal commercial opportunities, the Liberian government ratify the border agreements, and a French physician be appointed Director of Hygiene in Monrovia. The British and Germans also agreed, provided there was adequate provision for maintaining their economic interests.[85]

Negotiations soon began for a multinational loan sponsored by American banks. The Liberian government appointed Falkner, the American commission's head, its financial representative and negotiator. A multilateral receivership for customs was created, and an American, Reed Page Clark, appointed general receiver, with full authority to administer the country's treasury. French, German, and British receivers would assist him. The receivership (which lasted until 1926) would control Liberia's customs and tax receipts earmarked for repaying the loan.

Negotiations dragged on, slowed by European reticence and complicated by an incident on the Sierra Leonean border involving the Liberian Frontier Force. Grebo clans in 1910 rebelled and even appealed to the British governor of Sierra Leone to proclaim a protectorate over them. The natives cited specifically the depredations committed by this abominable force—the Liberian Frontier Force.

Finally, in 1912, a consortium of American and European financial institutions agreed to a loan of $1.7 million, at 5 percent interest, maturing in forty years. The purpose, according to the loan agreement, was to adjust "the indebtedness of the [Liberian] Republic" and to settle "claims or concessions." The "eventual balance of the proceeds" to be "used for productive purposes." With the loan, the government would manage to at last pay off the $900,000 or so in principal and accrued interest on the 1871 and 1906 loans.[86]

—⁂—

The Germans, before the loan actually materialized, however, almost derailed it. Frustrated in their inability to find a suitable niche for their imperialist aspirations in Liberia, they seized upon a relatively minor incident. One September night in 1912, "someone, presumably a Liberian, threw stones at some foreigners in Monrovia." By the time news of the attack circulated in Europe, it had been blown out of proportion "into a riot endangering the lives of all foreigners in Monrovia." The town was "torn by riots" the government could not subdue. Given these alarming reports, the bankers, not surprisingly, hesitated to move ahead with the loan.[87]

The American chargé d'affaires in Monrovia deflated the exaggerated accounts, opining that the "rumors had been started deliberately by German merchants." Another incident, a minor uprising at River Cess, which the government had easily put down, had, he reported, been "instigated by Germans in that region."[88] The German government, nonetheless, seized upon the incidents, and, sensing an opportunity to intervene, ordered a cruiser to Monrovia. A few days before the *Bremen* arrived, a German gunboat, the *Panther*, steamed into the harbor. Ironically, it was the same *Panther* that a year earlier precipitated an international crisis at Agadir, a small port on the Moroccan coast. It had been sent there allegedly to protect German interests threatened by French expansion.

President Barclay and Secretary Johnson feared the worst. According to one source, Germany also complained that a Liberian officer "deliberately insulted a German naval officer." Kaiser Wilhelm's officers demanded a "full apology" from Liberia, dismissal of the officer, and a "guarantee never to employ him again."[89] According to Duignan and Gann, while the statement could not be documented, "there can be little doubt that the German Empire would have welcomed an excuse," apparently any excuse, "to intervene in Liberia."[90]

This time the United States moved to counter the German threat. Secretary of State Philander Knox instructed the American ambassador in Berlin to "make it clear…that in view" of the consideration accorded Germany's position from the beginning of the negotiations with Liberia, the United States "feels justified" to expect Germany to have a "patient and liberal attitude."[91] To Liberia's relief, the threat from German imperialism before long became lost in the gathering clouds of an approaching world war.

One of the loan's key conditions required that Liberia reform its fiscal and domestic policies. Not an easy task at best, and made especially difficult when complicated by multilateral overseers who often found agreeing even on trivialities difficult. For example, after agreeing that Clark, the chief receiver, would be located in Monrovia, the British and German governments balked at the agreed-upon authority given the American chief receiver to assign their receivers to their stations. (The European receivers, as former consular officers, felt it beneath them to have an American who lacked any diplomatic rank give them orders.) Although ludicrous, the wrangling persisted until the United States instructed Clark to assign the receivers to posts of their choosing.

As another outcome of the commission's report, the United States agreed to sell arms to Liberia and to reorganize and command the frontier force. The American government assigned three black US Army officers to advise, train and command the reequipped LFF. After arriving in Liberia on May 1, 1912, they worked unofficially under the supervision of Major Charles P. Young, the US military attaché in Monrovia.

Liberia's Military

From the very first, the American-Liberian settlers faced threatening attacks from hostile natives. In defense, Jehudi Ashmun in August 1822 formed a militia of all able-bodied males from among the tiny group. The colony relied largely on hastily formed "home guard," units augmented mainly by American assistance. By 1846, the size of the militia had grown to two regiments. After independence, the republic struggled to deal with a near-continuous series of wars, rebellions, and disorders with and among the various tribes. The interior hinterland and borders were particularly vulnerable.

In response to threats of British and French intervention, the government undertook to organize the hinterland and establish effective control there. The French in 1907 threatened that they would intervene with their own forces if Liberia couldn't field "a frontier force to protect her boundary."[92] The British government echoed the call for a constabulary of some kind to guard the border and preserve order. The Arthur Barclay regime responded by creating the Liberian Frontier Force (LFF) on February 6, 1908 to patrol the borders—and more important—prevent disorders in the hinterland that invited intervention.[93]

The record of the LFF was checkered. As the agency for tax collection and the enforcer of government fiat, it understandably commanded little popularity among the tribal people. Although effective in putting down disturbances in the border areas, its conduct proved so undisciplined and its tactics so ruthless they stirred up unrest. Most Americo-Liberians shunned such unpleasant duties as extracting forced labor so that recruits came mainly from the various tribes. The Krahn tribal people became an important source of men for the force. (One would lead the coup that made him Liberia's first indigenous African ruler.)

The Treasury unfortunately could not regularly pay the expenditures involved. Therefore the unpaid and poorly supplied soldiers lived on their own from what they could steal and extort. They might collect annual hut taxes several times a year, depending on the requirements of troops in a given area. Corrupt district commissioners used the LFF to raid and pillage villages and steal livestock. They employed troops under their authority to round up men for forced labor on roads and government farms and for porterage. Reports of abduction of women by soldiers were common. In 1910 the Grebo clans rebelled and even appealed to the British governor of Sierra Leone to proclaim a protectorate over them, citing specifically the depredations committed by "this execrable force."

Responding to the 1909 commission's recommendation Liberians asked specifically that Lieutenant Benjamin O. Davis be assigned to reorganize and command the LFF. Davis at that time was one of a handful of black officers in the regular army and the US military attaché in the American legation in Monrovia. Davis, though relatively young and junior, had acquired valuable experience serving in the Spanish-American War and the Philippines. In his attaché assignment, he had become highly knowledgeable about Liberia. Though he was considered a wise choice for the assignment, the War Department turned down the request since it could find no legal authority that would enable the department to second Davis (who, incidentally would rise to become the US Army's first black general) to the Liberian government.

Instead the US government in 1912 assigned three black US Army officers to advise, train and command the reequipped LFF: Dr. Wilson Ballard, who received the rank of LFF major, and Arthur A. Brown and Richard H. Newton, both captains. They reported unofficially to Major Charles P. Young, the US military attaché in Monrovia. Combat veteran of the Indian wars, the war with Spain, and the Filipino insurrection, and a military attaché in Haiti, Young was "known as a man of unusual tact, steel determination, and tireless energy, who maintained discipline with a firm hand and was respected by his subordinates as well as his superiors."[94]

Born in 1864 to former slaves, Young, the third African American to graduate from West Point, had already racked up an impressive record in the Philippines and as the military attaché in Haiti. (After completing his stint in Liberia, he later would gain even greater renown in Pershing's 1916 Mexican expedition and World War I. He returned, as a colonel, for a second tour of duty in Liberia, where he died January 8, 1922, while on a reconnaissance mission in Lagos, Nigeria.

The LFF would show its mettle under American command in crushing the Kru revolt of 1915, in which rebel forces were decimated and ringleaders captured and hanged. The force would also reveal a troubling appetite for corruption, extortion, brutality, and abuse of residents, especially in its enforcement of the hut tax.

The LFF's ability to continue operating there despite the loathing it generated among the tribal people lay in the government's policy of recruiting its officers almost exclusively from the Americo-Liberian population or from the tribal elite who enjoyed firm links to the Americo-Liberian ruling class. Appointed on the basis of patronage, they had no motivation to change the status quo. The tribal people in the ranks also had little incentive. The authority of a uniform coupled with the "carte blanche opportunity to exploit the community" in which they were stationed "more than compensated" for their low pay. For obvious reasons the LFF segregated the men tribally and followed a policy of not posting men to their home areas.[95]

In 1962 the Liberia Frontier Force became the Liberian National Guard (part of what is now known as the Armed

Forces of Liberia) and turned over its ordinary police functions to the National Police Force. Its military structure gradually evolved "along more professional lines and modernized in many respects." An American officer-training program contributed to a "rising emphasis on efficiency and technical performance." Nevertheless, the "enlisted ranks—five or six thousand strong—were not regarded as an efficient fighting force" and enjoyed only "low esteem in the minds of politicians, journalists, and scholars alike." Even the Americo-Liberian military brass and tribal communities, according to Professor Liebenow, viewed the military "with contempt."[96]

The Americo-Liberian establishment—to their later regret—saw little threat to their rule from the military. The growing unrest among the military stemming from the government's illegal use of military forces to quell civil disturbances, the failure of national guard troops (who "sympathized with the plight of their own relatives and friends") to fire on demonstrators in the 1979 rice riots, and alleged plots by senior military officers should have raised a warning flag. But the most serious threat, even more widely ignored (and not only by Liberians), was the mounting dissatisfaction of the enlisted tribal soldiers with the gap between their lives and those of their officers and the Americo-Liberian society at large. The miserable hovel that served as quarters for Sergeant Doe, his wife, and four children—"a roofless hovel the size of a toolshed, with no door, no plumbing, a dirt floor, and windows without glass"—provided a visible exclamation point to this disparity. It became a symbol of Liberia's "revolution."[97]

As his twelve years in the anything but comfortable president's chair wound down, Barclay must have breathed more than just a sigh in relief. He and his administration had been buffeted from beginning to end by financial disaster, tribal violence, and European predations—all of which threatened to bring the republic crashing down. Only a man of Barclay's ability and perseverance, aided, of course, by the rivalry among the Europeans themselves, could have enabled the country to survive, despite the loss of much of its territory—and a substantial part of its sovereignty.

Barclay had won election in 1904 on the slogan "Internal Development."[98] Determined to open up the country, he had attacked the "closed door" policy in his initial inaugural address. He reminded his fellow Americo-Liberians that "Liberia was purchased for us [the Americo-Liberians] from its native inhabitants by Europeans," (the name given to Americans as well as to Europeans). Further, "the colony was founded by Europeans... and its expenses paid by" their money. The president went on to lambaste the 1865 Ports of Entry Law, which he claimed was probably passed "at the dictation of Liberian traders, then all-powerful with the electorate." He concluded with the warning that Liberians could only save and develop" their hinterland "by the help of the European trader."[99] Barclay did manage to nudge the Liberian door ajar. But, despite his best efforts, he could not muster sufficient legislative support to fully achieve his goal. That would have to wait more than three decades or so.

One way to attract the capital and expertise Liberia needed, he knew, was to award concessions to foreign investors. As the country (and Barclay) would discover, this machinery did not always work to the benefit of its citizens as a whole. But it would stimulate economic growth, though this was growth that an American university team of experts would later term "Growth Without Development."

Barclay also introduced measures to blunt the threat of imperialistic dismemberment. He managed to resolve the long-standing border disputes with Liberia's British and French colonial neighbors, although at a high cost in territory. To undercut complaints about the lack of peace and order in the hinterland, due to the government's failure to exercise "effective occupation," Barclay oversaw the creation of the Liberian Frontier Force and introduced an administrative system, termed "indirect rule," into the interior. He extended citizenship (though without the right to vote in 1904) to tribal natives. [100]He hoped these measures would still the natives' readiness to wage war against the government, Americo-Liberian settlers, or their fellow tribesmen. But serious tribal uprisings still marred his time as president. And the threat of European encroachment still lingered.

Barclay, like most of the leaders who came before him—and after—struggled unsuccessfully to crack the Liberian financial nut. The foreign loans he obtained and the foreign financial experts he enlisted, or was obliged to enlist, proved no lasting solution. In fact, they usually added to the problem. Interestingly, Barclay was mindful of the toxic futility of foreign loans. He was quoted in 1909 to the effect that loans would not help Liberia "unless they be invested in reproductive works, likely to lead to a large increase in revenues, through the development of the country." Such was seldom the case in Liberia. Moreover, he continued, if "obtained purely to assist the revenues by increasing receipts they are simply ruinous, and will augment, not ease, the financial strain."[101] He learned this lesson the hard way.

To raise domestic revenues, Barclay introduced a tax in 1910 on individual dwellings occupied by indigenous people. This toll, known as the "hut tax," infuriated natives, particularly in the hinterland, and added relatively little income to the government's coffers. Besides the hut tax, the government during this period depended primarily on revenue from duties on Liberia's principal exports: coffee, palm oil, palm kernels, piassava, rice, sugarcane, and timber. Meanwhile, the public debt continued to climb. By 1910, it had reached $1.3 million, of which almost $1 million was owed on the 1871 and 1906 foreign loans.[102]

Yet, on balance, there can be little argument over whether Arthur Barclay served Liberia well. His administration marked a turning point in Liberia's history. The decades-old conflict between mulattoes and blacks ended; indigenous Africans became citizens, if not voters; he introduced indirect rule and the Liberian Frontier Force and improved administration. (His "hut" tax, of course, angered the country's tribal people.) Barclay also sought to open the country's "closed door" by repealing the 1865 Ports of Entry law, entering into concession agreements, attracting international loans and revoking restrictions on owning real estate. The Naturalization Act of 1876 was repealed, and the four-year waiting period for "alien" Africans to obtain citizenship was reduced to one year.

> The constitution that established the republic in 1847 stipulated "none but persons of color shall be admitted to citizenship" (Article V, Section 13) and restricted ownership of real estate to citizens (Article V, Section 12). The 1907 amendment replaced "persons of color" with "Negroes or persons of negro descent" (thereby opening ownership of real estate to non-Liberian citizens). The Naturalization Act of 1876 also was repealed in 1907. The old act required "alien" Africans to spend at least four years in the republic before they could be granted citizenship. The naturalization period was reduced to one year. The restrictive act had been passed during the second administration of President Payne, when the "closed door" Republican Party dominated Liberian politics.[103]

Arthur Barclay only began the process (the Ports of Entry law remained on the books until his descendant, Edwin Barclay, became president), but his efforts earned him the sobriquet "father of the open door." Finally, and, most important, the Republic of Liberia, although a bit reduced in size, still remained on the world's map, one of Africa's only two independent countries.

Although he bade farewell to the President's House, Barclay did not abandon his career in public service. He served in several subsequent administrations as secretary of state, treasury, war, and interior, as president of his old alma mater, Liberia College, during 1914–17, and as Liberia's representative on the League of Nations' three-member committee investigating the country's forced labor scandal at the end of the 1920s and early 1930s. Liberia's fifteenth president died at home in Monrovia July 10, 1938.

Edward Wilmot Blyden, after his failed mission in France and Britain, retired in 1906 to his Sierra Leone home. He continued to struggle with health problems—"weak eyes" and a "disordered liver," among others—and at eighty years of age, died February 7, 1912. A renowned figure worldwide, whom many consider one of Africa's greatest nineteenth-century intellectuals, Blyden is credited, along with Alexander Crummell and Orishatuke Faduma (W. J. Davies), with providing the "main inspiration for the various Back-to-Africa" movements that arose in the late nineteenth and twentieth centuries.[104]

He strongly supported colonization as a means of "regenerating" the "negro race." His pan-African and pan-Negro philosophy influenced most of the continent and beyond. Blyden was a pioneer in developing west African cultural nationalism; he promoted the establishment of an independent African church and was a tireless advocate for creating a west African university.

His arrival in Africa, in the opinion of one admirer, "infused Liberian life not only with a flamboyant public figure but with an intellectual of much more than Liberian, or even West African stature."[105] A biographer called him "the greatest nineteenth century black intellectual." A historian "termed him an 'African celebrity.'"[106]

Edward Wilmot Blyden died almost penniless and was buried at the Freetown Race Course Cemetery.

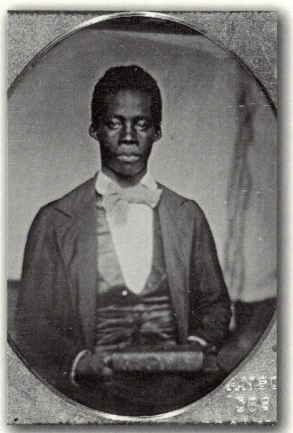

Edward Wilmot Blyden holding a book. Prints and Photographs Division, Library of Congress LC---USZ6-1944

After Liberia, Sir Harry Hamilton Johnston busied himself in writing. His forty books, most written after 1906, included a massive two-volume tome titled *Liberia*, an autobiography, and works ranging from a biography of David Livingstone to treatises on Bantu, histories, and four novels, which he only began writing when he was sixty years old. One, entitled *Mrs. Warren's Daughter*, deals with the suffragette movement in Britain. Although he was largely forgotten as "Kilimanjaro Johnston," some of his novels apparently were best sellers.

Johnston lacked a commanding presence that would match his character. Photographs show a somewhat delicate-featured, gentle man, perhaps of average or slightly less than average height, but sporting the standard-issue British colonial mustache. One political journalist (presumably not a Johnston supporter) during a political campaign wrote of "his vigorous little body, made taut by mountaineering," and a voice that lacked "depth and organic volume."[107] His brother thought him tactless, and, although a supporter of women's suffrage, given to caricaturing women. He quotes a lady neighbor's summation of a discussion with Harry about religion: "His trouble seems to be regret that he is not God."[108] But few could deny his ascendant role in virtually all things African in the decades preceding the First World War.

In 1925 Johnston suffered two strokes. He died August 31, 1927, at Woodsetts House in Nottinghamshire. One of his funeral wreaths, in recognition of his Liberian sojourn, bore the following: "A tribute of the deepest respect from the President of Liberia." No UK government official attended at graveside. A plaque in the church of Saint Nicholas in Poling, West Sussex, where he is buried, extols him as an "administrator, soldier, explorer, naturalist, author, and painter." Attesting to his exploits as a naturalist, a rare species of the giraffe family he discovered in the Congo's densest forest—the Okapi—is named *Okapia johnstoni*. Alex summed up his brother's contributions: "Not content with adding some four hundred thousand square miles to the [British] Empire, he added greatly to our knowledge of its territories."[109]

During this first decade of the twentieth century, each of these remarkable figures left his own indelible mark on Liberia, and on the course of Liberia's history. Arthur Barclay, in addition to his rich life of public service, left the country still another legacy. His family, according to Liebenow's extensive study of family linkages within the Liberian establishment, probably had the "greatest resiliency on the national scene." It included "two presidents, several justices of the Supreme Court, and a host of diplomats, legislators, and cabinet members," not to mention the wife of President William V. S. Tubman (1944–71).[110]

CHAPTER 14

One for the Record Book

—⚘—

JANUARY 1 AND 2, 1912. It was a sight never before seen in Monrovia. The streets awash in color. Some two thousand natives—Grebo, Kru, Mandingo, Kpelle, Krahn, Bassa, even Mano, Gio, Krahn, and nearly half a dozen others, chiefs, headmen, retainers, and tribesmen—crowding into downtown. Clusters of Americo-Liberians in their formal black attire almost lost in the colorful landscape, as if coveys of blackbirds had mistakenly alighted midst a giant colony of tropical plumage.

All watched the proceedings with keen interest and listened intently to the speakers, especially the newly elected sixteenth president of Liberia, Daniel Edward Howard. It was the first inauguration Liberia's native chiefs or their tribesmen ever attended. In his address, the president, fluent in a number of native languages,[1] stressed agriculture and education, and talked of giving the tribesmen "equal rights."

When, on the second day, Howard and his vice president, Samuel George Harmon, "donned attire similar to that worn by the native chiefs," the crowd erupted in boisterous approval. According to an observer, "the incident occasioned much good feeling." The same observer noted, "They talked nothing but peace and prosperity, and promised to do all in their power to make the new administration a highly successful one."[2]

The gods, apparently, had at last smiled on Liberia. All pointed to a brighter future. How could they have been so wrong?

—⚊ɯ⚊—

Daniel Howard seemed to be the right man for the job. Born in the town of Buchanan, Grand Bassa County, on August 4, 1861, he worked his way up through the civil service to become secretary of the True Whig Party. Someone thought him a "natural leader of men. Frank, honest, and decisive, he may be truly described as the Mark Hanna of Liberian politics." With his fluency in native languages, Howard had proved very influential with the indigenous population.[3]

But the inauguration huzzahs had scarcely died out when later in the year, the Kru at River Cess once more rebelled against the trading restrictions imposed by the Ports of Entry law. The Buchanan-area Bassa (a related tribe) soon joined the fray, burning several villages along the coast. Then, in 1913, several tribal communities living along the border with Sierra Leone, sparked by the despised hut tax and the notorious Liberia Frontier Force's abusive tactics, revolted against the government. Although quelled by American-led detachments of the frontier force, the threat of rebellion still smoldered.

In the fall of 1915, the Kru people along Liberia's coast, also inflamed by the hut tax and the LFF's predations and sensing the government's precarious position, launched a more serious threat to the Americo-Liberian hegemony. Declaring themselves British subjects, they asked for protection and demanded that Great Britain annex the area. Reportedly they hoisted the Union Jack in at least eight villages.[4]

When the 1915 rebellion broke out, Monrovia urgently called upon the United States in August for a naval vessel "as a moral aid in assisting the Government" in preserving order among "the restless and disaffected coastal tribes."⁵ In response, Washington radioed the cruiser USS *Chester*, then en route to Turkey, to alter its course and head for Liberia. Its stores included five hundred rifles and 250,000 rounds of ammunition purchased from the US government for delivery to Liberia. Awaiting the US warship's arrival, Great Britain unexpectedly offered the services of the HMS *Highflyer* then anchored at Monrovia. Taken aback, and questioning British motives (and concerned about preserving Liberian neutrality), the government turned down the offer with thanks.⁶

The *Chester* arrived on November 8, and after taking aboard a Liberian commission of inquiry and a "strong detachment of the Frontier Force," sailed down the coast to the scene of the uprising. Richard C. Bundy, the American chargé d'affaires in Monrovia, dispatched a message from shipboard on November 23 to Washington saying that negotiations for settling the conflict had collapsed and fighting had begun. A week later he reported the port of Sinoe had been taken and reopened, with a loss of two soldiers and twenty tribesmen.⁷

The belligerent Kru fighters surrendered, their ringleaders were captured and hanged, and the rebellion ended. Under American command the LFF had showed its mettle. Bundy denied Kru rebel charges that landing parties from the *Chester* participated in the fighting.⁸ The ship finally left Liberian waters in the latter part of March 1916. Subsequently, a United States naval officer assigned to investigate the incident reported that heavy taxation and the petty tyranny of Liberian authorities and appointed clan chiefs largely provoked the revolt. His report also criticized the Liberian government for failing to make reforms it had promised in its relations with tribal Africans.

Not surprisingly, protests against government authority would continue in subsequent years. Many villages along the coast would be deserted as tribal people fled into the interior.[9] Other tribal Liberians became restive as well. From 1913 to 1916 there were no less than seven conflicts of varying intensity between the tribal Liberians and Americo-Liberians.

The Liberian government, even in the organized areas on the coast, had difficulty enforcing its sovereignty over tribal groups that refused to accept its authority. The country's vast interior posed an even greater challenge. As early as 1869, the government created a cabinet-level Department of the Interior to administer native African affairs in the area it termed the "hinterland," the region that lay outside the four organized counties and two districts. In his 1868–69 and 1874 expeditions to the interior, Benjamin Anderson had already started securing treaties in which various chiefs submitted themselves to Monrovia's authority. However, the lack of funds limited any serious government effort to establish "effective control." (To colonial powers, legitimate claims to new territory required "effective occupation," meaning governance of it.)[10]

The Americo-Liberians' first real step toward imposing effective control over the region came in 1907. President Arthur Barclay introduced a system of "indirect rule," which had been employed by the British in India and various parts of Africa. In the system the government administered tribal areas through familiar traditional rulers.

Indirect Rule

Under indirect rule, each of sixteen designated tribal clusters was placed under the supervision of a paramount chief appointed by the central government. Essentially artificial, this structure separated many related clans and introduced divisions that had not been present before, thus thwarting the rise of potentially threatening alliances. The government's ability to impose the system and secure the acquiescence of the chiefs speaks more to the fragmentation of the tribes and their traditional rulers at that time than to the government's military and administrative prowess.

For administrative purposes, the system divided the hinterland into five districts, supervised overall by a commissioner general, who, in turn, reported to the secretary of the interior. A district commissioner in charge of each district oversaw the chiefs and looked after government interests. He also advised the paramount chiefs, represented the government before the tribal customary court, and decided cases in which customary usage conflicted with Liberian law. The officer's principal duties, however, consisted of collecting taxes, supplying contract labor from his district, and preventing incursion by foreigners. Tax collections covered district administrative costs, and although the government in Monrovia reportedly only received a relatively small percentage of the hut taxes collected, they still accounted for nearly one-third of its total revenues. The hinterland districts did not receive any government-supplied services, including schools.

The government expected chiefs, in discharging their duties, to follow local customs as customary law, provided they did not conflict with Liberian statute law or the public interest. Liberian law, for instance, prohibited slavery, which, in various shapes, indigenous Africans had long accepted. In 1912 the Liberian government adopted a separate uniform legal code, the Hinterland Regulations. These laws applied to tribal Africans living in the five districts, as well as to those living in the coastal counties.

Monrovia recognized the existing indigenous political units—mostly petty chiefdoms comprising only a few villages—as legal entities. These entities, which the government called clans, were essentially geographic and did not necessarily correspond to the traditional local political groupings. In addition, a number of them—each under a chief—were combined into larger areas through familiar traditional rulers who were co-opted into the government. In practice, however, Monrovia disregarded hereditary rulers, replacing them first with elected chiefs and later with chiefs appointed directly by the government.

The government looked upon these clans and chiefdoms as comprising a limited number of recognized tribes. The law recognized individual indigenous Africans as corporate members of their respective groups rather than as individual citizens of Liberia. The chiefs spoke for their subjects. Land belonging to a clan was owned communally but allocated to individual clan members. It could be alienated only with the agreement of the chief.

Although several chiefs, representing their respective tribal groups, were elected to the Liberian legislature, the political system actually operated to deny tribal Africans full citizenship. Only by renouncing his tribal affiliation and assimilating into Americo-Liberian culture and society could a native African participate fully in the country's political life. As a consequence, the system only helped widen the gap between Americo-Liberians and indigenous Africans.

—⋙—

While the outbreak of the First World War in 1914 ended any immediate threat to Liberian sovereignty from the European colonialists, it would take "its toll on the economy of a country already devastated by internal strife, mismanagement and, gross official corruption."[11] A beleaguered President Howard reported in his message to the legislature in March 1915 just how bad conditions had gotten. Liberia's economic lifeblood flowed from trade with Europe, especially with Germany. Half a dozen years before the war, for example, 347 ships called at Liberian ports. Some 233 were German. By 1915, the total number from all nationalities had plummeted to two. Exports fell from $1.3 million in 1913 to $618,500 in 1917.[12] No exports. No imports. No government revenue from customs. German ships also had employed about twenty-one thousand Kru tribesmen as deckhands.

The badly strapped government in August 1914 stopped paying all of its civil servants, except those working in customs. The frontier force was whittled down to six hundred men—no funds to meet the payroll. Schools closed. Even missionaries were forced to curtail their programs. Servicing foreign loans was impossible. And the outlook for the future, if anything, looked still bleaker. President Howard did manage to obtain $100,000 in credit from the Bank for British West Africa in 1917—given the state of Liberian finances, hardly a drop in the bucket. When the government went back for additional funds, the bank insisted on applying conditions, such as appointing bank officials to government positions. The Liberians balked.

—⋙—

President Howard initially attempted to keep Liberia neutral in the conflict that had engulfed Europe. On August 10, 1914, he issued a proclamation of neutrality. However, the government allowed all of the belligerents to use the cable and wireless facilities built earlier—the French on South Beach connecting with Europe and the African coast (plus a wireless station in Monrovia), and the Germans on Cape Mesurado connecting to Europe and Brazil.

Liberian sympathies, though, lay more with Britain and the United States, and as the war progressed, the country experienced a mounting distaste for Germany's conduct in it. Growing pressure from Washington after the United States entered the war on April 6, 1917, also weighed heavily on the government. Liberia occupied an important strategic location. Moreover, a neutral Liberia might well offer a source of supplies for German U-boats that preyed on Allied shipping in the Atlantic and could act as a center for German espionage activities.[13]

The United States prodded Liberia to join the Allied side and continued to push even harder for the government to carry out the reforms demanded. A week after the American declaration of war, the US secretary of state, Robert Lansing, dispatched a forceful diplomatic note prodding Liberia to take these actions.

On May 8, Liberia severed diplomatic relations with Germany, citing its submarine-enforced blockade (which stifled Liberian trade) as a primary cause. In addition, Liberia accused the German government of "upholding the rule of Force as against the Rule of Right," and "consistently [disregarding] accepted rules of civilized warfare." In addition, German authorities forced Liberian laborers working in German colonies to "serve in their colonial military service," usually abroad.[14] The Liberian government next ordered all German property in Liberia to be liquidated.[15] Liberia declared war on Germany on August 4, 1917, and even supplied three thousand men to serve in France.[16]

The war came to Liberia's front door on April 10, 1918. An eyewitness in Monrovia recounted that "about 4 o'clock in the morning," he and other hotel guests were "aroused and informed that a large German submarine had appeared in the bay" and the town was expected to be "bombarded immediately." The U-boat commander demanded that "the German and French cable stations and the French wireless station should be destroyed before noon."[17] Despite much bustle among the Liberian authorities, they could not produce a decision before the deadline.

The German captain, "to show that he meant business, blew up the Liberian navy, which consisted of one two-masted schooner," the *President Grant*. But the government held fast and delivered a reply that it was "unable to conform with the German wishes." With typical German punctuality, the commander "opened fire on the French wireless station" at the appointed hour. "But his shooting was very bad, and for an hour and a half shots landed all over town." Four women were killed, and three persons injured. Other than the wireless station, "damage was slight."[18]

To help ease the pain Liberia suffered because of the war and as a bonus for joining the Allied cause, the US Treasury on September 9, 1918, extended a $5 million credit to Liberia. The two governments began negotiating the terms and general purpose of the loan, but for some reason only about $36,000 was ever drawn down.[19]

At the war's conclusion, Liberia attended the Paris Peace Conference that began in January 1919, signed the Treaty of Versailles in June, and became a member of the League of Nations. Germany was forced to give up the special rights and privileges in Liberia it had obtained earlier, including nominating a German receiver of customs.

President Howard, doubtless chafed and worn from the ill winds that seemed to blow on Liberia from every direction, at least could now savor the sight of Liberia seated at the peace conference table with the other Allies and signing the treaty in the grandiose Palace of Versailles. For the first time, the world's great powers were treating Liberia as "one of them," a sovereign country, rather than some semicivilized, quasi-American colony of blacks. But the desperate condition of the country's economy must have left a bitter taste in Howard's mouth.

His secretary of state, Charles Dunbar Burgess King, who led the Liberian delegation, would return home after signing the peace treaty on June 28 to find himself Howard's successor. While still in Paris, he had been elected Liberia's seventeenth president in May. King's vice president, Henry Too Wesley, a Grebo, became the first native African in the country to be elected to high office. On January 5, 1920, the inaugural got underway.

King was born in Freetown, Sierra Leone. His parents, members of the Yoruba tribe in Nigeria, had been rescued from a slave ship and resettled in Sierra Leone. As a child, Charles migrated with them to Liberia. After completing his education, he embarked on a political career, rising through the ranks of the True Whig Party to fill the office of attorney general and other high-level government positions. He served as secretary of state during Howard's entire twelve years in office.

King was no stranger to Liberia's long-standing ills, but he could have had little inkling of what lay in store for the republic and for himself personally—a contentious encounter with one of modern black history's most flamboyant characters, the introduction of an economic enterprise that would dramatically alter the face of Liberian fortunes, an election that would land him in *The*

Guinness Book of Records, and his presidential term's abrupt ending in scandal.

As President King settled in to his new responsibilities, preparations had begun for another celebration of a black leader. This one would be a massive gathering in New York City. The leader—a charismatic thirty-three-year-old Jamaican named Marcus Garvey.

—∞—

August 1920. New York's streets are hot. No beer, nor other alcohol—Prohibition. The August 3 *New York Times* reports "a mass meeting" the previous night "in Madison Square Garden...of a thirty-day convention to take up the problems of the negro race." Some twenty to twenty-five thousand "negroes made the big hall rock when they yelled for an Africa free from the Strait of Gibralter [sic] to the Cape of Good Hope—an immense negro republic."

Garvey, "clad in cap and gown of purple, green and gold," received such an ovation he could not begin to speak for five minutes. He declared, "we shall now organize the 400,000,000 negroes of the world into a vast organization to plant the banner of freedom on the great continent of Africa." He continued, "we will begin by framing a bill of rights" and a constitution "to guide the life and destiny of the 400,000,000." His Universal Negro Improvement Association (UNIA), according to the story, was said to have "more than 1,000,000 members." Delegates to the convention reportedly came from "all over the United States, Canada, Central America, and the West Indies," and included an "African Prince, several chiefs and descendants of chiefs."[20]

W. E. B. Du Bois, who would become an implacable enemy, saw Garvey during the month-long convention in Liberty Hall, "a long, low, unfinished church basement roofed over," the UNIA headquarters in Upper Harlem. He described him as "a little, fat black man, ugly, but with intelligent eyes and big head...seated on a plank platform beside a 'throne,' dressed in a military uniform of the gayest mid-Victorian type, heavy with gold lace, epaulets, plume, and sword."[21]

President General of the Republic of Africa Marcus Garvey on parade, 1926. NYWT and S Collection, Prints and Photographs Division, Library of Congress LC---USZ62-107995

The "President General" was presiding over the investiture of other "Republic of Africa" officers. Du Bois believed "a casual observer might have mistaken it for the dress rehearsal of a new comic opera. But it was not; it was a serious occasion... part of a great 'back-to-Africa' movement and represented self-determination for the negro race and a relieving America of her most difficult race problem by a voluntary operation."[22] It seemed that Paul Cuffe's vision of a "Province of Freedom" and Edwin Blyden's idea of "providential return" to Africa might at last be fulfilled.

By the time the first convention of the Universal Negro Improvement Association ended on August 31, Marcus Mosiah Garvey arguably was the most widely known Negro in a large part of the world—famous to many, particularly of his race—infamous to many others, particularly whites. Unbeknownst to him, in Akron, Ohio, an equally dynamic figure, a captain of American industry, Harvey Firestone, worked on plans that would indelibly change the fortunes of both Liberia and Garvey.

—⁂—

But for now, the stark reality of Liberia's desperate financial straits absorbed President King fully. Liberia had accumulated some $189,000 in arrears on the 1912 loan and owed the Bank for British West Africa $100,646 (having exceeded the 1919 agreed ceiling of $100,000) and the US government $35,000. In addition, overdue LFF salaries amounted to another $118,544, and an internal floating debt came to $600,000. Big money at that time for a small country such as Liberia.

By the end of 1920, the president decided the country must draw upon the $5 million credit the US Treasury Department had established for Liberia in 1918. He appointed a mission, comprised of F. E. R. Johnson, associate justice of Liberia's supreme court; John L. Morris, Liberia's minister in Washington; and Gabriel L. Dennis, a prominent Liberian businessman, to bring home the completed loan agreement.

The mission, headed by King himself, arrived in New York March 6, 1921, aboard the US Mail Steamship Company's *Panhandle State*. King, "dressed in the full regalia of his office… [and] his hat decorated with bird of paradise plumes, attracted much attention." He was "hopeful...the already protracted negotiations would be consummated soon," so the money could finance an extensive program of harbor improvements, road construction, telephone and telegraphic facilities, and industrial schools.[23] The Liberian legislature had given King full powers and authority to conclude and sign the agreement laying out the loan's administrative arrangements.

The commission adjourned to Washington, where they met with Secretary of State Charles Evans Hughes on March 19 and President Warren Harding on April 21. According to Hughes's testimony the following year before the House Ways and Means Committee, they agreed on measures to safeguard the loan money and government revenues from the rampant corruption in Liberia, and on procedures for handling expenditures and repaying other creditors. Repaying Britain, France, and Germany would enable the government to eliminate them "from participation in...Liberia's financial and other public affairs."[24] American experts would control all government revenues and expenditures, and US officers would command the frontier force. The plan called for twenty-two American experts to carry out these tasks.

The proposed loan met with surprisingly strong resistance in the Congress, despite the fact that both the preceding Democratic Wilson and current Republican Harding administrations favored it. A lengthy January 22 conference at the White House, which included President Harding, Secretary Hughes, and House and Senate leaders, concluded that the delay in extending the credit had been justified; the Liberian government hadn't met all of the terms regarding the loan's repayment and the management of the country's finances. But, since all the conditions now had been satisfied, "the United States had a moral obligation to make the loan."[25]Critics in

Liberia and Europe, however, did not agree. The US government had to fend off charges that the loan would virtually make Liberia "an American colony" by pointing out that it "would be used largely to repay advances made by French and British financiers."[26]

The minority Democrats led the opposition. They alleged the loan would be for the benefit of American banking interests, to which the administration answered, "All tommyrot." Liberia's external debt totaled about $1.6 million, of which American citizens held only about $50,000 to $60,000; most was in the hands of Europeans. But the House Ways and Means Committee nonetheless deferred action on the measure.[27] The committee's minority report trumpeted that it was "decidedly in the best interests of the United States 'to notify all nations of the world that we have ceased to be a 'Lady Bountiful' and that henceforth no foreign nation can obtain a loan from the United States Treasury.'"[28] The country once more was well along on its road to isolationism.

Senate debate turned markedly caustic. Democratic senator Pat Harrison of Mississippi charged that if the loan went through, five "American negroes" would benefit to the tune of $650,000 in fees. The five included a former Harvard football player, William H. Lewis; Howard University secretary and treasurer Emmet J. Scott; and former American minister to Liberia Ernest Lyon.

Nebraska senator George W. Norris gave a speech dripping in sarcasm. In mock seriousness, he orated,

> [The world waited] in trepidation during the war [World War I], waiting to see on what side Liberia would fight...and when Liberia joined the Allies 'everybody knew the war was practically settled...[In] no war in all history had the hosts of Liberia ever been defeated or the Liberian navy been conquered. The Kaiser turned from a dark brunette to a pale blond. His hair stood on end and his mustache straightened out when Liberia entered the war.'[29]

President Harding put in a good word for the loan in a letter to the Senate, and Secretary Hughes declared that failure to make the loan would be lamentable" for both the United States' world position and more lamentable for Liberia."[30] But the loan was dead.

—∿—

Prior to the 1920 UNIA convention, Garvey had chosen the Republic of Liberia, the only independent Negro country in Africa other than monarchial Abyssinia (today's Ethiopia), as the site of his first colonization project. According to Rhode Island University professor Robert G. Weisbord, he sent Elie Garcia to Liberia in the first part of 1920 to discuss the proposed venture. Garcia promised, among other things, that the UNIA would help Liberia by all means possible to liquidate its foreign debt.[31]

An understandably interested President King had his secretary of state, Edwin Barclay, reply. On June 14 he wrote that the government appreciated the UNIA objectives Garcia had outlined. The Liberian government, Barclay continued, "have no hesitancy in assuring you that they will afford the Association every facility legally possible" to carry out "its industrial, agricultural and business projects" in Liberia.[32] Westbord relates that Barclay, in fact, had earlier in March even told UNIA officials that the government would "be glad to have your Association occupy...certain settlements already laid out"[33] To finance the venture, Garvey, in October 1920, announced the Liberian Construction Loan for repatriating blacks to Africa. A sixteen-man UNIA delegation left for Liberia on February 16 the following year.[34]

In a speech at Albert Hall in London, Garvey later would claim that he "had completed an agreement with the Liberian government [to obtain] four sections of the little country" on which the association could start the "experiment in helping to build Liberia and make her a worthy and worthwhile Negro state in West Africa."[35] According to him, the four delegations he sent to Liberia met the president and government officials, and, based on Liberian "urgings," UNIA "spent fully half a million dollars in buying machinery and materials." To transport these items and would-be colonists, Garvey said UNIA paid close to $260,000 for a former German liner. The association hired civil, mechanical, and mining engineers.[36]

All was in readiness to launch this historic effort to redeem Africa and black people throughout the world. Colonists supposedly would begin arriving later in the year; rumor had it that three thousand would depart for Liberia in November 1924. But when three UNIA representatives landed at Monrovia in July 1924 with proposals for six communities, the authorities arrested and deported them "the minute their ship reached Monrovia."[37] And in August the government sent a message to Washington that Liberia was "opposed to Garvey's Negro Plans."[38] The government abrogated the agreement with UNIA and kept, Garvey alleged, "nearly $200,000 worth of materials."[39] Moreover, Garvey fumed that the Liberians gave Firestone Rubber Company the one million acres of land set aside for the UNIA colony.

What had gone wrong? According to Garvey, Firestone's agent, after finding "it was possible to grow rubber in Liberia...influenced President King...to abrogate a sacred agreement" and give the land to Firestone.[40] That he might face competition in vying for the favors of Liberia hadn't occurred to Garvey.

Even before the massive 1920 convention, Marcus Garvey had landed on a number of government watch lists—of potential troublemakers, rabble-rousers, and "Bolshies" eager to spread "commie revolutions." (Attorney General A. Mitchell Palmer's notorious "Red Scare" raids, race riots, and widespread Negro unrest provided an appropriate backdrop.) Arriving in New York from

Jamaica aboard the SS *Tallac* on March 23 or 24, 1916, Garvey, penniless, moved in with a Jamaican family in Harlem. He managed to find a job as a printer. As a soapbox orator, speaking each night on a Harlem street corner, he soon attracted something of a following for his UNIA and "Back to Africa Movement."[41]

In less than two months, on May 9, Garvey moved onto the stage of Saint Mark's Church Hall in New York to give his first US public lecture. It ended in a disastrously dramatic exit. He fell off the stage. Undeterred, he next embarked on a monumental year-long speaking tour that carried him through thirty-eight states, returning to New York City only in May 1917. He had delivered his message to huge crowds of blacks all over the country eager to hear his message of hope. Thirteen of them organized a New York branch of the association.[42]

On July 1, 1919, rumors spread through East Saint Louis to the effect that a black man had killed a white. In the tightly wound relations existing between the two races, that was enough to ignite a riot the next day that left thirty-nine dead and hundreds injured. An incensed Garvey on July 8 mounted the podium at Lafayette Hall in Harlem to denounce the riots in a speech, referring to "the conspiracy of the East St. Louis riots" as "one of the bloodiest outrages against mankind." The situation would continue to worsen, so that the summer of 1919, which witnessed twenty-six race riots, was dubbed the "Red Summer."[43]

Not surprisingly, the Justice Department's Bureau of Investigation got wind of Garvey on June 3, 1918, via a written report of his nightly outdoor meetings on Harlem street corners. On July 12 the bureau requested that its New York office send all information on Garvey to Washington and alerted the Chicago office to monitor Garvey and other black activists. They soon came under the watchful eye of J. Edgar Hoover,[44] and a Marcus Garvey dossier joined those of other potentially dangerous rabble-rousers in the bureau's files.

Publication of Garvey's *Negro World*, which began August 17, 1918, as the official organ of the Universal Negro Improvement Association, heightened Hoover's suspicions. The newspaper preached Garvey's philosophy and carried news concerning black people in the United States and around the world (but no advertisements typically found in most Afro-American publications for such products as hair straighteners and skin lighteners). At its peak, the *Negro World*, with a circulation of two hundred thousand, was the most widely read black newspaper in the United States and boasted a wide readership in Central America, the Caribbean, Canada, Europe, and Africa, as well.[45]

Garvey's cry for independence from white colonial rule and "Africa for the Africans" scared many colonialists. Between February and August of the following year, authorities in numerous countries confiscated copies of the newspaper. The governor of British Honduras (now Belize) banned it, the governor of Trinidad termed it seditious, and the acting governor of Jamaica instructed the postmaster to detain copies of the publication.[46] On September 10, the colonial secretary in Great Britain handed the West Indian government authority to introduce legislation to suppress the *Negro World* as well as other publications they judged seditious. Copies of the banned newspaper nevertheless continued to be distributed by students, merchant marine sailors, and others.

The black leader's next adventure (or, better, misadventure) involved what would at first appearance look to be a bold and imaginative enterprise—the establishment of a black-owned ocean shipping line. He envisioned such a line promoting commerce among black communities worldwide, carrying raw materials, manufactured goods, other products, and passengers among black communities in America, the Caribbean, and Africa—the linchpin in a global black economy.

Garvey incorporated the Black Star Line with a capitalization of $500,000 maximum in June 1919. Individuals could purchase up to two hundred shares valued at five dollars each. Investors eagerly bought shares at UNIA meetings and conventions, from traveling agents, and through advertisements and mailed circulars. The new company launched its first ship, the SS *Yarmouth*, which Garvey planned to rename the *Frederick Douglass* in October. But on October 14, a disgruntled former employee, George Tyson, shot and wounded Garvey. He claimed Garvey had swindled him out of a $25 debt. Garvey recovered. Tyson committed suicide in his jail cell the next day.[47] The *Yarmouth* remained unrenamed.

With an all-black crew, under a black sea captain, Joshua Cockburn, the *Yarmouth*'s first charter involved transporting a cargo of whiskey from New York to Havana as Prohibition took effect in the United States—probably not exactly the kind of commerce Garvey envisioned. The thirty-two-year-old vessel reportedly required coast guard aid on January 19 when it was found sinking 101 miles outside New York harbor.

While enthusiastic crowds of Cubans greeted the ship with flowers and fruit when it finally arrived in Havana, the operation proved a disaster financially. The *Yarmouth*'s other two voyages proved equally rewarding in terms of welcoming crowds and equally disastrous in terms of financial returns. The voyages exhausted the old ship, built in 1887 and sailed as a coal carrier in the First World War. The Black Star Line paid $165,000 for it. The ship brought $6,000 when sold for scrap in December 1921—its name still unchanged. The line purchased two other vessels, the SS *Kanawha* and SS *Shadyside*, an excursion boat; they fared no better. The Black Star Line lost between $700,000 and $1.25 million and collapsed in April 1922. Many of Garvey's supporters who invested lost their life's savings.[48]

Although the Black Star Line provided a powerful symbol to masses of dispossessed black people, it also proved to be Garvey's undoing. J. Edgar Hoover and the Bureau of Investigation had been searching for a way to deport the black troublemaker ever since he appeared on Harlem's streets. In September 1919 the bureau had instructed its New York office to try to establish "sufficient evidence against Garvey to warrant" initiating "deportation proceedings." The following month Hoover suggested investigators look into prosecuting Garvey for his role in the Black Star fiasco as a basis for such action.[49]

Garvey and two other Black Star officers were charged with using the mails to defraud investors. Prosecutors dropped charges against his two colleagues but brought Garvey to trial May 18, 1923. Found guilty, he was sentenced on June 21 to five years in prison and fined $1,000, plus court costs. Denied bail, Garvey languished in New York's the Tombs prison for three months before being released while his case was appealed. On September 25 immigration authorities started putting together a case for Garvey's deportation.[50]

While awaiting a decision from the circuit court of appeals, Garvey still went about his duties as the supreme leader of his crusade for black power. In an August 2 story, the *New York Times* reported that "Marcus Garvey, President General of the African Republic and head of the Universal Negro Improvement Association," opened the fourth UNIA convention that would last a month. "Shining sabres" guarded him as he "stood in a gorgeous uniform on a reviewing stand in front of 54 West 135th Street yesterday afternoon surrounded by a glittering staff of 3,500 negro men and women which set a large part of Harlem wild with enthusiasm."[51] The following month, in a meeting in Liberty Hall, the Reverend James M. Webb, a negro preacher from Chicago, "hailed Garvey as a 'new Moses.'"[52] Garvey's middle name coincidentally happened to be Mosiah.

Reality, however, soon caught up with Garvey. On February 2, 1925, the circuit court of appeals upheld his sentence. Arrested on February 7 at the 125th Street train station in New York, Garvey was sent to the Atlanta federal penitentiary. He faced spending the next three and one-half years behind bars and deportation to Jamaica after that. His greatest disappointment, however, lay in what he termed the great Liberian "double cross."

Garvey's competition, Harvey Firestone, relished the role. Harvey Samuel Firestone was born December 20, 1868, in a farmhouse in Colombiana, Ohio. (The farmhouse was later moved to Henry Ford's Deerfield Village, a historic park in Dearborn, Michigan.) After completing high school, he worked for a buggy company producing rubber tires for carriages. Recognizing that the automobile, rather than buggies and carriages, would dominate future transportation, Firestone, at the age of thirty-one, moved to Akron, Ohio, America's burgeoning rubber capital.

With only limited cash (some say only $10,000), he established the Firestone Tire and Rubber Company in 1900 with twelve employees. He became associated with Henry Ford. As the supplier of original tires on Ford cars, Firestone, by 1910, was producing more than a million tires yearly. The company became one of the largest tire manufacturers in America. And Firestone, Henry Ford, and Thomas Edison—considered at that time three of the top leaders in American industry, part of an exclusive group known as "The Millionaires Club"—became fast buddies. Not even the "President General of the Republic of Africa" could stand up to such high-powered competition.

But, why would Harvey Firestone be interested in obtaining land in Liberia? The answer could be traced to a singular program the British government initiated in the aftermath of the First World War.

Fed by the automobile fever sweeping the United States at the turn of the twentieth century, world demand for rubber seemed insatiable. (Consumption in the United States climbed from 61 percent of world output in 1915 to 76 percent in 1924.) Supplies of wild rubber from the Amazon, Congo, and west Africa could not meet the demand.

Attention turned to managed plantations, particularly in the British colonies of Malaya and Ceylon, which possessed ideal growing conditions. Before 1904, the world could count only about fifty thousand acres of plantation rubber. Growers made large investments to develop plantations that soon were producing the largest share of the world's rubber output. Demand, however, continued to outstrip production and prices rose accordingly until World War I approached. Prices then plunged from $3.06 per pound in 1910 to sixty-six cents in 1914 and to seventeen cents by 1919. Output, meanwhile, had more than doubled between 1915 and 1919. Worldwide, stocks accumulated.

Awash in a sea of surplus raw rubber, the British rubber industry was seized with near panic. Some feared American interests might even acquire the entire industry. Compounding the fear, the US government had taken to insisting the United Kingdom repay what it owed the United States as a war debt. And the British Exchequer had difficulty in obtaining funds even to pay the interest.[53]

Then the secretary of state for colonies, Winston Churchill, had a brainstorm---- a rubber cartel that would support the commodity's price by restricting the amount traded. An eight-man committee, headed by Sir James Stevenson, came up with a plan. Stevenson (who was joint managing director of the Johnnie

Walker whiskey company) served Churchill as his personal business advisor. In its June 22 report, the committee, proposed that any exports by British colonial producers above 60 percent of their 1920 output be taxed at a higher rate than the 60 percent portion. When the world price rose to a level deemed "adequate," it would be "stabilized." The Dutch government, despite substantial rubber plantations in the Dutch East Indies, declined to participate in the plan, which took effect on November 1, 1923.[54]

Rubber prices rocketed. By July 1925 they hit $1.032 per pound, three times higher than the targeted stabilized price. Americans, who owned 80 percent of the world's automobiles, complained loudly.[55] Secretary of Commerce (later president) Herbert Hoover called such controls on raw materials "a growing menace."[56] The irascible colonial secretary shot back that "the British Government... [would] not remove restrictions on output." Period![57]

Harvey Firestone became the restrictions' most relentless opponent. He told Hoover the United States should produce its own rubber.[58] His blunt criticism of the British plan ruffled the feathers of his more moderate, less Anglophobic, fellow rubber manufacturers. Some even maintained that the rubber price "was not excessive." Hoover, nonetheless, agreed with Firestone. The commerce secretary wanted plantations located close to the United States.[59] Others, including the US secretary of war, John W. Weeks, favored the Philippines,[60] although opponents ridiculed the notion.

Firestone had already begun to look for suitable places to establish his plantation. Toward the end of 1923, he engaged M. A. Cheek, a Firestone representative in Singapore and veteran of twenty years in the rubber trade, to fly to the Philippines, accompanied by two rubber experts, Donald A. Ross and Samuel Wierman. They dismissed the Philippines as a possible location when they learned the government had enacted a law barring any individual's owning more than 2,500 acres of land, an area too small for the production levels Firestone envisioned. Next, they ruled out Mexico, where a 1917 law prohibited large-scale ownership of land. Too politically volatile, anyway.

Firestone's attention shifted to Africa and Firestone in 1923 queried the American chargé d'affaires in Monrovia, Solomon Porter Hood, regarding possible rubber production in Liberia. Hood responded favorably: a supply of cheap labor, close connections with the United States, and the fact that rubber already was being grown on a small scale at the Mount Barclay Rubber Plantation. The four Englishmen who operated the plantation abandoned it in 1910, and it reverted back to the government, which now would be prepared to grant concessions to any firm willing to take it over.[61]

Liberia's good relations with and heavy dependence on the United States particularly appealed to Firestone. He lost little time in dispatching William D. Hines, his private secretary, Ross, and Cheek to consult the Liberian government and to check out conditions for rubber growing in general, and, more specifically, at Mount Barclay. "Liberians were generally delighted to meet the Firestone Team and looked at the proposal as the best thing that ever happened to the Republic." At a working meeting with King and Barclay, it was decided that Firestone should be allowed to produce rubber in the country, depending on the outcome of a one-year experiment on Mount Barclay Plantation. Hines, Ross, and Cheek also "secured tentative approval for a lease of one million acres of land to Firestone for rubber production."[62]

After their return to the United States, Firestone on December 10, 1924, showed a draft contract to the State Department: one for leasing the Mount Barclay Plantation---a million acres of land (representing 10 percent of Liberia's arable land at that time) for ninety-nine years at six cents per acre—and another for a loan of

$5 million to Liberia. Secretary of State Hughes assured the rubber magnate that he could count on such "diplomatic assistance" as might be needed and appropriate.[63]

> When the Liberian leaders received Firestone's agreement, they reportedly were furious. The proposed $5 million loan (to be repaid in forty years), had never been discussed at the meetings in Liberia, nor had provisions for recruiting three thousand white workers and allowing imports of all articles for the plantation duty-free.[64] They rejected the proposed agreement, particularly because it packaged the loan and rubber contracts together. And the government did not want to assume an obligation to any company doing business in Liberia. Moreover, the Liberians understandably still had an aversion to foreign loans of any kind, since as President King cautioned in his 1924 inaugural address, they carried "too many political entanglements."[65]
>
> Firestone agreed to negotiate the $5 million loan separately and to cut the number of white employees to be recruited by half. The company also would pay a duty on rubber the company exported. In return, Liberian officials agreed that the company might import "recreational materials, welfare articles, and hospital equipment" duty-free. But negotiations with the Liberian government on the terms and conditions of the loan stalled. Even Sidney DeLa Rue, the American general receiver of customs in Monrovia, personally visited Harvey Firestone in Akron to clarify outstanding issues between the two parties. But the impasse continued. Finally, both Firestone and Liberian president King formally requested the American government's intervention.[66]

However, the US State Department, anxious to avoid being tarred as imperialistic, moved cautiously. And for good reason.

William Castle, the State Department division chief, for example, noted the financial advisor stipulated in the agreement would be designated by the US president and enjoy almost as much power as most heads of state. He would approve the budget each year, and without his consent, the government could not borrow money. The American president also would recommend four officers to lead the Liberian Frontier Force, the State Department would arbitrate any issues arising from the agreement, and Liberia would use the loan to repay outstanding debt to the United States.[67]

Castle cautioned that "the people who are always smelling out imperialistic schemes will be able to say that we forced a loan" on Liberia to gain control. The State Department, fearing possibly losing the project, joined the negotiations anyway. The Liberians were told, "it would be tragic to turn down the loan since it was needed for development."[68] As a concession, Firestone agreed that a separate company, the Finance Corporation of America, with the New York National Bank as fiscal agent, rather than the rubber corporation, would make the loan.

The negotiations at last were completed on March 18, 1925. On October 15, a pleased Harvey Firestone trumpeted that Firestone Plantations Company would invest $100,000 in Liberia. Outcries of imperialism from Professor Raymond Buell, W. E. B. Du Bois, and others promptly arose.[69] Both the US State Department and the Commerce Department's secretary Hoover defended the action. Government support for private US investment was American policy. Liberian president King and secretary of state Barclay came under fire from opponents within their country, many who saw the agreement as capitulation to an imperialist United States. Notwithstanding, the *Star*, a Monrovia newspaper edited by President King's personal secretary, on March 31, 1926, rationalized that Liberians should "accept the loan because 'the investment of large American capital in foreign countries demands protection to that capital.'"[70] The Liberian legislature ratified the agreement with Firestone on December 8, 1926.

It appeared that Firestone, at last, would have his rubber plantation.

Amid the lingering cries of American imperialism, Firestone engineers began clearing land and building roads and bridges for the plantation, followed by "a modern hospital staffed by American physicians and nurses," plus "additional roads, sanitary villages for Liberian employees, an electrical power plant and, a telephone system."[71] The company "collaborated with the Harvard University's Medical School in 1926 and 1927 to conduct an extensive health survey" of the appalling health conditions that regularly took many lives, especially of Europeans, in Liberia and other parts of Africa. It sponsored a survey by Yale University School of Forestry of Liberia's vast forests.[72] Company stores sold employees "necessities and little luxuries at prices within their range…Though its major objective was to increase the company's business and profits, the company's policies and methods were on the whole enlightened."[73]

Firestone's incursion into Liberia would mark a major turning point in the country's history and set in motion a transformation of the economy that would fundamentally transform Liberia. It would begin not only "a revolution in the country's economy," but a revolution "in the ways of life of many of its people," as well.[74]

The transformation of the Liberian economy, however, would not come easy, nor would it be without controversy. In the negotiations for the project, Firestone had insisted that the government supply labor for the plantation, but the workers "must be contented and recruited without coercion."[75] Little did the

Americans suspect that such a requirement, in the context of the relations overall between Liberia's Americo-Liberian leaders and its indigenous population, would spark a crisis of country-shaking proportion.

Meanwhile, Marcus Garvey unleashed a stream of withering criticism of the Liberian leadership, whom he now despised. He also lashed out at their partner in the "great Liberian double cross," whom he alleged was no less than the US government. He named Secretary of Commerce Herbert Hoover as the point man in a government conspiracy that had persuaded Liberian president King to rebuff Garvey and lease the land to Firestone. Garvey even linked the plot to his imprisonment after being convicted of mail fraud.

In his 1928 Albert Hall speech after his release from prison, he accused Hoover of having "railroaded" him "to prison." It was, he said, convenient in 1924 "to rush me to prison, because… I was able to make not only trouble for [President] Charles King, but for Firestone as well for double-crossing us in Liberia." He charged that "Firestone and the then American government knew" he had "enough influence…to prevent" King's third-term election in 1927."[76] Garvey never revealed what information he had, except he wrote later in his magazine, the *New Jamaican*, that King "saw the possibility of getting graft from Harvey Firestone."[77]

Garvey insisted that ratification of the Firestone agreement by the Liberian president and senate depended upon King's re-election. Without King in the president's chair, Firestone's project would be dead. And Firestone and the United States would have lost a valuable source of rubber. "They," Garvey complained, "thereupon railroaded me for five years and kept me there for six months" after King was reelected. He pointed out that President Calvin Coolidge had the power to commute his sentence or pardon him. Despite efforts of various groups and individuals (including Malcolm X's father, Earl Little), Coolidge waited until November 18, 1927, to commute Garvey's sentence and at the same time sign his deportation order. King was reelected president in May 1927.

W. E. B. DuBois paints a vastly different picture, writing that Garvey's own flaming oratory was to blame. "Without consulting the Liberians," DuBois asserted, Garvey rashly announced that his headquarters would move to Liberia in January 1922.[78] "He apparently was ready to assume partial charge of their state," DuBois continued, where he would "make a start...with industrial enterprises," and then, from there, "penetrate all of Africa and gradually subdue it." And, "instead of keeping this plan hidden and working cautiously...toward it, he yelled and shouted and telegraphed it all over the world."[79] All the while, he "openly and wildly [talked] of 'Conquest' and of telling white Europeans in Africa to 'get out!' and of becoming a black Napoleon."[80]

Reactions were not long in coming. A short time after Garvey had been convicted of mail fraud in June 1923, the British Foreign Office issued instructions that he was not to be allowed to visit any British West African colony.[81] Aroused European governments, fearing a spread of nationalism would end their colonial rule in Africa, pressured Liberia to deny Garvey any foothold there. And President King left no doubt about his position in his December 9, 1924, message to the Liberian legislature: the UNIA's announced objective was "to use Liberia as its base for dissemination of its propaganda of racial hatred and ill will." But, "Liberia's doors would be securely closed to a movement which planned to launch 'a race war against friendly states in Africa.'"[82]

Immediately after he was released from the Atlanta federal penitentiary, authorities hustled Garvey aboard the SS *Saramacca*, bound for New Orleans and Panama. From the deck the "President General of the Republic of Africa" delivered a farewell address in New Orleans on December 2, 1927, to hundreds who had "rushed to the docks to see him off." [83]Deported from the United States, Garvey was never to return.

Upon his arrival in Jamaica (aboard the SS *Santa Marta*, to which he transferred in Panama), he received "a hero's welcome." Barred from visiting Africa and American countries still under colonial rule, Garvey traveled to London, where he established temporary headquarters for his Universal Negro Improvement Association at the end of April 1928. Still smarting from the treatment meted out by the Coolidge administration, especially Herbert Hoover, he urged, in a *New York Times* article, "the four million negro voters" in the United States to cast their ballots for Alfred E. Smith in the upcoming presidential election.[84]

Back again in Jamaica the following year, Garvey began publishing a daily newspaper, the *Blackman*, and then sadly witnessed the demise of his premier newspaper, the *Negro World*, in October 1933. Frustrated by life in Jamaica, he decided two years later to move to London, leaving his wife, Amy Jacques Garvey, and two young sons behind in Jamaica. On or about January 20, 1940, Garvey suffered a cerebral hemorrhage, paralyzing his right side and affecting his speech. In one final "Mark Twainish" humiliation, a London correspondent reported Garvey's "premature death" in the May 18 issue of the *Chicago Defender*. Upon reading the account, he suffered another cerebral hemorrhage, or possibly a cardiac arrest, and died on June 10, 1940 at the age of sixty. But the onetime "President General of the Republic of Africa" and aspiring "Black Napoleon" would have to wait more than twenty years before being returned home on November 10, 1964. He was declared Jamaica's first national hero the next day and buried in the Marcus Garvey Memorial in Kingston's National Heroes' Park.[85]

Despite suffering defeat and disparagement in his lifetime, Marcus Garvey would after death emerge as the ultimate victor in his struggle for black "freedom and redemption." His son, Marcus Jr., declared that he "laid down the basic principle of Black Power, that the Black man must create his own Black institutions under Black leadership."[86] Toward this end, according to Marcus Jr., he founded the African Orthodox Church and believed in a black God.[87]

Garvey's movement amounted to more than "back to Africa"; it was a "plan for total African redemption."[88] One can only wildly imagine what Liberia and the rest of Africa might have looked like, what course history might have taken in Liberia and the rest of Africa had Harvey Firestone found a site for his rubber plantation in, say, Panama or the Philippines rather than Liberia, and Garvey had been allowed to carry out his program.

Even though he fell short of that grandiose goal, Marcus Garvey still influenced many leaders of Africa's liberation from colonialism. Kwame Nkrumah was one. When Ghana's prime minister, he even launched the Black Star Steamship service in Garvey's honor. Jomo Kenyatta and other African leaders also felt Garvey's influence, as did champions of black power and the back-to-Africa movement. "In a very real sense, as far as the British Empire is concerned, Garveyism," Professor Weisbord claims, "triumphed. Whitehall had good reason to be worried."[89] On a final ironic note, Weisbord writes, "Garvey, the passionate apostle of 'back to Africanism,' never did set foot on African soil."[90]

In Monrovia, President King's fortunes also began to tilt downward. The agreements with Firestone came under heavy fire, not only from outside the country, but internally as well. The loan agreement especially smacked of American imperialism, where the proconsul wore the mantle of financial advisor, attended by a bevy of other American advisors. Critics denounced the plantation agreement as unconstitutional since the lengthy lease violated the Liberian constitution's alien land clause; the exemptions granted Firestone from duties on imported goods encroached on the legislature's power to tax; and the arbitration provision usurped the authority of the Liberian courts. The dispute over the role of foreign capital in the republic's development, which had earlier roiled the country, broke out again.

In the 1927 election campaign, the Open Door policy became an issue for King and his vice presidential running mate, Allen Yancy. The People's Party, which had sprung up in 1923, chose Thomas J. R. Faulkner, a popular mayor of Monrovia during the First World War, as its candidate for president. Faulkner played heavily on the theme of an open door, arguing that the Firestone deal was a violation of the policy.

He apparently frightened King and the long-ruling True Whig Party sufficiently to stampede them into what first appeared to be a massive landslide in King's favor—243,000 votes for King against 9,000 for Faulkner. There was one problem, however. The Liberian constitution inconveniently limited suffrage country-wide to only 15,000 qualified voters.[91] (Years later this discrepancy would catapult the 1927 election into *The Guinness Book of Records* [1982] as the greatest election fraud ever reported.)[92]

An incensed Faulkner refused to surrender. Writing in the July 1929 *Baltimore Afro-American*, he accused King not only of "massive vote fraud" but of "complicity in forced labor procurement" and permitting slavery, as well.[93] The defeated candidate repeated his accusations in a lengthy letter to Sir Eric Drummond, the League of Nations secretary general, which the *New Republic* published in full in February 1930. (The eminent Raymond Buell, almost two years earlier, had aired reports that "slavery and forced labor existed in Liberia on a large scale.")[94]

Faulkner charged that indigenous Africans were forced to work as many as nine months on roads and other projects without compensation. They "had to furnish their own food and tools," and, adding injustice to injustice, were obliged to feed the frontier force soldiers who had conscripted them and the officials who supervised them. And, government officials benefited or profited from many of the projects, while headmen and chiefs who failed to produce their quota of recruits received heavy fines. He accused high officials, particularly Allen C. Yancy (also spelled Yancey), Liberia's vice president, of profiting "at ten dollars per head." Tribesmen understandably fled, leaving "whole districts depopulated."[95]

Reports of frontier forces depredations and abuses by government authorities in tribal areas surfaced periodically. In the eyes of many, although the "Liberian constitution continued to be modeled on that of the United States...Liberia administered its indigenous people in a manner reminiscent of the way in which the worst of European colonial powers governed their African possessions."[96] Seldom did any of these actions occasion corrective steps. But, on the other hand, few, if any, bore the marks of orchestration by top Liberian officials as those of the Fernando Po scandal did. And none had as great an impact on the country.

—⚏—

The origins of the scandal stretched back to an agreement made with the Spanish government in 1912 to supply laborers mainly to Fernando Po, a Spanish island off the west coast of Africa. Under the terms of the agreement, Spain would pay Liberia $45 per "boy" for the first three thousand recruits. For each additional 1,500 "boys" exported, a $5,000 bonus would be paid. Perennially near-bankrupt Liberia, of course, welcomed the revenue.[97] Because of appalling conditions, Liberia cancelled the agreement in 1921, but renewed it in 1928, when Spain's Sindicato Agrícola "guaranteed [Liberian laborers] good care, humane treatment, proper housing, adequate wages, and return to Liberia" after the contract expired.[98]

Unfortunately, the government's recruiting, mainly by the frontier force, depended largely upon coercion. Vice President Yancy, Buell alleged, sent frontier force soldiers to "catch boys." Armed LFF raiders would swoop down on tribal villages, force local chiefs to produce "boys" ostensibly to work on projects in Liberia. Instead, they would be herded aboard a steamer bound for Fernando Po to labor in cocoa plantations there.[99] He recounts that "a government official reportedly arrested a group of natives whom he took to the coast, presumably to put them in jail, but "instead shipped them to Fernando Po." Recruiters reportedly had received five dollars for each boy.[100] Despite reports from American officers in Liberia of deplorable conditions of laborers sent there and of extensive human "trafficking" by Liberian authorities in the interior, the US government took no actions to halt the abuses.[101]

After creation of the League of Nations, interest began to build in the continuing evil of slavery worldwide. At the insistence of Sir Arthur Maitland, Great Britain's delegate, the League Assembly in 1924 appointed a committee to investigate. Their report identified nineteen areas of the world where slavery persisted. Liberia was one. The previous year, a British colonial officer in Sierra Leone, Henry Fenwick Reeves, published a scathing indictment of Liberian leaders' treatment of the country's indigenous people in the hinterland.

What finally caught the attention of official Washington, however, was a dispatch from the US minister in Monrovia in February 1929 warning of the potentially disastrous impact Liberia's labor exports posed for the Firestone Plantation. The exports of labor made it increasingly difficult to obtain workers for the plantation. The American diplomat reported that Vice President Yancy had shipped 318 "boys" to Fernando Po in the previous two months alone.[102]

When Herbert Hoover was elected US president in 1928, he chose a tough Wall Street lawyer, Henry L. Stimson, as his secretary of state. Upon learning of the charges against Liberia, the new secretary dispatched a scathing message on June 8, 1929, to the American chargé in Monrovia to bring to the attention of President King and other Liberian officials. The "United States," he exploded, was "profoundly shocked" at the "development of a system which seems hardly distinguishable from organized slave trade." The frontier force enforced the system, while high Liberian government officials "furnished their authority and influence." Stimson demanded prompt reform, in a "thinly veiled threat of intervention, if Liberia did not quickly and thoroughly 'clean house.'"[103]

Edwin Barclay, Liberia's secretary of state, brushed off the charges as "an old story." But, he said, "we will investigate," although it would be difficult to get very far since the charges failed to pinpoint any specific incident.[104] Stimson, incensed by the Liberians' dilatory response, sent a second note complaining that "nothing had been done to carry out reforms and no action had been taken to punish the guilty officials."[105]

In addition to Faulkner, the chiefs and subchiefs of two chiefdoms in Maryland County filed a complaint against the King administration. They alleged that tribal Liberians had suffered forced recruitment and been sent to work on plantations in the then-French colony of Gabon and the Spanish island of Fernando Po. American missionaries and expatriates working in Liberia supported the charge, adding that several thousand men were being forcibly recruited, under threats of beatings and severe punishments against their chiefs and people if they refused to work on the plantations. Gabon and Fernando Po plantation owners, paid forty-five dollars to the recruiting officials and relatives of President King for each man recruited.

The *New York Times* reported a brief announcement by the US State Department on August 10, 1929, that an international commission of inquiry, appointed by the Liberian president, would investigate allegations of widespread "forced labor conditions" in the Republic of Liberia.[106] The three-man commission, headed by Dr. Cuthbert Christy, included former Liberian president Arthur Barclay and Dr. Charles Spurgeon Johnson, a University of Chicago alumnus, distinguished sociologist, and first president of historically black Fisk University. P. G. Wolo, a tribal Kru man and graduate of Harvard University, would serve as the commission's secretary.

Christy, the League of Nations' choice to lead the inquiry, at first blush appeared unusual, if not unsuited, for the assignment. A medical doctor who qualified at the University of Edinburgh, Cuthbert Christy had logged extensive time beginning in the 1890s in Africa and Asia, as a British military doctor in northern Nigeria, a special medical officer in India for plague, a member of a 1902 Uganda Sleeping Sickness Commission and 1903 Congo medical expedition, and other postings. He also gained notice, and a Royal Geographical Society medal, as an explorer in the Sudan, Nyasaland, and Tanganyika after service in the First World

War. Shortly following his stint on the Liberian inquiry commission, Christy, now a diplomatic celebrity, would die in May 1932 at nearly seventy years old. A buffalo gored him while he was on a zoological investigation in the Congo. (His book *Big Game and Pygmies: Experiences of a Naturalist in Central African Forests in Quest of the Okapi* would become a collector's item, fetching as much as £200 for a copy.)

The commission's terms of reference posed several questions for its members to pursue: Was there any slavery (as defined in the 1926 antislavery convention, which Liberia had signed) in Liberia? And did the Liberian government or its citizens participate in or encourage such slavery? Was slavery or compulsion involved in recruiting Liberian labor for export? To what extent was compulsory labor employed for either public or private undertakings in Liberia? Did the government approve recruiting laborers by using the Liberian Frontier Force or other officials to recruit laborers?

After arriving in Monrovia, the commission began its labors on April 7, 1930, and by September 8 had completed its extensive inquiry. The commissioners interviewed more than three hundred witnesses from all over Liberia, including more than one hundred residents of the hinterland, a large number of paramount chiefs and subchiefs, and three cabinet members.[107] The witnesses, according to a *New York Times* report, "testified with a frankness born of desperation."[108]

The *Times* said the commission uncovered "a shocking condition of affairs in Liberia."[109] Although traditional slavery, "with slave markets and slave dealers no longer" existed, tribal domestic slavery did. Any slave, though, could, at least in theory, win his freedom by bringing a lawsuit against his master or owner. A quasi-slavery custom called "pawning," however, found widespread practice. A person, "usually a child relative," was, in effect, sold into servitude for an indefinite period—during which time the unfortunate "pawn" received neither pay nor privilege.[110]

Forced labor, both inside and outside the country, drew the commissioners' strongest censure. In the tribal areas, chiefs regularly recruited local labor to work on roads, schools, barracks, civil compounds, and other projects, and to serve as porters. With the arrival of Firestone, local chiefs also recruited labor for the rubber plantations, for which they received payment. Abuse of the system was common. Government officials routinely diverted these laborers to "private use on their farms and plantations without pay."[111] Particularly damning, the commission found "a large portion of the contract laborers shipped to Fernando Poo [sic] and French Gabon from the southern counties of Liberia... [had] been recruited under conditions of criminal compulsion scarcely distinguishable from slave raiding and slave trading, and frequently by misrepresenting the destination."[112]

The testimony of a number of the commission's witnesses portrayed a "bloody trail of raided villages, torturing, burning, beating and other outrages...a picture of the worst slaving horrors of a century ago." The report recounted one of the various tortures," in which LFF soldiers "tied ropes around" some "workers [who had] incurred [their] special displeasure" and "hauled them up to the beams above. Then they lighted fires beneath them, into which they threw pepper." Presumably, "the little trick, well known in Liberia as "putting in the kitchen" or "over the fire" caused the workers pain and difficulty in breathing.[113]

Drawing on the commission's report, the *New York Times* reported that another witness, a Grebo native, testified how, in March 1929, soldiers came at night to his town, "knocking at doors and capturing and tying all men and women occupants," terrorizing the town. Many men escaped but returned since the soldiers held their women. They were then marched to Cape Palmas, without food or adequate clothing, and delivered to Mr. Yancy...[who] placed a large number of them in a big house, where they awaited the arrival of the steamer."[114]

Village women suffered as bad or even worse. LFF soldiers forced them to help build barracks at numerous sites in the interior. Moreover, one woman testified the soldiers violated them, with tragic consequences for children so conceived. Since customary tribal law required each mother to prove that her husband fathered any child born to her (clearly impossible in these cases), she tearfully recounted, they had to kill the newborn children. She begged the commission to protect the village women from these attacks by LFF soldiers.

One witness reported how he and fellow tribesmen managed to retaliate against frontier force troops who had raided nearby villages, appropriating women, "waylaying women and people on the pathways and robbing them." Tiring of such outrages, village "professional poisoners took them [the perpetrators] in hand." Three "died and seven others were incapacitated either seriously or permanently."[115]

The commission's report pulled no punches in assigning responsibility. The "Vice-President and other high officials...as well as county superintendents and district commissioners," had sanctioned the Liberia Frontier Force's "compulsory recruitment of labor" and using the LFF for "physical compulsion on road construction, for the intimidation of villagers, for the humiliation and degradation of chiefs, for the imprisonment of inhabitants, and for the convoying of gangs of captured natives to the coast, there guarding them till the time of shipment."[116]

Among those cited was Postmaster General Samuel Alfred Ross, who served as King's vice president in 1920–24. Earlier, as a senator, he allegedly used the LFF "to loot the village of Setra Kru," and while superintendent of Sinoe County, "personally flogged to death a tribal chief, [and] had five tribal officials hanged without trial."[117] He conveniently died December 10, 1929, before any sanctions against him could be taken.

—⁂—

The commission of inquiry called for sweeping reforms in Liberia. It urged the government to adopt a policy of the open door to business from the outside world. But it aimed primarily at the "radical reconstruction of the Liberian Government's policy toward the natives." This would entail breaking down the historical barrier between the "civilized" Americo-Liberians and the "uncivilized" masses of African natives and resurrecting the chiefs' tribal authority. The administration of the interior should be wholly reorganized, replacing current district commissioners and revising the lines that separated the hinterland districts from those along the coast.

The report demanded an end to "pawning" and domestic slavery, halting the export of laborers to Fernando Po and other foreign destinations, curtailing hinterland road construction (one of the main sources of abuses in the compulsory labor system), and tightening control of the Liberian Frontier Force (and revising its mission). As something of a postscript, the commission recommended encouraging better-educated American blacks to immigrate to Liberia to help Liberians work out their problems.[118] The report, if he read it, must have brought a smug smile of satisfaction to Marcus Garvey's face.

President King assured the State Department at the end of September that the government would enact the commission's recommendations, and the next month he informed the League of Nations that Liberia had declared all domestic slaves of native tribes free and also had abolished "pawning."[119] Stimson, however, wanted more. He noted that two months had elapsed since the report's submission but no actions had been taken against guilty officials, all of whom remained in office.

On November 17 the US State Department dispatched a scathing message in which the secretary expressed his outrage, calling the report "a shocking indictment of the Liberian government's policy of suppression of the natives, permitted, if not actually indulged in, by nearly all the high officials of Liberia, including the Vice President." He warned that "international opinion [would] no longer tolerate those twin scourges of slavery and forced labor," and threatened that unless the Liberian government instituted "a comprehensive system of reforms, loyally and sincerely put into effect," it would "result in the final alienation of the friendly feelings which the American government and people have entertained since nearly a century ago."[120]

Although King's "tacit admission of Liberian guilt" outraged "many leading Americo-Liberians,"[121] a "citizens non-partisan league" met in Monrovia on October 10 to draw up a petition to the legislature calling for King to resign.[122] A Liberian legislature committee, appointed to review the report, recommended that King resign, Yancy be impeached, two members of the House of Representatives be expelled, six Ministry of Interior employees be fired, and three frontier force officers be prosecuted. The legislature unanimously approved the recommendations.[123] The body also passed several reform measures, banned pawning, repealed the Ports of Entry Law, and provided for hiring foreign administrative officers.

The *New York Times* on December 5 reported that President King and Vice President Yancy had resigned. The secretary of state, Edwin Barclay, had assumed the office of president. The paper noted that while the evidence against Vice President Yancy and Postmaster General Ross proved particularly damning, any direct connection on President King's part "was never proved, but his responsibility was demonstrated."[124] King retired to a private rubber plantation.

By the time William Tubman became president in 1944, the former president had become something of an elder statesman, serving Liberia in various public offices. He was Liberia's first envoy extraordinaire and minister plenipotentiary to the United States and its first permanent representative to the United Nations. He finally retired from public life in 1952 but remained active in the Protestant Episcopal Church and the Masonic lodge. He died in 1961 at the age of ninety.

The republic had once again escaped an onslaught—but only barely. And another was on its way.

CHAPTER 15

Boss of the Whole Show

—⚞—

ON DECEMBER 5, 1930, SAMUEL Reber Jr., the American chargé d'affaires in Monrovia, received a message from Washington instructing him "to proceed cautiously in dealing" with the Liberian government in the wake of the resignation of President King and Vice President Yancy.[1] Confusion reigned about their status and the reforms. The tension in the air was palpable. The nervous British chargé even asked his government for a warship to cruise off the coast, as a "precautionary measure."[2]

A crowd of Monrovians collected early in the morning outside the Executive Mansion hoping for some kind of reassurance. As the sun began to fill the street, one person in the group apparently sighted the red, white, and blue flag, with its single white star and eleven red and white stripes, fluttering in the morning breeze. He began to sing, "The Lone Star forever! The Lone Star forever!" Others joined in: "O long may it float over land and over sea. Desert it never! O shout for the Lone Star banner, All hail." All seemed to know the familiar "National Flag Song" Edwin James Barclay had composed years before as a teenager.

Edwin Barclay, King's secretary of state, had stepped in to assume the presidency, but the US State Department, and others, had doubts about the action's legitimacy. After further investigation, Reber reported that Barclay had been duly chosen in accordance with Liberian law to serve until a new election was held.[3] In any event, given Barclay's anti-American reputation, the prospect of dealing with him as president of Liberia was not something to be relished. The department further instructed Reber "not to deal with the new government until it had demonstrated willingness to implement the inquiry commission's [proposed] reforms swiftly, to punish offenders, and to pledge not to retaliate against those Africans who had cooperated with the commission."[4] The *New York Times* on March 15, 1931, carried widespread reports of such reprisals.

On the first of June 1932, the newly installed American minister in Monrovia, Charles E. Mitchell, cabled Washington. Edwin Barclay had been elected president and James S. Smith vice president for regular four-year terms. The State Department told Mitchell the United States would withhold formally recognizing the new government "until it had made satisfactory progress" on the reform program and the country's public health conditions.[5] These conditions, which historically had posed a deadly menace to the population, particularly whites, had become a major issue. Yellow fever ran rampant, virtually unchecked. After it claimed the lives of two expatriate employees, the local branch of the Bank of British West Africa withdrew from Liberia, "owing to the alleged complete lack of sanitation."[6] Other similar examples would not be difficult to find.

And the economy once again neared total collapse. To the world, Liberia appeared to be a failing, if not failed state. Barclay moved to stem the fall, appealing to the League of Nations for help. The league's council in January 1932 appointed a special Committee to Examine the Problems Raised by the Liberian Government's Request for Assistance. Eight countries, even including non-league member the United States, agreed to participate. The committee recruited three foreign experts who sailed to Liberia in early 1932: Henri Brunot, a French administrative officer in the league and former governor of the Ivory Coast; a

Dutch financial expert, Mynheer Lighthart; and Dr. Melville D. MacKenzie of the league's health section. An officer from the neighboring British Gold Coast colony already was in Monrovia working on a preliminary health campaign, targeting yellow fever in particular.[7]

The league's experts, however, reported in May that the government was not taking any steps to check the fever. Equally alarming, they saw Liberia's finances in chaos and concluded that conditions there were so chaotic the "small republic [was] in danger of disintegrating."[8]

———

In a short time they pinpointed a major source of Liberia's economic woes. It was the concessions Firestone had obtained from the previous government—whose chief negotiator had been none other than Edwin Barclay. By the time the first latex began to drip from Firestone's trees planted in 1926 and 1927, rubber's price had plummeted from forty-eight cents per pound in 1926 to five cents in the early 1930s.

All of Liberia's exports, pummeled by the worldwide Great Depression, dropped by almost 40 percent, from $1.5 million in 1927 to less than $1 million in 1930.[9] The sharp decline in government revenue, mainly from export duties, put Liberia once again in financial jeopardy. A familiar scenario unfolded. The government could maintain only the barest minimum of operations, not paying employees even a single penny for months on end.[10] The team of experts concluded that unless the terms of the Firestone 1926 loan and planting agreements were modified, Liberia's financial illness would not only continue, but would even grow worse.

A simple calculation showed why. Based on fifty thousand acres initially having been planted, the rubber would come into full production five years later, estimated at four hundred pounds per acre. Firestone could then export about nine thousand tons for roughly $10.9 million at the prevailing price of five and one-half cents per pound. The 1 percent royalty on the exports, plus Firestone's annual rent of six cents per acre on the area planted, would bring the government a meager $13,300. Even assuming an almost four-fold rise in rubber prices to twenty cents per pound, the amount would still total only about $43,000, not even enough to cover the almost $53,000 in salaries of the officials responsible for servicing the loan.[11]

The costs associated with the 1926 loan—amortization and interest on the loan bonds, on top of the generous salaries paid the fiscal officers it required—took an increasingly heavy bite out of the shrinking revenue pie. Rising from 20 percent of the government's total income in 1928, they consumed a whopping 55 percent in 1931.[12] And, W. E. B. DuBois estimated that the loan expenses in 1932 devoured almost the government's entire revenue that year.

Upon their return to Geneva, Henri Brunot and his team presented their recommendations to the Committee on Liberia. They included raising the annual rent for the concession from six cents to fifty cents per acre and declaring a moratorium on loan payments by Liberia until revenues reached $650,000 yearly. Viscount Cecil of Chelwood, the committee's chairman, told the American member, "Everyone admitted that some modification" of the Firestone agreements "was both necessary and possible."[13] Some member countries suggested that it might be "unreasonable to ask Liberia to reform without [first] attacking the root of the evil," namely, deciding "whether the Firestone Company would remain in Liberia or not?"[14] The rubber company objected vigorously. And, the American financial advisor steadfastly insisted on payments agreed to in the 1926 loan.

Based upon the Brunot team's report, Lord Cecil drew up a League of Nations plan of assistance, which the council approved in May 1932. They proposed that Liberia outlaw all compulsory labor, except on communal projects in the hinterland, and suspend education taxes imposed on Africans. But when they recommended that Liberia engage twenty foreign nationals to help the country carry out a league-dictated development plan, Brunot and his colleagues stirred up an international hornets' nest. To implement the plan, they advocated what they termed a league program of "practical assistance and not merely...advice."[15]

The plan called for the country to be divided into three regions, each to be administered by a provincial commissioner, assisted by a deputy commissioner. The commissioners would be responsible to the president of the republic. However, any presidential administrative directive to them concerning hinterland administration would be subject to the approval of the chief advisor, a foreigner appointed by the league. No frontier force would be allowed in the hinterland, unless requested by a commissioner. Foreign commissioners would be permitted to remain in place as long as the chief advisor deemed them needed. Moreover, the chief advisor's recommendations would carry the force of law, unless the league, sans the Liberian delegation's vote, decided unanimously to overrule him.[16]

On the economic side, a financial advisor and his assistants would make all decisions dealing with the economy. They would approve all withdrawals of funds from the treasury. The Liberian government could not dismiss the financial advisor without the league's approval. The estimated cost of the plan, including the foreign advisors' salaries, totaled approximately $150,000, which it was assumed would come from the $2.5 million of undisbursed funds in the $5 million Firestone loan.[17]

Critics sternly cautioned that this proposal would lay "the foundation for...[an] abortive attempt by the League of Nations to assume complete control of Liberia."[18] In effect, the Republic of

Liberia would be reduced to a mere league mandate. Not surprisingly, some of the most heated objections came from Firestone, who viewed the whole exercise as a European attempt to disrupt an independent American rubber supply.[19]

The American rubber baron turned immediately to his old ally in the fight against the Rubber Restriction Plan that had fueled creation of the Liberian plantation in the first place. In a letter to now-president Herbert Hoover, Firestone warned "that unless the State Department takes a firm stand" and blocks the League of Nations from carrying out "their proposed Plan...of placing Liberia under their control, this independent source of rubber supply will be placed in great jeopardy, and eventually taken from the United States." The rubber magnate concluded with a little political jab to prod Hoover to action, writing that should Liberia fall under the league's control, "the administration will be embarrassed with the Negro race in this country [the United States]."[20]

This time, however, the American administration did not jump through Firestone's hoops. Time had changed the landscape. The restriction scheme had been lifted; rubber was readily available at market prices, and, moreover, the US State Department supported international rather than unilateral action to resolve the Liberian crisis.[21] The administration sought to keep a balance in its approach to Liberia, "trying," as the chief of the department's Western European Affairs Division put it, "to carry two pails, one filled with Negro votes and the other with Firestone contributions."[22]

Firestone received a two-sentence response from the White House, "assuring him of President Hoover's continued American interest in his Liberian enterprise." Period. Full stop.[23]

To Firestone's complaint that the league's plan "did not have sufficient provision for predominant or exclusive American participation," Secretary of State Stimson sharply retorted that the US government did not intend to assume "direct accountability for" any African country, "even at the request of the inhabitants themselves." He reminded Firestone that, based on the department's earlier analysis, the plan "provided a framework" that could afford protection to "legitimate Firestone interests." Moreover, if the rubber company head persisted in his opposition, he should be prepared "to accept responsibility for the...unfavorable public opinion" that would inevitably arise both "within and outside the United States."[24]

A chastened Firestone immediately met with US officials and dispatched a message to the Committee on Liberia in Geneva, promising to send a representative soon "to work out an agreement that would be mutually beneficial to the Republic and his company."[25] However, Firestone backtracked and instead sent J. T. Lyle, vice president of Firestone's Finance Corporation of America, to Monrovia. His visit and meeting on December 14, 1932, with President Barclay produced zero positive results. In fact, Liberia issued a statement prior to Lyle's visit saying that the country would not make any financial commitments to any party other than the League of Nations. Stalemate.

Barclay and the Liberian legislature also were far from enthralled with the league's assistance plan. But faced with the specter of disastrous financial collapse and piqued by Firestone's intransigence, they appropriated a play from Brunot's playbook. Unfortunately, it would be one that would draw the United States into the fray—and not on Liberia's side. The Liberian president signed a moratorium act on December 23, 1932, temporarily suspending payments on the Firestone loan, retroactive to June 30, "until the Republic's income reached $650,000 annually for two years in succession."[26] The legislative resolution also called for drastically reducing the numbers and salaries of the foreign financial experts.

The US government "expressed its profound dismay" at Liberia's unilateral repudiation of the loan agreement, and announced it would halt all economic assistance, as well as lodge complaints against any subsequent foreign loans to Liberia.[27]

Some suggested more severe sanctions. The American minister in Monrovia, Charles Mitchell, recommended that "Liberian leaders be 'disciplined' for allegedly humiliating and insulting the American government and its nationals."[28] Harvey Firestone allegedly wanted the US government to intervene directly and send in American troops.[29] Everett Sanders, his lawyer and chairman of the Republican National Party, reportedly called for an American warship to be sent to Liberian waters to protect Firestone interests. The Firestone group in Liberia, according to some sources, even sought to overthrow the government and openly advocated restoring ex-president King. (He had surfaced as Harvey Firestone's personal lawyer in Monrovia.) The rubber company's headquarters reportedly recalled one of its top officials from Liberia because of the rogue conspiracy.[30]

Few of these sanctions had any immediate impact on the Liberians. But when the foreign financial advisor in Monrovia refused to authorize the government to withdraw any funds under the depository agreement, President Barclay shot back that "no one [i.e., Liberia] can be expected to commit suicide because of the theoretical legal rights of another."[31] Graham Greene recounts how the advisor, an elderly American who had served successfully in Saudi Arabia and the Philippines, now found himself without any work. He "lived on in Monrovia at a reduced salary with nothing to do but shoot at bottles and hit billiard balls."[32] Then in January 1933, Barclay dismissed, in clear violation of the loan agreement, the supervisor of internal revenue, W. A. Travelle, another American. The war was on.

Barclay not only thumbed his nose at the international community, he also began flexing his muscles domestically. In the summer of 1932, he initiated a series of actions designed to harass and intimidate real and imagined enemies. Private newspapers were suppressed. Offending editors critical of the regime could find themselves in jail, charged with libel or even treason. While not unusual in the country's history, such suppression, historian Svend Holsoe suggested, "only became systematic" during Barclay's administration.[33]

In addition, the president "allegedly created, or approved the creation" of an organization of young men, playfully called the "President's Cowboys." Their job: to bully suspected administration opponents.[34] The American chargé in Monrovia described one incident in which the Cowboys raided the home of an attorney while he was in court. "[Rumors] circulated he would be arrested." Fearing the worst, the lawyer fled to the American legation for refuge.[35]

The administration didn't hesitate to accuse prominent political opponents—including ex-president King and Thomas Faulkner—of "betraying Liberia." Even Liberian Supreme Court justice T. E. Beysolow was accused of accepting a bribe from Firestone to strike down Barclay's moratorium on the 1926 loan. He found himself the uncomfortable subject of one of the so-called "grapevine" posters that prominently carried scurrilous attacks on and threats to Barclay's enemies. The justice "and his colleagues were warned to be careful or face death." Other posters featured leading Liberians accused of "frequenting the homes of 'white Americans…tattling, plotting, scheming against the government for a few dirty dollars.'" Such enemies, according to the posters, deserved "to be excoriated and made white [a very derogatory slander in Liberia] and ostracized."[36]

Barclay, of course, denied any involvement. However, authorities allowed the posters to remain in place for forty-eight hours before removing them, and the government failed to ever condemn the attacks or those responsible for them. Little doubt lingered in the minds of the public as to who was behind them. And the message was sufficiently clear to put an end to most serious opposition to the "boss of the whole show."

As a footnote, four years later a bizarre scheme unfolded. On September 1, 1939, a George Randolph and Sylvester Whitehead sought American help in overthrowing the Liberian government. The two plotters purportedly represented an Afro-American Navigation Association, located at 225 West 146th Street, New York City. They alleged that the Americo-Liberian establishment had made conditions "intolerable" for black Americans wanting to immigrate to Liberia, primarily to help Americo-Liberians maintain their favored status and privileges there. They boasted that if the US government would supply them a small vessel, within six months they would overthrow the Barclay government and establish a "liberal administration." Henry Villard, the State Department's chief of the African and Near Eastern Affairs Division, whom they had contacted, launched an investigation. The organization and its New York address proved fictitious, the two men unemployed.[37]

—⚬—

Born January 5, 1882, into one of the country's "most remarkable family dynasties", hard-knuckle politics came quite naturally to Edwin James Barclay. His paternal grandparents and their children immigrated to Liberia from Barbados. His father, Ernest, served as Liberia's foreign minister, and his uncle, Arthur Barclay, was Liberia's fifteenth president. Other relatives included "various justices of the Supreme Court, senators, and cabinet members.[38] Edwin himself had been a circuit judge, minister of education, and minister of justice. He also was known as a poet and musician.

The British novelist Graham Greene met President Barclay on a trip to Liberia's interior in 1935. Greene was somewhat surprised since "no president before Barclay had dared to tour the interior." His predecessor, Charles King, had passed quickly through a part of the area, carried in a hammock and guarded by two hundred soldiers, on a visit to Sierra Leone; Barclay had only thirty men with him. The difference lay in a recently completed native "pacification" program, the work of the infamous frontier force colonel Elwood T. Davies. [39]

Greene described the president at that time as a "middle-aged man...with curly greying hair in a thick dark suit, a pinned and pinched old school tie and a cheap striped shirt." After the president's African veneer—"lovely, vivid and composed, slipped away"—the author observed, "one was left with the West Indies, an affable manner, and rhetoric, lots of rhetoric. But there was a lot of energy, too." Greene saw him as "a politician in the Tammany Hall manner, but something new" on the West African coast. While Barclay was likely "out to play his own game," Greene thought he "was going to play it with unexampled vigour and the Republic would at least pick up some chips from his table."[40]

The author asked the president "whether his authority was much the same as the American President's." Barclay replied that "it was more complete. 'Once elected...and in charge of the machine'—words ran away with him—'why then, I'm the boss of the whole show.'"[41] And he played that role to the hilt, so much so that he had "some claim," Greene wrote, "to be known as the Republic's first dictator."[42] Besides being "the most dictatorial of all Liberian presidents," many in the international community added, Barclay also enjoyed the "reputation of being a racial nationalist."[43]

His domestic political opponents cried foul, but for a different reason. "There was a kind of unwritten law," Greene noted, "that the president could take two terms of office and then he had to let another man in to pick the spoils." And the president, as the "boss of the whole show," had the newspapers, the civil service, and, as President King had shown, the printing press and means to stuff ballot boxes to near overflowing. But Barclay, "beaming with gold-rimmed benevolence," proudly pointed out at least "how he had cleaned" the civil service up and, removed it "from political influence."[44]

Opponents complained Barclay "wasn't playing fair" because "he was treating politics seriously." Either they must have been speaking with tongues in cheek, or they thought better of describing to a British journalist the President's Cowboys and grapevine posters as "playing unfair." Although Greene did not swallow the president's "sweetness and light" fully, he wrote that he "had to admit" Barclay "had energy and courage...and his hands were comparatively clean." At least in the forced labor scandal, where the League of Nations commission had exonerated him.[45]

But, his administration had not been exonerated from responsibility in one of the most heinous episodes in Americo-Liberian relations with native African Liberians. Like most of the other tribes in Liberia, the Kru and Grebos had never brought themselves to fully accept Americo-Liberian dominance. Periodic outbreaks of uprisings, revolts, and wars dotted their relations. More than once they defied the Monrovian government's authority, even openly declaring themselves British subjects. They chafed under the restrictions the Ports of Entry law imposed on their trade. They refused to pay the hut tax and hated the frontier force and most Liberian administrators. Although Liberia's tribesmen were granted "citizenship" in 1907, it was largely a hollow gesture since they still were denied the right to vote.

Greene reported that he "never came across a single native who had a good word for the politicians in Monrovia." He added, "Everywhere in the north I found myself welcomed because I was white, because they hoped all the time that a white nation would take the country over."[46]

When Barclay assumed the presidency, the Americo-Liberian establishment still smarted from the worldwide ignominy of condemnation over the Fernando Po affair. The damning testimony the natives provided particularly stuck in the Americo-Liberian craws. Many of Barclay's True Whig Party supporters demanded punishment. The president also recognized that to attract and utilize foreign investments, "internal peace and tranquility... [were] conditions precedent."[47]

As the first step to achieve this "peace and tranquility," he decided it was time to establish the government's authority over dissident tribesmen. The rebellious Kru in the eastern coast area and the Gola in the west-central region provided the prime targets. On May 20, 1931, he ordered a frontier force expedition, commanded by Colonel Davies, to the rebel-controlled areas. They were to demonstrate the government's power to enforce its authority over the insurgents in a convincing manner, sufficient to deter other tribal groups from flouting Monrovia's rule.[48] Among other things, they were to collect overdue taxes from the natives and disarm them.

Davies, a black mercenary from North America, pursued his orders with a zeal rivaling that of Attila the Hun. He and his men reportedly destroyed every village they encountered along the Kru coast, ruthlessly killing at random, raping, pillaging. One of his soldiers recounted how they had attacked a village where they killed some one hundred or so residents, mutilating bodies, which, he wrote, "was awful to look at."[49]

Finally, the *New York Times* reported in an October 25, 1936, article, "one of the most cruel wars ever fought in Africa" had ended with the capture of King Nimley, the Kru rebel leader. Nimley, with a dozen other tribal chiefs, in 1932 "established an autonomous territory 100 miles square on the Liberian coast." The *Times* went on to report that twenty thousand natives had died, "many of them starved, mutilated, or eaten in the jungle struggle...hundreds of native villages...burned and families driven into the jungle to die from exposure and starvation."[50]

News of the expedition's atrocities soon reached Monrovia and the outside world. Outrage in Europe and the United States mounted; governments filed strong protests with the Liberian government. Britain's Foreign Office charged that Davies's actions "were tyrannical and high-handed in an inexcusable degree."[51] In response, Barclay appointed a three-man commission, composed of two Americo-Liberians and W. A. Travelle, the American inspector of revenue, to investigate. Villagers in the affected areas testified that Davies ordered their villages torched, trapping "old men, women, and children," who were burned to death. Towns were completely deserted as residents fled from anticipated attack. Many natives refused to testify out of fear of reprisal or from their hostility to the government.[52]

Despite these findings, the commission's report let Davies and his men off lightly, concluding that they had "acted with great caution in carrying out their duties," and "that Colonel Davies tried to do the best he could under the circumstances."[53] Travelle, whom Barclay would later fire from his inspector of revenue position, however, disagreed in a minority report. He charged that the frontier force soldiers "acted in an exceedingly brutal and oppressive manner," wantonly attacking and burning towns without warning, with "extremely great loss of lives and property."[54]

Travelle's dissent spurred the United States and its European friends to launch still another inquiry, this time by the British consul in Monrovia. D. G. Ryding would visit the interior and report to the League of Nations.[55] The consul surveyed a number of affected areas. At Sasstown, which had been the center of the most serious fighting, he found leveled villages, destroyed rice farms, and women, children, and old people near death after the young men had fled Davies's marauders. In his May 1932 report to the league, known as the *British Blue Book*, Ryding described how "the plantation town of Wolokri [in the Sasstown area]...was attacked in the night" as the inhabitants slept. "The soldiers," he wrote, "crept into the banana plantations, which surround all native villages," and fired round after round "into the huts," ruthlessly killing women and children.[56]

One unfortunate woman, "who had that day" delivered twins, "was shot in her bed." The twins died in the flames "when the village was fired by the troops." Forty-one villages reportedly were burned, 141 people killed, including forty-five women and children, and many women raped. An estimated twelve thousand natives fled their villages and farmlands. Ryding concluded that the Americo-Liberian administrators could not govern the African natives and recommended that the country be placed under "white rule."[57]

But the disturbances and investigations still would not go away. Frontier force soldiers attacked those Africans who had cooperated with Ryding's investigations. Many were too frightened to go back to their villages. The league sent Dr. Melville MacKenzie (the yellow fever expert) to try to persuade the displaced Kru people to return to their homes by guaranteeing them peace and protection, as well as plans for reconstructing their battered villages. The rebellious but naive Krus accepted the promise and turned over their weapons to MacKenzie. But, it was a promise the league could not keep.[58]

Graham Greene on his journey through the interior actually met—in a remote upcountry village named Tapee-Ta—the notorious Colonel Davies. Recounting the atrocities described in the *British Blue Book*, Greene wrote that he had felt "a little uneasy" at the prospect of meeting the colonel, whom he "pictured...

as something rather ferocious."⁵⁹ But upon seeing him, the author noted that "even at a distance there was something attractive about" the man who had come to be known as "the dictator of Grand Bassa. He had personality. He carried himself with a straight military swagger, he was well dressed in a tropical suit with a silk handkerchief stuck in the breast pocket. He had a small pointed head and one couldn't at that distance see the gold teeth which rather weakened his mouth."⁶⁰

In a couple of lengthy, unexpectedly pleasant, chats over whiskies, Davies sketched his background: "He had once been a private in the American army," serving in "Pershing's disastrous Mexican expedition," [and] later in the Philippines. He left the United States, came to Liberia, and "was very soon appointed medical officer of health," although he apparently didn't have "any kind of medical degree." President King appointed him "Colonel Commandant of the Frontier Force," and when King was forced to resign, Davies "managed to switch his allegiance to Mr. Barclay."⁶¹

Gingerly broaching the subject of the Kru war, Greene noted "the Colonel" surprisingly "took up the subject with enthusiasm." From Davies' version, Greene observed that "as far as I could make out the operation" in which Colonel Davies allegedly committed the atrocities, "had turned on a cup of Ovaltine rather than on rifles or machine-guns." By Davies's account, the town when he entered was "quite empty except for women and old men." Greene wrote that he would "have expected Colonel Davis [Greene's spelling] to have set fire to the town while his men raped the women: but no." Instead, he had "called for the oldest man, made him sit down, gave him a glass of Ovaltine… made friends with him, and had him send messages to the warriors [who had been sent out of the village to ambush Davies] to return in peace." The colonel confided that he always had "'a glass of Ovaltine at the end of a day's trek.'"⁶²

The British consul's report "that six children had been burnt alive," Davies said, had most "gone to his heart." Greene, obviously enchanted by the colonel, could not believe him responsible for a woman being shot while in her bed just after being delivered of twins, and her children burnt alive; or for "children cut down with cutlasses; the heads and limbs of victims carried on poles; for otherwise Colonel Davis had to be pictured as a monster, and a monster one simply couldn't believe him to be, as he flashed his gold teeth over the whisky, a bit doggish, a bit charmingly shy and small boy."[63]

Davies was never punished.

As the controversy surrounding the Kru war and Colonel Davies subsided, Liberia's disputes with Firestone, the US government, and the League of Nations continued. Firestone and the US government still objected to Liberia's moratorium on payments on the 1926 loan. Liberia disputed the need in the first place for any loan at all. Firestone refused to cooperate with league officials until Barclay repudiated his actions. Liberia opposed the league's proposal to give sweeping powers to foreign advisors in its plan of assistance and would not accept a chief advisor from the United States or any European country that had a colony bordering Liberia. And Firestone opposed the plan's concentrating power in non-American advisors.[64]

In early 1933, prior to newly elected president Franklin Delano Roosevelt's inauguration, Liberia's secretary of state sent a memorandum to the League of Nations; it claimed the government had not sought the 1926 loan and only agreed to accept it because of pressure from quarters supporting Firestone interests. The memo blamed Liberia's current economic calamity largely on the loan and the officials Firestone's subsidiary, the Finance Corporation of America, appointed to manage it.

Firestone rose to the challenge with its version of the circumstances surrounding the loan: Liberia needed the loan primarily to retire $60,000 of internal debt, to eliminate the 1912 customs receivership imposed on Liberia, and to insure adequate funds were available to the government to enable it to function in an orderly manner. Second, Firestone had no primary interest in extending a loan itself to Liberia. And, in fact, had asked the US government to advance a loan, which it flatly refused to do. Finally, King, while president, "publicly had claimed in 1928 that the American government did not seek any special political rights or economic privileges in his country."[65]

To counter the charge that the loan had gone largely to pay the foreign experts or otherwise been wasted, Firestone submitted an accounting to league officials. It showed 90 percent of expenditures had been applied to reduce Liberia's financial obligations incurred before the loan. Moreover, the government had failed to implement most of the experts' recommendations for curbing the financial crisis: most importantly, trimming the budget, especially by reducing the government's workforce and the size of the frontier force; taking measures to increase revenues by imposing penalties under existing laws for delinquent tax payments; prosecuting those who failed to pay customs duties; and going after officials guilty of misappropriating official funds.[66]

To what extent the government could have taken extreme cost-cutting measures in the face of the Great Depression, the impending League of Nations enquiries, and continuing disturbances in the hinterland is open to question. The prevailing political climate and the shakiness of the King administration would have made it difficult, at best, to carry them out without creating greater political and economic chaos.

Firestone's argument also did not fully dispel the charge critics made that Liberia had been pressured into accepting the loan. He insisted that he had considered the loan an essential condition to embarking upon the plantation venture, a needed protection against possibly future capricious government actions. When the Liberian government stubbornly refused to accept a Firestone loan, and the US State Department refused to step in to offer financing, he managed to enlist the latter's help in persuading Liberia to agree to the project and the Finance Corporation loan arrangement. [67] The department stressed that getting the Firestone operation successfully underway would significantly benefit Liberia by opening the door to additional investors, inviting them in to contribute to the country's development. In any event, American persuasion proved sufficient to get Liberia aboard the Firestone train.[68]

When critics such as Professor Buell and W. E. B. DuBois zeroed in on alleged "coercion" by the US government, President King had stepped forward with his denial statement. Now, seven years later, Firestone resurrected it to ward off attacks by Barclay, the man who had served as King's secretary of state and principal negotiator in the deal with Firestone. While Marcus Garvey in his excoriation of King implied that bribery might have played a role in King's acceptance of Firestone, no convincing evidence ever surfaced.

Arguments and counterarguments, charges and countercharges that flew back and forth between Monrovia and Akron achieved little to break the Firestone-Liberian deadlock. Firestone still insisted that the chief advisor proposed in the League's plan of assistance must be an American. Barclay still held out for a weakened plan in which the chief advisor would not be an American and would not come from any countries that had colonies bordering Liberia.

Both sides began to look to Washington, where the new Democratic administration was settling in. Early in 1933 DuBois, a longtime black pebble in Firestone's rubber sneakers, led a delegation of ten prominent black Americans, including Mordecai

W. Johnson, president of Howard University, and Walter White, secretary of the NAACP, to meet with William Phillips, the acting US secretary of state.[69]

The group pushed for the American government to recognize the Barclay regime and approve a chief advisor in the League's plan of assistance, one who "would be acceptable to Liberian authorities." Phillips's response was to assure the delegation that "the United States government" still maintained "its traditional policy of keen interest in the welfare of Liberia and the Liberian people."[70] Since the response, not surprisingly, did not wholly satisfy most black Americans, various groups continued to advocate for US support to insure Liberia remained "an independent political entity."[71]

After the State Department completed a reassessment of the relationship between Liberia and the United States, President Roosevelt took action. First, he met the Firestone train head on, saying, "Firestone went into Liberia at his own financial risk and it is not the business of the State Department to pull his financial chestnuts out of the fire except as a friend of the Liberian people."[72] He agreed to the United States cooperating with other countries in Liberia, but with the "clear understanding we are not guaranteeing any monies or making our continued interest depend on Firestone's financial interest."[73] And, he added, the United States would not insist on the chief advisor in the plan of assistance being an American.[74]

Firestone got the message. And Barclay, while holding off the league, busily carried out most of the reforms prescribed in the plan of assistance, including those demanded by the United States as quid pro quo for recognition. Officials in the hinterland could no longer force natives to serve as unpaid porters. Actions of the notorious Liberian Frontier Force were sharply curtailed, and employing force and raiding villages to collect taxes ended.[75]

The Liberian president also managed to block attempts of government officials to increase their salaries, demanded "an across-the-board reduction in government appropriations," and even ordered that legislators paid more than $300 monthly take a cut of 10 to 20 percent in their salaries. Many people lost their jobs. But, despite strong opposition, including threats of impeachment and removing the secretary of the treasury, the "boss of the whole show" was sufficiently "entrenched in power" to push ahead.[76]

The American minister in Monrovia, Lester A. Walton, Charles Mitchell's replacement, reported, "Tempers so frayed, friendship strained, personalities indulged in, bluntly written communications exchanged and reports circulated about threats of resignation, impeachment and removal from office."[77] But Barclay remained firm, convincing many people, particularly foreigners, of his ability to lead the country, even in perilous and chaotic times.

The year 1935, while disastrous for Ethiopia, Africa's only other country ruled by Africans, would prove to be a banner year for Liberia—and Edwin Barclay. The previous year rubber prices had begun to rise again. Barclay had managed to drag out the fights both with Firestone and the League of Nations proposed plan of assistance without capitulating to either one. Once again, it appeared the republic had skirted calamity, and one could envision a future, although the smell of future war hung heavy, even in the air of Africa.

Barclay, nonetheless, must have leaned back in his presidential chair, smugly savoring the fruits of his stubborn defiance of the world's great powers, even the League of Nations. Firestone and

Liberia worked out new supplementary agreements to the existing loan and planting agreements, in which the rubber company agreed to advance Liberia $650,000 for making payments on its outstanding debt, reduce the interest rate on the 1926 loan from 7 to 5 percent, and exempt Liberia from making interest payments whenever the republic's annual income fell to $450,000 or less. The financial advisor's annual salary was reduced to $9,000, and the salaries of the other loan officials were also cut. In return, Liberia "would waive import and export taxes on plantation products" and grant Firestone mineral rights to its leased lands.[78] On balance, Firestone still emerged from the extended fray with a very attractive arrangement, even better than the original one. In March 1935 the two parties signed the supplementary agreements.

> The 1935 Supplementary Agreement, an addendum to the original 1926 accord, by and large proved a "sweet deal" for Firestone: a modest 1 percent tax on exports of its products (rubber), but freedom for ninety years (1935–2025) from any and all taxes (except document stamps) or any other charges on imports (motor vehicles limited to 150 units) and exports for company operations and for developing the concession area. Expatriate employees also would be exempt from direct or personal taxes. The company, in addition, obtained exclusive mineral rights (even including diamonds, which Firestone's Harbel plantation was thought to contain) to its leased lands, with any royalties limited to 10 percent. Plus, the rubber company secured the right to build and operate an air transportation system.
>
> And the cost to Firestone for these rights and privileges? A bargain-basement price of $650,000 in Liberian government bonds (at par) issued under the 1926 Loan Agreement with Firestone. (With the transaction, the bonds were then retired.) Cash payment to the government? Zero.

Game to Harvey Firestone. He had legally managed to thwart President Barclay's suspension of Liberia's payments to the company on the 1926 loan by in effect accepting repayment in rights and privileges. And though Firestone would never use its exclusive mineral rights, they deterred others from undertaking any mining ventures.[79]

On May 28, 1935, the League of Nations dropped its plan of assistance for Liberia and ended further help.[80] And on June 11, the United States formally recognized the Barclay administration.[81] Domestically, Barclay was riding equally high. Not only did he win reelection on May 7, he also pushed through an amendment to the constitution extending the presidential term from four to eight years. He and his vice president, Daniel N. M. Falus, would serve until January 3, 1944.

—⚉—

President Barclay perhaps thought Liberia must at last be on its way to economic development and modernity. But anyone looking at the state of the country would have entertained serious doubts. The Monrovia Graham Greene described in 1935, for example, had progressed little from what Edward Blyden viewed in 1866; if anything, it had gone backward—very much like the roads the novelist had encountered up country.

Blyden was enthralled with the burgeoning capital city, begun only forty-five years earlier—four main streets with residences occupied by the Americo-Liberian elite, all "substantial structures of stone or brick, and the dwellings two stories high," government buildings, the Baptist, Presbyterian, Trinity (Episcopal), and Methodist churches, and the "Methodist Seminary, occupying what may be called the acropolis." A "fine street intersects" the four streets "and descends" from the seminary "gradually a full mile to the sea-shore on the south."[82]

Greene years later also saw Monrovia as "like a beginning" but, in contrast to Blyden, he saw a beginning which…[had] come to little beyond the two grassy main streets intersecting each other and lined with broken-paned houses all of wood and of one storey except for the brick churches, one little brick villa belonging to the Secretary of the Treasury, the three-storeyed Executive Mansion where the President lived, the State Department opposite and the unfinished stone house of ex-President King.[83]

Signs of thwarted beginnings abounded:

> Telephone poles along the main street and…the one motor road towards Mount Barclay and the Firestone Rubber Plantations, but the telephone service no longer exists. The residential street runs gently uphill towards a waste of scorched rock and sand…and here and there among the rocks are planted the beginnings of stone houses, sometimes only the foundation laid, sometimes several storeys, so that these unfinished buildings have the appearance of houses gutted by fire.[84]

Anyone with money to spare invested in buildings, which, Greene explained, seldom progressed beyond "the foundation and first storey" before the owner's funds were depleted.[85]

The interior, Liberia's vast hinterland, also appeared to have changed little since Benjamin Anderson's 1868 pioneering explorations—except, perhaps, for the unwelcome presence of Liberian administrators, frightening forays of the Liberian Frontier Force, and, of course, the Firestone rubber plantations. Greene found that only paths still connected one place to another in "the immense forest, which covers the Republic within a few miles of the coast." Like Anderson almost seventy years earlier, he traveled "more than three hundred miles through dense deserted forest," with twenty-five carriers, who "walked naked except for loin cloths," carrying "fifty-pound cases" on their heads, though "their legs were thin as a woman's...[and] their arms...childishly thin."[86]

They found most of the villages also remained pretty much the same as Anderson described them, including secret societies—the Poro for men and Sande for women—and witchcraft. In the absence of any formal schools, traditional "bush schools" still dominated village life. Families tilled a few acres of land, growing rice and cassava, largely for themselves, possibly some cocoa, coffee, and palm oil. No doctors or clinics, only traditional medicine, to counter the ever-present yellow fever and malaria.

The Poro and Juju

Graham Greene, in his delightful account of his journey across Liberia in 1935, recounts that secret societies were "more firmly rooted in Liberia than in any other country on the West Coast [of Africa]." He mentions the Leopard, Snake, and Alligator societies of the men and the Terrapin society of the women, and relates some of the local lore about them. How, for example, some Liberians believed Charles Dunbar King, the president forced to resign in 1930 because of the forced labor scandal, belonged to the Alligator society. He and several members of his cabinet allegedly sacrificed a goat to enhance their and the country's fortunes. However, since traditionally a human should have been offered, many thought a subsequent accident in which a boatload of young Kru tribesmen drowned represented the alligator's dissatisfaction with the sacrifice.[87]

Documented accounts of ritualistic murders and witchcraft, or juju as it is called in west Africa, abound. Greene describes how in a village he visited, everyone knew that four men had come to the village looking for a victim to satisfy "their ritual need of the heart, the palms of the hands, the skin of the forehead, but no one knew who they were."[88] In the 1930s the government court-martialed and executed fifty Leopard society members, "heart men" who had kidnaped a number of people and cut out their organs to use in their rituals. Even in the 1955 election campaign, Tubman supporters accused challengers Barclay and Coleman of seeking to eliminate the president by using juju. The two challengers in turn charged Tubman's followers of hiring heart men who at night seek victims (Barclay and Coleman in this instance) for their hearts to use in making juju.[89]

Two secret societies----the Poro for men and the Sande for women---- dominated village life in west Africa, most notably in Liberia and Sierra Leone. They flourished particularly among Gola, Vai, Dei, and Kpelle tribal people, Professor Liebenow notes, the "rituals and sanctions of Poro within these ethnic groups [took] "precedence over all secular associations and institutions. The Council of Poro elders, meeting in the sacred grove," could override "the decisions of secular chiefs" and undercut their authority. "The council [had] the power of life and death over members who violated its secrets, and the initiation of young men into the Poro [marked] their entry into adulthood."[90]

The Poro societies during the traditional era functioned as the village government, "controlling such antisocial behavior as incest, murder, arson, and looting by warriors." In addition, they secured villagers' cooperation in "defense, cultivation, house building, bridge construction," and other community undertakings. The Poro's primary sanction resided in "the fear and awe" a "visit of one of the masked figures instilled in the women, children, and uninitiated youths."[91] Its ultimate sanction? The death penalty. The two societies in addition served the community's educational needs by sending young boys and girls at extended intervals to separate "bush schools"—four years for the boys, three for the girls.

After the government extended its mandate into the tribal hinterland, it banned the societies. However, the ban against the Poro and Sande was lifted once the authorities felt sufficiently in control over them. The government allowed them to continue as an essential element in tribal society so long as they did not interfere with schools, clinics, or other institutions or otherwise conflict with Americo-Liberian interests. They became another instrument of Americo-Liberian control.[92] Poro society masks used in its rites are prominent in most museums of African art.[93]

Poro Society mask. Author's collection.

Transport still relied on native carriers and one's own feet since only the fringes of the hinterland possessed any roads. Graham Greene, on his 1935 trek through Liberia, bemoaned the lack of drivable roads. The problem, he decided after passing "an unfinished concrete bridge near Grand Bassa, on the coast southeast of Monrovia, "marking where the road had once reached" but now had vanished, was that roads in Liberia "went backward."[94]

Although there had been plans and proposals from various foreign interests over the years, the country still awaited a railroad and an adequate seaport. Expectations for schools and medical clinics, even in the coastal regions, much less the hinterland, had faded long ago

President Barclay's answer to Liberia's development relied to a large extent on foreign investments, an Open Door policy. In his first inaugural address in January 1932, he picked up his uncle Arthur's refrain when the latter was president, promising to "encourage the investment of reproductive foreign capital" according it "such facilities that while the investor may be satisfied, the economic status of our people will at the same time be improved."[95] He promptly obtained repeal of the infamous Ports of Entry Law and the Transportation Act, both of which curtailed foreigners' economic activities, and the government signed concession agreements with Dutch, Danish, Polish, and German investors.

Despite his efforts, the country still languished. Even though the League of Nations had given up on its plan of assistance, threats to Liberia's integrity continued to arise. According to Marxist writer and activist George Padmore, a small coterie of Liberians, mainly retired government officials, even petitioned the president to invite the United States to assume governance of Liberia. Barclay, of course, dismissed the request.[96] And Benito Mussolini's thirst for an Italian African empire, which soon would consume Ethiopia, stirred fears of a new scramble for Africa. Adding to this angst, the Italian government in 1935 made an unprecedented demand that its "nationals in Liberia be granted all the privileges of Liberian citizenship."[97] Barclay refused, but some worried that Italy's demand might be the prelude to greater demands. Then, the following year, the prime minister of South Africa, James Hertzog, suggested that the League of Nations give Nazi Germany a mandate over Liberia. This, he reasoned, would satisfy Germany's colonial lust, and, at the same time, solve Liberia's financial and social problems.[98]

But Barclay's (and Liberia's) luck held out. Under a three-year plan initiated in 1934, Liberia's foreign trade volume expanded, the tariff schedule was revised, and internal taxes were collected more systematically. Helped by favorable rubber prices, revenue in the first six months of 1936 registered a 31.8 percent rise compared with the same period in 1935. The $344,361 total allowed the government to pay the $46,475 interest due July 1 on its outstanding bonds and to continue making payments on its Firestone loan. (The government already had lifted its moratorium the previous year and resumed payments.)

The American minister in Monrovia, Lester Walton, cautioned, however, that the increased income did not "mean the country" was "enjoying an excess of prosperity." But at least it suggested the government was paying greater attention "to the efficient administration and development of the country." Walton described the president's plan, a substitute for the rejected league plan, as providing "for a balanced budget [and] reorganization of internal administration," as well as promoting agriculture, expanding educational facilities, building roads, and improving public health conditions. Seven foreign experts, of whom five were American, included Maxwell Sabin, the group's head, a financial advisor, military aide, economic advisor, supervisor of revenue, auditor, and public health administrator. Hopefully, they would help bring Barclay's plan to fruition.[99]

Firestone reportedly expanded, too, opening new plantations and boosting its work force to between five thousand and six thousand rubber cultivators. Minister Walton reported that Liberia enjoyed its "healthiest financial condition in its history."[100] In August 1938 the United States and Liberia signed a friendship, commerce, and navigation treaty, and in October the light cruiser USS *Boise* anchored at Monrovia on her maiden cruise to pay a courtesy visit. The ship's complement attended ceremonies celebrating Liberia's founding and presented some of the bunting from which the first Liberian flag was sewn.[101] Barclay received a message on July 26, 1939, from President Roosevelt, "on the anniversary of the foundation of the Republic of Liberia," extending "cordial congratulations and sincere best wishes for the nation's progress and prosperity."[102] The United States "was still interested in the little African country."[103] Liberia would need that interest and more.

———∽∽∽———

As war verged ever closer, President Barclay in the spring of 1939 began to consider contingency plans. He found Liberia's options in the event of a European war distressingly limited. The expense of building up a sufficient defense force put that avenue out of the question. Although he thought formally tying Liberia's defense to a foreign power or powers risky in terms of the country's independence, it was Liberia's only alternative. Both Harvey Firestone and American secretary of state Cordell Hull advised him that the best course of action would be for Great Britain and France to issue a joint declaration warning that a German attack on Liberia would be considered an attack on their own colonies. Hull indicated that the United States would not be willing to establish air or naval bases on Liberian soil and squelched the idea of inviting, as a precaution, French troops into the republic; such a move, he thought, might provide an unfriendly power an excuse to attack Liberia.[104]

The actual outbreak of war in September, followed by reports of German submarines spotted off the northwestern African coast—including one in Liberian waters—and purported German planning to invade Liberia on the pretext of protecting resident German nationals there spurred the government's efforts to seek help. The British response on July 8: "His Majesty's Government" declared it "could not remain indifferent if Liberia were the victim of unwarranted aggression" with the objective of establishing "a foreign power on her territory."[105]

December 7, 1941, suddenly pushed Liberia into the forefront of American strategic thinking. Harvey Firestone's great venture in Liberia to escape the British rubber restriction scheme now assumed a large dimension in American planning. With one fell swoop, the United States had lost, as Milo Perkins, director of the newly minted Office of Economic Warfare, put it, "practically all of our rubber."[106] Virtually all of America's allies suffered similar loss.

Not only did Liberia's rubber make her a valuable asset; her geographic location proved equally valuable. At this time, transatlantic flying was still relatively new. "The shortest way across the Atlantic with reasonable safety was between the continental 'bulges' of South America and Africa." Liberia had the good fortune to lie on what became "one of the most important airways of the world."[107]

Pioneering Pan American Airways negotiated with the Liberian government for constructing a modern airport shortly before Pearl Harbor, and in February 1942 the government granted the United States "the right to construct, control, operate and defend...military and commercial airports in the Republic," and, if necessary, provide for their defense. The agreement, negotiated by Roosevelt's special envoy, Colonel Harry A. McBride, also committed the United States to extend "aid to Liberia for its protection, including necessary equipment for road construction, money for defense purposes, assistance in the organization and training of Liberian military forces."[108] And that aid was not long in coming.

On June 17, 1942, Private First Class Napoleon Edward Taylor, a Negro of Baltimore, Maryland, had the honor of being the first man of the first American expeditionary force "ever to set foot in Africa." He had "rehearsed a one-sentence greeting...to be delivered" upon landing. As soon as the beat-up old canvas-topped lighter carried him and the other troops from their ship to a dock "somewhere in Liberia," he jumped off and recited, "'Liberians! We are here to join hands and fight together until this world is free of tyrannical dictators.' The only Liberians around, a half-dozen black-skinned boatmen assisting with the unloading, stopped, looked and listened. One of the group walked over and shook hands. The others silently resumed their work."[109]

The airport, named Roberts Field (sometimes written Robertsfield) in honor of Liberia's first president, would go up quickly. And the predominantly black contingent numbering over one thousand US Army combat engineers, with antiaircraft guns, machine guns, and other assorted weaponry—along with behaviors that riled many of the local population—soon would be ensconced in their new home.[110]

Germany, as expected, protested this flagrant violation of Liberian neutrality. Liberia ignored them and in effect entered the war (although it would not formally declare war with Germany and Japan until January 1944).[111] President Barclay requested "extensive powers to deal with war emergencies."[112] President Roosevelt on March 11, 1942, issued a statement from the White House cautioning that the "defense of Liberia was vital to the defense of the United States and authorized the extension of lend-lease aid to the Republic."[113] The German consul, vice consul, and seventy-six resident nationals left Liberia, as ordered by the government, November 5 at 11:00 a.m., aboard a French plane bound for Abidjan, then onward to Germany.[114]

Not long after, on November 7 and 8, American troops landed at Casablanca in Morocco and Oran in Algeria. As Operation Torch progressed, Winston Churchill, Roosevelt, and representatives of allies met in Casablanca January 14 to 24 to decide further strategy. At the meeting's conclusion, the two world leaders motored to Marrakech; then the American president flew to Bathurst in British Gambia and on to Roberts Field, Liberia.

When the two DC-4s carrying the president and his party set down on January 28, 1943, Roosevelt was welcomed to Liberia by an impressive group headed by President Barclay and including US military brass; the American chargé in Liberia, Frederick Hibbard; the Firestone Plantations general manager, George Seybold; and an array of Liberian and foreign dignitaries. After all, Roosevelt's visit marked an historic first—the first time a sitting American president visited a black African country.[115] (Of course, the first "official "visit had to wait until 1978 when President Jimmy Carter stopped on his way to Nigeria. Roosevelt's visit was to review the American troops in Liberia.)

A dispatch from an accompanying press officer described the brief visit: "The presidential party, after freshening up, were escorted to the officers' mess hall, where President Barclay, Liberian Secretary of State Clarence L. Simpson," and other notables greeted them. "After lunch President Roosevelt and President Barclay got into a jeep and bounced out to the parade ground where the Forty-first Engineers and a part of the defense detachment...were lined up at attention. The band rendered full honors and played both national anthems, after which the Presidents toured up and down the lines making a careful inspection." Seybold then drove them "through African villages with their picturesque circular adobe huts with straw thatched roofs" to the "great rubber plantation." On the "sixty-nine thousand acres under intense cultivation," the party saw "thousands of acres of new rubber shoots," and tapping the mature trees was "in full swing."[116]

The Liberian president seized the opportunity to broach a subject close to his heart: construction of a port in Liberia that could be converted to a naval base, if needed, for US warships (and incidentally would be an inestimable boon to Liberia). Roosevelt reportedly agreed.[117] Before bidding farewell, he also invited Barclay to visit him in Washington. Six months later, on May 26, the Liberian president, accompanied by William V. S. Tubman, would come knocking on the White House door. Tubman, elected to succeed Barclay only three weeks earlier, would leave one of the most telling imprints on Liberian history during his twenty-seven years in office (1944–70).

Roosevelt warmly welcomed the two Liberian leaders, who, at his request, stayed the night at the White House. They were the first Negro guests ever to do so, and the first to be entertained there since President Theodore Roosevelt had Booker T. Washington to lunch in 1901. Their host had instructed an aide, Edwin Watson, to ensure President Barclay received all the courtesies normally given a visiting head of state. He also had his staff organize a demanding schedule of social functions, visits, and even appearances at the US House of Representatives and Senate for the two black dignitaries.

The next day Barclay, accompanied by Tubman, went first to the Senate. Vice President Henry Wallace introduced the Liberian president, who expressed his "high appreciation of the courtesy shown" in allowing him "to observe for a few minutes the process of lawmaking in the United States." The senators in the chamber (about half of the total membership) gave him a standing ovation; many "shook hands with him and exchanged greetings."[118]

At the House of Representatives, Sam Rayburn, Speaker of the House, introduced Barclay as "the President of one of the few democracies existing outside the Western Hemisphere." Barclay "expressed his pleasure at being the guest of the House," and "conveyed greetings from Liberian citizens to members of Congress."[119] The Liberian leader drew warm applause from both sides of the chamber, particularly when he said, "We have neither large armies, air forces, nor navies to contribute, but we have something that is important in the prosecution of war—natural resources and a strategic position." And Liberia would make both "available to the Allies."[120]

At a press conference at Blair House, to where they had moved after their overnight stay in the White House, Barclay answered questions from the press, emphasizing the shared interests of Liberia and the United States.

Finishing off the day, Secretary of State Cordell Hull hosted a dinner at the Carlton Hotel.[121] The next day the Liberians visited Howard University, in Washington, founded for blacks in 1867 by a Civil War hero and funded by the US government, then traveled to Akron, Ohio, where they called in at Firestone's company headquarters and toured the manufacturing facilities. Company officials purportedly were obliged to lodge Barclay and his party in a private railroad car since they could not find suitable accommodations available to the colored visitors.[122] Before returning to Washington, the group stopped at Wilberforce University, in Wilberforce, Ohio, a historically black school founded by the African Methodist Episcopal Church in 1856.

Upon returning to Washington, President Barclay met with Henry Villard, chief of the State Department's Division of African and Near Eastern Affairs, and Harry Hopkins, one of Roosevelt's closest aides. The ever-acerbic president did not hesitate to express his utter disappointment in his visit to the United States. Although he appreciated the hospitable and courteous treatment afforded him, he had expected to have serious discussions about the port that President Roosevelt had agreed to when he visited Liberia.

Emphasizing that "he was a very busy man,"[123] Barclay said that, had he realized his trip would be almost completely devoted to social events, he would have remained at home. Regarding the proposed port project, the Liberian government would oppose any site chosen primarily to benefit the Firestone plantations. Thus, he wanted to be on record as opposing the site at Marshall, which would primarily do just that. Instead, he would favor a location on the Saint Paul River (on Monrovia's outskirts).

Barclay didn't stop with the port. Not one to mince words, the Liberian president charged on: the misbehavior of American soldiers in Liberia, an American education expert who propagated unacceptable ideas "modelled on old-time British Colonial methods," and American lend-lease aid that benefited Liberia little because American military officers employed the lend-lease equipment to construct "roads without considering the needs of Liberia or even consulting Liberian officials regarding their location." He also bared his intention to rein in Firestone in Liberia to counter the widespread feelings that Liberia "was being run for the benefit of the rubber company."[124]

President Barclay and his party on June 4 departed by train to New York City. The dynamic mayor of New York, Fiorello La Guardia, met them at Pennsylvania Station with a warm welcome. The Liberians were whisked off to view a shipyard and other points of interest. On June 6 in the Hospital for Joint Diseases at Madison Avenue and 124th Street, President Barclay underwent what publicists termed a minor operation on one of his legs. Mayor La Guardia visited him in the hospital two days later.

Unfortunately, Barclay still could not leave the hospital to attend a dinner on June 12 at the Hotel Roosevelt where he was to be the guest of honor. Some one thousand guests came. Fortunately, William Tubman, the president-elect, was able to attend in Barclay's place. The New York mayor spoke of the "'opportunity and hope for something real, the hope that a small country can protect itself against outside interests of greed and exploitation...It will be a great responsibility," he continued, "for the President-elect to see that Liberia is reserved for the people of Liberia and not for the profit of some foreign corporation."[125]

William Tubman accepted that challenge. And the Republic of Liberia stood ready to embark on a Tubman reign of twenty-seven years.

CHAPTER 16

"Uncle Shad"

—⚏—

IT WAS THE LARGEST FUNERAL ever seen in Liberia. Countless numbers of mourners came to pay their last respects or to breathe a sigh of relief. After twenty-seven years, William V. Shadrach Tubman, the Republic of Liberia's eighteenth president, lay dead. Loved by most, feared by many, Tubman, "helped by the Second World War," had brought a "poor and backward" Liberia "into the mainstream of twentieth-century economic life."[1] But such progress came at a cost. While his policies of national unification and an open door to foreign investments were crucial, the strain of unbridled growth and "Tubman's dictatorial inclinations" shattered social peace and crippled economic development.

—⚏—

On July 4, 1971, the president had flown to London for a two-month vacation in England. After coasting unopposed to his seventh presidential election four years earlier, he had worked hard and needed a rest. He also wanted to have a prostate problem, not unusual for a man of his age, looked at. The president checked into a London clinic and underwent a prostate operation, presumably for cancer. Close associates later said the operation was successful—Tubman even chatted with them afterward—but something went terribly wrong. Complications developed, and the president unexpectedly died from a hemorrhage the afternoon of July 23.²

Crowds paying their respects to their beloved leader jammed the modern, multistoried Executive Mansion in Monrovia, an edifice he constructed. "Uncle Shad" not only had ruled the republic as president for longer than any other person, but for most Liberians had come to be "a friend, a father, a provider, and arbitrator of family quarrels, one who assuaged the stricken hearted," one whose footprints were "larger than life."³ Unlike his predecessor, Edwin Barclay, the "dignified 'aristocratic' intellectual...often accused of being haughty," Shad Tubman inherited from his American-born mother "the easy, friendly and forthright manner so characteristic of the Americans." His noted Methodist minister-cum-politician father "instilled in Tubman respect for religion and a taste for politics."⁴

President William V. Tubman after being crowned "King of the Bassas" at a political rally. Tuan Wreh, *The Love of Liberty* ...

Tributes poured in from all over the world eulogizing the dead president. US senator Hubert Humphrey portrayed him as a "statesman, a great President, and a beloved human being."⁵ African leaders described him as "a great champion of African dignity, the untiring fighter for the liberation of African territories and the most eminent founder of the OAU [Organization of African Unity]."⁶ Others trumpeted how his introduction of the

Open Door policy set the economy on a modern path, and his Unification policy brought the tribal masses into the country's political, social, and economic mainstream. They called him the "Maker of Modern Liberia."

But to others, this revered but overpowering leader represented "political bossism at its zenith."[7] It represented suppression, ofttimes brutal, of political expression and criticism; corruption on a massive scale; and a paranoia that spawned assassination plots and a repressive security system. From this perspective, Tubman's administration was a dictatorship in which "the politics of force and fear were built into the political life of the nation, and the mechanism for its application was developed to a high degree of perfection."[8]

Tubman, one of six children, was born on November 29, 1895, in Harper City, Maryland County, to Elizabeth Rebecca Barnes and Alexander Tubman. Grandparents Sylvia and William Shadrach Tubman were freed by Georgia slave owner Richard Tubman (who donated $10,000 to help cover their resettlement expenses). After their arrival in 1837 aboard the bark *Baltimore*, they settled in Cape Palmas. Tubman's maternal grandparents, Martha Anne and Nathan Barnes, also freed slaves from Georgia, likewise settled in Cape Palmas in 1872, along with daughter Elizabeth, Shad's mother.[9]

Cape Palmas, in Maryland County, lies at the extreme southeastern tip of Liberia, where it meets the former French colony the Ivory Coast. The Maryland State Colonization Society in 1833 established the county as a colony, Maryland in Liberia. When Shad was born in 1895, Cape Palmas probably retained much of what English explorer Richard Burton saw on a visit in 1862. Burton described "the little settlement" as "not unpicturesque"; when he and his party landed, they found "sundry large stone buildings, Mr. Macgill's and Mr. Potter's stores," and black carpenters and coopers at work.[10] Climbing up the headland, they passed a wooden structure, "at once a post-office and custom-house, which [looked] much like a large hen-coop perched upon a ladder."[11] They came upon "Marshall's Hotel, a lumber building on the cliff, commanding a pretty view. The inner rooms [were] furnished with tables, sofas, and easy chairs; the mats and rugs [were] neat and clean, and cocoas, white-washed after the fashion of Philadelphia and Baltimore, [shaded] the front."[12]

They "walked to the Mission House...a large building with ample piazzas and shady verandahs," in front of which stood a "flagstaff, with cleats nailed on instead of ladder and rungs." It bore "the arms of Liberia, stripes and a Lone Star, stolen from Texas and not paid for."[13] Burton met with the Reverend C. E. Hoffman, a New Yorker, the Episcopalian missionary in charge, and visited Saint Mark's Hospital, "then approaching completion" as the first hospital in Liberia.[14]

Isolated from Monrovia and the centers of settler society by some 270 miles along the coast, Maryland lay in the territory of the Grebo, one of "the outstanding examples of indigenous resistance to Liberian occupation."[15] Settlers fought the Grebo in at least five conflicts between 1856 and 1910. One of the most serious took place in 1875–76; Tubman's uncle died in that conflict. By one account, after retreating government forces left his body on the battlefield, Grebo tribesmen dissected it and scattered his remains about.[16] Before the war, in 1874, local Cape Palmas people allegedly beat the future president's grandfather to death when he interrupted a native ritual by kicking away a "bowl of sassywood [poison] they had brewed to administer to four tribesmen accused of...witchcraft."[17] Mrs. Henries, Tubman's biographer and ardent admirer, even maintains that as Shad was being born, hostile tribesmen fighting each other threatened the newborn's safety.[18]

To young Tubman growing up in Maryland County violent encounters with local tribal people must have seemed a part of everyday life. In 1910, when only fifteen years old, he saw action against the Grebos and subsequently in "the ferocious" seven-year-long Sasstown War against the Krus, plus skirmishes in 1915 and 1917. In 1914, he even organized a "rag-tag unit," the "Tubman Volunteers," that was later absorbed into the regular army.[19]

Despite this background, Henries believed that "the spirit of peace" Shad's parents engendered in the home infused in him an "innate desire for peace [that] was evident in all his activities."[20] As he matured, the future president must have come to the realization that the only avenue to a durable peace would require what he termed "unification"—bringing together the disparate ethnic, social, and political groups making up the Republic of Liberia.

With his father, Alexander, an ordained Methodist minister, and his mother, Elizabeth, involved in missionary work, Tubman naturally enrolled in the Methodist Church's Cape Palmas Seminary. After graduating in 1913, he attended Cuttington College and Divinity School, and in 1916 worked as court recorder and, briefly, collector of internal revenue in Maryland County. He taught at the seminary from 1914 to 1920 at the salary of $12.50 per month. Since his father had become a politician of some stature, representing Cape Palmas in the Liberian House of Representatives and serving as Speaker, young Tubman set his sights on a career in politics. He studied law, was admitted to the Maryland County bar in 1917, and became county attorney two years later. In 1923, at the age of twenty-eight, Shad Tubman was elected to the Liberian Senate, the youngest senator in Liberian history.[21]

One story has it that Tubman so impressed President Charles King with his "eloquence at a Masonic banquet" that King supported his election to fill the senate seat made vacant by H. Too Wesley's elevation to the vice presidency.[22] Given the nature of Liberian politics at that time, endorsement by the president, head of the True Whig Party, virtually assured a candidate of winning. King's action prompted a long-term friendship between the two. This friendship, along with Tubman's family ties to Vice President Allen C. Yancy, his cousin, would later figure prominently in Tubman's resignation from the senate in 1931, when the scandal over forced labor and slavery forced the two leaders out of office in disgrace.

Early on in his career, Tubman became a Freemason. At that time being a member of that prestigious body conferred the highest social status imaginable and delivered an open "invitation to the corridors of power." The ambitious, up-and-coming young politician "joined every Masonic order in sight." He served as "Grand Master of Masons of Liberia, 33 degree...and General Grand Patron of the Order of the Eastern Star of Africa," as well as district supervisor of lodges of the Grand Order of Odd Fellows.[23] Adding to his impressive list of accomplishments, Tubman became a "distinguished lay preacher...and was selected in 1928 to represent Liberia at the Methodist Church's Quadrennial Conference meeting in Kansas City, Kansas."[24]

But Tubman did not neglect the common man either. Dubbed the "poor man's lawyer," he defended many for nominal fees or free of charge. Before long, Shad Tubman had developed a substantial grassroots constituency in his home county. And some in the political community began to think Tubman had a guardian angel.

Nor did he slight his military duty, as his participation in the wars and skirmishes against the Maryland County native tribes attest. When the forced labor–slavery affair swallowed up King and Yancy in 1931, Tubman resigned his senate seat and defended his cousin Yancy in a Liberian court. The ex-vice president was found guilty of extortion. This might well have spelled the end of the political road also for Tubman. But he fared better than cousin Yancy. The League of Nations investigation absolved him of any serious wrongdoing; as the lawyer of several chiefs, he had only failed to "manifest due diligence and act squarely with them in this matter."[25]

Even then, Tubman faced stiff opposition from within the True Whig Party when he sought to regain his senate seat in 1931. The party, trying to distance itself from the disgraced leaders, refused to endorse Tubman as its candidate for the post. Instead, party leaders named Joseph T. Gibson, a lawyer, as the True Whig official candidate—despite the fact Tubman "had defeated him ten votes to one" earlier in a party convention.[26]

The move outraged Tubman's supporters, who "destroyed the voting booths on election day...[and] took to the streets...[shouting] 'No Tubman, no Election.'" As a consequence, Maryland County lost the representation of its four representatives and one of its two senators in the legislature until 1934. A bye-election filled the vacancies, and Shad Tubman reclaimed his Senate seat. Three years later President Edwin Barclay appointed him associate justice of the Supreme Court, where he would serve for the next six years.[27] Tubman might well have languished in this politically comfortable post for much longer but for his guardian angel's working still another political miracle.

———※———

As Barclay's fourteen-year tenure neared its end, the president began his search for a successor. The most likely candidates, James F. Cooper and Clarence Lorenzo Simpson, hailed from Montserrado County, the county crowned by the national capital, Monrovia, and the home of almost all of the country's presidents, including Barclay.

Initially, President Barclay reputedly leaned toward Cooper, a wealthy rubber planter and secretary of the interior in President

King's cabinet. The president's endorsement, of course, would virtually guarantee his nomination in the party convention. According to a Tubman biographer, however, Cooper's authoritarian bearing and ruthlessness when interior secretary stirred a determined opposition. They warned Barclay that were Cooper elected president, "he would immediately jail" him (Barclay).[28] That Cooper could air more than enough of Barclay's dirty laundry presumably gave the president pause.

The other favorite, Barclay's secretary of state, Clarence Lorenzo Simpson, a mulatto, now seemed a virtual shoo-in. Simpson's father had immigrated from the United States, and his mother, a native African, came from so-called Vai tribe royalty. His supporters touted his mixed descent, saying it would prove a valuable asset to him as president by personifying "national unification." His position as secretary general of the party, a post of considerable influence, also would work to his advantage in vying for the votes of delegates.

William Shadrach Tubman, on the other hand, entered the fray as a relatively unknown outsider, far removed from the widely influential elite clique who ruled Montserrado County politics. Tuan Wreh, a Liberian journalist and Tubman biographer, maintains that although "he was known in Monrovia as a senator representing his faraway Maryland County" and as Barclay's selection to the Supreme Court, "Tubman was nonetheless a small potato in Liberian politics at this stage." In the search "for an astute, able, trusted national leader," he "was not even thought of"—at least initially.[29]

Wreh suggests that the Reverend S. T. A. Richards, the editor of a local publication, *The Friend*, proposed him in an article titled "Tubman for More Democracy" as "the most logical man to succeed Mr. Barclay."[30] Besides Richards, "more than fifteen months before the convention in 1943," Liebenow writes, the editor of a leading Liberian newspaper, *African Nationalist*, "picked Tubman as the leading aspirant." The editor noted Tubman had "the whole of Maryland County, and not a minor part of Montserrado, and everywhere his name is heard," adding, "it has a captivating charm, because he is a natural mixer of men, good manners, and some persons say—liquers."[31]

Once the convention got underway, Tubman supporters reportedly "launched a whispering campaign" that threatened frontrunner Simpson's popularity. They argued that "since most Liberian Heads of State had hailed from Montserrado County," it was time to give an opportunity "to someone" from another county, "especially from one that had not yet produced a Head of State," such as Maryland.[32]

Simpson's men, now aroused, fought back, and the meeting took on all the makings of a grand melee. To restore some semblance of harmony, the matter was handed to a party caucus, which in effect meant incumbent President Barclay, for resolution. He announced his choice of Tubman. What exactly motivated his choice is unclear.

Had the president "not come in to bestow the accolade on Tubman," Wreh believed, "Simpson could have fought for the True Whig nomination to the bitter end." And, Wreh added, had he done so, he might well have "caused a crisis and a split in the ranks of the True Whig Party."[33] But he didn't. Instead, Simpson accepted the consolation prize of running for vice president on the ticket with Tubman, giving up, in his words, "the opportunity of a life-time to achieve the ambition I had nurtured for…years and the greatest which any Liberian politician could have."[34]

The True Whig Party conventions on paper looked impressively democratic, especially to outsiders. In truth, however, they, like the entire party apparatus, actually served primarily to ensure the True Whigs' one-party rule—and domination by a relatively small clique of Americo-Liberian families (whose membership might change from time to time). This one-party system came to fruition in 1883 with Hilary R. W. Johnson's election and lasted until the coup in 1980. Liebenow viewed it, along with other institutions, such as the church and Free Masons, as vital to the solidarity Americo-Liberians needed to survive the threats "tribal rebellion and European incursions" posed to their rule.[35]

The general election in May 1943 proved lively, probably more than most Liberian contests. Rubber magnate Cooper, unsuccessful in his presidential quest with the True Whig Party, decided to try his hand with the opposition Democratic Party. Teamed up with vice presidential candidate Senator R. A. Sherman of Grand Cape Mount County, they, Wreh noted, "gave both Tubman and the outgoing President Barclay...a good run for their money." It was a campaign that saw, "as is usual in Liberian politics...a lot of mudslinging and character assassination." Cooper garnered support from the minority Americo-Liberians and intellectuals in the coastal belt, while "the predominantly tribal rural masses" threw their support behind Tubman."[36]

After the votes were counted, President-elect Shad Tubman wrote Barclay on May 10, "the Whig candidates were unanimously carried at each of the polls here. As a matter of fact, there was no organization of the Democratic Party at this end."[37] The opposition newspaper, *Weekly Mirror*, vented the heavily defeated and irate Cooper's reaction in an editorial: "The voting on Tuesday, May 4, 1943 was the most partial, the most unfair, the most brazenly corrupt and domineering in the long shady record of the True Whig Party and in the history of the Republic."[38] Surprisingly the editorial made no reference to the 1927 election that was so patently fraudulent it was catapulted into the record books. Of course, most old timers would add that a "fair election" was an alien concept in the First Republic.

Fraud or not, January 3, 1944, found William V. S. Tubman raising his right hand to take the oath of office as the Republic of Liberia's eighteenth president. In his inaugural address, the new president laid out what observers called a "well-balanced political, social and educational blueprint for Liberia under his leadership." His eloquence drew a "thunderous ovation" and even swayed foes.[39] He pledged "to stimulate and encourage the development of courageous and fearless manhood," preserve "in full force" the country's "democratic superstructure, and by wise and constitutional measures seek to promote intelligence among the people as the best means...to see to it that Liberty and Law march hand in hand." The government "must be in the hands of the people."[40]

The new president declared his administration would "strive" for "assimilation and unification" of the country's "various populations." He avowed that "Liberia must be a place for all Liberians to live in alike—all to stand equally privileged, responsible and protected by like administration of law. All classes of...[Liberia's] people must be made to fuse and coalesce into a solid whole."[41] A stirring speech, but, one that many Liberians in later years would look wistfully back upon.

To the surprise of many, however, he followed through on his radical vow. He would push through a constitutional amendment in 1945 granting—for the first time in history—native people in the hinterland the right to elect representatives to the national legislature. President Tubman on May 7, 1946, also extended the right to vote to women.[42]

—∽—

The new administration quickly got down to business. One of its first acts was to declare war on Germany and Japan—little more than a formality at this point in time. It next produced an ambitious "Overall Plan to Develop the Republic of Liberia for 1946–1950." Besides political reforms, the plan called for outlays for education; roads and bridges; light, power and water; and a nominal amount for agriculture. It also included $3.5 million for the country's centennial celebration of its independence, and a postwar building program. Estimated total cost—$23 million.[43]

The government's annual revenues during 1941–45, however, ranged only between $1.2 and $1.9 million, and expenditures seldom left any surplus and often produced a deficit. Tubman's development plan, without significant foreign financing, represented little more than pie in the sky. And, the United States, Liberia's sole source of foreign assistance at that time, was not yet prepared to commit funds.

Although forced to scuttle his plan, the president managed to rescue one of the primary objectives—celebration in 1947 of Liberia's one hundred years of independence. In his annual message to the legislature in 1950, he declared that "the Centenary, which was one of the major items of the Plan, was the first to receive consideration and you [the legislature] enacted the Centennial Tax and 15% Surtax Acts. With these, we were successful in executing the Centennial Program." The president proudly continued, "Centennial and Executive Mansion Pavilions as well as the Centennial Monument were constructed in the capital, and the Executive Mansion" was "completely remodeled and renovated." In each county, a centennial monument also was completed.[44]

Committing Liberia's scarce resources to these uneconomic projects raised many eyebrows among both friends and critics. How serious was he about development? But perhaps President Tubman read the Americo-Liberian community's mood and aspirations at that time better than his critics—and sensed an opportunity to solidify his leadership in that community. Mrs. A. Doris Henries, in her biography of the president, captured some of his devotion, possibly sanctified by his status as a lay preacher, to the centennial celebration. She wrote that "President Tubman resolved on a celebration which would honor the achievements of the founders and pioneers of this infant Republic," hopefully with the help of friendly foreign countries. When none came forward, "Liberia alone had to assume the entire financial responsibility."[45]

And the responsibility proved not insignificant for Liberia's resources at that time. At the opening of an imposing "pavilion on the inauguration grounds and another near the Executive Mansion," Mrs. Henries wrote, the "president led in a Sunday service of 'devotion and thanksgiving.'" Nineteen countries sent representatives, Mrs. Henries directed two historical plays written for the occasion, a centennial choir sang music composed for it, and three young Liberian writers read poems they had penned for the event.[46]

Topping off the grand celebration, Raphael O'Hara Lunier, US minister plenipotentiary and envoy extraordinary, presented a plaque on which a pair of clasped hands reaching across the ocean from America to Africa symbolized the friendship of the United States and Liberia.[47]

Tubman pronounced the centennial celebration a success. To Liberia's largest population, the indigenous Africans who had battled the Americo-Liberian settlers from the very first step they took on African soil, the celebration was an affront.

But Tubman already had initiated a program to win over the allegiance of that population. On February 14, 1944, he announced his Unification policy. The president insisted that the republic "must be composed of men [including native tribesmen] who are equal under the law and have the same rights and privileges." This, he declared, "is fundamental to the Unification Policy."[48] The Americo-Liberian old guard were stunned.

According to Professor Liebenow, they assumed that "Tubman, like most of his predecessors, would ignore the fiery campaign rhetoric" about reforming the political system. They couldn't have been more wrong. They hadn't counted on the strength of the independent political base he would develop "among both tribal people and the lower-class Americo-Liberians." And they underestimated the strength of his resolve. Nor had they reckoned with his "remarkable familiarity with the intricacies of the Liberian political system"—compliments of his politician father—and his knowledge of "the sins of omission and commission of all the leading politicians of the day"—thanks to his service as defense lawyer in the Fernando Po labor scandal.[49]

The House of Representatives was expanded to allow natives in the three hinterland provinces, as well as tribal areas within the coastal counties, to elect delegates who would give them "regular informal representation."[50] Representation in the Senate was still excluded, and real property ownership and race continued as requirements for voting. (But to qualify, a native would only have to own a hut on which he paid tax.)

The expansion of tribal people's rights continued in successive Tubman administrations, and culminated in 1964 with junking the provincial system established during Arthur Barclay's rule. Tubman introduced four new counties to replace the Eastern, Central, and Western Provinces that made up the predominantly tribal Hinterland Administration. These new counties—Grand Getah, Nimba, Bong, and Lofa—would function on a par with the five old settler counties along the coast. Each would enjoy full representation in the House of Representatives and two senators in the upper house. The counties and other subdivisions, however, continued to exist "largely as electoral areas for the national legislature," or units for maintaining law and order and collecting taxes. They enjoyed relatively little autonomy, and the "superintendents of counties and territories and the district commissioners were 'chief executives' of their respective areas in only a limited numbers of government functions."[51]

Acutely aware of previous presidents' failure by and large to connect effectively with the indigenous Africans, Tubman made a point when first elected to establish a rapport with them. In 1946 he started holding regular meetings to "listen to complaints and grievances"[52] and take immediate administrative actions where warranted. The president would visit each of the principal government facilities in the hinterland. In each, he would hold what he called "executive council" meetings during which residents and chiefs could seek redress for wrongs, propose new health and education programs, submit boundary disputes for arbitration, and request presidential help in various other matters.[53]

In the absence of legal restrictions and judicial precedents, Tubman would summarily dispense justice. In many instances, the judgments went against established interests, including cases of illegal acquisitions of land, an issue of particular sensitivity to tribal people. The punishment he handed out could be severe. The impact on the natives, few of whom had ever even seen a Liberian president, was profound. For many, the government, and even the country named Liberia had seemed distant. For Tubman, who adapted earlier administrations' use of such forums to settle intercommunal disputes, they served as a means of dispensing instant justice and exerting his "personal authority in the interior."[54]

President Tubman also began "national unification councils," where chiefs and government officials met to discuss matters of mutual concern. The first council in June 1954 met in Harper, the president's Maryland County hometown. Although it recorded no concrete results, it gave "an enormous psychological boost for a society troubled by ethnic problems."[55] The second met in Voinjama, in Western Province, in 1958, and the third four years later in Sanniquellie, in Central Province. Here, Tubman laid out his proposed reorganization of the interior into four new counties with a status matching that of the older settler-dominated five coastal counties.

The Unification program, however, did not wholly close the economic, social, and political gaps between the Americo-Liberians and the native African Liberians. Even Tubman, in his seven terms, never once chose a full-blooded native African to run with him as vice president—in spite of the availability of qualified men. The few cabinet and ambassadorial appointments he handed out to them were essentially token.[56] And, Tubman adamantly defended the observance of two holidays ethnic tribal people considered an affront: Pioneer Day, honoring the initial band of settlers from America; and Matilda Newport Day, celebrating a heroine who reputedly secured victory for the newcomers in their first encounter with hostile natives.[57]

Neither did his notion of unification extend to changing the national motto, "The love of liberty brought us here," which clearly referred to the descendants of freed slaves from America who founded the republic at the expense of resident indigenous Africans, or the constitution's preamble that spoke only of "We the People of the Republic of Liberia [who] were originally the inhabitants of the United States," sans any mention of the country's vast majority of native Africans. Despite the many shortcomings of the Unification program in practice, it nonetheless marked a major milestone in the republic's history.

The program reflected a new posture of promise in Americo-Liberian relations with the vast native majority. For the first time, Professor Lieberman noted, a native African Liberian could walk through the doors of the Executive Mansion to offer suggestions or present petitions of grievances to the country's president.[58] The meetings and policy reforms, however, were "as much an effort [by the president] to build an independent political base" as they were a "response to social and economic conditions of the society and the international environment."[59]

—⚛—

Even before his election in 1943, Tubman had begun to envision a comprehensive set of policies for "national growth and development" that he would follow as president. A February 1947 *Harper's Magazine* article by Earl Parker Hansen reported after an interview with President Tubman that "no one sees more clearly than... [he] the hard fact that a nation with a ruling class of 15,000 and a subject people one hundred times as large is headed for disaster in the modern economic world." Tubman's thinking continued to evolve as he confronted these issues firsthand as president. His address to the First Unification Council in 1954 encapsulated his vision: a modernized, prosperous, and unified Liberia, where, he insisted once again, "justice, equality, fair dealing, and equal opportunities for every one from every part of the country regardless of tribe, clan, section, element, creed or economic status" would prevail.[60]

To capture that vision, however, required "infrastructure, modern managerial and technological know-how, trained manpower and, above all, capital"—all sadly lacking in Liberia.[61] Raising enough capital domestically was not an option. Local savings institutions able to attract private savings did not exist. In 1943, the sole bank in the country, the Bank of Monrovia, was a Firestone subsidiary. Neither could public savings be counted on; government revenues seldom even covered its expenditures.

Given the paucity of domestic financing available, Tubman, harkening back to President Arthur Barclay, concluded that the country had little choice but to rely on private foreign investors.

To this end, he would pursue an aggressive exploitation of Liberia's natural resources by expanding the award of concessions to foreign investors. Importantly, these foreign investments also would provide job opportunities in the modern sector. He reasoned that with better education and improved transportation links to the interior opening the way, and employment opportunities beckoning, tribal people would migrate from their village life to the new, modern Liberia. Those remaining on the farms could then begin replacing their subsistence-based agriculture with modern technology and produce for the commercial market.

It would mean opening Liberia's door to foreigners. Just how far to open that door had exercised the Americo-Liberian establishment from the republic's earliest days and figured in presidential elections. Edwin Barclay, Tubman's predecessor, had set the door further ajar with the repeal of the Ports of Entry Law, which had limited foreigners' trading and discouraged "productive foreign capital" investments.[62]

Tubman felt that Liberia must step up the pace. In his January 3, 1944, inaugural address, he put out a welcome mat when he announced that Liberia would "encourage the investment of foreign capital in the development of the resources of the country, preferably on a partnership basis, and would be given protection and fairness of treatment."[63]

But many of the establishment, particularly in the conservative rural areas, still feared that an open door would undermine their solidarity and threaten their economic and political hegemony. And they ultimately would be reduced to a small minority in a sea of native African Liberians. Many, nevertheless, realized that the country could not long continue as it had, lurching from one economic crisis to another. The world, including Africa, was moving too rapidly and too radically to allow the republic the luxury of status quo, especially a luxury that largely benefited only a narrow, elite band of the country's population.

—⚄—

Some help actually had already arrived, as part of the American response to the Second World War. Liberia and the United States signed a defense area agreement in 1942, and the United States built an airport, Roberts Field, as an air force base. Able to handle large bombers (with an 11,000 foot runway, the longest runway in Africa for many years). It also played an important role in transporting military equipment and supplies to the African and Asian theaters, and after the war became a key link in international air travel (particularly for Pan American Airways). American military personnel now stationed in Liberia built roads linking Monrovia with the airport and an alternate airport in the southeastern part of the country.

Perhaps even more crucial, the lack of an adequate harbor hampered Liberia's efforts to exploit its resources. Large ships were forced to anchor offshore and resort to loading and unloading cargo and passengers by lighters. Firestone had planned to build a port but gave up because of the cost. President Edwin Barclay had ardently pursued the matter in his two meetings with President Roosevelt in 1943, and the two governments concluded an agreement on December 31 promising American funding. Construction began, and the Port of Monrovia was inaugurated in 1948.

Such an ambitious development program, though crucial for Liberia's modernization, posed serious risk. Tribal people's greater involvement "in the cash and wage economy could lead to demands for political participation"—and threaten Americo-Liberian rule.[64] The president no doubt recognized that as roads, bridges, and other communications projects were built, tribal people would come into greater contact with other Liberians. These hinterland residents also would gain access to goods and services, including teachers, medical personnel, and agricultural extension workers, hitherto denied them. As Liebenow points out, with new work opportunities, they would earn cash with which they could buy manufactured instead of locally crafted goods and accumulate money for their children's schooling.[65]

Tubman argued that such development was "actually a necessary tool in maintaining Whig control and supremacy."[66] Making these improvements would enable the Americo-Liberian rulers to manage any political demands from the tribal population stirred up by rising expectations. The real risk lay in the government's ability to keep pace with the rise of these expectations. The status quo alternative, however, could, Tubman felt, jeopardize Liberia's future as a viable country. The president's decision must have looked much like a forest fire where firemen, in the hope of preventing the fire's spread, take the risk of purposely setting a secondary fire—optimistically called a "controlled" burn.

Tubman's planners produced another five-year plan, for 1951–55, with an even larger price tag than the earlier scheme—$32.6 million. It, too, faltered. The lack of data and trained personnel made any realistic planning (even estimating costs) impossible. But the telling obstacle turned on financing, more precisely the government's inability to provide funds and the unwillingness of the United States to participate financially.[67] Tubman's visionary scheme for pursuing unification through development would have to wait.

He didn't have to wait, however, to begin consolidating his political power base and widening his popularity with the ordinary people. He became a master at subverting, to his advantage, the

Liberian constitution's system of checks and balances patterned on the American model. An amendment to the constitution in May 1935 extended the president's initial term from four to eight years, and Tubman engineered another amendment in 1949 to allow the incumbent to serve an unlimited number of succeeding four-year terms. It opened the political door to what some would term a "cult of the presidency." "Lifetime presidency" proved a more telling term. Tubman would be elected to five more consecutive terms, serving a total of twenty-seven years until death removed him from office.

During these years, Tubman would take steps as commander in chief to ensure the military's loyalty to him. On the civilian side, his power of appointment (with the Senate's advice and consent) made sure Liberia's ambassadors, judges, and other public officials owed him similar fealty. Despite the existence of a civil service system, Wreh claimed that "nearly all those in government service" under Tubman "were his direct appointees or had been appointed with his advice and consent. He looked upon civil servants as one of his sources of political support." [68] And the president "hand-picked many of his cabinets and government functionaries on the basis of family ties and political cronyism," with little or no regard to representing Liberian society as a whole. There was little room for "intellectuals, the critically inclined, and a large body of the educated elite" of indigenous Africans.[69]

Another source of what became Tubman's near-dictatorial powers lay in the traditional True Whig Party practice of allowing the president, as the party's standard-bearer, to decide which candidates would run for the House and Senate. Given the dominance of the True Whigs in what amounted to a one-party system, their election became a mere formality. Tubman, as head of the party, even "exacted from all public employees," whether party members or not, "tithes in support of his ruling Party"—in violation of the Public Employment Law. The president, Wreh alleges, managed "to use a portion of these collections to construct a True Whig Party headquarters in Monrovia costing $8 million."[70] Liberia's legislature also would contribute to Tubman's strengths on several occasions by granting him [sweeping] emergency powers, including suspension of the writ of habeas corpus.[71]

Professor Liebenow maintains that the only time opposition to the ruling party had "more than a theoretical chance" of winning elections was the thirty-five years from 1848 to 1883, the single "period of intense interparty competition in Liberia." Still, the Whig establishment deemed it important to keep at least what appeared to be active and viable elections. Particularly to the outside world, a vigorous election would confer an aura of legitimacy on the winner, and the energetic participation of the populace would validate the political system itself.[72]

The stretched-out ritual of entreating the president and other officers to stand for reelection, the spirited nominating conventions, the campaigns in which candidates and their "colorful and often humorous political posters" went into even the most distant and obscure villages, and the tense anticipation in tallying the votes—the entire election exercise—persuaded most observers that the opposition had at least an outside chance to win. But, in fact, little "was actually left to chance."[73]

The True Whig Party's bag of tricks included the three-member election commission, which could deny a candidate or party it deemed "unqualified" a place on the ballot. Although the body was supposedly nonpartisan, the president of Liberia chose the chairman and the two members, one "from a list... submitted by the opposition parties." Thus, the True Whigs, who controlled the presidency continuously from 1877, could shut out any party they feared—as they did the Reformation Party in 1951 and 1955, along with the Independent True Whig Party.[74]

And the Whigs had other tricks up their sleeves to draw on. In the 1943 election, for instance, the Barclay administration, which supervised the election, refused a Democratic Party request to station one judge and one clerk from that party at each voting booth to ensure against any irregularities. The refusal prompted outcries of unfairness, partiality, and possible fraud.

President Tubman also began to develop an extensive security apparatus that even the most iron-fisted regime might envy. As a starter, the legislature in April 1950 approved the appointment of public relations officers "so as to prevent the making of Liberian territories into fertile soil for the infiltration and germination of dangerous propaganda and subversive activity."[75] Biographer Tuan Wreh maintains that the operation began as "a social welfare and pension scheme" to help the unemployed, aged, handicapped, and retired government workers.[76] But, it changed into a "spying organization, which informed on citizens and aliens alike." A PRO informer might report any criticism, or even opposing views, of the administration or Tubman personally. A dossier rich with such adverse reports could have damaging results for the individual concerned.

A Tubman "crony, Jacob W. N. Seyon Cummings," headed the organization, often satisfying "his own personal grudges," for example, by accusing enemies of assassination plots. According to Wreh, Cummings led a troop of soldiers during 1950, when Didwho Twe was organizing an opposition party for the 1951 presidential election. Cummings and his soldiers moved about Monrovia "beating up and dumping in jail peaceful citizens whose political views ran counter" to Cummings's own. Tubman later appointed him to the House of Representatives, then, after the legislative body expelled him for "unbecoming behavior," an advisor on tribal affairs. Although subsequently eclipsed by newer security agencies, the system of public relations officers persisted until President William Tolbert, who took office in 1971, abolished it.[77]

Tubman next saw to the creation of four more security organizations: the National Intelligence and Security Service (NISS), National Bureau of Investigation (NBI), Special Security System (SSS), and Executive Action Bureau (EAB). The legislation establishing the SSS offers a glimpse at the unbridled power these organizations wielded. In providing security for the president and his family, their residence, and official documents, as well as carrying out other security-related functions, the service could obtain any and "all information" it deemed necessary from any person or body. And, an agent could arrest anyone who was committing a crime "or who may reasonably be suspected of the commission of a crime."[78]

—∞—

Tubman brooked no serious opposition—not even from a seventy-two-year-old light-complexioned, distinguished-looking gentleman with a cicatrix (a mark denoting him a Liberian Kru tribesman) on his forehead: Welleh Didwho Twe, often known as D. Twe. One of Liberia's most famous revolutionaries—a hero to many, but to the president, a menace—Twe was branded early in his career as a "troublemaker." His steady stream of criticism of the Americo-Liberian establishment and championing the rights of Liberian Africans earned him four years of self-imposed political exile in Sierra Leone. After his 1936 return to Liberia, both President Barclay and Tubman tolerated him as no more than a toothless old dog nipping at their heels. But not now that an opposition party, the Reformation Party, had chosen Twe to challenge Tubman in the 1951 presidential race.

Twe, born in Monrovia on April 14, 1879, to Klao (Kru) parents, attended the American Methodist and Trinity Episcopal schools and Cuttington College and Divinity School in Cape Palmas. In 1894, at the age of fifteen, he left for study in the United States, helped by William Wallace Grout, a US congressman from Vermont. During his sixteen-year stay in the United States, the young African tribesman attended an array of educational institutions: Saint Johnsbury Academy in Vermont; Cushing Academy in Ashburnham, Massachusetts; and Rhode Island State College in Kingston. Topping off his American educational sojourn, Twe studied agriculture at Columbia and Harvard Universities.[79]

When thirty-one, Twe returned to Liberia in 1910, but he would revisit the United States periodically.[80] Elected to the House of Representatives from Montserrado County in 1927, the Kru tribesman expressed his contempt for the Americo-Liberian ruling elite by introducing bills viewed as attacks on their society. He soon was branded a "troublemaker."

In 1929, Twe introduced a bill in the legislature to end "slavery and forced labor"; he wrote that the bill, if enacted, "would have saved Liberia from [the] international disgrace" that arose from the League of Nations investigation. He was charged with sedition and expelled from the legislature.[81]

Edwin Barclay, who succeeded King as Liberia's president, lost no time in pursuing Twe and other troublemakers. Following attempts on his life, Twe took refuge in neighboring Sierra Leone in November 1932. From there he continued his troublemaking, in 1934 even advocating a Kru revolution in Liberia and establishment of a "Kru Republic."[82]

Writing to an English friend, Twe argued that the Kru could accomplish this feat and "hold their independence intact till recognition" and "the arrival of [the] white League of Nations specialists." But "the Kru people" needed "at least six machine guns and 500 rifles with sufficient ammunition." This constituted "the only obstacle in the way to free a million people from oppression."[83] The scheme gained little traction, however.

Anxious to ward off Twe's challenge, Senator R. F. D. Smallwood blocked the new party's registration, claiming it had failed to meet the election law's deadline for registration.

Despite the government's refusal to qualify their candidates, Twe and his supporters persisted. Monrovia pulsed with excitement as they marched in "a colorful mass parade through the principal streets...with placards denouncing Tubman and extolling their candidate." In his April 10, 1951, acceptance speech, Twe told his followers and the country that "old practices and election frauds" had to be discarded. "The colonial peoples everywhere in Africa will be affected by our action in this election either for good or bad."[84]

The aspiring presidential candidate penned a letter to President Tubman on April 16 asking again that he be placed on the ballot and the election date be extended. He was, Twe added, "in a better position to save Liberia" than was Tubman. The president's less than civil response, dated 18 April, came shortly: "For the present time, my reply to your note is that you are inherently a traitor to your country, a consummate liar, a senile visionary, a sophisticated bigot and an uncompromising egoist, the truth of which you will be made to realize.

Faithfully yours,

Wm. V. S. Tubman."[85]

The threatening tone of the enraged president's letter was not merely the empty venting of his spleen. He began searching for a way to extract this increasingly painful "thorn in his flesh." And soon found one. Twe's supporters had sent "a petition entitled 'An Appeal for Justice and Relief from Political Suppression in Liberia'...to the UN Secretary-General Trygve Lie in New York" on April 17, 1951."[86]

Tubman once again proved to be the craftier player in this political chess match. After his reelection—he won without any opposition candidates on the ballot (Charles Simpson had bowed out of the race to be appointed ambassador to the United States)---- Tubman and his new vice president, William R. Tolbert, were inaugurated on January 7, 1952. He hadn't, however, forgotten Twe's brazen challenge to him and the True Whig Party.

The government charged Twe and his key colleagues with sedition. While Twe sought refuge in neighboring Sierra Leone, the government arrested and convicted his followers, alleging "that by communicating with the UN the 'defendants did hereby invite foreign interference in the domestic affairs of the Republic of Liberia with the intent...to overturn, subvert, and affect'" the country's stability.[87] In June 1953 the court sentenced them to three years in prison, the maximum term allowed. (Subsequently, Tubman, convinced they no longer posed a threat to him, gave them reprieves before they completed their sentence.)[88]

Twe reportedly escaped capture on his rubber estate by, according to his inspired Kru supporters, magically transforming "himself into a white cat at his farmhouse..." while the security forces searched in vain" for him. Twe offered an equally fanciful explanation that he had evaded capture by hiding in the woods for four months, helped by "two beautiful and trustworthy maidens, whom the friendly African chiefs had provided" him.[89] He traveled the final leg of his journey to Sierra Leone, apparently without incident or divine help, by canoe.

From there, the challenger "watched his chances of toppling Tubman evaporate." The Tubman juggernaut simply proved too formidable for him to pull off an upset victory. As Wreh points out, "No Liberian President...[had] ever been defeated in office, and Tubman could not tolerate the idea of being the laughing-stock of the voters." And, while the challenger "made an impressive showing with his American-style campaigning," the president refused "to stick to the rules of the game."[90]

D. Twe gave up politics and took advantage of an amnesty to return to Liberia. When Twe died on March 19, 1961, at eighty-two years of age, Shad Tubman, ever the good politician, "attended his glittering state funeral."[91] After all, the two "had one thing in common": each had been married to the same woman, Araminta Dent, Tubman's first wife.[92]

—⋙—

The strength of Didwho Twe's presidential campaign, largely driven by his Kru tribal brethren, must have shaken Tubman. But, with his style of leadership and his Unification policy, he had "single-mindedly built a personal political following among both repatriate and indigenous Liberians."[93] The latter posed few serious threats, given that any unity among the sixteen or so tribes in Liberia historically had been limited to intertribal alliances, usually temporary. Some were traditional enemies. Even within tribal groupings, divisions hostile to one another were common. Moreover, it was generally known that Tubman had most of the traditional leadership in his pocket; "tribal chiefs," especially, could be found on President Tubman's PRO payroll.

They saw him as the country's first president who appointed "country people" to high positions in the Liberian government. They would proudly point to a large house known as Native Mansion at the corner of Warren Street and Camp Johnson Road, which Tubman built "for traditional leaders." Tubman's leadership style, coupled with his rapport with the tribal people, gained him admiration from many Liberians.[94]

One paramount chief enthusiastically acclaimed, "President Tubman really turned this country around. We tribesmen can now mix up with the civilized people freely and nobody is looking down on us. We can now eat at the same table, shake hands and dance with the civilized men and women. God will bless him to live long. We want you to be President until you die."[95]

On balance, Uncle Shad Tubman's political future appeared secure, and the country was awash with glowing promises of economic and social benefits for all Liberians from the wave of foreign investments and concessions his Open Door policy had set in motion. Liberia at last seemed poised to enter a long-awaited golden era of development.

CHAPTER 17

A New Era

—⟁—

MONDAY, JANUARY 7, 1952, DAWNED bright in Monrovia. Crowds had gathered along the streets and around the Executive Mansion in anticipation. President William Shadrach V. Tubman, having served eight years as the republic's chief executive, prepared to embark on his second term, which would be of only four years' duration. He and all the "notables" (an accolade reserved for the elite of the Americo-Liberian establishment) attending followed Tubman's strictly enforced dress code. The spectacle of black men, formally dressed in tails and top hats and sporting ivory-topped canes, wilting in Monrovia's sweltering heat, left an indelible impression—almost a caricature of American inaugurals—on many observers and spawned many jokes about "Top Hats and Tom Toms."

The occasion, even more festive than most, featured the arrival of the US attack transport *Monrovia* and its six hundred marines who paraded down the capital's main streets. A jubilant Shad Tubman told the assembled masses he was "'happy to confirm' that Liberia's internal and external debts had been 'fully liquidated'" and they were at that time "the masters of [their] fiscal affairs."[1] It was a rare event, unprecedented in the country's fiscal history. The government had at last paid off the hated 1926 loan that "had hobbled" Liberia to "Firestone's control."[2] (The 1954–55 budget also was balanced.) The triumphant Tubman followed up by leading a motorcade miles into the "interior" during the week.

—⁂—

Tubman, with the election safely behind him, focused again on economic development. When his initial plan proved undoable, a disappointed Tubman in 1947 had turned to American businessman and politician Edward Stettinius for help. Stettinius played an important role in American foreign relations in the World War II era. As lend-lease administrator from 1941 to 1943 and under secretary and secretary of state from 1944 to 1945, he knew about the port and other aspects of Liberia's relationship with the United States. He and Tubman became close personal friends, and Stettinius became greatly interested in and sympathetic toward Africa's sole republic.

After leaving the US government, he founded a consulting firm, Stettinius Associates-Liberia, that came up with an innovative approach to Liberia's economic development. A Liberian company jointly owned by Stettinius Associates and the Liberian government would undertake to develop "the human and material resources of the Republic of Liberia." The Liberia Company would bring private American "capital and specialized knowledge" to bear on exploiting Liberia's natural resources, raise the people's "levels of living," and improve "their opportunities for economic and social advancement."[3]

In a statement of understanding, the partners laid out an incredibly ambitious series of objectives. They covered virtually the country's whole economy—from the banking system to agriculture and fishing to mining and timber and the entire infrastructure. It even foresaw establishing a company to import and export commodities, carry on internal trade in consumer goods, and act as the Liberian government's official procurement agency. They also planned a foundation for advancing higher education, particularly medical and technological training, sending Liberians to the United States for study.

In one unprecedented fell swoop, the Liberia Company acquired the legal rights to, "in short...develop the country." Dutch economist F. P. M. Van der Kraaij, in his in-depth study of the Liberian economy, concluded that never "before in the history of the country, had a single private, and largely foreign-owned company been given so many powers and so much confidence." He marveled that "one century after the creation of the 'independent and sovereign State of Liberia' its development was handed over. A most remarkable decision indeed."[4] And one that spoke of the mutual trust that Tubman and Stettinius held for one another.

Unfortunately, Tubman's guardian angel must have taken leave before his daring program got fully under way; Edward Stettinius Jr. died unexpectedly on October 31, 1949, in Greenwich, Connecticut. An American company, the Liberian Development Corporation—of which Juan Trippe, Pan American World Airways founder and Stettinius's brother-in-law, owned a substantial share—stepped in to purchase the local company. With the change in ownership, the government negotiated a new agreement in December 1949 that limited the Liberia Company's responsibilities and obligations and reduced its activities.

Stettinius, in addition, left another important contribution to Liberia's treasury—an arrangement in which Liberia registered maritime vessels that sailed the oceans flying a Liberian flag of convenience. As a result, Liberia, by 1959, could boast the third-largest maritime fleet in the world. He also guided passage of a 1948 corporation law that offered a tax haven for foreign companies that registered in Liberia but operated elsewhere.[5]

In April 1951, two years after Stettinius's death, Shadrach Tubman's guardian angel apparently returned to duty. And doubtless was smiling when the first shipment of iron ore from the Bomi Hills mine arrived at the port in Monrovia—"the beginning of a new era for Liberia."[6] Soon after, a column in the *New York Times* reported that a "battered Liberty ship [the *Simeon Reed*] had sailed" from Monrovia for Baltimore on June 5, 1951, with the first ten thousand tons of Liberian iron ore.[7] It was the long-awaited manna from heaven.

With each boatload of Liberian iron ore, government revenues soared, from $3.9 million in 1950 to $11.2 million in 1953 and $32.4 million in 1960. Foreign businesses, especially American, picked up the scent of money to be made, so that by the end of the 1960s, some fifty US firms would be represented in Liberia. Besides the American rubber and iron ore interests, they included banking, oil exploration, engineering and construction, petrol suppliers, motor vehicles, and construction and agricultural equipment and parts.[8]

The March 28, 1949, issue of *Time* magazine featured on its cover Lieutenant Colonel Lansdell Christie, West Point class of 1922, retired. The accompanying article explained how Christie learned about a "Devil Mountain" rich in iron ore when he served in Liberia in 1942, during the US Army's construction of Roberts Field. While there, Christie met William Tubman; the two became fast friends. After discharge from the army, Christie returned to Liberia to seek his fortune in the iron ore he had heard about. He applied to the government for a mining concession. That his friend Tubman now was the newly elected president of Liberia doubtless gave him encouragement.

> The presence of iron ore deposits in the Liberian hinterland had not gone unnoticed even in earlier times. An account

in 1555 mentioned natives putting it to use, and explorer Benjamin Anderson in 1868 noted "beds of specular iron ore, which the natives [broke] into fragments and [used] for shot."[9] It was, however, a Dutch geologist named Terpstra who stumbled on the Bomi Hills deposits in 1934 while searching for diamonds. Interested more in glittering stones, he turned his discovery over to W. H. Muller and Company, also Dutch, to continue exploring for iron ore. After finding the area to be intolerably difficult terrain, accessible only by footpaths—and failing to reach agreement with the government on royalties and taxes—Muller abandoned the project, only to have still another Dutch company take it up.[10]

This company, impossibly named Noord Europesche Erts en Pyriet (better known as NEEP), continued the exploration and surveys, and in 1937 reached agreement with the government on a concession. But then President Edwin Barclay balked, reputedly because his administration suspected that NEEP actually was a front for German financial interests. The official explanation for the rejection: "Nazi-funds." In actual fact, according to Van der Kraaij, the financial interests turned out to be Jews who had fled Nazi Germany to Amsterdam.[11]

Now the United States entered the chase.[12] The real reason for Barclay's backing away from NEEP, Raymond Buell reported, stemmed from pressure the State Department applied on the Liberian president. In any event, the Liberian government, reportedly on the department's suggestion, gave the rights to further exploration to US Steel. Once again, in 1938, exploration stopped. The American company saw the absence of a harbor too formidable an obstacle.

The onset of the Second World War soon changed the equation. President Barclay, on his trip to the United States in 1943, now managed to secure US agreement to build a port with lend-lease funds. To complement the agreement, signed on the last day of 1943, he also obtained a commitment for a US geological survey team to survey Liberia's iron ore resources. The port not only would facilitate development of the iron ore, but also fulfill a long-standing strategic desire for an American naval base on Africa's west coast.[13]

American concern about the need to seek new sources of iron ore also had begun to grow. Mounting demand for war production would speed depletion of the Mesabi Range deposits, the country's principal supplier. Seeing Liberia as a potential source for iron ore, as well as rubber and other important commodities, the US Foreign Economic Administration in November 1944 dispatched a mission to help Liberia "increase its production of...strategic materials."[14]

On August 27, 1945, Lansdell Christie strode out of a dingy government office in Monrovia with a concession to mine the Bomi Hills site. The ore there proved incredibly rich; it "assayed 68% iron," compared with an average 51 percent in the US Mesabi Range.[15] Christie, born in Brooklyn, New York, on November 20, 1903, "had made a small fortune operating a barge line in New York." But he lacked sufficient capital and technical expertise to swing such a potentially large undertaking as an iron ore project. He incorporated the Liberia Mining Company Ltd. and enlisted the Muller Company, the Dutch firm that had flirted with the project in the 1930s. Dutch government exchange restrictions limited Muller's investment in the new company, but a number of Dutch individuals came on board in technical and administrative positions.

Christie's concession gave him exclusive exploration rights on about three million acres located within a forty-mile radius of the Bomi Hills, plus exclusive mining rights for all minerals, excluding gold, platinum, and diamonds, on up to twenty-five thousand acres. In return, he would pay the Liberian government an exploration tax of $100 per month, which would increase to $250 after the three-and-a-half-year exploration period expired. In addition, the government would levy an annual five-cents-per-acre surface tax that would rise gradually to twenty-five cents and a royalty of five cents per ton of exported ore. The concession would be exempt from all other taxes.[16]

The agreement would not go unopposed, however. A number of Liberian citizens argued that it was tilted too heavily in favor of Christie and would seriously restrict Liberia's share of the benefits from the iron ore exports. A group of judges and two journalists felt strongly enough about the concession to submit a signed petition to the president opposing it. Tubman promptly dismissed the judges and jailed Albert Porte, one of the journalists. So much for opposition.[17]

The Port of Monrovia opened on July 26, 1948. Christie and company tackled the remaining obstacle to exporting the ore—a railroad connecting the port to the mining operations in the Bomi Hills. Given the cost of the project (and the fact, according to the *Time* magazine article, that Christie had already spent $1.5 million on the mine, including a forty-five-mile-long road to Monrovia), he sought additional financing. His success in persuading the Republic Steel Corporation in March 1949 "to come in on his deal" put him on *Time*'s March 28 cover. The American corporation bought Muller's and some of Christie's shares, ending up owning approximately twenty thousand shares—59.2 percent of the company. The outlay for the railroad, about $10 million, would represent private investors' principal investment in the project.

The magazine reported that Christie and Republic hoped in two years "to be shipping 1,000,000 tons a year from Monrovia to Republic and other US steel mills." While the exact amount of deposits had yet to be determined, the two parties estimated "it upwards of 30 million tons, enough to make the deal highly profitable for both of them, as well as for Liberia."[18] The Bomi Hills "Devil Mountain," Liberia's first iron ore mine, did prove highly profitable. Van der Kraaij claims that "within a few years" the initial $10 million investment "had been earned back," and income to the "owners totaled nearly $140 million" between 1951 and 1977.[19] The mining company's annual income from the ore until 1960 "exceeded the total revenues of the Republic of Liberia."[20]

Lansdell Christie's subsequent lifestyle would attest to the mine's profitability. He became a Democratic Party activist, serving as a New York delegate to the Democratic National Convention and sharing his largesse with the party as its largest individual contributor in the 1956 electoral campaign. Christie and his wife also became noted art collectors. They purchased one of Fabergé's most famous eggs for their collection in 1961. Lansdell Kisner Christie died, a wealthy "mining industrialist," in Locust Valley, New York, on November 16, 1965.

Uncle Shad Tubman did not forget his old friend. In his "Tribute on the Passing Away of Lansdell Christie, Friend of Liberia," he wrote that he wished "to point out as clearly as possible to the people of every class and range of Liberia, the unselfish, deep and immovable love and interest that this great man, Lansdell Christie, entertained for the development of this country, and prosperity of its people, particularly its common people."[21]

The Liberia Mining Company closed the gates at the Bomi Hills mine on March 31, 1977. Bomi Hills, which Liberians began calling "Bomi Holes, became a ghost town." But even before the gates were shut, this first venture had led to a succession of gates being opened at other mines. Additional deposits of ore were discovered in the Bea Mountains, only about nine miles from Bomi Hills, and in an area along the Mano River some forty-five or fifty miles distant. This time, however, the government proved far less giving in awarding concessions for exploiting the new discoveries. The realization that the government had handed foreign-owned Liberia Mining a virtual gold mine of earnings while offering Liberia little more than a relatively modest tax and royalty income—and a depleted mine—reignited the outrage the Firestone concession provoked two decades earlier.

A new corporation, the National Iron Ore Corporation (NIOC), established in 1957, followed a different pattern. The government assumed 50 percent, and the Liberia Mining Company 15 percent of the equity. The remaining $3.5 million worth of shares went to Liberian Enterprises Ltd., a company that Christie and some of his associates formed. Liberian Enterprises encouraged Liberians to buy shares from it in the new mining company by extending them interest-free loans. Tubman at least could say that Liberians owned about 70 percent of the new mining company. Of course, he didn't reveal which Liberians.[22]

> The government in 1958 granted the corporation a concession on the Mano River ore, and production began in 1962. Two Lansdell Christie companies managed the operation. By the end of 1977, the Mano River mine had shipped ore worth nearly $290 million out of the country. But during this sixteen-year period, the government realized only $2.5 million—less than 1 percent—from the sales. Exploration and surface taxes during 1968–77 added a modest $16,000.

Not only had the government exempted the Liberia Mining Company from paying tax on the income from its 15 percent equity interest in the NIOC, but it inexplicably failed to collect royalties from the corporation and exempted it, its shareholders, and management companies from all taxes and charges other than the exploration and surface taxes.[23]

A lengthy array of issues and disputes—assets, taxes, accounting practices, to name a few—marked the government's relations with the mining companies. An investigation in 1964, for example, reported that "a number of dubious arrangements and practices [followed by Liberia Mining] in that year had already been found prejudicial to the interests of Liberia."[24] The government, however, failed to take any actions against the company at that time, nor even after another report in 1974 repeated the allegations. While such failures might be laid at the doorstep of institutional weakness—insufficient trained and qualified people and inadequate administrative machinery—the Liberian political appointees at the top "had been well aware of the issues involved." But they did little to correct them.[25]

Among these political appointees, "the country's best known and wealthiest lawyer, Richard A. Henries...represented the mining company's legal interests in Liberia."[26] Henries, coincidentally, happened also to be the Speaker of the House of Representatives, and, according to Liebenow, "the most hated of the Old Guard," a Liberian J. Edgar Hoover. He allegedly knew "where every political skeleton in the system was hidden"—and used this sword of Damocles to his advantage.[27] One of the two members representing the government on the mining company's board of directors at that time was Secretary of the Treasury Charles D. Sherman. (He also was one of the few foreign-trained economists in Liberia.) The second member also had impressive credentials. Nevertheless, their approval of questionable company practices reportedly had been "little more than a formality."[28]

The board members failure to take corrective actions undoubtedly hid irregularities and various violations that adversely affected Liberia's national interests—while, no doubt, advancing their own personal ones. Another impediment to the government's taking a strong stand against the Liberia Mining Company, some argue, was the close friendship between President Tubman and Lansdell Christie. Only after Christie died in 1965 and Tubman in 1971 did the Liberian Treasury Department act firmly to force the mining company to revise its questionable accounting and other dubious practices.[29] In any case, the specter of widespread corruption would haunt Americo-Liberia's ruling elite down to the very end of their reign.

Having made it safely through the 1952 reelection storm, President Tubman turned his attention once again to his push for economic development. He saw the five-year plan extended in 1953 to cover nine years, 1951–60, and the projected expenditures almost doubled to $73.6 million.[30] This time, the president, in his October 23, 1953, annual message to the legislature, boldly asked that "the financing of this Program" not depend on "gifts or benevolence but upon the guarantee" of Liberia's own natural resources, both those "already being exploited, and others that are in the exploratory state."[31] With demand for Liberia's iron ore mounting, he now felt he could afford a touch of boldness.

The government built roads, constructed public buildings, and improved communications facilities—financed mainly by loans from contractors. It also stepped up spending on education and medical services, particularly in the interior, and on sanitary amenities—financed from government revenues and US assistance—to improve the capital's abominable health conditions. Tubman also presided over what had become a routine yearly government expansion. Existing departments had to be expanded and new ones added to accommodate the new employees he hired to an already corpulent civil service.[32] (Patronage still figured importantly in Tubman's recipe for presidential survival.)

It looked as if the good times would never end. Strong demand for Liberia's rubber and iron ore kept prices up. And the easy availability of the prefinanced contractor credit added to the heady, euphoric atmosphere. Even aid donors picked up their interest in Liberia. An agreement signed December 30, 1950, with the United States provided for $30 million in Point IV economic aid. The two countries merged existing health and economic missions into a joint Liberian-American Mission. Projects included demonstration farms, malaria control centers, school improvements, teacher training, natural resources surveys, and establishment of a bureau of statistics. The American Export-Import Bank extended a $6 million loan for roads and construction of a water and sewerage system for Monrovia.[33] The Europeans, particularly Germany, the UN and World Bank also were active. In 1954, for example, Liberia signed an eighty-year concession agreement for eighty thousand acres with the Africa Fruit Company, a firm from Hamburg, Germany.

Liberia now was on the world economic map, but Tubman aspired for even wider recognition. An invitation by American president Dwight Eisenhower to visit the United States provided Tubman such an opportunity. The Liberian president, now the world traveler, readily accepted. He welcomed the visit as a chance to showcase Liberia's progress to the world at large—and make the case for greater assistance.

When his ship, the *African Dawn*, docked at the Farrell Lines pier in Brooklyn on the morning of October 16, 1954, ten years had passed since William Tubman, with President Edwin Barclay, last visited the United States. Since then America had emerged from the dark and uncertain days of World War II. An air of confidence and goodwill epitomized by President Dwight D. Eisenhower prevailed, notwithstanding the mounting Cold War and Senator McCarthy–style "witch hunts" domestically. The American economy hummed, turning out all manner of goods for consumers worldwide, including weapons and other military wares for the struggle against communism.

To feed these demands, the United States was looking for assured raw material sources and for friends and allies in its Cold War challenges. Liberia fitted neatly into the American quest; it offered hints of ample deposits of natural resources and a president who vigorously opposed communism and communist states. All in all, it proved a good time for President Tubman to visit.

Richard C. Patterson, New York City's commissioner of commerce and public events, welcomed Tubman and his sizeable entourage of senior officials. After a two-night stay at the Waldorf Astoria Hotel, the Liberian president and entourage on October 18 set out on a grueling four-week program. First stop, Washington, DC, where Vice President Richard Nixon met their private plane at National Airport. During the automobile ride into the city, Tubman and his party glimpsed what the visit might be like. The *New York Times* reported that "military bands played along the route" and "spectators cheered the party at the White House gate." Clearly, this would be a very special trip. Even the *Times* would cover the visit with more than a dozen pieces.

At the White House, where Tubman would stay, President Eisenhower welcomed the Liberians as visitors from a country in which Americans had "taken deep and abiding interest." That evening the president and Mrs. Eisenhower hosted a dinner for fifty guests. President Tubman reciprocated the next evening when he entertained his hosts at the Liberian embassy.[34]

After a three-day stay in Washington that featured discussions on stepping up aid to Liberia, Tubman and several of his company left by train for the Midwest. Their week-long itinerary included a stop at Akron, Ohio, the home of both the Firestone and B. F. Goodrich rubber companies. (Goodrich later would announce that Liberia had granted it a long-term concession for rubber on six hundred thousand acres, to complement the Firestone enterprise, now more than two decades old.)

The train with Tubman's special coach pulled into New York's Grand Central Terminal five minutes late, at 8:20 a.m. on October 28. Limousines whisked the president and his party, which included Clarence L. Simpson, Liberia's ambassador to the United States; Henry Ford Cooper, ambassador to the United Kingdom; and several government ministers to their suite at the Waldorf Towers. Tubman "tipped his gray homburg to the crowd" waiting outside, and the Liberians began a four-day whirlwind visit with a "full-dress New York City welcome."[35]

At 12:05 p.m., the ticker-tape parade began. Accompanying Tubman, "contingents from the armed services and Fire and Sanitation Departments, with their bands and color guards" marched up Broadway. "At City Hall Plaza, while color guards stood at attention and after bands had played the Liberian and US national anthems, Mayor Robert Wagner presented President Tubman with an honor scroll and the city's red-ribboned Medal of Honor." He extolled the Liberian president "for fusing a people of various traditions into a united, prosperous and happy nation."[36]

During the luncheon at the Waldorf Astoria, the mayor continued the accolades, saying the world's peoples "could look to Liberia 'as a shining example of democratic life.'"[37] Any Liberians at home who read this probably wondered if the Americans might have confused Liberia with some other country. In the evening Ambassador Simpson, along with the Liberian Mining Company and the Farrell Lines, hosted a reception, also at the hotel, in Tubman's honor.

The following morning, Tubman and party, the *Times* reported, spent seventy-three minutes at the United Nations. After meeting with Secretary General Dag Hammarskjold, who gave them a personally guided tour, the Liberian president addressed the General Assembly. He urged member nations "to surrender a part of their sovereignty...to help establish a lasting peace." The president, who also was a Methodist lay preacher of some renown, even found time to visit the American Bible Society headquarters at Park Avenue and Fifty-Seventh Street before enduring still another dinner at his hotel. This time Averell Harriman, the Democratic candidate for New York governor; James A. Farrell, president of the Farrell Lines; Lansdell Christie, president of Liberian Mining Company; and Tubman addressed the two hundred guests. Tubman assured them that Liberia welcomed more private investments in his country.[38]

Taking a break, the president traveled to Oxford, Pennsylvania, to receive an honorary bachelor of laws degree from Lincoln University, founded in 1854 to train leadership in Liberia. In resuming his tour, Tubman inadvertently became entangled in American politics. With the 1954 US midterm elections looming on November 2, he hastily revised his original schedule. Fearing a backlash that might jeopardize the negotiations with the Republican Eisenhower administration on aid, "a perplexed...Tubman canceled 'controversial' trips to Hyde Park" to lay a wreath on President Franklin Delano Roosevelt's tomb and to Harlem for "a service and reception at the Abyssinian Baptist Church, where Democratic representative Adam Clayton Powell" was the pastor. "Instead, he toured Rockefeller Center" and lunched at the Waldorf Astoria as a guest of four religious and medical groups associated with Liberia.[39]

Before departing the city on the final leg of his trip, Tubman enjoyed a VIP tour of the New York harbor aboard a private yacht, the *Big Pebble*, and a luncheon hosted by the commissioner of the New York Port Authority. After the B. F. Goodrich Company gave a private dinner, the presidential party left Pennsylvania Station at 10:25 p.m., bound for Alabama and a week-long visit in the South. During this time, Tubman called at the Tuskegee Institute in Tuskegee, Alabama, a near-sacred institution for Liberians who greatly revered Booker T. Washington. During his two-day stay, the college awarded him an honorary doctor of laws degree. He continued on to Atlanta, Georgia, his mother's home city. While there, Morehouse College, a highly respected traditionally black school, conferred still another honorary degree on the Liberian visitor. During his American sojourn, Tubman would net some eight or nine honorary degrees.

The governor of Georgia, Herman Talmadge, known as a staunch segregationist (and considered by many a rabid racist) put in a surprise appearance at the Morehouse convocation. The press, understandably skeptical, refused to believe Talmadge had actually invited Tubman "to see the progress Negroes" had made in Georgia. And that he had accepted.[40] The governor finally convinced the nonbelievers by showing them his written invitation to the Liberian president and Tubman's acceptance. Talmadge, however, carefully avoided meeting the president face to face.[41]

At last, President Tubman decided it was time to head for home. The president "cut short his tour of the Southern states and returned quietly to New York City." Before he and his group sailed on the Panama Line's *Ancon*, Tubman, responding to reporters, offered "words of admiration for the United States and an optimistic report of Negro life in the South." When asked what impressed him most in his visit, he answered promptly, "'the liberty and freedom of the press'...adding that he considered it 'the most powerful influence of the United States, even above the

Congress.'" He also "said he was 'optimistic' about the ultimate success" of the negotiations over extending the US aid programs in Liberia.[42]

At 5:00 p.m. on November 11, the *Ancon*, with 146 passengers aboard and flying the Liberian flag, headed for Haiti. After landing on November 15 and going through another round of official receptions, Tubman and party would continue aboard a British cruiser to Jamaica, then on to Dakar by freighter, and finally arrive at home about the first of December.[43]

Monrovia welcomed a jubilant Shad Tubman, pleased that his long trip had proved a thumping success. In view of the president's troubled relationship with Liberian journalists, many doubtless scoffed at his parting statement in New York about freedom of the press. Others faulted his casting the country's lot with the United States in the Cold War, although many realized this was the price Liberia must pay to gain full access to American assistance. Tubman's thoughts, however, focused more on the upcoming presidential election less than six months away.

In a speech he gave after the True Whig Party nominated him for a third term, Tubman claimed that he had "decided to retire at the end of [his] second term [and] sit on the side lines helping when [he] could, giving support to [his] successor." But, he continued, "it soon became evident that my personal desires were clashing with the wishes of the majority and my patriotic responsibilities. I decided in favour of the majority—to serve the nation."[44]

Many Liberians unquestionably wanted Tubman to continue serving "to finish the good work that he [had] started." But it was equally clear that many opposed his reelection for a third term—and a large number were vehemently opposed. At the head of this group stood the man who had first made Tubman president, Edwin Barclay. It would be "Liberia's biggest and most publicized presidential campaign."[45]

Resistance to a third term for Tubman began to grow as early as 1953 when the Reverend S. T. A. Richards (the same Reverend Richards who had first proposed Tubman's candidacy ten years earlier) demolished the argument that the president should stay on in order to "finish the good work he started." He wrote that to accomplish this objective, Tubman "would have to live as long as Liberia [existed] and remain in office quite as long."[46] After leaflets opposing a Tubman third term, signed by an anonymous "Aboriginal Youth," started circulating in Monrovia, the president denounced them as subversive: "Nothing less than communist infiltration," the work of "a little group of political malcontents who have always been insurgent and firebrand rebels by nature."[47] He mobilized his administration and the True Whig Party to fight a "new opposition party"—the Independent True Whig Party—which grew out of a meeting of about one hundred Liberians in Edwin Barclay's home in September 1954. Barclay was elected its standard-bearer and S. David Coleman national chairman of the new party.

In a speech he delivered in Monrovia on August 27, 1954, ex-president Barclay attempted to explain his reentry into the political arena in opposition to his onetime protégé.[48] Despite his "'sincere desire' to continue 'to be free from the burden'" of the presidency, he said, and his mistaken "support" of Tubman, he felt compelled to once again take up the fight for reform. In a lengthy catalogue of Tubman administration abuses, the former president added that he had "observed with pain...the structure of public morality, financial integrity, and social welfare," which he had struggled "to found and erect, being ruthlessly torn down...behind a façade of so-called modern developments and purported improvements [and] being replaced by organized corruption, graft and financial irresponsibility."[49]

Barclay didn't mention his more personal motives: Tubman's befriending and appointing enemies who allegedly "plotted to assassinate him [Barclay] and other high government officials," abandoning Barclay's strict neutrality during World War II, taking "credit for the Open Door policy which Barclay had conceived," and scrapping Barclay's amendment to the constitution limiting presidential terms to two, in favor of Tubman's own amendment removing any strictures—thus enabling him to stay on in the Executive Mansion until he died.[50]

―∭―

The new opposition party kicked off its campaign with a demonstration in Monrovia. Led by the Liberian Frontier Force band, Independent True Whig stalwarts marched past the Executive Mansion three times while President Tubman peeked from upstairs windows. Barclay proclaimed that he and his supporters were "sure of a sweeping victory"—if the elections were "conducted democratically." It was an "if" many considered so unlikely that the secretary to the Liberian Senate took to ridiculing it in a humorous little verse that circulated.[51]

Tubman struck back by firing suspect government employees, sending them notice in "his green-colored official letters," for what he called "administrative reasons." Several Barclay supporters were arrested, charged with sedition, some for carrying a banner on which Tubman was pictured upside down "with the slogan 'To hell with Tubman.'" (Tubman supporters had displayed—without incident—a similar theme "showing Barclay upside down and plunging headlong into a blazing pit" accompanied by "To hell with Barclay and Coleman."[52]

Charges and countercharges flew from one side to the other. While Tubman loyalists accused Barclay's followers of resorting to juju (black magic), the latter charged that Tubman and his men hired so-called "'heartmen'—killers" who prowled the streets at night looking for victims whose hearts would be used "to make juju and native medicine." As a result, Monrovia streets supposedly "were always deserted around 6 p.m. as people scurried home, fearing to become their victims."[53]

The results of the May 3, 1955, elections surprised few. An official tally awarded Tubman 244,873 votes to the 1,182 reported for Barclay and his running mate, former attorney general Nete Sie Brownell, and sixteen (one of which Tubman reportedly cast) for Didwho Twe's old Reformation Party candidate, William Oliver Davies-Bright.[54] Tubman's True Whig nominees for the legislature also swept the county contests. In Montserrado, the largest county, 55,854 votes versus a miserable 570 for Barclay's Independent True Whigs. In Grand Cape Mount, the story proved much the same: 11,423 votes to the opposition candidates' 138. In the three remaining counties, the results were even more lopsided. In Grand Bassa, Sinoe, and Maryland, the ruling-party candidates garnered 17,240, 27,502, and 17,604 votes, respectively. Opposition candidates netted a total of zero votes. It was, in the opinion of most observers, "the most venomous [election] in Liberia's history."[55] But this one didn't make the record book.

Despite the apparent drubbing, Edwin Barclay refused to concede. Instead, he charged Tubman had "violated every constitutional and legal right" of the Liberian people, denying them their free choice of who should represent them. President Tubman, he alleged, employed "a network of armed soldiers to coerce, intimidate and terrorize electors. He had ballots pre-marked and packed into the ballot boxes before the election was due to open." Tubman and his officials, Barclay supporters claimed, blocked inclusion of an Independent True Whig representative on the Election Commission, denied representatives access to polling booths, particularly when ballots were counted, and destroyed ballots marked for Independent True Whig party candidates.[56]

The *New York Times*, too, reported "an unusual concentration of troops in Monrovia" on voting day, and, "according to witnesses," voting irregularities in the hinterlands, "including the casting of votes by small boys and the issuance of premarked ballots to voters." The New York paper, in addition, mentioned that prior to the May election, "fanatics in the True Whig Party wrecked the printing plant of a newspaper published by the opposition Independent True Whig party."[57]

Following up on his challenge, Barclay on May 6 lodged a formal protest, and a few days later a bill of exceptions, with the House of Representatives. The president replied by submitting to the House a seventy-seven page, fifteen-thousand-word assault on Barclay's protests, including a vicious personal attack calling attention to Barclay's having been born out of wedlock, noting he was "a bastard who [did] not believe in God." Tubman also tried to pin criminal responsibility on Barclay for acts that took place during the latter's tenure in office.[58] Barclay responded in kind as the war of words roared on, accusing Tubman of numerous outrages, of his even offering $20,000 for Barclay's "liquidation," and lesser amounts for the heads of the other party leaders.[59]

The incumbent president, however, held all of the high cards in the contest. Upon his recommendation, the legislature passed an act on June 28, 1955, outlawing the Independent True Whig and Reformation Parties. The legislators also imposed a penalty of $19,097 on Barclay to defray the expense of the special legislative session convened to deal with the dispute.[60] A wealthy rubber plantation owner who also received a $7,500 annual annuity as a former president, Barclay finally paid the levy—under protest.

Four months later, in the late afternoon of November 6, 1955, seventy-three-year-old Edwin J. Barclay died from pancreatic cancer at the Firestone Hospital in Liberia after a brief illness. In keeping with his wishes, he was "given a quiet but dignified burial...at his rubber estate on the Farmington River."[61] William V. Shadrach Tubman would live on for another sixteen years as Liberia's president.

These ensuing years, however, would witness little loosening of his grip on the country. If anything, he would squeeze even harder. More telling, questions increasingly would arise about Tubman's development strategy based on his Unification and Open Door policies. The growth clearly would be seen. But the development would be scarcely visible.

CHAPTER 18

Growth without Development

—∽∾∽—

IN JANUARY 1961 A TEAM of economists from Northwestern University arrived in Monrovia. At the Liberian government's behest and financed by the US aid program, their task was "to analyze the structure of the Liberian economy and measure its performance in order to suggest policies for development."[1] The seven-man team, headed by Robert W. Clower and aided by four short-term consultants and Northwestern resident staff, spent almost two years (from January 1961 through August 1962) in the country. They reported their findings to the government and the US Agency for International Development (USAID) and in 1966 produced a book aptly titled *Growth without Development*.

—∽∾∽—

As the 1950s wound down and Liberia moved into the 1960s, Tubman's development strategy was both succeeding brilliantly and failing dangerously. His Open Door policy had brought a rush of foreign investments and rapid growth in the economy overall. Liberia during the 1950s witnessed a virtual tsunami of investments. In those years, except for Japan, it boasted the fastest-growing economy in the world. (Between 1954 and 1960, real gross national product increased 12.5 percent yearly in Liberia, and 13.3 percent in Japan.)[2]

Van der Kraaij, who has written extensively on Liberia's economy, noted that "[in] a period of less than twenty years at least forty foreign companies concluded concession agreements with the Government." They included eleven for mining, seven in agriculture, six in timber, and five for agro-industry.[3] Private foreign capital in the early 1960s flowed into Liberia at about $75 million annually, mostly (about $60 million) for iron ore ventures.[4] The $215 million investment in the Liberian American Swedish Minerals Company (LAMCO), according to one of the company's top executives, made it the largest private industrial project in Africa as of 1962.[5] By the time Tubman's reign ended, Liberia would become the world's third-largest exporter of iron ore: exports rose from 0.2 million long tons in 1953 to 95.4 million in 1960.

Host to the biggest rubber plantation and latex factory in the world—Firestone's Harbel plantation covered sixty-nine thousand acres, plus another thirteen thousand acres at Cavalla—Liberia also could lay claim to having the world's largest mercantile maritime fleet (even if the vessels only flew a Liberian flag out of convenience). Government revenue reversed its perennial shortfall and in 1960 reached an unprecedented $32.4 million, compared with $3.9 million in 1950 and $11.2 million in 1953.[6] To Tubman and many, it looked like the "sudden prosperity would continue indefinitely."[7] And, capping this remarkable economic performance, Liberia, under Tubman, now had also become a recognized player on the international stage.

But, while Tubman saw his Open Door strategy working extremely well in promoting foreign investment and growth, critics saw it failing in advancing the country's development and unification. And even the seemingly successful growth strategy had worrying cracks in its façade. For one thing, diversification of the economy proceeded very slowly. Despite the country's ample forest resources, significant timber exports would not begin until 1967. Exports of industrial diamonds (which neighboring Sierra Leone frequently claimed had been smuggled from across its borders) remained small, as did traditional exports of tree crops, mainly coffee, cocoa, palm kernels, and papaya.[8]

Moreover, the country's heavy dependence on exporting only two raw materials—rubber and iron ore—left the economy painfully vulnerable to the vagaries of world markets. Unfortunately there were few processing and secondary industries and services developed that could provide alternative employment and lessen this vulnerability. The presence of sizeable foreign enterprises fueled wholesale and retail trade and construction and service industries in surrounding areas but made only limited impact beyond. The hotels, bars, theaters, dry cleaners, garages, and barbershops that serviced the larger companies' employees offered relatively little employment. And the local businesses that produced such items as beer, soft drinks, ice cream, bakery goods, soap, and paints were generally small. Most consumer goods, in any case, were imported.[9]

But possibly the most serious flaw in the Tubman strategy concerned agriculture and village life. Ninety-five percent or more of the country's population, the tribal people in the interior, remained fettered to a village life based on subsistence agriculture. Clower called these people on the 150,000 or so tribal farms that occupied more than a third of the country's total land area "illiterate and backward people." They cultivated the land at a low level of efficiency, "more as a way of life" than a means of producing food.[10]

This way of life essentially depended on the nuclear family made up "of a man, his wife or wives" (polygamy was "the ideal, although not the norm"), and his children. Pawns, "slaves, apprentices" and others, voluntarily or otherwise, were also considered part of the household, usually of "important men in a community." Pawning, where "a man placed one of his relatives (and occasionally himself) in servitude until a debt had been paid," was "a fairly common practice throughout West Africa."[11]

As sons took wives from other villages, families grew into villages. Some migrated to different locales to found new communities. "Migrating strangers [might] be given permission to farm" if they accepted the authority of the headman, called "the 'owner of the land.'" With time a cluster of such villages might be grouped together into a "town." Nonetheless, the family was "the most significant social [and usually economic] unit for an indigenous Liberian."[12]

The traditional village in 1960 most Liberians—the indigenous tribal African Liberians—still called home probably had changed little from the villages British novelist Graham Greene described on his trek across Liberia twenty-five years earlier. At that time, he wrote, "[Nearly] all the villages at which I stayed had...a hill, a stream, palaver-house and forge, the burning ember [for lighting fires] carried round at dark, the cows and goats standing between the huts, the little grove of banana trees like clusters of tall green feathers gathering dust."[13]

He continued, saying he "never wearied" of these villages, "the sense of a small courageous community barely existing above the desert of trees, hemmed in by a sun too fierce to work under and a darkness filled with evil spirits." Here, he encountered "wealth [in]...a little pile of palm-nuts, old age sores and leprosy, a few stones in the centre of the village where the dead chiefs lay...a man in a mask with raffia skirts dancing at burials." He marveled at the villagers's "kindness to strangers, [despite] the extent of their poverty and the immediacy of terrors." To him "[their] laughter and their happiness seemed the most courageous things in nature."[14]

Farms typically were small—usually one or two acres given over primarily to growing rice and cassava, mostly for the family's own consumption. In addition, scattered stands of trees produced palm kernels, coffee, and cocoa—traditional Liberian exports—for a bit of cash.

Most tribal farmers followed a system of slash and burn, in which they prepared their land by clearing it and burning the brush or trees on it. Usually after two or three years of cultivation, fertility declined, and they would move on to another area and repeat the process. Land ownership, in the sense in which land could be sold and permanently transferred to another party, was an unknown concept.

An array of domestic activities—"hunting, weaving, tapping palm wine, clearing roads, practicing medicine, building houses, blacksmithing, etc."—rounded out their village lives.[15] An American sociologist described how women and girls began each day at dawn, bringing water to heat for the men's baths, sweeping the living area and disposing of trash. While men prepared the fields for planting, the women kept busy carrying heavy loads of firewood, fetching water, and from late afternoon to early evening, pounding rice and cassava, making palm oil and palm butter, and preparing the evening meal. And, once the rice was planted, they helped weed and tend the crops, and, finally, joined in the harvest.[16]

Besides their work in the field, men occupied themselves making repairs on their huts and readying tools for the next day's work. Some might meet with friends in the village palaver hut and enjoy gourds of palm wine. By dusk, the last farm workers usually arrived back in the village ready to have their evening meals. On nights with a new moon, however, village residents would turn out to enjoy themselves. A drummer would beat out a rhythm, dancers would form a circle, and the dancing would begin, with each person in turn performing a solo in the center of the circle. The dancing, enhanced by palm wine, and, on occasion, cane juice, could last well into the night.[17]

Clower estimated that out of Liberia's roughly one million inhabitants, about 750,000 depended on subsistence farming. Of these, about five hundred thousand, he judged, were old enough to work. A much smaller group grew cash crops, other than rubber, for export. Every able-bodied tribal person seven years or older, the professor opined, probably worked on one of the estimated 150,000 tribal farms sometime in the year. But, surprisingly, the Northwestern economists found that a typical farm occupied considerably less than one full man-year of work, so that only about 15 percent of the total subsistence population were fully employed during the whole year. Only harvest time fully occupied the entire tribal labor force.[18]

Largely absent from this seemingly idyllic life, however, were the schools, clinics, roads, and the amenities and goods that more developed communities enjoyed (a perception that increasingly penetrated even remote villages). And more immediately, "the tranquility and routine pattern of village life [was] sometimes interrupted by the sudden appearance of a government official, messenger, or soldier, demanding palm wine and food."[19] Villagers, though customarily hospitable, seldom welcomed such visits; they usually spelled trouble. In fact, encounters with the government—in virtually any shape or form—counted as one of the most distressing aspects of life in rural Liberia.

An informal survey by Clower and his associates pointed up the strong aversion tribal Liberians felt toward the government.

Interestingly, their hostility did not extend to President Tubman. While most of the people interviewed "closely associated" the government with the Tubman administration, "the president's personal esteem often [made] him immune to criticism." Any government transgression they attributed to the "fault of 'big men' around" the president. And, on the other side, they gave him the credit for any "good deeds" or improvement.[20] Tribes hailed him "as a superior chief" and pledged "their wholehearted support."[21]

However, the usual face of the central government in the interior was not that of Shad Tubman, but that of the district commissioner, the DC, the highest official in the interior with whom tribal Liberians normally would "have personal dealings." As the official in charge of a county, he was, for most of the people in that county, "the government," and they would ascribe any act he took, either favorably or unfavorably—whether handing down court decisions, building needed schools, and clinics, or misappropriating government funds—to the government.[22]

At best, most county government officials ranked low in the estimation of the population they supposedly served. Residents saw tax officials as "undesirables" who "ate tax money" and demanded "rice and chicken" from the villagers, but who, if "handsomely dashed" [bribed or tipped], stood ready to falsely lower tax assessments. At border crossings, customs officials frequently imposed illegal fines on goods villagers imported. Other government employees, such as medical and agricultural personnel, health inspectors, teachers, usually won "praise for their assistance," even though they sometimes resorted to graft.

Tribal people, Clower and his associates found, also "generally respected" their paramount, clan, and town chiefs, even though they, too, "abused traditional rights," taking "goods and services for their own personal benefit, without providing commensurate service" to their fellow tribesmen. Clerks and administrative personnel, however, had no such respect for their superiors. To keep their jobs, they had to do "frequent favors" for and make "dashes" to their supervisors, as well as submit to numerous "collections in the name of the government or government sponsored projects."[23] But the government personnel feared most in the interior were Liberian soldiers. Every locale had suffered their demands for "rice, chickens, cattle, money, and various services." Everyone had "stories of brutality" if their demands went unmet.[24]

Workers in the central government weren't immune to exploitation either. New recruits often found the paymaster withheld their first month's pay as dash. Sometimes they experienced delays in receiving their pay, or it simply disappeared.[25] Some paymasters, too, if a worker failed to answer when his name was called, withheld his pay until he "paid $0.50 or $1 'dash.'" One reported that to get a better job, he "had to bring the department head one chicken (valued at $2.50) and $2 cash." And, refusal to pay periodic dashes of fifty cents or a few dollars to a supervisor, overseer, or headman could cost a worker his job.[26] The Northwestern team interviewers listened to bitter complaints about the government practice of "forcing employees to contribute to organizations, projects, congratulatory parties, the True Whig Party, and various church groups," particularly when the funds were often misappropriated.[27]

One of those interviewed summed up the sentiments of many when he joked, "We don't know which is the worst humbug—up country or down here [in Monrovia]. Up there, government forces you to work for nothing and takes your rice; down here, they may give you a job for two cents, but they always eat one cent of it."[28]

Besides the "unofficial" burdens on tribal villagers, the government imposed an onerous, but legal, levy on their produce and labor. In addition to a hut tax, five dollars that was paid in money, taxes in kind generally ran "approximately 100 pounds of rice per family" each year "in most places." Though this charge might seem "small by comparison with the extra-legal levies imposed by itinerant soldiers, visiting agricultural agents, self-styled 'agents' of government, and irresponsible district commissioners and clan and paramount chiefs," it still could prove costly to the family.[29]

The tax took the form of "requisitioning"—simply "demanding agricultural crops and livestock from tribal areas without any form of compensation." Failure by the villager to meet the demand carried a penalty. Complying, however, often so reduced a family's rice stocks that by the season's end, they were forced to buy the staple in the village market, or from the Lebanese traders who roamed the interior. Clower relates that in one chiefdom consisting of approximately five thousand huts, a high official requisitioned a yearly quota of 5,600 bags of rice from the residents, a total of 560,000 pounds.[30]

And the recipients of such largess? Tribal people told the Northwestern University group they firmly believed that "high ranking national officials, district administrators, chiefs, revenue agents, agricultural agents, and soldiers" mainly benefited from [these] requisitions. It was even rumored that one official sold rice "to Lebanese traders who in turn" sold it back "to the people who [had] planted and harvested the crop."[31]

—⚏—

A financial crisis in 1963 laid bare the emptiness of the government's agricultural program. Rice, the mainstay of Liberians' diet, occupied a special place in their lives. But the country's farmers, given the existing system, simply could not (or would not) produce enough rice to feed the mounting population. As a result, rice imports accelerated from 2.3 million pounds in 1942 to 163.2 million pounds in 1979.³² But when the flow of foreign earnings from rubber and iron ore exports began to slow, the administration faced a very serious situation. In an effort to stem rising public outrage, the president in 1964 launched Operation Production Priority Number One, designed to mobilize farmers in "self-help" to expand agricultural output 100 percent—or more.

The president on occasion liked to emphasize that nothing was "more important than" that Liberians "become self-sufficient, particularly in [their] food requirements."³³ Unfortunately, the Operation Production scheme failed gloriously. A staff of only two men covered the entire country, and Tubman, who would make "on-the-spot grants to honorary county chairmen," found the program useful for patronage. Lowenkopf cites one instance in which $5,000 of a $14,000 grant went for a car for the local chairman.³⁴ Typical of the government's bungling, the Agricultural Credit Corporation that was set up in 1962 couldn't make loans to farmers because it didn't accept crops as collateral.³⁵

The few successes came only when the government resorted to coercion. The president warned chiefs that anyone who failed to meet his quota would be fined $2,000. If that didn't work, a new chief would replace him. Clower relates how authorities even rounded up vagrants in Monrovia and dispatched them to work on farms in the hinterland. But, rice production still continued to fall short. Imports of rice continued to rise.³⁶

Clower explains that "even the most eloquent advocate of economic progress [could] not demonstrate the advantage of growing two grains of rice where only one flourished before if the prospective grower [knew] that both grains [would] go to someone else."³⁷

Villagers, on top of the many other demands, also were subject to so-called "labor recruitment"—in most instances, actually forced labor—without regard to any economic loss the farm family might suffer as a result. The practice doubtless awakened memories in the president, and many other Liberians, of the Fernando Po slave labor scandal that provoked an unprecedented League of Nations investigation and subsequent resignations of President King and Vice President Yancy in 1930.

After Firestone settled in Liberia in 1926, the country's first large concession, the company discovered that it could not always attract sufficient unskilled labor, mainly tappers, to work on its plantation at its prevailing wage rate. To relieve seasonal shortages, a government-approved system, codified in the laws, of recruiting labor came into play. Paramount chiefs of selected districts received monthly compensations for each tribesman employed. The Firestone Harbel plantation, for example, depended upon seven districts, each with a quota, to supply more than 80 percent of its average employment. In one year, the seven district chiefs, combined, received $2,055 monthly remuneration.[38] No other country in Africa at that time still recruited labor in this manner for private employment.

According to the Northwestern study, in 1960 more than 40 percent of the country's workers in the modern sector—about thirty-five thousand—labored in rubber production. Of these, at least one-half of the rubber tappers had been forcibly recruited, because, according to the economists, wage rates proved too low to otherwise attract them. Firestone and Goodrich paid tappers forty-five cents per day, plus free housing, medical care, elementary school education, and subsidized food that came to between one-fourth and one-third of their annual pay, but still insufficient to entice many to leave village life). The eight thousand or so who worked on independent Liberian rubber farms received only thirty-seven cents.[39]

Northwestern University interviewers found laborers, fearing retribution, "extremely reluctant to describe the recruiting system." But one did venture to admit that to leave his assigned job before being dismissed would bring him "trouble, real trouble." He said "the clan chief would grab" him, impose a fifty-dollar fine, and "put [him] in the guard house" if he didn't pay.[40] Some of the tribal workers, especially seasonal ones, would voluntarily leave their village for outside jobs "to escape labor recruitment and obligatory corvée (local government road maintenance, messenger service, etc.) for which little or no wages [were] paid."[41] Others would buy off the two or three months' work "by dashing a chief or district commissioner."[42]

Although the mining companies, which employed fewer than six thousand unskilled people, paid only a few cents more, along with supplements, they attracted more than enough workers. Only the rubber industry suffered seasonal shortages.[43] But, because of the industry's size, it exerted a major influence in the entire economy and provided the main reason for the forcible recruitment of tribal workers. (The Northwestern University economists estimated that if recruitment were abandoned, within a year the wages of unskilled labor would almost double to at least seventy cents per day.)[44]

These low wages for unskilled workers, coupled with the dismal prospects they faced for advancing to better-paying positions, deterred tribal people from abandoning subsistence agriculture for wage-paying jobs. The reason wage rates remained low, Clower noted, could be found in the Tubman government's "unofficial policy" to keep them low—below the level set in a free market.[45]

The policy, of course, not only upset Tubman's development program by discouraging subsistence farmers from moving into the modern sector, but made the hated "involuntary labor recruitment under government auspices" necessary. Otherwise, the rubber industry would suffer a severe labor shortage.[46] Neither

Firestone's American shareholders nor the eight thousand or so Americo-Liberian rubber farm owners—whose numbers included most important politicians and government officials—nor other sundry beneficiaries of the arrangement wished to see it changed. But among tribal Liberians, it added to their growing resentment.

And, as iron ore mining expanded, the workers (mostly tribal Liberians) increasingly pushed their demands for higher wages in strikes. The first major strike, in 1961, involved workers at the LAMCO mining concession. Monrovia registered a general strike in September of that year. A series of other confrontations followed, culminating in a strike by twenty thousand workers on Firestone's Harbel plantation. Five major disputes erupted in 1966, including one in February involving the plantation's entire rubber-tapping force. It forced the government to employ "riot police and army units" to restore control.[47]

Clower viewed these disturbances as "symptomatic of economic malaise" in which "the government responded to expressions of economic discontent," by "arming the President with stringent emergency powers against rebellion and subversion, and arming the military with more troops and guns"—not with measures to improve the material lives of the protesters.[48]

Put simply, most unskilled tribesmen in Liberia appeared to be headed for a lifetime of low-paying jobs at the bottom of the labor heap—despite a growing demand for skilled and professional Liberians. Foreigners, namely other Africans, Americans, Europeans, and Lebanese filled the gaps.[49] The problem for these unskilled Liberian tribesmen, according to Clower, rested primarily in their woefully inadequate education—almost half the elementary teachers had only an eighth-grade education; only 15 percent of their pupils reached the sixth grade, their literacy rate less than 10 percent. Few could qualify for high school, vocational training, or university. And more than 90 percent of those who did complete vocational training chose to work for the government rather than the private sector.[50]

Tubman made education, vocational training, and health key planks in his development platform. Budget appropriations for education grew dramatically, and by the time he died, the number of government schools had expanded from a mere 251 in 1944 to more than 1,000; elementary schools were enrolling more than six and a half times more students, and secondary schools almost two and a half times more.[51] Tubman also took advantage of US government–sponsored scholarships to send Liberians abroad to study in American schools. They were mainly Americo-Liberians who enjoyed a virtual monopoly on higher education, including foreign scholarships.[52]

Although the education explosion in the hinterland continued through the late 1970s, according to a 1978 National Education Survey, it still left about one-third of elementary-age children and one-half of children of high school age without a school to attend.[53] The literacy rate by 1974 had risen to 14 percent but still remained low by world standards.[54]

> Teachers overall continued in short supply, and more than 70 percent of those in service remained untrained. The system still depended upon expatriates to fill vacant positions and upon mission schools, which historically had shouldered most of the education burden. (Until 1950 Christian missions accounted for over 80 percent of primary and secondary education.[55] Even in 1960–61, they still enrolled some fifteen thousand students, about one-quarter of the total.) Only some 20 percent of high school graduates could obtain vocational training or go to college. Non-Liberians continued

to largely fill the demand for highly skilled workers—master mechanics, carpenters, masons, electricians, etc.[56] Most government schools, mainly in the hinterland, offered no modern education, and scores of them lacked access even to water and toilets. (Although 173 had flush toilets, 762 used only pits, and 48 had to do with only pails).[57]

For tribal people and others outside the Americo-Liberian elite, the entire system had the hollow ring of an educational Potemkin village.

Tubman's development program relied on roads to open up the hinterland and facilitate movement of villagers into the modern economy. At the beginning of the twentieth century, Liberia had no "modern" roads, railroads, or seaports. Coastal mangroves and swamps, tropical jungle, torrential rains, and forbidding soil had doomed two attempts by American concessionaires to build a railroad at the end of the nineteenth century and discouraged would-be road builders. In the absence of pack animals, travelers and shipments of goods followed trails or footpaths, usually accompanied by carriers. In some areas, the trails dwindled to little more than narrow paths cloaked by dense jungle. Most travelers required hammocks, which four men normally carried.

Tubman learned firsthand about traveling in the interior. Describing trips he made soon after becoming president in 1944, he said that while being "carried by hammocks on the shoulders of the tribal people," he saw the misery and hardship "this means of travel imposed"—carriers injured, fainting, and some so tired and resentful, they "threw down their loads and hammocks and [escaped] to the bush." He recounted that upon hearing the men sing as they trudged along, he asked what they were saying. "They were telling of their woes and hardships, [the] burden of carrying hammocks...the rigors of traveling through dense forests, of being bitten by scorpions and snakes, wounded by stones and stumps of trees."[58]

The president also observed "hundreds of people infected with yaws, sleeping sickness and diverse diseases;...the urgent and imperative need of hospitals, clinics and schools." He noted the country's "interior cut off from" the coastal areas, and "tribes isolated from tribes because of the lack of roads, transport, and communication."[59]

A Ford Motor Company shipping clerk in Michigan sparked construction of the country's first road. A large crate labeled "Liberia" arrived by accident in Monrovia in 1919. The clerk had mistakenly routed a Ford Model T meant for the agent of a British trading firm in Nigeria. When it was decided that shipping the car on to Nigeria was too risky, Harry A. McBride, the US receiver of customs in Liberia (stationed in Monrovia under the terms of the 1917 American loan) bought the automobile. After he confined his rides largely to Monrovia's streets for several years, the arrival of the Firestone Rubber Company rescued him. The company helped extend the road from Monrovia to Kakata, near the Firestone plantation, so that now, McBride had forty-four miles of "highway" on which to race his Model T.[60]

Even in 1945, Liberia still had only 206 miles of roads, none paved or hard surfaced, and mostly in poor condition. By 1952 the figures had risen, though only slightly, to twelve miles of paved, forty-two miles of surfaced, and 293 miles of unimproved roads. As the economy accelerated in the 1950s, the pace of highway construction quickened, and by 1961, the country could boast a total of 1,163 miles of roadways—291 miles paved, 741 miles surfaced, and 293 miles unimproved. Concessions built another seven hundred miles of private roads, most of which were also open to public use.[61]

Like roads, other communications also improved: a government-owned radio station in the late 1950s; followed by a second station, owned by a religious denomination, and a television station in the early 1960s. Transistor radios became increasingly available, even in remote villages. While these changes may have stimulated a faint sense of what Dr. Amos Sawyer, political science professor and dean at the University of Liberia, termed "Liberianese" (i.e., a "common set of national aspirations"), they also "sharpened the awareness of deep social divisions and polarity."[62]

—⚭—

By 1969, nearly 3,000 miles of road, of which 1,200 miles were hard surfaced, now spread over Liberia. They mostly connected areas in the hitherto remote interior with Monrovia, with the iron ore mines and rubber plantations. In fact, the three main hinterland counties at that time accounted for 46 percent of the total network. Although few branched out sufficiently to serve as farm-to-market roads, they had a pronounced effect in introducing modernization.[63]

Most obvious was a pointed increase in private rubber farming, initially along the paved road from Monrovia. As new roads were built, Martin Lowenkopf judged that farms multiplied in areas along them as much as fifteen times. Besides rubber, coffee and cocoa production for export also rose significantly, although still in relatively small volumes. The roads "created a new, if small, economically independent class of Liberians."[64]

But, as the Northwestern team's report cautioned, "Roads that bring good government to backward areas are clearly a blessing; roads that bring bad government may be a curse."[65] While these new roads brought certain social and economic benefits to isolated tribal groups, they also brought more "unofficial tax gatherers (including soldiers and agricultural extension workers), more labor recruitment, more petty corruption and graft, and more official tax levies for the building of offices and homes for government officials."[66] On his interior trips, President Tubman had witnessed, in his words, "soldiers routing the people" and the "enmity generated between them," as well as "commissioners receiving monthly supplies of food...for soldiers, messengers, and other interior personnel without giving just compensation."[67]

Most purchasers of land along the roads—for rubber farming, business, or speculation—belonged to the Americo-Liberian establishment. And most of the purchases displaced small farmers who were tribal Liberians. Many of these "dispossessed tribal occupants" reluctantly turned to voluntary wage labor as workers on the new rubber farms and the larger concession plantations and in the iron ore mines. The shifts of these "dispossessed tribal occupants...upset traditional economic patterns" for the hinterland people and added to the budding restlessness of the population at large.[68]

The combination of new roads and rising rubber prices during the Korean War spurred nontribal (and some "civilized" tribal) people to acquire these lands and begin growing rubber. Firestone, in addition, contributed seedlings and technical advice, gratis, and sold equipment to them at cost on interest-free credit.[69] As a result, the number of Liberian rubber growers shot up to four thousand in 1967, an eightfold increase over 1950. The farms employed some eighteen thousand workers, many of them the "dispossessed former tribal occupants," often recruited involuntarily and usually poorly paid, even, according to Lowenkopf, below the legal rate.[70]

Despite constitutional safeguards protecting tribal lands from being sold to nonaborigines for private use, these restrictions went "largely ignored."[71] Besides individual tribal farmers, "entire communities" occasionally were "swallowed up in government grants to foreign concessions" or "sold to non-tribal individuals."[72] Already in the 1930s, a number of well-placed Americo-Liberians, including Presidents Charles King and Edwin Barclay and Vice President Clarence Simpson, had acquired land and established farms.

By 1967, sixty-four of them owned farms larger than one hundred acres. The largest owners included President Tubman, with 1,600 acres, and Vice President Tolbert, with 600-plus acres.[73] The president even called attention in his 1964 inaugural address to the fact that some members of the ruling class "had acquired estates of up to twenty-thousand acres, for as little as fifty cents an acre." He failed to mention it was the president's office that authorized such transfers.[74]

Professor Liebenow, on a field trip to Liberia and Sierra Leone in 1960–61, became, in his words, "fascinated by the inner dynamics of the Liberian political system—largely ignored by other scholars...the intricate web of politics in [a] modern-day version of a Renaissance Italian city-state." This fascination, fed by subsequent visits to west Africa, matured into his becoming a leading authority on Liberian politics and history—and one of the Tubman regime's severest critics.[75]

Liebenow claimed that these "illegal" acquisitions and "outright thefts of land...under both Tubman...and Tolbert constitute one of the major 'land grabs' in African history, in a class with the land seizures by white settlers in South Africa, Zimbabwe and Kenya during the colonial era."[76]

Despite Tubman's development program, Liberia remained a country divided into two different worlds: One, home to the vast majority of Liberians, anchored to a traditional tribal society, based on a largely stagnant agriculture. The other centered in a modern or money economy. Dominated by foreign concessions, it included a relatively small circle of Americo-Liberians at the top, and a labor force—mostly "unskilled, low-paid, illiterate, and of tribal origin"—earning less than fifty cents per day, at the opposite end of the spectrum.[77]

Both domains, however, increasingly felt the tremors of change. Despite the barriers, a widening stream of tribal people Americo-Liberians had labeled "uncivilized" found their way into the world of money, wages, and Western goods and became "involved directly in the modern economy," even if only for limited periods of time.[78] The Northwestern University group thought they numbered "at least 100,000 and perhaps as many as 250,000." Permanent wage employment probably proved the exception rather than the rule. But "permanent rather than temporary migration from tribal areas" became "increasingly common."[79]

Cities and towns gradually sprang up around mines and plantations, growing from small rural villages or from nothing into trading towns and county capital towns. Lowenkopf observed that between 1950 and 1970, over one-fourth of Liberia's largely rural population migrated to these locations.[80] Monrovia's population, according to some estimates, swelled from about two hundred thousand in 1962 to about four hundred thousand ten years later.[81]

The city's population, probably like most other urban centers, now consisted mainly of three strata: tribal people, tribal people in transition, and Americo-Liberians (including descendants of recaptives and civilized tribal people). In this new setting, tribal people "gained access to modern social services," and mixed with individuals from other ethnic groups, even foreigners. Soon, Lowenkopf thought, an individual no longer concerned himself primarily with "tribal identities and structures."[82] A tribal association or labor union replaced the tribal community that traditionally had dominated his life. Now he worked for cash, and where once his land and other property had been owned communally, it now was personal. His occupation and class, not merely his ethnic identity, gradually influenced whom he associated with. As the future would painfully attest, however, tribal allegiances and ethnic identity, often of fierce intensity, did not easily nor fully disappear.

Nonetheless, a "slow but steady transformation in tribal people's way of life" had begun. But time was running out. The Northwestern economists feared the country's "iron ore reserves," the financial fount upon which development depended, would "be exhausted before" Liberian agriculture progressed sufficiently to sustain the development.[83] The "ingrained cultural habits" and the government's detrimental "political procedures and institutions" posed obstacles that even Tubman would not be able to overcome, at least in time to still the rising expectations of the many who were rapidly wearying of Americo-Liberian domination.[84]

After nearly two years in the field, the Northwestern team completed their extensive survey and delivered the results to the Liberian government. Their message was not one the country's leaders, especially the president, wanted to hear. While they accepted that Liberia had achieved one of the most rapid rates of economic growth in the world, fueled by an enormous rise in the output and export of primary commodities by foreign concessions, the team concluded that most Liberians benefited little.

The country's economic bonanza, the university economists noted, produced "novel indicators of change...[that were] everywhere to be seen: more foreigners, more taxes, more Western goods to buy, more mining companies, more rubber farms." But, "by far the largest proportion of the fruits of development" had disappeared into expenditures that benefited "only a handful of Liberians," mainly those who might appreciate such extravagances as the new Treasury Building, costing $2.5 million; the new Executive Mansion, costing $15 or $20 million; and the new law courts building, costing $5 million.[85] Clower remarked that it "was as though a country club [had] suddenly expanded its revenues." The "graft and preferential treatment" did not differ markedly from other countries, but what made "the Liberia case so critical" was the fact that the benefits went "to a very close-knit minority."[86]

One last jab by the American economists struck at the very heart of the Tubman regime, and the entire Americo-Liberian world of dominance and privilege. Despite what might have been a genuine desire on Tubman's part to see Liberia ultimately develop into a nation in which all its citizens shared a sense of community, of nationhood. Liberia lacked "a sense of national purpose—a widely and deeply felt desire for national betterment, a sense of personal identification with the national task of economic and social emergence from the tribal past."[87]

Clower and his colleagues continued,

> The rubber tapper working for 45¢ a day and receiving medical care from Firestone, the stevedore getting 10¢ an hour but paying $10 per month for a single room in a slum dwelling, the tribal farmer who [had] come to learn that the presence of government officials meant only additional requisitions on his rice—these workers may be pardoned for displaying a lack of

personal concern with the Open Door Policy and speeches extolling National Unification. There is nothing in their everyday experience to indicate that their traditional masters are in any way more concerned with their welfare than in the old days.[88]

In 150 years of rule, the Americo-Liberian overlords had yet to transform Liberia into a nation.

Moreover, given the entrenched Americo-Liberians' system of defending their dominant position—through the True Whig Party, the power of the presidency, the intertwined complex of family connections, and other establishment institutions such as the church and Masonic lodge—the likelihood of real change appeared dim at best. The Northwestern team decided that with the "political and social arrangements" then prevailing, "offering economic advice to Liberian leaders [was] rather futile."[89]

CHAPTER 19

Master of Liberia

—⋙—

"BRODER" SHAD, AS SOME OF his devoted followers called him, was at the top of his game. Dapper, affable, cigar-smoking, gregarious, known for generous donations to worthy (and politically advantageous) causes, Tubman for many typified the Liberian politician's politician. According to an entry in *Current Biography 1955*, he liked "people and [was] easily accessible," especially enjoying "dancing, singing in barber-shop quartets and entertaining at the Saturday Afternoon Club," a popular venue frequented by the Americo-Liberian establishment in Monrovia.[1] His unsurpassed ability to maintain a submissive legislature, to retain a chain of both Americo-Liberian and African supporters personally and politically loyal to him, and to employ an effective security network that quashed opposition made Tubman what Tuan Wreh called "the unchallenged master of Liberia."[2]

That he also adored good living went unquestioned. One critic summed up the times: "Tubman's long Havana cigar, his presidential yacht, his top hat and tail coat, his free spending, quaffing of good wine and chasing pretty women were the trademarks of his period in office." But, on the other side, Tubman "was a stickler of protocol and formality...Any one approaching him on a business day had to wear coat and tie." And on ceremonial occasions, he insisted on "European-style formal dress," although this demand often "made Liberia...into a laughing stock."[3] In his defense, an

English journalist, David Williams, observed that Tubman had "an eagle eye for proper dress not for its own sake but because he" believed Liberia could not "afford slackness in anything."[4]

The story of his presidential yachts circulated widely in the country. Mrs. Henries glowingly reported in her biography that Tubman "was the first [and would be the last] President to be presented with a yacht by the Government of Liberia."[5] The 463-ton *Edward James Roye*, purchased in 1951 for $150,000, sported an international crew—and an annual budget of $125,000. It even warranted a separate bureau in the Ministry of Foreign Affairs.[6] When the vessel, after having struck rocks off Cape Palmas, became unseaworthy, the *Liberian*, which later also collided with the rocks, replaced it. The *Hoffman River*, used only once in seven months, was sold after the government had shelled out $250,000 for maintenance.[7]

During his twenty-seven years in office, Tubman purportedly amassed substantial wealth. Besides his four-thousand-acre Totota estate and another three thousand acres in Maryland County, he owned buildings in Monrovia that he allegedly rented—at inflated rates—to government ministries. His Totota estate even boasted a private zoo, and a "palace" in the Congotown quarter of Monrovia reputedly cost $500,000 to build and furnish. Upon Tubman's death, his son William Jr. estimated his father's real estate holdings at approximately $4 million.[8]

When rumors circulated in 1968 that he had acquired a large fortune and a Swiss bank account, Tubman answered that he did "not have a single cent in any bank in Switzerland." He said, "All I have earned during my life I have given to the poor, the sick, the needy, for the building of churches and schools throughout the nation and for support to hundreds of students."[9] Although he enjoyed only a modest yearly salary of $25,000, the president had access to other funds, notably an official entertainment allowance and the special fund for the public relations officers program, for supporting politically attractive causes. And historically, expenditures by Liberian presidents never faced audit.¹⁰

Additionally, Tubman's birthday became a rare opportunity for neglected areas to obtain financing for needed roads, bridges, schools, telephones, and the like. The money came from the government as part of the birthday celebration. The hosting county or other jurisdiction usually would express its appreciation, often by naming or renaming local features. The Bomi Territory on Tubman's seventy-sixth birthday renamed its Bomi Hills capital, the site of Liberia's first iron ore mine, "Tubmanburg."¹¹

> Mrs. Henries proudly pointed out that next to Independence Day on July 26, President Tubman's birthday, November 29, was "celebrated throughout the country with great enthusiasm." Festivities in the capital "lasted all day and far into the night. Champagne was a conspicuous gift, while other presents were continually heaped upon the Chief Executive. Never before [had] a Liberian President been thus honored and showered with tokens of deepest love and esteem." She noted how "each county seemed to try to surpass the others in honoring" the president. The county of Grand Bassa, for example, for his birthday in 1960 entertained him and presented him "with a Chrysler sedan." The following year, Maryland County gave him a boat, and Sinoe County, for his sixty-seventh birthday the next year, an airplane.¹² On subsequent birthdays, the president was even presented "a series of public buildings; a library, a cultural center, and then a military academy."¹³

After the tumultuous 1955 elections, there was no real opposition movement or presidential candidate. Former circuit court judge William Oliver Davies-Bright, who also happened to be the pianist at the Methodist church where Tubman was a lay reader, ran as an opposition candidate. He garnered a total of sixteen votes versus Tubman's 244,937. In 1959 he managed to poll fifty-five votes, while the president received 530,566.[14] Tubman was re-elected without opposition—even from Davies-Bright—in 1963, 1967, and 1971 (when he died before his inauguration).

But, as Tubman's rule stretched on and on, disaffection among some elements in the country began to weaken their allegiance to him. Many Liberians grew weary of the excesses and the regime's suppression of opposition—even of virtually any criticism. Some feared that a "cult of the presidency" had developed as Tubman "unrelentingly pursued personal power."[15]

More ominous, Liberia's overwhelming majority, the indigenous Africans, displayed a growing discontent, despite—or possibly due to—the changes being wrought in their traditional way of life by Tubman's development strategy. Plots against him and the regime, real or imagined (some possibly concocted by the security establishment to prove their value) seemed to occur regularly, providing justification for repeatedly extending emergency powers to the president. These emergency powers, first granted by the legislature in 1942, and renewed numerous times, became a potent weapon in the hands of President Tubman.

The first attempt on the president's life unfolded on June 22, 1955. Paul Dunbar, to escape a rainstorm, ventured into the Executive Pavilion, "where Tubman was celebrating his re-election."[16] Dunbar, an unemployed "former police crack marksman," carried a .38-caliber Smith and Wesson revolver in his hip pocket. According to James Bestman, the president's security chief, Dunbar had drawn his gun, aiming it at President Tubman's back, and fired, but the security officer managed to deflect the assassin's shot.[17]

Dunbar, in his deposition taken for the trial, related the event differently. According to him, he came inside the pavilion and stood with a group of Liberian Frontier Force officers. Bestman apparently spotted the revolver in his pocket and "yelled that [he, Dunbar,] had come to shoot the President." In the scuffle with Bestman and the army officers, the gun fired twice without hitting anyone.[18] Liberian authorities allegedly forced Dunbar to implicate the leaders of the Independent True Whig Party in the plot.

The *New York Times* reported, "The days following the June 22 assassination attempt were ones of terror, especially for leaders of the Independent True Whig party."[19] Thirty persons were arrested and charged with sedition and treason, plotting to overthrow the government by assassinating Tubman and other "high dignitaries, burning the arsenal, stirring up insurrection and inciting rebellion." All complained of police brutality. The party's legal advisor was "arrested and dragged through the streets of Monrovia at the end of a chain fixed to a jeep." Others reportedly "were stripped to their under-shorts and forced to jog through the streets at gun-point."[20]

―◆―

S. David Coleman, the party's national chairman, and his son, John, had traveled to their family farm in Clay-Ashland the day of Dunbar's arrest. After the two fired on a police-army posse sent to arrest them, killing two and wounding five, the posse set fire to their farmhouse. The two Colemans escaped and made their way to the Bomi Hills, hoping to make it across the border to Sierra Leone. But Liberian security forces spotted them on a sugarcane farm.

According to the police commander, Captain Saydee Totaye, "I opened fire and the first shot hit [Coleman] on the right side of his chest which went through him and shattered his brains. I then...hit [John] on the hip. When he fell down, I ran nearer, took his father's rifle and shot him through the left eye."[21] Tubman reportedly ordered their decomposing bodies "dumped" at an army installation, the Barclay Training Center in Monrovia, where "thousands of Monrovians came" to view them.[22]

Seven of the persons charged went to trial in August. Six were found guilty, and Judge Pierre on January 4 the following year sentenced them to be hanged on the twenty-seventh of the month. One, Soko Brown, who turned state's witness during the trial, received a pardon and was set free.[23] Upon appeal, the Supreme Court upheld the remaining six defendants' convictions in February 1958, but Tubman ultimately ordered each of them reprieved. Paul Dunbar, conditionally pardoned in April 1958, was later found guilty of inciting workers at the Liberian American Swedish Minerals Company iron ore mine "to rise in insurrection." He died in the notorious Camp Belle Yallah of some unnamed illness in September 1961.[24]

Another of the political prisoners, Booker T. Bracewell, who had been a promising lawyer, ran afoul of the Tubman machine again after being released in 1960. The hapless Bracewell, it was charged, had schemed "to obtain $1 million from the Russian Embassy" in neighboring Guinea "in order to bribe the Liberian Army to stage a coup against the Tubman regime and to finance his own political party." He allegedly "had left Liberia dressed as a woman...and that on arriving in Guinea...had promptly proclaimed himself 'President of Liberia in Exile.'" Sentenced to twenty years' imprisonment, he also "died of natural causes" in Camp Belle Yallah.[25] The last of the "conspirators" released, former solicitor general S. Raymond Horace, was not freed until July 7, 1965. He reportedly had refused "to recant and repent to Tubman—the precondition for presidential clemency and release."[26]

By the end of 1955, President Tubman, convinced he had survived death at the hand of an assassin through divine intervention (presumably his guardian angel) was grateful for the opportunity it offered to punish his political foes. He felt confident as he addressed the legislature in his December 23 annual message. The economy, he announced, had generated a record $15 million income for the government, thanks to favorable iron ore and rubber prices.[27] Foreign governments and investors looked with growing favor on the country and its potential. The future looked rosy.

This euphoria carried over into the new year and into his inauguration on January 2, 1956. German contractors had failed "to complete a new $2,000,000 capitol building in time" for the ceremony—a failure for which the president had taken them to task in his message to the legislature. But even this offense and an inopportune tropical downpour on an unseasonably hot and humid day could not dampen the "colorful festivity in the capital city of Monrovia."[28]

The president and vice president "renewed their oaths inside the Centennial Memorial Pavillion, which was jammed with 3,000 persons," and then "marched to the music of massed bands beneath bright floral arches and strings of flags and pennants crisscrossing the way." Thousands "more stood in the rain outside and along the route of the Presidential march." In spite of the weather, the dress followed Tubman's strict formal code, so "there was many a damp top hat before the day was over. The only diplomatic representatives not in formal clothes were those of the Soviet Union, who appeared in dark business suits."[29]

In his inaugural address, President Tubman "stressed the need for world peace" to enable less-developed countries to advance. For Liberia, he outlined a four-year program that called for doubling the output of "rubber, rice, lumber, cocoa, coffee, palm oil and kola nuts"—the country's main agricultural products—and for creating "a national production council" to expand "agricultural and commercial production." On the financial side, he proposed eliminating the remaining "short-term Government debt," as well as raising revenue by 20 percent. Tubman underscored the importance of foreign development assistance, especially in exploiting Liberia's mineral resources. He particularly noted the aid extended by the United States in recent years.[30]

The inaugural festivities would "continue for eight days with fireworks and an inaugural ball and banquet, African dancing, an agricultural fair and other events." In addition to "representatives of thirty-five foreign countries," tribal chiefs from all over Liberia attended the occasion.[31]

The presence at Tubman's inauguration of these representatives of thirty-five foreign countries attested to Liberia's rise in the hierarchy of nations following the end of the Second World War. The welcome to foreign investors promised by Tubman's Open Door policy, coupled with Liberia's abundant supplies of natural resources—not to mention the drive of the opposing Cold War blocs to recruit friends and allies—fueled this rise. Tubman sensed the time was ripe for Liberia to spread its diplomatic wings and assume a more visible role in world affairs.

> The Soviet delegation's presence at the inauguration provoked considerable "interest and speculation," particularly given that the Soviet Union had turned down Liberia's invitation to the inauguration four years earlier. "Nearly everyone...

was wondering whether" the appearance this time was "just another of the friendly visits Soviet officials" were making to various countries, "or whether there may be some deeper significance." Some speculated that the Soviet envoy might be exploring establishing a mission in Liberia for economic assistance. Most concluded it was "a fairly obvious indication of the Soviet Union's interest in Africa and its desire to spread Soviet influence on the African continent."[32]

At a diplomatic reception the day before the inauguration, the head of the delegation, Alexander P. Volkov, read a message from Marshal Kliment E. Voroshilov, chairman of the Presidium of the Supreme Soviet, to President Tubman. He hoped the presence of the Soviet delegation would "serve the cause of establishing friendly relations between the Soviet Union and Liberia."[33]

Tubman "'expressed pleasure' at the message and said he also hoped for friendly relations between" the two countries. In a forty-five minute meeting on January 6 with the president Volkov proposed negotiations leading to the establishment of diplomatic relations between the two countries. He said the USSR was prepared to offer aid to Liberia. Later that day Tubman told the US ambassador that when he (Tubman) met Volkov in the next few days, he would tell him, "the economic and other relations between the US and Liberia are neither for sale nor barter with any country. Liberia had all the aid it can use and if it needs more it will make its request to the US government" [34]

Although the president sought to "project an image of Liberia as a non-aligned state," it clearly was not. His "foreign policy was out-and-out anti-Russian and anti-Communist."[35] He would not tolerate any political, diplomatic, or economic contacts with any of the communist powers. He feared they used "such contacts to indoctrinate the workers, peasants, youth and army...and endanger the capitalist system." He "resolutely opposed...the socialist doctrine of state ownership of private property."[36]

George Padmore, Liberia's new ambassador to the United States, in presenting his credentials on April 7, 1956, went out of his way to reaffirm its allegiance to Western values. He asserted that the Liberian government had "not agreed" to conclude a treaty of friendship with the USSR, "or to accept economic assistance." The president rejected an invitation to visit the Soviet Union because, he said, "he had other commitments."[37]

"This automatic compliance with the American line, reducing Liberia almost to the level of a vassal, disgusted many of Tubman's countrymen who felt that he was behaving like an Uncle Tom."[38] Liberia had landed firmly in the American camp in the Cold War. It would be a relationship that would stretch well beyond Tubman and his successors.

—w—

The president stepped up his campaign of personal diplomacy aimed at securing the republic a place on the international map. In 1955 Liberia sent representatives to attend the epoch-defining Conference of Asian and African States in Bandung, Indonesia. And on September 7 the following year, he began a tour of seven European countries, boarding a French liner at Monrovia's Freeport, "escorted there by a mile-long procession of trade unionists, school children, frontier force detachments and bands"—and "with assurances from Liberian politicians they would not 'stab him in the back.'"[39] Tubman's itinerary even included the Vatican, where Pope Pius XII received him in a private audience.[40]

Ending a busy diplomatic year, the government in December announced that Liberia would open legations in the Union of

Soviet Socialist Republics, in both communist and nationalist Chinas, in Egypt, and in the Gold Coast.[41]

With Liberia's and Tubman's fortunes clearly on the rise, visits to Monrovia by important world figures—such as US vice president Richard Nixon—would become more commonplace. The vice president, accompanied by Mrs. Nixon, "arrived in steamy Liberia" on March 7, 1957, "in a top hat, cutaway and striped trousers in accordance with the rigid protocol of Africa's oldest republic." According to a *New York Times* report, Nixon, playing the good diplomat, remarked that since he came from California, he felt "right at home" with the ninety-degree temperature in the shade, though "unlike California, the air was sticky with humidity."[42]

The Liberian vice president, William Tolbert, met the visitors at Roberts Field, where the two vice presidents reviewed an honor guard of Liberian Frontier Force soldiers, outfitted in US Army uniforms "and tasseled red fezzes." When they started the fifty-six-mile drive to Monrovia, however, the "air conditioning in their Cadillac broke down." Undeterred, they drove with the windows down, fighting the clouds of dust kicked up by other vehicles. They stopped six times along the way "at villages to shake hands with beaming Liberians" waving US and Liberian flags.[43]

To the relief of the Nixons, when they finally arrived at the Executive Mansion, they found "a large air-conditioned White House in the center of Monrovia," complete with red carpet. President Tubman, along with the military band he had had flown down from the ceremony at Roberts Field, greeted his guests and then escorted them upstairs to meet local officials and members of the diplomatic corps. They were ushered into "a drawing room with glass chandeliers and paneled walls bearing pictures of past Presidents. The room," according to the press report, "looked like one in an antebellum mansion in the South of the United States."[44]

The host, of course, had not neglected the entertainment. The *Times* reporter again: "Liberians from the bush...who outnumber the descendants of the American freedmen by fifty to one put on the best show of the day." He described how "Country Devils," who wore masks and grass skirts, "danced to drum music in little circles among thousands of calico-clad spectators while pretty girls from the Mandingo tribe strutted in bright colored wrappings." One of the "Devils" moved about in calico trousers on stilts about eighteen feet high. A state dinner at the Executive Mansion, the "outside walls lit with horizontal fluorescent tubes," closed the festivities.[45]

The following day, Paramount Chief Yeleweyan Bandi Wuobama robed Nixon in a "black and white gown of authority and put a red hat on his head," investing him "as a paramount chief." Twenty other paramount chiefs and Vice President Tolbert witnessed the investiture ceremony, which gave the American "the right to take as many wives as he [wished]." Contributing to the eventful two-day visit—one the Nixons likely would not soon forget—smoke had poured from one of the four engines on their plane when it landed at Roberts Field. The engine was rendered "unusable," but the US Air Force came to the rescue, flew in a new one, and the Nixons departed on schedule.[46]

As the Cold War intensified, President Tubman accelerated his international diplomacy. He was determined not to let the world forget Africa, and Liberia in particular. One unusual brainwave came to him in January 1960, when he discovered Washington's National Zoo had two female pygmy hippopotamuses, but no male. He dispatched an expedition to find and capture one, a kind of hippo "found only in Liberia." The captured animal was loaded on the Farrell Lines' 6,116-ton *African Glade*, bound for New York City and the Washington Zoo, the gift of President Tubman to President Eisenhower.[47] There is no record of the impact Tubman's gift made on US-Liberian relations, but the Liberian president followed up with a visit in October the next year to New York City and Washington.

―⁂―

In Washington he met with President John F. Kennedy. They "exchanged views on the…international situation and the relations between the two countries." Kennedy congratulated the Liberian leader on his success in arranging meetings of African states. He also assured him of American assistance in establishing "a strong central planning agency," expanding education and health facilities, and possibly in constructing the Mount Coffee hydroelectric project.[48]

An approving *New York Times* editorial described Tubman's "winding up a busy week [in New York]…with an active day in which he [would] address the U.N. General Assembly, entertain the U.N. leaders at lunch, receive an honorary degree from Fairleigh-Dickinson University at Teaneck, and be entertained at dinner by officials of the Bethlehem Steel Corporation."[49]

June the following year found the peripatetic Tubman traveling once again, on a ten-day state visit to Israel. In a joint communiqué with Premier David Ben-Gurion, he thanked the Israeli leader for "Israel's contribution to [Liberia's] development."[50] Then, on July 10 Tubman "stepped from a special train at [London's] Victoria Station," to begin a four-day state visit. He "was met by Queen Elizabeth and other members of the royal family and by Prime Minister Macmillan and the Earl of Home, the Foreign Secretary." After he inspected "a guard of honor from the Coldstream Guards, the president rode through the rain in an open carriage with Queen Elizabeth."

That evening, the queen hosted a state dinner at Buckingham Palace for the president and Mrs. Tubman.[51]

Liberia, Tubman was no doubt convinced, had arrived at its proper place in the family of nations. His personal diplomacy must be working.

—⋙—

Closer to home, the president began to reach out to other African countries. Liberia historically had provided support, such as "assistance and travel documents," to political activists like Hastings Banda, the "Father of Malawi"; Joshua Nkomo and Herbert Chitepo, who led the fight against white rule in Southern Rhodesia; and others in the 1950s.[52]

When Kwame Nkrumah of the Gold Coast (today's Ghana) burst upon the African political landscape preaching a radical nationalism, followed by Egypt's Abdul Nasser and Sékou Touré in Guinea, Tubman stepped up his efforts to foster greater moderation among emerging African states. Soon, Liberia arose as the leader of the moderate Monrovia Group, actively engaging in diplomacy and holding regional conferences on economic and political cooperation. Liberia promoted "landmark" meetings of independent African countries, including ones at Saniquellie in 1959 and Monrovia in 1961 that led up to the historic May 25, 1963, conference in Addis Ababa. There, thirty-two African states formed the Organization for African Unity (OAU). (The OAU was disbanded on July 9, 2002, and replaced by the African Union)

> The Addis Ababa conference was preceded by two preparatory meetings. On July 15–19, 1959, the heads of state and government of Ghana, Guinea, and Liberia met in Sanniquellie, Liberia. At Sanniquellie they drew up and signed the Declaration of the Principles of a Future Community of Independent African States. The Monrovia conference, which began on

May 8, 1961, drew representatives from nineteen independent African countries. (Morocco, Guinea, Ghana, the United Arab Republic, and Libya turned down the Tubman-issued invitation.) At the meeting President Tubman recommended that Africans adopt "a permanent machinery for consultation."[53]

The United States, embroiled in the Cold War, quite naturally welcomed these actions. Tubman was credited with promoting the cooperation among African states that led to OAU's creation. His actions "helped carry Liberia to the center of the African international stage."[54] (The OAU in 1979 would elect Tubman's successor, William Tolbert, chairman at its summit meeting hosted by Liberia.) And in 1960, United Nations members elected Liberia to the Security Council, the first black African country so honored. In 1970 Angie Brooks Randolph, a Liberian, became the only African woman elected president of the UN General Assembly. She presided over the assembly's twenty-fourth session. Liberia, under William Tubman's leadership, clearly had arrived on the international scene.

On the home front, however, the outlook was less promising. The financial bubble burst in 1963, punctured when the post-Korean War boom in rubber and iron ore collapsed. Against income of less than $40 million that year, Liberia faced $33.6 million in debt service alone. Basking in the glow of an expected rosy future, the government between 1959 and 1963 had run up almost $135 million of public debt, not including another $34 million in interest. (When Tubman took office in 1944, the debt figure stood at $1.3 million, and by the end of 1959, it was only $589,000.)[55]

The ensuing construction spree spent more than $50 million on roads and public buildings, including the $20 million new Executive Mansion, a new $2 million–plus Capitol building, and even $1 million for a Masonic lodge building. For the Executive Mansion, the president simply instructed the architect, "It should be awesome." In response to critics, he said, "It is too fabulous for a country with economic and financial resources such as ours...It is too good for me to live in, but not good enough for a President of Liberia."[56]

Fueling the meltdown, government agencies outside the Treasury's purview obtained short-term loans at high interest rates. Tubman, continuing his resolve to keep Liberia at the forefront of world affairs, ordered "setting up a costly network of diplomatic missions in newly independent African countries," plus others such as Haiti, Taiwan, Israel, the Vatican, and Jamaica—on top of his own expensive trips abroad. As a result, money spent on international relations jumped twenty-fold between 1946 and 1961. And outlays for security, especially the feared public relations officers program, continued to grow. The program's 1956 budget already totaled more than the budgets of the Agriculture and Commerce Departments combined. (Even Tubman's inauguration the same year cost more than those two departments received.)[57]

Taxes went uncollected, while public funds were misspent or embezzled.[58] Van de Kraaij cites an example in which the legislature in March 1952 passed a yearly one-dollar-per-capita tax on all citizens between twenty-one and sixty years old. Six years later, the Bureau of Internal Revenue admitted that it had never collected one dime of the tax because it had never received a copy of the act. The drop in commodity prices, the loans, the overspending, the incompetence, mismanagement, and corruption all added up to "a financial crisis unprecedented in the history of the country" where they were almost an annual event.[59]

The International Monetary Fund, which Liberia had joined in 1962, helped to reschedule the debt. The government initiated an austerity policy that included drastic cuts in expenditures and measures to improve tax revenues and find new sources, even to enact a detested austerity tax. But substantial budget deficits continued, and political unrest and strikes in the rubber and iron ore sectors followed.[60]

―⁂―

Adding to the unrest, the Liberian military, which traditionally had eschewed political actions, came under fire; the government (supposedly) uncovered a plot in February 1963 involving a former commanding officer of the Liberian National Guard. The officer, Colonel David Y. Thompson, allegedly "invited a number of army officers to join in killing the President and overthrowing his regime." Liberian secret police discovered the conspiracy, which the president described to a shocked meeting in Lofa County. Thompson, he charged, "'organized a civilian group called "the club"...composed principally of Klemoweh Grebos, some Vais, Krus, and a few citizens of Arthington.'"[61]

He continued that Thompson and two junior army officers "undertook to provide ['the club'] with arms and destructive weapons" for their conspiracy.[62] Thompson was jailed on February 3, 1963, charged with "sedition, conspiracy, and disloyalty." In October a court-martial board found the colonel guilty. After serving time at the Barclay Training Camp and the Belle Yallah prison, Thompson, nearly three and a half years later, "was granted a reprieve and freed."[63]

Some Liberians believed the army harbored many grievances against the government—the low pay, inadequate education and accommodations for both officers and men and their families, obsolete weapons, the desultory military training they received, and the fact that "it was being used to suppress the people, a role it disdained." They noted that such a lengthy catalog of complaints "would have given" the military, "had it been sufficiently provoked...a pretext for halting civilian rule." But Tubman, the master politician, "had the army in his pocket," and his mastery increased "as he picked off officers one by one, accusing them of plotting, with nobody speaking up in protest." Thus, most concluded that "the Thompson plot was a frame-up."[64]

The president next turned his wrath on what he termed "some of the young, impressionable and irresponsible...[Liberians] who seem to be still obsessed with the idea of tribalism...that the land of and territory of Liberia belong to them and that they had been deprived of their heritage." Further, he charged, they believed "the only way to retrieve the situation [was] to engage in subversive activities, treason and sedition and overthrow the Government by force and murder, establish a socialist system of government, expropriate the properties of those who by their many years of labour, sacrifice, toil and sweat" had acquired them. The president claimed some of the country's most prestigious schools, namely Cuttington College, the University of Liberia, and the College of West Africa (Liberia's oldest secondary school), were disseminating this unpalatable doctrine. And if these institutions failed to "take appropriate action, the Government" would do so.[65]

In this vein, Tubman's security service in 1962 learned that a "band of college and high-school students had formed a Youth Solidarity Movement that held 'secret meetings' at various places." At these meetings a Ghanaian embassy officer allegedly delivered "brainwashing instruction on Communism and on the revolutionary overthrow of the government."[66]

Despite their protests that they "only met to make a comparative study of the socialist systems of Ghana, Guinea and Mali," and with only flimsy evidence against them, ten were convicted of sedition. The circuit court in Monrovia sentenced them to fifteen years in the Barclay Training Center stockade. However, the president, in his customary act of mercy, granted them reprieves on January 9, 1965, after they had served less than four years.[67]

The regime discouraged students studying in communist countries and tried to keep visitors and any other interchanges between Liberia and communist bloc nations to the minimum.[68] Tubman proved to be one of America's staunchest allies in Africa. And Liberia would become an important strategic center for American interests in Africa, both political and economic.

But the paranoia and fears persisted, stoked by a rash of industrial disputes and strikes in the country and military coups in neighboring Nigeria and Ghana. The legislature in 1966 extended the president's emergency powers, even expanding them. He could, for example, suspend the right of habeas corpus, have arrested without warrant "any person considered dangerous to public safety." In addition, anyone who led a strike without prior authorization would be considered "guilty of an attempt to overthrow the government." He also "could conscript able-bodied citizens for military service" or "labor for all economic, social and industrial services and for defense." The president could even move the "seat of government...to any area deemed safe."[69]

Prior to the 1963 enactment of the Labor Code, all strikes in Liberia were illegal until first submitted to a labor court. Unfortunately, the government never got around to creating such a court. After 1963, any proposed strike had to be put before a government-established labor-practices review board. When faced with an impending strike, however, the board either would fail to announce any decision, or else unduly delay an announcement or even neglect to meet at all. And in the unlikely event the board decided against a company, no means of enforcing a judgment existed.[70]

The government, however, did not oppose "labor unions per se"; they "opposed only effective unions."[71] For example, Tubman's twenty-nine-year-old son in 1960 became head of the Liberian CIO (not affiliated with the American organization). Prior to assuming that position, he worked as public relations consultant for the Liberia Mining Company, and he even continued, while union chief, in a similar capacity for LAMCO, Liberia's second-largest private employer. To celebrate his taking on the leadership of the union, the government generously gave the CIO the building housing its headquarters, along with a $5,000 cash gift. The president's social secretary and former member of the House of Representatives headed Liberia's only other trade union.[72]

Despite the administration's attempts to thwart such actions, strikes, both organized and unorganized, multiplied. A dozen or more erupted in 1961 alone. In a general strike in September of that year, the government, in a pattern that would characterize future responses, deployed troops against unorganized violence, arrested union leaders on charges of sedition, and claimed that a "foreign conspiracy" had fomented the outbreak. (Unsurprisingly, the union-initiated strike on September 11, 1961, occurred while the union's head was out of the country.) Similar clashes in 1963 and 1966, major strikes at the Firestone and Goodrich rubber plantations and the LAMCO iron ore mine in Nimba, shook the Tubman regime even further.[73]

—⚏—

The paranoia-driven plots against Tubman peaked in January 1968. At a reception Liberia's foreign service customarily gave in his honor, Tubman addressed the country's ambassadors (who had been recalled for the event). Henry Boima Fahnbulleh,

Liberia's ambassador to Kenya, Tanzania, and Uganda, listened intently as the president extolled the envoys for their good performances abroad—that is, except one. The president hinted that the offending ambassador, without naming him, would be dismissed for serious misbehavior. The assemblage grew quiet, and one almost could make out anxious murmurs of "Is it I?" "Is it I?"[74]

A cloud of uncertainty and fear hung over the entire diplomatic corps, and Tubman's startling announcement unleashed a wave of public speculation. Monrovia buzzed with rumor.

The *Liberian Age,* one of the country's major newspapers, asked, "Who is that undiplomatic diplomat?"[75] The answer came after a month of anxious waiting, during which the allegation of misconduct and dismissal had escalated into something far more serious. Ambassador Fahnbulleh was arrested at his home on February 13, charged with sedition.

The president at a press conference later that day alleged that the ambassador "had been 'carrying on acts of sedition which amounted to treason.'"[76]

The March 7 indictment named Fahnbulleh "'the leader and promoter' of an underground movement whose avowed aim was to overthrow the government.'" A newspaper headline screamed, "Facts against Fahnbulleh are 'Hair-Raising.'"[77] The *New York Times* account of his trial, which began June 10 in Monrovia, described a plot bordering on the fantastic. Fahnbulleh was "accused of having conspired with Chinese Communists to overthrow…Tubman's regime." They would "replace the minority rule of the Americo-Liberian aristocracy with a government of…'aborigines' [tribal Africans]."[78] If convicted, Fahnbulleh, a member of the Vai tribe, could face a death sentence.

A secret memorandum, allegedly written by Fahnbulleh, outlined a scheme "to organize an underground movement for 'educating the 'sons of the soil' [the indigenous African Liberians]" about their exploitation by President Tubman and his Open Door Policy". To get the movement underway, "at least ten Communist Chinese experts" would be introduced covertly into Liberia. They also would help to find jobs for "foreigners of purported leftist sympathies" to support the movement.[79]

The prosecution, in addition, charged Ambassador Fahnbulleh with having written anonymous letters in January 1968 to the Israeli, American, and Nigerian ambassadors to Liberia. The letters accused the Liberian government "of having entered into a secret pact with the United States Government 'for repatriating 50,000 American Negroes called Black Muslims...to increase the near extinct Americo-Liberians.'"[80]

Remarkably, the authorities made public the vitriolic description of the government the purported letters painted: "a feudal, fascist regime, Americo-Liberian ruled state, persecuting her aborigines to abject serfdom under our cow-dung unification policy..."[81] They accused the regime of "'squandering' native lands that it had converted to large rubber plantations, of being 'the most corrupt dictatorship, tyranny and exploitation' in Liberia's history."[82]

For good measure, the prosecution threw in further charges. Among them that Fahnbulleh planned to confer with then-exiled former president of Ghana, Kwame Nkrumah. He also was charged with writing a book criticizing Americo-Liberian domination of the country and "a poem of 'an exciting nature' entitled Awake Captain." Finally, he was charged with turning over the keys of the Liberian embassy to a personal friend, an East Indian gynecologist named Dr. Yusef Ali Eraj.[83] The country understandably was electrified.

Ambassador Fahnbulleh dismissed the affair as a "'concocted plot' by someone who wanted to get his job."[84] But, he felt that he already had been found guilty before his trial. The odds were against him. When asked whether or not he, being a lawyer himself, might act in his own defense, he replied that he had little choice since he could not find a lawyer willing to do so. "They are all afraid," he said.[85] Tubman, however, reportedly was disturbed by the bad image of Liberia that a public trial, in which "the accused had no other counsel to defend him," would create. Shortly afterward, three attorneys, "as a result of pressure from above, offered their services."[86] The trial was scheduled to begin on June 10, 1968.

In the meanwhile, the beleaguered Fahnbulleh, one of a growing number of tribal Africans who had managed to join the Americo-Liberian establishment, found that even "friends and colleagues who had earlier cherished his friendship now thought it imprudent to speak out on his behalf, or even to visit him or his family." Not one of the three major newspapers in Monrovia cautioned "the public to withhold judgment" on his guilt or innocence until after the trial. Instead, "responsible members of the government and the public at large" took his indictment and jailing "as a signal to mount a massive attack against him."[87]

Liberian legislators kicked off the attack. Visiting President Tubman at the Executive Mansion on March 12, they assured him of their "continuous and unflinching support," and condemned Fahnbulleh's alleged "diabolical" and "subversive" acts.[88] Then on April 30, thousands of True Whig Party members paraded in Monrovia's streets. "Representatives from Grand Bassa, Nimba, and Bong Counties and the River Cess Territory noisily reaffirmed their loyalty" to the president and "irrevocable support of his unification and integration policy." They shouted, "Tubman is the right man for the nation," and would he "kindly...accept yet another term of office [which would be his seventh]...Tubman thanked the people for the honor their 'spontaneous' gesture had bestowed upon him."[89]

At a mass rally later that day at the Antoinette Tubman Stadium, the president issued "a stern warning to students and professors," both Liberian and foreign, who "engaged in subversive activities." Another "monster parade on the following day" saw "party members and residents of Maryland, Sinoe, and Grand Gedeh counties, and of Sasstown and Kru Coast" join the call for "Tubman to accept a seventh term as President," pledging "their unswerving loyalty to" his "dynamic and illustrious leadership and administration." They "described [Tubman] as Dr. Love and Unity instead of Dr. Tubman because of the numerous benefits of his administration." In response, "the President, wearing his Bassa [Tribal] King leopard-skin gown stressed how dear the Unification and Integration Policy was to him."[90]

And the Tubman support machine continued its roll. The next day, May 2, "more than 10,000" students and teachers from all over the country swarmed into the capital for "a massive parade." It was "the fourth large public demonstration held in Monrovia that week" supporting the president. "Students carried banners and brandished placards reading: 'We want education not subversion and denouncing alleged subversion.'"[91]

William A. Fernandez, president of the Cuttington College Student Association, read a statement in which he said, "It is with sincerity and confidence that I express the full support [of Tubman] of at least 99.9 per cent of the students of higher learning in this country. A few thoughtless scribblings," he continued, "written...on toilet walls, cannot and do not support a meaningful representation of the total thinking of Liberian youth."[92]

A crucial piece in Tubman's support network fell into place with publication of an article by an "aborigine," D. Nyeka Chie, in the *Liberian Star* on May 2, entitled "We Are Not Ingrates." Chie wrote, "We, the aborigines of Liberia love President Tubman as we love ourselves...[and we stand] solidly behind our indefatigable, great, dynamic and implacable leader, who is everybody's President." He concluded, "God bless President Tubman and save the State."[93]

As a final exclamation mark to the "Tubman love feast," that apparently "continued unabated," the *Liberian Star* on May 2 carried a lengthy poem by Delsena Draper, the president of a women's club. Its title? "Why Liberians Must Love Tubman."[94]

The jury found Fahnbulleh guilty of treason. The judge sentenced him to twenty years' imprisonment in the Barclay Training Center stockade with hard labor. His property was confiscated. After Tubman died in July 1971, Fahnbulleh petitioned the new president, William Tolbert, for a reprieve. Tolbert freed him on December 1, 1971.[95]

In the waning days of the Tubman era, the president still maintained a heavy travel schedule, striving to keep Liberia in the forefront as one of Africa's leaders. In March 1968 the seventy-three-year-old Tubman visited Washington for talks with US president Lyndon Johnson. Other trips took him to Europe. The Liberian legislature had to grant permission for each of his absences from the country. Their frequency and length—rest leave "from the seat of government in 1952, three months in 1956, 1958, and 1960"—"caused delays and disruptions" in the government's operations. There was no "decentralization or delegation" of authority. "Any expenditure over $25 [later raised to $100] needed his personal approval," and "he controlled and spent these public funds as his personal property."[96]

While in Washington, he spoke at the National Press Club on March 28, 1968, saying, "'No African can remain indifferent to the indignities and inhumanities' being perpetrated by white minority leaders in parts of Africa.' [He pointed, in particular to], 'obstinate pockets of tyranny and suppression [that still remained in] Southern Rhodesia, South-West Africa and the Portuguese colonies.'"[97]

Curiously, if one disregarded the oppressors' skin color, his speech could well have applied to the relations between Liberia's minority Americo-Liberian leaders and the country's African masses who viewed the Americo-Liberians as colonial masters. And, despite Liberia's booming growth, economic storm clouds had continued to gather, adding further to the tensions between the two.

In his 1968 New Year's Day address on his inauguration, the president sought to explain the reversal in the country's fortunes and defend the government's actions, especially its economic austerity program. The administration understandably tried to put the best face possible on the painful conditions in the country and their impact on the various parts of the population, regardless of race or class. Some of Tubman's most loyal minions tried. But it was a near-impossible task. All one had to do was look with open eyes.

The description of life in Liberia, for example, penned by the chairwoman of the Liberian Women Social and Political Movement (who also happened to be the wife of Speaker of the House Richard A. Henries) illustrates the Tubman regime's smoke screen that cloaked actual conditions in the country. Mrs. Henries depicted the 1967 countryside in glowing terms. Signs of prosperity abounded: Buildings "changing from mud huts with thatched roof to concrete buildings…Radios [found] in every village. Cars and trucks [owned] by tribal and non-tribal dwellers… shoes and stylish clothes…books and newspapers everywhere. Electricity. Telephones."[98]

According to her, Monrovia had "become a modern city" where the government was housed "in beautiful structures," and on strorefronts "electric lights of many designs and colors...[glittered] all night." One could find "streamlined theatres" that catered "for the tastes of all," as well as renovated churches and improved sports and educational facilities. "Zinc and wooden dwelling houses [had] been torn down and replaced by beautiful homes...Hotels of various shapes, sizes and comfort...located in convenient spots." Cars and buses sped "over paved streets." For all of these improvements and "the good things and opportunities of life the people of Liberia have been grateful to President Tubman."[99]

Alfred Friendly Jr., a correspondent for the *New York Times*, in May 1968 described a vastly different Monrovia, where, for example, "the two fountains...on each side of the nine-story... Presidential Palace" would play, while "no one else in the neighborhood [had] water. When official motorcades [careened] through the capital's commercial center, lesser traffic [was] diverted to rutted back streets past houses of corroded tin and automobile hulks among weeds." He felt "these contrasts" were "a fair index of the contradictions" that had come to plague Liberia under Tubman. While the country had made some improvements, the "extravagance, notably in spending for the symbols of power" were glaring.[100]

—⚘—

As the 1960s came to a close, a feeling of stagnation permeated the government. Some observers sensed the Tubman era fading, "symbolized by the 'old man's' halting gait, blurred speech and general loss of physical vigor."[101] Nonetheless, when Martin Lowenkopf of Stanford University broached the subject of succession in 1964, "one old hand observed, 'You are making a false assumption. What makes you think the old man is ever going to die?'"[102]

But, as one periodical observed, the ensuing retrenchment "reflected a regime then striving simply to survive."[103] Shad Tubman would survive another three years—until his final journey to London ended in a medical clinic on July 23, 1971.

A brief notice on September 9, 1971, in the *New York Times* announced that "a memorial service for President V. S. Tubman of Liberia...would be held on Friday, Sept. 17, at 5 P.M., at the New York Cultural Center, 2 Columbus Circle. Dr. Peter Sammartino, president of the center, will preside. The Liberian Ambassador, S. Edward Peal, will deliver the eulogy."

CHAPTER 20

After Tubman, What? A Summing Up

—⚏—

MRS. HENRIES, IN HER BIOGRAPHY of President Tubman, described a monument in Voinjama, Lofa County, the site of one of the president's initial "unification council" meetings. Dedicated January 7, 1961, it featured a statue of President Tubman. An inscription below recorded the "memory of great achievements resulting from [his] Unification and Integration Policy."[1] Another erected in 1956, the Tubman Monument Honoring Freedom from Foreign Debt, celebrated Liberia's paying off the notorious loan from Firestone in 1952. A plaque on it read, "This memorial erected by the people of Liberia is dedicated to the great relief brought to the country by the Tubman Administration in the retirement of the [Firestone] Loan with its humiliating and strangulation effects on the economy of the Nation."[2] Still another monument elsewhere honored his Open Door policy.[3]

The monuments and numerous thoroughfares and public structures named after him or members of his family attested to his widespread popularity—among tribal Liberians as well as Americo-Liberians. And, thanks to him, in 1946, grateful Liberian women could vote for the first time.

—⚏—

Most observers agree that the country as a whole undeniably benefited from Tubman's rule. But, the Americo-Liberian class in particular had the "decidedly good fortune" to have found "its hero" in warding off modern-day challenges to its dominant position. "Tubman—frequently over the strenuous opposition of many of his fellow Americo-Liberians"—including those who had prospered under his rule—had demonstrated a remarkable "talent for political imagination and manipulation far exceeding any of his predecessors."[4]

His Open Door policy even drew in foreigners whom nineteenth-century Americo-Liberians had feared as an "overt threat to" their supremacy (but who actually served as "witting or unwitting partners" of the Americo-Liberians in exploiting "the tribal masses").[5] His extending "suffrage and representation to the tribal hinterland" at least gave "the semblance of greater access for the tribal people to the citadels of political, social, and economic power in Liberia." And, at the same time, Liebenow argues, Tubman "skillfully injected Liberia into world affairs" and neutralized the "potential hostility of his neighboring African leaders."[6]

Tubman's evolutionary approach to change also was helping erode "the many historic barriers to legal, political, and social equality." Public arrogance toward tribal people was becoming less frequent, and the "flagrant abuse" of their rights "largely curbed." The Unification program "encouraged the tribal people to take a measure of pride in their antecedents, their art and language, and even in their traditional names." (Ambassador Henry Freeman, for instance, became Ambassador Henry Fahnbulleh.)

As a popular political figure, Tubman had "evidenced warmth, humor, and the ability to render substantive justice" and did "much to bridge the gap separating the two communities." The "tribal people [had] at last come to realize that the President of Liberia [was] also their President."[7]

Still, covert discrimination in government service and social relationships persisted. And legal and cultural distinctions—in "marriage and divorce, jurisdiction of tribal and statutory courts, and the occupation of land in the interior"—continued to separate the communities. Tribal kin on one side and the Americo-Liberian elite on the other, for example, often rejected Westernized tribal youths' "claim to civilized status." This rejection made it difficult for them to obtain the certificate exempting them "from compulsory labor, porter service, and the jurisdiction of tribal courts."[8] More worrisome, tribal people "still [tended] to regard themselves as Bassa, Kpelle, or Loma [or other tribe]," rather than Liberian, "reserving that [national] title for the Americo-Liberians."[9] The sense of nationhood remained little more than a distant banner.

Despite significant progress in narrowing the fault that divided the communities, a 1954 image created in the *New York Post* somehow persisted: "Symbolic of the distance separating Liberia's oligarchy...from the native tribesmen is the Sunday procession to church with the Americo-Liberian gentry in long-tailed coats, carrying canes, followed by poorly clad boys carrying hymn books."[10]

Trying to reduce a character as complex as Shad Tubman to simple black and white would do him, Liberia, and history a great disservice. Professor Liebenow thought Tubman cast himself "in the role of a charismatic leader" able to "breach the social and tribal schisms within Liberia." He enjoyed "greater popularity with the tribal people than any President before him." His "accessibility and dispensation of personal justice, his respect for tribal customs, the ceremonial aspects of his Unification Policy, and his informality on public occasions" greatly appealed to the tribal masses. And his fellow Americo-Liberians, at least the ruling elite, came to applaud the financial benefits his Open Door policy had delivered them, particularly since they came "without unduly mobilizing the tribal people in political terms."[11]

No other leader on the scene could challenge the president's leadership. Liebenow viewed him as "the dominant figure in Liberian national politics." But he maintained that "the President [was] not a dictator," but more accurately, "the presiding officer of the Americo-Liberian ruling class" who increasingly had "become the managing director of a moderate social revolution."[12]

But few would deny that he altered to a surprising degree much of Liberia's government and economy—and fundamentally affected the lives of its people. Although he was not a dictator, he is credited with bringing "the cult of the presidency" in Liberia to full fruition—an ascendancy that came at the expense of the legislature's and judiciary's decline. And the Americo-Liberian community acquiesced; they found a strong presidency effective in warding off both external and internal threats to their supremacy.[13] Illustrative of the extent of Tubman's control over the legislature, Vice President Tolbert remarked at the opening of the 1960 session, "The House and the Senate could not consider any measures during the first month; the president was still in Europe and 'we didn't know what his thoughts are.'"[14]

> Although a provision in the constitution upheld the independence of the three branches of Liberia's government, "the judges of both the Supreme Court and subordinate courts were in fact subject to control by the other two branches." According to Liebenow, removing judges "by joint resolution of the Legislature was a fairly common occurrence. Two justices of the Supreme Court, for example, were removed in 1957." Moreover, most judges at every level lacked legal experience and training.[15]
>
> Given the absence of systematic codification before the 1950s, uncertainty clouded what the law actually was. When added to bias, improper instructions to juries, and bowing to

"unscrupulous lawyers" on the part of judges, it made for a distinctly "unjudicial" atmosphere. Perhaps the most serious problem, though, lay in the excessive time it took to bring "cases to completion." The expense, loss of time from work and business, and the toll on family and friends discouraged many a critic or reformer from turning to the courts. "Litigation, in fact, was one of the most effective weapons for keeping the politically and socially dissident Liberians in line."[16]

—⚒—

Government jobs and patronage provided Tubman another avenue to cement his hold on the presidency. When he moved into the Executive Mansion in 1944, he inherited a "poorly trained and corrupt civil service" whose "administrative inefficiency and dishonesty undermined the very system it was designed to serve."[17] But Tubman took no steps to reform it. Instead, he parlayed the civil service into a vastly expanded body built on patronage and allegiance to "Broder" Shad and the True Whig Party—and still incompetent and given over to corrupt practices.

When he became president in 1944, government workers numbered fewer than 1,200. Despite efforts by successive Tubman administrations to contain the number, by 1979 it had swollen to almost thirty-eight thousand. That meant almost one out of every four permanent employees in the entire wage sector worked for the government. The number of ministries rose "from only a handful...to nearly twenty." Some "dozen government agencies and 26 public corporations," none of which existed in 1944, employed many of them.[18] Virtually all were beholden to Uncle Shad Tubman to various degrees in one way or another.

Senior executives in the public service, Professor Liebenow maintains, didn't bother with competitive testing, "impartial criteria for hiring and firing," or any semblance of training, either before or during employment. Their first obligation was to the president and the True Whig Party. An obligation they could fulfill by attending rallies, by voting, by "public displays of loyalty to the president," and by making the yearly contribution to the party ("which was automatically deducted" from their salary), as well as the occasional extra contribution they might be asked to make. Their second obligation was to support their patron or patrons, mainly in bureaucratic power struggles, even in those involving the employee's own superiors.[19] Any obligation to running an honest and efficient government responsible to the country was rare.

Most low-level employees received little or no training. However, the quality of Liberian education and training in the schools was of such low quality it hardly mattered. And even the upper-echelon civil servants who went abroad usually returned with scant qualifications for the position they would fill upon returning to Liberia.

The undue emphasis on legal and political studies led to the neglect of subjects needed to make a government operate efficiently: "agriculture, engineering, accounting, business administration," and other "technical" subjects involved in government programs. And, even if a Liberian student did opt for such a course, "there was no guarantee" that, upon return to Liberia, he or she would be placed where the training would be put to good use. Such inept personnel management, plus the corrosive effect of patronage, led many to disillusionment in the existing system and to the perception of politics as "the most rewarding profession in the long run."[20]

Both Tubman's personal charisma and popularity and his "seemingly endless tenure...made him personally indistinguishable from the presidency." Using the increased revenue from iron ore and the other concessions, he not only expanded the physical and social infrastructure, he also doled out "public funds as private gifts to whomever he pleased."[21]

As a result, Liberian politician and academician Amos Sawyer claims, the presidency "became, directly or indirectly, the ultimate source of individual livelihood." Whether seen as a gratuity in the form of cash from the bulging satchel carried by one of Tubman's aides, "or from earnings from private agricultural estates or peasant farms, all incomes were perceived to be derived from President Tubman. Accordingly, all praises went to him."[22]

This practice, Sawyer argues, "not only institutionalized graft as an instrument of political manipulation but also made this form of corruption a national virtue expected of the good leader."[23] Tubman, to be fair, did believe in limits. According to one story, "he used to point to his wrist and then to his shoulder and say, 'Up to here, O.K., up to there, no.'"[24]

In return, the public showered Tubman with adulation: witness the "erection of presidential statues at various points in the country, the naming of bridges, streets, and public buildings after the president or members of his family; the requirement that the president's picture be displayed in every commercial establishment; and the observance of public holidays to commemorate significant events in his life"—and, of course, the lavish gifts and the festivities that each host county felt compelled to offer on his birthday.[25]

Summing up, President William Vacarat S. Tubman left an indelible mark on Liberia and the course of its history. Even his critics concede the magnitude of his accomplishments. An introduction (on the book jacket) to Tuan Wreh's highly critical account of Tubman's presidency reads much like a public relations blurb:

"His character was larger than life. He was, needless to say, an ambitious politician, but his ambitions for his country were basically benevolent."

Tubman the statesman wanted to make Liberia into a modernized, prosperous country, recognized as a regional, if not international, leader in the world. Tubman the politician wished to be admired, respected, and at least liked, if not loved. Tubman the Americo-Liberian wanted to perpetuate the group's preeminence in the country's social, political, and economic life. To do so required that the republic be preserved. Its failure would spell the end of the long-playing Americo-Liberian hegemony. Tubman the egoist feared that such failure would reduce to ashes his legacy as one of Liberia's greatest leaders. And as a footnote, for Tubman the bon vivant, failure while he was still in office would spell a most unhappy end to the good life he enjoyed as president.

In 1944 Liberia was a poor and backward country; Tubman, helped by the Second World War, brought it into the mainstream of twentieth-century economic life. Materially and educationally, standards improved rapidly."[26] Amos Sawyer, also a political opponent, added, "Citizens generally look upon the Tubman years as the golden years of twentieth-century Liberia. Some analysts have even referred to the Tubman years as the era of 'modernization.'"[27]

> When he assumed the presidency, Tubman faced not only a poor and backward country, but one shackled economically by Firestone and US government control as well. The 1926 loan agreement with the rubber company made any new loans to the government subject to Firestone's approval and required that all tax revenues be deposited in a Firestone-owned institution. The American fiscal advisor to the government approved the government's budget each year and virtually controlled the Treasury's inflow of revenues (although in actual fact largely

confined to the Monrovia area).²⁸ Iron ore and Tubman's open door enabled Liberia to lift these yokes. Finally, an astute President Tubman managed to leverage the US interest in Liberia, sparked by the Second World War and the country's natural resources, into substantial economic and military assistance and the role of an ally throughout the Cold War.

The comprehensive set of policies for "national growth and development" Tubman initially outlined in 1943 reflected his experience growing up in Maryland County, and, as a young man, developing his persona in the local politics there. He doubtless could hear the rumblings of nationalism, self-determination, economic progress, and equality that had begun to sweep the less developed world like a threatening whirlwind. He realized, too, that the tribal people of Liberia, who looked upon their Americo-Liberian rulers as colonial masters, would not be deaf to these sirens in the brewing storm. While "the Americo-Liberians could not prevent change, they could at least attempt to control it."[29]

The race Tubman embarked on—bringing "off an evolutionary rather than a revolutionary transformation of the social fabric"—however, proved a risky strategy.[30] The government's long-standing exploitive practices coupled with the fast-moving changes then occurring, particularly in the interior, and fueled by the rising expectations of much of the population, proved a deadly mix. Astute observers could sense the wave of restlessness and disaffection gathering on the horizon, particularly among the country's African majority. And, as the administration grew more paranoid, the president, though still popular, seemed increasingly feeble in his attempts to calm the threatening wave. Liebenow noticed in 1967 "clear signs that the regime [was] far from confident it could 'exercise total control'" over the unfolding drama.[31]

As evidence, he pointed to the administration's "overreaction to criticism" by jailing or reprimanding journalists, dismissing teachers, and declaring foreigners persona non grata for "trivial indiscretions or slights against the president's or ruling elite's reputation." It also meant resorting to greater violence in the attempted assassinations and the "plot or alleged plot to overthrow" Tubman during his extended visit to Switzerland in 1967.[32] Equally disturbing were the government's attempts to suppress the labor movement, not only by quashing growth of "a vigorous and independent labor union leadership," but by its "swift and violent" reaction to the September 1961 riots in Monrovia and a series of strikes in 1966 in which the "police dealt ruthlessly with the strikers and their leaders."[33]

The degree of violence and the government's overreaction apparently so shook Tubman that he proclaimed the last week of February 1966 a national week of prayer and fasting. The president appealed to "all Liberians to gather in places of worship 'with lowly and contrite hearts, garbed in sackcloth and ashes or ordinary apparel, and pray for the peace of our country.'"[34]

Signs of public discontent spread even to Sinkhor, a "fashionable suburb of Monrovia's elite." Associated Press writer Arnold Zeitlin reported that a "rash of graffiti"—such as "Shameless Dog" and "Death to Congo Bitches"—appeared on compound walls in April 1968. ("Congo," an appellation similar to "honky," which American blacks applied to whites, referred to descendants of the Americo-Liberian settlers.)[35]

Liebenow points out that the regime's elaborate security system, coupled with "rewards to cooperative tribal leaders," had managed by and large to keep the lid on public dissatisfaction during the first decade of Tubman's rule. But the economy's subsequent rapid growth and the "greater freedom of movement by tribal peoples seeking employment," which led to "polyglot urban centers," had stretched "to its limits" the regime's capability to control the populace.[36] Feeling the effects of the "momentum of modernization," indigenous African Liberians grew "dissatisfied with the slow progress" in improving the opportunities offered them: migrant tribal workers dissatisfied with life on the farm after having seen Monrovia (and other urban centers); trained Liberians, many educated overseas, who coveted the jobs foreign managers occupied; restless students and disgruntled teachers who wanted more rapid change.[37] Many, especially "youthful Liberians," felt "disillusioned and embittered by political cynicism and hypocrisy." Tubman's response? A "reign of political terror."[38]

> Out of 36,130 people employed in the economy's modern sector in August 1961, only 4,960 Liberians filled skilled jobs, mainly lower and midlevel. Some 955 foreigners claimed the top positions.[39] In the absence of reforms, Clower saw foreigners continuing "as [managers and] straw-boss skilled supervisors and Liberians as illiterate semiskilled workers."[40] The government's failure to insist upon the economy's "Liberianization," Professor Liebenow thought, would at some point cause a "violent reaction...by both the tribal element and the lower ranks of the Americo-Liberian community."[41]
>
> Increasing numbers of migrant tribal workers posed an even greater menace. Some experts anticipated that by 1968, as much as one-third of Liberia's tribal population would "be involved in some phase of the money economy." And, these migrant workers could not be expected to continue being "satisfied with the unskilled or semiskilled jobs...offered them." Upon return visits to their village homes, after having seen the prosperity of other Liberians and the better life it afforded them, they would find it "difficult to accept the mounting taxes, the extortions from itinerant soldiers, and

the illegal demands for labor made by officials and private Americo-Liberians alike."[42]

Distribution of income dramatically highlighted the differences within the population. Drawing on the Northwestern University team's work, Liebenow estimated that three-quarters of Liberia's national income went to foreign businesses (mainly the concessions) and foreign individuals, plus the Americo-Liberian political elite. The remaining 25 percent was thinly spread among 97 percent of Liberia's population—the tribal people and lower-class Americo-Liberians.[43]

Despite these disturbing signs, most observers dismissed the threat of an imminent serious storm. Leadership had yet to emerge among the opposition, and in its absence, "discontent among the masses" leading to "revolutionary change" appeared unlikely—at least for the time being.[44] Similarly, the Americo-Liberian establishment saw little threat to their rule from the Liberian National Guard. Rising disgruntlement among the enlisted tribal soldiers, when they compared their lives with those of their officers and of Americo-Liberian society at large, went largely ignored by the regime—much, as they later would discover, to their great misfortune.

While the final verdict had yet to be decided, the odds, nevertheless, appeared to be turning against Shad Tubman, the "master of Liberia," and the Americo-Liberian establishment. "The frequency of [their president's] extended health leaves and his age" compelled many Liberians "to ask the long avoided question: 'After Tubman, what?'"[45] And this time there would be no jocular rejoinder about his seeming immortality. The issue had been settled in a London clinic and a hasty transfer of power in Monrovia in July

1971. But, on balance, one was left with the sadly empty feeling of a possibly grand opportunity lost.

Vice President William Tolbert, having waited in the wings for some twenty years, now would face the task of fulfilling Tubman's vision of creating a modern, unified Liberia and a nation—while at the same time maintaining Americo-Liberian dominion. Had he better read the pulse of Liberia's African masses or consulted a good astrologer, Tolbert might well have suffered second thoughts before accepting the job.

CHAPTER 21

Blood on the Sand: The End

—⚍—

THE BORROWED VOLKSWAGEN RACED MADLY along the road toward Monrovia. The man behind the wheel, Vice President William Tolbert, knew it was a race against time. And time was running out, his future at stake. Liberian secretary of state Rudolph Grimes had received a telegram in Monrovia earlier that day telling of Tubman's unexpected death in London. Upon receiving the news, the vice president had immediately gone into action. When his car broke down, he borrowed the VW, grabbed some nuts, candy, and a thermos of coffee—Liberian coffee that many in the last century had thought the world's best—to fortify himself for the hard drive ahead.

It was customary during President Tubman's frequent and often extended absences from the country for Secretary Grimes, the head of the cabinet, to execute the affairs of the government. Grimes, a graduate of Harvard Law School, with a master's degree from Columbia University in international affairs, founder and first dean of the University of Liberia's School of Law—and an ambitious member of a prominent Liberian family—had moved quickly to be installed as acting president. He argued that since Tolbert had left for his farm at Bellefanal, some two hundred miles away in Bong County, he could not be expected to return to the capital within the twenty-four-hour limit specified for succession in the Liberian constitution. Other cabinet members, notably

Postmaster General MacKinley DeShield, one of Tolbert's confidantes, however, objected and managed to stall Grimes's scheme.[1]

—⚍—

As Tolbert sped along, his thoughts must have turned back to earlier times. When, at the age of twenty-two, having graduated summa cum laude from Liberia College (later the University of Liberia), he began his government career in 1935—as a typist in the Treasury Department. The following year, he married Victoria David, the daughter of a Supreme Court associate justice, and became a government disbursing officer. During the seven years he held the job, he willingly carried out additional official duties on top of his regular responsibilities. He stepped up his work in the Baptist church (which he later would serve as an ordained minister and in 1965 be elected the first African president of the Baptist World Alliance). He also took an active role in the True Whig Party, the only political game in town.

Young Tolbert charted his course carefully. His destination? The political life, which for Americo-Liberians was their first choice of vocations. In 1943, at thirty years of age, he took his seat in the legislature representing Montserrado County. Born May 13, 1913, in the rural town then called Bensonville, only some thirty miles from Monrovia in Montserrado County, William Richard Tolbert Jr. was, in contrast to Tubman, no outsider in the Liberian political landscape. Another asset he could draw upon: he came from one of the country's largest and most affluent families. At least one source of the family's status could be traced back to his father, William Richard Tolbert Sr.

> When nine years old, the president's father, William Sr., immigrated to Liberia with his father, Daniel Frank Tolbert, mother, and three siblings in 1879. Daniel, a former slave from

Charleston, South Carolina, belonged to a group of 206 black South Carolinians called the African Exodus Association. They purchased a ship, the *Azor*, in which they sailed to Liberia in April 1878.

William Sr. apparently thrived in his new home. As he grew up, he became fluent in Kpelle, joined traditional bodies such as the secret Poro society, and "became a prosperous coffee grower and rice farmer." Besides marrying President Tolbert's mother, Charlotte Augusta Hoff, of Cape Mount, Liberia, he acquired a number of tribal wives by customary marriage. According to President Tolbert's nephew, Dr. Richard Tolbert, he reportedly fathered over fifty offspring.[2] Thus, another source claims, the vice president and his younger brother, Stephen, could count "an estimated seventy half-brothers and sisters through their father's tribal marriages."[3]

William, the president-to-be, and Victoria, for their part, contributed six daughters and two sons to the already crowded Tolbert clan. Their younger son, also William, "a congenitally armless child," the Tolberts adopted "during an official visit" to Liberia's interior.[4] The other, Adolphus or A. B. Tolbert, would follow his father's path to the House of Representatives, where he chaired the Foreign Affairs Committee and also served as ambassador at large. He would gain a degree of perhaps unwelcome notoriety from a television interview he gave in 1979 regarding his grandiose political ambitions, and, the following year, from his unsuccessful attempt to escape the military coup that toppled his father by seeking refuge in the French embassy in Liberia.

—⚋—

In his eight years in the House of Representatives, Tolbert diligently served his Montserrado County constituents, carrying out his responsibilities without much fanfare. He came to epitomize the "good soldier" in the ranks of the True Whig Party. Few figured him for high office. President Tubman would later praise him "as a man with a singleness of purpose and deep conviction for justice and fair play and a man of *guarded ambition*" (emphasis added).[5]

When Tubman chose the relatively unknown representative from Bensonville to be his vice presidential running mate in 1951, Tolbert became the youngest man in the country's history to be elected to that office. Many scratched their heads in bewilderment. And subsequently, during the 1960s, amid much of the speculation about "a possible successor to Tubman, few focused" on Tolbert, whom many called 'the 'invisible vice president,' who quietly and obediently served with Tubman during five of his six terms in office."[6] Many Whig politicians, notably House Speaker Richard Henries, "regarded him as little more than Tubman's errand boy."[7]

Some observers thought "Tolbert's possible succession would constitute a mere holding operation for Tubman's son," Shad Jr. By any measure, the president appeared to be grooming him for the presidency. Educated in the United States at Harvard and Rutgers Universities, Shad Jr. was president general of the Liberian Congress of Industrial Organizations, appointed chief of cabinet in 1964, and elected to the Senate. Many saw the son as following his father's successful political model: building a popular image identified with the fortunes of the lower middle classes and tribal people, particularly those living in Monrovia—those who probably posed the most serious threat to the regime. And Shad Jr.'s 1961 marriage to Vice President Tolbert's daughter, Wokie, bonding the two families in the kind of alliance that typified the Americo-Liberian elite, confirmed spectators' belief that he was the anointed one.[8]

In any case, in 1971 few "regarded William Tolbert as anything more than an interim successor who would quickly have to be shunted aside in favor of a stronger, more astute political craftsman," one who could meet the requirements of the "radically altered" presidency that twenty-seven years of Tubman's rule had imposed on the office. As a minimum, the candidate should be equally acceptable to both the Americo-Liberians and the indigenous tribal population—someone not "too closely identified with the primary interests of either one." He also should appreciate the "pomp and ceremony" most "aristocratic-minded Whigs" expected of their leader. But at the same time, he should "be able to move with ease among the masses" and "establish an empathetic joking relationship" with them in the manner that highlighted Tubman's popularity with the tribal people. "On most counts, at least before 1971, Tolbert failed to measure up to the Tubman image."[9]

And now, despite these odds, William Tolbert stood at the verge of becoming Liberia's nineteenth president. He could scarcely believe it.

After a furious drive in the borrowed VW following news of Tubman's death, Tolbert arrived back in Monrovia early in the evening of July 23. Still in his informal short-sleeved safari attire, the vice president was sworn in as Liberia's acting president. At his official inauguration on January 3, 1972, the Whig Party old guard was aghast when he appeared wearing a blue, open-necked cotton safari shirt. The dress, which became known as the "swearing in" suit, replaced the formal top hat and morning coat with tails Tubman had insisted everyone wear to inaugurations, ceremonies, and other public functions.

Liberians would soon discover that this largely symbolic action would be but the first of many, and more significant, changes the new president would introduce.

Some described the Baptist preacher-president as affable, baldish, heavyset, "bespectacled, and scholarly looking."[10] Professor Liebenow, in a 1960 interview, "found him to be reserved, humorless, and a bit of a 'stuffed shirt' who was ill at ease on social occasions."[11] Like many, if not most Liberians in higher government positions, Tolbert had availed himself of the opportunities his office afforded to become a wealthy rubber planter, rice and coffee grower—and "chairman of the board of directors of the Mesurado Group Companies Inc., a large fishing and refrigeration enterprise" his brother Stephen Tolbert founded.[12]

Even though Tolbert appeared younger than his fifty-eight years, few, if any, had expected the "dynamism" he showed on becoming president. "[The] pace he set in bringing about governmental reforms" soon earned him the nickname "Speedy."[13] "If we can manage to speed things up in this country," he remarked in a *Time* magazine article (April 23, 1973), "I don't care what they call me."[14] Clearly, the True Whig Party old guard were in for a ride they had not reckoned on.

After he'd been in office three months, the *New York Times* reported that the new president, having emerged "from the deep obscurity of 19 years in Mr. Tubman's shadow," had "made a promising start toward reform and faster change," displaying "both political skill and idealistic rhetoric."[15] Tolbert had dropped his "austere style of speaking" in favor of a more "folksy style," particularly in talking with tribal people. (Tolbert reportedly was the first president to speak an indigenous language, Kpelle, although Frederick Starr noted that President Daniel Edward Howard was fluent in several native languages.)[16] A foreign diplomat voiced the consensus view that "something very refreshing is happening in Liberia."[17] Even his local critics thought he "was one leopard who did change his spots."[18]

Abandoning the formality of Tubman's top hats and tails—a "conservative formalism...based on an imitation of the West, and, in particular, the United States"—was largely symbolic. But it represented a far more fundamental break both in domestic as well as foreign policy. Tolbert set about to do no less than "de-Tubmanize" the presidency, dismantling "Tubman's political and security apparatus," and replacing the former president's "patronage network with a system of civil administration."[19]

He started with releasing all political prisoners and "extending the 'hand of forgiveness,' a traditional Liberian gesture, even appointing several to high office."[20] More important, in the wake of heated attacks in the press, he disbanded the notorious public relations officers organization, substituting a social welfare program in its place. He also disbanded the National Intelligence and Security Service and the Executive Action Bureau. Local newspapers hailed "the return of press freedom."[21] Tolbert, in addition, moved to lower the voting age to eighteen years, and to reduce the power of the traditional chiefs, while proposing a more democratic system for electing them.

The new president next shook up the civil service by introducing standardization and the merit system for public employees.[22] Since the country's civil servants traditionally tended to avoid putting in a full day's work, he took to making surprise early morning visits to government offices. In "his first few weeks in office, [he] dismissed a Cabinet Under Secretary for corruption, suspended two much-hated officers of the secret police forces, replaced the director of the civil service and two of the powerful superintendents, or governors of counties." He also fired the secretary of commerce who had approved Tubman's creation of a private monopoly for importing rice, and G. Flama Sherman, minister of education, who was absent from his desk at eight o'clock on one of the president's surprise morning visits. He also did away with the odious yearly deduction of a month's pay from civil servants' salaries as a contribution to the party.[23]

Even the military was not immune; Tolbert replaced four hundred older men with young recruits from urban areas. The poor training that many of the new recruits received at the Tubman Military Academy, coupled with their tribal background, provoked a significant change in the military establishment's character—a change that would later haunt the administration.[24]

Tolbert sought to project the impression, particularly to external aid agencies such as USAID, the IMF, and the World Bank, of the bureaucracy's rising efficiency. However, such gestures too often merely reinforced the image of a president meddling in details while neglecting more important issues of "economic planning, fiscal conservancy, and rampant corruption."[25]

The energetic president declared "war on ignorance, poverty and disease," unveiling a series of programs—with slogans such as "Total Involvement for Higher Heights" and "From Mat to Matresses" (a scheme "meant to lift the poor from the sleeping mats in their huts and shacks onto mattresses in solidly constructed public housing estates"). He called for new schools and clinics, expanding local businesses, lowering Liberian reliance on foreign-owned companies and imports, and achieving self-sufficiency in rice. Tolbert also took long-overdue steps to raise the financial contributions of foreign concessions to the Liberian economy—renegotiating new agreements, requiring audits, and stressing accountability to the government.[26]

On completing the balance of Tubman's term, Tolbert was elected to four more years on his own. He and his vice president, Methodist bishop Bennie D. Warner, were inaugurated on

January 5, 1976. Tolbert, aiming at further reducing his predecessor's "cult of the presidency," successfully campaigned for a constitutional amendment that barred a president from serving more than eight years in office. Having staved off attempts by the legislature to repeal the amendment, when party stalwarts who opposed the limits raised the issue again in 1979, Tolbert answered, "I will serve my country as long as I have life. I do not have to be President to do so."[27]

In its relations with African countries, the new administration supported Tubman's initiatives. In May 1975 Liberia signed the treaty establishing the Economic Community of West African States. Tolbert served as chairman of the OAU from 1979 until his death the following year and played host to the organization's summit meeting in 1979. He maintained cordial relations with the United States (whom he supported in the war with Vietnam), but toned down his predecessor's strongly anticommunist, pro-West position. Adopting a more nonaligned stance, Liberia opened formal diplomatic relations with the Soviet Union, the communist People's Republic of China, Cuba, and several other Eastern bloc countries.[28]

On the economic front, however, Tolbert could find little cheer. Unluckily for him, Tubman's guardian angel did not transfer his (or her) allegiance to the new president. The hearty demand for Liberia's rubber and iron ore that had sustained Tubman's programs now was sluggish. The Organization of Petroleum Exporting Countries' oil embargo in 1973 would add further disarray in the world economy; it helped spark a global recession and contribute to economic stagnation in Liberia and much of sub-Saharan Africa.

Annual growth in Liberia's overall output slipped from 5.4 percent on average each year in 1965-73 to 2.0 percent in 1973-80. Increases in average per capita income dropped even more precipitously. Exports in the same period registered similar decline, and as the economy slackened, the government resorted to borrowing on an alarming scale. The total external debt of $158 million in 1970 ballooned to $573 million in 1980. Interest payments on external public debt that year amounted to $23 million (compared to $6 million in 1970).[29]

Despite the faltering economy, the new administration's break with precedent proved popular—at least "with young people" who said they had "resented the idea that their country resembled" a Negro fraternal organization's "running convention."[30] Tolbert managed to upgrade the University of Liberia and appoint a commission to review the continuing use of the country's motto ("The love of liberty brought us here"), flag, and national anthem—all symbols offensive to non-Americo-Liberians. As further evidence of Tolbert's interest in the national Unification policy, the administration created a series of modern courts to replace tribal ones. The president in 1971 also decreed that paramount, clan, and town chiefs be elected for fixed terms instead of being appointed for indefinite tenures. In addition, they would receive fixed salaries rather be paid a portion "of the poll taxes collected in their areas." In still another sop to the country's restive youth, Tolbert urged the nine newly created seats in the House of Representatives be reserved for True Whig candidates eighteen to twenty-eight years old.[31]

Expanding suffrage and representation and reforming the government's administrative framework, however, "did not bring about an actual realignment of political power." Local officials still enjoyed little real power; that remained in the national government, particularly in the president. While the regime presented "a façade of mass participation in the political process" to the world outside, decision making in the True Whig Party—and government—"remained firmly under the control of the Americo-Liberian minority."[32]

Nonetheless, the Tolbert reforms whirlwind, as might be expected, stirred up considerable dust. Opposition mounted. Much of the Americo-Liberian establishment was up in arms. Even family members upbraided him. His brother Frank later "would accuse him of 'opening the gates of Hell' by consorting with natives."[33] Leading rival families within the Americo-Liberian elite not only opposed the reforms, they decried the Tolbert clan's ascendancy in the country's economic as well as political sphere. The most glaring examples: brother Frank Tolbert, president pro tempore of the Senate; brother Stephen, finance minister; son A. B. Tolbert, ambassador at large and chairman of the House of Representatives Foreign Affairs Committee; and a host of daughters, sisters, and sons-in-law occupying important positions in the government and private sector.[34]

Despite his whirlwind start in "humanizing the presidency," Tolbert's momentum began to wane as he was seduced by the allure of the office—"all the trappings of royalty...the processions of limousines, the long lines of schoolchildren along his route of return from the airport, and the erection of statues and other monuments in his honor."[35] To future president Ellen Johnson Sirleaf, "his [Tolbert's] was a true development agenda; he tried to the best of his ability to create a government of true reform... But even one short year into his administration it was becoming clear...many of his plans would be hijacked by the system, never to materialize."[36] Tolbert, Amos Sawyer claimed, in seeking to de-Tubmanize Liberia, failed to successfully develop "viable political infrastructures as alternatives."[37] Whatever the reasons, more doubts surfaced about the system's capacity to adjust quickly enough to allow an "evolutionary rather than a revolutionary" social transformation.[38]

As the whirlwind slowed, the patience of the urban underclasses, the tribal people in their villages, and the students and educated Liberians who chafed at the slow pace of change and limited political expression was fraying. On the opposite side, many Americo-Liberians felt Tolbert's vacillating leadership posed serious risks for themselves as a group. The president and his colleagues feared this concern, coupled with resentment toward the Tolbert family, might incite some of the old guard to attempt unseating him. Trapped between these two potentially disastrous scenarios, paranoia soon settled over the Executive Mansion like a huge blanket.

The president's public appearances became more guarded, and he mingled less and less among the people. His stirring pronouncements underlining the urgent need for overhauling the system began to sound hollow and "patently insincere." Particularly when the stark on-the-ground "realities differed so drastically" from the incessant drumbeat of praise for the president from the government-controlled news media, from the endless delegations of tribal people, and from "the pulpit pronouncements of Whig politicians-cum-pastors."[39]

Tolbert also displayed a growing sensitivity to public criticism of himself or his family. Albert Porte, a longtime Liberian critic and pamphleteer, felt the sting of Tolbert's ire when Porte in 1974 criticized the president's brother, Minister of Finance Stephen Tolbert, for trying to "buy the country."[40] Stephen, who had acquired extensive holdings in various Liberian enterprises, brought a "crippling civil damages suit [with the president's acquiescence] against Porte."[41] The trial's outcome was never in doubt. The presiding judge? Chief Justice James Pierre, who happened to be Stephen Tolbert's father-in-law.

Another bizarre incident involved son A. B. Tolbert, who apparently enjoyed "dynastic ambitions." Appearing on the CBS *60 Minutes* television program "taped in Liberia in December 1979," the younger Tolbert boasted not only that "he would be the next president of Liberia, but that he hoped to become the president of *all* of Africa someday!"[42]

"Bentol," however, provided some of the most striking evidence of the turn—not for the better—Tolbert's administration had taken. Professor Liebenow relates that when he visited the Tolbert family's hometown, situated a few miles from Monrovia, in 1960, it was still called Bensonville. It was little more than a humble village, with a dirt road as its main street, "houses built on stilts, constructed of wood and corrugated iron," and "shutters instead of glass windows. It probably had changed little since the 1860s, when Tolbert's grandfather and other immigrants from South Carolina and the West Indies had settled there."[43] Little had changed—that is, until Tolbert became president.

During the nine years of his presidency, Bensonville had become Bentol, renamed for its illustrious native son, and Liebenow thought it "had taken on all the negative imagery of a Palace of Versailles in the days of the Bourbons." It now was "a city with more than a score of opulent villas lining the well-lighted, carefully manicured boulevards. Each member of the Tolbert clan" enjoyed his own private estate, complete with "a high, steel picket fence and an elaborate security system." The "city" even boasted "a private zoo and an artificial lake for motorboat racing and waterskiing." Its imposing new post office and other public buildings, to serve a relatively small population, suggested it had displaced Monrovia as Montserrado County's county seat.⁴⁴

The contrast with Monrovia was glaring. A *New York Times* correspondent found the capital city, not long after Tolbert became president, a "curious mixture of peeling old pillared houses reminiscent of the United States South, some modern office buildings," a multimillion-dollar "seven story presidential mansion that [looked] like a Miami Beach resort hotel, tin shacks and comfortable new houses for the upper class." And though on "Sundays the streets...filled with the strong, pure voices of church congregations...even on that day Lebanese, Syrian and Turkish bar girls and prostitutes [stood] in the doorways of saloons to lure sailors inside for a drink." Incidentally, the bar area he noted was "on a road with the phonetically appropriate name of Gurley Street."⁴⁵

After nine years of Tolbert's rule, the capital city remained much the same. Any comparison of Bentol, "on the one hand, and the squalor of Monrovia's slums and the general poverty of any up-country village, on the other, could—in the words of one of [Liebenow's] Liberian friends—'be described in a single phrase: utterly obscene!'"⁴⁶

―⁂―

Tolbert, his reform zeal largely depleted, now faced a veritable wave of dissent, particularly from disillusioned "younger Liberians, both tribal and Americo-Liberian." The wave had built during Tubman's long presidency but had temporarily subsided in the hope for reform Tolbert initially generated. At first, he apparently was sympathetic to the dissenters' demands. But on the other hand, he was mindful of the stubborn opposition of the True Whig Party's old guard, such as the Masonic lodge. The lodge's influential leaders, alarmed "by the rapid pace of change...insisted Tolbert deal harshly and convincingly with dissent." Neither the president nor the old guard Whig leadership could fully adjust "to the idea of sustained, organized opposition" to their continued domination of Liberia's politics.[47]

Tolbert, according to Liebenow, "wavered aimlessly between conciliation and repression." One moment, he made concessions to the reformers. The next day he might reverse himself "in a stemwinding speech intended to arouse the flagging spirits of the party faithful."[48] His vacillation projected an image of weakness and provoked "general dissatisfaction." It seemed Tolbert could not "please anyone for very long in the last two years of his rule."[49]

In one of his concessionary moods, the president invited the leaders of the Progressive Alliance of Liberia (PAL), an organization formed by Liberian students in the United States, to return home and register as an opposition party, the first since 1955. The PAL, headed by Gabriel Baccus Matthews, a graduate of City University in New York, sought to reform Liberia by returning to "African principles and values" in a "kind of pragmatic African socialism." Ellen Johnson Sirleaf called him "the Godfather of Liberian Democracy," who would be "remembered as one of Liberia's greatest sons."[50] Recruits to the organization would consist largely of "students both at home and abroad, low income and unemployed workers in Monrovia, and the small rural cultivators."[51]

The president, however, tilted back the other direction: closing the universities, prosecuting journalists and pamphleteers, jailing opponents, and using troops to quell labor disturbances. The legislature supported his stance, granting him (as it had, most notably, Tubman) emergency powers, including suspending the right of habeas corpus. Measures introduced earlier added limits on strikes by labor unions, students, and others; restricted public meetings and marches; and narrowed new organizations' ability to enlist members. Legislators redefined "treason" and "sedition" so that they covered virtually any "unauthorized discussion of public issues" or action that could be interpreted as encouraging tribalism or sectionalism, "with intent to divide the country."[52]

The conditions that sustained Americo-Liberian dominance for almost 150 years clearly were fast deteriorating. Ellen Johnson Sirleaf thought "Liberian society more unsettled than it had ever been. What had been a largely docile, uneducated population of young natives had now been radicalized, bringing to memory all the cleavage and disadvantages of the past and using that as a political tool. It was a highly combustible time."[53]

And the economy offered little relief. The president in presenting his 1978–79 budget warned that the world recession seriously reduced earnings and government revenues from the country's iron ore and rubber exports, although he optimistically opined that better tax collection would produce higher government revenue. But imports clearly had to be held in check.

While the president and his ministers wrestled with a solution, the fetid air in Monrovia hung heavy, laden with towering, menacing clouds awaiting the arrival of the rains in early April. The oppressive heat and humidity seemed to squeeze the very life out of residents in the squalor of the tin shacks in the city's Kru town and the restive students in the University of Liberia and Cuttington College. At even the slightest jolt, raw emotions threatened to erupt like a coiled spring suddenly released. That jolt would come to be called the rice riots of 1979, or simply April 14.

> An old Chinese adage reads, "A meal without rice is like a beautiful girl with only one eye." In Liberia, as in much of the world, rice was the heart of each day's diet. Unless one had

eaten at least one meal with rice, he had not really eaten that day. According to the Food and Agriculture Organization of the United Nations (FAO), yearly consumption averaged an estimated 265–75 pounds per capita, constituting around one-half of a Liberian's total consumption of calories. Even before *Oryza sativa*, the variety most widely cultivated worldwide, was introduced from Asia, an African variety (*Oryza glaberrima*) is thought to have been grown in what is now Liberia.

With few exceptions, every subsistence farmer in Liberia grew rice, but primarily for the family's consumption. Whatever surpluses they produced never proved enough to satisfy the urban population. As long as this population remained relatively small, feeding them with imported rice presented relatively little problem. However, as the country's modernization picked up steam, the flow of tribal people from their village farms to urban centers increased—and the need to import rice rose exponentially. The urban population grew from 22 percent of the total population in 1965 to 35 percent in 1980, expanding at more than 6 percent yearly between 1973 and 1980. [54]

Imports of cereals, notably rice, between 1975 and 1980 rose at an average annual rate of 21 percent. Earlier, President Tubman also had struggled with the problem even though imports during the last decade of his tenure increased less than 5 percent yearly. But production still continued to fall short. And cereals imports continued to climb. By 1980 they totaled almost 100,000 metric tons.[55]

The roots of the problem, as Dr. Clower and his Northwestern University team had pointed out, lay in the inadequate incentives for local farmers to grow rice for consumption outside their own family. To encourage local production, Tolbert's agriculture minister, Florence Chenoworth, proposed raising the retail price from $22 to $30 per one-hundred-pound bag—an onerous burden on a hungry family in a country with only an $80 average monthly wage.

In March 1979, as Tolbert mulled over the proposal, Matthews seized on the issue. It offered the perfect opportunity to energize a sagging drive to gather signatures required for registering the PAL as a legal party. He applied for permission to hold a rally "to protest any price increase." But President Tolbert turned him down and in a personal meeting told Matthews that "citizens had the right to meet peaceably and to petition, [but] they did not have the right to demonstrate."[56]

Matthews, supported by students and some of the University of Liberia faculty, decided to go ahead anyway. He called for a rally at three o'clock on April 14. The *New York Times* reported, "A crowd began to gather at the Alliance's headquarters on Monrovia's main street shortly after dawn. By 10:00 A.M. it had swelled to more than 2,000 people." They soon found themselves confronted by soldiers, "some of them in tanks, with water hoses and tear gas." Neither deterred the protesters. A student-led group separated "from the main body and headed toward the Executive Mansion where the President was directing the security forces."[57]

Tolbert recounted what happened next in a subsequent interview. He said that when the water and tear gas failed to stop the demonstrators, his "next thought was to fire in the air." But that also failed. As the crowd neared the mansion, and a security person was injured, the defenders asked for the "authority to retaliate." Tolbert responded, "'Well, in that case, if you have to fire, fire'—a firing in the air wouldn't suffice—'fire down in the extremities'" to lessen the danger of fatalities. "That made no difference. Then everything got out of control." For "the first time he acknowledged that he personally, had authorized the security forces to fire into the crowds."[58]

The police and soldiers, thinking the disturbance under control, began to disperse. Then further rioting and looting broke out. Reportedly, in the ensuing twenty-four hours, the looters stripped about 163 stores, mainly those that sold groceries and appliances. They hit Lebanese shops in particular since most Liberians thought them largely responsible for escalating prices. According to the government, seventy-four persons died in the melee (although many observers thought the death toll ranged as high as 140 students and others), more than 400 were injured, and an estimated $35 million in property was damaged.[59]

An alarmed Whig leadership prompted Tolbert to ask neighboring Guinea president Sekou Toure to send troops to help restore order. The seven hundred troops he sent remained in Liberia for a full three weeks. "To many Liberians," their "most terrifying memory...was the sight of Guinean MiG fighters making low passes over the disturbed area."[60]

Authorities arrested thirty-nine persons in the days following. Matthews and thirteen others were charged with treason, a capital offense, but the police released the others. The government on April 19 announced the price of rice would *not* be increased. On the twenty-second, it declared the university closed until further notice. The day after the disturbances and shootings, Tolbert "characterized the leaders of the demonstration as 'wicked, evil and satanic men' who wanted to bring chaos and disorder in the country with the eventual objective of overthrowing the Government." In a subsequent interview, the president reiterated his accusation that to these men "the rice issue" was "merely an alibi," leaving the government "no alternative but to assert its authority."[61] Some observers, however, concluded "that any determined group of protesters could that day have easily stormed the Executive Mansion." Tolbert reportedly "was in a state of hysteria."[62]

The president appointed a thirty-one-member commission "to recommend measures aimed at preventing a recurrence of the disturbances." Dr. Amos Sawyer, at that time an assistant professor at the University of Liberia, told the commission the disturbances arose from "the disparity between rich and poor." On one side," he said, "were people 'characterized by affluence and an ostentatious life style,' 'and on the other were people 'parched by the wretchedness of poverty, dazzled by the endless possibilities available to the affluent, languishing in the squalors of the city and the harshness of the rural village.'"[63]

The commission on June 12 delivered Tolbert a highly critical report that recommended amnesty for the demonstration's leaders, plus "investigation of the Ministers of Justice, Agriculture, Defense and Finance and the director of police." It also urged the commission's life be extended so it might make broader recommendations on the inequities in the country and enable the government to draw up a code of conduct to reduce the conflicts of interest. An official close to Tolbert remarked that the president "was 'shell-shocked' as a result of the report."[64]

President Tolbert responded to the commission's findings in a national radio address on June 26. At that time, "he announced that the price of a 100-pound bag of rice would be reduced by $2," and "all those 'directly or indirectly involved or responsible for the April 14 civil disturbance' would be granted unconditional amnesty." Tolbert promised that "he would consider the commission's report 'most sincerely and objectively, and make changes... in the best interests of the people...courageously and effectively.'"[65] However, he did not extend the commission's life.[66]

The boiling cauldron of violence that had threatened Tolbert and the Americo-Liberian regime now quietened, at least for the time being. For one thing, a great white elephant temporarily distracted much of the country—even many of the dissenters. The OAU, which Liberians trumpeted as one of the signal achievements of their own President Tubman, had decided to hold its 1979 annual summit meeting in Monrovia. Although the conference, held each year in a different member country, graced the host—at least in the eyes of most Africans—with an aura of prestige, a sense of having "arrived," the most lasting legacy inevitably turned out to be near bankruptcy. Each host country tried to outdo the other in the hospitality it extended; the meetings left a trail of white elephant skeletons that stretched across the entire continent.

> The Monrovia conference, which would last from July 7 to July 20, proved no exception. Tolbert pulled out all financial stops: a conference center and OAU village, a resort hotel, fifty-two VIP chalets, a new airport terminal and Ministry of Foreign Affairs building, lighting for the sixty-kilometer road from Roberts International Airport, a new bridge, and other infrastructure. One estimate put the cost of the hotel and chalets alone at about $200 million. In addition, each of the fifty-plus delegations were furnished seven cars, color television sets, and other "amenities." Given the impoverished state of the Liberian exchequer, the bulk of the financing came from foreign loans—usually on terms not favorable to Liberia.[67]

But Tolbert considered such expenses a minor cost, compared with his elevation to the chairmanship of the OAU, a position he had looked forward to "as a capstone in his long political career." He felt cheated out of the satisfaction this moment in time should have given him—cheated by being "plunged into his deepest domestic political crisis."[68]

"April 14, 1979," Professor Liebenow avowed, "marked the beginning of the end." In the threatening storm clouds, one could discern the growing strength of opposition from at least two civilian groups and a third force—the military—beginning to flex its muscles waiting in the wings.[69] The president risked far more than just relinquishing his prized chair at the head of the OAU table.

With the taste of April 14 still fresh, the PAL sensed the weakness of the Tolbert regime and determined to exploit it by registering as a legal political party looking to run for the presidency in 1983. Although Tolbert appeared to welcome the move, he allowed a lower court judge to block PAL's registration. In the face of a threat by Matthews to marshal another demonstration in the streets, however, the president in January 1980 again backed down.

The PAL leadership now decided to adopt a more appropriate name—the Progressive People's Party (PPP). Soon thereafter Matthews, for whatever reason, precipitously urged a crowd at a March 7 late-evening rally to march to the Executive Mansion and demand an audience with the president. Tolbert, however, was away up country. Matthews conveniently seized on the chief executive's absence as an excuse to issue a call for a countrywide general strike the following day, demanding Tolbert's resignation as president.

This time, an outraged Tolbert declared that from then on, he intended to be "tough and mean and rough." He would "carry out the law to its fullest," and if in the past he had been lenient, he asked "the people to forgive" him; he would not be lenient anymore. And he felt certain he had "the support of the Liberian people."[70]

President Tolbert on March 10 described for the legislature how the police the previous week had foiled "a plot to overthrow his Government." The plotters had tried "to cut off the capital from the outside world," he said, by putting up "road blocks in and around Monrovia," attempting "to burn down the telecommunications building, destroy a new bridge and take over the government information services." The police, he reported, intercepted Matthews and his followers "near the executive mansion shortly after midnight," while Tolbert was away. The authorities arrested nearly forty persons and charged them with sedition and treason. Matthews reportedly took refuge in the Vatican embassy but was "turned over to the Government by the Roman Catholic bishop of Monrovia."⁷¹

While Tolbert could count little on the Liberian people at large, he at least had the vigorous support of the True Whig Party faithful. Delegations from all over the country crowded the Executive Mansion, petitioning the government to exact the full penalty of the law from the accused, ban the PPP, or "declare Liberia a de jure one-party state under True Whig leadership." Thirty-eight dissidents remained in prison, their trial, "in one of those diabolical symbolic twists of which True Whig leaders were often capable," scheduled to begin April 14, the anniversary of the rice riots.⁷²

Among those arrested on March 10 was George (G. E. Saigbe) Boley, "in his early thirties...one of Liberia's promising young men." A tribal Liberian with a PhD from the University of Akron in the United States and an American wife, he had returned to Liberia not long before and become an assistant minister of education. Along with some twenty others, he found himself locked up in the Barclay Training Center, the notorious military facility in downtown Monrovia. Here he slept on a bare concrete floor, received twenty-five lashes each morning, ate "one scant meal a day," and was not allowed a bath, nor any visit from his family. But what really got his and his fellow prisoners' attention was the rumor that they would be executed on April 14, the anniversary of the rice riots.⁷³

Sanford J. Ungar, an American journalist and educator, visiting Liberia not long before the 1980 coup, portrayed Monrovia as a "steamy, grimy, torrid port city," which the poorest of the poor found "less escapable than in some other African capitals." It was a city where malaria reigned endemic and usually ran rampant, "the air...dense with industrial and automobile pollution, and one...[was] liable to be mugged or robbed, night or day." It was swollen with "youngsters who...[had] streamed into the capital from the underdeveloped countryside," looking "as if their expectations...[had] dwindled into a constant search for the next meal." Concealing all this was "an overlay of elegance and pomp; piazzas and limousines, pillared mansions and debutante balls, a marble Masonic temple that would look right at home in an American small town."[74] (The temple would be sacked and its statuary destroyed in the 1980 coup, but it would still loom as a shell on a hill at one end of Monrovia—as a home to squatters.)[75]

The city on Friday, April 11, 1980, differed little from Ungar's portrait. The sky felt heavy enough to totally collapse on the streets below, its warm, fetid air portended bad juju at work. Not long after midnight, shots rang out in the vicinity of the Executive Mansion, and shooting broke out around the seven-storied building. Several military installations also witnessed sporadic outbursts of gunfire. It soon became clear that the president and his aides were under attack.

But it wasn't until Samuel Doe, an unknown army master sergeant, a so-called uneducated, uncivilized aborigine of the Krahn tribe in eastern Liberia, announced over Monrovia Radio that a coup had toppled the Tolbert government. An "Army Redemption Council [composed of Doe and other enlisted men] had seized control." He explained that the "'rampant corruption and continuous failure by the Government to effectively handle the affairs of the Liberian people left the enlisted men no alternative.'"[76] Rumors abounded but no one was sure what all of this meant.

A subsequent announcement referred to Doe as "head of state," and visitors to the Executive Mansion reported that he "was running the country from an outside building, assisted by other enlisted men who referred to him as 'Mr. President.'"[77] At the age of twenty-eight, he apparently had become the youngest head of state (at least de facto) in Africa. (He also would sit in President Tolbert's cherished chairman's seat, the youngest person to occupy it, at the next OAU meeting.)

The *New York Times* thought the coup had "been a spur-of-the-moment decision, carried out by no more than 30 people." Doe, it seemed, "belonged to a special battalion, part of a group trained by the United States Special Forces" a year earlier and assigned to guard President Tolbert.[78]

However, few Liberians and no foreigners appeared to know Master Sergeant Doe, particularly his political and philosophical beliefs. His colleagues in the Liberian National Guard reported "that he always seemed career-oriented and apolitical...that he always chafed at the thought that his own progress upward through the military might be hindered because the highest officer positions always went to" Americo-Liberians.[79]

Doe delivered his words "in a slow resonant voice that [seemed] to hold great appeal." He would thrust his fist "forcefully into the air" as he addressed the crowds. His shoulders would be "thrown back, almost arrogantly as he [swaggered] through swarms of people who [thronged] to see him on his frequent trips through Monrovia's poorer neighborhoods." Born in eastern Liberia, the "son of a schoolmaster, he dropped out of school in the 11th grade for...economic reasons," then enlisted in the Liberian National Guard, the country's armed force. He "quickly developed a reputation as a skilled sharpshooter and an agile hand-to-hand combat fighter," skills that led to his selection for the Special Forces training. [80]

Although described as "not a tall man, about 5 feet 10 inches... his high-heeled boots and peaked cap, along with his upright posture [lent] him the appearance of someone much taller." His associates said he was "a stickler for neatness; his uniforms...always well pressed," and insistent that his "aides appear neatly dressed in public." The sergeant, they reported, was "not gregarious," and had "few friends beyond his brigade." While he had no hobbies, he was fond of swimming and running.[81]

In periodic radio announcements, "interspersed with American rock music and African songs," the new president ordered "riotous soldiers" who were engaged in looting, mainly of Lebanese and Indian merchants, and robbing and beating Liberians and foreigners, "to return to their units or be shot." Some had commandeered vehicles in which they raced around the city, celebrating by firing their weapons in the air.[82]

Although Doe reassured the public that the situation was under control, "he ordered a dusk to dawn curfew"[83] and reportedly approached the United States for help. Colonel Robert Gosny, who headed a six-man team advising the Liberian Defense Ministry, supposedly worked out new security plans with the defense minister.[84]

Two days later, on April 14, the new president delivered a twelve-minute speech on television. Dressed in green fatigues, complete with a hand grenade hanging from a pocket, with an army-issue cap and sunglasses, Doe explained that he and his fellow soldiers, all enlisted men, some of whom stood behind him with loaded rifles, overturned the old Americo-Liberian regime because "privilege had held our people down for too long." He "promised 'a new society' and a Government run 'without discrimination.'" He added, "Gone forever are the days of who you know and Do you know who I am?" Now, it would be "What can you do?"[85]

He reaffirmed the policy espoused by the previous two regimes of promoting foreign investment, respecting private property and free enterprise, as well as improving food, transportation, and housing. And to insure the solidity of his power base, he threw it a meaty little bone—doubling the military's minimum pay to enlisted ranks to $250 monthly, and paying all government workers at least $200 per month.[86]

Sergeant Doe also told the Liberian News Agency that President Tolbert had been killed in the predawn capture of the Executive Mansion. No details, however, were available (and the circumstances surrounding Tolbert's death still remain murky). The *New York Times* reported Tolbert was shot three times to the head, and Mrs. Tolbert was arrested. According to the president's nephew, Dr. Richard Tolbert, the president "was assassinated at the door to his bedroom."[87] Sanford Ungar's account takes the macabre story a step further: soldiers shot and killed the president upstairs in his quarters, disemboweled him, "stuck a bayonet through his head, and, after displaying his body in the morgue at the John F. Kennedy Hospital, buried it in a mass grave."[88]

Questions arose as to how the coup leaders, despite supposedly heavy security, gained access to the Executive Mansion so easily.[89] And why had Tolbert remained there that Friday night instead of following his usual practice of spending the weekend at home in Bentol (about thirty miles from Monrovia)? Rumors in the country suggested evidence of ritual ceremonies (which were not uncommon, even among the Americo-Liberian elite) had been found in the mansion after President Tubman's death in London. Spending the night in the building would bring him bad luck—which sadly it did.[90]

On April 15 soldiers reportedly dumped the bodies of Tolbert and twenty-seven others killed in the fighting from a truck or cart "into a swampy common grave on the edge of Monrovia's Palm Garden Cemetery."[91] Those buried included Brigadier General Charles Railey, chief of the palace guard.[92] Crowds who had gathered at the mass grave reportedly threw rocks at the bodies.

A week after the coup, Sergeant Doe toured some of Monrovia's poorer neighborhoods, where thousands greeted him. They struggled to touch him; "when he smiled the crowd roared and when he waved they cheered." A handyman said, "We were all ready for someone like Doe…We all were ready to erupt, and Tolbert never saw this."[93]

President Doe on his first day in power had ordered all government officials "to report to the executive mansion."[94] Ninety-one visibly shaken individuals—"former officials, judges, army and police officers, administrators and relatives of the late President"—ended up in a military base in the city. Hearings determined who would face trial on charges of corruption and misuse of public funds or on more serious counts of treason and violation of human rights.[95]

A five-man military tribunal sealed the fate of thirteen ministers and other top officials, finding them guilty of "high treason, rampant corruption and gross violation of human rights." The tribunal, after a kangaroo-style trial, in which the defendants were not allowed any defense counsel nor given any details of the charges against them, sentenced them to death.[96]

The group, a veritable "who's who" of the Americo-Liberian elite, included Frank E. Tolbert, presiding officer of the Senate and the slain president's elder brother; former foreign minister Cecil C. Dennis Jr.; Speaker of the House Richard A. Henries; F. Reginald Townsend, former chairman of the True Whig Party; Minister of Justice James Chesson; Supreme Court Chief Justice James A. Pierre; Finance Minister James T. Phillips; David Franklin Neal, minister for economic planning; Budget Director Frank Stewart; Cyril Bright, agriculture minister; John A. Sherman, trade minister; Charles T.O. King, member of the House of Representatives; and Clarence Parker, True Whig Party treasurer.[97]

Conspicuous by his absence was President Tolbert's son, A. B. Tolbert. He had managed to elude arrest on April 13 by taking refuge in the French embassy, hoping to escape to the Ivory Coast and the protection of his father-in-law, President Félix Houphouët-Boigny. Two months later, however, Doe's soldiers on June 14 burst into the embassy compound and took him to the Barclay Training Center.

In a surprising radio interview that day, he bemoaned, "I was arrested while I was praying," then during the interview, he pleaded for mercy from his captors, assuring them he "was 100 percent for the revolution."[98] Months later, however, Doe's deputy, Thomas Weh Syen, allegedly shot young Tolbert to death before he was brought to trial. Ironically, the following year, the same Weh Syen, along with four other original People's Redemption Council (PRC) members, met a similar fate in the Barclay Center. A secret military court convicted them of plotting to kill Doe and assume power themselves.[99]

In another ironic twist of fate, Doe's soldiers during the coup had seized the Barclay Training Center and flung open the cells to free Tolbert's political detainees—on April 12, two days before the date the detainees, rumor had it, would be executed. Moreover, Joseph Chesson, the Liberian justice minister who had zealously jailed the opposition leaders—including George Boley, the promising young returnee from the United States—now found himself facing execution.

Boley, however, had the good fortune that Doe had attended the Marcus Garvey School at night in Monrovia and had been in one of Boley's English classes. Doe and Boley also hailed from the same part of the country. The new young president, who had never even completed high school, never been outside Liberia, and spoke only halting English, asked his former teacher to serve as his minister of state for presidential affairs.

> According to Sanford Ungar, Boley occupied an office next to Doe's in the Executive Mansion for ten months. Now a person of importance, he gained back the weight he had lost while imprisoned in the Barclay Training Center and began wearing stylish, hand-tailored suits. The president "rarely made a move without consulting him." And, after office rivals in 1981 persuaded Doe to demote him to the less important post of minister of posts and communications, Boley, ever the survivor, managed to regain Doe's confidence. He became minister of education, then secretary general of Doe's newly minted National Democratic Party.[100] Even after Doe's downfall, Boley in 1994 would again turn up in Liberia, this time as "General" George Boley, commanding a motley collection of young men, women, and children, one of the warring factions in the country's civil war.

The former Tolbert ministers and officials, however, were not so lucky.

As morning dawned on Tuesday, April 22, dark and foreboding clouds filled the sky over the Barclay Training Center on Monrovia's beachfront, where hundreds of soldiers and thousands of civilians had gathered. The mood, however, was festive. A phalanx of media readied their cameras and audio equipment. Reporters, summoned to the beach from a seven-minute-long press conference with President Doe—in which he answered a total of two of the dozen questions submitted—positioned themselves. They had been encouraged to record in words, pictures, and on film the gruesome ceremony that would soon unfold.[101]

A newspaper account related that the crowd "stared at four 20-foot poles silhouetted against the ocean whitecaps." At 2:30 p.m. a truck arrived with two large mechanical hole drillers to add five more poles. At 3:30 a bus pulled up to a sandy dune on the beach. "Nine thick wooden posts had been lined up along the dune 10 feet apart."[102] Thirteen dazed and dispirited individuals climbed from the bus, attempting to avoid looking toward the wooden posts. Nine of the thirteen were "stripped to the waist, and tied, one to each post and facing away from the sea. A single long green rope was used."[103]

"Soldiers in battle fatigues, mostly armed with submachine guns, milled around the posts jeering at the prisoners who were tied by their waists. It took half an hour for their officer to get them to move far enough back to make room for the firing squad." The firing squad took up their positions, a "soldier with a rifle in front of each post at a distance of 15 yards." Frank Tolbert and seventy-two-year-old Richard Henries, Speaker of the House, "apparently fainted, and the firing squad killed them as they sagged to the ground on the [green] rope." Only former foreign minister Cecil Dennis and Reginald Townsend, ex-chairman of the True Whig Party, "appeared calm as they faced their executioners."[104]

When "the order was given, each soldier fired several times. When the "first shots missed Dennis and some others…he appeared astonished." Other soldiers then "opened up with bursts of machine-gun fire for several minutes amid wild cheering from the soldiers and from civilians lined up some distance from the beach. The nine bodies were cut down and left at the foot of the stakes." Soldiers brought the remaining four prisoners forward and tied them to the posts. After "another volley rang out," a staff sergeant moved from body to body emptying "the magazine of his weapon into the bodies, [then] turned to a reporter standing next to him and said that those put to death had 'no right to live' because they had made Liberians suffer for years, killing people and stealing our money."[105]

"By all accounts," following the executions, "there was jubilation throughout the country, literally dancing in the streets."[106] The so-called country people, the indigenous Liberians, danced as they sang, "Congo [Americo-Liberian] woman born rogue. Country woman born soldier." For 150 years Americo-Liberian women bore the country's "rogue" rulers, but the native women bore soldiers who now were in control.[107]

Even non-Liberians welcomed the change in the country's rule, although most abhorred the executions. They thought that at last a native African Liberian would lead the country and presumably right the great imbalance created by more than 130 years of Americo-Liberian dominance over the vastly larger indigenous population.

—⚛—

Three days later the government declared martial law and "suspended the 133-year-old Constitution 'until further notice.'" All legislative and executive powers were vested in [the] People's Redemption Council, headed by Doe, with seventeen enlisted men as members.[108] The president also presided over a fifteen-member cabinet, which included nine civilians, "mostly from the two political organizations that opposed President Tolbert, the People's Progressive Party [formerly the PAL] and the Movement for Justice in Africa."[109] Doe chose Ellen Johnson Sirleaf, who had served as a finance minister in the Tolbert regime, to head the Liberian Development Bank. She would go on to cause Doe acute political indigestion and would later on be elected president, the first woman to head an African state.

When Sergeant Doe and his cohorts ended the first republic in April 1980, Liberia had existed as a colony, a commonwealth, and a republic for 159 years. By all odds, it represented a remarkable record of survival—from hostile Africans who launched a near-continuous series of tribal wars intent on wiping out the small colony of American blacks; from the ever-present fevers and frequent starvation that devastated them; from European powers hungry for new lands and resources in their nineteenth-century scramble for Africa; and even from a righteous twentieth-century League of Nations intent on governing Liberia in the wake of a forced labor scandal. Equally remarkable, through much of its history, the country teetered on the edge of financial disaster but somehow endured.

The immediate causes of the downfall are not hard to find. Ungar alleges that the "Tolbert family's greed was a key factor in the downfall of a system that might otherwise have survived for another generation."[110] Corruption in Liberia, as in other African countries, was a traditional way of life. "In terms of corruption," though, Ungar maintains that Liberia had become "a leader in Africa and the Third World. Under Tubman's benign dictatorship, there were limits." According to "an old saw of Liberian politics 'when Tubman stole a dollar, he would give ninety cents back to the people' in the form of food or minor amenities. Tolbert, however, 'would return ten cents.'" Most Liberians thought the president's lawyer son, A. B. Tolbert, had prospered greatly at the public trough, and rumors circulated that the president himself had as much as $200 million stashed in the United States; his brother Frank acknowledged assets of $500,000-plus.[111]

Besides corruption and nepotism, the government's historic mistreatment of its indigenous people and suppression of any opposition deemed a threat to the Americo-Liberian elite unquestionably played the major role. Tolbert's downfall marked the end of the long-running colonial Americo-Liberian dynasty, but the seeds for its eclipse clearly had been sown long before Sergeant Doe appeared on the scene. The Americo-Liberians simply failed to forge a nation out of and in association with the mix of tribal Africans they ruled. They came as unwelcome foreign colonizers and stayed on, unwilling to give up their dominant position and the life it afforded them—fearing they would drown in a sea of "uncivilized African aborigines."

And their fear of drowning was not confined to African aborigines. The 1847 constitution limited to "negroes or those of negro descent." [112] The exclusion from citizenship of all other races, coupled with the limited supply of Negroes willing and able to immigrate, protected the Americo-Liberians from foreign competitors but condemned them to remain a very small minority ultimately unable to sustain its superior position in the country.

Initially, one is struck by the similarities between Liberia's and North America's early colonial histories: the expansion of settlements, the acquisition of territory by treaties (and other means), the existence of tribal-governed territories or reservations, the lengthy series of tribal wars. But the similarities fade in the end results. Europeans overwhelmed North America's indigenous peoples with waves of new settlers and the introduction of devastating diseases. The Americo-Liberians, on the other hand, did ostensibly rule the colony but remained a separate occupying presence until overthrown.

—⚬—

If the United States had taken on Liberia as a bona fide colony, would it have made the difference? The argument that some Liberians advanced was "yes." The Liberian ambassador to the United Nations, Charles T. O. King, in a speech on March 23, 1957, shocked many, given the prevailing, often-venomous denunciations of colonialism. The *New York Times* reported that King declared Liberia "lagged materially behind...because it had always been independent and had never reaped the advantages of colonialism." King, responding to comparisons with newly independent Ghana, said it was "the difference between the home of a man who [had] everything by his own sweat and toil...and that of a man who [had] enjoyed a large inheritance."[113]

He pointed to Ghana's "better roads, better schools, better harbor facilities, a more highly developed industry, agriculture and public revenue." Because the United States didn't "care about a colony on the coast of Africa," he complained, "we [Liberians] were left alone and struggling, to vegetate in the midst of developing European colonies." He attributed this divergence in the foreign interests of the European and American powers to the former's hearty appetite, especially during the nineteenth century, for raw materials, while the United States had relatively little such interest in Liberia until the Firestone rubber plantation.[114]

—⚬—

Liberia began as an experiment, America's first attempt to deal with its problem of race, an issue that still grips the United States even today. By that measure, the experiment failed. Some saw

Liberia as the missionary stepping-stone from which Africa could be Christianized (and civilized) but wasn't, although Liberia's founding contributed importantly to ending slavery and the slave trade in that part of west Africa.

Finally, after most of the continent had been consumed as colonies by acquisitive European powers in the nineteenth century, many Americans, including ardent advocates of "back to Africa," saw Liberia, the sole independent republic in Africa governed by black people, as a different experiment. This one hopefully would demonstrate their capacity to govern while espousing democratic values and advancing the economic welfare of their entire population. Again, the experiment by that measure could hardly be deemed a sparkling success—at least, until recently.

The inglorious end to Americo-Liberian dominance brought high hope for a better future. But it unfortunately failed to hasten the salvation of the Liberian people. They adopted a new constitution in 1984 and held elections, but still would endure two decades of brutal rule, of warring tribes and military factions, and a devastating civil war that threatened Liberia's very existence as an independent country before they could hope, even hesitantly, for a brighter future. And even that future trembled under the crushing weight of the 2014 Ebola epidemic, the largest in history.

Probably the light that shines brightest for that future are the women of Liberia. Ellen Johnson Sirleaf, who, in addition to serving under Tolbert and Doe, helped found an opposition party, was imprisoned for describing Doe and his cohorts as "idiots" in a speech in the United States, and then escaped to the United States, and lived in exile until she returned to Liberia to run for president against Charles Taylor in 1995. She lost that election but was finally elected president in 2005—the first female president in Africa.[115] Dubbed "Africa's Iron Lady" by the foreign press and "Ma Ellen" by fellow Liberians, she persistently spoke out against "violence and corruption, and ultimately transformed the government."[116] Sirleaf won reelection to another six-year term in 2011.

One can only hope that America's troubled African stepchild, having suffered a painfully uncertain childhood, will now emerge as a mature, diverse nation ready to take its rightful place in the family of nations.

EPILOGUE

ELLEN JOHNSON SIRLEAF STEPPED DOWN as president of Liberia at the end of her second tem in 2017. An election on October 10 of that year chose Senator George Weah and Vice President Joseph Boaki as candidates to replace her. In a run off election to decide her successor on December 26 Weah, also a soccer star, was elected president.

APPENDIX A

Time Line

1619
First shipload of African slaves arrives at Jamestown, Virginia.

1661
Virginia legislature legally recognizes slavery.

1795
Paul Cuffe born on Cuttyhunk Island, Massachusetts.

1807
United States bans slave trade, effective January 1, 1808.

1816
American Colonization Society founded in Washington, DC.

1820
First Colonization Society settlers cross the Atlantic on the *Elizabeth*, land in Sierra Leone.

1821
Lieutenant Robert Stockton and Dr. Eli Ayres purchase land for the Colonization Society on Cape Mesurado December 15.

1822
First colonists reach Cape Mesurado January 7. Land initially on Perseverance Island, move onto mainland April 25. Elijah Johnson rallies settlers to establish colony. Jehudi Ashmun arrives on brig *Strong*, leads in repulsing native attacks in November–December.

1823
Dr. Eli Ayres and sixty-one colonists arrive. Disaffection, "intrigue and rebellion rife." Ashmun's leadership threatened.

1824
Liberia and Monrovia (formerly Christopolis) named officially. Gurley and Ashmun draw up new plan of government.

1825
Colony acquires new lands (Grand Bass and New Cess).

1826
Additional land acquired in Cape Mount and Junk River areas. Trade Town War.

1827
US Navy delivers group of 124 recaptives to Liberia.

1828
Ashmun returns to United States, dies in New Haven, Connecticut. Lott Carey killed in gunpowder explosion.

1829
Joseph Jenkins Roberts and family aboard the *Harriet*, dock at Monrovia.

1832
Port Cresson colony founded. War with Dey and Golah.

1834

One-hundred twenty-six settlers arrive at Port Cresson colony at Bassa Cove. James Hall, with twenty-eight Maryland Colonization Society settlers, lands at Cape Palmas.

1835

Port Cresson settlement destroyed by Bassa tribesmen.

1836

Thomas Buchanan takes charge of Bassa Cove colony that replaced Port Cresson settlement.

1838

Thirty-seven settlers land at mouth of Sinoe River to establish Mississippi in Africa. Josiah Finley, governor of the colony, murdered by tribesmen. Greenville established as capital. Gola-Dei War (1838–40).

1839

Liberia becomes Commonwealth of Liberia. Colonization Society on January 5 adopts constitution, appoints Thomas Buchanan first governor. The colony elects Joseph Jenkins Roberts lieutenant governor.

1841

Governor Buchanan dies. Roberts acting governor.

1843

Britain questions Liberia's sovereign power to enforce commercial regulations and collect customs duties. US secretary of state responds: Liberia occupied a "peculiar position" with the United States.

1844–45

Roberts visits United States. Additional land acquired by purchases and treaties.

1847
Independence declared July 26 and Constitution of the Republic of Liberia adopted. Joseph Jenkins Roberts elected first president (inaugurated January 3, 1848).

1848
England and France extend recognition to republic (followed later by other countries). Admiralty presents Liberia a naval vessel, the *Lark*.

1849
Roberts reelected president. Gurley visits and prepares report on colony.

1850
Two German trading houses open in Liberia. Quarrels erupt among Vai, Dei, and Golah.

1851
Roberts reelected to third presidential term. Edward Wilmot Blyden arrives in Monrovia. Liberia College founded. Maryland colony governor John Russwurm dies.

1853
Roberts elected for fourth term. Maryland declared independent Republic of Maryland.

1854
On visit to Europe, Roberts proposes annexing Sierra Leone.

1856
Stephen Allen Benson inaugurated president. Napoleon III presents arms and equipment for one thousand men and a naval vessel to Liberia. Grebo-Maryland War 1856–58.

1857
Maryland joins Republic of Liberia February 28.

1858
George Seymour and James Sims explore Liberian interior.

1862
US president Lincoln extends recognition to Liberia September 23.

1864
Daniel Bashiel Warner inaugurated president. Appoints Edward Blyden secretary of state.

1865
Three-hundred forty-six immigrants, including Arthur Barclay, arrive from Barbados. Ports of Entry Law restricting foreign trade to six designated ports enacted.

1868
James Spriggs Payne, Liberia's fourth president, inaugurated. Benjamin Anderson embarks on lengthy exploration of hinterland, reaches fabled city of Musardu.

1869
True Whig Party founded. Constitution amended to lengthen president's and vice president's terms from two to four years.

1870
Edward James Roye begins presidential term. Anderson's account of his journey to Musardu published.

1871
Disastrous British loan. Roye proclaims extension of presidential term. Deposed from office, Roye escapes from prison

while awaiting trial. Dies under mysterious circumstances. Vice President James Skivring Smith serves as president for remainder of term.

1872

Roberts again serves as president.

1873

Worldwide financial panic lasting six or more years helps fuel Liberia's financial deterioration. Roberts reelected.

1874

Anderson undertakes second hinterland expedition.

1875

Grebo Reunited Kingdom Revolution 1875–76. US President Grant dispatches USS *Alaska* to support government.

1876

Roberts dies January 3, after returning from England. James S. Payne, a mulatto, inaugurated as the last president elected under the Republican Party banner (the party would disappear by 1899).

1878

Anthony William Gardiner takes office as president. British renew demand for compensation for damages by Liberian troops inflicted on British traders in disputed area along Sierra Leone border.

1879

US Navy commodore Robert W. Shufeldt arbitrates Liberian–Sierra Leone boundary dispute but fails to resolve differences. Grebo uprising in Maryland. USS *Ticonderoga* and *Essex* stand off-shore as revolt collapses.

1881
Expedition punishes Kru for involvement in affair of wrecked German steamer *Carlos*.

1880
Flow of new immigrants reduced to a trickle. (The Colonization Society would end active support of immigration and be officially dissolved in 1964.)

1882
Sir Arthur Havelock and gunboats from Sierra Leone appear at Monrovia to advance demands in Gallinas. Liberian Senate, led by Vice President Alfred Russell, erupts in stormy opposition to a draft agreement with Britain ceding disputed territory. Widespread public outcry: yielding "would be national suicide."

1883
Sierra Leone occupies disputed Gallinas territory. President Gardiner resigns, succeeded by Russell, who serves out Gardiner's unexpired term. Tribesmen plunder two wrecked foreign ships.

1884
Hilary Richard Wright Johnson becomes country's first president born in Liberia.

1885
Sierra Leone boundary dispute settled with Mano River the border. Great Britain formally annexes Gallinas territory.

1891
French claim Cavalla River as Liberia's boundary with Ivory Coast.

1892
Joseph James Cheeseman inaugurated president. Liberia protests but accepts French boundary demands.

1893
Grebo attack Harper in Third Grebo War.

1896
President Cheeseman dies. Is succeeded by Vice President William David Coleman.

1899
French officer surveying territory acquired by France questions veracity of Benjamin Anderson's account of his explorations.

1900
President Coleman resigns under pressure for using military to quell intertribal conflict and expanding government administration in interior. Rev. Garretson Wilmot Gibson succeeds him.

1903
Boundary with Sierra Leone demarcated.

1904
Arthur Barclay inaugurated president, attacks Liberia's "closed door." Sir Harry Johnston assumes managing directorship of Liberian Rubber and Liberian Development Companies.

1906
Arthur Barclay begins second term as president. British banking consortiu extends Liberia £100,000 loan to ward off financial collapse.

1907

Constitution amended to replace "persons of color" with "Negroes" to qualify for citizenship, and lengthen presidential term from two to four years. Naturalization Act of 1876 repealed. Barclay signs treaty fixing Liberia's boundary with France's Ivory Coast. Indirect Rule introduced.

1908

Upon reelection, Arthur Barclay begins four-year term as president. Bowing to British demands, Liberia establishes frontier force. Liberian commission visits Washington to enlist American assistance, followed by Sir Harry Johnston, who meets with President Theodore Roosevelt on Liberia's behalf.

1909

Barclay, fearing mutiny or coup, fires defiant Major Cadell. Roosevelt, alarmed at risk of Liberia's falling to a colonial European power, dispatches high-powered commission (headed by Booker T. Washington) to investigate conditions there.

1910

Commission recommends United States help Liberia reorganize its finances, resolve border disputes with Britain and France, and extend financial aid to the government. Government introduces "hut tax." US President Taft sends USS *Birmingham* to support government in major Grebo war.

1912

President-elect Daniel Edward Howard inaugurated. Multinational syndicate makes $1.7 million loan, secured by Liberian customs and tax receipts. American military advisors arrive in Liberia to assist frontier force. Tribal revolts against Ports of Entry Law, hut tax, and frontier force abuses.

1914
Outbreak of World War I, which devastates Liberian economy and fuels financial crisis.

1915
Kru rebellion threatens government rule in coastal areas, as tribe members declare themselves British subjects and demand that Britain annex the areas. United States dispatches USS *Chester* to help frontier force quell rebellion.

1918
Liberia declares war on Germany. Monrovia shelled by German submarine.

1919
Liberia attends Paris Peace Conference and joins League of Nations.

1920
Charles Dunbar Burgess King begins first term as president. Marcus Garvey announces back-to-Africa project in Liberia. President King arrives in United States to finalize $5 million US loan, but virulent congressional opposition blocks approval.

1923
Garvey found guilty of mail fraud, sentenced to five years in prison. To protect British colonial rubber growers facing enormous surplus, Britain introduces Stevenson Plan to limit output. William Tubman elected senator, youngest in Liberian history.

1924

American rubber manufacturer Harvey Firestone objects to British plan and chooses Liberia for new rubber plantation as alternative source. Liberian government abrogates agreement with Garvey on his colonization project.

1926

Liberia and Firestone Rubber Company sign agreements for $5 million loan and one million acres of land (which had been set aside for Garvey's undertaking). Garvey, along with other critics, denounce Liberian president and United States for the agreement.

1927

King reelected president in a contest *The Guinness Book of World Records* counts as world's most fraudulent election. Garvey deported after serving three and one-half years in prison.

1928

Harvey Firestone initiates first broadcasting in Liberia.

1929

Defeated presidential candidate J. R. Faulkner accuses President King of "massive vote fraud," involvement in forced labor procurement, and permitting slavery.

1930

King appoints international commission of inquiry. Finds domestic slavery, forced procurement of labor, and widespread frontier force atrocities; calls for sweeping reforms. President King and Vice President Allen N. Yancy forced to resign. Secretary of State Edwin J. Barclay assumes presidency.

1931

Frontier force expedition, commanded by notorious Colonel Elwood T. Davies, begins ruthless campaign of terror in Kru and Gola areas. Atrocities provoke British and American outrage. First Firestone rubber plantings come into full production.

1932

Barclay elected president for regular four-year terms. Repeal of 1865 Ports of Entry and Transportation Laws. Economic and financial crisis. Temporarily suspends payments on Firestone loan. Presidential campaign harasses and intimidates opposition.

1933

US government, incensed by moratorium on loan repayment, breaks off diplomatic relations, halts all economic assistance. Barclay imposes deep cuts in government spending. Liberia lays blame for economic woes on Firestone loan. President Roosevelt halts US support to Firestone.

1934

Rubber prices recover. Barclay initiates three-year plan for development.

1935

Constitution amended to lengthen presidential and vice presidential terms from four to eight years. Barclay elected for eight years. Firestone and Liberia sign new agreements. United States formally recognizes Barclay administration.

1936

Rubber prices climb 32 percent in first six months.

1942

US signs defense pact, extends lend-lease aid to Liberia. Roberts Field constructed. First American soldier of first US expeditionary force in Africa lands June 17.

1943

President Roosevelt arrives at Roberts Field from Casablanca Conference. Barclay and President-elect Tubman visit Washington and New York. Spend night at the White House and visit Senate and House of Representatives.

1944

William Tubman inaugurated Liberia's eighteenth president. Announces Open Door policy and unification program. Liberia formally enters Second World War on side of Allies.

1945

Native people in hinterland gain right to elect representatives to national legislature. Lansdell Christie establishes Liberia Mining Corporation to develop Bomi Hills concession.

1946

Constitution amended to extend suffrage to women. President unveils ambitious 1946–50 development plan, including expensive independence centennial celebration. Tubman initiates program of meetings with native chiefs and people.

1947

Former US secretary of state Edward Stettinius and Tubman form jointly owned Liberian Development Company.

1948

Port of Monrovia inaugurated.

1949

Constitution amended to allow incumbent to serve an unlimited number of four-year terms as president. Christie persuades Republic Steel to join Liberia Mining Company.

1950

Legislature approves creation of Public Relations Officers (PRO) program. Liberia and United States sign agreement for $30 million Point IV assistance.

1951

Reformation Party presidential candidate Willeh Didwho Twe disqualified. Tubman wins reelection—without opposition. First shipment of Liberian iron ore from Bomi Hills mine ushers in a new era of foreign investments and rapid economic growth.

1952

Tubman announces Liberia's debts, including hated 1926 Firestone loan, had been "fully liquidated," a rare event unprecedented in the country's fiscal history.

1953

President Tubman calls for almost doubling 1951–60 development expenditures, to be financed from Liberian resources.

1954

Tubman embarks on extensive twenty-six-day trip to United States, where he receives VIP treatment. Independent True Whig Party organized. First Unification Council.

1955

Tubman elected to third term, defeating Barclay with 99.5 percent of the votes .Barclay dies a few months later. Tubman steps up Liberia's diplomatic campaign, touring European countries and opening legations. First attempt on president's life thwarted.

1956
Independent True Whig Party members arrested for treason. Police kill party's national chairman and son attempting to flee. Thirty-five foreign countries, including the Soviet Union, attend presidential inauguration Government goes on spending spree, constructing public buildings and roads, improving education and medical services.

1957
US vice president Nixon and wife visit Liberia, entertained lavishly at Executive Mansion.

1959
Tubman, with 99.99 percent of the votes, reelected president over O. Bright Davies. Steps up diplomatic efforts in Africa as leader of moderate "Monrovia group." Proposes an Association of African States.

1960
UN members elect Liberia as first African country on Security Council. Tubman presents rare pygmy hippopotamus to President Eisenhower.

1961
First major strike (at Liberia's largest mine) followed by general strike in Monrovia. President and Mrs. Tubman visit United States where President Kennedy assures him of American support. Tubman addresses UN General Assembly.

1962
Tubman makes another series of state visits. Liberia joins International Monetary Fund. Financial bubble bursts with collapse of post-Korean War boom. Security service alleges students meeting secretly in plot to overthrow the government.

1963
Tubman reelected without opposition. Thirty-two African states form Organization of African Unity (OAU). Government (supposedly) uncovers plot by army officers to assassinate president and overthrow the regime.

1964
Hinterland tribal provinces converted to four counties.

1966
Legislature expands president's emergency powers. Special Security System introduced. Riot police and army units put down massive strike by Firestone rubber workers. Report, "Growth without Development," concludes most Liberians benefited little from rapid economic growth.

1967
Tubman reelected sans any opposition. Doubts arise of regime's ability to fully control country's transformation into modern economy.

1968
Tubman dramatically reveals plot allegedly to overthrow government. Mass rallies and parades organized to show support for Tubman.

1971

Tubman reelected, but dies in London July 23 after serving twenty-seven years. Vice President William R. Tolbert sworn in as president sets about to de-Tubmanize the presidency.

1972

Amendment to constitution lowers voting age from twenty-one to eighteen. Liberia establishes formal diplomatic relations with the Soviet Union and Romania.

1973

Sluggish demand for rubber and iron ore, coupled with OPEC oil embargo, sparks global recession and economic decline in Liberia. Large-scale borrowing causes external debt to balloon.

1975

Constitution amended to limit presidential term to eight years. Tolbert continues Tubman's foreign policy.

1976

After completing balance of Tubman's term, Tolbert elected to serve four more years as president.

1977

Bomi Hills iron ore mine closes. Reform zeal largely depleted, Tolbert faces wave of dissent.

1978

Survey finds about one-third of elementary and one-half of high school–age children still without a school to attend.

1979
April 14 rice riot kills as many as 140. Gabriel Matthew and followers charged with treason. OAU meets in Monrovia, elects Tolbert chairman.

1980
Coup led by Sergeant Samuel Kanyon Doe topples government. Tolbert assassinated April 12. Doe announces end of the old republic April 14. Thirteen ministers and prominent Americo-Liberians executed on Monrovia beach April 22.

APPENDIX B
Colonial Agents, Governors, and Presidents 1820–1980

Pre-Liberia Agents (1820–21)
Rev. Samuel Bacon 1820
Samuel A. Crozer 1820
Jonathan B. Winn 1821

Colony—Agents (1821–39)
Rev. Joseph B. Andrus 1821
Dr. Eli Ayres 1821–22, 1823, 1824
Jehudi Ashmun 1822–28
Richard Randall 1828–29
Dr. Joseph Mechlin 1829–34
John B. Pinney 1834–35
Nathaniel Brander 1835
Dr. Ezekiel Skinner 1835–36
Anthony D. Williams 1836–39

Commonwealth—Governors (1839–47)
Thomas Buchanan 1839–41
Joseph Jenkins Roberts 1842–48

First Republic—Presidents (1848–1980)
Joseph Jenkins Roberts 1848–56
Stephen A. Benson 1856–64

Daniel B. Warner 1864-68
James S. Payne 1868-70
Edward J. Roye 1870-71 (deposed)
James S. Smith 1871-72 (served remainder of Roye's term)
Joseph Jenkins Roberts 1872-76
James S. Payne 1876-78
Anthony W. Gardiner 1878-83 (resigned)
Alfred F. Russell 1883-84 (served remainder of Gardiner's term)
Hilary R. W. Johnson 1884-92
Joseph J. Cheeseman 1892-96 (died in office)
William D. Coleman 1896-1900 (served Cheeseman's unexpired term, elected, resigned)
Garrison W. Gibson 1900-04 (served Coleman's unexpired term, elected)
Arthur Barclay 1904-12
Daniel E. Howard 1912-20
Charles D. B. King 1920-30 (forced to resign)
Edwin J. Barclay 1930-44 (served King's unexpired term, elected)
William V. S. Tubman 1944-71 (died in office)
William R. Tolbert 1971-80 (served Tubman's unexpired term, elected, assassinated)

(Sources: Sir Harry Johnston, *Liberia;* J. Gus Liebenow, *Liberia: The Quest for Democracy*; Frederick Starr, *Liberia: Description, History, Problems* [Chicago: Privately printed, 1915]; http://en.wikipedia.org.wiki/Colonial_Heads_of_Liberia.); American Colonization Records, Library of Congress, Manuscript Division, Washington, DC)

NOTES

CHAPTER 1. THE MULATTO "MARINEER"

1. Rosalind Cobb Wiggins, *Captain Paul Cuffe's Logs and Letters, 1808–1817: A Black Quaker's "Voice from within the Veil"* (Washington, DC: Howard University, 1996), 102.
2. Ibid., 99.
3. Ibid., 102.
4. Ibid.
5. Ibid., 103.
6. Ibid., 104–5.
7. Ibid., 106.
8. *Times* (London), August 2, 1811.
9. Sheldon Harris{ XE "Sheldon Harris" }, *Paul Cuffe: Black America and the African Return* (New York: Simon and Schuster, 1972), 32. An 1812 engraving from a drawing by an English MD, John Pele, hangs in the New Bedford Whaling Museum. It suggests some Negroid features, but the engraving could just as easily be the profile of a country squire.
10. Ibid.
11. Allen Johnson and Dumas Malone, eds., *Dictionary of American Biography*, vol. 2, (New York: Charles Scribner's Sons, 1958), 585.
12. Sierra Leone was founded on land (bordering what later would be Liberia) purchased from an African chief by British

abolitionists in 1787. Initially a free settlement for the "Black Poor" of London, many of whom were Black Loyalists who escaped enslavement and fought for the British. The Sierra Leone Company in 1792 took over what became the crown colony of Sierra Leone and its capital, Freetown. After the British prohibition of the slave trade in 1807, captives rescued from slaving ships by the Royal Navy were settled there.

13. Charles Johnson, Patricia Smith, and the WGBH Series Research Team, *Africans in America: America's Journey through Slavery* (San Diego: Harcourt & Brace), 1998, 36.
14. US Department of Commerce, Bureau of the Census, *Historical Statistics of the United States*, Bicentennial Edition, part 2 (Washington: GPO, 1975), 1168; and Robert William Fogel, *Without Consent or Contract: The Rise and Fall of American Slavery*, (New York: WW Norton, 1989), 29–30.
15. David McCullough, *John Adams* (New York: Simon & Schuster, 2001), 132.
16. Ibid.
17. Ibid., 131.
18. Ibid., 132.
19. Johnson et al., *Africans in America*, 9.
20. Ibid., 16.
21. Ibid., 38.
22. William W. Hening, *The Statutes at Large: Being a Collection of All the Laws of Virginia from the First Session of the Legislature in the Year 1619* (Charlottesville: University Press of Virginia, 1869), quoted in Johnson et al., *Africans in America*, 48.
23. Rhett S. Jones, "The African Diaspora in British North America in the Time of Paul Cuffe," introduction in *Captain Paul Cuffe's Logs and Letters, 1808–1817* (Washington, DC: Howard University Press, 1996), 2.
24. Ibid., 3.
25. Ibid., 7–8.

26. Department of Commerce, *Historical Statistics of the United States*, 1168.
27. Christine Arato and Patrick L. Eleey, *Safely Moved at Last: Cultural Landscape Report for New Bedford Whaling National Historical Park*, vol. 1 (Boston: National Park Service, 1998), 2. Known commonly as Quakers, the Religious Society of Friends originated in seventeenth-century England. Each congregation holds meetings, generally once or twice weekly, for worship; periodic business meetings regulate religious discipline and society administration. One or more congregations constitute what is termed a Monthly Meeting. One or more Monthly Meetings comprise a Quarterly Meeting, and the Quarterly Meetings within a specified geographical area make up a Yearly Meeting.
28. *The History of Prince Lee Boo, to Which is Added the Life of Paul Cuffe, a Man of Colour, also, Some Account of John Sackhouse, the Esquimauxi* (Dublin: J. Jones, 1822), 147. See also "The History of Prince Lee Boo: The Life of Paul Cuffe, A Man of Colour," *Enterprise* (Falmouth, MA), February 13, 1991.
29. Paul Cuffe, *Cuffe's Journal, Letters, and Scrapbook* New Bedford, MA: Free Public Library, microfilm,147.
30. Remarkably, his book of accounts and his exercise book, in which childish scrawls, with practice, practice, practice, gradually morph into legible handwriting, are preserved in the New Bedford library. See *Cuffe's Journal*.
31. Local records note he purchased 120 acres in Westport, on the mainland just west of Bedford Village, in December 1766 for 650 milled Spanish dollars—a very tidy sum at that time.
32. Wiggins, *Cuffe's Logs and Letters*, 47.
33. *Enterprise* (Falmouth, MA). See also Wiggins, *Cuffe's Logs and Letters*, 45–70.
34. Arato, Safely Moved, 8. Joseph Rotch launched New Bedford's whaling trade in 1767. "By 1775 there were close to 75 vessels

and 1,000 seamen engaged in the town's flourishing maritime industries." It soon displaced Nantucket to rule as the world's capital of whaling from 1830 to 1860. (Petroleum disovered in Pennsylvania in 1859 doomed whale oil as the world's fuel of choice. New Bedford would no longer light "the lights of China.") Shipbuilding grew equally fast. New Bedford, led by shipbuilding and snd whaling, and prominent antislavery Quakers, also spawned a remarkable half-black man---the spiritualfather of Liberia.

35. Wiggins, *logs and letters*, 264-65.
36. Ibid. See also Wiggins, *Logs and Letters*, 48–70.
37. Wiggins, *Logs and Letters*, 48.
38. Jones, "The African Diaspora," 10–12.
39. Robert William Fogel, *Without Consent or Contract: The Rise and Fall of American Slavery* (New York: WW Norton, 1989), 124, Figure 19.
40. Department of Commerce, *Historical Statistics of the United States*, 1168.
41. See *Remarks on the Colonisation of the Western Coast of Africa by the Free Negroes of the United States, and the Consequent Civilization of Africa and Suppression of the Slave Trade*. (New York: WJ Burroughs), 9.
42. See Johnson et al., *Africans in America*, 107–11.
43. Ibid., 108.
44. Ibid., 110.
45. Ibid.
46. Ibid., 254.
47. Ibid., 256.
48. Ibid., 288.
49. Ibid., 289.
50. *Washington Post*, March 22, 2013.
51. Abraham Lincoln, *The Collected Works of Abraham Lincoln*, ed. Roy P. Basler, vol. 5 (New Brunswick, NJ: Rutgers University Press 1953), 37.

52. Johnson and Malone, *American Biography*, 585.
53. *Weekly Reader* (Boston), November 4, 1817.
54. Harris, *Paul Cuffe*, 22–23; and *Enterprise* (Falmouth, MA). See also Wiggins, 51.
55. Harris, *Paul Cuffe*, 25.
56. Johnson and Malone, *American Biography*, 585.
57. *History of Prince Lee Boo*, 163.
58. Johnson et al., *Africans in America*, 197–98.
59. Ibid., 194–95.
60. Ibid., 195.
61. Ibid., 196.
62. See "Birchtown, Nova Scotia," http://en.wikipedia.org/wiki/Birchtown_ Nova_ Scotia; and *Black Loyalists, Our History, Our People*, http://blackloyalists.info.
63. Sir Harry Johnston, *Liberia*, vol. 1 (1906; repr., New York: Negro Universities Press, 1969), , 122.
64. Peter Duignan and L. H. Gann, *The United States and Africa: A History* (New York: Cambridge University Press and the Hoover Institution, 1984), 81.
65. Boston King, "Memoirs of the Life of Boston King, a Black Preacher," from *The Methodist Magazine*, March–June 1798, electronic edition prepared by Antislavery Literature Project, accessed November 15, 2015, http://antislavery.eserver.org/narratives/boston _ kingbostonkingproof.pdf/; see also http://blackloyalist.com.

Chapter 2. Captain Cuffe and the "Province of Freedom"

1. Rosalind Cobb Wiggins, *Captain Paul Cuffe's Logs and Letters, 1808–1817: A Black Quaker's "Voice from within the Veil"* (Washington, DC: Howard University, 1996), 56.
2. See ibid., 56–57.

3. Ibid., 57.
4. Ibid., 77.
5. Paul Cuffe to John James and Alexander Wilson, 10 June 1809, quoted in Wiggins, *Logs and Letters*, 80.
6. Wiggins, *Logs and Letters*, 73–75.
7. James Pemberton to Cuffe, 8 June 1808, quoted in Wiggins, *Logs and Letters*, 77.
8. Abraham Lincoln, *The Collected Works of Abraham Lincoln*, Roy P. Basler, ed., vol. 5, (New Brunswick, New Jersey: Rutgers University Press, 1953), 371.
9. Ibid.
10. Wiggins, *Logs and Letters*, 94.
11. See Robert William Fogel, *Without Consent or Contract: The Rise and Fall of American Slavery* (New York: WW Norton, 1989), 211, 212, 216.
12. Wiggins, *Logs and Letters*, 78.
13. Ibid., 74.
14. Ibid., 107.
15. Ibid., 107–9.
16. Cuffe to Nathan Lord, 19 April 1805, quoted in Wiggins, *Logs and Letters*, 342.
17. Philip S. Foner, *History of Black Americans, from Africa to the Emergence of the Cotton Kingdom* (Westport, CT: Greenwood Press, 1975), 582.
18. Ibid.
19. Wiggins, *Logs and Letters*, 115.
20. Ibid., 114.
21. *Times* (London), August 2, 1811.
22. Wiggins, *Logs and Letters*, 59.
23. Cuffe to William Allen, 12 May 1812, quoted in Wiggins, *Logs and Letters*, 224.
24. Wiggins, *Logs and Letters*, 210.
25. Ibid., 211.

26. Ibid.
27. Ibid., 212.
28. Ibid., 212–13.
29. Ibid., 213.
30. Ibid.
31. Ibid., 252–53.
32. Foner, *History of Black Americans*, 583.
33. "Peter Bestes and Other Slaves Petition for Freedom (April 20, 1773)," in Herbert Aptheker, ed., *A Documentary History of the Negro People of the United States*, vol. 1, 7–8, accessed November 14, 2015, http:// historyisaweapon.com/decon1/ four petitions against slavery.html.
34. Foner, *History of Black Americans*, 575–76.
35. 1Cuffe to John Murray Jr., April 1815, quoted in Wiggins, *Logs and Letters*, 66.
36. Cuffe to Allen, 1 April 1816, quoted in Wiggins, *Logs and Letters*, 409.
37. Cuffe to Nathan Lord, 19 April 1815, quoted in Wiggins, *Logs and Letters*, 341–43.
38. Cuffe to William Rotch Jr., February 1816, quoted in Wiggins, *Logs and Letters*, 403.
39. Wiggins, *Logs and Letters*, 396–97.
40. Ibid., 395.
41. Cuffe to William Allen, February 1816, quoted in Wiggins, *Logs and Letters*, 404.
42. "The History of Prince Lee Boo: The Life of Paul Cuffe, A Man of Colour," *Enterprise* (Falmouth, MA), February 13, 1991.
43. Cuffe to Jebediah Morse, 10 August 1810, quoted in Wiggins, *Logs and Letters*, 436–37.
44. Harris, *Black America and the African Return*, quoted in Foner, *History of Black Americans*, 583.

45. Cuffe to Stephen Gould, 20 September 1816, quoted in Wiggins, *Logs and Letters*, 455.
46. Samuel C. Aiken to Cuffe, July 23, 1816, quoted in Wiggins, *Logs and Letters*, 427–28.
47. Cuffe to Samuel J. Mills, August 6, 1816, quoted in Wiggins, *Logs and Letters*, 431–33.
48. Samuel Eliot Morrison, *The Oxford History of the American People*, vol. 2 (New York: New American Library, 1972), 262.
49. Cuffe to Robert Finley, January 8, 1817, quoted in Wiggins, *Logs and Letters*, 492–93.
50. Foner, *History of Black Americans*, 584.
51. Cuffe to Allen, December 19, 1816, quoted in Wiggins, *Logs and Letters*, 483–84.
52. Cuffe to James Forten, March 1, 1817 (unfinished), quoted in Wiggins, *Logs and Letters*, 509.
53. Paul Cuffe, *Cuffe's Journal, Letters, and Scrapbook*. New Bedford, MA: Free Public Library, microfilm.

Chapter 3. The American Colonization Society

1. Isaac V. Brown, *Biography of the Rev. Robert Finley, D.D.*, 2nd ed. (Philadelphia: John W. Moore, 1857), 240, http://openlibrary.org.
2. Ibid., 231.
3. Ibid., 93.
4. Ibid., 20.
5. Ibid.,
6. Ibid., 86–91.
7. Isaac V. Brown, *Memoirs of the Rev. Robert Finley, D.D.*, (New Brunswick, NJ: Terhune and Letson, 1819), 77, http://openlibrary.org.
8. Brown, *Biography*, 97.

9. Foner, *History of Black Americans: From Africa to the Emergence of the Cotton Kingdom*, (Westport, CT.: Greenwood Press, 1975), 586.
10. *National Intelligencer*, December 16, 1816.
11. Ibid., December 31, 1816.
12. Foner, *History of Black Americans*, 587.
13. Ibid.
14. *Daily National Intelligencer*, December 23, 1816.
15. American Colonization Society, "Constitution of the American Society for Colonizing the Free People of Color of the United States," *First Annual Report of the Colonization Society*, January 1, 1818, microfilm, reel 289, American Colonization Records, Manuscripts Division, Library of Congress.
16. Allen Johnson and Dumas Malone, eds., *Dictionary of American Biography*, vol. 2. (New York: Charles Scribner's Sons, 1958), 365–66.
17. Foner, *History of Black Americans*, 587.
18. Brown, *Biography*, 178.
19. Ibid.
20. Foner, *History of Black Americans*, 589.
21. Bushrod Washington, "Address to American Colonization Society," January 8, 1820, microfilm, reel 289, American Colonization Records, Manuscripts Division, Library of Congress.
22. Foner, *History of Black Americans*, 588.
23. American Colonization Society, *A Memorial to the United States Congress*, February 1, 1820, Washington, http://pbs.org/wgbh/aia/part3. See also Albert Blaustein and Robert Zangrando, eds., *Civil Rights and the Black American: A Documentary History* (New York: Washington Square Press, 1968).
24. Ibid.
25. See Foner, *History of Black Americans*, 589.

26. Ibid., 590.
27. Ibid.
28. Ibid., 593.
29. Ibid.
30. Ibid., 591.
31. Rhett S. Jones, "The African Diaspora in British North America in the Time of Paul Cuffe," introduction to *Captain Paul Cuffe's Logs and Letters 1808-1817,* by Rosalind Cobb Wiggins (Washington, DC: Howard University Press, 1996), 32.
32. John B. Boles, *Black Southerners 1619–1869* (Lexington: University Press of Kentucky, 1984), 136, quoted in Jones, *African Diaspora,* 32.
33. Gary B. Nash, *Forging Freedom: The Formation of Philadelphia's Black Community, 1720–1840* (Cambridge: Harvard University Press, 1988), 219, quoted in Jones, *African Diaspora,* 32.
34. Boles, *Black Southerners,* 135, quoted in Jones, *African Diaspora,* 29.
35. Ibid.
36. Jones, *African Diaspora,* 35–37.
37. Ibid., 37.
38. Allen to Cuffe, January 25, 1817, quoted in Foner, *History of Black Americans,* 591.
39. Samuel Bacon, *Extracts from the Journal of the Reverend Samuel Bacon, Agent to the Colonization Society,* January 31, 1820, microfilm, reel 302, American Colonization Records, Manuscripts Division, Library of Congress.
40. Ibid.
41. Ibid.
42. See "Roll of Emigrants That Have Been Sent to the Colony of Liberia, Western Africa by the American Colonization Society and Its Auxiliaries, to September, 1843, &c.," transcribed from "Information Relative to the Operations of the United States Squadron on the West Coast of Africa,

the Condition of the American Colonies There, and the Commerce of the United States Therewith," 28th Congress, 2d. sess., S. Doc. 150, serial 458 (Washington: GPO, 1843), http://ccharity.com.
43. Elijah Johnson, *Extracts from the Journal of Elijah Johnson, Esq.*, February 6, 1820, microfilm, reel 302, American Colonization Records.
44. Ibid.
45. S. Bacon, *Journal*, February 4, 1820.
46. Samuel A. Crozer, *Journal*, January 20, 1820, microfilm, reel 304, American Colonization Records.
47. Crozer, *Journal*, March 20, 1820.
48. S. Bacon, *Journal*, April 5, 1820.
49. Ibid.
50. Ibid., April 6, 1820.
51. Ibid.
52. Daniel Coker, "Extract from a part of a journal" [thought to be Daniel Coker's], April 10, 1820, microfilm, reel 304 (?), American Colonization Records. See also Daniel Coker, *Journal of Daniel Coker: A Descendant of Africa*, (Baltimore: Edward J. Coale, 1820), http://inmotionaame.org/texts/.
53. S. Bacon, *Journal*, April 7, 1820.
54. American Colonization Society, *Fourth Annual Report*, 1821, microfilm, reel 289, American Colonization Society Records.
55. S. Bacon, *Journal*, April 9, 1820.
56. Ibid., April 10, 1820.
57. Ibid. April 11, 1820.
58. Ibid.
59. *The Fourth Annual Report of the American Society for Colonizing People of Colour of the United States*, 1821, Daniel Murray Pamphlet Collection, Library of Congress.
60. S. Bacon, *Journal*, April 10, 1820.
61. "Roll of Emigrants."

62. Christian Wiltberger, Papers of Christian Wiltberger, July 2, 1820, microfilm, reel, 289, American Colonization Records.
63. Ibid.
64. Ibid.
65. Ibid., Wiltberger to father, March 29, 1821.
66. Ibid., diary, January 27, 1821
67. Ibid., February 9, 1821.
68. Ibid., March 8, 1821.
69. J. B. Winn to A. Grant, March 8, 1821, American Colonization Records, microfilm, reel 289.
70. Grant to Winn, March 8, 1821, American Colonization Records, microfilm, reel 289.
71. Wiltberger, Papers, March 9, 1821.
72. Ibid., March 15, 1821.
73. Ibid., April 17, 1821.
74. Ibid., March 10, 1821.
75. Duignan and Gann, *United States and Africa*, 62.
76. Ibid., 83.
77. Wiltberger, Papers, April 17, 1821.

CHAPTER 4. THE SEARCH FOR A HOME

1. See Christian Wiltberger, Diary, March 20, 1821, Papers of Christian Wiltberger, American Colonization Society Records, microfilm, reel 289, Manuscripts Division, Library of Congress.
2. Ibid., Diary, 20 and 23 March 1821.
3. Ibid. Letter to father, March 1821.
4. Ephraim Bacon, *Abstract of a Journal Kept by. E. Bacon, Assistant Agent of the United States, to Africa: With an Appendix, Containing Extracts...* (Philadelphia: S.Potter & Co,, 1821), 12, http//babel.hathitrust.org.
5. Ibid., 13.

6. Ibid.
7. Ibid.
8. Ibid., 14.
9. Ibid.
10. Ibid., 16.
11. Ibid.
12. Ibid., 16.
13. Ibid., 17.
14. Ibid., 21.
15. Ibid., 22.
16. Ibid.
17. Ibid.
18. Ibid., 23.
19. Ibid., 25.
20. Ibid., 26.
21. Ibid.
22. Ibid., 26–27.
23. Ibid., 29.
24. Daniel Coker, *Journal of Daniel Coker: A Descendant of Africa* (Baltimore: Edward J. Coale, 1820), 16, http://inmotion-aame.org/texts/
25. Ephraim. Bacon, *Abstract of a Journal*, 47.
26. Ibid., 48.
27. Ibid., 19.
28. Ibid., 50.
29. Ibid.
30. Ibid., 52--53.
31. Daniel Coker, diary, April 21--September 1821, microfilm, reel 304, American Colonization Records.
32. Ibid.
33. Ibid.
34. Ibid.
35. Ibid.

36. Ibid.
37. Thomas Coates Stockton, *The Stockton Family of New Jersey, and Other Stocktons* (Washington: Carnahan Press, 1911), 111.
38. Ibid., 112.
39. Ibid., 128.
40. Glenn D. Bradley, *Winning the Southwest: A Story of Conquest* (Chicago: A. C. McClurg, 1912), 47.
41. Ibid.
42. American Society for Colonizing Free People of Colour, *Fifth Annual Report* (Washington DC: Printed at Davis and Force, 1822), 60, http://babel.haithitrust.org.
43. Amos Jones Beyan, *The American Colonization Society and the Creation of the Liberian State, 1822–1900* (Lanham, MD: University Press of America, 1991), 65.
44. Ekichard West, *Back to Africa: A History of Sierra Leone and Liberia* (New York: Holt, Rinehart and Winston, 1970), quoted in Beyan, *American Colonization Society*, 114.
45. Stockton, 112.
46. G. E. Saigbe Boley, *Liberia: The Rise and Fall of the First Republic* (London: Macmillan, 1983), 26.
47. Ibid.
48. Charles Henry Huberich, *The Political and Legislative History of Liberia*, vol. 1 (New York: Central Book, 1947), 195–96, quoted in Fred P. M. Van der Kraaij, *The Open Door Policy of Liberia: An Economic History of Modern Liberia*, vol. 1 (Bremen: lm Selbstveriag des Museums, 1983), 5.
49. Richard F. Burton, *Wanderings in West Africa*, vol.1, (1863; repr., New York: Dover, 1991), 277–78.
50. Sir Harry Johnston, *Liberia*, vol. 1 (1906; repr., New York: Negro Universities Press, 1969), vol. 1, 94.
51. Ibid., 101–2.
52. Jehudi Ashmun, *History of the American Colony in Liberia from December 1821 to 1823* (Washington: Printed by Way and Gideon, 1826), 8.

53. Jehudi Ashmun, *Memoir of the Life and Character of the Rev. Samuel Bacon* (1822; repr., Freeport, NY: 1971), 115.
54. Ashmun, *History*, 12.
55. Ibid.
56. Ashmun, *Memoir*, 115.
57. J. Gus Liebenow, *Liberia: The Quest for Democracy* (Bloomington: Indiana University Press, 1983), 27.
58. Ibid., 37.
59. Ashmun, *History*, 13.
60. Ibid.
61. Ibid.
62. Ibid., 14.
63. "View of Liberian History and Government," Africa Within, http://africawithin.com/tour/liberia/hist.govl.htm
64. Ibid.
65. Johnston, *Liberia*, vol. 1, 130.
66. Ibid.
67. "Roll of Emigrants That Have Been Sent to the Colony of Liberia, Western Africa by the American Colonization Society and Its Auxiliaries, to September, 1843, &c, from Information relative to the operations of the United States squadron on the west coast of Africa, of the American colonies there, and the commerce of the United States therewith," 28th Congress, 2nd session, 1843.
68. Ashmun, *History*, 15.
69. Ralph Randolph Gurley. *Life of Jehudi Ashmun, Late Colonial Agent in Liberia*. (Washington, DC: James C. Dunn, 1835), 116.

Chapter 5. Liberia Is Born

1. Ralph Randolph Gurley, *Life of Jehudi Ashmun, Late Colonial Agent in Liberia*. 2nd ed. (New York: Robinson and Franklin, 1839), 20.

2. Ibid., 35.
3. Ibid., 41.
4. Ibid., 51–52.
5. Ibid., 27.
6. Ibid., 125–26.
7. Ibid., 126.
8. J. Gus Liebenow, *Liberia: The Quest for Democracy* (Bloomington: Indiana University Press, 1983), 33.
9. Ibid.
10. Ibid.
11. See also Central Intelligence Agency, http://cia.gov. for slightly different estimates based on the 2008 census.
12. See Robert W. Clower, Mitchell HaRwitz, and A. A. Walters, *Growth without Development: An Economic Survey of Liberia* (Evanston, IL: Northwestern University Press, 1966), 333.
13. Gurley, *Life of Jehudi Ashmun*, 132–33.
14. Jehudi Ashmun, *History of the American Colony in Liberia from December 1821 to 1823* (Washington: Printed by Way and Gideon, 1826), 29.
15. Gurley, *Life of Jehudi Ashmun*, 147–48.
16. Ibid., 149.
17. Ibid., 148.
18. Ibid, 12.
19. J. H. T. McPherson, *History of Liberia* (abridgement of 1891 PhD diss., Johns Hopkins University, 2004), 12, http://www.fullbooks.com/History-of-Liberia.
20. Ibid., 150.
21. James Barnett Taylor, *Biography of Elder Lott Cary, Late Missionary to Africa* (Baltimore: Armstrong & Berry, 1837), 8.6
22. McPherson, *History*, 12.
23. Gurley, *Life of Jehudi Ashmun*, 196.

24. Ibid., 209.
25. Ibid., 155.
26. See Robert William Fogel, *Without Consent of Contract: The Rise and Fall of American Slavery* (New York: WW Norton, 1989).
27. Gurley, *Life of Jehudi Ashmun*, 222–23.
28. Ibid., 231
29. Ibid., 167.
30. Ibid, 233.
31. Taylor, *Biography*, 2.
32. Peter Duignan and L.H. Gann, *The United States and Africa: A History* (New York: Cambridge University Press and the Hoover Institution, 1984), 84.
33. Taylor, *Biography*, 16.
34. Gurley, *Life of Jehudi Ashmun*, 387–88.
35. Ibid., 393.
36. Ibid.
37. Ibid., 394–95. Relatively few monuments or public features—other than Ashmun Street, a principal thorough in Monrovia—honor his name.
38. Ibid., 395.
39. Taylor, *Biography*, 12.
40. Ibid.
41. Ibid.
42. Ibid., 15.
43. Ibid., 17.
44. Ibid.
45. Ibid., 19–20.
46. Duignan and Gann, *United States and Africa*, 387n16.
47. Fogel, *Without Consent*, 253.
48. Duignan and Gann, *United States and Africa*, 85. The Bassa Cove colony was founded by Quakers of the Pennsylvania and New York Young Men's Colonization Societies in July

1835. It replaced the previous Port Cresson colony started in December 1832 by the Pennsylvania and New York societies and destroyed by tribesmen in June 1835. Bassa Cove was incorporated into Liberia April 1, 1839.
49. Ibid.

CHAPTER 6. FROM COLONY TO COMMONWEALTH

1. Sir Harry Johnston, *Liberia*, vol. 1 (1906; repr., New York: Negro Universities Press, 1969), 180.
2. C. W. Tazewell, ed., *Virginia's Ninth President, Joseph Jenkins Roberts.* (Virginia Beach, VA: WS Dawson, 1992), 29.
3. Ibid., 11.
4. Ibid.
5. Ibid.
6. Ibid., 17.
7. Ibid.
8. Ibid.
9. Ibid., 6.
10. Ibid.
11. Ibid., 20.
12. Ibid., 19.
13. Ibid., 7
14. Ibid., 20.
15. Ibid.
16. "The Cost of African Colonization," *The Handbook of Liberia* (Monrovia: Government Printing Office, 1940), 279, quoted in Hassan B. Sisay, *Big Powers and Small Nations*, (Lanham, MD.: University Press of America, 1985), 187. The $2,558,907 total includes funding ($417,433) for the Maryland, New York, Pennsylvania, and Mississippi State Societies projects.

17. Peter Duignan and L.H. Gann, *The United States and Africa: A History* (New York: Cambridge University Press and the Hoover Institution, 1984), 86.
18. Tazewell, ed., *Virginia's Ninth President*, 20.
19. Ralph Randolph Gurley, *Life of Jehudi Ashmun, Late Colonial Agent in Liberia*, 2nd edition (New York: Robinson and Franklin, 1839), 155.
20. J. Gus Liebenow, *Liberia: The Quest for Democracy* (Bloomington: Indiana University Press, 1983), 25.
21. Alan Huffman, *Mississippi in Africa* (New York: Gotham House, 2005), 19.
22. See ibid., 153–56 and book rear cover.
23. Ibid., 154.
24. Duignan and Gann, *United States and Africa*, 85.
25. Huffman, *Mississippi in Africa*, 155.
26. "Arrival of the Brig Mail, and Sailing of the Ship Saluda," *The African Repository and Colonial Journal* 15 (1839): 80.
27. Huffman, 155.
28. Ralph Uwechae, ed., *Makers of Modern Africa: Profiles in History* (London: Africa Books, 1991), 656.
29. Quoted in Tazewell, *Virginia's Ninth President*, 34.
30. Ibid.
31. Ibid.
32. Ibid.
33. Ibid.
34. Ibid.
35. Ibid., 34–35.
36. *The Twenty-Ninth Annual Report of the American Colonization Society with the Proceedings of the Board of Directors and of the Society at its Annual Meeting*, January 29, 1846, Washington, 39.
37. Ibid.
38. Ibid., 20.

39. Carl Patrick Burrowes, *Power and Press Freedom in Liberia, 1830–1970: The Impact of Globalization and Civil Society on Media-Government Relations* (Trenton, NJ: Africa World Press, 2004), 60.
40. *The Thirtieth Annual Report of the American Colonization Society with the Proceedings of the Board of Directors and of the Society at its Annual Meeting,* January 21, 1845, Washington, 37.
41. Ibid.
42. Ibid.
43. See "Despatches from Liberia," 15–20; Burrowes, *Power and Press Freedom,* 60.
44. Joseph Jenkins to Robert McClain, January 29, 1847, *African Repository* 23 (1847): 132.
45. See Charles Henry Huberich, *The Political and Legislative History of Liberia,* vol. 1, (New York: Central Book, 1947), 821.
46. Ibid., 822.
47. Roberts to the Constitutional Convention, July 6, 1847, microfilm, reel 154, American Colonization Society Records, Manuscripts Division, Library of Congress.
48. Huberich, *Political and Legislative History,* vol.1, 823.
49. Ibid.
50. Ibid.
51. Ibid., 825.
52. See Ibid.
53. Ibid., 833.
54. In Convention, Declaration of Independence, as quoted in Ibid., 828-32.
55. Ibid., 833.
56. Ibid., 837.
57. Ibid., 838.

Chapter 7. From Commonwealth to Republic

1. Carl Patrick Burrowes, *Power and Press Freedom in Liberia, 1830–1970: The Impact of Globalization and Civil Society on Media-Government Relations* (Trenton, NJ: Africa World Press, 2004), 59.
2. Ibid.
3. Ibid., 60.
4. See succeeding section, *Liberian Political Parties*, 254-55.
5. See J. Gus Liebenow, *Liberia: The Quest for Democracy* (Bloomington: Indiana University Press, 1983) 88–89.
6. Ibid., 89.
7. Burrowes, *Power and Press Freedom*, 17.
8. Liebenow, *Quest for Democracy*, 89.
9. Ibid.
10. Charles Henry Huberich, *The Political and Legislative History of Liberia*, vol. 1, (New York: Central Book, 1947), 846.
11. Ibid., 846–47.
12. Sir Harry Johnston, *Liberia*, vol. 1 (1906; repr., New York: Negro Universities Press, 1969), 162.
13. C.W. Tazewell, ed., *Virginia's Ninth President: Joseph Jenkins Robert* (Virginia Beach, VA: WS Dawson, 1992), 40.
14. Johnston, *Liberia*, vol. 1, 227.
15. The United States formally recognized Liberia on September 23, 1862, when the American minister to England, Charles F. Adams, was empowered to conclude a treaty of commerce and navigation with the government. The United States delayed recognition because of Southern opposition in Congress. Haiti was recognized at the same time. President Lincoln appointed Abraham Hanson Commissioner and Consul General. He presented his credentials on February 23, 1864.
16. Tazewell, *Virginia's Ninth President*, 41.
17. *Liberia*, vol.1, 226–27.

18. Ibid.
19. Richard F. Burton, *Wanderings in West Africa*, Two Volumes Bound as One, vol. 2 (1863; *repr.*, New York: Dover Publications, 1991), 8.
20. Ibid., 9.
21. Ibid., 8.
22. Ibid. For a full and colorful account of the slave trade, see Johnston, *Liberia*, vol.1, ch. 7.
23. Roberts, "Appeal to the Government and People of the United States." *African Repository* 25 (1849): 233, http://books.google.com.
24. Burton, *Wanderings in West Africa*, vol. 2, 10.
25. Ibid.,, vol. 1, 279.
26. Ibid., 10.
27. Roberts to Rev. W. McLain, January 7, 1846, microfilm, reel 177B, American Colonization Society Records, Manuscripts Division, Library of Congress.
28. Roberts to the American Colonization Society, October 9, 1847, microfilm, reel 154, American Colonization Society Records, Manuscript Division, Library of Congress.
29. In a letter in October the previous year, Roberts had alerted the Colonization Society that "on the authority of a French officer, stationed near Grand Cape Mount," the British were planning on some sort of action. Though he somewhat discounted the report, Roberts felt "something" was "in anticipation, and unless a powerful effort be made," the Cape Mount area would be lost, "which would indeed be a great calamity." The governor's premonition would, of course, prove right on the mark. Roberts to Rev. William McClain, Secretary and Treasurer of the A.C.S. the American Colonization Society, October 19, 1846, *African Repository and Colonial Journal* 23, no. 1 (1847): 26–27.

30. Burton, *Wanderings in West Africa*, vol. 1, 277.
31. Ibid., 278.
32. Theodore Canot, *Revelations of a Slave Trader; or Twenty Years Adventures of Captain Canot*, ed. Brantz Mayer (New York: D. Appleton and Co., 1856). Quoted in Johnston, *Liberia*, vol.1, 174.
33. Johnston, *Liberia*, vol. 1, 174.
34. *New York Times*, February 6, 1852.
35. Ibid.
36. Ibid.
37. See ibid.
38. See Tazewell, *Virginia's Ninth President*, 17–18.
39. William C. Burke to Robert E. Lee, August 20, 1854; and Rosabella Burke to Mrs. Robert E. Lee, August 21, 1854, *African Repository* 31 (1855).
40. J. H. T. McPherson, *History of Liberia,* Johns Hopkins University Studies in Historical and Political Science. 1891, 15. E-book released 2004, accessed December 11, 2015, http://guttenberg.org.
41. Sarah Joseph Hale, *Liberia, or Mr. Peyton's Experiments*, (New York: Harper & Brothers, 1853), 205.
42. William W. Findlay to Joseph A. Wright, March 8, 1853, *Indiana Historian* (2000), 12.
43. Samuel Webster to Morris and Birtch, January 12, 1853, *Indiana Historian* (2000), 13.
44. Jasper Brush, "Letter to Colored Friend in New York," 7 April 1852. Quoted in Hale, *Liberia*, 260.
45. McPherson, *History of Liberia*, 18, repeating the observations of a German official, Carl Ritter.
46. Tazewell, *Virginia's Ninth President*, 41; and McPherson, *History of Liberia*, 18.
47. *New York Times*, May 12, 1853.
48. *Chicago Daily Tribune*, February 11, 1856.

49. See Tazewell, *Virginia's Ninth President*, 48–49.
50. "Address of Hon. Joseph J. Roberts, Ex-President of Liberia," *African Repository* 14 (1869), 111.
51. Ibid., 103, 113.
52. Ibid., 113.
53. Ibid., 115.
54. Ibid., 117.
55. Ibid.

CHAPTER 8. THE REPUBLIC ESTABLISHED

1. For an upbeat 1869 review of Liberia's progress in the almost half century since its founding and its promise for the future, see "Address of Hon. Joseph J. Roberts, Ex-President of Liberia," *African Repository and Colonial Journal* 14, no. 1 (1869), 117.
2. Sir Harry Johnston, *Liberia*, vol.1 (1906; repr., New York: Negro Universities Press, 1969), 234.
3. Richard F. Burton, *Wanderings in West Africa*, Two Volumes Bound as One, vol. 2 (1863; repr., New York: Dover, 1991), 289.
4. See J. H. T. McPherson, *History of Liberia*. Johns Hopkins University Studies in Historical and Political Science. 1891, 15. E-book released 2004, accessed December 11, 2015, http://guttenberg.org.
5. See Carl Patrick Burrowes, *Power and Press Freedom in Liberia, 1830-1970: The Impact of Globalization and Civil Society on Media-Government Relations* (Trenton, N.J.: Africa World Press, 2004), 17; and David Sharit, *The United States in Africa: A Historical Dictionary* (New York: Greenwood Press, 1989), 189.
6. Andrew H. Foote, Papers of Andrew H. Foote 1822–1890, microfilm 19,988, reel 2 (manuscript of *Africa and the American Flag*), Manuscripts Division, Library of Congress, 131.
7. Ibid., 130.

8. Ibid., 156.
9. Ibid.
10. Ibid., 157.
11. Ibid., 132.
12. Peter Duignan and L. H. Gann, *The United States and Africa: A History* (New York: Cambridge University Press and the Hoover Institution, 1984,), 85.
13. Johnston, *Liberia*, vol. 1, 234.
14. Ibid., 237.
15. See *Maryland Colonization Journal* 8, no. 24 (1857). Sir Harry Johnston in his *Liberia*, vol.1, p. 237, gives the annexation date as February 28. *Wikipedia* says March 18.
16. Duignan and Gann, *United States and Africa*, 85.
17. James Fairhead, et al., eds., *African-American Exploration in West Africa: Four Nineteenth-Century Diaries* (Bloomington: Indiana University Press, 2003), 28.
18. Ibid., 3.
19. Ibid., 45.
20. Ibid., 3.
21. Ibid,. 48-49.
22. Ibid., 1, 4.
23. "Address of Hon. Joseph J. Roberts, Ex-President of Liberia," January 19, 1868. American Colonization Society, Washington, *African Repository* 14 (1869): 113–14.
24. Ibid., 113.
25. "Monrovia in 1866," *Cavalla (Liberia) Messenger*, *African Repository* 42 (1866): 327–29.
26. Ibid.
27. Amos J. Beyan, *African American Settlements in West Africa: John Brown Russwurm and the American Colonization Efforts* (New York: Palgrave, 2005), 60.
28. J. Gus Liebenow, *Liberia: The Quest for Democracy*. (Bloomington: Indiana University Press, 1983), 89-–90.

29. Arthur Barclay, "Annual Message to the Legislature of the Republic of Liberia," Monrovia, 1909, 108.
30. Joseph J. Roberts, "Forty-Ninth Annual Report," *African Repository and Colonial Journal* 11, no. 2 (January 1866): 43.
31. See Daniel Bashiel Warner, "Annual Address to the Legislature," *African Repository*, 42 (1866), 100–101; and Johnston, *Liberia*, vol. 1, 241–49.
32. Warner, ibid.
33. Ibid. Nevertheless, the law gave the Americo-Liberians a major advantage at the expense of native traders.
34. Johnston, *Liberia*, vol. 1, 248–49. See also See succeeding section, *Liberian Political Parties*, 254-55.
35. J. B. Pinney to President Abraham Lincoln, November 22, 1862, Abraham Lincoln Papers, series 1, General Correspondence, 1833–1916, Library of Congress.
36. Edith Holden, *Blyden of Liberia*, (New York: Vantage Press, 1967), 96.
37. Ibid., 100.
38. Ibid., 97.
39. Ibid., 107.
40. "Annual Message of President Warner," December 11, 1865, Monrovia, *African Repository*, 42 (1866): 9.
41. "Information about Going to Liberia" (published first as an American Colonization Society Brochure 1848), *African Repository*, 42 (1866): 237–41.
42. Ibid.
43. Ibid.
44. Ibid.
45. Ibid., 239.
46. Ibid., 241.
47. Holden, *Blyden of Liberia*, 19–21.
48. Edward Wilton Blyden, *Liberia's Offering* (New York: John A. Gray Press, 1862), ii.

49. Holden, *Blyden of Liberia*, 22.
50. Blyden, *Liberia's Offering*, ii.
51. Blyden to William Coppinger, September 13, 1884, microfilm, reel 166, American Colonization Records, Manuscripts Division, Library of Congress.
52. Edward Wilmot Blyden to J. B. Pinney, February 1851, *African Repository* 27 (1851): 266.
53. Ibid.
54. Holden, *Blyden of Liberia*, 30.
55. Ibid., 36.
56. See Holden, *Blyden of Liberia*, 38–40.
57. Ibid. 45.
58. "Items from *The Liberia Herald*," *African Repository* 30 (1854): 92–93.
59. Holden, *Blyden of Liberia*, 37.
60. Blyden to William Gladstone, April 20, 1860, quoted in Holden, *Blyden of Liberia*, 67.
61. See Holden, *Blyden of Liberia*, 65–66.
62. Blyden to Rev. J. J. Wilson, March 13, 1861, quoted in Holden, *Blyden of Liberia*, 78.
63. Ibid., 79.
64. Ibid., 69.
65. Ibid., 73.
66. Blyden, "Discourse," Presbyterian Church on 7th Avenue, New York City, July 21, 1861, quoted in Holden, *Blyden of Liberia*, 80.
67. Holden, *Blyden of Liberia*, 91–93.
68. Ibid., 91.
69. Ibid., 138.
70. Ibid., 130.
71. Blyden to B. V. R. James, April 13, 1866, quoted in Holden, *Blyden of Liberia*, 138–39.
72. Blyden, "The Duties and Responsibilities of a Pastor of a Church," *African Repository* 42 (1866): 246.

73. Pieter Boele van Hensbroek, "Confronting the European Challenge: Discourses in 19th Century African Political Thought," *African Political Philosophy, 1860–1995*, (Groningen, The Netherlands: Center for Development Studies University of Groningen, 1948), 20.
74. Holden, *Blyden of Liberia*, 161.
75. Van Hensbroek, "Confronting the European Challenge," 49.
76. Ibid., 52–53.
77. Donald A. Ranard, ed., "Liberians: An Introduction to Their History and Culture," *Culture Profile* no. 19 (Washington: Center for Applied Linguistics, 2005), 10–12.
78. See Blyden to Dr. Walter Lowrie, January 15, 1876, quoted in Holden, *Blyden of Liberia*, 328.

CHAPTER 9. A SCANDAL, COUP, AND MYSTERY

1. *Newark Advocate*, April 22, 1984.
2. David Sharit, *The United States in Africa: A Historical Dictionary* (New York: Greenwood Press, 1989), 88.
3. F. P. M. Van der Kraaij, *The Open Door Policy of Liberia: An Economic History of Modern Liberia* (Bremen: Im Selbstverlag des Museums, 1983), vol. 1, 24.
4. See Frederick Starr, *Liberia: Description, History, Problems,* (Chicago: Privately published, 1913), 199–202; and "Annual Message of President Roberts" December 9, 1872, *African Repository* 49 (1873): 173.
5. "Annual Message of President Roberts," December 9, 1872, *African Repository* 47 (1872): 173.
6. See ibid.

7. Ibid.
8. Ibid., 174.
9. "Liberia Not Prospering," quoted in Edith Holden, *Blyden of Liberia* (New York: Vantage Press, 1967, 179–80.
10. *New York Tribune,* June 9, 1871, quoted in Holden, *Blyden of Liberia,* 180.
11. Sir Harry Johnston, *Liberia,* vol. 1 (1906; New York: Negro Universities Press, 1969), 260–61.
12. Ibid., 261.
13. "The Drowning of President Roye," *African Repository* 48 (1872): 220–26.
14. Ibid.
15. Equally mysterious is what exactly happened to the money from the loan. Most would-be sleuths believe not more than £20,000 ($100,000) reached Liberia. Some say only £8,000 ($40,000) made it. See Van der Kraaij, *The Open Door Policy,* vol. 1 ,25.
16. "President Edward J. Roye (1870–1871)," *Liberia Past and Present,* http://liberiapastandpre.org/EJRroye.htm; also Johnston, *Liberia,* vol. 1, 261–62.
17. Holden, *Blyden of Liberia,* 179.
18. See "President Edward J. Roye (1870–1871)," http://liberiapastandpresent.org.EJRoye.htm.
19. Johnston, Liberia, vol. 1, 262. Anderson refused to return to Liberia unless he was guaranteed freedom from prosecution.
20. For a full account of the loan and its consequences, see Johnston, Liberia, vol. 1, chapter 15; and Starr, Description, History, Problems, 199–202.
21. Henry W. Dennis to Dr. William McLain, May 6, 1871, quoted in Holden, *Blyden of Liberia,* 175. Also see Holden, 175–185.
22. Ibid.

23. Ibid.
24. J. B. Pinney to McClain, June 6, 1871, Holden, *Blyden of Liberia*, 177.
25. Rev. Dr. Joseph Tracy to McLain, Holden, *Blyden of Liberia*, 181.
26. Pinney to McLain, Holden, *Blyden of Liberia*, 177.
27. Ibid.
28. Ibid., 177–78.
29. Ibid.
30. Tracy to McLain, quoted in Holden, *Blyden of Liberia*, 181.
31. William Coppinger to H. W. Dennis, quoted in Holden, *Blyden of Liberia*, 181.
32. Tracy to McLain, quoted in Holden, *Blyden of Liberia*, 179.
33. Blyden to Coppinger, quoted in Holden, *Blyden of Liberia*, 206.
34. "Address of Hon. Joseph J. Roberts, Ex-President of Liberia," January 19, 1868, American Colonization Society, Washington, *African Repository* 4 (1869): 103–17.
35. Blyden to Coppinger, quoted in Holden, *Blyden of Liberia*, 206.
36. Ibid., 207.
37. "Inaugural Address of President Roberts," January 1, 1872, *African Repository*, 48, no. 4 (1872): 103–6.13
38. Roberts to American Colonization Society, May 1, 1872, quoted in *African Repository*, 48, no. 5 (1872): 254.
39. "Inaugural Address of President Roberts," January 5, 1874, *African Repository* 50, no. 1 (1874), 193–94.
40. Ibid., 197.
41. Roland Oliver and G. N. Sanderson, eds., *The Cambridge History of Africa*, vol. 6, (Cambridge: Cambridge University Press, 1981), 226.
42. Ibid.
43. *New York Times*, October 12, 1875.

44. *New York Times*, November 25, 1875.
45. Ibid.
46. *New York Times*, December 3, 1875.
47. Oliver and Sanderson, *Cambridge History*, 226. William Wade Harris, popularly known as Prophet Harris, the "Black Elijah" of west Africa, was a Grebo tribesman from Liberia. His prophetic mission during 1910–29 "attracted tens of thousands of West Africans...especially in the Ivory Coast" away from traditional native religions "into Christianity and modernization." See also David A. Shark and Jocelyn Murray, *Prophet Harris, the "Black Elijah" of West Africa: Thought of William Wade Harris* (Leiden: E. J. Brill, 1994).
48. Roberts to Dr. [Walter] Lowrie, January 15, 1876, quoted in Holden, *Blyden of Liberia*, 328. Lowrie was a member of the American Colonization Society's Executive Committee and secretary of the Board of Foreign Missions.
49. Johnston, *Liberia*, vol. 1, 264. According to Johnston, Roberts had just attended a colleague's funeral when a "tornado burst with an awful downpour of rain."
50. Rev. John Maclean, Introduction of Ex-President Roberts in a Meeting in Jersey City, New Jersey in 1869, *Evening Journal* (Jersey City, NJ), quoted in *African Repository* 45 (1869): 234.
51. Johnston, *Liberia*, vol. 1, 236.
52. Pieter Boele Van Hensbroek, "Confronting the European Challenge: Discourses in 19th Century African Political Thought," *African Political Philosophy, 1860-1995* (Groningen, the Netherlands: Center for Development Studies University of Groningen, 1948), 31.
53. Blyden to Dr. Lowrie, January 15, 1876, quoted in Holden, *Blyden of Liberia*, 328.
54. J. Gus Liebenow, *Liberia: The Quest for Democracy* (Bloomington: Indiana University Press, 1983), 91.

55. See Donald A. Ranard, ed., *Liberians: An Introduction to Their History and Culture*, Culture Profile No. 19, April 2005. Washington, DC: Center for Applied Linguistics, 10–12.
56. Liebenow, *Quest for Democracy*, 90.
57. Ibid., 91
58. Ibid., 92.

CHAPTER 10. THE 1870s: COMING OF AGE

1. Sir Harry H. Johnston, *Liberia*, vol. 1, (1906; repr., New York: Negro Universities Press, 1969), 274.
2. J. Gus Liebenow. *Liberia: The Quest for Democracy*. (Bloomington: Indiana University Press, 1983), 19.
3. H. Johnston, *Liberia*, vol. 1, 274.
4. J. Gus Liebenow, *Liberia: The Evolution of Privilege* (Ithaca, NY: Cornell University Press, 1969).
5. Carl Patrick Burrowes, *The Americo-Liberian Ruling Class and Other Myths: A Critique of Political Science in the Liberian Context*, occasional paper no. 3, (Philadelphia: Temple University, 1989), 4.
6. Liebenow, *Quest for Democracy*, 19, table 2.
7. Ibid., 49.
8. "Death of Commodore R. F. Stockton," *African Repository* 42 (1866): 349.
9. "Address of Hon. Joseph J. Roberts, Ex-President of Liberia," January 19, 1868, American Colonization Society, Washington, *African Repository*, 14 (1869): 104.
10. Hassan B. Sisay, *Big Powers and Small Nations: A Case Study of United States-Liberian Relations*, (Lanham, MD: University Press of America, 1958), 106–107.
11. Ibid.

12. J. B. Pinney to the American Colonization Society, February 10, 1833, *The African Depository and Colonial Journal* 9 (1833): 60. Quoted in Johnston, *Liberia*, vol. 1, 25.
13. Ibid.; and Liebenow, *Quest for Democracy*, 48–49.
14. Liebenow, *Quest for Democracy*, 48–49.
15. Jehudi Ashmun, Journal, August 21, 1821, in *American Colonization Society, Sixth Annual Report*, appendix, 30. Quoted in Boley, *Rise and Fall*, 23; and Liebenow, *Quest for Democracy*, 49.
16. Joseph Mechlin Jr. to Rev. R. R. Gurley, April 1832, quoted in *African Depository and Colonial Journal* 8, no. 5 (1832), 135. The letter also gives an interesting account of one of the tribal wars.
17. Liebenow, *Quest for Democracy*, 49.
18. See ibid.
19. Ibid., 48.
20. Konia Kollehlon, "Life in Liberia," in Ranard, *Liberians: An Introduction*, 4.
21. Liebenow, *Quest for Democracy*, 48.
22. Ibid.
23. Ibid.
24. Ibid., 27.
25. Ibid.
26. Rosalind Cobb Wiggins, *Captain Paul Cuffe's Logs and Letters, 1808–1817: A Black Quaker's "Voice from within the Veil"* (Washington, DC: Howard University, 1996), 115.
27. Alan Huffman, *Mississippi in Africa* (New York: Gotham Books, 2005), 155.
28. Ibid.
29. Ibid.
30. Ibid.; and Liebenow, *Quest for Democracy*, 22.
31. Ibid., 21.

32. Ibid., 22.
33. Ibid.
34. *Liberia Herald*, April 17, 1854.
35. Peter Duignan and L.H. Gann, *The United States and Africa: A History*, (New York: Cambridge University Press and the Hoover Institution, 1984), 118. See also US Department of State, *Papers Relating to Foreign Relations of the United States 1872–1873*, 330–37, and *1879*, 699–701. James Milton Turner, the first black US Foreign Service officer, served as consul-general to Liberia 1871–78. Highly critical of the Americo-Liberians and colonization, Turner was recalled at the government's insistence. See Gary Kremer, *James Milton Turner and the Promise of America* (Colombia: University of Missouri Press, 1991); and *Liberian Politics: The Portrait by African American Diplomat J. Milton Turner*, ed. Hanes Walton Jr., James Bernard Sr., and Robert L. Stevenson.
36. "Legislature-House Bills," *African Repository* 49 (1873): 212.
37. "Liberian Affairs," *African Repository* 49 (1873): 307.
38. "A Coffee Huller for Liberia," *African Repository* 49 (1873): 21.
39. Liebenow, *Quest for Democracy*, 21.
40. Amos J. Beyan, *African American Settlements in West Africa: John Brown Russwurm and the American Colonization Efforts* (New York: Palgrave, 2005), 61.
41. Ibid.
42. Liebenow, *Quest for Democracy*, 23.
43. Ibid.
44. US Department of State, *Papers Relating to the Foreign Relations of the United States 1882* (Washington: GPO), 611. The entire series of these papers, which began in 1861, can be viewed on the US Department of the Historian website, www.history.state.gov/historicaldocuments. University of Wisconsin–Madison Libraries Digital Collections, www.digicoll.library.wisc.edu.

45. Anthony W. Gardiner, "Message of President Gardiner," *African Repository* 49 (1873): 110.
46. Liebenow, *Quest for Democracy*, 21.
47. See ibid., 22–23.
48. Ibid., 22.
49. Ibid.
50. G. E. Saigbe Boley, *Liberia: The Rise and Fall of the First Republic* (London: Macmillan, 1983), 32.
51. Duignan and Gann, *United States and Africa*, 195.
52. James Fairhead, et al., eds., *African-American Exploration in West Africa: Four Nineteenth-Century Diaries* (Bloomington: Indiana University Press, 2003), 1.

CHAPTER 11. THE UNKNOWN HINTERLAND

1. Geysbeek, Tim. "Brief Sketch of the Life and Character of the Late Hon. Benj. J.K. Anderson, M.A., PH. D., K.C" *History in Africa*. African Studies Association 34 (2007): 46. Geysbeek quotes from an obituary probably written by Anderson's son, Benjamin John Knight Anderson, discovered in 2000 at the University of Chicago's Regenstein Library.
2. Ibid., 46 n9, 46 n21.
3. Donald A. Ranard, ed., *Liberians: An Introduction to Their History and Culture,* Culture Profile No. 19 (Washington, DC: Center for Applied Linguistics, 2005), 7.
4. Ibid.
5. Ibid., 46.
6. Ibid., n28.
7. Ibid., 51.
8. Ibid., 47.

9. James Fairhead, et al., eds., *African-American Exploration in West Africa: Four Nineteenth-Century Diaries* (Bloomington: Indiana University Press, 2003), 3.
10. Ibid., 23.
11. See Ibid., 24.
12. Ibid.
13. Tim Geysbeek, "The Anderson-d'Ollone Controversy of 1903–04: Race, Imperialism, and the Reconfiguration of the Liberia-Guinea Border," *History in Africa* 31 (2004): 186.
14. Peter Duignan and L.H. Gann, *The United States and Africa: A History* (New York: Cambridge University Press and the Hoover Institution, 1984,), 118 n2.
15. See Fairhead et al., eds., *African-American Exploration*, particularly chapters 1 and 5, for an excellent account of Anderson and his and others' expeditions. The book also includes a very useful background to colonization and the creation of Liberia.
16. Benjamin J. K. Anderson, "The Country East of Liberia," *African Repository* 46 (1870), 132. Note: "The Country East of Liberia" is a series of excerpts from Anderson's book, *Narrative of a Journey to Musardu, the Capital of the Western Mandingoes*, contained in this volume of *The African Repository*.
17. Ibid., 278.
18. Ibid., 133–34.
19. Ibid.
20. Ibid., 134.
21. Ibid.
22. Ibid., 135.
23. Ibid.
24. Ibid.
25. Ibid., 137.
26. Ibid., 136.
27. Ibid., 137–38.
28. Ibid., 297.

29. Ibid.
30. Ibid., 140.
31. Ibid.
32. Ibid., 145.
33. Ibid., 162. The overabundance of and variety in spelling tribal names is daunting. Some of the most common are:Pessey=southern Kpelle; Barline, Barlain, Berlu, Gbalein=Kpelle; Boozie=Loma or Toma; Mandiko, Manduka, and Manduko=Mandingo. See also chapter 5, 129-31.
34. Ibid., 180.
35. Ibid., 158
36. Ibid, 181–82.
37. Ibid., 182.
38. Anderson, "Country East," 186.
39. Ibid.
40. Ibid., 187.
41. Ibid.
42. Ibid., 188.
43. Ibid., 190–91.
44. Ibid., 191.
45. Ibid., 213.
46. Ibid., 214.
47. Ibid.
48. Ibid., 215.
49. Ibid.
50. Ibid.
51. Ibid., 217.
52. Ibid.
53. Ibid.
54. Ibid.
55. Ibid.
56. Ibid.
57. Ibid., 218.
58. Ibid.

59. Ibid., 218–19.
60. Ibid., 219.
61. Ibid.
62. Ibid.
63. Ibid., 220.
64. Ibid.
65. Ibid., 221.
66. Ibid., 243, 245.
67. Ibid., 244.
68. Ibid.
69. Ibid.
70. Ibid., 246.
71. Ibid., 245.
72. Ibid., 247.
73. Ibid.
74. Ibid., 247
75. Ibid., 247.
76. Ibid., 248.
77. Ibid., 248
78. Ibid., 249
79. Ibid., 281.
80. Ibid., 259.
81. Ibid., 263.
82. Ibid., 263.
83. Ibid., 300.
84. Ibid., 265
85. Ibid., 265
86. Ibid., 248.
87. Ibid., 278
88. Ibid., 279.
89. Ibid., 266
90. Ibid., 299.
91. Ibid., 301.

92. J. Gus Liebenow, *Liberia: The Quest for Democracy* (Bloomington: Indiana University Press, 1983), 26.
93. Duignan and Gann, *United States and Africa*, 118.
94. Anderson, "Country East," 133.
95. Sir Harry H. Johnston, *Liberia*, vol. 1, (1906; repr., New York: Negro Universities Press, 1969), 254.
96. Geysbeek, "Brief Sketch," 47.
97. Ibid., 48 n16; and Fairhead, et al., 72.
98. Geysbeek, "Brief Sketch," 48.
99. See Geysbeek, "The Anderson-d'Ollone Controversy," 187.
100. Geysbeek, "Brief Sketch," 48, n15.
101. Ibid., 278.
102. Anderson., "The Country East," 261.
103. Ibid., 262.
104. Duignan and Gann, *United States and Africa*, 118.
105. Johnston, *Liberia*, vol. 1, 274.

CHAPTER 12. THE SCRAMBLE

1. Thomas Pakenham, *The Scramble for Africa: White Man's Conquest of the Dark Continent from 1876 to 1912* (New York: Avon Books, 1991), 239.
2. Ibid., 241.
3. Ibid., 254.
4. See Sir Harry H. Johnston, *Liberia*, vol. 1, (1906; repr., New York: Negro Universities Press, 1969), 242-43. Johnston in Chapter IV provides a full account of the dispute and the problems the 1865 Ports of Entry Law later generated on the borders with both British and French possessions.
5. Peter Duignan and L. H. Gann, *The United States and Africa: A History* (New York: Cambridge University Press, 1984), 121.

6. US Department of State, Office of the Historian, *Milestones 1866–1898: Commodore Robert W. Shufeldt's Voyage to Africa, the Middle East, and Asia, 1878–1880* (Washington, DC), 2, http://history.state.gov/milestones/1866-1898/commodore-shufeldt.
7. Duignan and Gann, *United States and Africa*, 121.
8. Sixty-Sixth Annual Report of the American Colonization Society, April 1883, *African Repository*, 59, no. 2 (1883): 40.
9. George B. Cartland, "Havelock, Sir Arthur Elibank (1844–1908)," *Australian Dictionary of Biography*, vol. 9, 2015, http://adb.anu.edu.au/biography/havelock/.
10. US Department of State, *Papers Relating to the Foreign Relations of the United State 1882* (Washington: GPO), 612.
11. Duignan and Gann, *United States and Africa*, 121; see also Nathaniel R. Richardson, *Liberia's Past and Present* (London: Diplomatic Press, 1959), 121; J. H. T. McPherson, *History of Liberia* (Baltimore: Johns Hopkins University, 2004), 24.
12. Edith Holden, *Blyden of Liberia* (New York: Vantage Press, 1967), 180.
13. Ibid., 380.
14. Ibid., 381.
15. Ibid., 383.
16. Ibid., 382.
17. Ibid., 383.
18. Sixty-Sixth Annual Report, *African Repository*, 59.2 (1883), 40.
19. "British Aggression in Liberia," *African Repository*, 58.3 (1882), 91.
20. "Liberia's Peril," *African Repository*, 58.3 (1882), 94.
21. Sixty-sixth Annual Report, *African Repository*, 40.
22. Anthony W. Gardiner, "Annual Message to the Legislature," Monrovia, December 6, 1882, quoted in Smith to Frelinghuysen, *Foreign Relations of the United States 1882*, 612.

23. US Department of State, *Papers Relating to the Foreign Relations of the United State 1882* (Washington: GPO), *612*.
24. *US Foreign Relations 1882*, 610.
25. Ibid., 615–16.
26. Johnston, *Liberia*, vol. 1, 279.
27. The country would be reduced in size to approximately forty-three thousand square miles, about the size of Portugal. J. Gus Liebenow, *Liberia: The Quest for Democracy* (Bloomington: Indiana University Press, 1983), 28.
28. Ibid.
29. Duignan and Gann, *United States and Africa*, 121.
30. Kevin Skillington, *Encyclopedia of African History* (New York: Routledge, 2004), 820.
31. McPherson, *History of Liberia*, 38.
32. Holden, *Blyden of Liberia*, 381.
33. Duignan and Gann, *United States and Africa*, 119.
34. Ibid, 120.
35. Ibid, 119.
36. Ibid, 120.
37. Pakenham, *Scramble for Africa*, 205.
38. Ibid.
39. Ibid., 756.
40. Ibid.
41. Johnston, *Liberia*, vol. 1, 290.
42. Ibid., 291.
43. Ibid., 292.
44. Duignan and Gann, *United States and Africa*, 122–23.
45. Ibid.
46. Liebenow, *Quest for Democracy*, 124.
47. Ibid.
48. Duignan and Gann, *United States and Africa*, 124.

49. Bruce W. Jentleson and Thomas G. Paterson, eds. *Encyclopedia of US Foreign Relations*, vol. 3. (New York: Oxford University Press, 1997), 65–66.
50. Tim Geysbeek, "The Anderson-d'Ollone Controversy of 1903–04: Race, Imperialism, and the Reconfiguration of the Liberia-Guinea Border," *History in Africa* 31 (2004): 186.
51. Ibid., 187.
52. Ibid.
53. Ibid., 186–87.
54. Ibid., 190.
55. Ibid., 8–9.
56. Liebenow, *Quest for Democracy*, 26.
57. Ibid., 28.
58. Ibid., 98.
59. Johnston, vol. 1, *Liberia*, 276.
60. Ibid.
61. Ibid.

CHAPTER 13. THE BARCLAYS OF BARBADOS

1. Edward Wilmot Blyden, "Monrovia in 1866," *African Repository* 42 (1866): 328–29.
2. F. P. M. Van der Kraaij, *The Open Door Policy of Liberia: An Economic History of Modern Liberia* (Bremen: Im Selbstverlag des Museums, 1983), vol.1, annex 2n118.
3. Ibid., n120.
4. Alex Johnston, *The Life and Letters of Sir Harry Johnston* (1929; repr., London: Kessinger, 2010), 253.
5. Ibid., 41.
6. Ibid.
7. Ibid., 91.
8. Ibid., 137.

9. Ibid., 152.
10. Sir Harry Johnston, *Liberia*, vol. 1, (1906; repr., New York: Negro Universities Press, 1969), 382.
11. Sir Harry Hamilton Johnston, *The Story of My Life* (Indianapolis: Bobbs-Merrill Co., 1923), 371, 402.
12. Ibid., 288.
13. Anthony W. Gardiner, "Annual Message to the Legislature," Monrovia, December 6, 1882, quoted in *Papers Related to Foreign Relations of the United States 1882* (Washington: GPO), 614
14. Van der Kraaij, *Open Door Policy*, vol. 1, 30.
15. Ibid.
16. C. T. O. King, "Liberia before Europe," in *Weekly News* (Sierra Leone), *African Repository* 66 (1890): 125–26.
17. Ibid., 30 and n85.
18. See H. Johnston, *Story of My Life*, 416.
19. See Benjamin Brawley, *A Social History of the American Negro*, 1921 (New York: AMS Press, 1971), 199.
20. A. Johnston, *Sir Harry Johnston*, 251.
21. Ibid., 252.
22. H. Johnston, *Story of My Life*, 373.
23. Ibid., 404.
24. A. Johnston, *Sir Harry Johnston*, 405.
25. H. Johnston, *Story of My Life*, 375.
26. Ibid., 407.
27. Ibid.
28. See Ibid., 408.
29. Ibid., 407.
30. See Frederick Starr, *Liberia: Description, History, Problems* (Chicago: Privately published, 1913), 202–205. See also Van der Kraaij, *Open Door Policy*, vol. 1, 35. Some of the latter's details vary from Starr's. The annual interest on the loan, for example, is given at £30,000 rather than $30,000.
31. Ibid., 204.

32. Ibid.
33. Ibid., 203.
34. Ibid. See also J. D. Fage, et al., *The Cambridge History of Africa*, vol. 7 (Cambridge: Cambridge University Press, 1970–85), 456.
35. Starr, *Description, History, Problems*, 205 quoting the investigation's findings.
36. Raymond W. Smock, ed., *Booker T. Washington in Perspective: Essays of Louis R. Harlan* (Jackson: University Press of Mississippi, 1988), 78.
37. H. Johnston, *Liberia*, vol. 1, 408.
38. Ibid.
39. G. E. Saigbe Boley, *Liberia: The Rise and Fall of the First Republic* (London: Macmillan, 1983), 35.
40. Pieter Boele Van Hensbroek, "Confronting the European Challenge: Discourses in 19th Century African Political Thought," *African Political Philosophy, 1860–1995* (Groningen, the Netherlands: Center for Development Studies University of Groningen, 1948), 48.
41. Hakim Adi and Marika Sherwood, *Pan-African History: Figures from Africa and the Diaspora Since 1787* (London: Routledge, 2005), 12.
42. Van Hensbroek, "Confronting the European Challenge," 52.
43. Starr, *Description, History, Problems*, 116.
44. Ibid., 110.
45. Ibid.
46. Ibid., 116.
47. Ibid.
48. J. Gus Liebenow, *Liberia: The Quest for Democracy* (Bloomington: Indiana University Press, 1983), 28.
49. Starr, *Description, History, Problems*, 121.
50. Liebenow, *Quest for Democracy*, 28.

51. US Department of State, *Diplomatic and Consular Messages*, vol. 9 (Washington: GPO, 1909), 255–57.
52. Starr, *Description, History, Problems*, 118.
53. Ibid., 119–20.
54. See Robert L Keiser, *Liberia: A Report on the Relations Between the United States and Liberia* (Washington, DC: GPO, 1928), 29, quoted in Starr, *Description, History, Problems*, 120; and Hassan B. Sisay, *Big Powers and Small Nations: A Case Study of United States-Liberian Relations* (Lanham, MD: University Press of America, 1958), 29.
55. Starr, *Description, History, Problems*, 120.
56. Ibid., 142.
57. Smock, *Booker T. Washington*, 79.
58. Starr, *Description, History, Problems*, 122.
59. Peter Duignan and L. H. Gann, *The United States and Africa: A History* (New York: Cambridge University Press and the Hoover Institution, 1984), 195.
60. Starr, *Description, History, Problems*, 123.
61. Sisay, *Big Powers and Small Nations*, 29. See also John Mitchell, "America's Liberian Policy" (PhD diss., University of Chicago, 1955), 62–63, microfilm 57005396.
62. H. Johnston, *Liberia*, vol. 1, 408.
63. Duignan and Gann, *United States and Africa*, 196. The commission, appointed March 4 by President William Howard Taft, consisted of Richard P. Falkland, George Sale, and Emmet J. Scott. They arrived in Monrovia May 8 and spent thirty days in Liberia and Sierra Leone.
64. Ibid., 197.
65. Smock, *Booker T. Washington*, 79.
66. Duignan and Gann, *United States and Africa*, 196.
67. Smock, *Booker T. Washington*, 79.
68. Ibid.
69. Ibid.

70. "Affairs in Liberia," Commission's Official Report to the President of the United States, *Senate Executive Documents*, United States Senate, 61st Congress, 2d session, 1909 (Washington DC: GPO), 14–19.
71. Smock, *Booker T. Washington*, 78.
72. H. Johnston, *Story of My Life*, 383–384. See also Duignan and Gann, *United States and Africa*, 195.
73. Duignan and Gann, *United States and Africa*, 187.
74. Ibid., 195.
75. *New York Times*, August 10, 1908.
76. Smock, *Booker T. Washington*, 79.
77. Keiser, *Liberia: A Report*, 698.
78. H. Johnston, *Story of My Life*, 388.
79. Starr, *Description, History, Problems*, 248–249.
80. *Foreign Relations of the United States 1910*, 699–700.
81. Knox to Commission, April 13, 1909, *Foreign Relations of the United States 1909*, 700.
82. Starr, *Description, History, Problems*, 273–74.
83. United States Senate, "Affairs in Liberia," *Senate Executive Documents*, 61st Cong., no. 452d sess., no. 457, 14–19, quoted in Duignan and Gann, *United States and Africa*, 196.
84. Ibid.
85. See Sisay, *Big Powers and Small Nations*, 31.
86. Raymond Leslie Buell, *Foreign Policy Reports: The Reconstruction of Liberia* (New York: Foreign Policy Association, 1932), 804.
87. Duignan and Gann, *United States and Africa*, 199. See *Foreign Relations of the United States 1911*, 654–62.
88. Duignan and Gann, *United States and Africa*, 199.
89. Ibid.
90. Ibid., 200.
91. Ibid.
92. Ibid., 121.

93. See H. O. Akingbade, "The Role of the Military in the History of Liberia, 1822–1947" (Ph.D. thesis, Howard University, 1976).
94. Ibid., 198.
95. Liebenow, *Quest for Democracy*, 180.
96. Ibid., 178–79.
97. Sanford J. Ungar, *Africa: The People and Politics of an Emerging Continent* (New York: Simon and Schuster, 1989), 91.
98. Van der Kraaij, *Open Door Policy*, vol. 1, 32.
99. Ibid., 33.
100. See Liebenow, *Quest for Democracy*, 74.
101. Arthur Barclay, "Annual Message to the Legislature of the Republic of Liberia" (Monrovia, 1909) quoted in Van der Kraaij, *Open Door Policy*, vol. 1, 32 and n107.
102. By 1910 public debt had reached $1,289,570, consisting of $443,025 in principal and unpaid interest on the 1871 loan, $464,640 on the 1906 loan, plus $381,905 in treasury notes. Boley, *Liberia: Rise and Fall*, 35.
103. Van der Kraaij, *Open Door Policy*, vol. 1, 32 and n94.
104. Van Hensbroek, 31.
105. Ibid., 47.
106. Ibid.
107. A. Johnston, *Life and Letters*, 260.
108. Ibid., 288.
109. Ibid., 339
110. Liebenow, *Quest for Democracy*, 110.

CHAPTER 14. ONE FOR THE RECORD BOOK

1. See Frederick Starr, *Liberia: Description, History, Problems* (Chicago: Privately published, 1913), 98.

2. Liberian Forum, "Liberia Background: Liberian Presidents," last modified 01/05/2015, http://www.liberianforum.com/history.htm.
3. Starr, *Description, History, Problems,* 97–98.
4. Ronald W. Davis, *Ethnohistorical Studies on the Kru Coast,* Liberian Studies, Monograph Series, no. 5 (Newark: University of Delaware, 1976), 54, cited in F. P. M. Van der Kraaij, *The Open Door Policy of Liberia: An Economic History of Modern Liberia,* vol. 1 (Bremen: Im Selbstverlag des Museums, 1983), 37.
5. Robert E. Keiser, *Liberia: A Report on the Relations Between the United States and Liberia* (Washington: GPO, 1928), 161.
6. See Duignan and Gann, *The United States and Africa: A History* (New York: Cambridge University Press and the Hoover Institution, 1984), 200.
7. Ibid.
8. See Dugnan and Gann, *United States and Africa,* 404 n39.
9. See F. P. M. Van der Kraaij, *The Open Door Policy of Liberia: An Economic History of Modern Liberia* (Bremen: Im Selbstverlag des Museums, 1983), vol. 1, 37.
10. See Thomas Pakenham, *The Scramble for Africa: White Man's Conquest of the Dark Continent from 1876 to 1912* (New York: Avon Books, 1991), 253–54.
11. G. E. Saigbe Boley, *Liberia: The Rise and Fall of the First Republic* (London: Macmillan, 1983), 37.
12. See Van der Kraaij, *Open Door Policy,* vol. 1, 38.
13. See Boley, *Liberia: Rise and Fall,* 37.
14. Nathaniel R. Richardson, *Liberia's Past and Present* (London: Diplomatic Press, 1959), 129.
15. Ibid, 130.
16. See Solomon Porter Hood to Secretary of State, February 17, 1924, *Documents in Affairs of Liberia,* Decimal File 882.00/738, reel 12, cited in Hassan B. Sisay, *Big Powers and Small Nations:*

A Case Study of United States-Liberian Relations (Lanham MD: University Press of America, 1958), 33.
17. *New York Times,* June 14, 1918.
18. Ibid.
19. *New York Times,* March 29, 1922.
20. *New York Times,* August 3 1920.
21. 1W. E. B. Du Bois, "Back to Africa," *Century* February 1923, quoted in John Henrik Clarke, ed., *Marcus Garvey and the Vision of Africa* (New York: Vantage Books, 1974), 105-106.
22. Ibid.
23. *New York Times,* March 7, 1921.
24. Ibid.
25. *New York Times,* January 25, 1922.
26. *New York Times,* March 7, 1922.
27. *New York Times,* March 29, 1922.
28. *New York Times,* November 29, 1922.
29. *New York Times,* November 25, 1922.
30. *New York Times,* March 20, 1922.
31. See Robert G. Weisbord, "Marcus Garvey, Pan-Negroist: The View from Whitehall," in Clarke, *Marcus Garvey,* 421–27.
32. Barclay to Garcia, June 14, 1920, in Amy Jacques Garvey, ed., *The Philosophy and Opinions of Marcus Garvey,* (London: Frank Caee & Co.), 365, quoted in Weisbord, 423.
33. Weisbord, 423.
34. See "Marcus Garvey Timeline," *American Experience,* http://www.pbs.org/wgbh/amex/garvey/timeline/index.html.
35. Marcus Garvey, "Speech at Royal Albert Hall," June 6, 1928, quoted in Clarke, *Marcus Garvey,* 293.
36. Ibid.
37. See Clarke, *Marcus Garvey,* 104; and Garvey, "Royal Albert Hall," in Clarke, *Marcus Garvey,* 284–99.
38. *New York Times,* August 27, 1924

39. Du Bois, in Clarke, *Marcus Garvey*, 105–19.
40. Garvey, "Royal Albert Hall," in Clarke, *Marcus Garvey*, 293.
41. *Wikipedia*, s.v. Marcus Garvey, last modified 2014, http://en.wikipedia.org/wiki/Marcus_Garvey; and "Marcus Garvey Timeline," *American Experience*,
42. "Marcus Garvey Timeline."
43. Ibid. Actually, these outbreaks would be only a prelude to the disaster known as the 1927 Tulsa, Oklahoma, race riot, one of the worst in the nation's history. According to the *Washington Post* (May 27, 2012), a rumor that "a young black male had improperly touched a white female elevator operator" sparked the onslaught. "About 300 people---90 percent of them African American---were killed [and] more than 1,200 houses destroyed, along with dozens of office buildings, restaurants, churches and schools."
44. Hoover headed the Justice Department's Alien Enemy Bureau. He became head in 1919 of the Bureau of Investigation's "Radical Division" and in 1924 director of the Bureau (renamed the Federal Bureau of Investigation in 1935).
45. Ibid.
46. Ibid.
47. Ibid.
48. See Hugh Mulzak, "Memories of a Captain of the Black Star Line," from *A Star to Steer By* (New York: International, 1963), in Clarke, *Marcus Garvey*, 127–38.
49. "Marcus Garvey Timeline."
50. Ibid.
51. *New York Times*, August 2, 1924.
52. *New York Times*, September 15, 1924.
53. Ibid., 49.
54. Ibid, 49; and *New York Times*, March 13, 1923
55. Sisay, *Big Powers and Small Nations*, 51.

56. *American Automobile Rubber Report* (Washington: American Automobile Office, 1926), 14, quoted in Sisay, *Big Powers and Small Nations*, 51.
57. *New York Times,* July 23, 1925.
58. Joseph Brandes, *Herbert Hoover and Economic Diplomacy: Department of Commerce Policy, 1921–1928,* (Pittsburg: University of Pittsburg Press, 1962), 118, quoted in Sisay, *Big Powers and Small Nations*, 52.
59. Sisay, *Big Powers and Small Nations*, 52.
60. Ibid, 53.
61. Ibid., 55.
62. Ibid.
63. Hughes to Harvey Firestone, December 22, 1924, *Documents in Affairs of Liberia*, microfilm, file 882.6176 F51/4, reel 20, quoted in Sisay, *Big Powers and Small Nations*, 56.
64. Sisay, *Big Powers and Small Nations*, 56.
65. US Department of State, *Papers Relating to the Foreign Relations of the United States 1925*, vol. 2, (Washington: GPO, 1943), 536, quoted in Sisay, *Big Powers and Small Nations*, 58.
66. Sisay, *Big Powers and Small Nations*, 58.
67. Ibid., 59.
68. Ibid., 58–59.
69. Ibid., 60.
70. Ibid., 59.
71. Duignan and Gann, *United States and Africa*, 221.
72. Ibid.
73. Ibid., 222.
74. Ibid., 221.
75. Alfred Lief, *The Firestone Story* (New York: McGraw-Hill, 1951), 165, quoted in Sisay, *Big Powers and Small Nations*, 67.
76. Garvey, "Royal Albert Hall," in Clarke, 294.

77. Garvey, "The Communists and the Negro," *The New Jamaican*, September 5, 1932, in Clarke, *Marcus Garvey*, 320.
78. Du Bois, "Back to Africa," in Clarke, *Marcus Garvey*, 112.
79. Ibid.
80. DuBois, "Marcus Garvey and His Critics," *The Crisis*, December 1920, 58–60; January 1921, 112–115, in Clarke, *Marcus Garvey*, 304.
81. See Weisbord, "Marcus Garvey, Pan-Negroist," *RACE* (London: Institute of Race Relations 1968), in Clarke, *Marcus Garvey*, 426.
82. Ibid., 424.
83. Clarke, "Commentary," in *Marcus Garvey*, 260.
84. *New York Times*, October 29, 1928.
85. "Marcus Garvey Timeline."
86. Marcus Garvey Jr., "Garveyism: Some Reflections on Its Significance Today," in Clarke, *Marcus Garvey*, 379.
87. Ibid., 382.
88. Clarke, "Commentary," in *Marcus Garvey*, 3.
89. Weisbord, "Marcus Garvey, Pan-Negroist," in Clarke, *Marcus Garvey*, 427.
90. Ibid., 426.
91. Raymond L. Buell, *Liberia: A Century of Survival 1847–1947*, African Handbook No.7 (Philadelphia: University Museum, University of Pennsylvania, 1947), 8.
92. Van der Kraaij, *Open Door Policy*, vol. 1, 470; and Buell, *Liberia: A Century*, 8n.
93. Carl Patrick Burrowes, *Power and Press Freedom in Liberia, 1830–1970: The Impact of Globalization and Civil Society on Media-Government Relations* (Trenton, NJ: Africa World Press, 2004), 159.
94. Buell, *Liberia: A Century*, 34.
95. Faulkner to Sir Eric Drummond, secretary-general of the League of Nations, *New Republic*, February 26, 1930, 256;

and US Department of State, *Report of the International Commission of Inquiry into the Existence of Slavery and Forced Labor in the Republic of Liberia*, State Department Publication no. 147 (Washington: GPO, 1931), 4–5, quoted in Duignan and Gann, *United States and Africa*, 202–203.

96. Peter Duignan and L. H. Gann, *The United States and Africa: A History* (New York: Cambridge University Press and the Hoover Institution, 1984), 201.
97. Sisay, 70; and Raymond L Buell, *Foreign Policy Reports: The Reconstruction of Liberia* (New York: Foreign Policy Association, 1932), 124.
98. Duignan and Gann, *United States and Africa*, 203.
99. Sisay, *Big Powers and Small Nations*, 70.
100. Raymond L. Buell, *The Native Problem in Africa*, vol. 2, section 14 (New York: Macmillan, 1928), 779–80.
101. Sisay, *Big Powers and Small Nations*, 71.
102. Ibid.
103. US Department of State, *Report of the International Commission*, 4–5 quoted in Duignan and Gann, *United States and Africa*, 203.
104. Duignan and Gann, *United States and Africa*, 203.
105. Buell, *Liberia: A Century*, 36.
106. *New York Times*, August 11, 1929.
107. Sisay, *Big Powers and Small Nations*, 75; and US Department of State, *Report of the International Commission*, 120.
108. *New York Times,* January 11, 1931.
109. Ibid.
110. Ibid.
111. Ibid.
112. US Department of State, *Report of the International Commission*, 134–35, quoted in Duignan and Gann, *United States and Africa*, 204.
113. 2*New York Times,* January 11, 1931.
114. Ibid.

115. *New York Times,* January 11, 1931.
116. US Department of State, *Report of the International Commission,* 134–135, quoted in Duignan and Gann, *United States and Africa,* 204.
117. Ronald W. Davis, *Ethnohistorical Studies on the Kru Coast,* 55–57, quoted in Van der Kraaij, *Open Door Policy,* vol. 1, 470 n137; and Buell, *Liberia: A Century,* 8.
118. *New York Times,* January 11, 1931.
119. *New York Times,* October 24, 1930.
120. The Department of State to the Liberian Consul General. November 17, 1930, *Foreign Relations of the United States 1930,* vol. 2 (Washington: GPO, 194,) 369–370, quoted in Sisay, *Big Powers and Small Nations,* 85.
121. Liebenow, *Quest for Democracy,* 58.
122. The Charge d'Affaires in Liberia to the Secretary of State, October 13, 1930, *Foreign Relations of the United States 1930,* vol. 3 (Washington: GPO, 1945), 361, quoted in Sisay, *Big Powers and Small Nations,* 85.
123. Sisay, *Big Powers and Small Nations,* 89; and Charge d'Affaires, October 13. 1930, in Sisay, *Big Powers and Small Nations,* 78.
124. *New York Times,* January 11, 1931.

Chapter 15. Boss of the Whole Show

1. The Secretary of State to the Charge d'Affaires in Liberia, December 5, 1930, *Papers Relating to the Foreign Relations of the United States 1930* (Washington: GPO, 1930), 381, quoted in Hassan B. Sisay, *Big Powers and Small Nations: A Case Study of United States-Liberian Relations,* (Lanham, MD: University Press of America, 1958), 90.
2. Sisay, *Big Powers and Small Nations,* 89.

3. The Department of State to the Liberian Consul General, December 19, 1930, *Foreign Relations of the United States 1930*, vol. 2 (Washington: GPO, 1930), 384–85.
4. Ibid., 318, quoted in Sisay, *Big Powers and Small Nations*, 90.
5. *New York Times*, June 2, 1931.
6. *New York Times*, January 11, 1931; F. P. M Van der Kraaij writes that the manager insisted the bank withdrew from Liberia because of a dispute over payments to the British-owned Liberian Rubber Company, in *The Open Door Policy of Liberia: An Economic History of Modern Liberia*, vol. 1 (Bremen: Im Selbstveriag des Museums, 1983), 422.
7. *New York Times*, June 2, 1931.
8. *New York Times*, May 20, 1932.
9. See "Reber to State Department, October 17, 1930, microfilm, file 882.51/2126, *Documents in Affairs of Liberia;* and Sisay, *Big Powers and Small Nations*, 91–92.
10. See Government of Liberia, Treasury Department, *Annual Report* 1926–1927, 29, in Van der Kraaij, *Open Door Policy*, vol. 1, 54.
11. See W. E. B. DuBois, "Liberia, the League and the United States," *Foreign Affairs* 2 (1933): 690, in Sisay, *Big Powers and Small Nations*, 92–93.
12. See DuBois, "Liberia, League, United States," 685, in Sisay, *Big Powers and Small Nations*, 91.
13. Ibid., in Sisay, *Big Powers and Small Nations*, 93.
14. Ibid., 95.
15. *League of Nations Report for Assistance Submitted by the Republic of Liberia* (Geneva: League of Nations, 1932) 15, in Sisay, *Big Powers and Small Nations*, 94.
16. See Sisay, *Big Powers and Small Nations*, 94; and League of Nations, *Documents Relating to the Plan of Assistance Geneva Proposed by the League of Nations* (Washington: GPO, 1933), 12–15.
17. Sisay, *Big Powers and Small Nations*, 94.

18. Ibid.
19. See ibid., 93–95.
20. Firestone to President Herbert Hoover, September 26, 1932, Hoover Presidential Papers, mss., box 991, Hoover Presidential Library, West Branch, Iowa, in Sisay, *Big Powers and Small Nations*, 95.
21. Memorandum on Secretary of State's Interview with Harvey Firestone, December 10, 1930, *Foreign Relations of the United States 1930* (Washington: GPO, 1930), 385–386, in Sisay, *Big Powers and Small Nations*, 95.
22. Frank Robert Chalk, "The United States and the International Struggle for Rubber, 1914–1941," PhD diss., University of Wisconsin, 1967, 194–95, in Sisay, *Big Powers and Small Nations*, 95.
23. Hoover to Firestone, October 6, 1932, Hoover Presidential Papers, mss., box 91, in Sisay, *Big Powers and Small Nations*, 95.
24. Henry Stimson to Firestone, October 5, 1932, Hoover Presidential, Papers, mss., box 991, Hoover Presidential Library, West Branch, Iowa, in Sisay, *Big Powers and Small Nations*, 95–96.
25. Sisay, *Big Powers and Small Nations*, 96.
26. E. O. Briggs, Memorandum, February 7, 1933, Hoover Presidential Papers, mss., box 51, Hoover Presidential Library. West Branch, Iowa, in Sisay, *Big Powers and Small Nations*, 97.
27. Sisay, *Big Powers and Small Nations*, 97. See Mitchell to Secretary of State, January 25, 1933, microfilm, file 882.01/31, reel 5, "Documents in Affairs of Liberia."
28. Chalk, "International Struggle for Rubber," 199–203, in Sisay, *Big Powers and Small Nations*, 97.
29. Van der Kraaij, *Open Door Policy*, vol. 1, 54-55, draws upon the accounts of Clarence Lorenzo Simpson's *Memoirs: The Symbol of Liberia* (London: Diplomatic Press, 1961), 141,

180–81, and Frank Robert Chalk, "The United States and the International Struggle for Rubber, 1914–1941," 31.

30. See Van der Kraaij, *Open Door Policy*, vol. 1, 55; Numandi Azikiwe, *Liberia in World Politics* (1934: repr., Westport, CT: Negro Universities Press, 1970), 334; and Harry Greenwall and Roland Wild, *Unknown Liberia* (London: Hutchison, 1936), 99. q

31. "Annual Message of His Excellency Edwin Barclay, President of Liberia," October 25 1933," mss, unorganized, MFA/N, National Archives, Monrovia, 3–6, in Van der Kraaij, *Open Door Policy*, vol. 1, 54.

32. Graham Greene, *Journey without Maps*, (1936; repr., New York: Viking Penguin, 1986), 237.

33. J. Gus Liebenow, *Liberia: The Quest for Democracy* (Bloomington: Indiana University Press, 1983), 93.

34. Chargé in Liberia to secretary of state, August 16, 1932, *Liberian Internal Affairs*, file 882.00/974, cited in Sisay, *Big Powers and Small Nations*, 112.

35. Ibid.

36. Mitchell to secretary of state, February 7, 1935, *Liberian Internal Affairs*, file 882.51/2144, in Sisay, *Big Powers and Small Nations*, 112.

37. Memorandum of a Conversation on Requested Assistance of the United States Government in Overthrowing the Government of Liberia, September 1,1939, file 882.00/1100, in Sisay, *Big Powers and Small Nations*, 128.

38. Liebenow, *Quest for Democracy*, 50.

39. Greene, *Journey without Maps*, 107. Greene spells the name "Davies."

40. Ibid., 105.

41. Ibid.

42. Ibid., 106

43. Raymond Leslie Buell, *Liberia: A Century of Survival 1847–1947*, African Handbook No. 7. (Philadelphia: University Museum, University of Pennsylvania, 1947), 9.
44. Greene, *Journey without Maps*, 106.
45. Ibid.
46. Ibid., 107.
47. 0First Inaugural Address of President Edwin James Barclay, January 4, 1932, cited in Van der Kraaij, *Open Door Policy*, vol. 1, 42.
48. See Sisay, *Big Powers and Small Nations*, 109, who refers to Mitchell to secretary of state, October 12, 1931, *Liberian Internal Affairs*, file 882.00/899.
49. Mitchell to secretary of state, November 5, 1931, *Liberian Internal Affairs*, file 882.00/899, quoted in Sisay, *Big Powers and Small Nations*, 109.
50. *New York Times*, October 25, 1936.
51. British aide memoire to secretary of state, February 23, 1932, *Liberian Internal Affairs*, file 882.00/921, quoted in Sisay, *Big Powers and Small Nations*, 109.
52. Samuel Beber to secretary of state, December 9, 1930, *Liberian Internal Affairs*, file 882.00/866 quoted in Sisay, 109.
53. Sisay, *Big Powers and Small Nations*, 110, quoting Mitchell to secretary of state, April 1932. *Liberian Internal Affairs*. file 882.00/930.
54. Ibid.
55. See Sisay, *Big Powers and Small Nations*, 110-111.
56. D. G. Ryding, *Report to the League of Nations, 1932* (known as the British Blue Book), *Liberian Internal Affairs*, file 882.00/964, 55–31, quoted in Sisay, *Big Powers and Small Nations*, 111.
57. Ibid.
58. Sisay, *Big Powers and Small Nations*, 112.
59. Greene, *Journey Without Maps*, 197.
60. Ibid., 200.

61. Ibid., 202.
62. Ibid., 203.
63. Ibid., 206.
64. See Sisay, *Big Powers and Small Nations*, 119; and League of Nations, *Documents Relating to the Plan of Assistance Proposed by the League of Nations* (Washington: GPO, 1933), 25–26.
65. Sisay, *Big Powers and Small Nations, 120*; and League, Plan of Assistance, 25-26
66. See Sisay, *Big Powers and Small Nations*, 120.
67. See Ibid.
68. See ibid., 120–21; and Chalk, 87–88.
69. They presented Phillips with a petition that accused whites of stymieing Negro progress by "loaning money to small [black] countries" and then "encouraging them to buy and spend beyond" their means to repay. The next step meant "finding or inventing some moral excuse for intervention, and taking charge of the country in the name of some white country and in the interest of a commercial" enterprise "whose chief and only object [was] profit. Charles H. Wesley, "Liberia Begins Its Second Century," *The Negro History Bulletin*, 12, (1948), 62, quoted in Sisay, *Big Powers and Small Nations*, 123.
70. Ibid.
71. Ibrahim K. Sundista, "The Dilemma: Afro-America and Americo-Liberia, 1933–1934," paper presented at the Liberian Studies Conference, Indiana University, April 8–10, 1976, 16, quoted in Sisay, *Big Powers and Small Nations*, 23.
72. Presidential memorandum to undersecretary of state, August 19, 1933, Franklin Delano Roosevelt Personal Papers, mss, box 676, Franklin D. Roosevelt Library, Hyde Park, New York, quoted in Sisay, *Big Powers and Small Nations*, 125.
73. Ibid.
74. *New York Times*, October 10, 1933.

75. See Report of W. A. Travelle, Supervisor of Internal Revenue, Republic of Liberia, December 3, 1931, *Liberian Internal Affairs*, file 882.51/2144, quoted in Sisay, *Big Powers and Small Nations*, 113.
76. Sisay, *Big Powers and Small Nations*, 125.
77. Walton to secretary of state, January 23, 1942, *Liberian Internal Affairs*, file 882.00/1156, quoted in Sisay, *Big Powers and Small Nations*, 126.
78. Sisay, *Big Powers and Small Nations*, 126, citing John Payne Mitchell, "America's Liberian Policy," PhD diss., University of Chicago, 1955, microfilm 57005396 (and Library of Congress 4455E, 221); and George Brown, *The Economic History of Liberia* (Washington: Associated, 1941), 211.
79. See Van der Kraaij, *Open Door Policy*, vol. 1, 55–56.
80. *New York Times*, April 12, 1934.
81. See Cordell Hull to President Roosevelt, May 28, 1935, Roosevelt Personal Papers, miss., box 676, cited in Sisay, *Big Powers and Small Nations*, 126.
82. Edward Blyden, "Description of Monrovia," *African Repository*, 42 (1866), 328–29.
83. Greene, *Journey without Maps*, 230.
84. Ibid.
85. Ibid., 231.
86. Ibid., 78–79.
87. Ibid., 173–77.
88. Ibid., 174.
89. Tuan Wreh, *The Love of Liberty: The Rule of President William V. S. Tubman in Liberia* (London: C. Hurst 1976), 67. Wreh also relates a 1970 case of an Ivory Coast witch doctor, a university law student, and General George Toe Washington, Tubman's military advisor. They were charged with conspiring to murder the minister of defense and army chief of staff. The story appeared in the *Liberian Star*, October 15, 1970.

90. Liebenow, *Quest for Democracy*, 328, chapter 14, note 1.
91. Ibid., 44.
92. See ibid., 84. The Americo-Liberian elite was wary of any outside influence that might undermine their authority among the tribal people. Liebenow maintains their attitudes even "toward missionaries began to sour" in the latter part of the nineteenth century. He says that "the government refused, until well into the twentieth century, to permit Christian missionaries to establish churches and schools more than fifty miles into the interior"; ibid., 53.
93. See Frank Willett, *African Art: An Introduction*. (New York: Thames and Hudson, 1971), 25.
94. Greene, *Journey without Maps*, 222.
95. "Annual Message of His Excellency Edwin Barclay, President of Liberia," October 25, 1933," mss, unorganized MFA/N, National Archives, Monrovia, quoted in Van der Kraaij, *Open Door Policy*, vol. 1, 74.
96. George A. Padmore, "Five Other Presidents of Liberia as I Knew Them: President Edwin J. Barclay, the Intellectual," *The Liberian Age*, December 1978. Padmore (1903–59), born Malcolm Ivan Meredith Nurse in Trinidad, was a widely known black communist on the international scene.
97. Peter Duignan and L. H. Gann, *The United States and Africa: A History* (New York: Cambridge University Press and the Hoover Institution, 1984), 205.
98. See ibid.; and Simpson, *Memoirs: Symbol of Liberia*, 198–99.
99. *New York Times*, August 30, 1936.
100. *New York Times*, July 27, 1939.
101. *New York Times*, October 17, 1938.
102. *New York Times*, July 27, 1939.
103. Duignan and Gann, *United States and Africa*, 20.
104. See Henry S. Villard, memorandum, May 26, 1939, *Foreign Relations of the United States 1939*, 585–86; and Secretary of

state to minister in Liberia, *Foreign Relations of the United States 1939*, 562, 590–93, cited in Sisay, *Big Powers and Small Nations*, 133–34.

105. The ambassador to the United Kingdom to the secretary of state, July 8, 1939, *Foreign Relations of the United States*, 1939, 601, quoted in Sisay, *Big Powers and Small Nations*, 134.

106. Milo Perkins, "Introductory Remarks by Milo Perkins, Executive Director of the Office of Economic Warfare," April 22, 1943, Roosevelt Personal Papers, mss, box 476, quoted in Sisay *Big Powers and Small Nations*, 135. See also

107. Duignan and Gann, *United States and Africa*, 304.

108. The president of Liberia to Harry A. McBride, February 14, 1942, *Foreign Relations of the United States 1942*, 364, 358, quoted in Sisay, *Big Powers and Small Nations*, 135–36. See also Duignan and Gann, *United States and Africa*, 254.

109. *New York Times*, December 4, 1942.

110. Sisay, *Big Powers and Small Nations*, 136.

111. *New York Times*, January 28, 1944.

112. See Sisay, *Big Powers and Small Nations*, 136, citing Simpson, *Memoirs: Symbol of Liberia*, 228.

113. President of Liberia to McBride, February 14, 1942, *Foreign Relations of the United States* 404, cited in Sisay, *Big Powers and Small Nations*, 135.

114. Chargé to secretary of state, November 5, 1942, *Foreign Relations of the United States* 1942, 430, cited in Sisay, *Big Powers and Small Nations*, 137.

115. See *New York Times*, January 29, 1943; and the Chargé d'Affaires in Liberia to the secretary of state, January 28 1943, *Foreign Relations of the United States 1943*, 656–57, cited in Sisay, *Big Powers and Small Nations*, 137–38.

116. *New York Times*, January 29, 1943.

117. See memorandum of conversation by Charles W. Lewis of the Division of Near Eastern Affairs, June 12, 1943, *Foreign*

Relations of the United States 1943, 680–81, cited in Sisay, *Big Powers and Small Nations*, 138.
118. Sisay, *Big Powers and Small Nations*, 138.
119. Ibid., 139; and *New York Times*, May 29, 1943.
120. Sisay, *Big Powers and Small Nations*, 139; and US Congress, House, 78th Cong., 1st sess., May 14, 1943 to June 14, 1944, *Congressional Record*: 4893.
121. *New York Times*, May 28, 1943.
122. Sisay, *Big Powers and Small Nations*, 139.
123. Memorandum of conversation by the assistant chief of Near Eastern Affairs, June 1, 1943, *Foreign Relations of the United States 1943*, 659–63, quoted in Sisay, *Big Powers and Small Nations*, 140.
124. Ibid.
125. *New York Times*, June 12, 1943.

Chapter 16. "Uncle Shad"

1. Tuan Wreh, *The Love of Liberty: The Rule of William V.S. Tubman in Liberia 1944–1947* (London: C. Hurst, 1976), front flap of book jacket.
2. Ibid., 120.
3. Stanton Peabody, ed., *The Liberian Age*, July 29, 1971, quoted in Wreh, *Love of Liberty*, 123.
4. Clarence Lorenzo Simpson, *Memoirs: The Symbol of Liberia* (London: Diplomatic Press, 1961), 241.
5. Wreh, *Love of Liberty*, 123.
6. Ibid., quoting Ivory Coast president Felix Houphouet-Boigny.
7. Ibid., 3.
8. Ibid., 27.
9. Ibid., 26.
10. Richard F. Burton, *Wanderings in West Africa*, vol. 1 (1863; repr., New York: Dover, 1991), 290.

11. Ibid., 291.
12. Ibid., 293.
13. Ibid.
14. Ibid., 301.
15. J. Gus Liebenow, *Liberia: The Quest for Democracy* (Bloomington: Indiana University Press, 1983), 27.
16. Wreh, *Love of Liberty*, 6.
17. Ibid.
18. A. Doris Banks Henries, *A Biography of President William V. S. Tubman* (London: Macmillan, 1967), 2.
19. Wreh, *Love of Liberty*, 8.
20. Henries, *William V. S. Tubman*, 2.
21. See Wreh, *Love of Liberty*, 7–8.
22. Ibid., 8
23. Ibid.
24. "William V. S. Tubman," *Current Biography Yearbook 1955* (New York: H. W. Wilson., 1955) 616.
25. Harvey Glickman, ed., *Political Leaders of Contemporary Africa South of the Sahara: A Biographical Dictionary* (New York: Greenwood Press, 1992), 292.
26. Wreh, *Love of Liberty*, 10.
27. Ibid.
28. Ibid., 2.
29. Ibid.
30. S. T. A. Richards, "Tubman for More Democracy," *The Friend*, 1944, quoted in Wreh, *Love of Liberty*, 2.
31. *African Nationalist*, November 8, 1941, quoted in Liebenow, *Quest for Democracy*, 97.
32. Wreh, *Love of Liberty*, 32.
33. Ibid., 33.
34. Simpson, *Memoirs: Symbol of Liberia* 237.
35. Liebenow, *Quest for Democracy*, 91.
36. Wreh, *Love of Liberty*, 33.

37. William V. S. Tubman to President Edwin Barclay, May 10, 1943, quoted in Wreh, *Love of Liberty*, 34.
38. Editorial, *Weekly Mirror*, quoted in Wreh, *Love of Liberty*, 34. See also Raymond Leslie Buell, *Liberia: A Century of Survival 1847–1947*, African Handbook No. 7 (Philadelphia: University of Pennsylvania Press, 1947). Professor J. Gus Lieberman in *Quest for Democracy* (94) wrote that even if an opposition party managed to make it to Election Day, "there was still no assurance that its partisans would be permitted to vote or that their votes would even be counted." And if they were counted and the party victorious, "there was no assurance that the victory would be officially recognized."
39. Wreh, *Love of Liberty*, 36.
40. "First Inaugural Address of President Tubman," Monrovia, January 4, 1944. Quoted in Wreh, *Love of Liberty*, 36–37.
41. Ibid., quoted in F. P. M. Van der Kraaij, *The Open Door Policy of Liberia: An Economic History of Modern Liberia*, vol. 1, Afrika Archiv, Band 17/1 (Bremen: Im Selbstverlag des Museums, 1983), vi.
42. See, ibid., vii; and Amos Sawyer, *The Emergence of Autocracy in Liberia: Tragedy and Challenge* (San Francisco: California Institute for Contemporary Studies Press, 1991), 207–208. According to Liebenow, "[only] the threat of European incursions compelled President Arthur Barclay in 1904 to extend citizenship to tribal residents of the interior" (*Quest for Democracy*, 47). Only in 1907 was the constitution amended to replace "people of color" with "negro." In any case this action was little more than an empty gesture since their voting was restricted.
43. Van der Kraaij, *Open Door Policy*, vol. 1, 306, table 29.
44. Tubman, "Annual Message to the Legislature," Monrovia, November 7, 1950, quoted in Van der Kraaij, *Open Door Policy*, vol. 1, 306.

45. Henries, *William V. S. Tubman*, 36.
46. Ibid.
47. Ibid., 37.
48. 6Tubman, "Unification Policy," policy statement, Monrovia, February 14, 1944, quoted in Wreh, 43.
49. Liebenow, *Liberia: Quest for Democracy*, 59.
50. Ibid., 63.
51. Liebenow, *Quest for Democracy*, 130.
52. Henries, *William V. S. Tubman*, 121.
53. See Liebenow, *Quest for Democracy*, 65–66.
54. Sawyer, *Emergence of Autocracy*, 208.
55. Ibid.
56. Wreh, *Love of Liberty*, 35.
57. Ibid.
58. See Lieberman, *Quest for Democracy*, 64–65.
59. Sawyer, *Emergence of Autocracy*, 207.
60. "The National Unification of Liberia: Hands Across the Country," Liberia Department of State, Bureau of Information, 1941, 10, quoted in Hassan B. Sisay, *Big Powers and Small Nations: A Case Study of United States-Liberian Relations*, (Lanham, MD: University Press of America, 1958), 149.
61. Van der Kraaij, *The Open Door Policy*, vol. 1, iii.
62. Ibid., n4.
63. Ibid., 461 n5.
64. Liebenow, *Quest for Democracy* 62.
65. Ibid.
66. Ibid.
67. Van der Kraaij, *Open Door Policy*, vol. 1, 322–23.
68. Wreh, *Love of Liberty*, 39.
69. Ibid.
70. Ibid., 41.
71. Ibid.

72. Liebenow, *Quest for Democracy*, 91.
73. Ibid., 91–92.
74. Ibid., 92.
75. Van der Kraaij, *Open Door Policy,*, vol. 1, 316, quoting the legislature's act "empowering and authorizing the President...to appoint liaison and relations officers in Counties, Provinces, and Districts," 515 n33.
76. Wreh, *Love of Liberty*, 27.
77. Ibid., 28–29.
78. Liberia, Special Security Service, "Synopsis of the Act of the Legislature," *Liberian Age*, February 26, 1966, quoted in Wreh, *Love of Liberty*, 29–30. President Tolbert disbanded the National Intelligence and Security Service and Executive Action Bureau and consolidated their functions into the National Bureau of Intelligence and Special Security Service, headed by a director general of security services.
79. Elwood Dunn, Amos J. Brown, and Carl Patrick Burrowes, *Historical Dictionary of Liberia*, 2nd ed. (Lanham, MD: Scarecrow Press, 2001), 339.
80. Wreh, *Love of Liberty*, 48; and Dunn et al., *Historical Dictionary of Liberia*, 177.
81. Didwho Twe to President William Tubman, April 16, 1951, quoted in Wreh, *Love of Liberty*, 53–54.
82. Dunn, et al., *Historical Dictionary of Liberia*, 339.
83. Ibid.
84. Didwho Twe, Acceptance Speech, United People Party, Monrovia, April 10, 1951, quoted in Wreh, *Love of Liberty*, 51–52.
85. William V. S. Tubman to Didwho Twe, April 18, 1951, quoted in Wreh, *Love of Liberty*, 54.
86. Wreh, *Love of Liberty*, 54.
87. Indictment of the defendants, quoted in Wreh, *Love of Liberty*, 54.
88. Ibid., 55

89. *New York World-Telegram and Sun*, March 31, 1952, quoted in Wreh, *Love of Liberty*, 56.
90. Wreh, *Love of Liberty*, 57.
91. Wreh, *Love of Liberty*, 57.
92. Ibid., 48.
93. Glickman, *Political Leaders*, 294.
94. American University, Foreign Areas Studies Division, *Area Handbook for Liberia*, Department of the Army, Pamphlet 550-38 (Washington: Government Printing Office, 1972), 196, quoted in "The Man Called d. Twe," by Siahyonkron Nyanseor, *The Perspective*, http://theperspective.org/2014/016, accessed February 25, 2016.
95. Ibid.

Chapter 17. A New Era

1. *New York Times*, January 9, 1952.
2. F. P. M. Van der Kraaij, *The Open Door Policy of Liberia, An Economic History of Modern Liberia*, vol. 1, Afrika Archiv, Band 17/1 (Bremen: Im Selbstverlag des Museums, 1983), 314.
3. Letter of understanding between the Liberian government and the Liberia Company, September 3, 1947, approved December 4, 1947, 1–2, quoted in Van der Kraaij, *Open Door Policy*, vol. 1, 84.
4. Van der Kraaij, *Open Door Policy*, vol. 1, 84.
5. Ibid., 313. The New York–based International Trust Company collected the fees—a welcome contribution to the country's foreign exchange coffer—from the ships and corporations, and acted as Liberia's maritime administrator.
6. Ibid., 167.
7. *New York Times*, June 11, 1951.
8. See Martin Lowenkopf, *Politics in Liberia: The Conservative Road to Development* (Stanford, CA: Hoover Institution, 1976), 61–63.

9. Benjamin J. K. Anderson, "The Country East of Liberia," *African Repository* 46 (1870), 227–28.
10. Van der Kraaij, *Open Door Policy*, vol. 1, 162–63.
11. Ibid., 163. See also letter of understanding between the Liberian government and the Liberia Company, September 3, 1947.
12. Raymond Leslie Buell, *Liberia: A Century of Survival 1847–1947*, African Handbook No. 7 (Philadelphia: University Museum, University of Pennsylvania, 1947), 48.
13. Van der Kraaij, *Open Door Policy*, vol. 1, 164. See also Buell, *Century of Survival*, 6, 99.
14. Buell, *Century of Survival*, 6, quoted in Van der Kraaij, *Open Door Policy*, vol. 1, 164.
15. *Time*, March 28, 1949.
16. Van der Kraaij, *Open Door Policy*, vol. 1, 166.
17. Ibid., 167.
18. *Time*, March 28, 1949.
19. Van der Kraaij, *Open Door Policy*, vol. 1, xviii.
20. Ibid., 171.
21. E. Reginald Townsend and Abeodu Jones, eds., *The Official Papers of William Tubman, President of the Republic of Liberia* (London: Longmans Green, 1968), 371–75, quoted in Van der Kraaij, *Open Door Policy*, vol. 1, 168.
22. Van der Kraaij, *Open Door Policy*, vol. 1, 190.
23. Ibid., 191.
24. Ibid., 187.
25. Ibid.
26. Ibid.
27. J. Gus Liebenow, *Liberia: The Quest for Democracy* (Bloomington: Indiana University Press, 1983), 189.
28. Murray Whinney, et al., Fourth Report, presented to A. B. Jalah, acting deputy commissioner of internal revenues, Republic of Liberia (Monrovia: May 20, 1964), 4, quoted in Van der Kraaij, *Open Door Policy*, vol. 1, 187.

29. J. Milton Weeks to LMC Ltd., September 13, 1971, quoted in Van der Kraaij, *Open Door Policy*, vol. 1, 188.
30. Van der Kraaij, *Open Door Policy*, vol. , 323, table 34.
31. Republic of Liberia, An Act Approving the Nine Year Program for the Economic Development of the Republic of Liberia, 1953, quoted in Van der Kraaij, *Open Door Policy*, vol. 1, 322 n47.
32. Van der Kraaij, *Open Door Policy*, vol. 1, 317.
33. See Charles Moritz, ed., *Current Biography Yearbook, 1955* (New York: H. W. Wilson, 1955), 617 and Van der Kraaij, *Open Door Policy*, vol. 1, 324-26.
34. *New York Times*, October 19, 1954.
35. *New York Times*, October 25 and 29, 1954.
36. *New York Times*, October 29, 1954.
37. Ibid.
38. *New York Times*, October 30, 1954.
39. *New York Times*, November 2, 1954.
40. *New York Times*, November 3, 1954.
41. *New York Times*, October 26, 1954.
42. *New York Times*, November 15, 1954.
43. Ibid.
44. Tuan Wreh, *The Love of Liberty: The Rule of William V. S. Tubman in Liberia 1944–1947* (London: C. Hurst, 1976), 65.
45. Ibid., 64–65.
46. "Why Third Term? Liberia Has Men," editorial, *The Friend*, Monrovia, November 7, 1953.
47. William V. S. Tubman, press statement, Monrovia, November, 1953 (?), quoted in Wreh, *Love of Liberty*, 64.
48. Ibid., 58–61.
49. Edwin J. Barclay, Acceptance Speech, Independent True Whig Party, Monrovia, August 27, 1954, quoted in Wreh, *Love of Liberty*, 58–61.
50. Wreh, *Love of Liberty*, 61–63.

51. Ibid., 66.
52. Ibid.
53. Ibid., 67.
54. Ibid., 68, 87. William Oliver Davies-Bright in the subsequent May 1959 presidential election fared somewhat better. He received fifty-votes. Of course, Tubman received 530,566.
55. Ibid., 58.
56. Ibid., 69.
57. *New York Times,* January 14, 1956.
58. Wreh, *Love of Liberty,* 72.
59. Edwin J. Barclay, press statement, Monrovia, May 1955, quoted in Wreh, *Love of Liberty,* 73.
60. Wreh, *Love of Liberty,* 73.
61. Ibid., 85.

CHAPTER 18. GROWTH WITHOUT DEVELOPMENT

1. Robert W. Clower et al., *Growth without Development: An Economic Survey of Liberia* (Evanston, IL: Northwestern University Press, 1966), v.
2. See Clower et al., *Growth without Development,* 24.
3. F. P. M. Van der Kraaij, *The Open Door Policy of Liberia: An Economic History of Modern Liberia,* vol. 1 (Bremen: Im Selbstveriag des Museums, Afrika Archiv, Band 17/1, 1983), 313.
4. See Clower, et al., *Growth without Development,* 35.
5. See ibid., 212, n11.
6. See ibid., 24.
7. Martin Lowenkopf, *Politics in Liberia: The Conservative Road to Development* (Stanford, CA: Hoover Institution, 1976), 61.
8. See J. Gus Liebenow, *Liberia: The Quest for Democracy* (Bloomington: Indiana University Press, 1983), 61–62.

9. Lowenkopf, *Politics in Liberia*, 70.
10. Clower, et al., *Growth without Development*, 244.
11. Liebenow, *Quest for Democracy*, 57. See chapter 3.
12. Ibid., 39–41.
13. Graham Greene, *Journey without Maps* (1936; repr., New York: Viking Penguin, 1986),79.
14. Greene, *Journey without Maps*, 79–80.
15. Donald A. Ranard, ed., *Liberians: An Introduction to Their History and Culture,* Culture Profile No. 19 (Washington, DC: Center for Applied Linguistics, 2005), 30; Clower, et al., *Growth without Development*, 232.
16. Ibid.
17. See ibid.
18. See Clower, et al., *Growth without Development*, 229–30.
19. Ranard, *Liberians: An Introduction*, 30.
20. Clower, et al., *Growth without Development*, 17.
21. A. Doris Banks Henries, *A Biography of President William V. S. Tubman* (London: Macmillan, 1967), 121.
22. Clower, et al., *Growth without Development*, 16.
23. Ibid., 17.
24. Ibid., 16.
25. Ibid., 20.
26. Ibid., 21.
27. Ibid., 20.
28. Ibid., 22.
29. Ibid., 232.
30. Ibid., 17–18.
31. Ibid.
32. Van der Kraaij, *Open Door Policy*, vol. 1, 426.
33. William V. S. Tubman, Annual Message to the Fourth Session of the Forty–Fifth Legislature, Monrovia, December 13, 1963, quoted in Lowenkopf, *Politics in Liberia*, 73.
34. Lowenkopf, *Politics in Liberia*, 74.
35. Ibid.

36. Liebenow, *Liberia: The Evolution of Privilege* (Ithaca, NY: Cornell University Press, 1969), 185.
37. Clower, et al., *Growth without Development*, quoted in Liebenow, *Evolution of Privilege*, ci.
38. See Clower, et al., *Growth without Development*, 310–11, table 102.
39. See ibid., 325.
40. Ibid., 297–98.
41. Ibid., 268.
42. Ibid., 296.
43. Ibid., 260, 325–26.
44. Ibid., 273.
45. Ibid., 150.
46. Ibid.
47. Lowenkopf, *Politics in Liberia*, 103–104.
48. Clower, et al., *Growth without Development*, 272.
49. Ibid., 260.
50. Ibid., 85, 260.
51. See Van der Kraaij, *Open Door Policy*, vol. 1, 386, table 57.
52. See also Liebenow, *Evolution of Privilege*, 79.
53. See Amos Sawyer, *The Emergence of Autocracy in Liberia* (San Francisco: Institute for Contemporary Studies Press, 1992), 359 n33.
54. Van der Kraaij, *Open Door Policy*, vol. 1, 395. Max Roser estimated world literacy at 42 percent in 1960 and 56 percent in 1970. Max Roser, "Literacy," published online at OurWorldInData.org, 2015. http://ourworldindata.org/data/education-knowledge/literacy.
55. See Liebenow, *Evolution of Privilege*, 180.
56. See Sawyer, *Emergence of Autocracy*, 359, 33; Clower, et al., *Growth without Development*, 263, 373.
57. Van der Kraaij, *Open Door Policy*, vol. 1, 387, 392, 394.
58. Tubman, speech to gathering of chiefs and tribal people of Kolshon, Lofa County in Voinjama, Liberia, January 5, 1951,

E. Reginald Townsend, ed., *William Tubman Speaks* (London: London Consolidated, 1959), 181, quoted in Hassan B. Sisay, *Big Powers and Small Nations: A Case Study of United States-Liberian Relations* (Lanham, MD: University Press of America, 1958), 149.
59. Ibid.
60. Van der Kraaij, *Open Door Policy* vol. 1, 397–98.
61. Clower, et al., *Growth without Development*, 32.
62. Sawyer, *Emergence of Autocracy*, 260–61.
63. Lowenkopf, *Politics in Liberia*, 75–76.
64. Ibid., 77.
65. Clower, et al., *Growth without Development*, 33.
66. Ibid.
67. Tubman, speech, January 5, 1951, Townsend, ed., *William Tubman Speaks*, 181, quoted in Sisay, *Big Powers and Small Nations*, 150.
68. Lowenkopf, *Politics in Liberia*, 77.
69. Ibid., 67.
70. Ibid., 68.
71. Ibid., 77, quoting Article V, Section 14 of the 1847 constitution.
72. Leon Weintraub, "Land and Power in Liberia" (paper presented at Second Conference on Social Sciences in Liberia, Bloomington, Indiana, May 1970), quoted in Lowenkopf, *Politics in Liberia*, 77.
73. Lowenkopf, *Politics in Liberia*, 67–68.
74. Liebenow, *The Evolution of Privilege*, 210.
75. Ibid., ix.
76. Liebenow, *Quest for Democracy*, 63.
77. Clower, et al, *Growth without Development*, 259.
78. Lowenkopf, *Politics in Liberia*, 106.
79. Clower, et al., *Growth without Development*, 238.
80. Lowenkopf, *Politics in Liberia*, 106.
81. Sawyer, *Emergence of Autocracy*, 259.
82. Lowenkopf, *Politics in Liberia*, 106.

83. Clower, et al., *Growth without Development*, 239.
84. Ibid., 244.
85. Ibid., 267 n3.
86. Ibid., 95, quoted in Liebenow, *Evolution of Privilege*, 187.
87. Clower, et al., *Growth without Development*, 267 n3.
88. Ibid
89. Ibid., 14, quoted in Liebenow, *Quest for Democracy*, 165–66.

CHAPTER 19. MASTER OF LIBERIA

1. Charles Moritz, ed., *Current Biography Yearbook, 1955* (New York: H. W. Wilson, 1955), 618.
2. Tuan Wreh, *The Love of Liberty: The Rule of William V. S. Tubman in Liberia 1944–1947* (London: C. Hurst, 1976), 23.
3. Ibid., 22–23.
4. David Williams, "Profile of a President—Tubman of Liberia," *Africa South*, quoted in ibid., 23.
5. A. Doris Banks Henries, *A Biography of President William V. S. Tubman* (London: Macmillan, 1967), 151.
6. Wreh, *Love of Liberty*, 18.
7. Ibid., 21–22.
8. Ibid., 25.
9. Ibid., 24.
10. Ibid., 24.
11. Ibid., 25–26.
12. Henries, *William V. S. Tubman*, 149–150.
13. J. Gus Liebenow, *Liberia: The Evolution of Privilege* (Ithaca, NY: Cornell University Press, 1969), 154.
14. Robert W. Clower, et al., *Growth without Development: An Economic Survey of Liberia* (Evanston, IL: Northwestern University Press, 1966), 9.
15. Moritz, ed., *Current Biography Yearbook 1955*, 294.

16. Wreh, *Love of Liberty*, 76.
17. J. Gus Liebenow, *Liberia: The Quest for Democracy* (Bloomington: Indiana University Press, 1983), 90.
18. Wreh, *Love of Liberty*, 77.
19. *New York Times*, January 14, 1956.
20. Wreh, *Love of Liberty*, 79.
21. Ibid., 81.
22. Ibid., 82.
23. *New York Times*, January 5, 1956.
24. Wreh, *Love of Liberty*, 85.
25. Ibid.
26. Ibid., 86.
27. *New York Times*, December 24, 1955.
28. *New York Times*, January 3, 1956.
29. Ibid.
30. Ibid.
31. Ibid.
32. Ibid.
33. Ibid.
34. Embassy in Liberia to the Department of State, January 6, 1956, *Foreign Relations of the United States 1955-1957, Africa,* XVIII, 136.
35. Wreh, *Love of Liberty*, 45–46.
36. Ibid., 46.
37. *New York Times*, May 3, 1956.
38. Wreh, *Love of Liberty*, 45.
39. *New York Times*, September 23, 1956.
40. *New York Times*, December 2, 1956. Liberia established formal diplomatic relations in 1972.
41. *New York Times*, September 9, 1956.
42. *New York Times*, March 8, 1957.
43. Ibid.
44. Ibid.

45. Ibid.
46. Ibid.
47. *New York Times,* July 2, 1962.
48. *New York Times,* October 22, 1961.
49. Ibid.
50. *New York Times,* July 2, 1962.
51. *New York Times,* July 11, 1962.
52. Harvey Glickman, ed., *Political Leaders of Contemporary Africa South of the Sahara: A Biographical Dictionary* (New York: Greenwood Press, 1992), 295.
53. *New York Times,* May 9, 1961.
54. Glickman, ed., *Political Leaders,* 293.
55. F. P. M Van der Kraaij, *The Open Door Policy of Liberia: An Economic History of Modern Liberia,* vol. 1 (Bremen: Im Selbstveriag des Museums, Afrika Archiv, Band 17/1, 1983), 315–18.
56. *West Africa,* October 26, 1963; Liebenow, *Evolution of Privilege,* 155.
57. Van der Kraaij, *Open Door Policy,* vol. 1, 316.
58. See ibid., 315–18.
59. Ibid., 317.
60. Ibid., 319–20.
61. Wreh, 102–103.
62. Ibid.
63. Ibid., 105.
64. Ibid., 105–106.
65. Ibid., 104.
66. Ibid., 46.
67. Ibid.
68. Ibid., 47.
69. Ibid., 41-42.
70. Liebenow, *Evolution of Privilege,* 89.
71. Ibid., 88.

72. Clower, et al., *Growth without Development*, 281 n12.
73. Liebenow, *Evolution of Privilege*, 89.
74. Wreh, *Love of Liberty*, 107.
75. *Liberian Age*, January 26, 1968.
76. *Liberian Age*, February 16, 1968.
77. Ibid.
78. *New York Times*, June 19, 1968.
79. Victor D. Du Bois, *The Trial of Henry Fahnbulleh, Part I: Background of the Trial*, West Africa Series, vol. 11, no. 3 (Hanover, NH: American Universities Field Service, 1968), 5. This three-part, eighty-five-page document, which details the entire affair (including photographs), offers a fascinating glimpse of the obsessed Tubman regime and the adulation many Liberians, especially tribal people, felt for him at this time.
80. Ibid., 5.
81. Ibid., 3.
82. *New York Times*, June 19,1968.
83. Victor Du Bois, *Trial: Part I*, 3.
84. Ibid., 5.
85. Ibid., 5.
86. Ibid., 15.
87. Ibid., 5.
88. Victor Du Bois, *Trial, Part I*, 3, quoted in *Liberian Age*, March 12, 1968.
89. *Liberian Star*, May 1, 1968, in Du Bois, *Trial, Part I*, 5–6.
90. *Liberian Star*, May 2, 1968, in Du Bois, *Trial, Part I*, 7–8.
91. *Liberian Star*, May 3, 1968, in Du Bois, *Trial, Part I*, 8.
92. Ibid., 8.
93. *Liberian Age*, 2 May 1968, quoted in Du Bois, *Trial, Part I*, 10–12.
94. Du Bois, *Trial, Part I*, 13–14.
95. See Wreh, *Love of Liberty*, 112.
96. Van der Kraaij, *Open Door Policy*, vol. 1, 515.

97. *New York Times*, March 29, 1968.
98. Henries, *William V. S. Tubman*, 178.
99. Ibid., 179.
100. *New York Times*, May 12, 1968.
101. Lowenkopf, *Politics in Liberia*, 169.
102. Ibid.
103. Glickman, 293.

CHAPTER 20. AFTER TUBMAN, WHAT? A SUMMING UP

1. A. Doris Banks Henries, *A Biography of President William V. S. Tubman* (London: Macmillan, 1967), 165.
2. Martin Lowenkopf, *Politics in Liberia: The Conservative Road to Development* (Stanford, CA: Hoover Institution Publications, 1976), 39; Henries, plate 237.
3. Ibid., 165.
4. J. Gus Liebenow, *Liberia: The Quest for Democracy* (Bloomington: Indiana University Press, 1983), 206.
5. Ibid.
6. Ibid., 207.
7. Ibid., 206–7.
8. Ibid., 209.
9. Ibid., 208.
10. *New York Times*, November 29, 1954; *Current Biography Yearbook*, 618.
11. J. Gus Liebenow, *Liberia: The Evolution of Privilege* (Ithaca, NY: Cornell University Press, 1969), 152.
12. Ibid., 152–53.
13. Ibid., 117; see also Amos Sawyer, *The Emergence of Autocracy in Liberia* (San Francisco: Institute for Contemporary Studies, 1992), 285.
14. Ibid., 127–28.
15. Ibid., 129.

16. Ibid.
17. Ibid., 130; F. P. M. Van der Kraaij, *The Open Door Policy of Liberia: An Economic History of Modern Liberia*, vol. 1 (Bremen: Im Selbstveriag des Museums, Afrika Archiv, Band 17/1, 1983), 204.
18. Van der Kraaij, *Open Door Policy*, vol. 1, 434.
19. Liebenow, *Evolution of Privilege*, 131.
20. Liebenow, *Quest for Democracy*, 131.
21. Sawyer, *Emergence of Autocracy*, 284.
22. Ibid., 285.
23. Ibid., 284.
24. *New York Times*, November 11, 1971.
25. Liebenow, *Evolution of Privilege*, 119–20.
26. Tuan Wreh, *The Love of Liberty: The Rule of William V. S. Tubman in Liberia 1944–1947* (London: C. Hurst, 1976), front and rear flaps of book jacket.
27. Sawyer, *Emergence of Autocracy*, 285.
28. Van der Kraaij, *Open Door Policy*, vol. 1, 394.
29. Liebenow, *Evolution of Privilege*, 77.
30. Ibid., 170.
31. Ibid., 215.
32. Ibid.
33. Ibid., 217.
34. *West Africa*, February 26, 1966; Liebenow, *Evolution of Privilege*, 218.
35. Liebenow, *Evolution of Privilege*, 217.
36. Ibid.
37. Ibid., 212.
38. Harvey Glickman, ed., *Political Leaders of Contemporary Africa South of the Sahara: A Biographical Dictionary* (New York: Greenwood Press, 1992), 295.

39. Robert W. Clower, et al., *Growth without Development: An Economic Survey of Liberia*. (Evanston, IL: Northwestern University Press, 1966), 135.
40. Ibid., 265.
41. Liebenow, *Evolution of Privilege*, 182.
42. Ibid., 213–14.
43. Ibid., 187; Clower, et al., 67.
44. Liebenow, *Evolution of Privilege*, 214.
45. Ibid., 219.

CHAPTER 21. BLOOD ON THE SAND: THE END

1. See Van der Kraaij, "William Tolbert," *Liberia Past and Present*, http://liberiapastandpresent.org/WilliamTolbert.html.
2. See Richard Tolbert, "Liberia: William R. Tolbert in the Pantheon of Great African Leaders," http://allafrica.com/stories/liberia.
3. Charles Moritz, ed., *Current Biography 1974* (New York: H. W. Wilson, 1974), 416.
4. Ibid., 418.
5. Ibid., 416.
6. J. Gus Liebenow, *Liberia: The Quest for Democracy* (Bloomington: IN University Press, 1983), 122-23.
7. Ibid., 124.
8. Ibid., 123.
9. Ibid.
10. Moritz, ed., *Current Biography 1974*, 418.
11. Liebenow, *Quest for Democracy*, 124.
12. See Van der Kraaij, "President Edward J. Roye (1870–1871)," *Liberia Past and Present*, http://liberiapastandpresent.org.
13. Moritz, ed., *Current Biography 1974*, 418.
14. Ibid.

15. *New York Times*, November 1, 1971.
16. See Frederick Starr, *Liberia: Description, History, Problems* (Chicago: Privately published, 1913), 98.
17. *New York Times*, November 1, 1971.
18. Liebenow, *Quest for Democracy*, 124. This was an elder Liberian's comment to Liebenow.
19. Amos Sawyer, *The Emergence of Autocracy in Liberia* (San Francisco: Institute for Contemporary Studies, 1991), 287.
20. Liebenow, *Quest for Democracy*, 125.
21. Tuan Wreh, *The Love of Liberty: The Rule of William V. S. Tubman in Liberia 1944–1947* (London: C. Hurst, 1976), 30. The notorious Colonel James P. Bestman, head of the SSS, and C. Wellington Campbell, the NISS chief, were dismissed and subsequently charged with "gross misuse of government funds."
22. Sawyer, *Emergence of Autocracy*, 287.
23. *New York Times*, November 1, 1971; and Liebenow, *Quest for Democracy*, 133. Tolbert also abolished the rice monopoly even though his son-in-law was an owner.
24. See Sawyer, *Emergence of Autocracy*, 287.
25. Ibid.
26. Ellen Johnson Sirleaf, *This Child Will Be Great* (New York: Harper Collins, 2009), 67.
27. William R. Tolbert, "Tolbert Rejects Another Term," *Monrovia Sunday Express*, November 2, 1979, quoted in http://www.en.wikipedia.org/wiki/william_R._Tolbert/jr.
28. See Liebenow, *Quest for Democracy*, 138.
29. According to the World Bank, the yearly growth of gross national product per capita in Liberia fell on average from 2.4 percent during 1965–73 to -1.5 percent in 1973–80. The bank judged that falling commodity prices, coupled with rising oil prices, was a major factor for low-income countries such as Liberia, but population growth, declining investment, and low returns on investment in the region were highly significant. *Sub-Saharan Africa: From Crisis to Sustainable Growth*

(Washington: The International Bank for Reconstruction and Development, 1989), 24–27, and Statistical Annex, 221–22, 252, 240–41, 252–53, 258.
30. *New York Times,* November 1, 1971.
31. Liebenow, *Quest for Democracy,* 125.
32. Ibid., 160.
33. Sirleaf, *This Child,* 68. Liebenow devotes an entire page each to diagramming the family and political nexus of the Tubman and Tolbert families in *Quest for Democracy,* 108–9.
34. See Liebenow, *Quest for Democracy,* 109.
35. Ibid., 121.
36. Ibid., 67.
37. 1568 Sawyer, 287.
38. Liebenow, *Quest for Democracy,* 134.
39. Ibid.
40. Albert Porte, *Liberianization or Gobbling Business?* mimeographed (Crozierville, Liberia: published by the author, 1974).
41. Liebenow, *Quest for Democracy,* 121.
42. Ibid. The italics are Liebenow's.
43. Ibid.
44. Ibid.
45. *New York Times,* November 1, 1971.
46. Liebenow, *Quest for Democracy,* 121–22.
47. Ibid., 173.
48. Ibid.
49. Ibid.
50. Sirleaf, *This Child,* 82.
51. Ibid., 174.
52. Ibid.
53. Sirleaf, *This Child,* 67.
54. The World Bank, Sub-Saharan Africa From Crisis to Sustainable Growth (Washington: The International Bank for Reconstruction and Development, 1989), 278.

55. The World Bank, *African Economic and Financial Data* (Washington: The International Bank for Reconstruction and Development, 1989), 157.
56. *New York Times*, May 30, 1979.
57. Ibid.
58. Ibid.
59. See *New York Times*, May 30 and July 20, 1979.
60. 1591 Liebenow, *Quest for Democracy*, 172.
61. *New York Times*, May 30 and July 20, 1979.
62. Liebenow, *Quest for Democracy*, 172.
63. *New York Times*, May 30, 1979.
64. *New York Times*, July 20, 1979.
65. *New York Times*, May 30, 1979.
66. *New York Times*, July 20, 1979.
67. Liebenow, *Quest for Democracy*, 170. Ellen Johnson Sirleaf added that an "ocean liner was rented as a floating hotel," in addition to "the multi-story Hotel Africa with a swimming pool [shaped] like the continent of Africa" and "fifty-one beach villas (one for each head of state expected to attend)." She reported the hotel now stood "gutted, forlorn, and empty" (*This Child*, 83).
68. *New York Times*, July 20, 1979.
69. Liebenow, *Quest for Democracy*, 174.
70. Kayode Awosaya, "How the Liberia Time Bomb Exploded," *New Nation*, 3 (1980), 5–7, quoted in Liebenow, *Quest for Democracy*, 175.
71. *New York Times*, March 11, 1980.
72. Liebenow, *Quest for Democracy*, 175–76.
73. Sanford J. Ungar, *Africa: The People and Politics of an Emerging Continent* (New York: Simon and Schuster, 1989), 88.
74. Ibid., 101.
75. Ibid.

76. *New York Times*, April 20, 1980.
77. *New York Times*, April 13, 1980.
78. *New York Times*, April 21, 1980.
79. Ibid.
80. Ibid.
81. Ibid.
82. *New York Times*, April 13, 1980.
83. Ibid.
84. *New York Times*, April 16, 1980.
85. *New York Times*, April 15, 1980. See also Sirleaf, *This Child*, 100.
86. Ibid.
87. Richard Tolbert, "Liberia"; Ellen Johnson Sirleaf, a former Tolbert minister of finance (who was destined to become president of Liberia) writes in her autobiography that the president was killed in bed. Another version (in Steven Ellis's *Mask of Anarchy*) maintains that soldiers discovered the president sleeping in his office, where they killed him.
88. Ungar, *Africa: People and Politics*, 90. Ellen Johnson Sirleaf relates in her memoir (page 97) that she was taken to the hospital where she viewed Tolbert's "brutalized" body.
89. In 2008 William Clarke, Tolbert's deputy minister of national security, testified that he and other top security officers stood outside the Executive Mansion during the assassination. He said that radio communication with a police officer reporting from inside the building failed because the battery in his radio went dead; Clarke thought the president had been killed. Clarke subsequently became director of police in the People's Redemption Council in Doe's government. William Clarke, testimony before the Liberian Truth and Reconciliation Commission, December 7, 2008;

and "Tolbert's Top Security Officers Stood by as He Was Assassinated," http://tcofliberia.org/press_release/59.
90. See, *Liberia Past and Present*, 1.
89. See Van der Kraaij, "President Edward J. Roye (1870–1871)."
90. *New York Times*, April 16, 1980; and Liebenow, *Quest for Democracy*, 186.
91. *New York Times*, April 16, 1980. Nephew Richard Tolbert asserts that his uncle was buried in an unmarked mass grave somewhere on Center Street in Monrovia.
92. *New York Times*, April 20, 1980.
93. *New York Times*, April 13, 1980.
94. *New York Times*, April 20 and 25, 1980.
95. *New York Times*, April 23, 1980.
96. Ibid.
97. *New York Times*, April 15, 1980.
98. Ungar, *Africa: People and Politics*, 107–8.
99. Ibid., 89.
100. Ibid., 90.
101. *Washington Post*, April 23, 1980.
102. *New York Times*, April 23, 1980.
103. *New York Times*, April 23, 1980.
104. Ibid.
105. Ibid.
106. Ungar, *Africa: People and Politics*, 90.
107. See Sirleaf, *This Child*, 95.
108. *New York Times*, April 25, 1980.
109. *New York Times*, April 25, 1980.
110. *New York Times*, April 21, 1980.
111. Ungar, *Africa: People and Politics*, 100.
112. Ibid., 99
113. The constitution was amended in 1907 to replace the word "color" with negro, thus enabling indigenous Africans to become citizens.Ungar, Africa: People and Politics, 100.

114. *New York Times,* March 24, 1957.
115. Ibid.
116. Sirleaf's autobiography, *This Child Will Be Great,* is a fascinating, easy read.
117. Veronica Arellano, *Library Journal Review* (Library Journals, 2010).

SELECTED BIBLIOGRAPHY

Beyan, Amos Jones. *The American Colonization Society and the Creation of the Liberian State, 1822–1900*. Lanham, MD: University Press of America, ca. 1991.

Boley, G. E. Saigbe. *Liberia: The Rise and Fall of the First Republic*. London: Macmillan, 1983.

Buell, Raymond Leslie. *Liberia: A Century of Survival 1847–1947*. African Handbook no. 7. Philadelphia: University Museum, University of Pennsylvania, 1947.

———. *Foreign Policy Reports: The Reconstruction of Liberia*. New York: Foreign Policy Association, 1932.

———. *The Native Problem in Africa*. 2 vols. New York: Macmillan, 1928.

Burrowes, Carl Patrick. *Power and Press Freedom in Liberia, 1830–1970: The Impact of Globalization and Civil Society on Media-Government Relations*. Trenton, NJ: Africa World Press, 2004.

Clarke, John Henrik, ed. *Marcus Garvey and the Vision of Africa*. New York: Vantage Books, 1974.

Clower, Robert W., George Dalton, Mitchell Harwitz, and A. A. Walters. *Growth without Development: An Economic Survey of Liberia*. Evanston, IL: Northwestern University Press, 1966.

Duignan, Peter, and L. H. Gann. *The United States and Africa: A History*. New York: Cambridge University Press and Hoover Institution Press, 1984.

Dunn, Elwood, Amos J. Brown, and Carl Patrick Burrowes. *Historical Dictionary of Liberia*. 2nd ed. Lanham, MD: Scarecrow Press, 2001.

Glickman, Harvey, ed. *Political Leaders of Contemporary Africa South of the Sahara: A Biographical Dictionary*. New York: Greenwood Press, ca. 1992.

Guannu, Joseph Saye, ed. *The Inaugural Addresses of the Presidents of Liberia. From Joseph Jenkins Roberts to William Richard Tolbert, Jr., 1848 to 1976*. Hicksville, NY: Exposition Press, 1980.

Holden, Edith. *Blyden of Liberia*. New York: Vantage Press, 1967.

Huberich, Charles Henry. *The Political and Legislative History of Liberia*. 2 vols. New York: Central Book, 1947.

Johnson, Charles; Patricia Smith; and the WGBH Series Research Team. *Africans in America: America's Journey through Slavery*. San Diego: Harcourt & Brace, 1998.

Johnston, Alex. *The Life and Letters of Sir Harry Johnston*. 1929. Reprint, London: Kessinger, 2010.

Johnston, Sir Harry H. *The Story of My Life*. Indianapolis: Bobbs-Merrill, ca. 1923.

———. *Liberia*. 2 vols. New York: Dodd Mead, 1906. Reprint, New York: Negro Universities Press, 1969.

Liebenow, J. Gus. *Liberia: The Quest for Democracy*. Bloomington: Indiana University Press, 1983.

———. *Liberia: The Evolution of Privilege*. Ithaca, NY: Cornell University Press, 1969.

Lynch, Hollis R. *Edward Wilmot Blyden: Pan-Negro Patriot, 1832–1912*. Oxford University Press, 1970.

McPherson, J. H. T. *History of Liberia*. Johns Hopkins University Studies in Historical and Political Science, 1891. E-book released 2004. http://guttenberg.org.

Ranard, Donald A., ed. *Liberians: An Introduction to Their History and Culture*. Culture Profile no. 19. Washington: Center for Applied Linguistics, 2005.

Sirleaf, Ellen Johnson. *This Child Will Be Great*. New York: Harper Collins, 2009.

Sisay, Hassan B. *Big Powers and Small Nations: A Case Study of United States-Liberian Relations*. Lanham, MD: University Press of America, 1958.

Starr, Frederick. *Liberia: Description, History, Problems*. Chicago: privately published, 1913.

Tazewell, C. W., ed. *Virginia's Ninth President, Joseph Jenkins Roberts.* Virginia Beach, Virginia: WS Dawson, 1992.

Van der Kraaij, Fred P. M., *The Open Door Policy of Liberia: An Economic History of Modern Liberia,* 2 vols. Bremen: lm Selbstveriag des Museums, 1983.

Wiggins, Rosalind Cobb. *Captain Paul Cuffe's Logs and Letters, 1808–1817: A Black Quaker's "Voice from Within the Veil."* Washington, DC: Howard University Press, 1996.

For a full listing of sources, refer to the notes.

A NOTE ABOUT THE SOURCES

———~m~———

MOST OF THESE SOURCES ARE available in the Library of Congress and other libraries, and on the Internet at such websites as forgottenbooks.com, babel.hathitrust.org, openlibrary.org, archives.org, Gutenberg.org, and books.google.com. The *New York Times* Archives (https://timesmachine.nytimes.com) is a valuable source for firsthand accounts.

African Repository (initially titled the *African Repository and Colonial Journal*), published 1825 to 1919, usually monthly, by the American Colonization Society, is a prime source for nineteenth-century history. It includes a wide range of materials—the society's annual reports, articles, correspondence, addresses, sermons, news items, obituaries, etc. The publication can be found in the Library of Congress, on the Internet, and possibly in a scattering of other libraries.

The Manuscript Division of the Library of Congress houses another key source for Liberia's nineteenth-century history, the Records of the American Colonization Society (1792–1964). The collection, on microfilm, comprises various unpublished manuscripts such as correspondence, diaries, journals, reports, financial contributions, and business papers. Among other useful primary resources in the library are US State Department publications such as *Papers Relating to the Foreign Relations of the United States*, country by country, year by year.

In addition, the National Archives in Washington, DC, holds a large number of documents relating to Liberia's history, namely Department of State records dealing with the internal affairs of Liberia from 1906 to 1947, dispatches from American ministers to Liberia from 1863 to 1929, *Papers Relating to the Foreign Relations of the United States 1963–1947*, and other records, reports, and correspondence.

ABOUT THE AUTHOR

—⁂—

DAVID GENE REESE RETIRED FROM the World Bank with more than fifty years' development experience in Asia and Africa. Although trained largely as an economist, he is (according to him) a "congenital" historian. While he worked with Liberia, he became fascinated with the country and its origins and history. The result? Ten years spent researching and writing this book.

INDEX

Adams, John Quincy, 66
African Institution, 45
African Methodist Episcopal (AME) Church, 67, 79
African Society, 48
Africa Squadron, *see* A "Peculiar Special Relationship," 146-48 (*see also* international slave trade)
agriculturists among immigrants, 240-49, 494 *see also* rice
airport (*see* Roberts Field)
Allen, Richard, 66-67, 79
Alligator, USS, Robert Stockton and, 94-96
American Colonization Society, 46, 50, 51, 54-68 *passim*, 595; establishment of, 54, 60-61; opposition to, 66-68 (*see also* Cultural Divisions among Free Black Americans, 69-70); as US agency for resettling recaptives, 65; halt of support to immigration by, 235; dissolution of, 235
Americo-Liberian rule, downfall, causes of, 588-91, 612
Anderson, Benjamin J. K., 190, 243, 252; early life of, 253-54; career of, 257-58; journey to Musardu, 260-79 *passim*, 280-83; 302-303, 306, 321, 363, 426-27, 474, 599, 600
Andrus, Joseph B., 673
Arthur, Chester A., 294
Ashmun, Jehudi, early life of, 108-110; arrival of at Cape Mesurado, 111; departure from, 126; death of, 130-31; 596
automobiles, 329, 382-83
Ayres, Eli, 96, purchase of land for Liberia colony by, 97-99; 102, 105, 106, 111, 112, 124-25, 148-49, 595, 596, 613

711

back-to-Africa movements, Blyden and "provident return," 238 (*see also* Cuffe, Blyden, and Garvey)

Bacon, Ephraim, search by for a site for the colony, 85-90; 91, 97, 613

Bacon, Samuel, 71-72, journal of, 74-78; 613

Bankston, 71, 75, 78, 79, 80

Barbados, immigration to Liberia from, 200, 313, 599 ; Barclays' arrival in Liberia from, 313-14

Barclay, Arthur, 303, 307, 314; early career of, 314-15; financial crisis, 317-18; reelection of, 323; and British finance and Harry Johnston, 328-30; and border disputes with France and Britain, 332-34; reforms of, 336-39; frontier force creation by, 336; and Mackay Cadell, 336-39; record, appraisal of, 353-56

Barclay, Edwin J., background and description of, 412-14; author of "National Flag Song," 403; and frontier force expedition, 414-15; and Firestone, 423-24; reelection as president, 425; US recognition of, 425 ; endorsement of Tubman by, 447-50, 487-89; as opposition candidate, 608, 487-89; refusal to concede election, 489-90; death of, 490, 605

Barclay Training Center, 520, 533, 539, 584, 585, 586

Bayard, Thomas F., as US secretary of state, opposition to French territorial claims, 300.

Benson, Stephen A., as second president of republic for four terms, 179, 184, 194

Berlin conference, 286 (*see also* The Scramble, 266-311)

Bethlehem Steel Corporation, 527; Christie and, 476

Birch, Samuel, 28

Birmingham, USS, dispatched to Liberia by President T. Roosevelt 342-43, 603

Bismarck, Otto von, 286, 298

Black Star Line, 378-80, 391 (*see also* Garvey)

Britain, (*see also* England and Great Britain)

Burgess, Ebenezer, survey of African west coast with John Mills, 64; presentation of report to American Colonization Society, 64

Blyden, Edward Wilmot, early life of, and as a young man, 201-208; arrival of in Liberia; correspondence with Gladstone, 206; professor at Liberia College, 208; secretary of state, 209; race, obsession with, 210, 230; "plan for rebirth of Africa," 210; "back-to-Africa,",356; "provident return," theory of, 238; as "African celebrity," 210; and Edward Roye, 211, 222-24; hatred toward, 222-25; in Freetown, Sierra Leone, 225, 331; as ambassador in London, 290-91; and Edward, Havelock, 291; border disputes with France and Britain and, 290-91, 332, 355; resignation of as a Christian minister, 332; favorable view of Islam, 331-32; death of, 356-57 (*see also* border disputes)

Boley, George, 578, 584-85

Brown, Moses, 40

Brown, Obadiah, 40

Buchanan, Thomas, as governor of Liberia, 136-39, 141, death of 136; 597, 613

Buchanan, town of, 115, 117, 254, 361

Buell, Raymond Leslie, 386, 393-94, 421, 474

Burgess, Ebenezer, search for site for colony, 64; 73, 81 (*see also Samuel Mills*)

Burton, Richard, 100, 170, 185, 257, 319; and Gallinas, 172-7; description of Cape Palmas by, 443-44

Cadell, Mackay, 336-39 (*see also* Liberia's Military, 349-52)

Canot, Theodore, 100, 173

Cape Mesurado, 72, 86, 97, 100, 101, 108, 112, 114, 122, 124, 203, 367, 561, 595, 596; arrival of settlers on, 102-103

Carey, Lott, 20, 122, 128, 132, 134, 147, 249, 596, 122

Carter, Jimmy, 436

Chester, USS, 342-43, 362-63, 604

China, 126, 525, 564, 618n34

Chinery, David, 215

Christie, Landsdell K., 473, 475-78, 480, 484, 607, 608 (*see also* iron ore)

Churchill, Winston, 382-83, 435 (*see also* rubber)

Clark, Reed Page, 345, 348

Clay, Henry, 60-61, 62

Cleveland, Grover, 300-301

coffee, 176, 178, 191, 194, 211, 232, 243, 248-9, 250, 284, 293, 329, 355, 427, 494, 496, 508, 522, 536-58, 561, 648n38

Coker, Daniel, 72, 75, 79,81-83,,91, 93-94, 96, 105

Coleman, William D., 306-307

colonization, cost of, 147
colonization movement, early advocates of, 30
colonization societies, state and local societies, 134-36, 149 (*see also* Maryland, New York, Mississippi, Louisiana, Pennsylvania, New Jersey state societies)
color, skin, 140, 167, 194, 210, 223-34, 236, 355 (*see also* Liberian Political Parties, 232-34)
Congoes (recaptives), 129, 194, 211, 229, 232, 240, 244, 247, 261, 263, 278
corruption, 222, 226, 311, 251-52, 284, 351, 366, 371, 443, 480, 549, 509, 530, 580, 591, 588-89, 583, 562-63
Councils, Executive, 455; Legislative, 137, 147, 153, 154-55, 164; Unification, 457, 543, 608 (*see also* unification)
Crozer, Samuel A., 71, 73,74,76,79, 80, 613
Crummel, Alexander, 197, 208, 223, 230, 259, 331, 356
Cuffe, Alice Pequit, marriage to Paul Cuffe, 17
Cuffe, Paul, birth of, 6; description of, 5-6; early life of, 15-17; marriage of, 17; voyages by, to Sierra Leone 1-5, 36-37; to Sierra Leone with immigrants, 45-48; to England, 37-38; the Friendly Society formed by, 35-36, 39,47; as a prosperous mulatto entrepreneur, 24-27; as a member of the Westport Friends Meeting, 24; Cuff's school constructed by, 24; as America's first wealthy Negro, 26; trips to Washington by, 40-43, 44; petition to Congress by, 43-45; and colonization, 50; American Colonization Society meeting, absence from, 61; and the international slave trade, 35-36: death of, 52
culture (*see* Cultural Divisions among Free Black Americans, 69-70)
Cuttyhunk Island, 6, 12, 15, 595

Declaration of Independence, Liberian, 159, 161-62, 228, 294
Doe, Samuel K., 352; government toppled in coup led by, 579-85 *passim*
Du Bois, W. E. B., 370, 371, 386, 389, 406,, 421
Duigman, Peter and Gann, L.H., on Havelock, 289, 339; on European designs on Liberia, 297-98

Elizabeth, voyage of to Sherbro Island, Sierra Leone, with first group of colonists, 71-73; 595 (*see also immigrants*)
Ethiopia, 207, 375, 423, 431
executions on the beach, 586-87 (*see also* Samuel Doe)

Fahnbulleh, Henry, Sr., trial and conviction of treason of, 534-39
Faulkner, Thomas J. R., 233, 301, 392-93, 411, 605
Fernando Po, 393-96, 398, 400, 415, 454, 502
fever, 63, 74, 75, 76, 91, 93, 106, 119, 121, 122, 132, 141, 42, 183, 236, 256, 310, 320, 382, 404, 417, 427, 588
finances, dependency of colony on colonization societies and US government, 251; of republic on import duties and taxes, 252 (*see also loans*)
financial crises, *see* Timeline, 595-612 *passim*
Finley, Robert, 55; background of, 56-58; influence of Second Great Awakening on, 58; colonization and, 59; establishment of American Colonization Society, role in, 59-61, "Father of," 62; president of University of Georgia, 62, death of, 63 (*see also* American Colonization Society; colonization, black opposition to (*see also* Cultural Divisions Among Free American Blacks, 69-70)
Firestone, Harvey S., 381; Herbert Hoover and, 383, 408-409; opposition to rubber restriction by, 383; Garvey and, 375-76, 388; direct intervention in Liberia, 410, and Roosevelt, 422
Firestone Rubber Company, 376, 384, 408, 409, 420-21; search for rubber plantation site, 383-84; plantation and loan agreement and, 386; and loan to Liberia, 405-407, `543; opposition to loan and, 392, 405, 420-21, 606, 608; Supplementary Agreement and, 605; League of Nations and, 419, 432, 433; labor and, 395, 398, 502, 504, 610
flag, 161; "National Flag Song," 403
Foote, Andrew H., 186-87, 188
Fourah Bay, Siera Leone, 99, 79, 85, 90-96 *passim*
France, and imperialism in Liberia, 302-304;
Franklin, Benjamin, 8

Freetown, Sierra Leone, 29, 31, 34, 38, 47, 64, 73, 78, 82, 85, 91, 93, 94, 225, 258, 296, 337, 357, 369

Friendly Society, Sierra Leone, 36, 39, 46, 47, 48, 52 (*see also* Paul Cuffe)

Frontier Force, *see* Liberia's Military, 349-52

Fugitive Slave Act, 202-203

Gallinas, 169,170-72, 185, 194-95, 285, 287, 289-90, 293-95, 299, 601 (*see also* international slave trade)

Gardiner, Anthony W., and border dispute with Britain, 195, 291-93; resignation of, 293-94

Garvey, Marcus, 370-72, 375-81, 388-91, 604-605; arrival in New York of, 377; J. Edgar Hoover and, 377; UNIA conventions, 375, 380; President-General of the Republic of Africa, as, 380; Black Star Ocean Line and, 378-80; back-to-Africa project in Liberia and, 375-76; abrogation of agreement by government, 376; acquisition of land by Firestone, 376; complicity of Herbert Hoover alleged by 388; the "great Liberian double-cross," 388; deportation of, 390; African redemption, plan of, 391; African Orthodox Church founded by, 391; back-to-Africanism, 391; adverse reactions to, 389; burial of, 391; influence of, 391; Kwame Nkruma, 391; Du Bois on, 370, 389; Marcus Garvey School, 585

Germany, and possible colonization of Liberia, 298-99

Great Britain, and ban on trade with US, 139; and voyage of Cuffe to, 37-39; and visit of Roberts to, 168-69; and border dispute with Liberia, 387-95 *passim*, 309, 326-27, 285, 350-52, 600-602 *passim*; and attacks on Liberian sovereignty, 138, 143, 165, 175, 152-53, 301, 340-41, 363, 309; and reforms in Liberia, 335-36; and Mackay Cadell (*see also* Liberia's Military, 349-52); and friendly relations with Liberia, 309-10; and death of Tubman in

Greene, Graham, 410, 413-15, 417-19, 425-26, 428, 430, 495

Greenleaf, Simon, 157-59, 180

Growth without Development, 492-514 *passim*

Gurley, Ralph, 106-107, 598, 596, 126-27

Harris, John Meyer, 287-88
Harris, Sheldon, 5, 48
Harvard University, 71, 157, 180, 374, 387, 391, 465, 556, 559
Havelock, Sir Arthur, 289-93, 295-96, 601
Henries, Richard, 479, 540, 559, 584, 586
Henries, A. Doris Banks, 444, 452-53, 516-17, 540, 543
Hoover, Herbert, 383. 386, 388, 395, 408 (*see also* Firestone)
Hoover, J. Edgar, 178, 180, 479. (*see also* Marcus Garvey)
Howard, Daniel Edward, 307, 360-61, 366, 368-69, 561, 603

immigrants, backgrounds and occupations of, 245
imperialism, *see* The Scramble, 286-311 *passim*
indirect Rule (*see* Indirect Rule, 364-65), 287, 317, 354, 355, 363, 549, 603
intellectuals, black, *see* Edward Blyden
International Monetary Fund, 570, 610
iron ore, 116, 148, 264, 272, 282, 321, 473-77, 478, 480, 493, 494, 501, 504, 508, 509, 512, 517, 520, 529, 531, 534, 549, 551, 564, 568, 571, 608

Islam, 210, 242, 264, 274, 332 (*see also* Blyden)

Jefferson, Thomas, on colonization, 7-8, 23, 12, 13, 59, 139, 150
Johnson, Elijah, 79, 105, 106
Johnson, Sirleaf, Ellen, 591-93
Johnston, Sir Harry (*see* also Africa's Renaissance Man, 319-21), 602-603, description of, 358; and Roberts, 167, 230; on race in Africa, 230; and Arthur Barclay, 318; on Ports of Entry Law, 196; on Roye, 221; as director in Liberian companies, 325; and loan from British financiers, 328; misspending funds, accusation of, 329; dispensed with by Barclay, 330; on decline of lighter Liberians, 236; on reverence for Queen Victoria, 310; and Theodore Roosevelt, 341-42; death of, 358

Kennedy, John F., 527, 609; Hospital, 582
Key, Francis Scott, 59, 61, 65 (*see also* American Colonization Society)
King, Charles Dunbar Burgess, 369, 428, 604; as president, 33,

372-73. 388-89,410-11, 413,428, 445, 510, 604-605, 614 (*see also* Marcus Garvey, Firestone Rubber Company)

King, Boston, 28-29, 30 (*see also* America's First Black Èmigrès, 28-30)

Kizell, John, 63, 74, 77; owner of Sherbro Island site of colonists' first landing, 73

LAMCO (Liberian American Swedish Minerals Company), 493, 504, 534

land, traditional tenure, 97, 149

League of Nations, Liberia as member of, 368; investigation by finds slavery in Liberia. 394-401; request by government for assistance of, 404-406; plan of assistance by submitted to government, 406-408; critics caution plan would lead to complete control of Liberia by, 407-408; proposal dropped by, 425

Lee, Robert E., 176

Liberia College 193

Liberia *Herald,* 161-62, 155, 186, 194, 200, 205

Liberia's Military, 349-52

Liberia Mining Company, 475, 478-79, 480, 483, 484, 534, 607, 608

Lincoln, Abraham, 191, 599; and colonization, 32,-33, 197

land, tenure of and conflicts over, 302

literacy, 505, 687n54

loans, 222, 251, 122, 123, 126, 154, 155, 166, 410, 478, 480, 501, 530, 550, 576

London *Times,* 5, 37

MacCarthy, Charles, as governor of Sierra Leone, 83

Maryland Colonization Society, 135, 149, 597

Maryland County, Liberia, 189, 195, 43, 444-45, 448-49, 455, 489, 516, 518, 551, 598, 599, 600

Maryland, Independent State of Maryland in Africa, creation of, 184-86, 189

Maryland, Republic of, 188

Matilda Newport Day, 456

Mills, Samuel J., as "father of foreign missions," 46; search for site for colony, 63-64; death of 64; 50, 63, 64, 73, 81 (*see also* Ebenezer Burgess)

mining and minerals (*see* iron ore)

Mississippi Colonization Society, 135, 149, 150, 245

Mississippi in Africa, 135, 149, 151, 241, 247, 257, 597

Monroe, James, 65, 66, 71, 80, 139, 146
Monrovia, Liberia, naming of by American Colonization Society, 127; by tribal people "The American Place," 250; and description of, 569, 579; and German U-boat attack on, mortality rates, 78 (see also fever)
multinational corporations (see Growth without Development, 492-514)

Nantucket, Massachusetts, 12, 16, 17, 24, 109
National Iron Ore Corporation, 478
Nautilus, voyage of to Freetown, Sierra Leone with (second group of colonista, 81 (see also immigrants)
New Bedford, Massachusetts, 12, 16, 24, 34, 43, 44
New England, slave population of, 7; anti-slavery sentiment of, 12
New Jersey Colonization Society, foundation of by Robert Stockton, 95
New York City, Negro uprising, 19; *See also* "The Book of Negroes"
New York Colonization Society, 135, 209

New York *Times*, 582, 473, 174, 482, 542, 490, 370, 228, 401, 541, 590, 561, 535, 415-16, 198, 380, 484, 527, 580, 573, 176, 397
New York *Tribune*, 216, 217
Nkrumah, Kwame, 391, 528, 536
Northwestern University (see Growth without Development, 492-514, *passim*)

Organization of African Unity (OAU), 442, 528-29, 564, 575-76, 580

Pakenham, Thomas, 298
Paris Peace Conference, 368
Pawning, 397, 400, 401, 495
Payne, James S., 231
People's Redemption Council (PRC), 584
Perry, Matthew C., 97, 151, 189, 202, 203
Perseverance Island, Liberia, disembarkation of first immigrants on, 101
Pinney, John B., 197, 202; correspondence of, 203-204, 223; visit to Liberia, 239, 613
political parties, *see* Liberian Political Parties, 232-35
Poro society, 255, 427-29, 558
Porte, Albert, 476, 567
Ports of Entry Law, 195, 197

Province of Freedom, 194, (see Sierra Leone and Paul Cuffe)

Quakers, and antislavery beliefs, 12; and abolition of the slave trade, 31; as one of New England's most influential and prosperous communities, 12; as Cuffe Slocum's and Paul Cuffe,'s religious affiliation, 13, 14; as supporters of Paul Cuffe's plans, and colonization 2, 34, 40-42

Quaker Meetings, see 617n27

race (see color, skin)

railroad, 476

recaptives, 194; social position of, 236; program for, 240-41; first delivery to Liberia of, 516. (see also Congoes)

recognition, of republic, by European powers, 168, 97, 598; by US, 635n15

Rhode Island, slave population of, 7; growing community of prosperous free Negroes and influential Quakers in, 12; prominent religious and political leaders residents of (see also Cuffe trips to Washington and voyages to Sierra Leone)

rice riots of 1979, see William Tolbert

Roberts, Joseph Jenkins, 596, 597, 598, 600; family of, 139-40; paternity and birth of, 39; work and education of, 140; and William N. Colson, 140-42; arrival at Monrovia, 141; as successful trader and businessman, 141-42; entry into politics 142; as commonwealth chief justice and lieutenant governor, 142-44; court cases defending Liberia's sovereignty won by, 143-44, 152-54; appointment as governor, 139; independence proposed by, 154-55; approval of independence and constitution guided by, 156-59; election as first president, 166-67; reelection, 156-59; and territorial expansion, 172-73; recital of republic's achievements by, 191; belief in God's desire to achieve great work in Africa through Liberia,, 227; Sir Harry Johnston on ethnicity and color of, 229-30; description of, 229-30; as president twelve years, 598, 600;

Roberts Field, 435-36, 459, 473, 525, 526, 607

Robertsport, 178

Roosevelt, Franklin, and Firestone, 422; message to Edwin,

Barclay, 432-33; defense of Liberia 435; visit to Liberia 436-37; visit of Barclay and Tubman, 437; seaport and, 438, 459

Roosevelt, Theodore, personal interest in Africa, 340; fact-finding mission to Liberia and, 340-45, 603; Harry Johnston and, 341-42

Roye, Edward J., childhood of, 212-13; arrival at Monrovia of, 213; as leading merchant in Liberia, 213, 246; political career of, 214; inauguration of as president, 214; British loan secured by, 216; constitution, attempt to amend by, 217; uproar against, 217; arrest of, 218; impeachment and conviction of, 218; escape from jail by, 218; drowning of, 218-19; Tubman on death of, 218; Sir Harry Johnston on money from British loan (*see also* The Drowning of President Roye, 219-21)

rubber, 116, 148, 243, 250, 318, 322, 323 (*see also* Firestone Rubber Company)

Russell, Alfred F., 293

Russwurm, John, as governor of Maryland colony, 184; as first black governor of colony, 185-87, death of, 188; 598

Ryder, D.G., and the British *Blue Book*, 416-17 (*see also* League of Nations, Arthur Barclay)

Sande society, *see* The Poro and Juju, 428-29

Scheffelin, Henry M., Anderson expedition, financing of, 260; as vice-president of New York Colonization Society Board of Managers, 260

Scramble for Africa, *see* The Scramble, 286-311; Berlin conference

Second Great Awakening, 58

Seymour, George L., 189-90, 259, 599

Seys, John, 155

Sherbro Island, Sierra Leone, 72, 73, 100, 66, 90, 64, 74, 80-84 *passim*

Shufeldt. Robert W., 288

Sims, James I., 189-90, 259, 599

slave uprisings, in New York City, 19; 20-22; Denmark Vessey, 21; Nat Turner, 21-22; George Washington's niece, fear of, 49-50; 83, 175, 184

slavery, in America, 7-8; abolition of by states, 19; by Africans, 263; League of Nations and, 295; (*see also* Slavery in America, 9-11)

slave trade, international, (*see also* Slavery in America, 9-11) 7, 34, 33, 35-36, 65, 89, 148, 167, 172, 595, 591; heavy involvement in by New England shipping, 7; description of in Gallinas, 170-74; abolition by Britain, 29; by US, 18; eradication by Liberia, 111, 128-29, 132-33, 137, 138, 169, 172-73, 180; opposition by native chiefs to eradication of, 99; Cuffe on, 32, 36, 42; Stockton and, 94, 96 (*see also* A "Peculiar" Special Relationship, 146-48)

Smyth, John H., 293, 297, 300

Soviet Union, 521, 522,-24, 525, 564, 609, 611

Special Relationship, 146-48

steamships, 250, 309

Stettinius, Edward, and the Liberia Company, 471-72

Stevenson Rubber Restriction Scheme, 182, 604. (*see also* rubber and Firestone)

Stimson, Henry L., 195, 300, 408-49

Stockton, Robert F., 86, 94-96, 98, 111, 112, 144, 148, 595. (*see also* slave trade)

Taft, William Howard, 340, 343, 345, 603

territorial expansion, 138, 149, 189; Burton on, 172 (*see also* Gallinas)

territory, Liberian, loss of, 310, 333-34

Ticonderoga, USS, 288-89, 600

Tolbert, A.B., "dynastic ambition" of, 568; refuge in French Embassy of, 584

Tolbert, Stephen, and Allen Porte, 567-68

Tolbert, William R., family and background of, 557-58; career of, 557, 558-59; as the "invisible vice president," 559; "swearing in" suit of, 560; description of, 561; reforms of, 562-63; social and economic programs of, 565-66; foreign policy of, 564; OAU and, 564, 576; resentment toward family of, 566; growing apathy of, 566-67; Gabriel Matthews and, 570, 573; and April 14 rice riots, 572-75; increasing paranoia of, 567; assassination of, 582-83

trade, between coastal areas and hinterland, 256; commodities in, 256; rivalry between tribal groups for, 256;